entre

Handbook of Educational Leadership and Management

Handbook of Educational Leadership and Management

Edited by
Professor Brent Davies and John West-Burnham

PEARSON
Longman

London • New York • Toronto • Sydney • Tokyo • Singapore
Hong Kong • Cape Town • Madrid • Paris • Amsterdam • Munich • Milan

PEARSON EDUCATION LIMITED

Edinburgh Gate
Harlow CM20 2JE
Tel: +44 (0)1279 623623
Fax: +44 (0)1279 431059
Website: www.pearsoned.co.uk

First published in Great Britain in 2003

© Pearson Education Limited 2003

© Barbara MacGilchrist 2003, Part Six: Learning, Teaching and the Curriculum, (Introduction)
   Learning and teaching in the intelligent school (Chapter 41)
© Thomas Sergiovanni 2003, A cognitive approach to Leadership (Chapter 2)
© Ron Glatter 2003, Governance and educational innovation (Chapter 22)
© Paul Black and Dylan Wiliam 2003, The development of formative assessment (Chapter 40)
© OECD 2003, The OECD schooling scenarios (Chapter 62)

ISBN 0 273 65668 6

British Library Cataloguing in Publication Data
A CIP catalogue record for this book can be obtained from the British Library

10 9 8 7 6 5 4 3 2

Typeset by Pantek Arts Ltd, Maidstone, Kent
Printed and bound in Great Britain by Biddles Ltd, Guildford & King's Lynn

The Publishers' policy is to use paper manufactured from sustainable forests.

Brent Davies would like to dedicate this
book to Barbara

John West-Burnham would like to dedicate
this book to Ingrid

CONTENTS

FIGURES

TABLES

INTRODUCTION

The field of educational leadership and management has expanded rapidly over the last 30 years from its early days of educational administration. This Handbook examines some of the major themes in the field and aims both to explore their current context and discuss how they are developing to meet the changing circumstances of the twenty-first century. We do not claim this book represents a comprehensive survey of the field, but we do believe it represents a major collection of insights and perceptions around ten major themes. Each of these themes forms a major part of the book and the ten sub-editors have brought together leading experts and practitioners to explore each area.

Part One, edited by John West-Burnham, focuses on the nature of leadership. Here Linda Lambert, Thomas Sergiovanni, Kenneth Leithwood, Rosanne Steinbach, Alma Harris, John West-Burnham, Peter Gronn and John Novak provide a perceptive and challenging set of ideas to reconceptualize the nature of leadership. This part seeks to help readers understand how our understanding of leadership is changing and to challenge emerging orthodoxies about the nature and purpose of leadership in education.

In Part Two, edited by Brent Davies, the traditional functional management processes are set in a broader strategic leadership context. In this part the leadership implications of strategy and planning, reengineering, marketing and finance are examined with case studies to illuminate the theory. With contributions from Brent Davies, Barbara Davies, Les Bell, Greg Barker, Derek Wise and Nick Foskett this section links leadership and management in an integrated way. It sees leadership and management as different sides of the same coin, and it seeks to provide a united framework to analyse some of the key processes in schools.

Part Three, edited by Mike Bottery, examines how the national and international policy context for educational leadership and management has developed and changed. With contributions from Mike Bottery, Ben Levin, Christopher Day, Nick Foskett, Peter Gilroy and Jenny Ozga this part provides a critical analysis of the developing policy framework and its potential future direction.

Janet Ouston in Part Four examines the fundamental changes in the relationships between governance structures and school leadership and management. This part draws on contributions from Ron Glatter, Stephen Gorard, Chris Taylor, Peter Earley, Michael Creese, Suzanne Hood and Keiko Watanabe. It maps the fundamental shifts that have occurred in relationships between parents, school governors and the schools themselves and draws implications for the future.

Guilbert Hentschke takes an in-depth look at the rapidly emerging private sector in education in Part Five. This part analyses the public/private interface in the form of the state, private for-profit and private not-for-profit sectors. It draws extensively on the experience of the USA as a template to examine UK and global trends in this field. It has contributions from James Guthrie, Jason Walton, Michael Sandler, Jeffrey Fromm, Guilbert Hentschke, Todd Kern, Dean Millot, Keith Collar, Renée Jacob, Kim Smith, Allan Odden, David Crossly, James Tooley, Pauline Dixon and Stephen Heyneman.

Part Six, edited by Barbara MacGilchrist, examines the leadership and management dimensions of the core purposes of schools: learning, teaching and the curriculum. With contributions from Patricia Collarbone, Frank Hartle, Russell Hobby, Peter Hill, Carmel Crévola, Dennis Lawton, Paul Black, Dylan Wiliam, Barbara MacGilchrist and Len Barton this provides a critical collection to re-examine these fundamental processes in schools.

Dean Fink and Andy Hargreaves in Part Seven look at the area of change in schools with a particular focus on sustaining change. This part considers the leadership necessary to sustain change in schools and also how to sustain that leadership. The concept of building both individual and organizational capacity for sustainability is a major theme of the section, drawing on the contributions of Andy Hargreaves, Dean Fink, Michael Fullan, Hugh Mehan, Amanda Datnow, Lea Hubbard, Ann Lieberman, Diane Wood, Louise Stoll and Lorna Earl.

Part Eight, edited by David Hopkins and Alma Harris, evaluates the contribution made by the school improvement and school effectiveness movements to increasing the quality of education in our schools. It moves on from this base to highlight how these insights may improve practice in the future. It draws on the expertise of David Hopkins, Pam Sammons, Karen Elliot, Mel West, David Reynolds, David Potter, Chris Chapman, Louise Stoll, Alma Harris and Charles Teddlie.

Patricia Collarbone in Part Nine focuses on leading and managing the critical resource of teachers. This part looks at the framework for developing and sustaining the quality of the teaching force in education. It draws on contributions from Ralph Fessler, Rochelle Ingram, Sara Bubb, Agnes McMahon, Linda Evans, David Clutterbuck, Vicki Phillips and Marilyn Crawford to provide valuable insights for leaders in education.

Finally, Part Ten, edited by Brian Caldwell, provides five insightful accounts of the future of education and schooling in particular. It considers the future of schools in a global, local and individual dimension and the impact on leadership of decentralization and centralization trends. The contributors – Hedley Beare, David Istance, Judith Chapman, David Aspin, Yin Cheong Cheng and Dan Gibton – provide a unique cross-section of ideas and opinions in the field. This aims to provide a catalyst for debate among colleagues and readers.

This handbook seeks to provide an accessible resource for all those involved in the leadership of schools. In drawing on the ten themes it aims not only to explain current practice but to provide a framework and insights with which to build a future understanding of the changing nature of leadership and management in schools. We wish the readers well in this venture.

BRENT DAVIES AND JOHN WEST-BURNHAM

ACKNOWLEDGEMENTS

The editors would like to express their thanks for all the hard work of the section editors – Mike Bottery, Janet Ouston, Guilbert Hentschke, Barbara MacGilchrist, Dean Fink, Andy Hargreaves, David Hopkins, Alma Harris, Patricia Collarbone and Brian Caldwell – who have made this handbook possible. We would also like to thank all the contributors who have given us such wonderful material.

The editors would like to thank Maureen Cornet for secretarial and administration support in producing this book, and Christopher Bowring-Carr for his outstanding editorial assistance.

PART ONE

Leadership

JOHN WEST-BURNHAM

Introduction

JOHN WEST-BURNHAM

Leadership is a multifaceted activity and so are the approaches to studying it. Few topics in the study of organizational life can have inspired such a diverse range of prescriptions, nostrums and intellectual constructs. The sheer volume of academic and quasi-academic activity in the area has led to authors and editors prefacing any new study with an apology for 'yet another study'. No such apology is offered here.

The study of leadership has to be a central component of any genuine debate about the future of education. One of the significant changes in educational policy across the world in the 1990s was the discovery of management by policy makers. This resulted in a wide range of attempts to offer a new panacea for all organizational ills and to create a new hegemony around a range of reductionist taxonomies and exhortations. The simplification of the concept of leadership into a series of instrumental behaviours and its adoption as a 'magic wand' has created an artificial and simplistic model redolent, at its worst, of the moral rhetoric of English public schools in the nineteenth century.

At the same time, it is necessary to offer a corrective to what might be called the over-intellectualization of the subject. Leadership is a fundamental social, organizational and political phenomenon. Whatever the abstractions of academic discourse, people aspire to be leaders, study to become leaders, are described as leaders and, on occasion, do actually lead. The academic debate therefore has to recognize the reality of actual practice and the pragmatic needs of those who are increasingly described as being in leadership positions.

Part One of this handbook seeks to achieve a balance between the legitimate demands of scholarship and practice. Each chapter addresses in varying degrees the imperatives of research, scholarship and practice. Each focuses on the relationship between theory and practice and offers conceptual frameworks to help develop understanding.

Linda Lambert's opening chapter offers a critique of the historically prevailing models of leadership and then develops a sustained analysis of the emerging syntheses that might inform the current debate about what leadership might become. Her systematic review of the significant literature in the field leads to a new conceptual framework that has echoes in the succeeding chapters – most importantly that leadership is, profoundly and fundamentally, about learning and relationships. Thomas Sergiovanni adds a powerful additional dimension in challenging the orthodox perspective of bureaucratic and personal authority and arguing for leadership 'based on ideas, values and purposes'. His commentary on the four types of error in discussing leadership provides an example of how scholarship can illuminate discourse and provides insights into professional practice.

Kenneth Leithwood and Rosanne Steinbach's rigorous analysis of the research literature demonstrates how leadership models can be informed and developed through systematic analysis; using the concept of social capital they illuminate a range of strategies that offer models of leadership that are both practical and relevant to a category of schools often neglected in debate about leadership. Alma Harris develops an equally radical critique by relocating the debate away from individual authority into a discussion of leadership being distributed across the school. She provides a vehicle to replace the rhetoric about the empowerment of teachers with specific strategies focused on 'the leadership capability of the many'.

John West-Burnham's chapter extends the discussion about the increasing complexity of the concept of leadership and relates it to the debate about appropriate models of learning. The penultimate chapter is Peter Gronn's subtle and detailed questioning of the very notion of leadership. His contribution is a salutary reminder that all of our discussions about leadership are, in the final analysis, social and cultural constructs that reveal abiding historical imperatives and political exhortations. It is only in the relationship between critical scholarship and professional understanding that the debate about leadership has any validity or future.

Part One ends with John Novak's meditation on the relationship between the role of leader and the person. Whatever constructs of leadership are presented, there has to be an abiding awareness of the need for personal integrity as the essential precursor to professional integrity. Leadership development cannot be divorced from personal development and, in the final analysis, effective leaders are effective people.

– CHAPTER 1 –

Shifting conceptions of leadership: towards a redefinition of leadership for the twenty-first century

LINDA LAMBERT

As we advance into this new millennium, we are compelled to examine the meaning and the influence of the concept of leadership. Questions arise that challenge and give form to such meanings: 'Are all children learning?' 'Are adults in our organizations learning as well?' 'Do citizens of our societies have access to a satisfying quality of life?' 'Is there equitable access to the resources and opportunities of societies?' Our answers to these questions leave us wanting.

Further, are these potential answers a function of leadership? To determine new relationships between the quality of living and learning and leadership it will be necessary to define (or redefine) leadership in new ways. Old paradigms and ancient archetypes have led us down narrow paths – paths limited by the notion that leadership and leader are the same. By situating leadership in the role, position and skill set of an individual, access to the work of leading has been restricted to those in formal authority. And, by situating leadership in the goals and actions of an organization's mission, we may miss the larger value issues.

Fortunately, in these transitional years into the new millennium, especially since 1995, leadership conceptions have been shifting. These shifts are opening possibilities that allow us to entertain new ways of thinking that enable us to struggle more effectively with our initial questions. This chapter offers four categories of leadership conceptions drawn from recent scholarship in the field and advances a theory of leadership that captures the leading edge of new thought. 'The categories and the theory enable us to emerge ahead of our accomplishments' (Steinbeck, 1941).

To 'emerge ahead of our accomplishments' is a tantalizing idea. Such emergence requires that we envision and forecast directions that are not yet fully realized. No concept is more in need of intense revisioning than the concept of 'leadership'. Leadership is being pulled and stretched, unlayered and rediscovered by those who think and write in this field. It is about time.

Shifting conceptions of leadership: four emerging categories

Let us step back a century and consider that from 1900 to 1990 we found a somewhat consistent picture of the conceptions of leadership (Rost, 1991, p. 180):

> *Leadership is good management. … Leadership is great men and women with certain preferred traits influencing followers to do what the leaders wish in order to achieve group/organisational goals that reflect excellence defined as some kind of higher-level effectiveness.*

Rost referred to this composite definition as the 'industrial leadership paradigm', which is hierarchical, individualistic, reductionistic, linear and mechanical – ideas that are worlds away from the needs of today's schools and society. By 1995 it would have been difficult to find anyone writing in this vein. Leadership had entered a new venue (although there are charges that some leadership preparation programmes in the USA are still based on those outdated ideas). The conversation about leadership is now broader, deeper and with a wider range of possibilities.

Four categories of perspectives on the concept of leadership are emerging from scholarship and practice (Lambert *et al.*, 2002). First, a call for the abandonment of the word and idea of leadership altogether, in favour of another word and idea. Second, reframing leadership by changing its defined personal qualities within a larger, but constant definition. Third, puzzlement about the meaning of the term – puzzlement from thinkers who were until now more sure. Fourth, redefining – allowing leadership to take on new meanings and suppositions.

A call for the abandonment of the word and idea of leadership

In the winter of 1997, at a conference of the California Staff Development Council, Tom Sergiovanni asked if I would give up the word 'leadership'. At the time, I replied that I might if he would consider giving up the word 'followership'. Neither of us responded definitively to those challenges by abandoning our fondness for the concepts, but the request has lingered. Block (1996) did abandon leadership in favour of 'stewardship', which he says:

> *can be most simply defined as giving order to the dispersion of power. It requires us to systematically move choice and resources closer and closer to the bottom and edges of the organisation. Leadership, in contrast, gives order to the centralisation of power.*

Europeans, who seldom use the word 'leadership', shudder from ancient abuses of the industrial or dictatorial practice and coinage.

In his recent reflections on leadership, Bennis (2000) includes a part entitled 'The End of Leadership'. Bennis calls for an abandonment of the archaic baggage that has situated leadership in top-down, hierarchical models, sensing that this core metaphor may be so burdened with old meanings that it cannot be saved.

Reframing leadership by changing its defined qualities within a larger, but constant definition

Although Bennis calls for an end to leadership, he proceeds to reframe leadership by changing the defined qualities of the leader (2000, pp. 153–7):

- The New Leader understands and practises the power of appreciation. The New Leader is a connoisseur of talent, more curator than creator.
- The New Leader keeps reminding people of what is important.
- The New Leader generates and sustains trust.
- The New Leader and the Led are intimate allies.

Thus Bennis remains in the second category of responses to leadership. According to this way of thinking, leadership is something that leaders do with or to others (followers, the Led). Most writers continue to use leadership and leader as inter-changeable. 'The problem with the organization is leadership', an analyst might claim when referring to a specific person, the 'leader'. 'The absence of leadership (a person in that role) resulted in confusion and continuing conflict.' Leadership means the sets of skills or actions held by a person in a particular role or position. What continues to change, however, is the collaborative, engaging language being used to describe the actions of the leader. Values of human endeavour are more explicit; control and manipulation are minimized.

These definitions play out in persistent patterns of process that characterize what leaders do or what leadership is. Whether a writer is describing leadership or leader, definitions typically fall into three parts: (i) what the leader does, (ii) for or with whom the action is taken, and (iii) towards what end the actions are taken. A few additional illustrative definitions from the work of these authors will clarify this three-dimensional analysis:

- Glickman (1998): leaders engage others in the development of schools as democratic communities, thereby invoking broad-scale participation and learning.
- Heifetz (1995, p. 15): leaders mobilize people to tackle tough problems. Leadership is solving tough problems.
- Palmer (1998, p. 160): leaders 'lead from the same model we have been exploring for teaching itself, creating a space centred on the great thing called teaching and learning around which a community of truth can gather'.
- Sergiovanni (1999, 2000): leaders bring diverse people into a common cause by making the school a covenantal community. Sergiovanni also describes and uses the concept of constructivist leadership (Lambert et al., 1995, 1997, 1998, 2002) and Palmer's (1998) ideas of spirituality as congruent with his own writings on moral leadership.
- Kellerman (1999, p. 10): 'leadership is the effort of leaders – who may hold, but do not necessarily hold, formal positions of authority – to engage followers in the joint pursuit of mutually agreed-on goals. These goals represent significant, rather than merely incremental, change'.
- Avolio (1999, p. 34): transformational leadership involves the process whereby leaders develop followers into leaders; the leader has a development plan in her or his head for each follower.

- Stoll and Fink (1996, p. 109): invitational leadership is 'about communicating invitational messages to individuals and groups with whom leaders interact in order to build and act on a shared and evolving vision of enhanced educational experiences for students'.
- Gardner (1990): leadership is the process of persuasion or example by which an individual (or leadership team) induces a group (followers) to pursue objectives held by the leader or shared with his or her followers. While this definition is more than a decade old, Gardner's work has been so influential in the field as to continue to deserve retention.
- Wheatley (1999, p. 130): on effective leadership:

> the Leader's task is first to embody these principles – guiding visions, sincere values, organisational beliefs – and then to help the organisation become the standard it has declared for itself. This work of leaders cannot be reversed, or either step ignored. In organisations where leaders do not practice what they preach, there are terrible disabling consequences.

These writers adhere to leadership as something carried out by an individual, with or for others, towards a specific goal or outcome. 'Transformational leadership' is consistently referred to as the most progressive of these descriptions in that it aims towards the deep transformation or emancipation of those led.

Early in the 1990s Leithwood (1992) predicted that transformational leadership would subsume instructional leadership as the dominant image of school administration. Two years later, Poplin (1994) observed that instructional leadership encompasses hierarchies and top-down leadership, where the leader is supposed to know the best form of instruction and closely monitors teachers' and students' work. She argued that instructional leadership had outlived its usefulness. In truth, now in the early years of the new century, the accountability climate has floated instructional leadership to the top once again. Two encouraging observations can be made. There is more puzzlement over what is meant now by 'instructional leadership' and people are realizing that there are a myriad of instructional leadership tasks, not all of which may need to be performed by the headmaster or principal (Olson, 2000). These new insights reveal a convergence of more traditional leadership thinking (as described above) and transformational and constructivist leadership perspectives (US Department of Education proceedings, 2001).

Puzzlement about the meaning of leadership

Puzzlement about the concept of leadership is a promising state of affairs. It is a sign of a concept in transition when thinkers in their own field are less sure and more speculative about the notion of leadership than they were in the early 1990s. The puzzlement about instructional leadership described above signals a shifting conception that is overdue.

In 1992 Barth said that leaders make happen that in which they believe while working with all in a community of leaders. Later, in the conversation (2001), Barth noted that this sounds somewhat self-centered and misses the notion of 'what is in the collective best interest'. How about 'assisting/engaging the group to bring to life what is in its best interest? ... or assisting the group to make happen what it believes in?' I ask. 'Oh well', he proclaims, 'I'm not sure what leadership is.' Unsureness, of course, may not be an apt description for thinking in transition.

With each product of their prolific pens, writers such as Barth and Sergiovanni raise new issues and ideas about the concept. Unsureness can lead to abandoning the concept (or at least the word) altogether, or it can lead to a redefinition. New definitions are gathering force on the horizon.

Redefining the concept of leadership

Some writers are redefining the concept of leadership and separating it from the interlocking sameness of leader. Foster (1989) was a pioneer in challenging traditional thought when he described leadership as 'the reciprocal processes among leaders and followers working toward a common purpose'. Since 1995, there have been multiple shifts in understanding:

- Roberts (in Senge's work, *Schools that Learn*, 2000, pp. 404, 414–18) describes constructivist leadership and proceeds to define leadership as problem solving (with Heifetz), engaging, leading learning, and learner rather than authority-based.
- Conzemius and O'Neill (2001) integrate constructivist leadership and the concept of 'leadership capacity' (Lambert, 1998) to describe 'leadership as the capacity of the school for broad-based, skilful participation in the creation and fulfilment of a vision focused on student learning'.
- Ackerman, Donaldson, and Van Der Bogert (1996) view leadership as a process, a quest, that entails learning to think and act as a leader in response to the ever-changing challenges of learning, and dealing with growing children and the adults who care about them. While the authors write primarily about the principal's learning quest, the definition does not demand that it be attached to a specific person in a specific role.
- Capra, who in 1995 adhered to the 'great man' theory of leadership (personal conversation), later suggested that 'In self-organising systems, leadership is distributed, and responsibility becomes a capacity of the whole. Leadership, then, consists in continually facilitating the emergence of new structures, and incorporating the best of them into the organisation's design'(1997, pp. 8–9).
- Gardner (1995, p. 22; in Sergiovanni, 1999, p. 169): leadership is:

  a process that occurs within the minds of individuals who live in a culture – a process that entails the capacities to create stories, to understand and evaluate these stories, and to appreciate the struggle among stories. Ultimately, certain kinds of stories will typically become predominant – in particular, kinds of stories that provide an adequate and timely sense of identity for individuals who live within a community or institution.

- Spillane, Halverson and Diamond (2001): 'distributed leadership' holds that leadership cognition and activity are situated within an interactive web of actors (leaders and followers), artefacts and situations. The situation, or context, is not an external force but an integral part of the leadership dynamic. Leadership is 'stretched over' leaders, followers and activities within a reciprocal interdependency. School leadership, therefore, involves the identification, acquisition, allocation, coordination and use of the social, material and cultural resources necessary to establish the conditions for the possibility of teaching and learning.

Those who are redefining leadership situate it in the processes among us, rather than in the skills or disposition of a leader. As a concept separate from, yet integrated with, leader, leadership stands as a broader notion, a more encompassing idea. This breadth is evident when we consider the connections or processes among individual leaders that are embedded in the context – the culture of an organization. These processes include problem solving; broad-based, skilful participation (leadership capacity); task enactment; conversations; and stories. Such processes engender a wave of energy and purpose that engages and pulls others into the work of leadership.

The transition from disillusionment, or abandonment, of the idea of leadership to puzzlement and redefining brings us to the need for an encompassing theory of leadership. This theory must form a broad umbrella that distinguishes leader from leadership, and embeds it in a learning and purposeful community.

Towards a theory of constructivist leadership

The fourth category – 'redefining' – is best captured by the theory of 'constructivist leadership'. Constructivist leadership is the reciprocal processes that enable participants in an educational community to construct meanings that lead toward a shared purpose of schooling (Lambert *et al.*, 1995). Learning and leading are intertwined because these conceptions arise from our understandings of what it is to be human. To be human is to learn and to learn is to construct meaning and knowledge about the world.

At the beginning of this new century, we can declare with some certainty that all humans bring to the process of learning personal schemas that have been formed by prior experiences, beliefs, values, socio-cultural histories and perceptions. When new experiences are encountered and mediated by reflection, inquiry and social interaction, meaning and knowledge are constructed. Learning takes place, as does adult development. When actively engaged in reflective dialogue, adults become more complex in their thinking about the world, more respectful of diverse perspectives and more flexible and open toward new experiences. Personal and professional learning require an interactive professional culture if adults are to engage with one another in the processes of growth and development.

The concept of constructivist leadership is based on the same ideas that underlie constructivist learning: Adults, as well as children, learn through the processes of meaning and knowledge construction, inquiry, participation and reflection. Table 1.1 draws a parallel between our knowledge of good constructivist teaching and learning and a projection of those practices into the realm of leadership. As leaders, we are compelled to develop a learning environment for adults that draws from the theory or epistemology base for human learning. For instance, it is essential to consider the learner's views, challenge beliefs, construct meaning and knowledge through reflection and dialogue, consider the whole or gestalt, and engage learners in assessments that consider the complexities of the broader context (e.g. leading beyond the classroom). In a similar way, Table 1.2 draws parallels between teaching habits of mind (Costa and Kallick, 2000) and leading. 'Leadership', then, becomes the processes of purposeful learning from which actions are drawn.

Table 1.1 *A comparison of constructivist teaching and leading*

Constructivist teachers	Constructivist leaders
Seek and value students' points of view.	Seek and value teachers' points of view.
Structure lessons to challenge students' suppositions.	Structure the notion of leadership to challenge teachers' belief systems.
Recognize that students must attach relevance (meaning) to the curriculum.	Construct meaning through reflection and dialogue.
Structure lessons around big ideas, not small bits of information.	Structure the life of the school around the whole picture, not a singular event, or small piece of information.
Assess student learning in the context of daily classroom investigations, not as separate events.	Assess teacher learning in the context of the complexity of the learning organization, not as isolated events.

Source: created by Janice O'Neil, University of Calgary; based on the work of Brooks & Brooks and Linda Lambert.

Table 1.2 *Teaching and leading habits of mind*

	Teaching	Leading
Modelling	Modelling of what we want students to do.If we want students to be thoughtful, we need to demonstrate what thoughtfulness looks like.	Modelling of leadership behaviours. If we want others to be leaders, we need to demonstrate what leadership looks like.
Coaching	Helping students to think through what they are trying to do. The teacher raises questions rather than tells students what to do.	Helping others to think through what they are trying to do. Teachers raise questions with each other rather than tell others what to do.
Scaffolding	Providing the content bridges necessary for the task, raising the necessary questions and giving students the opportunity to explore and perform the task.	Providing the content bridges necessary for the task, raising the necessary questions and giving others, particularly new teachers, the opportunity to explore and perform the task.
Articulation	Explaining what the teacher is thinking about so thinking is visible to the student.	Explaining what the teacher is thinking about so thinking is visible to colleagues and parents.
Reflection	Being reflective and thoughtful about the work. Raising evaluation questions. What went well today? Why? If I did this again, how would I do it differently?	Being reflective and thoughtful about the work. Raising evaluation questions. What went well today? Why? If I did this again, how would I do it differently?
Exploration	Modelling risk-taking so students understand that uncertainty is involved in all new learning.	Modelling risk-taking so others understand that uncertainty is involved in all new learning.

Source: adapted from Costa and Kallick, 2000.

Such learning demands the capacity for reciprocity – to be able to move outside oneself, to differentiate one's perceptions from those of another, to practise empathy, to move out of the self and observe the responses and thoughts of another. Reciprocity involves the mutual and dynamic interaction and exchange of ideas and concerns; it requires a maturity that emerges from opportunities for meaning-making in sustainable communities over time. This theory suggests a deep faith that, when individuals learn together in community, then shared purpose and collective action emerge – shared purpose and action about what really matters. These learning processes that enable us to construct meaning occur within the context of relationships. The creation and expansion of our possibilities and capacities for reciprocity occur in communities rich in relationships.

The discussion about relationships, purpose and community is in its essence a spiritual one. By 'spiritual', says Palmer (1998: p. 11):

> *I mean the diverse ways we answer the heart's longing to be connected with the largeness of life – a longing that animates love and work, especially the work called teaching (p. 5) ... The connections made by good teachers are held not in their methods but in their hearts – meaning heart in the ancient sense, as the place where intellect and emotion and spirit and will converge in the human self.*

Hilliard (1991) asked us more than a decade ago if we had the will to educate all children. This will must be found in the meaningful conversations in schools. Connectedness found in the conversations we have with each other includes essential questions framing the 'largeness of life':

- How do we relate to each other?
- What contributions are we making to each other and to the larger society?
- How do we create community? How do we create caring communities?
- What is our shared purpose?
- What does it all mean?

Meaning-making requires 'going to ground' – getting in touch with our inner terrain and therefore our most profound successes, puzzlements, mistakes and avoidances. When we confront our failures to teach all children, a form of remorse and anguish is inevitable. Such anguish can be survived and acted upon only in supportive communities, otherwise denial is the expedient response. Many of our urban schools live in a state of denial created by the lack of an authentic community in which to translate the knowledge of failure with many children into what Etzioni (1999) refers to as 'civic repentance', By civic repentance he means our capacity to acknowledge mistakes (privately and collectively), learn from them, get back in touch with our core values and restructure our lives as professionals. This process, not to be mistaken for the lingering guilt that can result in illness, challenges us to create Palmer's 'community of truth', a place where we can come face-to-face with the realities of our lives, embrace those truths and learn from them. Such a community requires the 'epistemological reality that knowledge is embedded in discursive community, and knowledge claims (any claim to truth) should therefore be evaluated and, where appropriate, modified in the context of co-operative enquiries with community members' (Etzioni, 1998, p. 64).

We need to stop thinking of roles or people as fixed entities and instead view them as relationships and as patterns of relationships that involve one another. Constructivist leadership is defined as a concept transcending individuals, roles and behaviours. Therefore, anyone in the educational community – teachers, administrators, other staff, parents, students – can engage in leadership actions.

There are some major assumptions that underlie this view of leadership:

- leadership is the reciprocal learning processes that enable participants in community to construct meaning leading toward a shared purpose;
- leading is about learning;
- everyone has the potential, the right and responsibility to serve as a leader;
- leading is a shared endeavour;
- leadership requires the redistribution of power and authority.

Why are these assumptions central to our work? Because the overwhelming body of research tells us that they connect directly to student and adult learning. Indeed, the purpose of schooling is to engage children and adults within patterns of relationships in school communities that serve as centres for sustained growth. Moral educational communities come into existence as people learn to grow together. The purposes referenced in the definition of constructivist leadership involve a commitment to the growth of children and adults as well as a commitment to communities and societies that support each other. The function of leadership must be to engage people in the processes that create the conditions for learning and form common ground about teaching and learning. Schooling must be organized and led in such a way that these learning processes provide direction and momentum to human and educational development.

Acts of constructivist leadership

An 'act of leadership', as distinguished from role leadership, is the performance of actions (behaviours plus intention) that enable participants in a community to evoke potential within a trusting environment; to inquire into practice, thereby reconstructing old assumptions; to focus on the construction of meaning; or to frame actions based on new behaviours and purposeful intention (Lambert *et al.*, 1995). Everyone in the school community can perform an act of leadership. Leadership is an inclusive field of processes in which leaders do their work.

Those who perform acts of constructivist leadership need:

- a sense of purpose and ethics, because honesty and trust are fundamental to relationships;
- facilitation skills, because framing, deepening and moving the conversations about teaching and learning are fundamental to constructing meaning;
- an understanding of constructivist learning for all humans;
- a deep understanding of change and transitions, because change is not what we thought it was;
- an understanding of context so that communities of memories can be continually drawn upon and enriched;
- an intention to redistribute power and authority, for without such intention and action none of us can lead;
- a personal identity that allows for courage and risk, low ego needs and a sense of possibilities (Lambert *et al.*, 2002).

Full participation leads to acts of leadership; being fully engaged in meaning-making activates one's drive toward purpose and community. One cannot help but lead; one is compelled to do so by the self-directed drive toward self-renewal and interdependency. Responsibility toward self and others surfaces as an essential developmental process. Freire's ideas (1973, p. 44) have long been persuasive: 'Humankind emerge from their submersion and acquire the ability to intervene in reality as it is unveiled'. They also need to construct and to reintervene in their realities: the next essential question is asked, ideas and traditions are challenged, people volunteer to lead, groups form, curiosity is aroused, and verbal and nonverbal interactions change. It is the participation processes that create the meaning and the understandings (the reality) to which people then commit themselves. Without these participatory opportunities, commitment is not possible – only compliance and disengagement.

This vision of the potential of educational leaders may not only seem ideal; it is ideal – and it is possible. Constructivist leadership enables human growth that was previously reserved for the few. Others were followers, relegated to second-class citizenship and second-class growth. In our traditional systems, growth was a limited resource; in ecological communities, interdependence and reciprocity require equal partners.

Constructivist leadership captures the emerging meaning expressed by the fourth category of leadership descriptions, 'redefining'. The stage is set to entertain other redefinitions as well.

Shifting conceptions of leadership

Based on what we now know about leadership at this point in our history, what can we safely say?

- The concept of leadership is in transition, yet there is a convergence of meaning around the characteristics of effective leaders and the cultural embeddedness of the notion.
- Leadership that is culturally embedded in a school's or organization's community is directly related to student learning, high productivity and high leadership capacity.
- Leadership is spiritually purposeful – it must be value-driven in order to accomplish purposeful learning among participants.
- The process of leadership must provoke us to new actions – to challenge old assumptions about who can learn, how, and why. Such provocation is initiated through inquiry, reflection, dialogue and a focus on results.
- Leadership is an open agenda, inviting thoughtful responses and redefinitions. The work is not done; the book is not closed.

These understandings are grounded in relationships, community, learning and purpose. Behaviours that emerge from such understandings can guide our pursuit of sustainable improvements in schools and organizations. It is essential that we redefine leadership so as to invest faith in the belief that leaders emerge, that leaders grow out of our purposeful work together. This process of redefinition is an open one. Since the mid-1990s, leadership has been bandied about in energetic and new ways; a ball in the air, it has been discarded, tossed around, repainted, reshaped. It has evoked lively discussion and stimulated many to wander into uncharted territory. Leadership is in transition. Among the trailblazers of this new path has been constructivist leadership, boldly separating itself from the 'one leader' and embedding itself within the patterns of learning relationships in schools and organizations.

REFERENCES

Ackerman, R.H., Donaldson Jr., G.A. and Van der Bogert, R. (1996) *Making Sense as a School Leader*, San Francisco: Jossey-Bass.

Aviolio, B.J. (1999) *Full Leadership Development*, Thousand Oaks, CA: Sage.

Barth, R. (1992) *Improving Schools from Within*, San Francisco: Jossey-Bass.

Bennis, W. (2000) *Managing the Dream: Reflections on Leadership and Change*, Cambridge, MA: Perseus Publishing.

Block, P. (1996) *Stewardship*, San Francisco: Berrett-Koehler.

Brooks, J.G. and Brooks, M.G. (1993) *In Search of Understanding: The Case for the Constructivist Classroom*, Alexandria, VA: Association of Supervision and Curriculm Development.

Capra, F. (1997) *Creativity and Leadership in Learning Communities. A Lecture*, Mill Valley School District, CA.

Conzemius, A. and O'Neill, J. (2001) *Building Shared Responsibility for Student Learning*, Alexandria, VA: Association for Supervision and Curriculum Development.

Costa, A. and Kallick, B. (eds) (2000) *Habits of Mind*, Alexandria, VA: Association for Supervision and Curriculum Development.

Etzioni, A. (ed.) (1998) *The Essential Communitarian Reader*, New York: Rowman and Littlefield Publishers.

Etzioni, A. (ed.) (1999) *Civic Repentance*, New York: Rowman and Littlefield Publishers.

Foster, W.F. (1989) 'Towards a critical practice of leadership' in Smyth, J. (ed.) *Critical Perspective on Educational Leadership*, London: Falmer Press.

Freire, P. (1973) *Education for Critical Consciousness*, New York: Continuum.

Gardner, H. (1995) *Leading Minds: An Anatomy of Leadership*, New York: Basic Books.

Gardner, J.W. (1990) *On Leadership*, New York: Free Press.

Glickman, C. (1998) *Revolutionising America's Schools*, San Francisco: Jossey-Bass.

Heifetz, R.A. (1995) *Leadership without Easy Answers, Cambridge*, MA: The Belknap Press of Harvard University Press.

Hilliard, A. (1991) 'Do we have the will to educate all children?' *Educational Leadership*, 51, 31–36.

Kellerman, B. (1999) *Reinventing Leadership: Making the Connection between Politics and Business*, Albany, NY: State University of New York Press.

Lambert, L. (1997) 'Constructivist Leadership Defined' in Wildman, L. (ed.) (1997) *School Administration The New Knowledge Base. The Fifth Yearbook of the National Council of Professors of Educational Administration*, Lancaster, PA: Techomic Publishing.

Lambert, L. (1998) *Building Leadership Capacity in Schools*, Alexandria, VA: Association of Supervision and Curriculm Development.

Lambert, L., Walker, D., Zimmerman, D., Cooper, J., Lambert, M., Gardner, M., Slack, P. J. (1995) *The Constructivist Leader*, New York: Teachers' College Press.

Lambert, L., Walker, D., Zimmerman, D., Cooper, J., Lambert, M., Gardner, M., Szabo, M. (2002) *The Constructivist Leader* (2nd edition) New York: Teachers' College Press.

Leithwood, K.A. (1992) 'The move toward transformational Leadership', *Educational Leadership*, 49(5), 8–12.

Olson, L. (2000) 'Principals try new styles as instructional leaders', *Education Week on the Web* (1 November).

Palmer, P. (1998) *The Courage to Teach*, San Francisco: Jossey-Bass.

Poplin, M. (1994) The restructuring movement and voices from the inside: compatibilities and incompatabilities. Seminar conducted at the meeting of the Association of California School Administrators, Palm Springs.

Rost, J.C. (1991) *Leadership for the Twenty First Century*, New York: Praeger.

Senge, P., Cambron-McCabe, N., Dutton, J., Kleiner, A. (2000) *Schools That Learn*, New York: Currency Press.

Sergiovanni, T. (2000) *The Lifeworld of Leadership*, San Francisco: Jossey-Bass.

Spillane, J.P., Halverson, R. and Diamond, J.B. (2001) 'Investigating school leadership practice: a distributed perspective', *Educational Researcher*, AERA.

Steinbeck, J. (1941) *Sea of Cortez, The Log from the Sea of Cortez*, New York: Viking Press.

Stoll, L. and Fink, D. (1996) *Changing our Schools, Linking School Effectiveness and School Improvement*, Buckingham: Open University Press.

U.S. Department of Education (17 January, 2001) Conversation on School Leadership, Washington, D.C. Proceedings.

Wheatley, M.J. (1999) *Leadership and the New Science*, San Francisco: Berrett-Koehler.

CHAPTER 2

A cognitive approach
to leadership

....

THOMAS SERGIOVANNI

Everyone wants a school management and leadership that is based on practices driven by valid theories. But validity depends on the cogency and relevance of these theories and practices. Cogency and relevance are the basic standards for determining what is true and what should be done as a result.

In this chapter I explore the cogency and relevance question as it applies to our understanding of schools as organizations and to the sources of authority we use for the practice of school leadership in these organizations. I argue that present conceptions of organization and of leadership, when applied to schools, are neither cogent nor relevant and thus may be invalid. A valid practice requires that we change our understanding of schools from formal organization to social organization[1] and change our emphasis from a leadership based on bureaucratic and personal authority to one based on moral authority. These changes in understanding promise to make leadership in schools more cogent and relevant. To this end I propose a cognitive approach to leadership based on ideas, values and purposes.

The four types of error

Cogency can be misplaced or misjudged. Misjudged cogency, the best known of these distinctions, refers to errors in practical judgements which result when standards or statistical limits are set too high (commonly known in scientific research as a Type I error) or are set too low (a Type II error). Though Types I and II errors are rarer than other types in schools, they are inevitable in the decisions we make for some students when all are treated the same. Avoiding this problem, for example, may require acceptance of the principle that standards and standardization are not the same thing. Acceptance allows for the setting of few rigorous uniform standards in some areas balanced by many different rigorous standards in other areas, thus creating an approach that would be more responsive to student interests and to culturally defined needs.

Misplaced cogency, too often neglected in our scientific tradition, refers not to errors of measurement or method but to the adequacy of problems addressed. Addressing the wrong problems, regardless of how careful and thorough the method, is referred to as a Type III error (Mitroff, 1974). A Type III error is made, for example, when subject-matter goals are chosen and assessed exclusively by the use of standardized tests because these goals are suited to this kind of testing.[2] Other, deeper and more rigorous, learning goals are forsaken because of the assessment difficulties they present. Portfolios, performance exhibitions linked to standards, and peer school quality reviews are rejected because they are more complex, even though if used they would allow for learning goals to be deeper and richer. John Tukey's admonition is important in avoiding the Type III error: 'Far better an approximate answer to the right question, which is often vague, than an exact answer to the wrong question, which can always be made precise' (quoted in Rose, 1977, p. 23).

Misplaced relevance refers to the development and use of cogent knowledge that is relevant to one type of problem but not to another. When this happens we commit the Type IV error (Dunn, 1980, p. 39). Using cogent knowledge about the distribution of resources borrowed from the corporate world in a family setting is an example. Within the corporate sector resources are usually distributed based on merit, thus providing incentives for people to work harder. The best producers get more resources than do their less productive neighbours. Promotion to head teller at the bank results from evaluations of performance and demeanour with the highest scoring person getting the job. But in the typical family resources are based on need. Within a limited budget, new shoes go to the child with the greatest need regardless of his or her performance in fulfilling household chores or his or her grades in school. Should the family decide to adopt a corporate strategy, a Type IV error would be made and eyebrows would be raised. No matter how cogent the knowledge base underlying corporate resource distribution patterns, their relevance for use in the family is questionable, as would be the case for the inverse. To the extent that schools should be more like families than corporations, school leadership is equally vulnerable to the Type IV error. The four types of error are summarized in Table 2.1. In today's world of school leadership it is Type III and Type IV errors that are of greatest concern, with the focus of this chapter being on Type IV.

Table 2.1 *Types of errors*

Type I	Misjudged cogency: an error in practical judgement that results when standards and/or statistical limits are set too high.
Type II	Misjudged cogency: an error in practical judgement that results when standards and/or statistical limits are set too low.
Type III	Misplaced cogency: an error in practical judgement that results when the wrong problem is addressed, regardless of cogency of method.
Type IV	Misplaced relevance: an error in practical judgements that results when cogent knowledge (knowledge that is relevant for one kind of problem but not for another) is used in the other problem.

School leadership and the Type IV error

Consider the following questions:

- Should schools be understood as formal organizations or communities?
- Should the sources of authority for school leadership be embedded in bureaucratic theories and in the leader's personality and interpersonal skill? Or should the sources of authority for school leadership be moral, embedded in ideas, conceptions of the common good, shared values and commitments, and the norms systems that evolve as a result?

The questions and their answers are connected. If schools are going to be considered as formal organizations, then the sources of authority for leadership should be embedded primarily in bureaucratic procedures and rules and/or in the leader's personality and interpersonal skill. But if schools are going to be considered as communities, then the sources of authority are likely to be more moral, being embedded in ideas, values, shared frameworks and conceptions of the common good. This idea-based leadership is decidedly cognitive in its orientation and effects.[3] The Type IV error occurs when schools should be considered as communities, but the leadership that is used in them has its roots in bureaucracy and personality. This is a common situation in schools across the globe. Avoiding this type of error will require that idea-based leadership be placed at the centre of school theory and practice, with bureaucratic leadership and personally based leadership moved to the periphery.

Ideas at the heart of community

The need for cognitive leadership in schools can be found in the ways that communities differ from formal organizations (Sergiovanni, 2001). Community has many meanings. But at root is the Latin *communis* and the Latin *communitas*. Both provide the themes for defining authentic community. *Communis* means common and *communitas* means fellowship. As Carey and Frohnen (1998, pp. 1–2) explain:

> A true community, one that lives up to its name, is one in which members share something in common – something important enough to give rise to fellowship or friendship and to sustain it. There may be many kinds of communities with varying ends or goals. But each must form around characteristics, experiences, practices, and beliefs that are important enough to bind the members to one another, such that they are willing to sacrifice for one another as 'fellows' or sharers of a common fate.

When individuals (students, teachers, parents) in schools that are understood as communities are bound together by shared ideas, values, beliefs and frameworks, then bonds of fellowship emerge that provide a moral climate that empowers the membership as a whole. For faculties this fellowship has two dimensions: a sense of collegiality that resembles a community of practice and an Aristotelian view of leadership that involves a moral commitment to care for and nurture one's colleagues. Thus, communities embody civic virtue – the willingness of individuals to sacrifice their self-interests on behalf of the common good. And this virtue is the reason why communities can be so powerful in uniting parents, teachers and students in common purpose. The research is clear that shared commitment to a common purpose provides a focus that contributes to school effectiveness (see, for example, Bryk and Driscoll, 1988; Hill, Foster and Gendler, 1990; Hill and Celio, 1998; Sergiovanni,1994, 2000).

In sum, communities share many common characteristics. They spring from common understandings that provide members with a sense of identity, belonging and involvement that results in the creation of a tightly held web of meaningful relationships with moral overtones. Further, communities can be thought of as having 'centres' that are repositories of shared values and other ideas that give direction, order and meaning to community life. These centres are the cultural heart of any community. Shils (1961, p. 1999) explains:

> The center ... is a phenomenon of the realm of values and beliefs ... which govern the society... In a sense, society has an official 'religion'... The center is also a phenomenon of the realm of action. It is a structure of activities, of roles and persons, within the network of institutions. It is in these that the values and beliefs which are central are embodied and propounded.

The role of ideas in developing a caring and effective community life within schools is seminal. Once accepted, ideas become reflected in norms. And norms provide the framework for the guidelines and directions that members are obliged to embrace as ideas become actions.

The sources of authority

Few issues are more important to effective leading than deciding what will be the reasons why others are being asked to follow. The right reasons will create a powerful leadership force that brings people together and points them in a common direction. The wrong reasons result in a leadership that does not count much and may even be harmful.

Let us examine our options by asking some questions.[4] Who should we follow? What should we follow? Why should we follow? In many schools *who* means the leader. *What* is the leader's vision or the expectations the leader has. The *why* question is a bit more difficult to answer. If an explanation were forced it might be something like this: 'Follow me because of my position in the school and the system of roles, expectations, and rules that I represent'. This is the simplest way to get things done in schools: rely on bureaucratic authority. An alternative response might be: 'Follow me because I will make it worthwhile if you do'. This is the most popular way to get things done in schools: rely on personal authority. Personal authority is expressed in the form of the leader's charisma, motivational abilities and human relations skills.

Few readers would advocate a leadership based primarily on bureaucratic authority, but leadership based on personal authority remains popular. Leaders like to think of themselves as being good motivators who know how to handle people and know how to get people to do the things that they should by being persuasive in personality or in style. But following a leader because of her or his personality or interpersonal skills is really a poor reason. Teachers, for example, ought to follow not because leaders are clever manipulators who know which motivational buttons to press, or are pleasant persons who are fun to be with, but because leaders stand for something, are persons of substance and base their practice on ideas.

When purposes are in place and shared values are cultivated, an idea framework evolves in the school that encourages teachers to respond by feeling a sense of obligation to embody these ideas in their behaviour. There is, in a sense, a moral authority that emerges, which compels them to participate in shared commitments and to be connected to others with whom these commitments are shared. The sources of authority and their relationship to leadership are depicted in Table 2.2.

Table 2.2 *Sources of authority for leadership*

Source	Assumptions	Leadership strategy
Bureaucratic authority in the form of:		
Hierarchy	Teachers are subordinates in a hierarchically arranged system.	'Expect and inspect' is the overarching rule.
Rules and regulations		
Mandates	Supervisors are trustworthy, but you cannot trust subordinates very much.	Rely on predetermined standards to which teachers must measure up or face sanctions.
Role expectations		
	Goals and interests of teachers and their supervisors are not the same; thus supervisors must be watchful.	Directly supervise and closely monitor the work of teachers to ensure compliance.
	Hierarchy equals expertise; thus supervisors know more than do teachers.	Figure out how to motivate them and get them to change.
	External accountability works best.	
Personal authority in the form of:		
Motivation technology	The goals and interests of teachers and supervisors are not the same but can be bartered so that each gets what they want.	Develop a school climate characterized by congeniality among teachers and between teachers and supervisors.
Interpersonal skills		
Human relations leadership practice	Teachers have needs, and if those needs are met at work, the work gets done as required in exchange.	'What gets rewarded gets done'; therefore expect and reward.
	Congenial relationships and harmonious interpersonal climates make teachers content, easier to work with and more apt to cooperate.	

Table 2.2 *Continued*

Source	Assumptions	Leadership Strategy
Moral authority in the form of:		
Felt obligations and duties derived from widely shared community values, ideas and ideals.	Schools are professional learning communities.	Identify and make explicit the values and beliefs that define the centre of the school as community.
	Communities are defined by their centre of shared values, beliefs and commitments.	
		Translate the above into informal norms that govern behaviour.
	In communities, what is considered right and good is as important as what works and what is effective.	Promote collegiality as internally felt and morally driven interdependence.
	People are motivated as much by emotion and beliefs as by self-interest.	Rely on the ability of community members to respond to duties and obligations.
	Collegiality is a professional virtue.	Rely on the community's informal norm system to enforce professional and community values.

Some principles for implementing idea-based leadership

This section discusses some principles that school leaders may find helpful as they seek to understand the importance of idea-based leadership and to apply this leadership in their practice.

The task of leadership is to provide purposing to the school

In his classic book *The Functions of the Executive*, Barnard (1938, p. 87) wrote: 'The inculcation of belief in the real existence of a common purpose is an essential executive function'. Inculcation of belief comes from the embodiment of purpose as school leaders act and behave.

Vaill (1984, p. 91) coined the word 'purposing', defined as 'that continuous stream of actions by an organization's formal leadership which has the effect of inducing clarity, consensus, and commitment regarding the organization's basic purposes'. During his research of organizations that, given their resources and previous history, were performing well beyond expectations, Vaill found that purposing was the common denominator. He explains that these high performing systems:

> are clear on their broad purposes and on near-term objectives for fulfilling these purposes. They know why they exist and what they are trying to do. Members have pictures in their heads which are strikingly congruent. Commitment to these purposes is never perfunctory, although it is expressed laconically. Motivation as usually conceived is always high. (ibid., p. 86)

When purposing is present in a school, shared expectations are understood; a value framework exists that enables the seemingly routine activities that characterize daily life in schools to take on special meaning and significance; norms are established that guide our behaviour; and an ideology emerges that helps the school to differentiate itself from other schools. As a result the school is transformed from a 'secular' workplace to a 'sacred' enterprise. Purposing is an essential ingredient in successful schools and an important characteristic of idea-based leadership.

Idea-based leadership can help to create the motivating conditions

The research on motivation to work (Herzberg, 1966; Hackman and Oldham, 1980; Peters and Waterman, 1982) reveals that highly motivating conditions are present when teachers and others:

- find their work lives to be meaningful, purposeful, sensible and significant, and when they view the work itself as being worthwhile and important;
- have reasonable control over their work activities and affairs and are able to exert reasonable influence over work events and circumstances;
- experience personal responsibility for the work and are personally accountable for outcomes.

Meaningfulness is an important outcome of idea-based leadership. Further, meaningfulness is also a key to wanting more control over one's work and being willing to take personal responsibility for what one does. Unless work experiences are sensible and meaningful there is no incentive to seek control or personal responsibility, so compromising teacher motivation and placing their commitment, loyalty to the school and job satisfaction at risk.

Seek to serve rather than be served

Traditionally leadership is thought of as an interaction/influence system within which leaders try to get followers to follow. Good followers are those who serve the leader's interests. When idea-based leadership is used, leadership itself is turned upside down. Leaders seek to serve rather than be served and ask other members of the school community to do the same. Thus, instead of 'follow me' because of my position or 'follow me' because of my personality, the usual stance for everyone is 'don't follow me, follow the ideas we share'. Leaders become head followers who join with others in a shared commitment to the school's idea framework.

Pay attention to the grammar of leadership

One responsibility that leaders have is to communicate the purposes, norms and other cultural artefacts that comprise a school's idea structure. How do I get the message out? This goal is often complicated by leadership being expressed in different ways – phonetically and semantically. The phonetics of leadership is what the leader does and the semantics of leadership is what this action means to others. To complicate matters, different actions of the leader have different meanings in different situations and for different people. For this reason the leader's eye must always be focused on the semantics. What meanings are being communicated by my actions? Focusing on the semantics helps in understanding that very often it is the little things that count. Simple routines and humble initiatives properly expressed can communicate important messages and high ideals. Even the daily routines of school life can be expressions of leadership. Spending lots of time in classes communicates that teaching and learning is important. Involving teachers in important decisions about their work communicates that they are valued. Emphasizing cleanliness in the school instils pride in the culture and lets students know that they too are valued. When actions communicate important messages and model important dimensions of a school's idea structure, leaders are expressing symbolic aspects of leadership. Key to symbolic aspects is focusing the attention of others on matters of importance to the school – on understanding the grammar of leadership.

Humility is a virtue in today's complex world of leadership

Leadership in today's schools requires a healthy dose of reflection on one's practice that comes from more humble, slow, low-keyed incremental approaches.[5] Humble leaders are not afraid of trial and error, providing it is focused rather than random (Etzioni, 1989). They know when to start searching for an effective solution. They check the feedback they are getting and modify their courses of action accordingly. They realize that early decisions made at one time change all the relevant conditions so that subsequent decisions based on the same assumptions no longer apply. They avoid committing to a course of action too early, preferring instead to commit to revising once underway. They are sceptical of strategic planning frameworks that are too grand in scope, too specific in content and too committed to a 'one best way'.

Two other features of humble decision making that can serve leaders well are reasoned procrastination and careful decision staggering (Etzioni, 1989). Both features challenge the image of the strong decisive leader who stays the course, valuing consistency above all. And, both features support the folk wisdom implicit in the truism 'Never make a decision on Friday'. Procrastination allows the collection of better information as new options emerge. And procrastination allows some problems to take care of themselves. Decision staggering, by making decisions in small increments rather than going all out, allows for monitoring progress and making adjustments as the process of decision making moves along. Leaders benefit when they widen the circle of decision making by including others. A wider circle, they reason, allows for more ideas to come to bear and for building commitment as decisions are made, rather than struggling to get people committed afterwards.

Conclusion

In this chapter I have argued that today's leadership theories are too rational and scripted to fit the messy world of schooling. Though these theories sound great they too often do not work well in the real world of practice and too frequently result in the making of Type III and Type IV errors. Dealing with the complexities of this world requires that teachers and administrators practise a leadership based less and less on personalities, less and less on their positions, less and less on mandates, and more and more on ideas. Leadership that counts is far more cognitive in orientation than it is personality based or rules based. Cognitive leadership works because it has more to do with purposes, values and frameworks that obligate us morally than it does with needs that touch us psychologically or with bureaucratic things that push us organizationally.

NOTES

1 I have in mind the school being thought of as a community, which is one kind of social organization. Examples of formal organizations are corporations, armies, unions and hospitals. Examples of social organizations are families, friendship cliques and communities. See for example Blau and Scott (1962).
2 A more familiar example is the person who searches under the streetlight for his car keys even though he lost them several metres away.
3 Cognitive in leadership means to perceive, to come to know, the process of knowing, to be aware of, to understand, to rely on sensibility, reason and wisdom. At root is ideas (values, understandings, frameworks, purposes). Idea-based leadership is decidedly cognitive. When this base of ideas is shared in community, members feel morally obliged to embody ideas in their practice.
4 This discussion follows Sergiovanni (1992a), pp. 203–14; Sergiovanni (1992b), pp. 30–9; and Sergiovanni (2001), pp. 28–34.
5 This discussion of humble leadership follows Sergiovanni (2001), pp. 12–13; adapted from Sergiovanni (1992), pp. 203–14.

REFERENCES

Barnard, C. (1938) *The Functions of the Executive*, Cambridge, MA: Harvard University Press.

Blau, P.M. and Scott, W.R. (1962) *Formal Organizations*, San Francisco: Chandler Publishing Co.

Bryk, A.S. and Driscoll, M.E. (1988) *The School as Community: Theoretical Foundations, Contextual Influences and Consequences for Teachers and Students*, Madison, WI: National Center for Effective Secondary Schools.

Carey, G.W. and Frohnen, B. (eds) (1998) *Community and Tradition: Conservative Perspectives on the American Experience*, Lanham, MD: Rowman & Littlefield Publishers.

Dunn, W.N. (1980) 'Reforms as arguments', International Conference on Political Realization of Social Science Knowledge and Research: Toward Two Scenarios, Institute for Advanced Studies, Vienna, Austria, 18–20 June.

Etzioni, A. (1989) 'Humble decision making', *Harvard Business Review*, 74 (4), pp. 122–6.

Hackman, J.R. and Oldham, G.R. (1980) *Work Redesign*, Reading, MA: Addison-Wesley.

Herzberg, F. (1966) *Work and the Nature of Man*, New York: World Publishing.

Hill, P.T. and Celio, M.B. (1998) *Fixing Urban Schools*, Washington, DC: Brookings Institution Press.

Hill, P.T., Foster, G.E., and Gendler, T. (1990) *High Schools with Character*, Santa Monica, CA: RAND Corporation.

Mitroff, I.I. (1974) *The Subjective Side of Science*, New York: Elsevier.

Peters, T.J. and Waterman, Jr., R.H. (1982) *In Search of Excellence*, New York: Harper & Row.

Rose, R. (1977) 'Disciplined research and undisciplined problems' in Weiss C.H. (ed.) *Using Social Research in Public Policy Making*, Lexington, MA: T.C. Heath.

Sergiovanni, T.J. (1992a) 'Moral authority and the regeneration of supervision' in Glickman, C. (ed.) *Supervision in Transition, The 1992 Yearbook of the ASCD*, Alexandria, VA: Association for Supervision and Curriculum Development.

Sergiovanni, T.J. (1992b) *Moral Leadership*, San Francisco: Jossey-Bass.

Sergiovanni, T.J. (1994) *Building Community in Schools*, San Francisco: Jossey-Bass.

Sergiovanni, T.J. (2000) *The Lifeworld of Leadership: Creating Culture, Community, and Personal Meaning in Our Schools*, San Francisco: Jossey-Bass.

Sergiovanni, T.J. (2001) *Leadership: What's in it for Schools?* London: Routledge/Falmer Press.

Shils, E.A. (1961). 'Centre and periphery' in *The Logic of Personal Knowledge: Essays Presented to Michael Polanyi*, London: Routledge and Kegan Paul.

Vaill, P. (1984) 'The purposing of high-performance systems' in Sergiovanni, T.J. and Corbally, J.E. (eds) *Leadership and Organizational Culture*, Urbana: University of Illinois Press.

CHAPTER 3

Successful leadership for especially challenging schools

KENNETH LEITHWOOD AND ROSANNE STEINBACH

No one close to schools thinks that providing them with leadership is an easy business. The work of those in formal leadership roles, heads for example, is hectic and fast-paced, demanding, by some estimates, as many as 150 decisions in the course of a typical day. This is a 10–12-hour non-stop sprint filled with brief encounters ranging in nature from trivial to occasionally life-threatening. But some schools are clearly more challenging than others and our purpose in this chapter is to clarify the nature of successful leadership in such schools. Much of the available evidence relevant to this purpose has been collected with heads or deputy heads in mind. Nevertheless, we do not limit ourselves to the leadership of a single person or role in this discussion. We have chosen, instead, to highlight classroom and school policies and practices associated with successful leadership from any source.

Our framework for thinking through this issue is summarized in Figure 3.1. As the figure indicates, there are two quite different trajectories that account for how much pupils benefit from their school experiences: a 'typical' and a 'preferred' trajectory. The starting point for both is the same – a set of potentially intransigent antecedents giving rise to our meaning of 'especially challenging schools'. Typically, these antecedents have a very large and direct impact on pupil outcomes, an impact that far outweighs the total effects of everything that schools do, hence the direct connection in the typical trajectory of Figure 3.1 between antecedent conditions and pupil outcomes.

We now know, however, that school leadership plays an unprecedented role in determining which of the two trajectories a school faced with these antecedents will follow (Gezi, 1990; Hatton, 2001; Scheurich, 1998). 'Typical' leadership does little to mitigate their corrosive effects on pupil outcomes; it also tolerates school conditions that neither add value to pupil learning, overall, nor address the inequities accounting for large gaps in the learning of different groups of students. This leadership is, in Englert's (1993) terms, either inactive or, at best, reactive in its relationship with the antecedents in Figure 3.1.

On the other hand, successful school leadership reduces the depressing effects of some of those antecedents dramatically, by acting both directly and indirectly to change them; this accounts for the nature of the relationships depicted in the preferred trajectory of Figure 3.1 between antecedents and both leadership and school conditions. Successful leadership also recasts some antecedents as levers for learn-

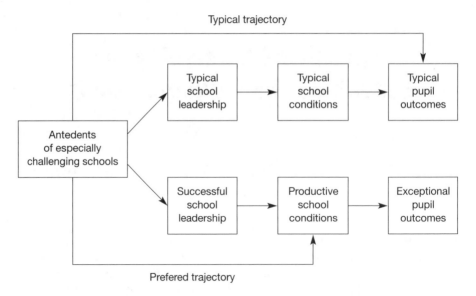

Figure 3.1 Processes accounting for student outcomes: typical and preferred trajectories

ing, and creates a productive set of school conditions in which virtually all students are able to learn in spite of some of these antecedents. With especially challenging urban schools in mind, Englert (1993, p. 2) claims that successful 'interactive' principal leaders:

> understand the urban context in order to create productive interchanges that will tap environmental resources of potential benefit to the school, insulate to some extent the school against unwanted forces, provide services and supports that can help compensate for unalterable negative influences that place students and the school at the risk of failure, and generally manipulate those alterable variables at the school's disposal.

Especially challenging schools

Family educational cultures

What do we mean by 'especially challenging schools'? Burned out or poorly prepared teachers, a history of underachievement, poor facilities, inadequate teaching resources, an uninvolved community – these all quickly come to mind (Portin, 2000; Englert, 1993). But many of the features typically associated with challenging schools can be traced to the nature of the family and student populations that they serve. Beginning with the now-famous evidence reported by James Coleman and his colleagues (1966), study after study has suggested that the socio-economic status (SES) of families explains more than half of the variation in student achievement (e.g. Rutter *et al.*, 1979). SES is highly related to other student-related effects such as violence, dropping out of school, entry to post-secondary education and levels of both adult employment and income (Dill and Haberman, 1995; Englert, 1993).

Schools serving low SES families often find themselves in an 'iron circle' that begins with the family's impoverished economic conditions. These conditions may be a consequence, for example, of unemployment, cultural, racial and/or linguistic factors, recent immigration, high mobility, family breakups and the like (Gezi, 1990: Dillard, 1995). Impoverished economic conditions decrease the chances of families struggling to survive in communities of high-density housing, with their members suffering from malnutrition, other health problems (Englert, 1993) and substance abuse (Portin, 2000). Low SES families are more likely to have low expectations for their children's performance at school.

A family's SES, however, only begins to capture what it is that defines our meaning of especially challenging schools. Some low SES families have children who do very well at school indeed, so there must be more to the explanation. In fact, SES is a relatively crude proxy for a set of family conditions and interactions considerably more powerful than SES in accounting for student learning (Lee, Bryk and Smith, 1993). Taken together, these conditions and interactions constitute what we will refer to as 'family educational culture'. These conditions and interactions vary widely across families, sometimes without much relation to family income or other social variables, although the relationship between SES and family educational cultures is both positive and significant.

At the core of family educational cultures are the assumptions, norms and beliefs held by the family about intellectual work in general and school work in particular. The behaviours and conditions resulting from these assumptions are demonstrably related to school success by a substantial body of evidence (Bloom, 1985; Finn, 1989; Rumberger, 1987; Scott-Jones, 1984). On the basis of such evidence, Walberg (1984) concluded that the basic dimensions of family educational cultures are family work habits, academic guidance and support provided to children, and stimulation to think about issues in the larger environment. Other dimensions resulting from Walberg's analysis include academic and occupational aspirations and expectations of parents or guardians for their children, the provision of adequate health and nutritional conditions, and physical settings in the home conducive to academic work.

Social capital

Our meaning of especially challenging schools, then, includes this understanding of family educational culture and the powerful role it plays in the opportunity that students have to take advantage of their school experiences. Schools serving large proportions of families with unhealthy or weak family educational cultures are especially challenging. But this is not the whole story; it does not identify the mechanisms that join particular types of family educational cultures with the ability of students to benefit from their school experiences. The primary mechanism, we argue, is 'social capital'. Variation in the strength of family educational cultures matters for pupils' success at school because it exerts a powerful influence on their acquisition of, and access to, social capital.

Our understanding of social capital is informed by treatments of the concept found, for example, in Coleman (1987, 1989) and more recently in Driscoll and Kerchner (1999); it is the 'assets' accrued by a person by virtue of his/her relationship with other persons and networks of persons. Depending fundamentally on the existence of high levels of trust, Driscoll and Kerchner suggest that these assets may take a number of forms, three of which seem quite relevant to this discussion: reciprocal obligations and expectations of one another held by members of a social group (for example the obligation a child feels to work hard at school in return for the obligation a parent feels to provide a happy, secure and stimulating home environment); the potential for information that inheres in social relations (for example a relative's knowledge of who best to contact in order to be considered for a job opportunity); and the existence of effective norms and sanctions that encourage some forms of behaviour and discourage others (for example norms held by the family about what constitutes respectful behaviour toward teachers, and appropriate disincentives for disrespectful behaviour).

We believe there is a fourth type of social capital that is especially important in accounting for a pupil's ability to succeed at school. This consists of the habits and dispositions evident in family members' individual and collective responses to intellectual and other everyday problems. When such habits and dispositions are productive, and when the form they take falls into what Vygotsky (Cole *et al.*, 1978) calls the child's 'zone of proximal development' (roughly, not too hard to understand but requiring learning to apply), they constitute an enormously valuable resource for children. Once acquired, such habits and dispositions serve not only instrumental problem-solving purposes, but they also contribute to the child's sense of self-efficacy. Considerable evidence suggests that a robust sense of self-efficacy generates persistence in the face of the challenges presented by the school curriculum – a key explanation for differences in pupil success (Bandura, 1986).

The old adage that 'it takes a village to raise a child' also reminds us that the nuclear, or even the extended family is not the only potential source of social capital for a child. Community agencies, caring neighbours, churches, clubs and the like are all capable of contributing to this form of capital. In the best of circumstances, these agencies together form 'strong' communities: communities based on familiarity, interdependence and commitment to a common purpose (Smrekar and Mawhinney, 1999); they may add to the capital provided by healthy family cultures or, in some cases, compensate for unhealthy cultures. But this means that schools serving children with unhealthy family cultures situated in weak community cultures face especially difficult challenges.

Estimating the value for schooling of the social capital a child possesses, however, is more complex than an economically dominated explanation suggests. This is because value depends on what the school chooses not to count as educationally useful social capital, as much as what it does count. Our meaning of especially challenging schools, then, also includes the full array of structural to overt responses by the school and its stakeholders to forms of social capital arising from linguistic, racial, religious and cultural diversity. Prejudice, bias, racism and most other sources of inequity are instruments for denying the value of some types of social capital – those types that are different from the types produced within the dominant culture, religion or race, for example. These types of social capital, typically 'written off' or 'discounted' by the school, often hold considerable potential for the child's education. But schools must chose to view them as resources rather than deficits.

The preferred trajectory of Figure 3.1, then, signifies the importance of school leaders recasting, as educationally useful, some types of social capital brought to the school by its pupils typically considered a deficit. The main reason for viewing such social capital in deficit terms is its deviation from the forms of social capital valued by the members of the dominant culture, race or religion.

Contributions of school leadership to especially challenging schools

In our introductory remarks, we claimed that successful school leadership has an important influence on the learning of students in especially challenging schools. But we provided no explicit evidence in support of that claim, something to which we now turn. In the past ten years a substantial amount of relevant empirical evidence has been published about leadership effects across all types of schools, as well as leadership effects in especially challenging schools.

Based on a series of both comprehensive and systematic reviews of evidence (approximately four dozen studies) across all types of schools, Hallinger and Heck (1996a, 1996b, 1998) concluded that the effects of school leadership on pupil outcomes were educationally significant – accounting for about a quarter of the variation in student achievement across schools explained by school factors. This was the case when 'mediated models' were tested by the research.

Mediated models assume that most effects of leaders on students, especially the effects of those in formal leadership positions such as heads or principals, are indirect. These leaders act in ways that, for example, help to build a consensus about the goals of the school, create more collaborative professional cultures or provide opportunities for teachers to develop further their instructional skills. According to the logic of mediated models, changes in these school conditions enhance the quality of education available to students, resulting in better learning on their part. Similar results have been reported by Leithwood and Jantzi (1999, 2000), specifically focused on the effects of 'transformational' approaches to school leadership (for a description of such approaches, see Leithwood, Jantzi and Steinbach, 1999).

Inner-city schools, many of which qualify as especially challenging, have been the focus of considerable research since the mid 1970s, much of it under the banner of the effective schools movement (Rutter *et al.*, 1979; Mortimore *et al.*, 1988). A substantial body of evidence has accumulated from this research, pointing to 'strong positive leadership' as one of most significant correlates of effective schools (Mortimore, 1993, p. 300).

For the purposes of this discussion, we were also able to locate a small number of additional recent studies about the effects of school leadership on a variety of student outcomes in especially challenging schools. In a qualitative study carried out in one school, Reitzug and Patterson (1998), for example, found that the principal empowered students by interacting with them directly. Based on four studies carried out in elementary schools with successful leaders, Scheurich (1998) concluded that Mexican-American elementary students can achieve exceptionally well academically – often superior to students in high-performing Anglo schools, in fact. Generally positive effects of successful leaders on student learning were reported by Hatton (2001) in the context of small, rural, disadvantaged elementary schools in New South Wales, and by Sebring and Bryk (2000) in the context of Chicago elementary schools.

In a secondary analysis of the effects of career assistant principals, Marshall *et al.* (1996) found that those who based their practices on an ethic of care were able to 'turn the worst kids around'. And finally, a review of ten studies carried out in inner city schools run by successful leaders (Gezi, 1990) found pupils' academic achievement to be at or near the national median on achievement tests. Pupils in these schools made large gains in maths achievement and modest but positive gains in reading. These different sources of evidence, together, make a compelling argument for the contribution to students' growth of successful school leadership in especially challenging schools.

Leadership and family educational cultures

The preferred trajectory in Figure 3.1 points to a direct relationship between school leadership and family educational cultures (among the 'antecedents' in Figure 3.1). This relationship acknowledges our claim that family educational cultures are alterable (unlike the components of SES). In this section we identify leadership initiatives known to produce such change.

Parent education programmes

Bringing the resources of families more forcefully to bear on the schooling of children has been the mission of many people for at least the last century. Following up earlier reviews of literature (Henderson, 1981, 1987), Henderson and Berla (1994, p. 1) declared that: 'The evidence is beyond dispute. When schools work together with families to support learning, children tend to succeed not just in school, but throughout life'. Henderson and Berla argue in their review that the best predictors of student achievement are the extent to which the child's family is able to create a home environment that encourages learning, express high but realistic expectations for the child's achievement and future occupation, and become involved in their children's education at school and in the community. Furthermore:

> When schools support families to develop these three conditions, children from low income families and diverse cultural backgrounds approach the grades and test scores expected for middle-class children. They are also more likely to take advantage of a full range of educational opportunities after graduating from high school. Even with only one or two of these conditions in place, children do measurably better at school.

Interventions with families that produce these impressive results often include material supports, emotional encouragement, information presentations, therapeutic guidance and skills development (Cheng Gorman and Balter, 1997). A central component of these efforts has been the development of parent education programmes. Such programmes encompass a wide range of activities, for example, group meetings to discuss parenting problems and learn new skills, newsletters for single parents, phone consultations, and the provision of audio, video and print resources. Three distinct orientations are evident among the more widely known parent education programmes (Dembo, Sweitzer and Lauritzen, 1985): reflective orientations designed to build parent awareness, understanding and acceptance of the child's feelings; behavioural orientations aimed at training parents to use specific techniques to control undesirable behaviour in their children; and Adlerian approaches which encourage parents to use natural and logical consequences to control behaviour, while maintaining a cooperative home environment.

As Cheng Gorman and Balter (1997) suggest, however, each of these approaches may be more or less culturally sensitive – that is, demonstrate more or less understanding and appreciation of the unique values, beliefs and customs of the parents to be served by the programme. Schools serving culturally diverse families will benefit from not just providing parent education programmes, but providing programmes that are accepting of non-traditional child-rearing practices, unique family structures, or preferred forms of social interaction, for example. Most fully developed parent education programmes are culturally 'adapted', at best, rather than culturally specific. Evidence suggests that parent education programmes at least adapted to family needs arising from cultural diversity can have effects on student achievement (Cheng Gorman and Balter, 1997) just as substantial as the effects typical programmes have on families who belong to the cultural majority. For leaders of especially challenging schools, the implication is not just to sponsor and encourage parent education programmes in their communities, it is also to hold such programmes to the standard of 'cultural sensitivity'.

School-linked, integrated social services

Extending, in a coherent and accessible form, the sources of social capital available to pupils is a primary purpose for the development of school-linked, integrated social services. This goal is accomplished by bringing together the full array of social, health, educational and other services from which pupils, families and their wider communities might benefit in a single location, usually the school. Volpe *et al.* (2001) identify at least four approaches to integrated social services that are evident in the literature: bringing together unconnected complementary services; overturning ineffective practices and policies; creating the means to promote and sustain integration; and rethinking the relationship between children/families and service providers. These are, respectively, client-centred, programme-centred, policy-centred and organization-centred approaches to integrated social services.

A more fundamental distinction among approaches to providing integrated social services, however, is based on the extent to which the actual demands of students and families, along with their cultures and languages, are addressed. Under the banner of 'full service schools', early efforts to provide social capital through integration of social services focused largely on the providers' supply of services to pupils, families and the wider community. But as Smrekar and Mawhinney (1999, p. 457) explain, this supply orientation has experienced limited success because it fails to acknowledge 'the fundamental social conditions that characterize whole urban neighbourhoods and communities'. Arising in its place is a model of integrated social services responsive to community members' demands for assistance, their empowerment in decisions about this assistance, and the congruence of such assistance with the cultures and languages of the community. This model views community cultures and languages as foundations to build on in collaboration with community members.

There are significant challenges to the implementation of culturally congruent social services of this sort that will meet the genuine demands and needs of pupils, families and other stakeholders. These challenges include adequately understanding the implications for services of the community's culture, and establishing and maintaining communication among all stakeholders, including a sufficiently broad array of stakeholders to address the fundamental need for community development and the like. Evidence (Volpe *et al.*, 2001; Smrekar and Mawhinney, 1999) suggests that successful leadership practices in response to such challenges include, for example:

- rethinking institutionalized practices that disempower the very groups of people that the new and expanded programmes are designed to reach;
- developing with all stakeholders a common vision and set of goals towards which to work;
- distributing leadership flexibly across roles (formal and informal leadership roles) and stakeholder groups, depending on the issues being faced and the locus of expertise required for dealing with the issues;
- ensuring adequate communication among all stakeholder groups, including proactive efforts at resolving the conflicts among groups that inevitably arise;
- awarding considerable power to pupils, parents and other community stakeholders in the process of making decisions about their needs and the types of services useful in meeting those needs;
- incorporating the parents' home language into the provision of services.

Through these leadership practices, school-linked, integrated services should provide seamless collaboration between families, schools and their communities and a new covenant for reconstructed systems that are 'designed for communication not control' (Harry, cited in Smrekar and Mawhinney, 1999, p. 456).

School policies and successful leadership practices

Figure 3.1 suggests that school conditions, both policies and practices, have a direct impact on pupils and are, in turn, directly influenced by those exercising school leadership. In this section, we identify policies and practices within the classroom and across the school that ought to be a priority for attention by those providing leadership to especially challenging schools. To be clear, however, our allocation of conditions to either the class or school level is a simplification that ignores, for the moment, the complex dependence of classroom practices on school-level norms and policies to be found in any real school.

Within the classroom, we focus especially on class size, student grouping practices, and curriculum and instruction. At the school level, we are concerned about school size, partnerships with parents, racism and sense of community; our concerns at the school level also encompass student retention and promotion policies and instructional programme coherence.

Within the classroom

Class size

By now there is little debate in the research community over the contributions to student learning of smaller elementary school class sizes. Recent summaries of this evidence (Finn *et al.*, 2001; Biddle and Berliner, 2002) conclude that class sizes below 20 students, accompanied by appropriate adaptations to instruction, produce increases in achievement and are most beneficial in the early primary grades with students who are economically disadvantaged. The advantages realized by smaller classes in the primary grades appear to be maintained even three or four years later.

Among the explanations for small class effects are improved teacher morale, more time spent by teachers on individual instruction and less on classroom management, along with fewer disruptions and indiscipline. Explanations for small class size effects also include greater engagement by students in instruction, reduced grade retention, reduced drop-out rates in secondary schools and increased aspirations among students to attend college (Finn, 2001).

Although school leaders usually have little control over the total numbers of students assigned to their school building, they are usually in a position to influence how those students are distributed across classes within the school. The benefits of smaller classes are unlikely to be realized if student allocation decisions aim at providing equal class sizes for most teachers. Assuming no increase in the resources available to the school, successful leadership practices, in this case, entail working with staffs towards reducing class size in the early grades with a corresponding increase in class size at the higher grades.

Student grouping

The grouping of students for instruction is influenced by decisions made at both the school and classroom levels and decisions at both levels often require intervention by those assuming leadership roles. This is because both heterogeneous and homogeneous-ability grouping practices are advocated for the accomplishment of the same goals.

At any point over at least the last 50 years, however, a synthesis of available empirical evidence would have suggested, quite unambiguously, that students having difficulty at school, especially those disadvantaged by their socio-economic backgrounds, learn more when they are working in heterogeneous rather than in homogeneous-ability groups (Oakes, 1985; Yonezawa, Wells and Serna, 2002). Relatively high expectations for learning, a faster pace of instruction, peer models of effective learning and a more challenging curricula are among the reasons offered for this advantage.

In spite of this evidence, over this same period, the bulk of teachers and administrators have enacted practices that separate students by ability; their argument is that homogeneous grouping produces greater learning by allowing for the concentration of instructional resources on the same set of learning problems. Implementing heterogeneous grouping practices in classrooms has been regarded by many teachers as very difficult. Nevertheless, this is one of the rare examples of professional 'common sense' being just plain wrong.

Changing the common-sense beliefs of teachers about heterogeneous grouping effects on the learning of struggling students requires those providing leadership to bring relevant evidence to the attention of their colleagues in accessible and convincing ways, to encourage actual trials with heterogeneous groupings under conditions that include opportunities for practice, feedback and coaching, and to help teachers generate 'the kind of assessment information that will make the impact of tracking and detracking more visible' (Riehl, 2000).

Curriculum and instruction

A considerable amount of evidence can be interpreted as suggesting that the best curriculum for socially, economically or culturally disadvantaged children will often be the rich curriculum typically experienced by relatively advantaged students. But this is not often the case. Rather, the typical curriculum experienced by the children under consideration here is narrowly focused on basic skills and knowledge and lacks much meaning for these students.

Why this should be the case has much to do with a widely mistaken understanding about the kind of curriculum from which these children will most benefit. In a comprehensive synthesis of empirical evidence, Brophy (n.d.) touches on the main features of a 'rich' curriculum, one similarly beneficial for most students no matter what their background. This is a curriculum in which the instructional strategies, learning activities, and assessment practices are clearly aligned and aimed at accomplishing the full array of knowledge, skills, attitudes and dispositions valued by society. The content of such a curriculum is organized in relation to a set of powerful ideas. These ideas are 'internally coherent, well connected to other meaningful learning, and accessible for application' (ibid., p. 7). Skills are taught with a view to their application in particular settings and for particular purposes. In addition, these skills include general learning and study skills, as well as skills specific to subject domains. Such metacognitive skills are especially beneficial for less able students who might otherwise have difficulty monitoring and self-regulating their own learning.

In especially challenging schools, instruction, as well as the curriculum, should meet the same standards of effectiveness that would be expected in schools serving relatively advantaged students. But such standards are not often met. A significant proportion of these schools lack minimally adequate instructional resources and are in physical disrepair. Many teachers do not find it satisfying to work with students in especially challenging schools; they move on to less demanding environments at the first opportunity (Englert, 1993). They cite the lack of psychic rewards from seeing their students succeed, feeling uncertain about their ability to meet the goals they have for students, and knowing when they have done so; rewards of this sort are more easily available to teachers in less challenging schools. These teachers often have low expectations for pupil performance and require their pupils to spend excessive time on drill and practice activities aimed almost exclusively at improving basic academic skills.

Brophy's (n.d.) synthesis of research suggests that effective instruction is conducted in a highly supportive classroom environment, one embedded in a caring, learning community. In this environment, most of the class time is spent on curriculum-related activities and the class is managed to maintain students' engagement in those activities. Effective instruction also includes questions 'planned to engage students in sustained discourse structured around powerful ideas', and teachers provide the assistance students need 'to enable them to engage in learning activities productively' (ibid., pp. 8–9).

In contrast to the features of effective instruction identified by Brophy, research by Cummins (1986) suggests that much of the instruction used with children designated as 'at risk' places them in a passive role. Such children, he argues, need to be encouraged to become active generators of their own knowledge, to 'assume greater control over setting their own learning goals and to collaborate actively with each other in achieving these goals' (ibid., p. 28).

At-risk children also may require 'culturally responsive' teaching (Riehl, 2000; Jagers and Carroll, 2002). This is teaching based on the premise that culturally diverse students pose opportunities instead of problems for teachers. Teachers adopting this perspective identify the norms, values and practices associated with the often diverse cultures of their students and adapt their instruction to acknowledge, respect and build on them.

Successful school leaders have high expectations for the quality of the curriculum and insist on adherence to such standards. These leaders promote culturally responsive teaching by demonstrating such teaching themselves in their relations with parents, teachers and students. Such instruction is fostered, as well, through examining the impact of various organizational alternatives (student grouping practices, for example) on the stratification of access to instruction and on student achievement, and by making appropriate changes that promote both equity and excellence for all students.

Across the school

School size

A considerable amount of evidence suggests that pupils in especially challenging schools benefit from being part of relatively small organizations (Lee and Smith, 1993; Lee, 2000). For elementary schools, the optimum size seems to be about 250 to 300 students, whereas 600 to 700 students appears to be optimal for secondary schools.

Especially for struggling students, smaller schools increase the chances of their attendance and school work being monitored. Smaller schools also increase the likelihood of students having a close, ongoing relationship with at least one other significant adult in the school – an important antidote to dropping out. Smaller school organizations tend to have more constrained and more focused academic programmes. Typically, they are also more communal in nature, with teachers taking more personal responsibility for the learning of each pupil. Summarizing the rationale for smaller schools, Lee, Ready and Johnson (2001, p. 367) argue that: 'Constructs such as social networks, social resources, caring, social support, social capital, cultural capital, and communal school organization are bound by a common idea. Students and adults in schools should know one another better'. There is, they go on to claim, 'general agreement on the importance of positive social relations for adolescents' academic and social development. Such relations are much more likely to develop in smaller schools'.

School leaders are not often in a position to determine the total numbers of students assigned to their school buildings. But they do have some control over the internal social structures of those schools. Because secondary schools often range in size from 1000 to 3000 students in the same building, creating schools-within-schools has frequently been recommended as a practical means for realizing the benefits of small units. While promising, however, this solution has not been nearly as widely implemented as is generally believed. Where it has been implemented, it is typically a response to uncommitted pupils – pupils with low attendance rates, high drop-out rates and generally low performance (Lee, Ready and Johnson, 2001).

Partnerships with parents

Site-based management policies prevail, by now, in the school systems of most developed countries (Leithwood and Menzies, 1998). These policies typically create new or expanded roles for parents in schools, arguably creating one of the biggest changes in the life of school administrators over the past decade (Murphy and Beck, 1995; Whittey and Power, 1997). But evidence suggests that the contribution of parent partnerships to student learning varies enormously across the alternative forms that those partnerships may take (Epstein, 1996). These forms range from parent involvement in the instruction of their own children, at one extreme, to direct participation in school decision making, at the other. No matter the size of the student population, when school leaders have a choice, involving parents primarily in the instruction of their own children is most likely to contribute to student growth.

Creating meaningful partnerships with parents in especially challenging schools is often quite difficult (Griffith, 2001; Hatton, 2001). It is difficult to 'mandate parent involvement with people whose time is totally consumed in a struggle to survive' (Crosby, 1999, p. 303). But when the educational culture of the student's home is weak, students benefit from the school's direct efforts to influence that culture in ways that acknowledge the circumstances faced by students' families .

Cummins's (1986) synthesis of evidence suggests that the failure of minority students at school can be traced to the relationships between educators and minority students and between schools and minority communities. To alter this pattern of failure significantly, Cummins argues, requires 'personal redefinitions of the way classroom teachers interact with the children and the communities they serve' (ibid., p. 16). Students need to become empowered and such empowerment includes both cognitive or academic skills and cultural identity.

Cummins's framework for empowering minority students includes, as one of its four 'structural elements', 'community participation'. 'When educators involve minority parents as partners in their children's education, parents appear to develop a sense of efficacy that communicates itself to children, with positive academic consequences' (ibid., p. 24). Cummins cites the effects of a study that entailed children reading to their parents at home as evidence of the dramatic effects such participation can have on achievement (the Haringey project in the UK).

Racism

A growing body of evidence suggests that racism lies behind a significant proportion of the cultural 'insensitivities' to which we have alluded (Carr and Klassen, 1997a, 1997b; Walcott, 1994). Furthermore, this evidence calls into question multiculturalism, the most prevalent response to diversity in many schools and districts, because:

> multiculturalism perpetuates a kind of colour-blind relativism that implies that although people's skin colour may be different, they are regarded in our society ... as equal and the same. This pretence both masks and denies the very real prejudice, conflict, and differential achievement of students in most schools. (Shields, Larocque and Oberg, 2002, p. 117)

In place of multicultural policies and practices, school leaders are now encouraged to engage in 'antiracism education' (Dei, 1996) to eliminate the marginalizing, oppressive, and self-destructive impact of racism on people of colour. Antiracism education works at several levels (Solomon, 2002). At the individual level, it attempts to eliminate behaviours that impact negatively on people of colour, while at the organizational level it critically examines and then alters the structures and policies that entrench and reproduce racism. As a general stance towards racism, school leaders are encouraged 'to analyze, challenge, and change power relations; advocate for equitable access of people of color to power and resources; and ensure their full participation in racially diverse societies' (Solomon, 2002, p. 176).

There is, as yet, little empirical evidence about successful leadership responses to racism in schools. Nonetheless, advocates of antiracism believe that school leaders should establish antiracism as an ethical and moral imperative in their schools, and persistently and explicitly reject assumptions of cultural and racial deficiency (Wagstaff and Fusarelli, 1995). They argue, as well, that school leaders should expect all staff to work toward equity, democracy and social justice for all students and their families. With staff, these leaders should systematically examine the content and process of schooling to eliminate racism, and provide opportunities for racial minorities to express the negative impact of racism on their lives (Shields, Larocque and Oberg, 2002). For antiracism education to be effective, it is argued that school leaders need to ensure that student social groups are well reflected in the teaching and support staffs; this is so because an ethnically diverse teaching staff has the potential to enrich the school's teaching and learning, and provide a voice for racial minority concerns (Solomon, 2002). School leaders will further antiracism education when they uphold antiracism principles and practices in the face of challenges from all stakeholders in the school. Shields, Larocque and Oberg (2002) suggest that this might be accomplished by building a 'community of difference' in the school – one that encourages respect, dialogue and understanding about differences rather than the shared norms, beliefs and values typically associated with the concept of community. Finally, advocates of antiracism argue that racism will be reduced as school leaders build alliances and coalitions with other equity-conscious groups and agencies in the broader community.

Sense of community

This section encompasses two school 'communities': the broad community of students, staff, parents and others; and the more specialized professional sub-community of teachers.

It is important to create a widely shared sense of community among all the school's stakeholders for two reasons. First, the affective bonds between students and teachers associated with a sense of community are crucial in engaging and motivating students to learn in schools of any type (Lee, Bryk and Smith, 1993). A widely shared sense of community also is important as an antidote to the unstable, sometimes threatening, and often insecure world inhabited by a significant proportion of the families and children served by especially challenging schools. A collective sense of belonging for those living with these circumstances provides psychological connections and identity with, and commitment to, others (Beck and Foster, 1999, p. 350). Individuals who feel secure and purposeful as a result of these connections, identities and commitments are, in turn, less susceptible to the mindset of fatalism and disempowerment that often arises from repeated episodes of loss (Mitchell, cited in Beck and Foster, 1999). Success at school depends on having goals for the academic, personal and vocational strands of one's life, as well as a sense of self-efficacy about the achievement of those goals. Feelings of fatalism and disempowerment discourage both the setting of such goals and the development of self-efficacy about their achievement.

A small but impressive body of evidence also suggests that pupils benefit when teachers in a school form a 'professional learning' subcommunity (Bryk and Driscoll, 1988; Newman and Associates, 1996; Louis and Kruse, 1995; Louis, Marks, and Kruse, 1996). Participation in such communities promotes instructional programme coherence across the school. It also stimulates growth in teachers' instructional skills, enhances teachers' sense of mastery and control over student learning, and builds teachers' sense of responsibility for student learning.

Conceptually and methodologically, the most sophisticated empirical study of the effects of professional learning communities has been reported by Louis, Marks and Kruse (1996). Two sets of conditions were found to contribute to a professional learning community in this study – structural conditions, and human and social resources. Structural conditions included small school size, relatively simple and non-specialized forms of school organization, time scheduled for teacher planning, and opportunities for teachers to exercise power and discretion in decisions about teaching and learning. Critical human and social resources were openness to innovation, feedback on instructional performance, and opportunities for professional development. Supportive leadership was also a key human resource:

> Whether exercised by principals or site-based teams, supportive leadership focuses efforts on issues related to school improvement: collegiality, shared purpose, continuous improvement, accountability, and responsibility for performance and structural change ... They act as a critical source of information on how to deviate from the existing situation. (Louis, Marks and Kruse, 1996, p. 763)

School administrators, in particular, help develop professional community through their attention to individual teacher development, and by creating and sustaining networks of conversation in their schools around issues of teaching and learning.

Retention and promotion policies

While student retention by course has long been a common practice in secondary schools, social promotion by grade has been a common policy in elementary schools until quite recently. Over the past decade, however, conservative policy makers in many jurisdictions have enacted a 'tough love' strategy for raising student performance, which often includes retaining students at grade until they meet minimum passing standards (often judged by the results of end-of-grade exams). Over all groups of elementary students, evidence strongly suggests that retention policies rarely produce improved learning and often have negative effects on learning as well as attitudes toward school and learning (Shepard and Smith, 1990; Foster, 1993; Reynolds, 1992; McCoy and Reynolds, 1999; Westbury, 1994; Darling-Hammond, 1998).

Some of this evidence seems contradictory, however, and this is because retention policies have dramatically different effects on different groups of pupils. For pupils with a relatively robust sense of academic self-efficacy, the raising of standards with clear sanctions for failure can be positively motivating. A robust sense of academic self-efficacy typically results in more work as a response to the threat of failure (Bandura, 1986). So those who have traditionally done well at school, acquired high levels of academic self-efficacy in the process, but are not trying as hard as they could may well benefit from such policies. In contrast, those who have often struggled at school and frequently experienced failure are likely to have developed a low sense of academic self-efficacy. For them, the most likely response to the threat of retention is to give up, and at the secondary level, to drop out of school altogether (Haney, 2001).

Successful leadership of especially challenging elementary schools requires the adoption of a differentiated or contingent grade promotion policy: one that allows for either retention or social promotion based on careful diagnosis of the reasons for a student's failure.

Instructional programme coherence

While the amount of evidence about instructional programme coherence is modest, Newman *et al.* (2001) report impressive effects on pupils' achievement in reading and mathematics in elementary schools serving communities experiencing high rates of poverty, social stress and racial diversity. For purposes of this exceptionally well-designed study, instructional programme coherence was defined as: 'a set of interrelated programs for students and staff that are guided by a common framework for curriculum, instruction, assessment, and learning climate and that are pursued over a sustained period' (ibid., p. 297). In contrast to excessive numbers of unrelated, unsustained improvement initiatives in a school, instructional coherence contributes to learning by connecting students' experiences and building on them over time. As pupils see themselves becoming more competent, their motivation to learn is likely to increase also. Similar effects can be expected for teachers as they work collaboratively toward implementing a common instructional framework.

Developing instructional programme coherence requires strong leadership, but leadership that fosters teachers' professional community and a shared commitment for the programme. Such leadership entails, for example: the decision to adopt or develop a common framework and to make it a priority for the school; to insist the framework is used by all teachers; strongly to encourage teachers to work with their colleagues to implement the framework; and to provide sustained training for staff in the use of the framework (Newman *et al.*, 2001).

Conclusion

Our starting point for clarifying the meaning of 'especially challenging schools' was to point to the interdependent nature of the relationships among family educational cultures, the development (and interpretation by the school) of social capital, and children's success at school. Unhealthy family cultures provide children with insufficient amounts of the social capital they require to succeed at school. So schools serving large proportions of children with limited social capital face special challenges in meeting their pupils' educational needs. Family cultures, and the social capital to which they give rise, are significantly influenced by the economic conditions of both the immediate family and the contiguous community in which the family is located. It is simply more difficult for adults in impoverished circumstances to provide the conditions that build children's social capital; while some adults manage remarkably well, they are clearly the exception.

Estimating the value for schooling of the social capital a child possesses, however, is more complex than an economically dominated explanation suggests. This is because value depends as much on what the school chooses not to count as social capital, as much as what it does count. Our meaning of especially challenging schools, then, also includes the responses of the school and its stakeholders to diversity in its many forms (linguistic, racial, religious and cultural). Prejudice, bias, racism and most other sources of inequity are instruments for denying the value of certain forms of social capital – the types not possessed by the dominant culture, religion or race, for example. These discounted forms of social capital often hold considerable potential in the child's education when schools choose to view them as resources rather than deficits, as we demonstrated earlier.

This complex conception of especially challenging schools has begun to identify two approaches to leadership. The first approach includes practices aimed at implementing policies and other sorts of initiatives that, according to the best evidence available, serve well those populations of children about which we have been concerned. Three sets of such policies and initiatives were examined. One set aimed to support family educational cultures directly by providing parent education programmes and school-linked, integrated social services. A second set of classroom-focused policies included reducing class sizes, using mostly heterogeneous student grouping practices, and building rich curricula delivered through sustained discourse structured around powerful ideas. Included among the third, school-focused set were school size, partnerships with parents, sense of community, promotion and retention policies and instructional programme coherence. This third set of school-level policies and practices aimed to keep school size relatively small, create productive partnerships with parents and build a strong sense of community in the school; this set of policies and initiatives also intended to base student promotion on both academic and social growth and ensure instructional programme coherence.

A second approach to leadership that has been developed here aims to ensure, at minimum, that those policies and other initiatives that we have examined are implemented equitably. This usually means building on the forms of social capital that students do possess rather than being restricted by the social capital they do not possess. Such an approach to leadership is referred to variously as emancipatory leadership (Corson, 1996), leadership for social justice (Larson and Murtadha, 2002) and critical leadership (Foster, 1989). Examples of specific practices associated with this approach, beyond those described to this point, include: heightening the awareness of school community members to unjust situations that they may encounter and how such situations affect their lives; providing members of the school community with the capacities needed to resist situations that generate inequities; and providing opportunities to become involved in political actions aimed at reducing inequities (Ryan, 1998).

The two approaches to successful leadership that have been described often seem to live in different worlds. The first is a mainstream world that acknowledges poverty but often seems insensitive to the consequences of diversity. The second is a world more in tune with sources of injustice but unconcerned about the full range of tasks faced by school leaders. Especially challenging schools demand both sets of leadership practices if they are to serve their pupils well.

REFERENCES

Bandura, A. (1986). *Social Foundations of Thought and Action*, Englewood Cliffs, NJ: Prentice-Hall.

Beck, L.G. and Foster, W. (1999) 'Administration and community: considering challenges, exploring possibilities' in Murphy, J. and Louis, K.S. (eds), *Handbook of Research on Educational Administration*, San Francisco: Jossey-Bass, pp. 337–58.

Biddle, B.J. and Berliner, D.C. (2002) 'Small class size and its effects', *Educational Leadership*, 59 (5), pp. 12–23.

Bloom, B. (1985) *Developing Talent in Young People*, New York: Ballantine.

Brophy, J. (n.d.) *Teaching: A Special Report Reprinted by the Laboratory for Student Success*, Philadelphia, PA: Mid-Atlantic Regional Educational Laboratory at the Temple University Centre for Research in Human Development and Education.

Bryk, A.S. and Driscoll, M.E. (1988) *The School as Community: Theoretical Foundations, Contextual Influences, and Consequences for Students and Teachers*, Madison: University of Wisconsin, National Centre for Effective Secondary Schools.

Carr, P. and Klassen, T. (1997a) 'Different perceptions of race in education: racial minority and white teachers', *Canadian Journal of Education*, 22 (1), pp. 67–81.

Carr, P. and Klassen, T. (1997b) 'Institutional barriers to the implementation of antiracist education: a case study of the secondary system in a large, urban school board', *Journal of Educational Administration and Foundations*, 12 (1), pp. 46–68.

Cheng Gorman, J. and Balter, L. (1997) 'Culturally sensitive parent education: a critical review of quantitative research', *Review of Educational Research*, 67 (3), pp. 339–69.

Cole, M., John-Steiner, V., Scribner, S. and Souberman, E. (eds) (1978) *Mind in Society: The Development of Higher Psychological Processes*, Cambridge, MA: Harvard University Press.

Coleman, J.S. (1966) *Equality of Educational Opportunity*, Washington, DC: Government Printing Office.

Coleman, J.S. (1987) 'Families and schools', *Educational Researcher*, 16 (6), pp. 32–8.

Coleman, J.S. (1989) 'Social capital in the creation of human capital', *American Journal of Sociology*, 94, pp. 95–120.

Corson, D. (1996) 'Emancipatory discursive practices' in Leithwood, K., Chapman, J., Corson, D., Hallinger, P. and Hart, A. (eds), *International Handbook of Educational Leadership and Administration*, Dordrecht, The Netherlands: Kluwer Academic Publishers, pp. 1043–67.

Crosby, E.A. (1999) 'Urban schools: forced to fail', *Phi Delta Kappan*, 81 (4), pp. 298–303.

Cummins, J. (1986) 'Empowering minority students: a framework for intervention', *Harvard Educational Review*, 56 (1), pp. 16–36.

Darling-Hammond, L. (1998) 'Alternatives to grade retention', *The School Administrator*, 55 (7), pp. 18–21.

Dei, G.J.S. (1996) *Antiracism Education: Theory and Practice*, Halifax, Nova Scotia: Fernwood.

Dembo, M.H., Sweitzer, M. and Lauritzen, P. (1985) 'An evaluation of group parent education: behavioral, PET and Adlerian programs', *Review of Educational Research*, 55, pp. 155–200.

Dill, V. and Haberman, M. (1995) 'Building a gentler school', *Educational Leadership*, 52 (5), pp. 69–71.

Dillard, C.B. (1995) 'Leading with her life: an African-American feminist (re) interpretation of leadership for an urban high school principal', *Educational Administration Quarterly*, 31 (4), pp. 539–63.

Driscoll, M.E. and Kerchner, C.T. (1999) 'The implications of social capital for schools, communities, and cities: educational administration as if a sense of place mattered' in Murphy, J. and Louis, K.S. (eds), *Handbook of Research on Educational Administration*, 2nd edn, San Francisco: Jossey-Bass, pp. 385–404.

Englert, R.M. (1993) 'Understanding the urban context and conditions of practice of school administration' in Forsyth, P. and Tallerico, M. (eds), *City Schools: Leading the Way*, Newbury Park, CA: Corwin Press, pp. 1–63.

Epstein, J. (1996) 'Perspectives and previews on research and policy for school, family, and community partnerships' in Booth, A. and Dunn, J. (eds), *Family–School Links*, Mahwah, NJ: Lawrence Erlbaum Associates, pp. 209–46.

Finn, J. (1989) 'Withdrawing from school', *Review of Educational Research*, 59 (2), pp. 117–43.

Finn, J., Gerber, S., Achilles, C. and Boyd-Zaharias, J. (2001) 'The enduring effects of small classes', *Teachers' College Record*, 103 (2), pp. 145–83.

Foster, J.E. (1993) 'Reviews of research: retaining children in grade', *Childhood Education*, 70 (1), pp. 38–43.

Foster, W. (1989) 'Toward a critical practice of leadership' in Smyth, J. (ed.), *Critical Perspectives on Educational Leadership*, London: Falmer Press, pp. 39–62.

Gezi, K. (1990) 'The role of leadership in inner-city schools', *Educational Research Quarterly*, 12 (4), pp. 4–11.

Griffith, J. (2001) 'Principal leadership of parent involvement', *Journal of Educational Administration*, 39 (2), pp. 162–86.

Hallinger, P. and Heck, R.H. (1996a) 'The principal's role in school effectiveness: an assessment of methodological progress, 1980–1995' in Leithwood, K., Chapman, J., Corson, D., Hallinger, P., and Hart, A. (eds), *International Handbook of Educational Leadership and Administration*, Dordrecht, The Netherlands: Kluwer Academic Publishers, pp. 723–83.

Hallinger, P. and Heck, R.H. (1996b) 'Reassessing the principal's role in school effectiveness: a review of empirical research, 1980–1995', *Educational Administration Quarterly*, 32 (1), pp. 5–44.

Hallinger, P. and Heck, R.H. (1998) 'Exploring the principal's contribution to school effectiveness: 1980–1995', *School Effectiveness and School Improvement*, 9 (2), pp. 157–91.

Haney, W. (2001) 'Response to Skrla *et al.*: the illusion of educational equity in Texas: a commentary on "accountability for equity"', *International Journal of Leadership in Education*, 4 (3), pp. 267–75.

Hatton, E. (2001) 'School development planning in a small primary school: addressing the challenge in rural NSW', *Journal of Educational Administration*, 39 (2), pp. 118–33.

Henderson, A. (1981) *Parent Participation and Student Achievement: The Evidence Grows*. Columbia, MD: National Committee for Citizens in Education.

Henderson, A. (1987) *The Evidence Continues to Grow: Parent Involvement Improves Student Achievement* (an annotated bibliography). Columbia, MD: National Committee for Citizens in Education.

Henderson, A. and Berla, N. (1994) (eds) *A New Generation of Evidence: The Family is Critical to Student Achievement*. Columbia, MD: National Committee for Citizens in Education.

Jagers, R.F. and Carroll, G. (2002) 'Issues in educating African-American children and youth' in Stringfield, S. and Land, D. (eds), *Educating at-risk Students: 101st Yearbook of the National Society for the Study of Education*, Chicago: University of Chicago Press, pp. 49–65.

Larson, C.L. and Murtadha, K. (2002) 'Leadership for social justice' in Murphy, J. (ed.), *The Educational Leadership Challenge: Redefining Leadership for the 21st Century*, Chicago: University of Chicago Press, pp. 134–61.

Lee, V. (2000) 'School size and the organization of secondary schools' in Hallinan, M.T. (ed.), *Handbook of the Sociology of Education*, New York: Kluwer/Plenum, pp. 327–44.

Lee, V., Byrk, A. and Smith, J.B. (1993) 'The organization of effective high schools' in Darling-Hammond, L. (ed.), *Review of Research in Education*, 19, Washington, DC: American Educational Research Association, pp. 171–267.

Lee, V., Ready, D. and Johnson, D. (2001) 'The difficulty of identifying rare samples to study: the case of high schools divided into schools-within-schools', *Educational Evaluation and Policy Analysis*, 23 (4), pp. 365–79.

Leithwood, K. and Jantzi, D. (1999) 'The relative effects of principal and teacher sources of leadership on student engagement with school', *Educational Administration Quarterly*, 35 (suppl.), pp. 679–706.

Leithwood, K. and Jantzi, D. (2000) 'Principal and teacher leadership effects: a replication', *School Leadership and Management*, 20 (4), pp. 415–34.

Leithwood, K., Jantzi, D. and Steinbach, R. (1999) *Changing Leadership for Changing Times*, Buckingham: Open University Press.

Leithwood, K. and Menzies, T. (1998) 'Forms and effects of school-based management: a review', *Educational Policy*, 12 (3), pp. 325–46.

Louis, K.S. and Kruse, S. (1995) *Professionalism and Community: Perspectives on Reforming Urban Schools*, Thousand Oaks, CA: Corwin Press.

Louis, K.S., Marks, H.M. and Kruse, S. (1996) 'Teachers' professional community in restructuring schools', *American Educational Research Journal*, 33 (4), pp. 757–98.

Marshall, C., Patterson, J.A., Rogers, D. and Steele, J. (1996) 'Caring as career: an alternative perspective for educational administration', *Educational Administration Quarterly*, 32 (2), pp. 271–94.

McCoy, A.R. and Reynolds, A.J. (1999) 'Grade retention and school performance: an extended investigation', *Journal of School Psychology*, 37 (3), pp. 273–98.

Mortimore, P. (1993) 'School effectiveness and the management of effective learning and teaching', *School Effectiveness and School Improvement*, 4 (4), pp. 290–310.

Mortimore, P., Sammons, P., Stoll, L., Lewis, D. and Ecob, R. (1988) *School Matters: The Junior Years*, Wells, Somerset: Open Books.

Murphy, J. and Beck, L.G. (1995) *School-based Management as School Reform: Taking Stock*, Thousand Oaks, CA: Corwin Press.

Newmann, F.M. and Associates (1996) *School Restructuring and Authentic Student Achievement*, San Francisco: Jossey-Bass.

Newman, F., Smith B., Allensworth, E. and Bryk, A. (2001) 'Instructional program coherence: What it is and why it should guide school improvement policy', *Educational Evaluation and Policy Analysis*, 23 (4), pp. 297–321.

Oakes, J. (1985) *Keeping Track: How Schools Structure Inequality*, New Haven: Yale University Press.

Portin, B.S. (2000) 'The changing urban principalship', *Education and Urban Society*, 32 (4), pp. 492–505.

Reitzug, U. and Patterson, J. (1998) '"I'm not going to lose you!": empowerment through caring in an urban principal's practice with students', *Urban Education*, 33 (2), pp. 150–81.

Reynolds, A.J. (1992) 'Grade retention and school adjustment: an explanatory analysis', *Educational Evaluation and Policy Analysis*, 14 (2), pp. 101–21.

Riehl. C.J. (2000) 'The principal's role in creating inclusive schools for diverse students: a review of normative, empirical, and critical literature on the practice of educational administration', *Review of Educational Research*, 70 (1), pp. 55–81.

Rumberger, R.W. (1987) 'High school dropouts: a review of issues and evidence', *Review of Educational Research*, 57 (2), pp. 101–21.

Rutter, M., Maughan, B., Mortimore, P. and Ouston, J. (1979) *Fifteen Thousand Hours: Secondary Schools and Their Effects on Children*, London: Open Books.

Ryan, J. (1998) 'Critical leadership for education in a postmodern world: emancipation, resistance and communal action', *International Journal of Leadership in Education*, 1 (3), pp. 257–78.

Scheurich, J.J. (1998) 'Highly successful and loving, public elementary schools populated mainly by low-SES children of colour: core beliefs and cultural characteristics', *Urban Education*, 33 (4), pp. 451–91.

Scott-Jones, P. (1984) 'Family influences on cognitive development and school achievement' in Gordon, E. (ed.), *Review of Research in Education*, 11, Washington, DC: American Educational Research Association.

Sebring, P. and Bryk, A. (2000) 'School leadership and the bottom line in Chicago', *Phi Delta Kappan*, 81 (6), pp. 440–43.

Shepard, L.A. and Smith, M.L. (1990) 'Synthesis of research on grade retention', *Educational Leadership*, 47 (8), pp. 84–8.

Shields, C.M., LaRocque, L.J. and Oberg, S. (2002) 'A dialogue about race and ethnicity in education: struggling to understand issues in cross-cultural leadership', *Journal of School Leadership*, 12 (2), pp. 116–37.

Smrekar, C.E., and Mawhinney, H.B. (1999) 'Integrated services: challenges in linking schools, families, and communities' in Murphy, J. and Louis, K.S. (eds), *Handbook of Research on Educational Administration*, 2nd edn, San Francisco: Jossey-Bass, pp. 443–61.

Solomon, R.P. (2002) 'School leaders and antiracism: overcoming pedagogical and political obstacles', *Journal of School Leadership*, 12 (2), pp. 174–97.

Volpe, R., Batra, A., Howard, C., Paul, N. and Murphy, S. (2001) *The Leadership/Followership Dimension in Integrating Schools and Community Services (Final Report)*, Toronto: University of Toronto, Institute of Child Study.

Wagstaff, L., and Fusarelli, L. (1995) 'The Racial Minority Paradox: New Leadership for Learning in Communities of Diversity', Paper presented at the annual meeting of the University Council for Educational Administration, Salt Lake City, October.

Walberg, H.J. (1984) 'Improving the productivity of America's schools', *Educational Leadership*, 41 (8), pp. 19–27.

Walcott, R. (1994). 'The need for a politics of difference', *Orbit*, 25 (2), pp. 13–5.

Westbury, M. (1994) 'The effect of elementary grade retention on subsequent school achievement and ability', *Canadian Journal of Education*, 19 (3), pp. 241–50.

Whittey, G. and Power, S. (1997) 'Quasi-markets and curriculum control: making sense of recent educational reforms in England and Wales', *Educational Administration Quarterly*, 33 (2) pp. 219–40.

Yonezawa, S., Wells, A. S. and Serna, I. (2002). 'Choosing tracks: "Freedom of choice" in detracking schools', *American Educational Research Journal*, 39 (1), pp. 37–67.

CHAPTER 4

Teacher leadership: a new orthodoxy?

ALMA HARRIS

Contemporary educational reform places a great premium upon the relationship between effective leadership and school improvement. Both the school effectiveness and school improvement research traditions highlight the importance of leadership in successful school development and change. The effective schooling literature affords a prominent place to the development of leadership in its accounts of the various factors that combine to make up effective departments and schools (Sammons, Thomas and Mortimore, 1997; Sammons, 1999; Harris, 1999; 2001). Similarly, school improvement research has consistently reinforced the importance of leadership in the pursuit of enhanced school and student performance (Mitchell and Sackney, 2001; Mortimore, 2000; Stoll and Fink, 1996; Southworth, 1995).

Effective leadership is widely accepted as being a key constituent in achieving school improvement. The evidence from the international literature demonstrates that effective leaders exercise an indirect but powerful influence on the effectiveness of the school and on the achievement of students (Leithwood, Jantzi and Steinbach, 1999). Whilst the quality of teaching strongly influences levels of pupil motivation and achievement, it has been consistently argued that the quality of leadership matters in determining the motivation of teachers and the quality of teaching in the classroom (Fullan, 2001; Sergiovanni, 2001). As Day et al. (2000 p. 6) note: 'whatever else is disputed about this complex area of activity, the centrality of leadership in securing school improvement remains indisputable'.

Goddard (1998, p. 4) notes 'there are as many definitions of leadership as those who write about the concept'. The literature on school leadership contains a bewildering array of definitions, theories and models. However, while constructions and understandings of the term 'leadership' vary in subtle and numerous ways, one simple but profound assumption prevails – that leadership equates with position or role. A preliminary glance at the research literature reveals that it is dominated by empirical studies derived from headteachers' self-report and description. It is premised upon individual impetus rather than collective action and offers a heroic view of leadership predominantly bound up with headship.

While it is clear that the idea of the head as the solitary, dynamic leader is inadequate for the new directions in educational reform, it still persists. Murphy (2000) notes that the 'great man' theory of leadership prevails in spite of a groundswell towards leadership as empowerment, transformation and community building. Possibly, this is because schools as organizational structures remain largely unchanged, equating leadership with status, authority and position. Gunter (2001) argues that the top-down transmission of what is known simply serves to reinforce a model of leadership that is premised upon individual, rather than collective leadership.

Teacher leadership offers a radical departure from the traditional orthodoxy of school leadership for two reasons. First, because it equates leadership with agency, focusing upon the relationships among people and crossing organizational boundaries. Second, because it sees leadership not simply as being about a role or function but rather as a dynamic between individuals within an organization. One of the most congruent findings from recent studies of effective leadership is that authority to lead need not be located in the person of the leader but can be dispersed within the school in between and among people (MacBeath, 1998; Day *et al.*, 2000). Teacher leadership is separated from person, role and status and is primarily concerned with the relationships and the connections among individuals within a school.

Teacher leadership

Within teacher leadership, 'leadership' and 'leader' are not the same (Lambert, 1998). This model of leadership implies a redistribution of power and a realignment of authority within the organization. It means creating the conditions in which people work together and learn together; where they construct and refine meaning leading to a shared purpose or set of goals. Evidence would suggest that where such conditions are in place, leadership is a much stronger internal driver for school improvement and change (Hopkins, 2000). In practice, this means giving authority to teachers and assisting teachers to use authority wisely. It also means relinquishing the idea of structure as control and viewing structure as the vehicle for empowering others. For teacher leadership to work, a high degree of trust between senior managers and teachers is required. As Evans (1998, p. 183) notes:

> Trust is the essential link between leader and led. It is vital to people's job, status, function, loyalty and it is vital to fellowship. It is doubly important when organisations are reaching rapid improvement which requires exceptional effort and competence, and doubly so again in organisations like schools that offer few motivators.

Teacher leadership is conceptualized as a set of behaviours and practices that are undertaken collectively. It is centrally concerned with the relationships and connections among individuals within a school. A key element in the model of leadership proposed is that the nature and purpose of leadership is 'the ability of those within a school to work together, constructing meaning and knowledge collectively and collaboratively' (Lambert, 1998, p. 5). Taking this stance, leadership is fluid and emergent, rather than as a fixed phenomenon (Gronn, 2000, p. 324). As Wheatley (1999, p. 2) notes:

> We have known for nearly half a century that self-managed teams are far more productive than any other forms of organising. There is a clear correlation between participation and productivity. There is both a desire to participate more and strong evidence that such participation leads to the effectiveness and productivity we crave.

Gronn (2000, p. 333) has suggested that distributed leadership is an idea whose time has come. First, it implies a different power relationship within the school where the distinctions between followers and leaders tend to blur. Second, it has implications for the division of labour within a school, particularly when the tasks facing the organization are shared more widely. Third, it opens up the possibility of all teachers becoming leaders at various times. It is this last dimension that has most potency and potential for school improvement because it is premised upon collaborative forms of working among teachers.

Research has consistently underlined the contribution of strong collegial relationships to school improvement and change. Little (1990) suggested that collegial interaction at least lays the groundwork for developing shared ideas and for generating forms of leadership. Rosenholtz (1989) argued even more forcibly for teacher collegiality and collaboration as means of generating positive change in schools. Collaboration is at the heart of teacher leadership, as it is premised upon change that is enacted collectively. Teacher leadership is premised upon a power redistribution within the school, moving from hierarchical control to peer control. In this leadership model the power base is diffuse and the authority dispersed within the teaching community. An important dimension of this leadership approach is the emphasis upon collegial ways of working. As West *et al.* (2000, p. 39) suggest:

> If this leadership potential is to be realised, then it will have to be grounded in a commitment to learn and develop that inhabits the structures of schools as well as the classroom – it is likely that the school will conceive and act differently from the traditional explanations of leadership and structure. This view of leadership, then, is not hierarchical, but federal. It is a view which is both tight and loose; tight on values, but loose on the freedom to act, opportunity to experiment and authority to question historical assumptions.

There is shared understanding and shared purpose at the core of teacher leadership. It engages all those within the organization in a reciprocal learning process that leads to collective action and meaningful change. In summary, teacher leadership is premised upon the belief that leadership potential is widely distributed amongst organizational members

School improvement

Successful school improvement is dependent upon the ability of individual schools to manage change and development. As Hopkins (2001, p. 2) suggests, 'real' improvement: 'is best regarded as a strategy for educational change that focuses on student achievement by modifying classroom practice and adapting the management arrangements within the school to support teaching and learning'. This necessitates building the 'capacity' for change and development within the school as an organization. Capacity building is concerned with creating the conditions, opportunities and experiences for development and mutual learning. Building the capacity for school improvement necessitates paying careful attention to how collaborative processes in schools are fostered and developed. In particular, it is concerned with maximizing teacher leadership and teacher learning. It suggests that where 'individuals feel confident in their own capacity, in the capacity of their colleagues and in the capacity of the school to promote professional development' (Mitchell and Sackney, 2000, p. 78) school improvement is achieved.

Building capacity for school improvement implies a profound change in understanding schools as organizations. Sackney, Walker and Hajnal (1998, p. 52) argue that:

> The post-modern era suggests a conception of organisations as processes and relationships rather than as structures and rules with conversation as the central medium for the creation of both individual meaning and organisational change. From this perspective, the image of schools as learning organisations seems like a promising response to the continuing demands for re-structuring.

This suggests a view of the school as a professional community in which teachers have the opportunity to learn from each other and to work together. In such communities leadership is distributed throughout the system and improvement occurs from an internal search for meaning, relevance and connection (Mitchell and Sackney, 2000, p. 139). Barth (1990) talks about creating a community of learners in which the prime purpose of the organization is to increase the capacity to bring about collective growth and development.

Capacity-building processes will obviously differ from school to school and from context to context. Of central importance in building learning capacity within organizations is the human perspective. By placing teachers at the centre of change and development there is greater opportunity for organizational growth. Building the capacity for improvement means extending the potential and capabilities of teachers to lead and to work collaboratively. This growth can only be achieved as part of a democratic process in which individual ideas and actions can be freely expressed. When schools operate democratically, then teachers will be more likely to contribute to their development in a positive way (Harris, 2002a).

Leithwood, Jantzi and Steinbach (1999, pp. 811–12) describe how school leaders provide opportunities for teachers to participate in decision-making and lead in school development. Their work highlights the following structuring behaviours:

- distributing the responsibility and power for leadership widely throughout the school;
- sharing decision-making power with staff;
- allowing staff to manage their own decision-making committees;
- taking staff opinion into account;
- ensuring effective group problem-solving during meetings of staff;
- providing autonomy for teachers;
- altering working conditions so that staff have collaborative planning time;
- ensuring adequate involvement in decision-making related to new initiatives in the school;
- creating opportunities for staff development.

Wenger's (1998) notion of communities of practice is also particularly helpful in understanding how teacher leadership can be generated within schools. It suggests that individuals derive their understanding of their work from the community of practice within which they carry it out. The members of the community have a shared understanding of the work and individuals are drawn into the community by a process of learning about the boundaries that define the collection of tasks that make up the practice. There are two important points about communities of practice. First, everyone is a member of more than one community of practice. Teachers, for example, are part of a wider community of teachers, which defines certain aspects of behaviour as legitimate, whilst also being members of a school. Second, teachers are simultaneously members of a school, of a subject area and an individual classroom. Through this multiple membership individuals transact the expectations of one community of practice into others.

Wenger (1998, p. 273) suggests that individuals derive their identity from their membership of, and participation in, communities of practice. He suggests that 'communities of practice become resources for organising our learning as well as contexts in which to manifest our learning through an identity of participation'. Hence, a learning community involves multiple forms of membership and participation. Consequently, to view leadership as a collective activity offers greater opportunity for organizational development, change and improvement (Harris 2001).

There is a body of evidence that demonstrates that teachers work most effectively when they are supported by other teachers and work collegially (Hargreaves, 1994). Collegial relations and collective practice are at the core of building the capacity for school improvement. In schools that are failing, the quality of relationships between teachers will almost inevitably require most immediate attention. The quality of relationships rather than resources or systems enables schools to develop and grow. It is the nature of communication between those working together on a daily basis that offers the best indicator of organizational health. Hopkins, West and Ainscow (1996 p. 177) note that: 'successful schools encourage co-ordination by creating collaborative environments which encourage involvement, professional development, mutual support and assistance in problem solving'.

If sustained improvement is to be achieved, teacher partnerships and other forms of collaboration need to be encouraged. This implies a form of professional development and learning that is premised upon collaboration, cooperation and networking. It implies a view of the school as a learning community in which teachers and students learn together.

Conclusion

Teacher leadership differs from the existing theories that dominate the leadership literature because of the specific focus upon developing various forms of human capital. It has implications for the division of labour within a school, particularly when the tasks facing the organization are shared more widely. It also opens up the possibility for all teachers to become leaders at various times. It implies a redistribution of power and a realignment of authority within the school as an organization. It suggests that leadership is a shared and collective endeavour that engages all teachers within the school (Harris and Lambert, 2003). It also implies that the context in which people work and learn together is where they construct and refine meaning leading to a shared purpose or set of goals.

Louis et al. (1996) found that in schools where the teachers' work was organized in ways that promoted professional community, there was a positive relationship with the academic performance of students. Research by Crowther et al. (2000) reveals that teacher leadership is an important factor in improving the life chances of students in disadvantaged high schools. Silns and Mulford (2002) similarly conclude that student outcomes are more likely to improve when leadership sources are distributed throughout the school community and when teachers are empowered in areas of importance to them. They argue that teachers cannot create and sustain the conditions for the productive development of children if those conditions do not exist for teachers. Empowering teachers in this way and providing them with opportunities to lead is based on the assumption that if schools are to become better at providing learning for students then they must also become better at providing opportunities for teachers to innovate, develop and learn together.

Barth (2000, p. 444) has suggested that 'all teachers can lead'. He proposes that if schools are going to become places in which all children are learning, all teachers must be leaders: 'The fact of the matter is that all teachers harbour leadership capabilities waiting to be unlocked and engaged for the good of the school'.

The question is how to enhance and develop teacher leadership in schools. The answer is not difficult to find but potentially more difficult to achieve. Work by Little (1993) suggests that where teachers learn from one another through mentoring, observation, peer coaching and mutual reflection, the possibilities of generating teacher leadership are significantly enhanced. By investing in the school as a learning community there is greater opportunity to unlock leadership capabilities and capacities among teachers. Sergiovanni (2001) observes: 'Rare is the effective school that does not have an effective head. Adding teacher leadership to the equation ensures that school improvement becomes a way of life in the school'.

Teacher leadership is premised upon the ability to empower others to lead. It is a shared commodity owned by those who work within the school and by those who work on behalf of the school. To cope with the unprecedented rate of change in schools in the twenty-first century requires alternative approaches to school improvement and school leadership. If schools are to be learning communities this cannot be achieved by operating with outdated models of change and school improvement. Similarly, it is unlikely that schools will become learning communities by clinging to singular, individual approaches to school leadership. A new understanding of organizational change and development is emerging, one that operates from the basis of complexity and change rather than rationality and stability. By association, new models of leadership are needed that reflect the leadership capability of the many rather than the few, and recognize that everyone in the school community has the potential to lead.

REFERENCES

Barth, R. (1990) *Improving Schools from Within: Teachers, Parent and Principals Can Make a Difference*, San Francisco: Jossey-Bass.

Barth, R.S. (2000) *The Teacher Leader*, Providence, RI: The Rhode Island Foundation.

Crowther, F., Hann, L., McMaster, J. and Fergurson, M. (2000) *Leadership for Successful School Revitalisation: Lessons from Recent Australian Research*, paper presented at the annual meeting of AERA, New Orleans, LA.

Day, C., Harris, A., Hadfield M., Tolley, H. and Beresford, J. (2000) *Leading Schools in Times of Change*, Buckingham: Open University Press.

Evans, L. (1998) *Teacher Motivation*, London: Cassell.

Fullan, M. (2001) *Leading in a Culture of Change*, San Francisco: Jossey-Bass.

Goddard, T. (1998) Of daffodils and dog teams: reflections on leadership', paper presented to the annual meeting of the British Educational Management and Administration Society, Warwick.

Gronn, P. (2000) 'Distributed properties: a new architecture for leadership', *Educational Management and Administration*, 28 (3), pp. 317–38.

Gunter, H. (2001) *Leadership in Education*, London: Paul Chapman Press.

Hargreaves, A. (1994) *Changing Teachers: Changing Times*, London: Cassell.

Harris, A. (1999) *Effective Subject Leadership: A Handbook of Staff Development Activities*, London: David Fulton Publishers.

Harris, A. (2001) 'Department improvement and school improvement: a missing link? *British Educational Research Journal*, 27 (4), pp. 477–87.

Harris, A. (2002a) *School Improvement: What's In It for Schools?*, London: Routledge.

Harris, A. (2002b) *Leading the Improving Department*, London: David Fulton.

Harris, A. and Lambert, L. (2003) *Building Leadership Capacity for School Improvement*, Buckingham: Open University.

Hopkins, D. (2001) *School Improvement for Real*, London: Falmer Press.

Hopkins, D. West, M. and Ainscow, M. (1996) *Improving the Quality of Education for All*, London: David Fulton Publishers.

Lambert, L. (1998) *Building Leadership Capacity in Schools*, Alexandria, VA: Association for Supervision and Curriculum Development.

Leithwood, K., Jantzi, D. and Steinbach, R. (1999) *Changing Leadership for Changing Times*, Buckingham: Open University Press.

Little, J.W. (1990) 'The persistence of privacy: autonomy and initiative in teachers' professional relations', *Teachers' College Record*, 91, pp. 509–56.

Little, J.W. (1993) 'Teachers professional development in a climate of educational reform', *Educational Evaluation and Policy Analysis*, 15 (2), pp. 129–51.

Louis, K.S., Marks, H. and Kruse, S. (1996) 'Teachers' professional community in restructuring schools', *American Educational Research Journal*, 33 (4), pp. 757–89.

MacBeath, J. (ed.) (1998) *Effective School Leadership: Responding to Change*, London: Paul Chapman Publishers.

Mortimore, P. (2000) *The Road to School Improvement*, Lisse, The Netherlands: Swets and Zetlinger.

Murphy, J. (2000) 'Transformational change and the evolving role of the principal' in Murphy, J. and Seashore, Louis K. (eds) *Reshaping the Principalship: Insights from Transformational Reform Efforts*, Newbury Park: Corwin.

Rosenholtz, S. (1989) *Teachers' Workplace*, New York: Longman.

Sackney, L., Walker, K. and Hajnal, V. (1998) 'Principal and Teacher Perspectives on School Improvement', *Journal of Educational Management* 22 (2) pp. 104–12.

Sammons, P., (1999) *School Effectiveness: Coming of Age in the Twenty-First Century*, Lisse, The Netherlands: Swets and Zeitlinger.

Sammons, P., Thomas, S. and Mortimore, P. (1997) *Forging Links: Effective Schools and Effective Departments*, London: Paul Chapman Publishing.

Sergiovanni, T. (2001) *Leadership: What's in it for Schools?* London: Routledge/Falmer Press.

Silns, H. and Mulford, B. (2002) 'Leadership and School Results' in *Second International Handbook of Educational Leadership and Administration*, Zurich: Kluwer Press.

Southworth, G. (1995) *Talking Heads: Voices of Experience*, Cambridge: University of Cambridge Institute of Education.

Stoll, L. and Fink, D. (1996) *Changing our Schools: Linking School Effectiveness and School Improvement*, Buckingham: Open University Press.

Wenger, E. (1998) *Communities of Practice: Learning, Meaning and Identity*, Cambridge: Cambridge University Press.

West, M., Jackson, D., Harris, A. and Hopkins, D. (2000) 'Leadership for school improvement' in Riley, K. and Seashore, Louis K. *Leadership for Change*, London: Routledge/Falmer Press.

Wheatley, M.J.(1999) *Leadership and the New Science*, San Francisco: Berrett-Koehler.

CHAPTER 5

Learning to lead

JOHN WEST-BURNHAM

The purpose of this chapter is to explore the relationship between the development of effective leadership and the nature of the learning process. Somewhat bizarrely, leadership and learning – two key concepts in any debate about education – are the two most elusive and problematic concepts. There is only limited consensus as to what they actually mean. Much of the debate around them is concerned with elucidation rather than application. The discourse that they generate is characterized by normative statements that are largely aspirational in character. Leadership and learning are seen as higher order activities that permit exhortation, prescriptions and aspiration rather than analysis and discussion. If there is a 'conceptual illiteracy' about each of these terms, there is an even greater problem when they are linked. The potential for obfuscation and reductionism becomes almost irresistible.

The reductionist and instrumental approach has tended to be the response to this conundrum. Talk of leadership and learning has tended to be expressed in terms of managing and teaching. Leadership has been defined in terms of super-management and learning has been seen as the successful completion of a series of events. There has been an implicit assumption that more and better management and attendance at more and better events equates with leadership and learning. This rationalistic fallacy leads to a disarming confidence that learning to lead is understood and under control.

This chapter will explore three issues: the nature of leadership, the nature of learning and strategies for leadership learning. However, it is impossible to approach such a discussion without a number of fundamental assumptions (or prejudices). The 'foundation principles' of this chapter are:

- learning is a unique, individual and subjective process;
- leadership is a distinctive, higher order activity, which provides the context and direction for management;
- leadership is a composite of knowledge, skills, experience and personal qualities in varying ratios according to time, place and personality;
- leadership is understood through relationships, not status.

The nature of leadership

The world would be a much easier place if the 'great man' theory of leadership was a serious proposition rather than a historical confidence trick. Leadership based on hierarchical status, the product of a hierarchical schooling system that produced in the few the confidence to lead and in the many the dependency that created the willingness to follow, has a beguiling simplicity. Such a model might have been pragmatically, if not morally, justifiable at a given time. The traditional view of headship in England, derived from the public schools of the nineteenth century, still has powerful resonances in the anglophone world.

However, the world has changed and the debate about the nature of leadership has started to change with it. At the most rarefied level this change is in response to our changing understanding of the laws governing the universe.

> In the old science, the Newtonian paradigm, nature is seen as simple, law-abiding and ultimately controllable. The whole science is about organised simplicity. In the new science, the quantum paradigm, nature is seen as complex, chaotic and uncertain. This science is about learning to live with and to get the fullest potential out of complexity. Attempts at control can be counterproductive. (Zohar, 1997, p. 43)

It is not unreasonable to propose that the historical model of leadership was an expression of the prevailing world view: essentially hierarchical, controlling and non-contestable. Wheatley (1992, p. 133) reinforces the conceptual leap that is needed to move from the old to the new paradigm.

> But if we can trust the workings of chaos, we will see that the dominant shape of our organisations can be maintained if we retain clarity about the purpose and direction of the organisation. If we succeed in maintaining focus, rather than hands-on control, we also create the flexibility and responsiveness that every organisation craves. What leaders are called upon to do in a chaotic world is to shape their organisations through concepts, not through elaborate roles or structures.

It is a profound conceptual leap from the new science to the new school term; from the abstract complexities of quantum mechanics, chaos theory, complexity and fuzzy logic to the pragmatic, immediate and very practical imperatives of ensuring that the school actually runs on the first day of term. And yet the first day of term is complex, chaotic and fuzzy (extremely so for some) and it works. The reality is, of course, that there are multiple perspectives operating and that no one person can control such an event, only set broad parameters. The day works because of what Johnson (2001, p. 20) calls emergent complexity, which shows: 'The distinctive quality of growing smarter over time, and of responding to the specific and changing needs of (the) environment'.

Virtually every organization works only because of emergent complexity – the truth is that most organizations, in their totality, cannot be managed; only aspects of the organization's life are amenable to management *per se*. For most of the time there have to be local initiatives operating within a broad consensus. In applying the concept of emergence to the evolution of cities, Johnson points out that: 'They are the sum of thousands of local interactions: clustering, sharing, crowding, trading – all the disparate activities that coalesce into the totality of urban living'. (ibid, p. 109).

And so it is for schools. It is physically impossible for one person to manage the complexity that is a school; what is required is leadership that meets the definition offered by Bennis and Townsend (1995, p. 6): 'Leaders are people who do the right things and managers are people who do things right. Leaders are interested in direction, vision, goals, objectives, intention, purpose and effectiveness'.

'Doing the right thing' is a task of great complexity and which is vested with high significance. The basis of this definition is clearly moral – the higher order activities which give the organisation shape and purpose and create the context in which all other activities take place. Leadership is therefore about making choices; the nature of schools as organizations means that they are understood through the decisions that are made (as opposed to products offered or symbolic roles that are discharged). Because of the social significance that is invested in education, decisions taken by educational leaders have profound implications relative to many other activities. Thus it can be argued that any process that seeks to develop educational leaders has to provide the means to function in the context of activities that combine high complexity with high significance. Figure 5.1 seeks to represent this relationship: quadrant 1 represents high-level leadership activity – work that is value-driven, person-orientated, strategic and creative; quadrant 2 represents the symbolic aspects of leadership; quadrant 3 describes the routine administration that is fundamental to every organizational role but has relatively low impact; quadrant 4 characterizes a great deal of management work – the operationalization of what emerges from quadrant 1. Clearly the learning and development needs relevant to each quadrant will differ considerably.

4	High complexity Low significance	High complexity High significance	1
3	Low complexity Low significance	Low complexity High significance	2

Figure 5.1 The nature of leadership work

Gardner (1995, pp. 302–4) highlights two aspects to this tension:

Unless we can find or form leaders who retain some links to expert knowledge, on the one hand, and some ability to communicate to non-experts on the other, our world is likely to spin even further out of control. By pretending that leadership will happen naturally or that leadership can be inculcated incidentally, we ensure that there will be an unacceptably low number of individuals who can fill the essential desiderata of leadership. And we make it less likely that leaders will emerge from less dominant groups and less privileged institutions in the society.

The crucial points here are, first, the distinctiveness of leadership being concerned with both the task and the process and, second, the importance of deliberate, systematic and targeted leadership development. There is another significant tension with regard to leadership development – the balance that has been achieved between over-intellectualizing the process and retreating into the comfort of reductionist and instrumental lists. There is a natural pragmatism that focuses on the operational aspects of the job rather than its essential nature and purpose – development strategies have to recognize this duality of demand. However, it is in the conceptually complex areas that the essence of leadership is to be found. A synthesis of the leadership themes set out in Hesselbein, Goldsmith and Beckhard (1996) and Chowdhury (2001) produces the following, unmediated, taxonomy:

Accountability	*Federation*
Beliefs	*Followership*
Change	*Futures*
Chaos	*Globalization*
Collaboration	*Individualism*
Communication	*Innovation*
Communities	*Integrity*
Complexity	*Knowledge*
Creativity	*Networks*
Culture	*Spirituality*
Distributed	*Stewardship*
Emotions	*Technology*
Empowerment	*Values*
Failure	*Vision*

These concepts are the emerging vocabulary of leadership, in essence the agenda for leadership development.

The nature of learning

If the nature of leadership is complex, problematic and elusive, then the nature of learning is even more so. Much of the discourse about learning characterizes it as an essentially passive process – the product of being taught, attending a course and being lectured by an expert. Historically a great deal of management development has been concerned with the transmission of information with little regard for its relevance, applicability or potential impact.

One way of trying to understand how leadership learning takes place is to use the image of a mental map – a conceptual framework. The purpose of leadership development is to increase the usefulness of the map by ensuring that it is an accurate depiction of the territory to be covered and that it is useful to the individual. The usefulness of any map is determined partly by its scale and partly by the information that it depicts (and how it is depicted). As leaders develop, so their personal mental maps become more sophisticated, more detailed and, often, more idiosyncratic. At the early stages of leadership development an atlas might be appropriate; this will be refined to a road map, which in turn will be developed into an A–Z street plan. However, the best maps are those that draw on generic information and personalize it to suit a particular purpose at a given time. Although the analogy can be pushed too far, it may be helpful to think of leadership learning as the process of creating personal meaning from a complex environment, with multiple reference points so as to facilitate a journey.

If leadership learning is about the creation of personal maps, then the process is subject to a number of variables that can be best expressed as propositions:

- to create new knowledge, leadership development has to recognize and respect prior knowledge;

- experience of itself has only limited value unless it is mediated by reflection and so modifies knowledge and behaviour;
- successful learning is a function of positive emotional engagement that will inform motivation and sustainability;
- all leadership learning will be processed through personal value systems that will determine significance, applicability and prioritization.

For leadership learning to lead to attitudinal change and so to significant behavioural change, all four factors have to be recognized and incorporated into any strategy. The absence of any one component will compromize the other three; for example, the lack of emotional engagement will severely inhibit learning from experience because it is the interpersonal and intrapersonal that actually allow us to make sense of our experiences. Equally, knowledge that is not applied to experience is impoverished and the absence of values makes all learning pointless.

However, these propositions about the process of learning are helpful only if they are set in the context of a meaningful definition of learning. The nature of learning can perhaps be best understood not as one process but rather operating in a number of modes. Table 5.1 argues that there are three modes of learning. Each is valid in its own right and they are non-sequential, but each mode has profound implications for the integrity of the potential impact of learning on the learner.

Shallow learning is perhaps the most common mode. It results in the ability to replicate information; experience is unmediated, the motivation to learn is extrinsic and it results in acceptance and dependence. Shallow learning characterizes a lot of 'educational' experiences from school to university and is very prevalent in training. Deep learning, by contrast, creates understanding – what happens when generic information becomes personal knowledge, which can then be transferred between contexts and over time. Experience is understood through reflection and the motivation to learn is intrinsic. Deep learning allows personal interpretation and creates a sense of autonomy and confidence.

Profound learning moves into a different level of significance altogether. Shallow learning results in the ability to apply a formulated response to a problem, if it is presented in the right way. Deep learning allows a range of responses to be formulated, tested and applied. Profound learning leads to the problem and solution being redefined. Profound learning is about the creation of personal meaning and so enhances wisdom and creativity. Experience is processed intuitively. The motivation to learn is moral and the outcome of profound learning is the ability and willingness to challenge orthodoxy. Such learning is sustained through interdependent engagement in problem solving and thinking.

Table 5.1 *Modes of learning*

Shallow	Deep	Profound
Replication	Understanding	Meaning
Application	Transfer	Creativity
Information	Knowledge	Wisdom
Experience	Reflection	Intuition
Extrinsic	Intrinsic	Moral
Acceptance	Interpretation	Challenge
Dependence	Independence	Interdependence

Shallow learning is exemplified in what might be called 'tourist' Italian. I have a limited vocabulary, some knowledge of grammar and can survive. Deep learning of Italian would allow me to engage in spontaneous and significant conversations. Profound learning would mean that not only could I engage meaningfully in the high points of Italian culture but possibly contribute to them. And the same applies to the practice of medicine, to the artist, to the joiner and the use of computers. There is a clear incremental shift – akin to the progression from novice to expert. The purpose of leadership development is to facilitate this growth.

But if leadership is about transformation, creating the future, vision and values and enhancing the quality of personal relationships, then it can be truly developed only through profound learning. Another important reason why leadership development has to focus on profound learning is the issue of sustainability – long-term learning, development and growth can be sustained only by intrinsic and moral motivation. This is fundamental to the notion of leadership as an interactive process – the change and development of leadership styles and strategies is possible only if learning is seen as axiomatic to any definition of leadership. Barth (2001, p. 119) quotes the anonymous dictum: 'The way to learn is by leading. The way to lead is by learning' and then goes on to exemplify it by describing an Aspiring Principals Programme (APP), which uses experienced principals as mentors:

> The distinguished principals are the very heart of the APP. In a real sense they are the APP. By enlisting these educators as mentors for aspiring principals, the program enables the veterans to pass on the wisdom of their craft. Of equal importance, the APP provides for these seasoned professionals a very sophisticated forum for their own professional development. Through writing, conversation, mentoring and networking, they reflect on and make visible the best of their practice and continually share it with the APs and other distinguished principals. (Ibid., p. 125)

Profound learning comes about because of the profundity of the experiences, relationships and resources that are made available to support it. A practical example of this model can be found in the issue of *managing* change. The first question to be raised is the problem of managing change (surely change involves leadership?) Shallow learning about the process of change would result in a formulaic presentation of the various academic models, the ability to describe personal experiences of change, engagement in the process because of external imperatives and an uncritical and unquestioning acceptance of the process. Deep learning in this context is manifested in the ability to develop a personal model of the change process that is a synthesis of a range of sources, and the ability to translate that model into action. Experience is mediated through reflection, which allows for personal interpretation and a sense of autonomy. Profound learning, however, results in the creation of personal meaning; integrating principles, values and practice so that behaviour is intuitive and the response to change is creative, challenging, ethically driven and integrative.

Deep and profound learning are rooted in social relationships; indeed it could be argued that learning exists only in a social construct. It is difficult to conceptualize any learning that does not involve some form of interaction with others; even solitary engagement with a text is a form of dialogue with the author. In discussing the work of Vygotsky and its implications for our understanding of pedagogy, Daniels (2001, p. 67) argues:

Teaching and assessment should be focused on the potential of the learner, rather than on a demonstrated level of achievement or understanding ... teaching should create the possibilities for development, through the kind of active participation that characterises collaboration, it should be socially negotiated and it should entail transfer of control to the learner.

This emphasis on 'potential', 'possibilities', 'participation', 'negotiation' and 'transfer of control' provide important insights into the nature of the social relationships for effective leadership leaning and, indeed, for all learning.

The centrality of learning as a set of relationships is reinforced by Lave and Wenger (1991, p. 98) in their discussion of communities of practice, which they define as:

A set of relations among persons activity, and world over time and in relation with other tangential and overlapping communities of practice. A community of practice is an intrinsic condition for the existence of knowledge, not least because it provides the interpretive support necessary for making sense of its heritage.

Thus leadership learning might be seen as induction into the community of leadership practice; it is a process that is rooted in the person: 'Because learning transforms who we are and what we can do it is an experience of identity. It is not just an accumulation of skills and information, but a process of becoming – to become a certain person' (Wenger, 1998, p. 215).

Leadership learning is therefore perhaps best seen as a series of complex relationships, often unpredictable, of varying levels of significance and multiple modes of engagement. While it might be possible to formalize aspects of this process, to create opportunities and to provide support, the process of learning to lead is, necessarily, as complex as the nature of leadership itself. If it proves possible to simplify a process in this context then it is probable that either learning or leadership have been compromised. Although Wenger is speaking of school students in the following quotation he might equally be speaking of school leaders:

Deep transformative experiences that involve new dimensions of identification and negotiability, new forms of membership, multimembership, and ownership of meaning ... are likely to be more widely significant in terms of the long-term ramifications of learning than extensive coverage of a broad, but abstractly general, curriculum. (Ibid., p. 268)

The 'deep transformative experiences' involve the creation of 'new' knowledge. In this context, again as for school students, it is wrong to perceive the acquisition of knowledge as the mastery of a curriculum. It is rather the engagement in relationships that creates knowledge. The engagement between the learners' pre-existing or personal knowledge and public knowledge is the dynamic process that leads to the creation of new knowledge, rooted in personal understanding. Knowledge is thus a personal construct, constantly adjusting as the learner impacts on the world as much as the world impacts on the learner.

Learning for leadership can therefore be described only as the formation of coalitions of perceptions, not as taxonomies of skills, knowledge and behaviours.

Strategies for learning to lead

The creation of a personal nexus – the complex interaction of a number of variables, to formulate a mental model of reality – has a parallel in what we are increasingly understanding about neurological functioning. Our perception of the world is the result of patterning in the brain – the building of bridges between brain cells in order to create a coalition of meaning. Profound learning is the result of a similar process – the creation of rich and significant patterns that make our mental models sophisticated, deep and capable of enrichment and elaboration.

To achieve such a level of learning requires a range of strategies to be in place:

- the development of a range of cognitive skills: analysis, logic and the interpretation of data;
- learning activities that are based on problem-solving in real-life situations;
- reflection on actual experience based on appropriate feedback;
- challenge derived from new ideas, confronting performance, etc.;
- coaching to help mediate the perceived gap between actual and desired performance;
- a sense of moral purpose, a vocation, a search for personal authenticity;
- the creation of a community of practice to support the above.

In practical terms the most powerful basis for profound learning is supported reflection – support being provided through coaching and mentoring, the use of a reflective journal, structured reading to inform the review and, perhaps most importantly, peer review and feedback on actual practice. The Leadership Programme for Serving Heads (LPSH) offers headteachers in England both a sophisticated conceptual framework to support review and support for analysis and action planning. However, LPSH is an event rather than a process and although it models excellent practice it needs to be part of a personal developmental process that is axiomatic to the leadership role. Perhaps one of the most significant components of such a process is the recognition that learning is a fundamental component of the job itself – not an adjunct or a bonus but a key element in the definition of the role. It is well known that leadership development, especially for headteachers, is the first casualty of any constraint on resources – time or money. This is not to argue for more time to be spent on courses but rather for the principles outlined above to become implicit to personal working patterns, for example:

- building review into meetings and all individual and team projects;
- scheduling time and space for regular reflection;
- establishing a structured and regular pattern of professional reading and creating opportunities to discuss and apply insights gained;
- regular meetings with a coach and/or mentor as part of a sustained (and sustaining) developmental relationship;
- acting as a coach/mentor to others;
- creating networks (virtual and actual) to nourish support and challenge.

All that has been written so far makes at least one fundamental assumption – that there is the personal motivation and desire to develop as a leader. Without this everything else is superficial. In essence, effective schools are led by effective people, school improvement is contingent on personal improvement and organizational development requires individual development. Most importantly, a learning organization (and what else can a school be?) has to be led by leaders who are learners.

REFERENCES

Barth, R.S. (2001) *Learning by Heart*, San Francisco: Jossey-Bass.

Bennis, W. and Townsend, R. (1995) *Reinventing Leadership*, London: Piatkus.

Chowdhury, S. (2001) *Management 21c*, London: Pearson Education.

Daniels, H. (2001) *Vygotsky and Pedagogy*, London: Routledge/Falmer Press.

Gardner, H. (1995) *Leading Minds*, New York: Basic Books.

Hesselbein, F., Goldsmith, M. and Beckhard, R. (eds) (1996) *The Leader of the Future*, San Francisco: Jossey-Bass.

Johnson, S. (2001) *Emergence*, London: Allen Lane, Penguin Press.

Lave, J. and Wenger, E. (1991) *Situated Learning*, Cambridge: Cambridge University Press.

Wenger, E. (1998) *Communities of Practice*, Cambridge: Cambridge University Press.

Wheatley, M.J. (1992) *Leadership and the New Science*, San Francisco: Berrett-Koehler.

Zohar, D. (1997) *Rewiring the Corporate Brain*, San Francisco: Berrett-Koehler.

CHAPTER 6

Without leadership?

PETER GRONN

The last two decades of the second millennium bore witness to what can only be described as a massive, worldwide resurgence of interest in leadership. While it is difficult to quantify the precise scale and scope of the mood of ebullience, by any standard this development was truly extraordinary. Anywhere one cared to look, the signs were evident. The rate of scholarly and popular publishing on leadership soared. The leadership phenomenon also received probably unprecedented attention in the print and visual media. The numbers of leadership gurus and their consultancies mushroomed. In universities, the establishment of leadership development centres with a national and global outreach quickly became de rigueur. And, in a lemming-like scramble for market edge, numerous university faculties frantically rebadged their courses and subjects with 'leadership' in preference to 'management' or 'administration' – although interestingly, despite the appeals of critics for leadership, rather than management education (e.g. Bennis and Nanus, 1985, pp. 219–21), the high-profile Master of Business Administration title remained pretty much immune from this contagion. Overall, however, a leadership industry of vast proportions emerged and boomed.

The key question is not so much why this remarkable phenomenon occurred, but, rather, why leadership? Why not something else? What is this mantra that leadership is the elixir for societies and organizations telling us? Or, consider the obverse situation: the possibility, not of a surfeit of leadership but of its absence – what would that be telling us? Would 'alarm about a "lack of leadership"', perhaps, be taken as 'a sign of increasing social despair and massive learned helplessness' (Barker, 2001, p. 478)? So deeply entrenched has the phenomenon of leadership recently become in the natural order of things in schooling and other sectors of society that this question is scarcely even contemplated by anyone, let alone asked. Nowadays, the idea that organizations might operate without leadership is an unthinkable iconoclasm bordering on heresy. Symptomatic in this regard is the recent reaction of a university vice-chancellor to criticism of a draft advertisement for a new faculty dean. When a colleague at a meeting attended by the author pointed out that there was no mention of leadership, a slightly embarrassed vice-chancellor apologized for the omission and assured everyone the oversight would be rectified by redrafting the document.

Yet this situation of supposed normality has not always been the case. In fact, just over two decades ago, leadership underwent a near-death experience, as Hunt (1999, p. 130), guest editor of a symposium on transformational and charismatic leadership in *Leadership Quarterly* reminded his readers:

To be active in the field as I was in the 1970s and 80s was to question its survival as a seri-ous area of academic interest. A number of us became very concerned. First we defended it ... but as the critical crescendo continued we began to have doubts ourselves ... Maybe the concept had outlived its usefulness. Could the concept of leadership wither away? Was it really, as many Europeans argued, a U.S. phenomenon, overemphasized because of our indi-vidualistic culture?

In retrospect, there was indeed a problem, which, in essence, was concerned with the legitimacy of leadership. There were two dimensions to the problem: the first concerned the performance of a particular set of social institutions, and the second was to do with the appropriate modes for representing the operation and perfor-mance of those same institutions. While the first of these two aspects (which may have partly been a trigger for the second) was mainly an American phenomenon, the second was of more general and enduring significance.

For both Bennis and Nanus (1985) and Gardner (1984), the crisis of the period typified by Hunt as the doom and gloom years for leadership lay with the gov-erned, rather than the governors, for somehow or other a culture conducive to 'reluctant followership' (Bennis and Nanus, 1985, p. 12) and an 'anti-leadership virus' (Gardner, 1984, p. 323) had taken root. Part of the difficulty, in Gardner's view, lay with institutional decentralization and the separation of powers at the heart of American federalism, so that with leadership dispersed among so many groups, a cacophony of fragmented voices was the norm. What had once been interpreted as the peculiar virtue of American democracy by the great nineteenth-century French observer Alexis de Tocqueville, had now, apparently become an inherent weakness. The price paid for this plural expression of liberty was an over-all incapacity to deal with transcendent questions, and the inability of any single American institution to instil social unity and over-riding moral purpose.

The antidote for what was perceived to be a malaise of follower disengagement, we know in retrospect, became a diet of 1980s' visionary inspiration in the guise of transformational leadership. Quite apart from the conventional scholarly criticism that it has attracted, this approach to leadership has reawakened the ongoing ten-sions with American cultural values that preoccupied Gardner. Keeley (1998, p. 125), for example, sees the concentration of influence in the hands of transforma-tional leaders as contrary to the view of one of the founding fathers, James Madison, which was that, in a democracy, 'inspired leadership can do as much harm as good'. Transactional leadership, by contrast, is asserted as being much better suited to a system founded on a separation of powers doctrine. Previously, Hook (1955) had voiced similar concerns about the so-called 'event-making' hero of history, who later became a prototype for the transformational leader. Undeterred, Bass (1998, p. 175), the leading advocate for transformational leader-ship, responded to Keeley with the claim that the checks and balances of power separation in a federal system promote gridlock, that can be cleared away only by the best of leadership that is 'both transformational and transactional'.

Coincident with these American cultural developments, the wider field of leader-ship spawned its own peculiar brand of melancholia – a rash of anti-leadership thinking. From the mid-1970s a number of scholars began voicing their disquiet. The first was Miner (1975, p. 200) who asserted that leadership had 'outlived its usefulness'. The field had lost its way, said Miner (1975, p. 198), for 'we simply do not know what we want to know'. As an alternative mode of representing schol-arly understanding of how organizations worked, Miner proposed the concept of control – control both external (through hierarchical, professional, group and task-related norms) and internal (as in self-control) to the individual. He was soon followed by a succession of doubters who were prominent in the fields of organizational behaviour and management, and who either exited the field completely or questioned its orthodox assumptions. These luminaries included Calder (1977), Pfeffer (1977), Kerr and Jermier (1978), Argyris (1979) and Mintzberg (1982).

Perhaps the most high profile rejection was Argyris's abandonment of leadership for action science (1979). He claimed that research in leadership was mainly additive or confirmatory in its significance (i.e. successive findings represented more of the same), rather than cumulative (i.e. the findings provided no qualitative advance in knowledge). If leadership research was to be useful, however, the knowledge it produced had to be connected with practitioners' theories-in-use, otherwise it would remain distant, remote and ornamental. Surprisingly, perhaps, Argyris even chastised himself for the folly of his own earlier forays in leadership, mainly because 'the theories-in-use that subordinates held were never mapped ... I never studied the learning system that they created' (ibid., p. 61). Much of Argyris's subsequent work helped lay the foundations for reflective practice, organizational learning and the rectification of defensive reasoning and routines amongst senior organizational leaders.

But the commentators whose criticisms had the most enduring effects were Calder (1977) and Kerr and Jermier (1978). Calder (p. 181) criticized his peers for 'little sense of really having achieved anything in the way of new or profound understanding of leadership beyond that available from everyday knowledge'. As an alternative he proposed to reorient the focus of research away from leadership, which he saw as common-sense lay terminology for interpersonal influence, towards the construct of attribution. Leadership subsumed a range of behaviour that could be accommodated equally well under alternative labels, yet it was the presumed causal potency of leadership in the minds of so many people that gave it its currency. Rather than legitimating this lay view, Calder saw it as the scholar's job to subject such assumptions to critical scrutiny. The purpose of attributions of leadership was that they served merely to 'make the perceiver's world more predictable and manageable', and they were triggered by inferences made on the basis of 'differences in behaviour which fit expectations of how leaders typically behave' (ibid., pp. 186–7, 190). Far from endorsing lay reasoning about leadership, the proper object of study was to investigate the cognitive processes through which people inferred causal potency on the basis of their observations of the situated behaviour of sets of actors. According to this line of reasoning, leadership was nothing more than a perception, albeit a culturally powerful one.

Pfeffer (1977) echoed Calder's scepticism and highlighted the processes by which leadership was socially constructed. He showed, for example, how social myths and institutional processes both fostered the legitimacy of particular attributions of leaders, and reinforced the assumption that leadership was somehow related causally to organizational performance. Such processes included various selection and inauguration mechanisms, and symbols and ceremonies. One way of reducing the powerful effects of these phenomena, he speculated, might be to choose leaders 'by using a random number table' (ibid., p. 110). Pfeffer's and Calder's efforts helped clear the ground for important subsequent work on cognitive attribution theory and information processing (Lord and Maher, 1993) and the phenomenon known as the 'Romance of Leadership' (Meindl, 1995).

Kerr and Jermier (1978) were the first writers to canvass the possible redundancy of leadership. There were occasions, they claimed, in which leadership could be nullified, substituted or rendered irrelevant. They suggested, for example, that because of factors such as individuals' predispositions, the inherent nature of tasks they performed and the processes in workplaces that affected employees' levels of performance and their relations with superiors, researchers were faced with 'a taxonomy of situations where we should not be studying "leadership" (in the formal hierarchical sense) at all' (ibid., p. 377). Thus, feedback on an individual's performance from peers or clients, or their self-motivation, could substitute for the (direct or indirect) influence of a formally designated leader. Leadership was also unnecessary when the work tasks were routine, well-rehearsed, unambiguous and known by heart. In fact, in a series of experiments, Kerr and Jermier (p. 398) suggested that in 12 of 24 posited occasions characteristics inherent in a task (e.g. its intrinsically satisfying nature) or in a subordinate (e.g. her or his ability) could substitute for both task-oriented or relationship-oriented leader behaviour. One possible implication was that other influences on task performance replaced face-to-face interaction with leaders. Another was that leaders influenced employees more indirectly through a variety of processes 'by making decisions that minimise[d] the need for the face-to-face exercise of power' (Jermier and Kerr, 1997, p. 99). Such findings narrowed significantly the scope of and need for direct leader influence, and complicated the identification of its locus and form.

Kerr and Jermier's (1978) arguments stimulated a string of subsequent endorsements of self-leadership and self-leading work teams (e.g. Manz, 1986, 1992; Manz and Sims, 1980; Manz, Mossholder and Luthans, 1987) as possible substitutes for leadership. Even so, reflecting two decades later, Jermier and Kerr (1997, p. 97) were disappointed with the overall reception accorded their substitutes idea, and believed that their peer commentators had not appropriately addressed the implications of their original claim.

Perhaps the most forcefully articulated antileadership view from this early period was advanced by Mintzberg (1982). From his perspective, a substantial amount of leadership research failed his Bill and Barbara test. Two friends, Bill and Barbara, were invited by Mintzberg to read and comment on the utility of a number of recent leadership writings. In most cases, these failed dismally, because they had tried to measure the unmeasurable. For Bill, for example, the test was that leadership was non-quantifiable, and to try to quantify it was rather like an art critic saying that 'if the ceiling of the Sistine Chapel were one foot higher and the index fingers of God and Adam one inch further apart, the impact would be 2 per cent less' (Mintzberg, 1982, p. 246). With a few exceptions, leadership researchers themselves had not been providing leadership to their natural constituency: practitioners. In fact since the 1960s, in Mintzberg's judgement:

> *Every theory that has since come into vogue – and I shall not name them for fear of losing all my friends – has for me fallen with a dull thud. None that I can think of has ever touched a central nerve of leadership – approached its essence ... Since the beginning, there seems to have been a steady convergence on the peripheral at best, and all too often on the trivial and irrelevant.* (Ibid., p. 250)

Mintzberg's immediate target, then, was leadership research. But what about leadership itself: did it matter? Mintzberg (ibid., p. 253) believed the answer was yes, although a number of his fellow academics took a contrary view. When he pressed one such colleague to reconcile his espoused view with his well-known politicking in deanship selection processes, the latter's embarrassed response was that he acted this way 'just in case!'. Facetiously, Mintzberg asserted that the only way to change such entrenched academic attitudes to leadership was to submit proposals for research funding and submissions to journals to initial 'screening by an intelligent practitioner' who would assess their relevance before approval (ibid., p. 259).

In the mid-1980s and on into the 1990s, neo-trait theories of leadership became the new orthodoxy. In this climate, antileadership arguments appeared only spasmodically. When they did, the cynicism to which they gave voice represented an almost mirror image reversal of the gusto with which the newly ascendant visionary, transformational and charismatic models were being proclaimed. Thus, for Bailey (1988), Vanderslice (1988) and Gemmill and Oakley (1992), the institutionalized leadership of high profile individuals had to be seen for what it was: a conspiracy to render followers inert, docile and compliant. This was because followers were invariably duped by leaders into uncritical devotion, they were disempowered by them and discouraged from taking responsibility for their own actions and they were deskilled by them by falling for the belief that they needed somebody else to tell them what to do.

Early in the new millennium, cracks have begun to appear once again in the leadership edifice, only this time the criticisms seem to be qualitatively different from those encountered previously. First, there has been a reaction to neo-trait theories. The first generation of trait theories had fallen into disfavour in the late 1940s, but the criticism of second generation trait theory reflects an unprecedented concern with leader-centrism and the monopoly or near monopoly of leadership by a single designated leader. Yukl (1999, p. 301), for example, has attacked transformational leadership as a reversion to a heroic archetype and for its failure to describe adequately the presumed direct influence of leaders on followers, while Beyer (1999, p. 318) deplores the neglect of context by transformational and charismatic theorists. She also notes 'the romantic oversimplification' of describing organizations 'as if they had only one leader as a source of leadership'. Second, some writers openly raise the possibility of jettisoning the category of 'follower' (e.g. Miller, 1998, p. 18), mainly on the grounds that as the basis of organizational authority switches increasingly from status to competence, organizations will comprise distributed systems of leadership with ensuing processes of 'negotiation between leaders'. Others, such as Lakomski (1999, p. 48) propose bypassing leaders and leadership altogether in favour of research into effective practice, in which theorizing is reduced to 'explaining how the relevant neuronal patterns are activated which facilitate organizational (or any other) action'.

What, then, of the future of leadership? In the most recent mainstream rebuttal of these dissenting voices, Shamir (1999, p. 51) interprets them as evidence of a recurring pendulum swing between so-called strong and weak theories of leadership, and he dichotomizes focused leadership and instances of what he terms 'leaderless collective action'. The former he labels 'strong' – or 'disproportionate social influence in which the party that exerts greater influence on others (the leader) can be identified' – whereas the latter (i.e. distributed leadership, leader substitutes) he deems 'weak'. In recognition of the fact that numerous workplaces are being reshaped by computer-supported cooperative work (CSCW) systems, and imperatives such as flexibilization and career boundarylessness, Shamir's response is to call for a new charisma (ibid., p. 64). His revamped neo-trait approach is designed to strip charismatic leadership of 'the perception of the leader as extraordinary or the attribution of super-human qualities to the leader'. The new charismatic leader should possess 'strong enough referent power to explain how leaders perform the integrative functions', offer answers to 'why' questions, increase organization members' commitment, and 'provide the psychological safety needed in times of change, all this without the support of permanent strong cultures, or other "substitutes"'.

But these more recent criticisms of leader-centrism surely portend a much more fundamental problem for leadership, for they are an acknowledgement of wholesale changes in the division of labour in the workplace. The tradition in leadership studies has always been to presume or to take for granted the existence of a binary division of workplace labour: i.e. a 'leader' and 'followers'. But for how much longer can this assumption be sustained? Ethnographers in the burgeoning field of workplace studies (Hutchins, 1996; Engeström, 1999), for example, are accounting for performance outcomes, including instances of complex computational problem solving, in settings across the human service and corporate sectors, with scarcely any hint of leadership as a causal factor. Moreover, a key implication of recent research in cognitive psychology and connectionism is that organizations may be analogous to autonomous, emergent and self-sustaining systems in the natural world, which are able to evolve and adapt without any central locus of control (Clark, 1999).

The key questions, it would seem, then, are: who needs leadership, and what do they need it for? To retain credibility and utility in the light of these intellectual developments, commentators will need to rethink or even dispense with many of the prevailing leadership assumptions. These include its individualism, its exaggerated sense of agency, its naïve realist ontology and its presumed causal potency. Most of all, leadership will need to be shredded of its pet dualistic terminology. What, for example, is the rationale for continuing to dichotomize the organizational world into two groups of people, leaders and followers, and then assuming their unproblematic correspondence to superiors and subordinates? This verbal dexterity should be seen for what it is: a fudging of roles. Why, finally, are we so uncomfortable with employment relations terms, such as employers and employees? And, if our focus is on overall sound organizational practice, why do we not simply refer to colleagues, peers or collaborators?

It would be premature, on the basis of this brief survey of developments, to conclude that leadership has run its race. On the other hand, complacency in the face of these emerging challenges would, at best, be a prescription for indifference to leadership and, at worst, the irrelevance of it in explaining the work of organizations. When confronted by a similar set of circumstances some two decades or so ago, the response, as we have seen, was for mainstream thinkers to rework their tried and true trait prescriptions. But such a response in the new millennium, one suspects, is much more likely to be received as a recipe for making do without leadership than as a formula designed to win the hearts and minds of scholars and practitioners.

REFERENCES

Argyris, C. (1979) 'How normal science methodology makes leadership research less additive and less applicable' in Hunt J.G. and Larson L.L. (eds), *Crosscurrents in Leadership*, Carbondale, IL: Southern Illinois University Press.

Bailey, F.G. (1988) *Humbuggery & Manipulation: The Art of Leadership*, Ithaca: Cornell University Press.

Barker, R.A. (2001) 'The nature of leadership', *Human Relations*, 54 (4), pp. 469–94.

Bass, B.M. (1998) 'The ethics of transformational leadership' in Ciulla, J.B. (ed.), *Ethics: The Heart of Leadership*, Westport, CN: Quorum Books, pp. 169–92.

Bennis, W. and Nanus, B. (1985) *Leaders: The Strategies for Taking Charge*, New York: Harper & Row.

Beyer, J.M. (1999) 'Taming and promoting charisma to change organizations', *Leadership Quarterly*, 10 (2), pp. 307–30.

Calder, B.J. (1977) 'An attribution theory of leadership' in Staw, B.M. and Salancik, G.R. (eds), *New Directions in Organizational Behaviour*, Chicago, IL: St Clair.

Clark, A. (1999) *Being There: Putting Brain, Body, and World Together Again*, Cambridge, MA: MIT Press.

Engeström, Y. (1999) 'Expansive visibilization of work: an activity-theoretical perspective', *Computer Supported Cooperative Work*, 8 (1), pp. 63–93.

Gardner, J.W. (1984) 'The anti-leadership vaccine' in Rosenbach, W.E. and Taylor, R.L. (eds), *Contemporary Issues in Leadership*, Boulder, CO: Westview Press.

Gemmill, G. and Oakley, J. (1992) 'Leadership: an alienating social myth', *Human Relations*, 45 (2), pp. 113–29.

Hook, S. (1955) *The Hero in History*, Boston: Beacon Press.

Hunt, J.G. (1999) 'Transformational/charismatic leadership's transformation of the field: an historical essay', *Leadership Quarterly*, 10 (2), pp. 129–44.

Hutchins, E. (1996) *Cognition in the Wild*, Cambridge, MA: MIT Press.

Jermier, J. and Kerr, S. (1997) 'Substitutes for leadership: their meaning and measurement – contextual recollections and current observations', *Leadership Quarterly*, 8 (1), pp. 95–101.

Keeley, M. (1998) 'The trouble with transformational leadership: toward a federalist ethic for organizations' in Ciulla, J.B. (ed.) *Ethics: The Heart of Leadership*, Westport, CN: Quorum Books, pp. 111–44.

Kerr, S. and Jermier, J. (1978) 'Substitutes for leadership: their meaning and measurement', *Organization and Human Performance*, 22, pp. 374–403.

Lakomski, G. (1999) 'Against leadership: a concept without a cause' in Begley, P.T. and Leonard, P.E. (eds) *The Values of Educational Administration*, London: Falmer Press.

Lord, R.G. and Maher, K.J. (1993) *Leadership and Information Processing: Linking Perceptions to Performance*, London: Routledge.

Manz, C.C. (1986) 'Self-leadership: toward an expanded theory of self-influence processes in organizations', *Academy of Management Review*, 11 (3), pp. 585–600.

Manz, C.C. (1992) 'Self-leading work teams: moving beyond self-management myths', *Human Relations*, 45 (11), pp. 1119–40.

Manz, C.C. and Sims, H.P. (1980) 'Self-management as a substitute for leadership: a social learning theory perspective', *Academy of Management Review*, 5 (3), pp. 361–7.

Manz, C.C., Mossholder, K.W. and Luthans, F. (1987) 'An integrated perspective of self-control in organizations', *Administration and Society*, 19 (1), pp. 3–24.

Meindl, J.R. (1995) 'The romance of leadership as a follower-centric theory: a social constructionist approach', *Leadership Quarterly*, 6 (3), pp. 329–41.

Miller, E.J. (1998) 'The leader with the vision: is time running out?' in Klein, E.B., Gabelnick, F. and Herr, P. (eds) *The Psychodynamics of Leadership*, Madison, CN: Psychosocial Press.

Miner, J.B. (1975) 'The uncertain future of the leadership concept: an overview', in Hunt J.G. and Larson L.L. (eds) *Leadership Frontiers*, Kent, OH: Kent State University Press.

Mintzberg, H. (1982) 'If you're not serving Bill and Barbara, then you're not serving leadership' in Hunt, J.G., Sekaran, U. and Schriesheim, C.A. (eds) *Leadership: Beyond Establishment Views*, Carbondale, IL: Southern Illinois University Press.

Pfeffer, J. (1977) 'The ambiguity of leadership', *Academy of Management Review*, 2, pp. 104–14.

Shamir, B. (1999) 'Leadership in boundaryless organizations: disposable or indispensable?' *European Journal of Work and Organizational Psychology*, 8 (1), pp. 49–71.

Vanderslice, V.J. (1988) 'Separating leadership from followers: an assessment of the effect of leader and follower roles in organizations', *Human Relations*, 41 (9): pp. 677–96.

Yukl, G. (1999) 'An evaluation of conceptual weaknesses in transformational and charismatic leadership theories', *Leadership Quarterly*, 10 (2), pp. 285–305.

CHAPTER 7

Invitational leadership and the pursuit of educational living

JOHN NOVAK

These are the times that try educators' souls.

Throughout the world, educators are being bombarded with mandates to change – the faster, the better. Trying to work with care and integrity in the midst of this transformational rush, many dedicated educators feel that business methods are being thrust upon them that are cutting out the heart of their educational sensibilities. Education, for them, is not a matter of profit and loss but a commitment to assist unique people to learn important things in order to live more meaningful lives. To ignore these commitments is to risk losing educational heart. To work with these commitments is to send the message that the educational life is worth living.

Invitational leadership is about promoting educational living. It is based on the premise that the heart of schooling is schooling with an educational heart, that is headed in a defensible direction and that is able to come to grips with vital issues. This perspective on leadership is centred on an approach that links educational relationships with a language of appreciation and transformation. The key elements of invitational leadership are its intrinsic connections to educational living and humanely effective school practices, its basis in an ethical theory of communication, and its application to different parts of an educator's life.

An educational perspective

> *To put it simply, there is no surer way to bring an end to schooling than for it to have no end.* (Postman, 1996, p. 4)

Education for a democratic society can be seen as an imaginative act of hope. This hope is based on a belief that people can learn to savour, understand and better more of their individual and collective experiences. That is, as a result of being more educated, people should be able to appreciate more of their daily life, be able sort out the world in more meaningful ways and be able to improve their personal and public lives. In other words, education for a democratic society is a commitment to the belief that people are capable of becoming more adept at educational living. This pursuit of educational living can serve as a moral compass with its own excellences and rewards and can differentiate educational pursuits from business and bureaucratic endeavours, which, understandably, have other goals and guiding ideals.

A key aspect of educational leadership is summoning, sustaining and surpassing imaginative acts of hope by keeping alive the active tension between the ideal of educational living and the actualities of school practice. The relationship between education and schools is similar to the relationship between love and marriage, or the relationship between justice and law. In each pair, the former is the ideal and the latter is the social institution. The two are not the same but need to be vitally connected for there to be ethical life in either. It is the job of educational leaders to keep the life processes going and to see that this educational ideal does not overwhelm or underwhelm those working in schools.

This educational ideal is overwhelming if it is so far removed from actual school practice that it seems to be merely a remote wish. This ideal is underwhelming if it does not call forth persistence, resourcefulness and courage. It is the art of educational leadership to reach the right 'whelm' level and have this ideal work to enable people to learn to savour, understand, and better more of their experiences in and out of school. The art of this perspective on leadership is aided by using key ideas and strategies of invitational education.

Invitational education

Leaders articulate and define what has previously remained implicit or unsaid; then they invent images, metaphors, and models that provide a focus for new attention. (Bennis and Nanus, 1985, p. 39)

Invitational education is a system of ethical assumptions, concepts and strategies for developing and sustaining imaginative acts of hope in schools and beyond. Based on the idea that education is an ethical activity in which human potential is called forth rather than dictated or manipulated, invitational education emphasizes the quality of doing-with, dialogical relationships. By focusing on the messages that are sent and received, it is a communicative theory of ethical practice that aims to create contexts where people want to be, want to learn and want to become wiser in the pursuit of educational living.

As an evolving theory of ethical practice, invitational education is based on five interlocking assumptions (Purkey and Novak, 1996, p. 3).

- people are able, valuable, and responsible and should be treated accordingly;
- educating should be a collaborative and cooperative activity;
- the process is the product in the making;
- people possess untapped potential in all areas of worthwhile endeavour;
- this potential can best be realized by places, policies, programmes and processes specifically designed to invite development and by people who are intentionally inviting with themselves and others, personally and professionally.

These assumptions take on a definite form when they are linked to a unifying metaphor based on humans in relationships.

Invitational education is based on the metaphor that involvement in the educative process is comparable to the act of inviting – of calling forth participation in activities that provide opportunities for savouring, understanding and bettering experiences. Invitational leadership is about bringing about, supporting and extending the quantity and quality of messages that promote enhanced living.

From a dialogical perspective, the heart of the educational practice is the invitation. An invitation can be defined as the summary of the content of messages communicated verbally, non-verbally, formally and informally through people, places, policies, programmes and processes. Inviting messages inform people that they are valuable, able and responsible and can behave accordingly. The structure of this system of thinking and acting can be better understood by looking at key concepts.

Foundations

Invitational education aims to provide an ethical and democratic context for schooling. Just as a Christmas tree provides a context for decorative ornaments, invitational education provides a context for the various activities undertaken in the name of schooling. This integrative context requires a solid foundation in order to work with depth and sensitivity.

Invitational education has three interlocking foundations:

- Democratic ethos: a belief that all people matter and can participate meaningfully in their self-rule.
- Perceptual tradition: a perspective emphasizing that people need to be understood according to how things seem to them.
- Self-concept theory: a viewpoint that all people are internally motivated to maintain, protect and enhance their perception of who they are and how they fit into the world.

These three foundations provide an ethical and political commitment to the development of human potential, a psychological focus on how individuals perceive and interpret events, and a motivational orientation that builds on the ongoing dynamics contained within each person.

Levels of inviting

People are never neutral in their interactions with others. Everything people do and every way they do it sends a message that either calls forth or shuns human potential. Attention to the messages people send and their resolve in sending those messages provide a four-level classification system for examining what takes place in and around schools. This four-level classification system can give an educational leader a language for discussing what is and what should be happening in schools.

Any message can be categorized as follows:

- Intentionally disinviting: done on purpose to negate someone's worth.
- Unintentionally disinviting: done without resolve but still negating another.
- Unintentionally inviting: done without reflection but having positive effects.
- Intentionally inviting: done on purpose for purposes that can be ethically defended.

It is the job of invitational leaders to fight the practice and legitimating of intentionally disinviting messages; to call attention to and change unintentionally disinviting conduct; to help articulate a deeper rationale for unintentionally inviting behaviours; and to cultivate, celebrate, and extend intentionally inviting practices. This cultivation, celebration and extension of messages applies to oneself and others.

Areas of inviting

How long can educators maintain an intentionally inviting commitment? Perhaps only as long as their hearts can endure. The strength of heart necessary for being intentionally inviting develops as an educator applies an inviting approach to oneself and others, personally and professionally. This means that an invitational leader needs to orchestrate the following:

- Inviting oneself personally: for example finding ways to celebrate everyday life, recharging one's batteries, maintaining one's sense of wellness.
- Inviting others personally: for example cultivating a solid support group, developing an imaginative social committee, joining an online chat group.
- Inviting oneself professionally: for example working on advanced degrees, doing action research, presenting at professional conferences.
- Inviting others professionally: for example developing new programmes; publicly recognizing contributions of colleagues, taking the school into the community.

Leading for educational living involves keeping each of these areas alive and creatively orchestrating a vital balance among them. This goal of leading for educational living can be managed in a systematic manner by attending to the relationships involved in educational leadership.

Leading and managing educational lives

Try, try, try to be inspired. If you cannot be inspired, at least be methodical.

Conceptually, an act of educational leadership involves a leader interacting with individuals so that values and knowledge are attained and extended. This process takes place within an educational community for the sake of the development of a particular type of society. These relationships can be seen as the educational LIVES model (Leaders, Individuals, Values and knowledge, Educational community and Society), with each relationship being seen in light of an important belief and strategy for invitational leadership (Novak, 2002).

Relating to the leader within

Invitational leaders must first of all be human and only after that professional. This type of leadership begins with personal beliefs that are then embodied in sustained and imaginative actions. And so, rather than trying to learn sequences of unanchored professional behaviours, invitational leadership begins by reflecting on the following personal beliefs about self, others, purpose and frame of reference:

- Self: work to feel connected with others and think in terms of 'we' rather than 'they'. This manifests itself in a sense of empathy.
- Others: strive to see people as able to learn important things. This manifests itself in a sense of efficacy.
- Purpose: work to attend to people's thoughts and feelings. This manifests itself in a sense of focus.

- Frame of reference: strive to think long-term rather than short-term. This manifests itself in a sense of perspective.

These personal beliefs get to the heart of the matter. They are translated, tested and refined as they are put into practice in the following ten skills of inviting:

- Preparing the environment: creating clean, comfortable, safe work areas.
- Preparing oneself: remembering what it is like to be invited and realizing one's strengths in doing this.
- Developing goodwill: acting in a trustworthy way and respecting confidences.
- Reaching a variety of people: attending to those who are often ignored.
- Reading situations: viewing what's happening from the perspective of the participants.
- Making invitations attractive: demonstrating care, competence and creativity in sending messages.
- Ensuring delivery: being clear about what is being invited.
- Negotiating alternatives: developing mutually agreeable options.
- Handling rejection: learning from what happened when what happened – was not what you wanted to happen.
- Following through: providing what was offered and celebrating success.

Developing these ten skills involves being persistent, being able to use many dimensions of one's personality and being able to face difficult situations.

Relating to individuals in conflict

Even if invitational leaders have people-oriented beliefs and develop the skills of inviting, they will still have to deal with conflict. Conflict is an inevitable part of life and can be a basis for change and growth. It also can be draining and painful. Invitational leaders seek to deal with conflict in straightforward ways that are consistent with the principles of invitational education and also effective. They seek to deal with conflict:

- at the lowest possible emotional level: being emotionally strained makes imaginative solutions less likely;
- with the least expense of energy: having less energy takes away from other endeavours;
- in an appropriate and caring manner: maintaining an inviting stance represents a deepening of educational integrity;
- in a potentially growth-producing way: seeking ways to turn difficult situations into educational experiences.

With these principles in mind, invitational leaders follow the 'rule of the six Cs'. The key is to start at the lowest level and use that C as thoroughly as possible and only move to the next level as necessary. Here is a sketch of each of the Cs in a potential conflict situation:

- Concern: decide if this is a situation that needs action now by you.
- Confer: meet in private, listen and get a personal commitment from the person to change.

- Consult: remind the person of previous commitment and help work out a plan.
- Confront: again, remind the person of previous steps and mention consequences that will follow if behaviour persists.
- Combat: take action to follow through on consequences.
- Conciliate: restore a noncombative quality to situation.

Will this approach work with all conflict situations? No. However, it can be helpful in many. Elementary school students at Cameron Park Elementary School in Hillsborough, North Carolina use the six Cs to handle problems that develop in the playground or classroom. Invitational leaders work to teach it to others so that it becomes the preferred way of dealing with conflict at their school.

Relating to valued knowledge

An invitation needs an object to complete its meaning. It is always an invitation to something. From the perspective stressed here, people are invited to learn to savour, understand and better more of their experiences. This is more apt to happen if people learn that they can learn and can feel good about who they are and what they are doing. This is a key part of the valued knowledge of an inviting school. Focusing on four aspects of self-concept-as-learner gives invitational leaders a key for examining what is taught and learned in their school:

- Relating: do people have a chance to trust, appreciate, and identify with their peers and with the school? Are they encouraged to become a part of a larger 'we'?
- Asserting: what degree of control do people have over their learning situations? Can people tell teachers when they are learning and not learning?
- Investing: are people encouraged to try new things? Can they identify with what they are doing?
- Coping: can people meet learning expectations? What happens when they do not?

Invitational leadership is about artfully orchestrating these four areas so that people are able to develop more of the desire and disposition to become life-long learners. This has a better chance to happen in an aligned educational community.

Relating to educational communities

Everything done in schools and every way it is done contributes to the success of students and to the quality of life of the educational community. Schools are ecosystems made up of people, places, policies, programmes and processes. Focusing on each of these and applying steady and imaginative pressure can enable people to work together to develop aligned educational communities.

- People: everyone in the school is an emissary for the school, for good or ill. Is there a sense of collegiality in the school in which all who work there are seen as competent and caring?
- Places: the maintenance and enhancement of a school send an ongoing message about the quality of the leadership that is taking place there. Do the signs posted in the school express courtesy and explanation?

- Policies: rules tell you about who is in charge and how things are done. How is the telephone answered at the school?
- Programmes: the curricular and extra-curricular activities should meet the wide spectrum of needs of the students. Are any school programmes elitist, sexist, racist, ethnocentric, lacking in educational integrity or just not working?
- Processes: the overall tone, feel and flavour of the spirit of the school tells you whether people are being done-with or done-to. Can people in this school say 'We are all in this together'?

Inviting leaders use teams made up of faculty, staff, students, parents and community members to address each of these Ps. The careful alignment of these teams can work to make the school 'the most inviting place in town'.

Relating to the larger society

Invitational leaders are advocates for educational living within and outside their schools. Their job as educational leaders is not merely to respond to the latest societal pressures but to work to direct these forces toward educational ends using educational means. For this to happen, it is important that their school members have wide and varied connections to the outside world and that the larger community is welcome within the school. Here are some ways for the school to connect with the larger community:

- create a colourful, informative, up-to-date website;
- write articles for the local newspaper or neighbourhood newsletter;
- organize displays of student work in local stores and agencies;
- involve students in community projects;
- contact radio and television stations to make announcements about the school;
- schedule a lunch meeting with local estate agents and show them around the school.

There is a variety of ways to involve the community in the school. This includes inviting parents and community members to participate in school programmes, school surveys and beautification projects. In addition, with the pressure to form partnerships with business groups, invitational leaders have an ethical responsibility to establish guidelines for these working relationships. These guidelines can deal with the following issues (Citizens Bank of Canada, 2000):

- Human rights: what is the human rights record of the company in regard to child or prison labour?
- Military weapons: to what extent is the company involved in the manufacture of weapons of mass destruction or torture?
- Employee relations: what is the company's record on employee health, safety, labour practices or employment equity?
- Environment: does the company have a progressive record on ecological issues?
- Sustainable energy: is the company involved in the production of questionable sources of energy?
- Tobacco: does the company manufacture and promote tobacco products?

- Treatment of animals: does the company test animals in the development of the goods it produces?
- Business conduct: does the school do its business in ethical ways?

All these issues are complex and involve many subtleties. In addition, each issue needs to be looked at individually in the light of deliberated ethical principles and reliable information. Invitational leaders promote educational living by inviting those in the school and business world to discuss these issues in informed and civil ways so that all can learn from the experience and fair, imaginative and ethical policies can be developed. This is not easy, but it cannot be ignored in an institution dedicated to educational living. In an educational world with mandates to change, it is not business as usual.

Final statement

Is that all there is, my friend?

Educational leadership is an ethical practice dependent on a heightened sensitivity to the importance of ideals and the subtleties of school practice. Business models of leadership miss their mark in schools if they do not touch the heart of these ideals and if they override these subtleties.

Invitational leadership focuses on summoning, sustaining and extending imaginative acts of hope by helping to develop the persistence, resources and courage necessary to keep alive the heart of educational living. An invitational theory of practice provides assumptions, concepts, strategies, and insights that attempt to connect with an educator's deepest commitments, best thoughts and creative plans for action. This theory of practice can be applied systematically to the personal, interpersonal, curricular, organizational and societal realms. By learning to think and converse in a language of appreciation and transformation, all involved in schools can work to become educational leaders for life. That is both the ends and means of invitational leadership. During these times of mandated change, should dedicated educators settle for anything less?

REFERENCES

Bennis, W. and Nanus, B. (1985) *Leaders: The Strategies for Taking Charge*, New York: Harper & Row.

Novak, J.M. (2002) *Inviting Educational Leadership: Fulfilling Potential and Applying an Ethical Perspective to the Educational Process*, London: Pearson Education.

Novak, J.M. and Purkey, W.W. (2001) *Invitational Education*, Fastback 488, Bloomington, IN: Phi Delta Kappa Educational Foundation.

Postman, N. (1996) *The End of Education: Redefining the Value of School*, New York: Vintage.

Purkey, W.W. and Novak, J.M. (1996) *Inviting School Success: A Self-Concept Approach to Teaching, Learning, and Democratic Practice*, Belmont, CA: Wadsworth.

PART TWO

Leadership and Management Processes

BRENT DAVIES

Introduction

Over the last ten years there has been a huge expansion in books on leadership, often playing down the critical role of management. In leading and managing organizations it is important to keep a balance between the two activities of leadership and management. Leadership ideas and direction that cannot be translated into action will be ineffective. Similarly, efficient management activities that do not have a sense of direction or purpose will not take the organization forward. What is needed is a balance.

A humorous view of why it is important to focus on both leadership and management is provided by the following quotations. The first, from the manager of the LA Dodgers baseball team, seemed to sum up the importance of management: 'We've been working on the basics because, basically, we've been having trouble with the basics' (Bob Ojeda quoted in Moe, Bailey and Lau, 1999, p. 68). It is important that the basics of good curriculum design, good teaching and learning strategies and safe, caring environments are established and maintained. Indeed, without these then little else can be achieved. However, it is important that we do not just replicate some formula for good practice year after year; we need to reassess and redirect our schools to be successful in the future as well as currently.

The second quotation is from Wayne Gretzky, arguably the most successful player in the history of the North American ice hockey league. When asked the secret of his success he gave a simple but telling reply: 'I skate to where the puck is going to be, not where it has been' (Moe, Bailey and Lau, 1999, p. 37). It is also important to develop leadership vision and direction so that the organization can meet the challenges of the future.

Part Two tries to merge good management and good leadership in a review of traditional management functions from a strategic leadership perspective. The four functions analysed here are:

- strategy: planning the direction of the organization
- reengineering: rethinking the school as an organization
- marketing: communicating the organization's values and purposes
- finance and budgeting: resourcing the organization.

Strategy in education has become a much used but little understood word. When seen in a planning context the increased demands for accountability by central governments has led to what many regard as obsessive short-term target setting. Strategy as seen by these centralized accountability frameworks is often little more than a series of short-term plans linked together. What is needed is a much more holistic approach to planning. Brent Davies and Barbara Davies develop a conceptual framework for developing strategic understanding in schools and go on to provide a model and a process of planning that can be utilized in schools. This model is supported by Les Bell's critical review of the direction strategy needs to take in schools.

To achieve strategic development, the historic incremental approaches of TQM and school improvement may prove inadequate to the task. An additional view of organizational development is required. To achieve it Brent Davies looks at re-engineering as a means of thinking differently about schools by using the lens of reengineering to focus on core processes rather than organizational structures. Having established a conceptual basis for this part, Greg Barker and Derek Wise, in two case studies, give insights into how two leading headteachers have used a reengineering perspective to change their schools.

Of course, none of this practice can be realized if there is not a good communication process operating in school. This process can be evaluated by using a marketing perspective. Brent Davies and Barbara Davies provide an analysis of marketing in schools. One of the key elements here is the importance of organizational mindset and culture in relationship to marketing. Taking up this challenge, Nick Foskett provides a critique of marketing and organizational culture and provides three strategic tools for leaders to deploy in their schools.

Finally, Part Two looks at the critical issue of resource management in schools to provide the means of financing a school's operation.

REFERENCE

Moe, M.T., Bailey, K. and Lau, R. (1999). *The Book of Knowledge: Investing in the Growing Education and Training Industry*, New York: Merrill Lynch & Co.

CHAPTER 8

Strategy and planning in schools

BRENT DAVIES AND BARBARA DAVIES

Strategy has become a key aspect of leadership in schools. It is seen as desirable and necessary for schools to master and engage in strategy. However, there is not always a common understanding of what strategy and strategic planning is in schools. This chapter will draw together some perspectives on strategy and articulate a model of planning for schools. It will then go on to consider how they can be applied in practice.

Mintzberg, Ahlstrand and Lampel (1998, pp. 9–15) articulate the well known five Ps for strategy, which provides a useful conceptual map of strategy. They see strategy as a plan, a pattern, a position, a perspective and a ploy. The definition of strategy as a plan is used when the organization's objectives are sequenced into a definable series of actions. The definition of a pattern is used when consistent behaviour is demonstrated over time, so the emerging pattern becomes the successful organization's strategy. Strategy as position is related to the organization defining its activities in one part of the market or service sector in which it operates. Strategy as perspective relates to the way that the organization looks at itself and its broader context. Strategy as a ploy relates to an organization ostensibly developing one approach to outwit an opponent, while in fact following a different approach. The first four Ps provide a different way of looking at strategy; the fifth is probably of less use in education and presents some ethical dilemmas.

What is clear is that when we talk about strategy it is useful to see it as a process, in that it sets the direction of the organization and by doing so focuses the efforts of the organization in a consistent and coherent way. The standard text for business students, Johnson and Scholes (1993), provides a good basic definition of strategy as: 'the direction and scope of an organisation over the long term: ideally, which matches its resources to its changing environment' (ibid., p. 11).

Strategic planning and strategic thinking are not the same

The danger of talking about strategy is that one confuses strategic thinking with strategic planning. Strategic planning can become a linear, incremental process that builds year on year. This process begins to direct the organization, rather than the organization directing the process, and the result is the school becomes immune to radical thought and challenge. This is the danger of strategic planning because it often does not break out of the existing paradigm of thinking. In Mintzberg's view (1994) there are dangers in assuming that events can automatically be predicted in any sort of detail or certainty. He maintains that the whole process is far too prescriptive and that strategic planning by the top leaders of an organization ignores the realities of planning experienced by those at the operational interface. Koch (2000, p. 131) considers the approach 'is rightly unpopular, and lives on only in primitive quarters'. This is ironic considering the emphasis on strategic planning, especially strategic school development planning, in the school sector.

What may be of more use is strategy as perspective – the way we look at things. This may encompass not only strategic thinking but also strategy as vision and strategy as learning. For a more detailed look at the various schools of thought in strategy, Mintzberg, Ahlstrand and Lampel (1998) outline ten schools of interpretation of strategy in 'Strategic Safari – a guided tour through the wilds of strategic management'. Garrat (1995, p. 2) sees 'strategic thinking' as:

> *The process by which an organisation's direction-givers can rise above the daily managerial processes and crises to gain different perspectives of the internal and external dynamics causing change in their environment and thereby giving more effective direction to their organisation. Such perspectives should be both future-orientated and historically understood.*

This perspective is shared by Mintzberg (1995, p. 67) who considers that: 'strategic thinking means seeing ahead. But, in fact, you cannot see ahead unless you can see behind because any good vision of the future has to be rooted in an understanding of the past.' As well as considering other aspects of strategic thinking Mintzberg makes the perceptive point (ibid, p. 70) that there needs to be the quality of 'seeing it through' if the thinking is to deserve the label strategic.

Having considered the dimensions of strategy, the limitations of strategic planning and the importance of strategic thinking, we need to consider how a strategic approach can be developed in a school. It is important for leaders in education to be able to establish 'mental models' of complex areas, not only to develop their own understanding but also to build understanding within others, in the organization. We need a model of strategy that will be of use as a frame of reference for education leaders and also a model of planning that can be applied to the complex world of schools.

A model of strategy

In a very perceptive conceptualization of strategy, Max Boisot (1995) provides a model for strategic management that is very applicable to the education sector (*see* Figure 8.1). The structure of his model has two axes. First, he maps change, which he considers in its dynamic form is best described as turbulence, ranging from low to high turbulence. Second, he maps levels of understanding of the nature and dimensions of that change and an organization's understanding of the ability to respond to change. Within this framework he plots four domains of strategy: strategic planning, emergent strategy, intrepreneurship and strategic intent.

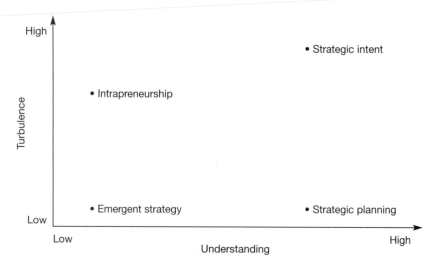

Figure 8.1 Typology of strategies
Source: Boisot, 1995, p. 40.

Strategic planning

Strategic planning is based on the premise that in broad terms (dealing with aggregated data) it is possible to plan over the medium term, say, three to five years, because the environment is predictable. With strategic planning it is assumed that the environmental context of the organization does not remain static but is changing at a rate slower than the organization can understand the change and act on it. It is also assumed that short-term changes are just that – they are not fundamental changes in the paradigm in which the organization exists. As considered earlier, words like proactive (looking forward and taking action), linear (there is a predictable path) and often incremental (the organization is building a strategy over time) are often associated with strategic planning. This is still true for significant parts of a school's activities. For example, student numbers in 4–11 or 11–18 schools are relatively stable and predictable. Whereas the intake year may fluctuate, it is a reasonable assumption that four-year-olds get older and become five-year-olds and then six-year-olds etc. So projections over three to five years have some degree of predictability, assuming a disastrous inspection report is not due! Similarly, having appointed three new staff, schools can assume incremental drift on salaries and the increased budget expenditure predicted, and also, of course, retirements of older members of staff in their late 50s or early 60s, which will reduce budget expenditure. A good example of predictable expenditure would be a repainting or refurbishment project spread over five years.

While educational change is a fact of life, key areas of the curriculum such as literacy and numeracy are likely to remain at the centre of both government and school agendas. This is why strategic planning is in the right-hand quarter of Figure 8.1. It is operating in an environment in which there is a moderate to low level of change (the fundamental nature of the organization has not been challenged) and there is a high level of understanding about the level of turbulence and how to understand its nature and its impact. In schools in the UK, with School Development Planning, and in states like Victoria in Australia, with School Charters, the features of strategic planning have been incorporated into an accountability framework. However, where it may be possible for detailed planning to work over a one- to two-year period, extending that linear planning in detail, as is often expected, to a third, fourth and fifth year, does not make those plans strategic; they are simply over-detailed wishlists with little or no relationship with reality.

To summarize, strategic planning takes place in stable, predictable parts of a school's environment, dealing with broad aggregated data within a three to five-year time frame.

Emergent strategy

Emergent strategy is best thought of as learning from doing. It occurs when an organization is presented with a change that although significant, is not fundamental to the existence of the organization and those in charge have little understanding of the changes and how best to implement them. In such circumstances a process of learning by doing, or trial and error, can be utilized. This, of course, can be a trial for others if the leader or manager makes many errors! As with strategic planning, while there is a significant change it is not of a magnitude that the organization cannot adapt to it. However, unlike strategic planning, this change involves a reactive process. The organization reacts by building on the initial limited or low level of understanding to develop a strategy.

This is an approach often deployed by school leadership when faced with multiple initiatives from central government. The schools are left with little time or choice as to whether or how to implement the change, but build up experience by doing rather than by planning ahead. A good example would be the introduction of performance management in the UK. Rapid introduction of the initial training forced schools to develop expertise as they went along. After going through one cycle of the performance management system, the school will have done some things well and can repeat that experience. It will then find the things that it has been less successful at and will not repeat those. Thus a pattern of successful experiences are built up and a strategy is formed.

Strategic planning is not a superior form of planning because it is proactive, nor is emergent strategy an inferior sort of planning because it is reactive. Each strategy is appropriate given the context of the level of understanding and the time frame within which the organization is operating.

Intrapreneurship

The term 'entrepreneur' describes a creative and dynamic individual who develops products and sells them to the external market. The term 'intrapreneur' describes the same creative and dynamic type of individual but one who trades within a larger organization. So the head of one of a number of divisions within a larger company would have autonomy to be creative to trade with other divisions of the company. Intrapreneurship describes the planning framework of decentralized management. With a turbulent and rapidly changing environment and little knowledge at the centre of the complexity of operating in one of the divisions, planning has to take a different form. The form it takes is one of laying down a very limited number of central requirements and allowing the sub-units considerable freedom in how to operate and how to achieve those central requirements. It can be applied to education either at the local or central government level or within the school.

National or state governments have used a combination of centralization and decentralization as part of their reform efforts. By instituting a raft of reforms or initiatives at the centre and facing the criticisms of how individual schools will cope with multiple implementation, they have solved (or avoided) the questions by simultaneously implementing a series of decentralized management schemes to increase schools' site-based decision-making powers to implement those reforms. The schools are then held accountable by a limited number of central accountability measures, such as test scores and inspection results. Thus coping with little understanding at the centre in a turbulent environment is achieved by giving additional power to the sub-unit and making responsible by increased delegated powers and responsibilities. These powers are, of course, limited by the imperatives to meet central targets.

At the individual school level, it is doubtful that any individual leader would attempt to understand every detail or aspect of major curriculum reform such as the National Curriculum in the UK. In practice he/she would delegate that responsibility to individual subject leaders and hold them accountable by some overall school requirement. So intrapreneurship is a strategic approach where the central unit copes with complexity by making the sub-unit responsible for limited central targets in a framework of increased decentralization and site-based management.

Strategic intent

Strategic intent allows an organization to plan in a turbulent environment with a broad understanding without the necessity to engage in obsessive detail in the planning process. Strategic intent involves the leader of the organization being able to articulate a limited number of strategic intents – to prevent loss of focus these should be no more than five. These intents involve significantly 'leveraging up' the organization's performance in critical areas. Therefore, with strategic intent, a capability and capacity-building process is necessary.

Strategic planning encompasses concepts like linear, predictable, rational and aggregated data. It can be summarized as, in broad terms, you know where you want to go and you know how to get there. However, in an increasingly turbulent environment, such planning is not always possible and strategic intent might be more useful. Strategic intent is described by Boisot (1995, p. 36) as 'a process of coping with turbulence through a direct, intuitive understanding, emanating from the top of the firm and guiding its efforts'. In simple terms, it could be said that you know broadly where you want go but not how to get there.

When using the concept of strategic intent, the school sets itself a limited number of intents and these are expressed in concrete terms. They are not vague 'visions', but specific areas of activity. They may be considered as visions into action. The leader in the school is aware of areas for fundamental change and improvement and know whats s/he wants to achieve but does not immediately know how to achieve them. A good example would be developing a success and high achievement culture across the whole school community. The challenge is in living with the ambiguity that organizational capability is developed first to understand the nature and dimensions of the area for development and then to build solutions. Strategic intent is about tackling deep-seated cultural change and fundamental rethinking by building organizational capability and competencies, rather than assuming that the school has a set of simple linear plans that it can put into action. This capability enhancement is based on increased knowledge and understanding as to *how* to perform at a higher level as well as *what* to perform.

To achieve strategic intent, it is necessary to go through four stages, as shown in Table 8.1. With a strategic planning approach it is possible to go straight to stage four. However, the capability-building process necessary in establishing a set of common strategic intents involves working through all four stages.

Table 8.1 *Building strategic intent: the ABCD approach*

Articulate	1	Strategic intent
Build	2	Images Metaphors Experiences
Create	3	Dialogue Cognitive map Shared understanding
Define	4	Strategic perspective Outcome orientation Formal plans

Source: Davies, 2001, p. 17.

Inspection frameworks seldom understand strategy, often seeing it as simply the addition of an extra year to an existing short-term planning framework. Certainly external inspection systems, such as the Office for Standards in Education (OFSTED), want planning frameworks with definable outcomes that can be measured. That precision is fine for some activities. However, when we come to activities that are more complex and culturally bound, and that deal, in the words of Hargreaves (2000, p. 2), with changing 'social and emotional understanding', such precision is not possible. With these deep-seated challenges of shifting organizational culture, setting intents while the organization builds an understanding both of the nature of the intent and the capability to undertake it, is the only way to achieve sustainable transformation.

The challenge is to be able to devote energy and direction to the establishment and development of strategic intents while 'fighting off' the reductionist approach of external inspection that wants definable outcomes at the start of every plan.

A planning framework for schools

Hoyle (1986) distinguishes between two types of theory: theory for understanding and theory for action. This is a useful concept; both Mintzberg, Ahlstrand and Lampel (1998) and Boisot (1995) provide theories for understanding. How do these theories for understanding translate into theories for action and practice? In the

UK experience, theories for understanding were articulated in early models of school planning and were given a significant emphasis with *Planning for School Development* (DES 1989) being supported later by *Development Planning* (DES, 1991). Writers such as Hargreaves and Hopkins (1991), Skelton, Reeves and Playfoot (1991), West and Ainscow (1991) and Puffitt, Stoten and Winkley (1992) and Davies and Ellison (1992) articulated the theme. Later work by MacGilchrist *et al.* (1995), Broadhead *et al.* (1996) and Fidler (1996) developed the field.

The earlier work as represented by DES (1989) assumed a circular process approach of audit – construction – implementation – evaluation, combined with a system's view of external influences and constraints. The limitations of this approach are two-fold. First, it assumes planning is a short-term operational activity since the model proposed did not have a strategic dimension. Second, it assumed a rational linear approach that in practice is not always feasible. This DES (1989) approach is reflected in the work of Hargreaves and Hopkins (1991) and West and Ainscow (1991). Later, National Professional Qualification for Headship Materials (DfEE, 2000) show only limited understanding of the need to set short-term planning in a medium-term strategic framework.

A different 'theory for action' approach is Fidler (1996). This is a highly rationalistic approach, largely drawn from the work of Johnson and Scholes (1984) in the business sector. Johnson and Scholes use the three-stage linear process of strategic analysis, strategic choice and strategic implementation. Their definition of strategy revolves around 'the longer term' but they never define this. As such it has the limitation of not integrating planning stages, operation, futures etc., and as witnessed by the DES (1989) it is linear and rationalistic in how it works throughout the three-stage process of choice, analysis and implementation.

What is required is a planning process that allowed a school (a) to operate at different levels of planning concurrently and not work from one level (i.e. operational) to the next (i.e. strategic), and (b) to reflect the realities of school management and not assume it is always possible to work through the process of analysis, plan, construction, implementation and evaluation in a sequential way.

To establish a planning process for schools we have used a planning framework from Davies and Ellison (2003) and added a planning process dimension to it. First, we will consider the Davies and Ellison model. Then we will consider how best to operationalize the model within a school planning process.

The planning model put forward by Davies and Ellison (2003) considers that planning operates at three levels, as represented in Figure 8.2. The model represents the concept that schools move through a series of planning activities concurrently, i.e. the model is not hierarchical. It is not neccesary to do the operational planning first and then move on up. While there is flow between the various strands, as represented by the arrows, the model recognizes that leaders in schools manage and lead concurrently at each strand. The definitions we use for each strand are as follows:

- Operational action plans: these have grown out of annual operating plans such as School Development Plans in the UK or School Charters in Victoria, Australia. While two years present a definable planning framework, many plans stretch to three years. We have doubts as to whether those plans can sustain the achievement of detailed objectives in the third year, given the

Figure 8.2 Planning model

Source: Davies and Ellison, 2003.

level of economic, social and technological change let alone the level of educational change.

- Strategy: this consists of strategic intent and strategic plans. Strategy, as described earlier, is seen as broad areas for action dealing with aggregated data on a three-to-five-year time scale. Adding an extra year of detail on to a two-year plan does not make it strategic; it merely becomes a wishlist. So strategic planning involves broad development areas where targets are known and the actions necessary to achieve those targets are also understood. We see strategic intents as involving targeted changes where the capability has first to be built, through a series of understandings and activities, before detailed planning can commence. Both are underpinned by strategic thinking.
- Futures perspective: we consider it is impossible to write a future plan in any sort of detail. It is better thought of in terms of engaging in a futures dialogue or conversation (see Hirschhorn, 1997, p. 123; Van Der Heijden, 1997, p. 41; and Caldwell, 1998, p. 210). By engaging in this dialogue or conversation a futures perspective can be developed. In terms of a time frame it is useful to relate this to the child's experience. It is worth thinking, not of some 'future' generations of children, but the children that have started this year and what we need to do for those children in the last year we are responsible for them. If a child starts a nursery or kindergarten at four years old, what experiences will the school have to provide for that child at 11? Similarly for a secondary or high school student, at 11, there is the challenge of what sort of education or world of work he/she will be moving on to in seven years' time. Thus a seven to ten-year framework is a useful starting point – not too far in the future (i.e. *Star Trek* type visions) but sufficiently separated from today's realities.

When translating these plans into an action framework, it is necessary to consider what these three strands of planning would look like.

Futures perspective

While it is very difficult to write a futures plan, it is useful to highlight two sets of futures thinking; one about how the external world is impacting on the school and the second how the school envisages it needs to develop over the longer term. The two need not relate to each other, but of course they may interrelate. These then form the basis of a futures dialogue or conversation. It could look something like Table 8.2.

Table 8.2 *Dimensions of futures thinking*

External factors	Internal factors
Increasing globalization and its impact on employability.	Increasing need for the school to be at the centre of the community – a community of learning for those in the school and the wider social and geographical area.
Increasing global tensions.	
Changes in the social capital in society.	Redefinition of the role of parents in the education of their children and the balance between home and school in the learning process.
Continued growth of technology.	
Greater understanding of the brain-based science of learning.	Changes to the internal architecture (the learning environment), even though the external architecture of the school may stay the same.
	The role of values and spirituality as means of making sense of self in a turbulent world.

The futures dialogue is not, of course, intended to provide an immediate answer to these challenges but to provide a basis to examine the backcloth of today's actions. This dialogue develops the school as an outward-facing organization that reexamines itself, and the broader world, over a period of time.

The strategic process

Figure 8.3 illustrates the stages in the strategic process.

Figure 8.3 The strategic process

Strategic analysis

This is the process of assembling the data and turning those data into useful information on which to base decisions. For a useful discussion of the various approaches and techniques available, see Davies and Ellison (2003). Having undertaken the analysis, the school will then be able to distinguish between those areas where it knows in a broad sense what it wants to do and how to do it – the strategic plan; and those areas where it knows what it would like to do but does not understand how to achieve it – the strategic intent.

Strategic intent

Strategic intent is not a vague aim or vision. It is a definable objective where building capability and capacity is necessary. First, it is necessary to understand the nature and dimension of the intent, then subsequently to understand how to translate that intent into action. As Hamel and Prahalad (1989, p. 65) state: 'Strategic intent promotes the concept of the learning organisation in that it sets a target that deserves personal effort and commitment towards building capability "to reach seemingly unattainable goals" '. Activities in each of the intent areas build our understanding of what is needed to achieve each intent and then, with that understanding, we can formulate a plan to sustain successful change. The sequence of the process is shown in Figure 8.4.

For example, a school decides it has four strategic intents to:

- create a success culture and celebrate success
- become a 'learning organization'
- create effective teams in school
- create a positive and aesthetic learning environment.

At first, creating an effective team seems straightforward. However, as staff work through a series of activities that affect how individuals perceive themselves and their relationship to others, fundamental attitude changes are involved. This is the process of building capability to understand first the nature and dimensions of the intent and then to accept it and finally to turn that into action. This is a slow process and needs a time frame to build the capability and capacity in the school. Thus a school would have a limited number (five or less) of strategic intent statements. These are in effect areas for development or work in progress. Only later, when a clearer picture emerges, can the intent be translated into a definitive planning process. Table 8.3 is an example of building a strategic intent statement, which works through the definition of activities to build understanding and capability to achieve that intent. As time goes on there will be a need either to redefine the activity or move to the normal plan.

Figure 8.4 The stages of strategic intent

Table 8.3 *Capability building measures in strategic intent*

Strategic intent 3: create effective teams in school and develop a shared understanding of an effective team	
Activities to build capability	Need to redefine (R) or to formal plan move (P)
Define what an effective team is (process)	
Develop a shared understanding of what an effective team does (action)	
Create an understanding of self and how that relates to others	
Provide opportunities for individuals to develop within teams	
Develop a mutually supportive/positive work environment	
Develop shared understanding of corporate responsibility	
Involve all staff (teaching, support, governors) in creating a shared view	
Involve all in values building. What are we committed to?	
Celebrate achievements of whole teams – feedback sessions	

Strategic plan

The strategic plan is concerned with broad areas of development over the medium term. It focuses on key activities that underpin all the school's activities. Therefore it is necessary for those designing strategic plans to draw together between three and five key areas to focus strategic improvement. In two leading schools in which we have worked, we have found the following examples of broad strategic categorizations:

School A :

- children's achievements
- support for learning and teaching
- leadership and management
- developing people.

School B:

- learning outcomes – pupil progress and achievement
- support for the quality of learning and teaching
- leadership and management processes.

The point of these categorizations is that they do not replicate the many factors found in operational plans but focus on broad strategic areas.

Operational action plans

Operational action plans take the five areas of the strategic plan and break them down into detail for that particular year's contribution, together with any other short-term plans. This is the area of traditional School Development Plans.

Individual staff plans

All schools will also have systems of individual staff targets, setting plans and pro formas linked to the performance management system. However, during the performance management review it is important to engage in a 'strategic dialogue' or 'strategic conversation'. To achieve this, the following three sets of questions should be asked:

Phase one:

- What contribution did you make to whole-school plans last year?
- What contribution did you make to your area of responsibility (subject, year group, key stage, etc.)?

Phase two:

- What contribution do you plan to make to whole-school plans next year?
- What contribution do you plan make to your area of responsibility (subject, year group, key stage, etc.) next year?

Phase three:

- What support do you need to achieve your targets for next year?

Integrating the planning process

It is also important to ensure that the planning initiative flows from the strategic level through the operational stage to individual teacher action plans. This is shown in Figure 8.5 which illustrates this flow from the strategic to the operational to individual plan for School A (a primary school) for the leadership and management element.

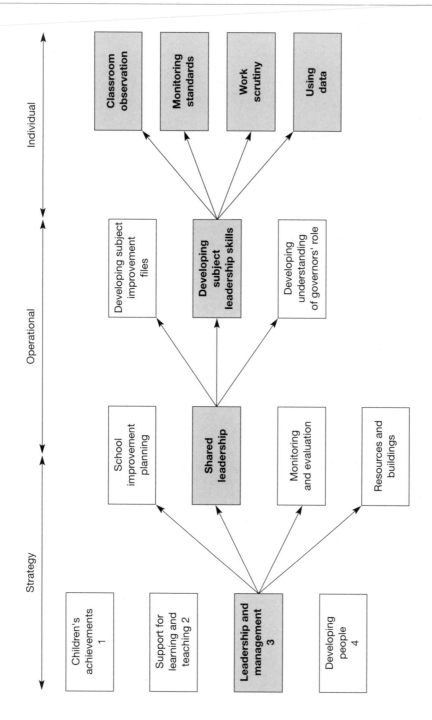

Figure 8.5 The strategic/operational flow

Conclusion

In this chapter we have established a strategic framework for planning in schools that sets the organization's activities in a broader context. We have linked this with examples of what these plans would look like in practice. This framework suggests that a school should have an improvement plan that has the following sections:

- a commentary on the nature of the school and its futures context;
- a strategic intent statement;
- a strategic plan;
- an operational action plan.

We hope that has provided readers with a framework to examine and validate their own planning practice. Developing a critical new perspective on planning is continued by Les Bell in the next chapter.

REFERENCES

Boisot, M. (1995) 'Preparing for turbulence' in Garratt, B. (ed.) *Developing Strategic Thought*, London: McGraw-Hill.

Broadhead, P., Cuckle, P., Hodgson, J. and Dunford, J. (1996) 'Improving primary schools through school development planning' in *Education Management and Administration*, 24 (3), pp. 277–90.

Caldwell, B. (1998) *Beyond the Self Managing School*, London: Routledge.

Davies, B. (2001) 'Rethinking schools and school leadership for the 21st century: changes and challenges', inaugural professorial lecture: University of Hull.

Davies, B. and Ellison, L. (1992) *School Development Planning*, Harlow: Longman.

Davies, B. and Ellison, L. (2003) *The New Strategic Direction and Development of the School*, London: Routledge/Falmer Press.

DES (1989) *Planning for School Development: Advice for Governors, Headteachers and Teachers*, London: HMSO.

DES (1991) *Development Planning – A Practical Guide*, London: Department of Education and Science.

DfEE (2000) *School Development Planning* (NPQH Materials Unit 1.3), London: Departmenr for Education and Employment.

Fidler, B. (1996) *Strategic Planning for School Improvement*, London: Pitman Publishing.

Garratt, B. (1995) *Developing Strategic Thought*, London: McGraw Hill.

Hamel, G. and Prahalad, C.K. (1989) 'Strategic intent', *Harvard Business Review*, May/June.

Hargreaves, A. (2000) 'The Three Dimensions of Educational Reform', paper given to the launch conference of the Global Alliance for School Leadership, Nottingham, May.

Hargreaves, D. and Hopkins, D. (1991) *The Empowered School: The Management and Practice of Development Planning*, London: Cassell.

Hoyle, E. (1986) *The Politics of School Management*, London: Routledge.

Hirschhorn, L. (1997) *Re-working Authority: Leading and Authority in the Post-Modern Organisation*, Cambridge, MA: MIT Press

Johnson, G. and Scholes, K. (1984) *Exploring Corporate Strategy* (3rd edn), Hemel Hempstead: Prentice Hall.

Koch, R. (2000) *The Financial Times Guide to Strategy* (2nd edn), London: Financial Times.

MacGilchrist, B., Myers, K. and Reed, J. (1997) *The Intelligent School*, London: PCP.

Mintzberg, H. (1994) *The Rise and Fall of Strategic Planning*, Hemel Hempstead: Prentice Hall.

Mintzberg, H. (1995) 'Strategic thinking as seeing' in Garratt, B. (ed.) *Developing Strategic Thought*, London: McGraw-Hill.

Mintzberg, H., Ahlstrand, B. and Lampel, J. (1998) *Strategy Safari – A Guided Tour through the Wilds of Strategic Management*, London: Prentice Hall.

Puffitt, R., Stoten, B. and Winkley, D. (1992) *Business Planning for Schools*, Harlow: Longman.

Skelton, M., Reeves, G. and Playfoot, D. (1991) *Development Planning for Primary Schools*, Windsor: NFER.

Van Der Heijden, K. (1997) *Scenarios: The Art of Strategic Conversation*, New York: John Wiley.

West, M. and Ainscow, M. (1991) *Managing School Development – A Practical Guide*, London: David Fulton Publishers.

CHAPTER 9

Strategic planning in education: a critical perspective

LES BELL

Over the past decade the use of the term 'strategy' in the context of educational leadership and management has come to encapsulate a range of activities associated with planning. Indeed, the term 'strategic' has become almost inseparable from the word 'planning', such that if planning is not 'strategic' then it is not regarded as planning in any meaningful sense. Furthermore, it is expected that departments, faculties and curriculum areas in schools will derive their own strategies from the overall strategic plan for their schools. These plans will fit together like so many musicians' parts, each making a predetermined if limited contribution to the symphonic whole. Only the head and a few senior staff, the conductors, will have a real sense of the nature of the performance – the overall plan. Thus strategic planning has come to be the only acceptable approach to planning and its utilization has become the only acceptable way for schools to face the future. Little consideration has been given, however, to the assumptions on which strategic planning rests or to alternative approaches to preparing for the future. This chapter will examine the conceptual assumptions that underpin strategy in education and the inherent weaknesses of these assumptions. The chapter will conclude by identifying an alternative approach to planning in schools.

Strategic planning: is it significant?

The extent to which strategic planning is possible in any organization has been discussed extensively in management literature (see Whipp, 1998, for a summary). The argument has been extended to education, where it has been noted that strategic planning is predicated on the capacity of the school to achieve organizational goals through a rational process that begins with analysis and finishes with implementation (Bell, 1998). This theory implies that planning and implementation are orderly and sequential and that schools can be shaped and controlled in such a way as to avoid the unintended consequences of change while realizing strategic objectives. This, however, may not be the case. Quinn (1980) and Pettigrew (1973) have exploded the myth that strategic planning evolves in a neat linear form from analysis to implementation. March and Olsen (1979), in their analysis of decision making in higher education, show that decisions and choices are often not made by a careful matching of means to ends. They are frequently the result of oversight, accident, flight or loose association, none of which is a rational or a strategic process. Thus the dynamics of schools as organizations are such that defining and implementing a strategic plan is extremely problematic.

To treat organizational activity as a rational response to an analysis of the environment is to assume that there is a range of actions that match environmental circumstances and from which rational choices can be made. The fallacious nature of this position was noted by March and Olsen (1979) when they argued that although organizations do act within environmentally constrained boundaries, a similar environmental situation may produce different organizational responses and the same organizational action may produce different environmental outcomes at different times. Even Hargreaves (1995), the architect of the school development planning process, recognizes that the planning model that underpins school development is defective because it is insufficiently responsive both to short- and long-term changes in the environment. Planning based on a coherent strategy demands that the aims of the school are challenged and that both present and future environmental influences inform the development of that strategy. There should be a clear and well-articulated vision of what the school should be like in the future. Planning, therefore, should be long-term and holistic.

Even more fundamentally, strategic planning in schools must be based on an analysis of both present and possible future states and presupposes the capacity to control the environment and not be controlled by it. Thus, organizationally acceptable means and desired ends must be irrevocably linked and unintended consequences avoided. Mintzberg (1994) has drawn attention to the mistake of assuming that means and ends can be linked in this way, that significant changes in the environment can be predicted or that organizations can make rational choices about ways in which to respond to their environments. Strategic planning requires staff in schools to be both proactive and interactive. They are proactive to the extent that they do not wait to respond to externally imposed changes. Rather, they plan for their own improvement and establish clearly their patterns of accountability. They should also be interactive in the sense that they do not take the external environment to be immutable but seek to influence and shape it by deploying resources to create change. These characteristics are not embedded in the school development planning process (Fidler, 1996).

Conceptualizations and weaknesses

There are four significant weaknesses in the current use of strategic planning in schools and colleges. The first derives from conceptualization of leadership and management upon which strategic planning is predicated. The emphasis on the centrality of the role of the head or principal in strategic planning has been noted above. The head is presented as the locus of management expertise and the individual who carries the burden of responsibility for planning. Thus headship is located within a hierarchical view of school management in which the head is the solitary, heroic and accountable leader who personifies and exemplifies the totality of leadership skills and managerial competences (Bolman and Deal, 1991). This is the myth of the hero-innovator reborn. It fails to acknowledge the dilemmas of leadership, particularly the extent to which successful planning in schools should be a collective rather than an individual responsibility, and it does not recognize the part played by individual teachers in implementing strategies for school improvement.

Leadership and management in all schools are inextricably linked. At its most strategic, planning involves formulating a vision for the school, in conjunction with the whole school community, based on strongly held values about the aims and purposes of education and their application to specific institutions, and then translating this into action. Leadership involves the embodiment and articulation of this vision and its communication to others in the form of a strategic plan. The fundamental flaw in this conceptualization of strategic planning is that it leads to the over-emphasis on the role of the head. Such an analysis assumes that heads will identify the vision and carry overall responsibility and accountability for the implementation of the strategic plan. Thus there is a failure to recognize that, just as the vision and the mission are derived from overarching values and beliefs, so the realization of plans based on them requires commitment from and the involvement of staff at the organizational and operational levels.

If strategic planning involves translating the vision into broad aims and long-term plans, then it is at the organizational level that the strategic view is converted into medium-term objectives, supported by the allocation of appropriate resources and the delegation of responsibility for decision making, implementation, review and evaluation. Here much of the responsibility for translating strategy into actions that may produce significant school improvement rests. In turn, the implementation of these medium-term plans requires them to be further subdivided into the totality of the delegated tasks that have to be carried out. At the operational level, therefore, resources are utilized, tasks completed, activities coordinated and monitored. It is at this level, in the classroom, that those tasks that may bring about improvements in pupil achievement must be carried out. Thus accountability, resource deployment and management and the responsibility for improvement are located here as much as in the previous two levels.

The three levels of management must work in harmony towards a common purpose if strategic planning is to be successful. This will happen only if all members of the school community share the vision and if values are largely communal. Each level of management depends on the other two. To emphasize one and ignore the others is fundamentally to misunderstand the nature of educational management. Headteachers cannot manage schools alone, nor can they carry the burden of motivating others to achieve objectives and complete tasks without significant support from colleagues. Heads and their staff must move towards inclusive forms of management and leadership that are holistic rather than fragmented and instrumental.

A second set of weaknesses in the current approach to strategic planning is derived from conceptualizations embedded in its ideological antecedents, namely school effectiveness. As Slee and Weiner (1998, pp. 1–2) point out: 'The effective schooling research, in conjunction with its operational branch – the school improvement movement – has been adopted by policy-makers pursuant to the resolution of ... the alleged crises in state education'. The difficulty here is that the discourse of effective schooling and school improvement overstates what planning can achieve, has an extremely narrow assessment of school effects and tends to reduce learning to limited, discrete, assessable and comparable segments of academic knowledge – witness the emphasis on literacy, numeracy and little else in the current strategic targets that are set for schools. Slee and Weiner note that: 'Students' achievements in pencil and paper limited and culturally specific tests are … used as the data for comparison and the compilation of published league tables' (ibid., p. 6).

Such reductionism makes simplistic assumptions about the nature and purposes of education and strategic planning related to it and suffers from an impoverished, mechanistic and narrow view of what counts as achievement. This ignores the impact of context and disregards the effects of differential funding, marketization, school selection policies and, above all, social and economic disadvantage. There are degrees of difference in the improvement that can be expected through schooling, however well planned this may be. Policy makers, therefore, must ensure that the ways in which differences are identified and incorporated into planning are not merely based on what can easily be tested and quantified.

The criteria adopted to measure performance and improvement often fail to take into account social and economic diversity. Gray and Wilcox (1995) conclude that they had yet to identify an effective school in which the environment was poor, the roof needed repair or where the school had serious staffing difficulties. Thus wider economic and social issues have to be addressed in the context of making judgements about educational achievement, yet the school effectiveness discourse takes no account of the limited impact that schooling alone might have on pupil performance. Thus strategic planning under New Labour should move away from simplistic notions of effectiveness towards a conceptualization of achievement that will take account of the rich educational experience to which our children are entitled in order to equip them to live in the coming century.

The school effectiveness discourse has a further weakness. It labels entire schools as good or bad, after measuring them against conformity to disconnected criteria, and brands entire institutions as failing when the anticipated conformity is not observed. This is an inappropriate level of analysis. Identifying schools as good or bad – that is, treating them as units of analysis in themselves – is problematic. This aspect of the school effectiveness discourse fails to recognize that it is not necessarily the difference between schools that affects achievement most significantly but the differences within them (Lingard, Ladwig and Luke, 1998). Even inspection reports from the Office for Standards in Education (OFSTED, 1992) confirm that in many failing schools examples of good practice can be found. Furthermore, it was noted as early as 1966 that the variations between schools had relatively little to do with individual pupil achievement and that achievement varied more within schools than between them (Gamoran and Berends, 1987). This is not to reject the view that schools can and should make a difference. It is to say, however, that the sources of differential achievement within schools must be carefully considered. Strategic planning must pay far more attention to this and less to inter-school comparisons through league tables and other differential performance indicators.

Perhaps the most significant weakness of all in the school effectiveness discourse is the fundamental vacuum at its very core. It lacks any clear conceptual rationale that links the characteristics that commonly describe an effective school with a dynamic model of school processes in such a way that it might be possible to establish and explain the relationships between those characteristics and improved performance. As Ouston (1998) has pointed out, the precise nature of the relationship between an effective head, the classroom performance of an individual teacher and the learning of a particular child is largely ignored in the school effectiveness literature. New Labour policy in this regard rests largely on exhortation and a battery of tactics, the precise outcomes of which are, at best, indeterminate. Strategic planning for school improvement, therefore, must rest on a much more fundamental understanding of the nature of management and leadership in schools than is the case at present.

Alternative approaches to planning for the future

The world view on which much strategic planning based on school effectiveness is predicated is one of order, simplicity and conformity, where everything operates according to specific, knowable and predetermined rules. This view, in turn, means that all activities should be rational, predictable and controllable. The search for truth in such a world view is a search for the rules that order that world. Gaining knowledge is based on the identification of alternatives and on the assumption that everything is a sum of its parts. Learning, therefore, is rooted in dissection, so that the parts can be isolated and understood. It is an individualistic process that proceeds in a linear way through analysis and the construction of generalizations based on empirical evidence. Its outcomes are presented as the disjointed acquisition of disconnected elements of knowledge and the limited acquisition of context-specific competences. The atomism, fragmentation and concern with predictability and control that shape this approach to strategic planning produce an underlying set of cognitive processes that are reductive, reactive and unable to cope with rapid change and uncertainty. This is because the cognitive processes that underpin this form of planning are rigid, inflexible, exclusive and, therefore, inappropriate. Thus strategy is reduced to the identification, by a small group of senior managers, of a long-term goal and the one way to achieve it – the implementation of which rests with the majority who had no part in its formulation.

It can be seen, therefore, that strategic planning, as it exists in most contemporary organizations including schools, is based on power and social relationships derived from modes of activity that are rooted in conflict and competition as the prime determinants of social order. It is also based on inaccurate assumptions about organizational dynamics, the predictability of the environment and the capacity to know about that environment. The world is required to be to be an orderly, predictable place where the whole is equal to, but no greater than, the sum of its parts. Change comes through planning, usually by those at or near the top of the organizational hierarchy. This top-down approach involves deploying strategy through the construction of a neat and linear alignment between ends and means, for others in the organization to implement.

In an unpredictable, rapidly changing environment, however, strategic planning of this sort is unhelpful as a way of enabling schools to prepare for the future. It inhibits creativity and imaginative thinking, it fails to employ much of the talent in the organization and it cannot readily take account of forces emanating from the external environment in a period of rapid and extensive change (Zohar, 1997). Does this mean that all attempts to develop insights into the future should be abandoned? Clearly not, since schools, like other organizations, cannot be left to drift aimlessly on a turbulent sea of change. How then, might the future be addressed?

So complex has the world become that it can be argued that those responsible for developing strategy in schools have little chance of knowing sufficient about the environment even if they wished to do so. Making accurate predictions on which to base planning becomes an almost impossible task. The rate and impact of technological change, the extent of social change and the global influences on local environments combine to make it impossible for schools to have a complete understanding of their environments. This, in turn, means that the knowledge base on which strategy can be based is totally inadequate (Davies, 1998). The environment cannot be totally known nor can it be predicted. As Handy (1994) has argued, we are faced with an unpredictable world in which the only certainty is uncertainty. Such an environment requires an approach to planning that can be based not on a set on immutable, externally imposed targets but on reaching agreement on a series of short-term objectives (Bell, 1998). It needs to take into account the nature of the questions that may be asked about the future, while recognizing that the answers to them may be either unknown or unknowable. It has to be recognized that in coping with the future, important information may not be available, important alternatives may be ignored and important possible outcomes neglected.

The capacity to retain a distinct separation between means and ends and to rely on the linear relationship between them is greatly reduced in this new environment. Thus plans will not be made and implemented. Rather, they will be made and remade endlessly as the school proceeds through a process of successive approximation to agreed objectives derived from policy, both of which may change before being achieved. Lindblom (1959) termed this approach to policy formulation and planning 'the science of muddling through'. It is, in spite of this terminology, an extremely sophisticated form of responding to unknown and perhaps unknowable organizational futures. For such an approach to planning to succeed, however, there must be an agreement within the school about basic values and broadly acceptable means, which are not rooted in the traditional hierarchical management model with its rule-bound inflexibilities and emphasis on the separation of functions. Work relationships must move towards being less hierarchical, more multifunctional and holistic, based on a wider distribution of power within the organization. Whole-school perspectives must be developed. These are too important to be left to a small group. It will then be seen that there are many ways of getting things done, each of which may be equally legitimate, and that co-operation, responsiveness, flexibility and partnership must replace our present inflexible structures. This is a most difficult and the most exciting challenge.

Perhaps a way forward can be found in the distinction between connected and separate modes of knowing, developed through an investigation into problem solving by women in management positions in schools (Tarule, 1998). Separate knowing is Newtonian. It seeks objectivity, is abstract, adversarial, critical, exclusive and detached from personal relationships. It is inherent in strategic planning. Connected knowing is a collaborative process of looking for what is right by accepting the validity of a range of different perspectives. Meanings are constructed and developed through reasoning with others through narratives rather than analysis, which take place within inclusive and communal relationships, the foundation of which is a commonality of experiences, not a defence of differences. Such connected knowledge, and the processes inherent within it, provide a foundation on which flexible yet inclusive policy formulation, based on different but shared values and perspectives, can be developed.

The emphasis will be on holistic policies that focus on integration rather than fragmentation, recognize that the sum is greater than the parts and celebrate the imaginative and the experimental. The mode of discourse will shift from debate to a dialogue that focuses on finding out rather than knowing, questions not answers, and proceeds through listening not criticizing, sharing rather than winning and losing and exploring new possibilities not defending established positions. The cognitive processes that support this approach are such that they enable each individual to make a distinctive contribution within a flexible framework rather than expecting a series of limited contributions, the sum of which make up the predetermined whole. Such an approach to strategic planning is far removed from the linear, rational, positivist methods rooted in the unequal distribution of power and a belief in the sanctity of order and control on which the employment of strategy is based. It requires a new form of leadership predicated on openness, collaboration and power sharing, where flexibility, creativity, imagination and responsiveness can flourish and genuine accountability for school improvement can exist.

REFERENCES

Bell, L. (1998) 'Back to the Future: the development of education policy in England', keynote address to the Australian Conference of Educational Administration, Brisbane.

Bolman, L.G. and Deal, T.E. (1991) *Reforming Organisations: Artistry, Choice and Leadership*, San Francisco: Jossey-Bass.

Davies, B (1998) 'Leadership in schools', inaugural lecture, University of Lincolnshire and Humberside: Lincoln.

Fidler, B. (1996) *Strategic Planning for School Improvement*, London: Pitman Publishing.

Gamoran, A. and Berends, M. (1987) 'The effects of stratification in secondary schools: synthesis of survey and ethnographic research', *Review of Educational Research*, 57 (4), pp. 415–35.

Gray, J. and Wilcox. B. (1995) *Good School, Bad School*, Buckingham: Open University Press.

Handy, C. (1994) *The Empty Raincoat: Making Sense of the Future*, London: Hutchinson..

Hargreaves, D. (1995) 'Self-managing schools and development planning – chaos or control?', *School Organisation*, 15 (3), pp. 215–17.

Lindblom, E. (1959) 'The science of muddling through' in Faludi, A. (1973) *Reader in Planning Theory*, Oxford: Pergamon Press, pp. 151–70.

Lingard, B., Ladwig, J. and Luke, A. (1998) 'School effects in post-modern conditions' in Slee, R., Weiner G. with Tomlinson, S. (eds) *School Effectiveness for Whom: Challenges to the School Effectiveness and School Improvement Movements*, London: Falmer Press, pp. 84–100.

March, J.G. and Olsen, J.P. (1979) *Ambiguity and Choice in Organisations*, Bergen: Universitetsforlaget.

Mintzberg, H. (1994) *The Rise and Fall of Strategic Planning*, Hemel Hempsted: Prentice Hall.

OFSTED (1992) *Framework for the Inspection of Schools*, London: HMSO.

Ouston, J. (1998) 'The school effectiveness and school improvement movement: a reflection on its contribution to the development of good schools', paper presented to the ESRC Seminar Series, '*Redefining Education Management*', Open University, Milton Keynes.

Pettigrew, A. (1973) *The Politics of Organisational Decision Making*, London: Tavistock.

Quinn, J. (1980) *Strategies for Change: Logical Incrementalism*, Homewood, IL: Irwin.

Slee, R. and Weiner, G. (1998) 'Introduction: school effectiveness for whom?' in Slee, R., Weiner, G. with Tomlinson, S. (eds) *School Effectiveness for Whom: Challenges to the School Effectiveness and School Improvement Movements*, Falmer Press: London, pp. 1–9.

Tarule, J. (1998) 'The characteristics of connected and separate modes of knowing', paper presented to the joint UCET/AATCDE seminar, London.

Whipp, R. (1998) 'Creative deconstruction: strategy and organisations', paper presented to the ESRC seminar series 'Redefining Education Management', Cardiff.

Zohar, D. (1997) *Rewiring the Corporate Brain*, San Francisco: Berrett-Koehler.

CHAPTER 10

Reengineering: rethinking the school as an organization

BRENT DAVIES

This chapter considers how reengineering can provide a 'lens' to consider the radical change necessary in schools as they seek to meet the challenges posed by current economic and social trends. Reengineering is often criticized as being just one of a whole series of fads or business fashions that purport to be the solution to a wide range of current problems. Reengineering is not a panacea but a perspective for examining the effectiveness of organizations. As a different paradigm, drawn from a business setting, it provides a valuable method of taking a fresh look at what schools do and how that might be radically reorganized to meet current challenges in a significantly different and more productive way. Indeed, reengineering 'mindsets' as well as organizational processes would seem a valuable 'lens' to view strategy, marketing and finance. This chapter develops a critique of reengineering in two stages. First, it looks at the principals of reengineering and then moves on to examine both parallels and applications of reengineering in the education sector. The following two chapters examine two case studies of reengineering, one in a primary and the other a secondary school.

Principals of reengineering

The key definition of reengineering was provided by Hammer and Champy (1993, p. 32) as 'the fundamental rethinking and radical redesign of business processes to achieve dramatic improvement in critical contemporary measures of performance'. Thus four elements are highlighted in the definition:

- fundamental rethinking
- radical redesign
- business processes (or in education: school and learning processes)
- dramatic improvement.

It is worth spending a little time unpacking each of these elements. First, reengineering is about fundamental rethinking. It avoids the incremental approach and starts with the proverbial 'clean sheet of paper' to reconceptualize the processes and their context. This links into the second element, that of radical redesign. Reengineering makes the assumption that past and current processes are inadequate so, while it is important to research why they are inadequate, more emphasis should be given to radical new solutions. Third, there is the key aspect of processes. Hammer and Stanton (1995, p. 17) consider that: 'We reengineer how work is done, how outputs are created from inputs. We cannot and do not reengineer organizational units'. Hammer (1996, p. xii) highlights the overwhelming importance of process as follows:

> Originally I felt that the most important word in the definition was 'radical'. The clean sheet of paper, the breaking of assumptions, the throw-it-all-out-and-start-again flavour of reengineering ... I have now come to realize that I was wrong, that the radical character of reengineering, however important and exciting, is not the most significant aspect. The key word in the definition of reengineering is 'process': a complete end-to-end set of activities that together create value for a customer.

The fourth element, dramatic improvement, is concerned not with making things 5 or 10 per cent better but with dramatic leaps in performance.

The need for reengineering

The question that most people ask is, 'Why is reengineering necessary?'. The answer is that in an era of rapid economic, social, technological and educational change, incremental improvement is inadequate to meet these challenges. This idea is summarized by Drucker (1993, p. 1): 'Every few hundred years in Western history there occurs a sharp transformation ... Within a few short decades, society rearranges itself ... its world view; its basic values; its social and political structures ... We are currently living through such a transformation.' This would suggest that if change in this period is only incremental, then it is unlikely to be sufficient. Not only are we experiencing a period of transformational change, but it is significantly more important for the education sector because the traditional factors of production (land, labour and capital) are being superseded by knowledge and information. In fact Drucker (ibid., p. 20) sees that 'knowledge is now fast becoming the sole factor of production'. It is argued from a reengineering perspective that in these circumstances traditional incremental improvement processes are no longer adequate to deal with the challenge facing the modern organization.

This situation is summed up well by Stoll and Fink (1996) who use as the title of their first chapter 'Good schools if this were 1965'. Gerstner *et al.* (1994) put forward the view that it is not that schools are doing bad things but that times have changed and radical shifts have taken place and schools have not adapted. The era in which we are living demands rapid and fundamental change, so that traditional incremental school improvement strategies may be inadequate to meet that challenge. In such circumstances, the necessary paradigm shift for educational leaders may be achieved by using the concepts and approaches from the reengineering movement.

A useful tool for conceptually mapping the need for and the timing of that reengineering is provided by Handy (1994), who makes use of the sigmoid curve, as shown in Figure 10.1. The concept behind the sigmoid curve is that all organizations go through periods when they develop and improve and also face the possibility of decline. The incremental nature of improvement is seductive. When

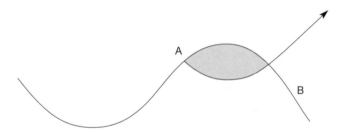

Figure 10.1 The sigmoid curve
Source: Handy, 1994, p. 51.

the leader of a school or part of that school takes over and makes a difference and things improve, the school's performance will move up to point A on the diagram. This is the seductive nature of incremental improvement; all the signals coming into the school are positive – things are going well and continuous improvement has been established. The danger is that the outside community will expect the same things to be repeated: 'Keep on doing what you are already doing' or 'My daughter has gone throughout the school and had a good experience – please replicate that experience for my son who is about to start'. The danger is not that the previous formula was wrong historically but that the outside world has changed and new approaches are necessary. Merely to continue with the previous approach will result in the school 'peaking' and then declining to point B. At point B of course it is difficult to change, because the decline results in lowered morale and resource problems. The best example in the business world in recent years of moving over the peak and into decline is Marks and Spencer, the major retail group in the UK. Repeating past retail formulae and ignoring the change in consumer demand, especially the focus on 'branded goods', led to a very significant decline in its fortunes.

In the school setting, successful schools should use futures thinking concepts. For the child just entering the school, the school needs to consider what will need to be provided for his or her last year, i.e. what will make the school successful in terms of its provision five or seven years later? Thus at point A proactive leadership should resist the temptation merely to repeat successful formulae from the past and instead go through a fundamental rethinking period (the shaded area) to make decisive changes to move on to the next sigmoid curve and move upwards. It is often the case with successful schools that they have organizational capital in terms of good relationships and goodwill to go through a period of fundamental reflection. This is not always the case once decline sets in.

So a key challenge for the leader in the school and those in leadership positions within the school to ask those 'outside the box' paradigm-shifting questions such as 'What would a successful school look like in five years' time and what processes would need to change to enable that to happen?' Within the school, similar questions could be asked about the nature of successful teaching and the use of technology or the curriculum in particular areas of the school. This fundamental rethinking must always focus on the radical redesign of organizational processes, especially learning processes, which are the core function of schools.

Reengineering v. traditional school improvement or quality management approaches

Another common question is 'How does reengineering differ from traditional school improvement or quality management approaches?'. The response must examine whether (a) school improvement or quality approaches are incremental and (b) the basis on which the improvement is being built is either appropriate or adequate in the first place. A useful analysis of the limitations of school improvement is provided by Barber (1996, p. 247):

> *The question is, however, whether this focus on school improvement, though a necessary step forward, will ever be sufficient. In my view it is deficient as a model of educational salvation in four respects. Firstly, even in improving schools, there are sufficient numbers of pupils who slip through the net of educational success. Secondly, though many improving schools work hard at relations with parents, the focus on school improvement casts the parents in the role of (perhaps supportive perhaps not) bystander ... Thirdly, the implicit assumption behind school improvement is that the aspirations of every learner can be met within one school ... this assumption becomes increasingly questionable and perhaps even absurd. Fourthly, school-improvement, with its important focus on making schools responsible, also fails to address sufficiently the overall inadequacy of British cultural attitudes to education and learning.*

Barber suggests moving the attention to the learner (reengineering the learning process!) with each child having an 'individual learning promise'. This is an individually agreed learning programme, with the child, the school and the parent reviewing progress and setting targets every six months. The focus is on that child's learning needs and not on the structure of the school. The learning should be considered in three contexts: learning at school, learning in organized out-of-school locations and learning at home. Barber's idea of shortening the school day and lengthening the learning day is an example of reengineering by refocusing on learning rather than concentrating on school structures or their reorganization. Barber's 'pupil learning resource credit' as a means of providing educational resources at home, together with the establishment of study-support centres funded through taxing child benefit, are radical ways of reengineering learning resources focused on the child and not on the institution of the school. What Barber suggests is a root-and-branch reengineering of the role of the school as a coordinator of learning.

Figure 10.2 outlines the radical shifts played by reengineering in contrast to an incremental approach of school improvement and quality initiatives.

The differences between reengineering and incremental approaches can also be seen in Table 10.1. This four-point taxonomy highlights the very fundamental and radical differences between the two approaches. As is highlighted, the radical challenges that reengineering poses to core processes are significantly different from the evolutionary, added-value approach of school improvement or quality movements. The difference is between the school improvement/quality frameworks and reengineering is that the former assumes that the design of the process is sound and that all it needs is some enhancement to solve current problems. However , if the context has changed dramatically since the process was designed, that design may be fundamentally flawed and incapable of delivering the required performance. Reengineering is then called for. Reengineering does not merely enhance the individual steps of the process but entirely reconsiders how they are put together.

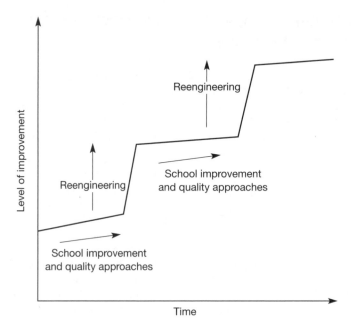

Figure 10.2 Reengineering v. incremental approaches
Source: based on Hammer, 1996, p. 83.

Table 10.1 *School improvement and reengineering: a conceptual framework*

Factors	School improvement	Reengineering
Type of Change	Evolutionary – a better way to do things	Revolutionary – a new way of doing things
Method	Adds value to existing processes	Challenges process fundamentals and their very existence
Scope	Encompasses whole organization	Focuses on core school processes
Role of technology	Traditional support, e.g. management information system, performance data	Used as enabler of learning

Source: based on Carr and Johansson, 1995, p. 16.

Reengineering in schools

While writers applied reengineering first to the business sector, there have also been attempts to cross over to the educational sector. Typical of the earlier writers was Drucker (1995, pp. 204–5) who examined reengineering in a knowledge-based education system:

Paradoxically, this may not necessarily mean that the school as we know it will become more important. For in the knowledge society clearly more and more knowledge, and especially advanced knowledge, will be acquired well past the age of formal schooling, and increasingly, perhaps, in and through educational processes that do not centre on the traditional school.

Bentley (1998, p. 1) advocated a reengineering approach:

It requires a shift in our thinking about the fundamental organisational unit of education, from the school, an institution where learning is organised, defined and contained, to the learner, an intelligent agent with the potential to learn from any and all of her encounters with the world around her.

There are valuable insights as to how a reengineering process looks at the learning processes rather than organizational structures. Typically schools are organized in the UK around structures that are based on traditional usage norms rather than the learning needs of the students. For example, Davies (1997, p. 27) provides a useful case study of applying reengineering thinking in a school:

A school in the UK, 'Moortown', is oversubscribed by 60 pupils each year. It is an 11–18 school with no other school nearby. The Local Education Authority refuses entry to these extra pupils each year, stating that the school is full to capacity. How does this relate to schooling in the future? A closer examination of the case study school reveals some interesting factors. The school opens for pupils for 190 days a year (i.e. 52% of the time), and during those days pupils operate an 8.30 am to 2.30 pm day (25% of the time). As a result the building, as a fixed asset, is used for 13% of the total possible time. This raises some interesting questions. Do children only learn in that 13% or does learning also take place in the other 87% of the time? The answer is obviously the latter. Once the perspective of schools being facilitators of learning and not the sole providers of education is accepted, then a little more creative thinking can be encouraged. Can Moortown school only be expanded by extra capital expenditure which produces buildings that are used only for 13% of the time? Or can different patterns of attendance for different age groups be used? Can staff have different working hours and conditions. Can greater use be made of technology so that 'learning' takes place when teachers are not there? Can other adults be used as coaches as well as fully trained staff? The ideas that can be generated are many but our traditional way of thinking usually does not encompass them. We need far more radical interpretations of possible future scenarios. Will all the children be attending five days in ten years' time? Will part of the lessons be conducted at home using the computer? Will traditional libraries become information centres bringing all pupils the best of the best all the time by using available technologies? Will the teachers work in support teams and facilitate the access to differing learning resources? Will the internal organisation in terms of buildings look like the traditional classrooms of four hundred years ago or be radically different? Redesigning learning processes needs a radical shift in the 'mind set' of our educational leaders.

This case study illustrates how traditional thinking can be redefined by a reengineering approach, which shifts the emphasis away from structures and buildings and on to the learning needs of the students.

I examined earlier the various definitions of reengineering. While the centrality of reengineering is a focus on process, to be successful reengineering also needs to reengineer 'mindsets' as well as processes. The way that we see education in the future is critical to adopting the appropriate strategies; using the 'lens' of reengineering is a beneficial if not necessary approach. How reengineering has taken place in practice in schools will be illustrated in the next two case studies by Greg Barker in the primary sector (4–11) and Derek Wise in the secondary sector (13–18). They show how reengineering can be applied to the core process of the school – that of teaching and learning. They also articulate how the four elements of reengineering – fundamental rethinking, radical redesign, a focus on process and dramatic improvement – can be achieved.

ACKNOWLEDGEMENT

Carfax Publishers are thanked for permission to adapt material from: Davies, B. 'Reengineering and its application to education', *School Leadership and Management* 1977, 17 (2), pp. 173–85.

REFERENCES

Barber, M. (1996) *The Learning Game*, London: Gollancz.

Bentley, T (1998) *Learning Beyond the Classroom*, Routledge: London

Carr, D.K. and Johansson, H.J. (1995) *Best Practice Reengineering*, New York: McGraw-Hill.

Davies, B. (1997) 'Rethinking the educational context – a reengineering approach' in Davies, B. and Ellison, L. *School Leadership for the 21st Century*, London: Routledge/Falmer Press.

Drucker, P.F. (1993) *Post-Capitalist Society*, New York: Harper Business.

Drucker, P. (1995) *Managing in a Time of Great Change*, Oxford: Butterworth Heinemann.

Gerstner, L.V, Semerad, R.D., Doyle, D.P. and Johnson, W.B. (1994) *Reinventing Education: America's Public Schools*, New York: Dutton.

Hammer, M. and Champy, J. (1993) *Reengineering the Corporation*, New York: Harper Business.

Hammer, M. (1996) *Beyond Reengineering*, New York: Harper Business.

Hammer, M. and Stanton, S.A. (1995) *The Reengineering Revolution – A Handbook*, New York: Harper Business.

Handy, C. (1994) *The Empty Raincoat: Making Sense of the Future*, London: Hutchinson.

Stoll, L. and Fink, D. (1996) *Changing our Schools*, Buckingham: Open University Press.

CHAPTER 11

Case study 1: reengineering teaching and learning in a primary school

GREG BARKER

Context

St Vincent's Catholic Primary School is situated in Warrington, Cheshire and caters for 4–11-year-olds and currently has 257 children on roll. Pupils enter the reception class with a broad range of attainments, which overall are about national average and there are no significant problems of behaviour or absenteeism. The school has, through its leadership and management processes, worked through several phases in order to raise standards. The first phase meant doing the same, but more of it; the second phase meant doing the same but doing it more effectively. The third phase was preceded by a period of reflection, focused on reengineering our teaching and learning processes.

Influences on reengineering mindsets and processes

The work of Senge (1990) shows us that our mental models – the way we perceive the world – largely determine the ways in which we think and act. Our mental models are constructed from our own learning experiences and, at St Vincent's, as we learnt more about learning, we began to realize that our existing mental models about learning were often inaccurate, misleading and sometimes even paralysing. Thus we had to engage in fundamental rethinking. Our new knowledge and understanding of learning equipped us to ask questions about our current processes and enabled us to see, as if through new lenses, the existing reality of the learning opportunities organized for our children and the quality of the learning environment created for them and for ourselves as fellow learners. This proved, at times, to be very unsettling, as our long-held beliefs about teacher effectiveness, and our existing mental models of such fundamental things as ability and intelligence, had to be challenged. This, inevitably, caused conflict, but as Fullan (1993, p. 36) states: 'You can't have organisational learning without individual learning, and you can't have learning in groups without processing conflict'. In reengineering terms, this 'fundamental rethinking' was the start of our journey.

Recently, the work of Davies and Ellison (1999) on school planning has helped me to develop a more holistic and more strategic view of school improvement so that, even in the turbulence that schools now find themselves, it is still possible to remain focused on the core purpose of helping our children to become effective lifelong learners. This holistic view of planning has been joined by a major catalyst that has transformed my thinking about teaching and learning: this is the work of Howard Gardner (1983, 1999) and his theory of 'multiple intelligences'. Suddenly, from a new perspective, I began to see myself as a particular type of learner with particular strengths and weaknesses in various intelligences and possessing particular biases in learning styles. Developing this more holistic view of myself as a learner then enabled me to perceive children and other learners in the same way.

A further process of fundamental rethinking came from reading Csikszentmihalyi (1990). Csikszentmihalyi's theory of optimal experience is based on the concept of 'flow', which he describes as: 'a state of mind which happens when people are so involved in an activity that nothing else seems to matter; the experience is so enjoyable that people will do it even at great cost, for the sheer sake of doing it' (ibid, p. 4). Csikszentmihalyi states that when people are in flow they are experiencing the ideal conditions for learning. He suggests that when goals are clear, feedback relevant, and when challenges and skills are balanced, attention becomes ordered and fully invested. Therefore, because of the total demand on psychic energy, a person in flow is completely focused:

> There is no space in consciousness for distracting thoughts, irrelevant feelings. Self-consciousness disappears, yet one feels stronger than usual. The sense of time is distorted: hours seem to pass by in minutes. When a person's entire being is stretched in the full function of body and mind, whatever one does becomes worth doing for its own sake; living becomes its own justification. (Csikszentmihalyi, 1997, p. 31)

As Figure 11.1 illustrates, the optimum conditions for flow are present when a person's skills are fully involved in overcoming challenge that is just about manageable and that optimal experiences usually involve a fine balance between one's ability to act and the available opportunities for action. Flow activities are described as those that allow a person to focus on goals that are clear, compatible and relevant, and immediate feedback is provided to inform how well one is

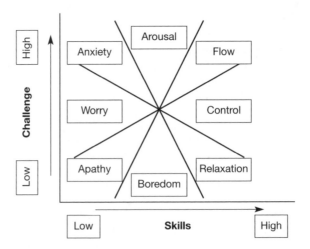

Figure 11.1 Finding flow

Source: Csikszentmihalyi, 1990, p. 31.

doing. *Flow: The Psychology of Optimal Experience* proved to be one of those rare, life-changing books, and as I absorbed the theories it expounded I began to build a reengineered perspective of what the educational provision at St Vincent's could be like. If we could translate the theories into practice, we could create the optimum conditions for all our learners, including the adults within the school.

The reengineering process

2

The task then, was to reengineer what we were doing so that our teaching took account of the new science of learning. It was as simple and as complex as that. We needed to reengineer the core purpose of the school – learning.

To make teaching a flow activity, the constituent elements for flow would need to be present. There would need to be fundamental rethinking and a radical redesign of our processes to achieve:

- Clarity of goals: clear and specific learning outcomes.
- Relevant and accurate feedback: assessment data.
- A feeling of being in control: we would set the targets and our deliberate actions would influence the outcomes.
- A clear focus upon which to concentrate: we would choose a particular focus, stick with it and monitor progress.
- High expectations: mutually agreed and clearly articulated challenging targets.
- Good communication and deep involvement: this would mean the involvement of teachers, teaching assistants, governors, parents and, of course, we would need to let the children in on the 'big secret'.

One of the key reengineering processes was 'learning about learning', which became the most significant focus for in-service training (INSET), or, more precisely, in-service learning. This would be conducted mainly through in-house INSET activities, which would enable us to reflect on our developing understanding of effective teaching and learning and to make a comparison with what was currently happening in our classrooms. The aim, therefore, was to translate the theory into practice, monitor the results and reflect on what emerged. In-house INSET was chosen as the main method to bring about change because of the fundamental belief that school development *is* staff development.

Change requires collaboration, and conflict is inevitable. However, through collaboration and good communication, ideas emerge and, because of the collegial nature of our school, there exists a collective confidence, which enables us to both question what we do and to share ideas. Through dialogue, we all get to know what everyone else knows and collectively, we build capacity, which ultimately leads to greater effectiveness, continuity and progression. There is also congruence in the philosophy of learning we hold for our children and that which we hold for our colleagues. For example, as one of the optimum conditions for learning is relaxed alertness, then that has to be a prerequisite for our colleagues as well as for our children. The presence of threat, no matter how subtle, must therefore be removed if deep learning is to happen. However, once good practice has been collectively defined and policy agreed, poor practice must always be challenged, but this must be done with both courage and compassion.

Our results showed that in 1997 we had been making progress in our end of Key Stage results (*see* Table 11.1). Attainment in science, however, was lagging behind and we, as well as the Office for Standards in Education (OFSTED), had identified it as a key area for improvement. There was, therefore, a demonstrable need for change and a collective sense of urgency to improve. Science then, became our initial focus for improvement. In reengineering terms we needed to move from incremental to dramatic improvement. Improvements came through consciously attending to the learning environment, systematically building in quality review time and improving our curriculum planning by utilizing multiple intelligences as 'gateways' to access learning. This proved to be effective and our end of Key Stage 2 results in 1998 (*see* Table 11.2) showed that achievement in science matched that in English and mathematics.

In the following year I became acquainted with, the work of Smith and Call (1999). I decided to use some of our Standards Fund to purchase copies of their book for all the teachers and teaching support staff and to use it a kind of training manual. This proved to be our reengineering text.

Drawing upon new and innovative thinking about learning from various sources, Smith and Call present a structured approach to organizing classroom learning in the form of 'the accelerated learning cycle'. The cycle has several components, the first, which actually runs throughout, emphasizes the importance of creating a supportive learning environment. It then proposes the worth of connecting new learning to prior knowledge and understanding and providing the learner with an overview of what is to come whilst, at the same time, emphasizing the importance of the new learning to the learner. Next, learning outcomes are clarified and targets are set. The teacher then presents information in visual, auditory and kinaesthetic modes to cater for the variety of learning styles. The learning

Table 11.1 *Key Stage 2 test results, 1996–7*

	1996 %	1997 %
Average Level 4 and above	57	67
English	46	74
Mathematics	57	71
Science	68	55

Table 11.2 *Key Stage 2 test results 1996–2001*

	1996 %	1997 %	1998 %	1999 %	2000 %	2001 %
Average Level 4 and above	57	67	77	90	96	92
English	46	74	77	91	97	94
Mathematics	57	71	77	83	94	86
Science	68	55	77	96	97	97

activities, which follow the teacher input, are designed to draw upon and develop a range of intelligences and are structured in such a way that ensures the learner has the opportunity to demonstrate learning. Finally, the cycle emphasizes the importance of review for recall and retention.

Reengineering outcomes

Adopting the structure of the accelerated learning cycle, and using the staff development model described above to develop an understanding of its rationale, has increased the effectiveness of our teaching. Teacher assessment and data analysis support this, as did the findings of the team of inspectors who conducted our OFSTED inspection in October 2001. The increase in the standard of attainment is the result of more effective teaching to promote deeper learning. What the results in Table 11.2 does not show is that the percentage of children attaining Level 5 in science in 1999 was 81 per cent.

At St Vincent's there is an acceptance that the quality of teaching and learning is at the heart of school improvement. There is a collective sense of responsibility to increase our effectiveness as leaders and educators. There is shared belief that real and lasting change only comes from what teachers and teaching assistants consistently do. Fundamental to the improvement process is the quality of the leadership in operation at various levels in the school.

Reengineering teaching and learning at St Vincent's School is proving to be exciting and challenging. Our teaching now gives children opportunities to access information in ways that suit their preferred modes of thinking and so caters for different learning styles. Our commitment to learn about learning has enabled us to view all children as intelligent and changed our mental model of ability from a single, unchangeable attribute to something more qualitative. This has enabled us to raise our expectations for all our children and challenge the notion that ability is somehow 'fixed'. Similarly, we encourage the children to raise expectations of themselves by promoting a positive, 'can do' philosophy. Our deeper understanding of emotional intelligence (Goleman, 1996) has heightened the level of importance we attach to creating a caring and supporting learning environment. In such an environment, the aim is to reduce the level of stress so all learners are more relaxed and yet alert and feel secure enough to take risks with their learning. The nurturing and maintenance of quality teacher–learner relationships is paramount; this is fostered in many ways but mainly in the numerous, daily encounters when teachers show genuine care and concern for the children and, indeed, pleasure in being in their company.

We have enhanced our curriculum planning to provide challenging activities that acknowledge multiple intelligences. These intelligences are used as 'gateways' to develop numeracy, literacy and scientific competencies. We teach the children about learning and the optimum conditions for learning, including the importance of diet, water, good health, exercise, the significance of emotional states, self-esteem and the views we have of ourselves as learners. We teach listening skills, give time for thinking and teach methods to promote retention and recall through review and novel ways of recording.

Developing a deeper understanding of the learning process has enabled us to make conscious decisions about teaching styles and the range of learning experiences we organize for the children. We have reengineered what we do and how we do it. This started after new understanding had been gained and when we could no longer live with the tension that came from knowing that our practice was not as effective as it could be. More fundamentally, we had ceased to believe in what we were doing because it no longer matched the needs of our children, our own needs, in terms of job satisfaction, and the needs of the school as a learning organization. In other words, it no longer fitted with our core values.

Such change is not easy. It is often painful, sometimes frustratingly slow, and to keep going requires tenacity and resolve. Part of the problem has been that, in some people's eyes, we were already successful. Why change a winning formula? Some were content with the way things were – they were comfortable with existing strategies because they appeared to be working. For some, therefore, there was little motivation to change. As I, however, learnt more and more about whole-brain learning and Gardner's work on multiple intelligences, I became discontented with the existing situation and the task became clear – there would have to be a significant development programme to introduce the staff to this new science of learning and to promote the introduction of accelerated learning techniques.

Change is difficult. It is difficult because we have to change peoples' habits, and, as we all know, it is very difficult to change our own habits, never mind the habits of others. Change, in terms of improvement, therefore, takes time. The government's fixation on short-term results can create further tensions and problems when trying to focus on fundamental change. This is why it has been so important to build a shared vision of the future and to adopt mechanisms for school development that encourage strategies for implementation to emerge (Davies and Ellison, 1999). Knowing where we want to be while, at the same time, being open to ideas that may help us to get there, generates confidence and reduces stress, even in these times of turbulence.

At St Vincents we are finding that reengineering teaching and learning is also influencing other processes. The transformation we are experiencing was preceded by leadership transformation. I changed, and it was learning that brought about that change. We are a transforming school, and in transforming schools transforming leaders transform their followers – the teachers. These, in turn, transform the children into effective lifelong learners.

We have raised standards of attainment by reengineering the teaching and learning processes – and reengineering our own mindsets.

REFERENCES

Csikszentmihalyi, M (1990) *Flow: The Psychology of Optimal Experience*, New York: Harper Perennial.

Csikszentmihalyi, M. (1997) *Finding Flow: The Psychology of Engagement With Everyday Life*, New York: Basic Books.

Davies, B. and Ellison, L. (1999) *Strategic Direction and Development of the School*, London: Routledge.

Fullan, M. (1993) *Change Forces*, London: Falmer Press.

Gardner, H. (1983) *Frames of Mind*, New York: Basic Books.

Gardner, H. (1999) *Intelligence Reframed*, New York: Basic Books.

Goleman, D. (1996) *Emotional Intelligence*, London: Bloomsbury.

Senge, P.M. (1990) *The Fifth Discipline*, London: Random House.

Smith, A. and Call, N. (1999) *The Alps Approach*, Stafford: Network Educational Press

CHAPTER 12

Case study 2: reengineering teaching and learning in a secondary school

DEREK WISE

Context

Cramlington Community High School is a 13–18 high school situated in the small town of Cramlington, Northumberland. Cramlington has a population of 30,000; it is a new town set up on a greenfield site to accommodate the urban overspill of a large city and regenerate an area blighted by the decline of the coal industry. As the only high school in the town it receives a fully comprehensive intake with perhaps fewer than expected high flyers but a skew towards the middle ability range. The key is to get the most out of these 'average' students.

When I became headteacher in September 1990 I was faced with a number of challenges. The most important of these was that the school was losing the confidence of the local community and we were, therefore, losing students to rival schools. The next six years were dominated by measures to raise the expectations of the staff and the aspirations of the students. In particular, we introduced a new timetable (four periods in the morning, two in the afternoon), a new curriculum to go alongside it, and staff held accountable for both discipline and results. We also improved the learning environment with carpeted classrooms, improved student toilets and social facilities. We publicly shared examination results and because the curriculum structure consisted of 90 per cent common core we were able to compare faculty areas with each other and to ask pointed but essential questions – such as why is this faculty/department/member of staff doing better or worse than that faculty/department/ member of staff, given that they have exactly the same students. With the students we shared data on their progress, set targets and celebrated success wherever we could find it. We established regular reviews of departments and guidelines for schemes of work and what we considered to be good teaching and learning. As a result of these reforms we impressed the school inspectors from the Office for Standards in Education (OFSTED) when they inspected us in January 1997, earning the accolade 'a very good school'. Rising examination results and an increasing number of students wishing to join us helped to confirm our growing reputation.

Starting the reengineering process

It is, of course, at this very juncture – when all the news is good – that the sigmoid curve (Handy, 1994, p. 51) warns you to start the new curve. I was aware that we had put our emphasis on teaching rather than learning, and on outcomes, in the form of exam results, rather than process. It is the reengineering focus on process(es) that was to become the cornerstone of all our activities. In the UK there is a danger that we reduce our role as educators merely to fitting learners to the curriculum and reduce the curriculum to preparation for the national tests. This model – where the content (curriculum) becomes so important that it is 'delivered' to the students who are then nationally tested – is unlikely to encourage many of our students to become independent learners. What we needed, I believed, was a model that would give our students the knowledge, skills and understanding necessary to take their first tentative steps into society but which would also make them independent lifelong learners, prepared for continuous training and retraining and able to appreciate how learning *per se* can be a consuming passion that will remain with them between employment and after employment.

If we were to develop such a model we needed to marry the needs of the learner and the process of learning to the content. If we were to be a school where 'learning is our business' we had to recognize that learning is a highly individual matter, and students learn in different ways with preferred styles to access and process information. The decision was taken, therefore, to start our new sigmoid curve by reengineering the learning process. We adopted the accelerated learning cycle (Smith, 1996) as a framework and planning tool to design lessons (*see* Figure 12.1). The cycle blends our developing knowledge of neuroscience, motivational theory and cognitive psychology to increase students' engagement in learning and their

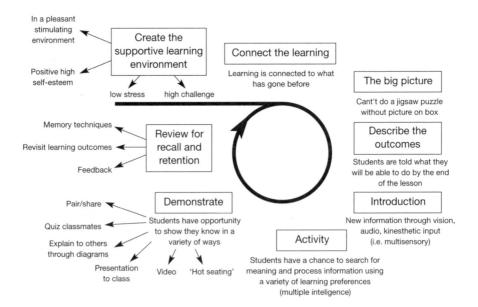

Figure 12.1 The accelerated learning cycle

Source: adapted from Smith 1996, p.11.

motivation to achieve. The cycle gives coherence, pace and rigour. Without the cycle, accelerated learning techniques can become a bag of tricks wheeled out to impress visitors. With the cycle as a framework and used as a planning vehicle, we get good practice put into the right order.

Our use of the cycle highlighted that we needed to identify and cater to each learner's uniqueness and thereby led to a number of key questions, which in essence led to a reorganization around process:

- How can we vary the conditions of learning to meet individual needs?
- How can we give our students the keys to unlock these new learning opportunities?
- How can we ensure our school has the capacity to continually improve in our quest to enhance student learning?

Reengineering the conditions of learning to meet individual needs

Changing the time variable

Intensive Study Weeks

We have become accustomed to a segmented curriculum in which lessons are packaged into single or double periods spaced throughout the week. This may work well for some students or subjects. However, it does not seem to match what we know about learning outside the formal educational structure. Learning here is often in-depth and intensive, with the opportunity to see things through from start to finish. Consequently we try to mirror this for six weeks of the year by suspending our segmented timetable structure and blocking or consolidating curriculum time. So, for example, over three-week periods students receive their subjects in blocks of time of half a day, a full day or even successive days. This arrangement facilitates an intensive investigatory approach, encourages fieldwork with sufficient time for debriefing, and promotes an in-depth 'hands-on' methodology, often through working with experts 'in residence'.

Investigation Week

Again, this is a different approach to learning, this time one that encourages teamwork, decision making, time management and research and presentation skills in solving a real-life problem. Its characteristics are that it is:

- purpose-centred – there is a real problem where the outcomes benefit others, not just the students;
- rigorous – it is multi-disciplinary but involves knowledge of the separate disciplines and develops investigation and research skills.

Investigation Week mirrors real work practices: students have to bid for an allocation of scarce resources and have deadlines to meet. Good teamwork is needed! Students have the responsibility to produce a real product for exhibition or presentation by the end of the week.

Both Intensive Study Weeks and Investigation Week are particularly helpful in meeting the needs of the kinaesthetic learner who learns best through movement, modelling and 'doing' via a 'hands-on' approach.

Changing the style of teaching variable

The style of teaching is changed via Intensive Study Weeks and Investigations Week. In our post-16 work, 20 per cent of the students' time per subject is based on independent learning. Students are timetabled into the Independent Learning Centre, where they are guaranteed access to a computer in a supervised environment. All subject departments set specific work for this 20 per cent of students' time. Homework, private study and reading around the subject are additional to this.

Changing the place variable

Learning in a school context is not always appropriate for all our students all the time. If we reconceptualize the role of the school as a broker of learning opportunities on behalf of its students then some learning will take place outside traditional school hours or the traditional school environment. We have, therefore, students who spend one or two days in the workplace on individually designed schemes, others who spend half a day a week at college on a vocational course, for example catering, and yet others who work from home on an online course. This can be seen in Figure 12.2.

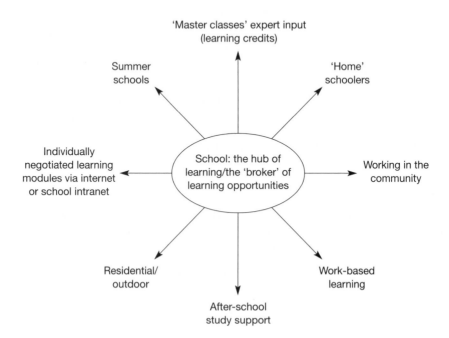

Figure 12.2 The school at the centre of the learning process

Redesigning student learning opportunities

To give our students the keys to unlocking these new learning opportunities we need to train them in their use. All our students in our intake year (Year 9) follow a Learning to Learn course in which they discover how their brain works, their individual learning preferences when it comes to accessing and processing information, ways to manipulate their learning environment, and skills such as mindmapping, concept mapping, use of graphic (visual) organizers and memory-enhancing techniques.

Increasingly throughout the curriculum we are using the students as a resource to help each other (peer tutoring) and provide each other with feedback. As teachers, we tend to think that it is us that should be giving feedback, but during a busy lesson we do not have enough time to give all our students as much feedback as they would like or need. Unless feedback happens during the lesson it can be too little, too late and too vague. A great shame – because our brain thrives on feedback.

The solution is simple. Use the great resource that we all have available to us in a lesson: the students! For example:

- pair share
- students correct each other's work against specifications
- groups evaluate other groups' work
- small group presentations are evaluated by the whole class
- students score their work against a checklist
- students present work to their group, which helps them edit it
- students give themselves a mark and then have to justify it to others.

Sustaining improvement in our key processes

We have introduced an innovative management structure that emphasizes quality assurance and continuous improvement and allows greater participation and involvement by all staff (*see* Figure 12.3). Participation is not simply based on status or seniority but on responsibility or the willingness to serve and be a creative thinker. The separation of the Operational Management Team from the Strategic Policy Team has proved to be a great success. Too often, senior management teams become bogged down in operational matters with little or no time to discuss important strategic issues. The separation of strategic and operational functions has resulted in a separation of the urgent from the important. No longer does the urgent drive out the important; both are now catered for. In addition, the various groups provide a unique 'time horizon' management structure:

- Operational Management Team: focusing on the next 0–12 months
- School Development Plan Team: focusing on the next 6–24 months
- Research and Development Team: focusing on the next 2–5 years.

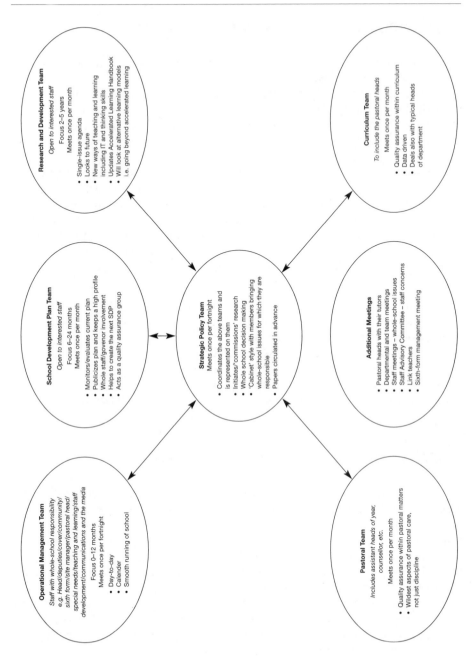

Research and Development Team
Open to interested staff
Focus 2–5 years
Meets once per month
• Single-issue agenda
• Looks to future
• New ways of teaching and learning
  including IT and thinking skills
• Updates Accelerated Learning Handbook
• Will look at alternative learning models
  i.e. going beyond accelerated learning

Curriculum Team
To include the pastoral heads
Meets once per month
• Quality assurance within curriculum
• Data driven
• Deals also with typical heads
  of department

School Development Plan Team
Open to interested staff
Focus 6–24 months
Meets once per month
• Monitors/evaluates current plan
• Publicizes plan and keeps a high profile
• Whole staff/govenor involvement
• Helps to create the next SDP
• Acts as a quality assurance group

Strategic Policy Team
Meets once per fortnight
• Coordinates the above teams and
  is represented on them
• Initiates/'commissions' research
• Whole school decision making
• 'Cabinet' style with members bringing
  whole-school issues for which they are
  responsible
• Papers circulated in advance

Additional Meetings
• Pastoral heads with their tutors
• Departmental and team meetings
• Staff meetings – whole-school issues
• Staff Advisory Committee – staff concerns
• Link teachers
• Sixth-form management meeting

Operational Management Team
*Staff with whole-school responsibility
e.g. Head/deputies/cover/community/
sixth form/site manager/pastoral head/
special needs/teaching and learning/staff
development/communications and the media*
Focus 0–12 months
Meets once per fortnight
• Day-to-day
• Calender
• Smooth running of school

Pastoral Team
*Includes assistant heads of year,
counsellor, etc.*
Meets once per month
• Quality assurance within pastoral matters
• Wildest aspects of pastoral care,
  not just discipline

Figure 12.3 The reengineered organizational structure

The School Development Plan Team, owing to its composition, is more likely than any senior management team to know whether the development plan is working on the ground. Its current plan is to produce a continually updated movie of the school development plan in action! The Research and Development Team has already proven to be invaluable, searching the world for world-class best practice and bringing it to Cramlington. Its members regularly visit the USA for this purpose and £3000 is put aside from the school budget to facilitate these visits. Currently, the team is doing action research into a number of different areas, including home-learning projects as a substitute for the traditional homework tasks and different ways for teachers to assess students' work, for example audio assessment and training students in self-assessment techniques. The team investigates, researches and develops new ideas, the most successful of which are absorbed into our normal practice.

Staff development

It is very difficult to have curriculum development without staff development. Too often staff development is left to one-off courses or takes place after school when everyone is tired. By rearranging the school week, we finish at 2 pm every Wednesday and staff are involved with developmental work, planning, reviewing and in-service training (INSET) between 2.15 and 4.15. These times are not used for the often dreaded departmental meetings: any administration or business can be dealt with by a bulletin. Only if INSET and planning time are regular throughout the year are we able to promote a culture of inquiry and collaboration in which teachers are involved in a constant dialogue about teaching and learning.

The emphasis we put on staff development to change and sustain school culture is also illustrated by other initiatives:

- an intensive in-house five-day INSET package, received by all staff after two years in the school, to promote further development;
- internal secondments of one week, for staff to research the impact of developments within the school or write new high-quality units of work for their departmental colleagues;
- learning coaches, who work alongside colleagues in the classroom to model, give feedback, encourage new practice and support its integration into our everyday practice; currently we have two such coaches, one in accelerated learning, the other in ICT.

Reengineering outcomes

So does it work? Whilst pleading the inevitable 'work in progress', the signs are very promising. In November 2000 the inspectors (OFSTED) returned and were even more impressed than before, describing us as 'a strikingly successful school' and an 'exciting place in which to learn'. The inspectors recognized our focus on learning:

There is a strong focus on what students should learn and lessons have clearly stated learning objectives. Lesson objectives are set out, explained and revisited at key points in lessons, and reviewed to sum up what students have learned at the end. Students understand that they are at school to learn and they are encouraged to be active learners. The range of methods used by teachers is diverse and retains students' interest and motivation whilst moving them quickly on ... Teachers present the work broken down into specific assignments in a stimulating and often imaginative manner. They seize the students' attention, connect the task with their previous learning and emphasise its relevance. Pacing the closely-structured lessons into fast-moving 'chunks' of identified time and learning activities breaks them up into manageable and appropriate periods and creates styles of working which lead to confident, effective learning. (OFSTED, 2000, p. 13)

In addition, the science department, which has been using accelerated learning techniques the longest, shows the greatest value-added of all the major departments. As a school we have moved the percentage of students who achieve five or more higher grade GCSEs from the mid-50s (1994–7) to the mid-60s (1998–2001). Perhaps even more important is that we have moved beyond reform to fundamental reengineering of what we do. We are in the business of creating butterflies, not faster caterpillars!

REFERENCES

Handy, C. (1994) *The Empty Raincoat: Making Sense of the Future*, London: Hutchinson.

OFSTED (2000) *Report on Cramlington High School*, London: Office for Standards in Education.

Smith, A. (1996) *Accelerated Learning in the Classroom*, Stafford: Network Educational Press.

CHAPTER 13

Marketing schools: an analysis for educational leaders

BRENT DAVIES AND BARBARA DAVIES

This chapter will define marketing and examine the perceptions of marketing that exist in schools, in order to provide a framework to guide leadership and management practice. It is important initially to distinguish between 'markets' as allocation systems and 'marketing' as a communication strategy. Although here we will mainly focus on the latter, we will briefly explore 'markets' as allocation systems first.

What are markets?

Generally it is possible to consider two basic ways, in a society, of allocating resources. First is the use of central planning, usually by a governmental body, where decisions of what to produce and how to allocate what has been produced is taken by a central planning authority. This system is operated through a decision-making process taken by government officials, whether elected or not, who determine what is produced. The 'old' communist Soviet Union provides examples of highly centralized planning approaches. Within the UK significant parts of the economy in terms of goods and services are centrally planned, for example defence, health care, in the form of the National Health Service, and education, in the form of state-provided education. These are examples of central planning playing the major role in terms of what is provided and how it is distributed.

An alternative to central planning, as a means of allocating resources, is to use market forces. Within a market the individual decisions of consumers and suppliers interact, through the price mechanism, to determine what is produced. Thus if consumers 'demand' a product, which is demonstrated by their willingness to allocate their financial resources to it, then suppliers will respond and produce a commodity that meets that demand. In practice, suppliers try to anticipate the demand by producing goods they think consumers will buy and communicate that to consumers through the marketing process. As Glatter, Woods and Bagley (1997, p. 7) assert:

> A key element in any functioning market must be that there are differences between the 'products' on offer and that these differences to some extent reflect and accord with the variety of needs and preferences amongst consumers.

How can this analysis of markets be extended? We believe for a market to exist several preconditions have to be satisfied. What would an education market look like? It would have some of the following features:

- a price mechanism;
- effective choice on the part of consumers (students, parents);
- relatively easy entry for new schools or educational providers;
- freely available, comprehensive information about different providers and their products;
- minimal regulation by government authorities.

What we see in education systems in the UK and overseas are only partial elements of these features surfacing in the various systems. It is useful to reflect on how movements in the five categories above are increasing or decreasing the influence of market forces on education in their context. In the UK over 90 per cent of children attend state schools, and only a small proportion of children are served by a 'market' system – those paying for independent education from a competing range of suppliers. However, in the state sector price can also be seen to be operating through the mechanism of the housing market where parents 'bid up' the prices of houses in the catchment area of desirable schools. Parents are given a choice of school, but this is dependent on availability of places and is therefore rationed by administrative criteria. Gorard (1999) questions whether all parents have this choice and identifies four areas of difficulty. Do parents have: (i) convenient geographical access to a range of schools, (ii) the ability to articulate their needs, (iii) the time and resources to consider all the alternatives, and (iv) the ability to interpret the data, and access to relevant data? Unless there is a positive response to all the questions the effect of market forces will be limited.

How easy it is for new schools to be set up is debatable. There is some evidence that the increased involvement of the private sector in the UK is bringing a diversity of providers into the system; this is also true of the charter school movement in the USA. The question still to be answered is whether this is a marginal change on the total level of provision or whether a significant number of schools will be involved so as to make a difference to the system. There is certainly much more information available for consumers in the UK, for example the school prospectus, the publication of examination and national test results and the publication of Office for Standards in Education (OFSTED) inspection reports.

So what can we conclude? There are increased parental contributions, increased choice and more information and these are examples of market forces operating within an essentially planned system. This part-market or market influence is often called a 'quasi-market' and is described by Levačić (1995, p. 26):

> For all its deficiencies of structure and information, the school quasi-market has become more competitive through more open enrolment in the context of surplus places in many areas, and parents now have more information, particularly if they choose to seek it out.

It is, therefore, possible to reflect that in the school sector education reforms have introduced elements of market forces so that quasi-markets or market influences are working in the system. This is the context in which schools operate.

How schools choose to communicate with their clients by the use of a systematic marketing approach will be considered next.

Marketing as communication

Davies and Ellison (1997, p. 3) define marketing in education as: 'the means by which the school actively communicates and promotes its purpose, values and products to the pupils, parents, staff and wider community'. Many teachers are suspicious or even hostile to the idea of marketing schools. Evans (1995, p. 4) suggests that in education 'marketing is not selling' and that 'marketing is not advertising'. He describes marketing as 'the management process of identifying and satisfying the requirements of consumers (parents/students) and society in a sustainable way'. All schools have reputations and those reputations are affected by what the school does. All schools need to communicate with parents and the wider community. All schools need to promote values and approaches to education. Marketing provides a coherent and systematic way of doing these things. If the value-laden 'marketing' sets up negative emotions, then 'communication strategy' or 'reputation management' can be used. The three Ws of marketing – why, who and what – can be used to frame this initial discussion.

Why are we marketing?

Two ideas statements can be used to answer this question. First, 'every school has a reputation and that reputation has to be managed' and, second, 'virtue does not bring its own reward but virtue with a good marketing strategy may'. What do we mean by these?

First, it is naïve to assume that by not marketing then the communication process is proceeding in a useful way or that the school's reputation is necessarily being enhanced. One of the common mistakes by oversubscribed or exclusive schools is that they have more than enough pupils and they do not need to market themselves. It could be, of course, that they are oversubscribed because they are good, or it could be that they are the least worst school in a particular area. Either way, it is still vital to address the needs and wants of the students and parents and to convey the values and key aspects of the education that the school is providing. By doing so, the quality of the relationship between the community and the school is enhanced and the school benefits from taking a proactive and responsive approach.

Second, virtue does not bring its own reward. It is necessary for schools to communicate their positive achievements and values and not leave a vacuum for others to fill. The negative press and perception of some politicians needs to be countered to give an accurate account of the many achievements of our schools. In an age in which information is increasingly available, and consumers of education can obtain the necessary information and use it to make choices, it is vital that the school is able to provide that information.

To whom are we marketing?

Davies and Ellison (1997) distinguish between the internal and external market as shown in Table 13.1. The significance of this classification is that it draws attention to the difference between external and internal marketing. There is a danger in concentrating on the external market: in the longer term, the strategy may be ineffective if, having persuaded various parties to interact with the school, they

Table 13.1 *Market segmentation in the education sector*

Internal markets	External markets
● Governors	● Prospective pupils
● Staff (teaching and support staff)	● Prospective parents
● Regular visitors and helpers	● Prospective staff
● Current pupils	● Former pupils/parents/staff
● Current parents	● Other educational institutions
	● The local community
	● Commerce and industry
	● Local education authority
	● OFSTED
	● Teacher Training Agency/General Teaching Council
	● National groups/organizations

Source: Davies and Ellison, 1997, p. 8

find that the rhetoric does not match reality. Considerable damage to the school's reputation may ensue. It is therefore very important to focus the marketing effort initially on the internal market. By doing this all those in day-to-day contact with the school are informed of and build up a clear perception of the school's values, achievement and major features and can communicate these to others outside the school when they come into contact with them. The power of the internal market can never be underestimated, since individuals and organizations will have their perceptions reinforced or denied on the strength of this interaction. The answer to the question 'To whom are we marketing?' is both the internal and external market, but we should start with the internal market.

What are we marketing?

The first response to this is that it is obvious and includes key aspects like teaching and learning, pastoral care and welfare, school climate/culture and extra-curricular activities. But it is important – bearing in mind the commentary on internal and external markets – that a limited and shared list is articulated by all those in the school. By linking marketing to choice of school, Gorard (1999, p. 31) establishes that parents have five possible reasons for their choice of school:

- Academic: a school is selected by parents because they believe that their child will thrive better academically at that particular type of school.
- Situational: a school is chosen because it is geographically convenient or because the child has established friendship groups at the school.
- Organizational: the perceived ethos of the school may be important. This may be evaluated through the use of school uniform, the physical environment, the way parents are treated when visiting the school, school and class size or a perception of how 'happy' the children are at the school.
- Selective: a desirable school could be one with high-ability children, either indicated through performance tables or in a school whose admissions are selected through ability. Selection could also be related to gender, religion, culture or social background.
- Safety and welfare: the importance of moral values, respect for others, absence of bullying and well-behaved children.

It is important for the school to undertake its own value definition of what it wants to articulate, taking into account some market research on the needs and wants of the community.

A strategic marketing framework

In the UK, following the reforms of the late 1980s and early 1990, a great deal of attention was paid to marketing in terms of publicity. Numerous books and courses sprang up, often concerned with disseminating good design and dissemination of publicity materials. Once schools had established the 'good prospectus', a more fundamental appraisal of the nature and dimensions of marketing took place. We believe a much more strategic approach is now necessary in schools. This strategic approach can be summarized in Figure 13.1.

Figure 13.1 The phases of the marketing process

Source: Davies and Ellison, 1997, p. 18.

Traditionally, because of demands to produce the school brochure or prospectus, many schools have become involved at the implementation phase first. While this is beneficial in that it produces the marketing materials that are necessary, it can be self-defeating if those materials are not based on a strategic process that integrates both the creation of strategic intent and strategic market analysis. Intent provides the driving force and analysis provides the direction for that force. Let us now consider each in turn.

Strategic intent

Strategic intent has been dealt with in detail in Chapter 8. We can use it here as a means of giving focus to the direction and purpose of the school and binding the staff into a common understanding of that direction and purpose. By creating that strategic intent for marketing purposes we can make use of three interlinking concepts:

- a strategic cause;
- creating and sustaining a client-focused culture
- creating and sustaining a proactive staff.

In each of these three categories the framework established for strategic intent will be used. This involves setting an intent to be achieved and developing capability and capacity in the school to deliver it. Putting these three elements together builds a key element of a successful marketing strategy: that of building the capability and capacity to be an outward-looking, value-driven organization.

Strategic cause

Strategic cause is a very powerful concept. It is developing a belief system that is shared by all those working within the school that gives them purpose and direction; this is then communicated to the external world. A cause embodies a vision. What is the school trying to achieve? What is its moral purpose? What difference will it make to children's lives and opportunities? This is the 'passion' part of education. What do we passionately believe in and what do we want to do to benefit children? Without this driving force, schools take on a functional process of delivering the curriculum and assessing the outcomes as agents of the local or national government. Schools are at their core moral communities and this should be reflected in their value system and sense of purpose and direction. Unless schools define their purpose and values, they have very little to communicate apart from transfer of such skills as literacy or numeracy.

Creating a client-focused culture

A useful response to questions from staff is: 'What is in the best interests of the children?'. The purpose of this question is constantly to reinforce the organizational imperative of focusing all the time on the core purpose of the school. By their very nature, schools are made up of various interest groups with different agendas and priorities. It is very easy over a period of time to provide structures and processes that meet the needs of the adults in the organization in the belief that if the adults are OK the children will be also. This is not the necessarily the case and the concept of 'producer capture' is relevant here. The producers of education, the teachers or the local education authority, organize things to suit their needs. It is an important lesson to reflect on the needs of the 'consumers' of education, i.e. the children. In a marketing sense, unless one can deliver quality education consistently to the child then there is little to communicate to the external world. Thus constantly reassessing the needs of the client is imperative.

Creating a proactive staff

The traditional view teachers have of themselves is often that they should be recognized for what they do. While this is true, it does not necessarily happen. Indeed, the lack of articulation and promotion has often led to a vacuum, with politicians and others filling the gap. We need to be proud of what we do and of our achievements, and articulate that with passion. This is not necessarily easy, but does need to be done consistently and positively. The impression that the outside world has is often formed by the teachers with whom they come into contact. A simple example can be found in what happens on a Friday night. Teachers call in for a drink at a bar and when told 'You look tired', they might respond with either: 'You would be tired if you worked at that dreadful school', or 'It's been a fantastic week in school. I'm looking forward to a break but can't wait to get back on Monday.' How staff represent themselves and the school is a cornerstone of effective marketing.

Strategic market analysis

Having created the marketing intent, it is then necessary to obtain the information on which to base the implementation strategy. Figure 13.2 illustrates the dimensions of the strategic marketing analysis process.

Market research can use two sets of concepts. The first is primary and secondary data. Primary data provide the required information that the school needs to collect. For example, the school could use a questionnaire to gather parent, teacher or pupil attitudinal data. Secondary data already exist, and the school has to locate and access them. An example of such data would be birth rates and predictions of student numbers.

The second similar but different set of concepts is aggregated and disaggregated information. Does the information exist in the school in an accessible form, i.e. is it all brought together (aggregated) or is it fragmented and needs bringing together (disaggregated)? An example of aggregated data is the return of standardized test school results from an external agency. An example of disaggregated data is the comments made to all the teachers at last night's parents' meeting, which need to be captured before all the ideas and comments are forgotten.

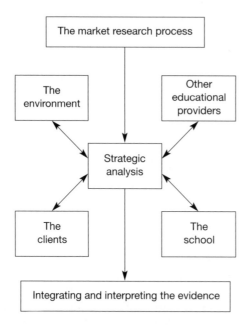

Figure 13.2 Strategic market analysis – a conceptual framework

Source: Davies and Ellison, 1997, p. 20.

The areas that need to be researched are:

- The environment: what is happening in the wider world? Developments in technology, employment and social trends provide the backcloth for more immediate planning activities.
- Other educational providers: these could be schools in the region or the growing number of technology-based educational providers. What are they doing well and what lessons can be learnt from that experience?
- The clients: the students and their parents. Do we really know what they want and does this conflict with what the professionals in the school believe they need? The wants and needs do not always coincide. The school needs to consider what managers should do to close the gap.
- The school: what information do we have on its strengths and weaknesses and how is it going to develop to enhance its provision in the future?

Once the analysis has taken place the critical leadership and management task is making sense of the data by integrating and interpreting the evidence to turn it into useful information. Several techniques are available; see, for example, Davies and Ellison (1999).

Strategic marking implementation

Marketing needs to be focused by answering two questions: to whom are we marketing and what methods are we using? We have already considered internal and external markets, which is a useful initial focusing device. When deciding the part or parts of the market on which to concentrate, the following methods can be used:

- oral communication
- prospectuses, brochures and flyers
- other written material
- the media
- advertising
- open evenings and other events
- technology-based communication, websites, promotional videos
- group promotion
- other communication techniques.

Several marketing or promotion books describe the mechanics of undertaking the above and readers will, from their own practice, by familiar with all of them. It is important to stress the first one, as it underpins all the others. It is possible to use four Ps to break oral communication to its component parts: pupils, parents, professionals and public. The existing pupils need to have their contribution to the school valued, value their school and have a pride in its achievement. This creates a positive culture in the school. If this 'culture' factor is missing then it is doubtful that the reality of the interaction with pupils will ever match the promotional claims for the school. Similarly, the attitude of the parents towards the school is critical in that the 'school-gate grapevine' is a powerful guardian of a school's reputation. Ensuring good communication and involvement and having a responsive approach will ensure that the message spread by the parents is a positive one.

When considering professionals, it is useful to take teachers as a case study. When someone applies for a post in a school, what is their experience? Do they receive a polite, helpful response for details when they phone up, or are they told the information is are not ready yet or told to send a stamped addressed envelope? Are they treated fairly at interview, and if they are not appointed are they debriefed and thanked for their contribution? Their experience will spread in the local educational community and determine whether the school attracts strong applicants in the future. Finally, of course, there is the general public. What is the school doing to promote positive messages about the school in the local press and community groups? How is it linking and supporting its local community? All these factors will be critical in supporting the reputation of the school.

2

Conclusion

Marketing can be defined as a coordinating function, ensuring that the relationships and the range and quality of the services on offer are of the highest standard. Marketing is also a series of techniques, the most important being the use of effective communication: 'Marketing will only work for those who really believe in listening and responding, it starts and ends with caring for people' (Sullivan, 1991, p. 4).

All schools market themselves whether they are conscious of it or not. Those who are aware of it, do it better. It is all about learning: learning about people's perceptions and needs and then acting on that learning to communicate the school's core purpose and values, both to the school community and to those outside.

Schools can be marketed in a socially, ethically and educationally responsible manner. There must be a clear conceptualization of marketing in the mind of the school leader. The main concepts are:

- define marketing for staff and others involved in the school community;
- use an appropriate model to analyse marketing practice in your school;
- engage in marketing based on values;
- involve all those in the 'internal market' in the marketing process;
- remember that you need to market 'marketing' in the school.

The marketing process needs to be seen as three essential stages: intent, analysis and implementation. The danger is to concentrate on the marketing approach and techniques that are part of the implementation stage and neglect the intent and analysis stages, which take a broader strategic view and link to wider leadership and management processes. To develop this concept further, the following chapter by Nick Foskett will extend that strategic perspective by examining marketing culture.

REFERENCES

Davies, B. and Ellison, L. (1997) *Strategic Marketing for School*, London: Financial Times/ Pitman.

Davies, B. and Ellison, L. (1999) *Strategic Direction and Development of the School*, London: Routledge.

Evans, I. (1995) *Marketing for Schools*, London: Cassell.

Glatter, R., Woods, P.A. and Bagley, C. (1997) *Choice and Diversity in Schools*, London: Routledge.

Gorard, S. (1999) 'Well that about wraps it up for school choice research: a state of the art review', *School Leadership and Management*, 19 (1), pp. 25–48.

Levačić, R. (1995) *Local Management of Schools*, Buckingham: Open University Press.

Sullivan, M. (1991) *Marketing your Primary School: A Handbook*, Harlow: Longman.

CHAPTER 14

Measuring marketing cultures in schools

NICK FOSKETT

In the context of educational leadership and management, an understanding of the significance of culture as a key component of educational organizations has emerged through the work of a wide range of authors from Deal (1988) to Handy (1986) and Hargreaves (1999). Culture is the third leg of any organization, alongside structure and process (O'Neill, 1994), and is an important element in framing how organizational change may be lead and managed. Culture is the product of a wide range of factors, but must be recognized as a conservatively dynamic element in the organization – while limiting change, it responds both to internally generated and externally imposed political, social and economic influences to produce a new profile over time.

Culture is also multifaceted in that we can identify culture at a number of levels (Prosser, 1999) – from the individual classroom, to teams within the school, to the whole school, and beyond to each level of operation (local, regional, national, international) within which the individual school functions. Sub-cultures and counter-cultures (Beare, Caldwell and Milliken, 1989) can be identified, too, which react and respond to each of the levels of culture on a continuing basis. Importantly, we must recognize that the precise set of cultures in any school will be unique and that understanding the impact and role of culture requires not just the importation of generic ideas but an analytical application of those ideas in the school's specific context.

Culture is both implicit and explicit in its expression. In its most explicit forms it is observable through the behaviours, actions, rituals and artefacts of an organization. In its implicit forms it appears in the attitudes and values of individuals and teams to change within their own environment and the touchstone for day-to-day decision-making. Indeed, it is culture that provides the basis for action in the circumstances where there is no direct line-management instruction about how to behave in a particular situation. In this respect culture is not simply an interesting but abstract aspect of schools as organizations. It is a key factor in facilitating or constraining change, and in a period when school improvement is a dominant theme, understanding culture as a prelude to managerial intervention is essential.

Hargreaves (1999) has identified three tasks for school managers in relation to culture:

- The diagnostic task: identifying the current culture(s) of an organization. This enables the identification of how things are done in a particular organization and whether there may be mismatches between internal culture and the requirements for change that are emerging from the external environment and from internally prioritized goals.

- The directional task: identifying the vision of what the culture should become.
- The managerial task: planning and implementing a strategy to achieve the 'new' culture.

In the context of this purpose of cultural analysis, Hargreaves (1999) also identifies a number of strategies for identifying and describing school culture and explores the applicability of such insights for managing change and promoting school improvement.

Organizational culture is always subject to processes of reconstruction, as the internal and external environment change. We explore here an approach to identify cultural change in schools in response to the increased autonomy that has characterized many national educational arenas in the last two decades. This metatrend of the decentralization of educational management from national authorities to regional/local authorities and/or to schools has been based on a range of ideological and managerial premises about enhancing the three Es of economy, efficiency and effectiveness. Central to this perspective are the clarion calls for raising standards, increasing the value for money from public sector education and enhancing national economic competitiveness.

Important operational features of this trend have been:

- the delegation of responsibility for resource management to local authorities or, very frequently, to individual schools;
- the delegation of accountability to individual teachers and headteachers/ principals for the acquisition of resources, the management of their deployment and the outputs achieved in terms of pupil standards;
- competitive environments both between schools and within them;
- an increased emphasis on management focused on and beyond the school boundaries.

Such changes are sometimes summarized in the shorthand term 'marketization', which reflects the movement of schools from what Carlson (1975) has termed the domesticated environment of centralized control to the wild environment of self-reliance and autonomy. It is not simply a process of creating markets though, and indeed the market element may at times be hard to identify. Rather it is the creation of an operating environment where schools have greater responsibility and accountability for their own affairs, and successes and failures, and must compete for scarce resources.

These major functional changes must be recognized as a project of cultural change, in which the 'demand side' of the operating environment (government, parents, pupils, and community) is prioritized over the supply side (schools) in terms of their influence on educational processes and outputs. This cultural change has both indirect and direct components. Indirectly, any organizational change will inevitably have impacts on the culture of schools, as staff at all levels are required to operate in different ways. However, we must recognize that cultural change in schools has itself been a key target for change, based on a belief that it has been restrictive and unhelpful in enabling governments to achieve wider social and economic gains through education. Decentralization is premised on a view that the three Es will be achieved only when schools at both institutional and individual level move towards a set of values based on a commitment to raising standards and a responsiveness to the needs and wants of pupils, parents and communities.

Such a cultural change can be characterized as a shift from a 'product orientation' to a 'marketing orientation'. Product-oriented organizations are those in which there is a primary concern with supplying a product or service that they have expertise in producing, with little or no consideration for the requirements or expectations of the client or customer, and may be seen as historically typical of most public services and private sector professional services. In contrast, a marketing orientation is one in which the customer or client is the central focus of day-to-day activities and the aim of the organization is to monitor continuously and respond to those needs and wants. In the context of schools this involves responsiveness to the statutory and policy requirements of government, external quality assurance demands (e.g. inspection or public examinations), professional bodies, local communities and, in many cases, the rights of parents and pupils to choose. As Foskett (1998, p.199) suggests:

> A marketing orientation has implications for the organization and its management structures. Marketing will not be confined to the marketing team but will be central to the organization's whole approach ... Such an organizational refocusing in schools brings an important cultural challenge, yet, in many dimensions, is not far removed from the traditional operating approach of 'good' schools, with their focus on comprehensiveness, community and partnership with stakeholders.

But what does such a marketing orientation look like in terms of the implicit and explicit facets of a school's culture? Cowell (1984) has considered the cultural characteristics of market-focused organizations in a wide range of professional, public sector and private sector environments, and his analysis has identified four broad groups of characteristics that will be present where marketing orientation is strong:

- an attitude of mind: in which the centrality of customer focus permeates the whole organization;
- an internal organization system: which ensures that responsiveness to customer wants and needs drives the operation of the organization;
- the integration of a range of activities that contribute to the marketing process: including marketing research, customer-driven product/service design, the planning of external communications, quality control in service/product delivery, evaluation of the whole marketing process and customer satisfaction;
- the use of an array of techniques and tools to support these processes: including, for example, SWOT analysis, buyer-behaviour analysis.

The terminology of Cowell needs some interpretation in the context of education, where the 'business discourse' is replaced by the 'discourse of education'. For example, 'customer-driven product design' may be seen in terms of a curriculum that meets government specifications (for example, a national curriculum) and also enables the specific needs of individual pupils to be met, for example in relation to special needs education or the use of a work-related curriculum rather than an academic curriculum for some pupils, or in the use of individual target setting and learning plans. Indeed, it may be more appropriate to reconfigure the term 'marketing oriented organization' and replace it with the phrase 'the responsive organization', which emphasizes more the relationships that lie at the heart of the concept rather than the economic processes that may be driving it.

Foskett (1995, 1998) has developed a methodology, based on Cowell's conceptualization, for measuring and mapping the development of a marketing/responsive culture in schools. A refined version of that model is presented here in a format that enables individual schools to use the tool for the process of self-evaluation and diagnosis. Table 14.1 places Cowell's classification in the context of schools, to highlight the elements of a marketing culture that might be significant. Table 14.2 enables each of the criteria to be assessed in relation to a three-level model that distinguishes a criterion as being strongly developed, moderately developed or weakly developed. Completion of the self-evaluation tool can either be undertaken on the basis of subjective judgements by informed people within the school or by an external evaluator, and requires the relevant level of development of each criterion to be assessed.

Table 14.1 *Marketing criteria*

Criterion	Components in a school context
A Attitude of mind	1 Senior staff emphasize responsiveness to external influences, e.g. on curriculum, finance, recruitment. 2 Teaching staff emphasize the same responsiveness to external influences. 3 Marketing and responsiveness are viewed as positive aspects of their roles by teachers and senior management. 4 Policy, planning and practice in school prioritize external accountability over internal preference. 5 There is strong internal promotion of the school's aims and vision by senior staff with respect to responsiveness. 6 Staff development, emphasizing external responsiveness and pupil-focused approaches, is a priority.
B Organizational systems	1 There is a clear system of responsibility for monitoring, responding to and implementing external and internal 'customer-driven' change. 2 Responsiveness, marketing and external relations management are integrated into school development planning. 3 The budgetary system is linked to accountability in relation to responsiveness, e.g. enhanced pupil achievement, pupil recruitment. 4 Internal quality assurance and evaluation systems provide feedback on the achievement of aims linked to responsiveness.
C Promotional tools	1 The school uses a wide range of external communication and promotional methods. 2 The aims and limitations of each method are understood by senior management. 3 The effectiveness of each method is evaluated.
D Analytical tools	1 Marketing research methods (formal or informal) are used to analyse the external environment and pupil/parent/community/government needs and wants. 2 All staff are aware of the school's 'market position' as a result of using such tools. 3 Strategic and operational planning is evidence based and uses the findings of external environment sensing.

Source: Cowell, 1975.

Table 14.2 *Marketing culture: self-evaluation*

Criterion	Strong development	Moderate development	Weak development	Notes
A1 Senior team (ST) responsiveness	ST always emphasize how the school is meeting external requirements	ST often emphasize how the school is meeting external requirements	ST occasionally emphasize how the school is meeting external requirements	Focus on public examination results, inspection grades, media image, new curricula
A2 Teaching staff (TS) responsiveness	TS always emphasize how the school is meeting external requirement	TS often emphasize how the school is meeting external requirements	TS occasionally emphasize how the school is meeting external requirements	As above
A3 Positive view of responsiveness	Staff are usually positive in attitude to responding to pupil/parent/external demands	Staff are sometimes positive in attitude to responding to pupil/parent/external demands	Staff are usually negative in attitude to responding to pupil/parent/external demands	Staff may see the need to emphasize exam results in a positive or negative way
A4 Planning prioritizes responsiveness over preference	Development plans mostly emphasize meeting externally imposed demands	Development plans sometimes emphasize meeting externally imposed demands	Development plans rarely emphasize meeting externally imposed demands	Plans may emphasize exam result targets, pupil recruitment targets, income generation targets
A5 Internal marketing of responsiveness aims	ST always promote in documents and meetings the achievement of responsiveness aims	ST sometimes promote in documents and meetings the achievement of responsiveness aims	ST rarely promote in documents and meetings the achievement of responsiveness aims	How far do ST seek to change TS attitudes to being responsive?
A6 Staff development to promote responsive	TS/ST strongly encouraged to undertake staff development to promote responsiveness	TS/ST sometimes encouraged to undertake staff development to promote responsiveness	TS/ST rarely encouraged to undertake staff development to promote responsiveness	Do development priorities focus on e.g. communicating with parents, target setting with pupils, designing new curricula, rather than subject knowledge enhancement?

Table 14.2 *Continued*

Criterion	Strong development	Moderate development	Weak development	Notes
B1 Environmental monitoring systems	Marketing, curriculum development and QA systems are clearly defined and operate well	Marketing, curriculum development and QA systems exist and usually work	Marketing, curriculum and QA systems are weakly established	Is there an active marketing committee? Is there a school curriculum review group?
B2 Integration of responsiveness, marketing and external relations into planning	School development documents strongly integrate responsiveness to external relations/marketing issues	School development documents show some integration of responsiveness to external relations/marketing issues	School development documents show little responsiveness to external relations/marketing issues	Do all sections of the school development plans show how the school is responding to external demands, e.g. for standards, curriculum change, etc.?
B3 Budgetary system driven by accountability	All budgets are allocated and reviewed according to development plans and targets	Some elements of budgets are allocated and reviewed according to development plans and targets	Few if any of the budgets are allocated and reviewed according to development plans and targets	Is funding (internal or external) linked to clear targets showing responsiveness?
B4 Internal evaluation systems to measure achievement of responsiveness aims	QA and annual monitoring systems are strongly developed and operational	QA and annual monitoring systems are partially developed and operational	QA and annual monitoring systems are little used	Does the school regularly review whether its responsiveness aims are being met?
C1 Use of a wide range of external communication and promotion	Many strategies are used for external communication, and PR/promotion is a high priority	Some strategies are used for external communication, and PR/promotion is seen as of some importance	Minimal emphasis on external communication, and PR/promotion is a low priority	Does the school actively use media links, produce highly professional brochures or use advertising?
C2 Aims and limitations of communications understood	Most staff recognize the aims of the strategy for communications and its importance to the school	Only staff directly involved know the aims of the strategy for communications, but most staff recognize its importance	Few staff understand the aims of the strategy for communications or recognize its importance	Do staff share the message of the school's aims and character and understand its identity?

Table 14.2 *Continued*

Criterion	Strong development	Moderate development	Weak development	Notes
C3 Communications evaluated	The impact and effect of external communications are usually measured/evaluated	The impact and effect of external communications are sometimes measured/evaluated	The impact and effect of external communications are rarely measured/evaluated	How far does the school know if its communication systems are effective?
D1 Marketing research used	The school often uses formal and informal methods of measuring the views, needs and wants of current and potential audiences	The school uses informal methods of measuring the views, needs and wants of current and potential audiences	The school uses few or no methods of measuring the views, needs and wants of current and potential audiences	Does the school seek to find out about its 'markets'?
D2 Staff are aware of 'market position'	Most ST and TS know who the key audiences are, know their needs and wants, and know what the school's aims are	Only some ST and TS know who the key audiences are, know their needs and wants, and know what the school's aims are	Few if any ST and TS know who their audiences are, know their needs and wants, and know what the school's aims are	Is there a shared view of the aims of the school and of its position in its various markets?
D3 Evidence-based planning uses evidence from environmental sensing	Data from marketing research and the external environment are usually used as a basis for choosing strategies and actions	Data from marketing research and the external environment are sometimes used as a basis for choosing strategies and actions	Data from marketing research and the external environment are rarely used as a basis for choosing strategies and actions	Is the school really responsive to (and value) objective evidence about the world outside?

From the completed results two forms of summary can be produced:

- A profile diagram (Figure 14.1): this provides a visual impression of the development of a marketing culture, and enables a comparison between schools or between time periods within a school.
- A simple descriptive numerical index: the Index of Marketing Cultural Development (IMCD) may be calculated by allocating a value of 2 to each criterion which is strongly developed, a value of 1 to each criterion which is moderately developed, and a value of 0 to each criterion which is weakly developed, providing a range of possible scores between 0 and 32. Based on a study of schools in a number of contrasting socio-economic and geographical locations in England in the mid-1990s, Foskett (1998) has shown that a mean value of IMCD for urban schools of 14.6 contrasts with a mean value of 6 for rural schools in relatively uncompetitive environments.

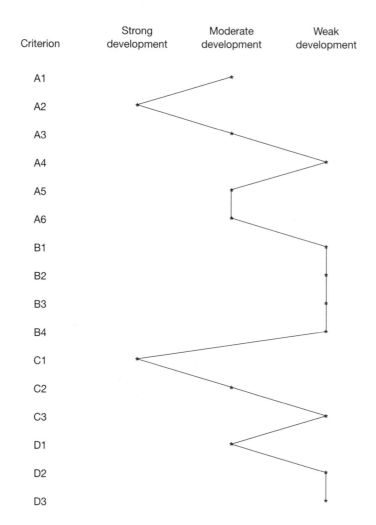

Figure 14.1 Marketing culture: development profiles

However, strong evidence in that study indicated a rapid evolution in all the schools involved, leading to increasing IMCD values over timescales of less than one year.

It is important to recognize that an analysis such as this simply describes the outcomes of complex processes involving many factors. On a national scale, the development of a marketing oriented culture will depend very strongly on the ideological perspectives and political processes that define the operational environment of schools. Foskett and Lumby (2002), for example, show how internationally there is a wide range of responses to the metatrend of decentralization and the emergence of self-managing schools. At its most extreme, marketization has been strong in schools in England and Wales, New Zealand, Victoria in Australia and in some parts of the USA, notably Chicago. More commonly, the emergence of some elements of decentralization has encouraged some degree of engagement with markets and responsiveness to external environments (for example in Indonesia and Argentina). Hence national contrasts in the emergence of a marketing culture in schools will be inevitable.

At the local and regional level, specific contextual factors will be important, and Foskett (1998) identifies the importance of:

- local demographic change
- the competitiveness of collaborative nature of the local school arena
- the socio-economic profile of the school's catchment area
- the budgetary environment of the school or local authority
- the political profile of the school catchment
- the school's geographical location.

At a micro level, a wide range of within-school factors will influence the cultural development, including:

- the school's history and development
- micro-political processes within the school
- the educational values and perspectives of staff and senior management
- the ideological perspectives of staff
- the existing organizational systems in the school
- the management skills of those in leadership positions
- the school's financial status and state
- pressures from the school's stakeholders.

Responding to the pattern of culture, which an analysis such as that presented here provides, requires careful consideration of the range of factors outlined above, and an identification of which of those are most capable of leverage in the direction that institutional aims require. Changing culture is certainly more difficult than changing structure or process, partly because the things to change are less clear and partly because it may be very deeply rooted in the attitudes, values and belief systems of those in the organization.

REFERENCES

Beare, H., Caldwell, B. and Millikan, R. (1989) *Creating an Excellent School: Some New Management Techniques*, London: Routledge.

Carlson, R. (1975) 'Environmental constraints and organisational consequences: the public school and its clients' in Baldridge, J. and Deal, T. (eds) *Managing Change in Educational Organisations*, Berkeley: McCutchan.

Cowell, D. (1984) *The Marketing of Services*, Oxford: Butterworth.

Deal, T. (1988) 'The symbolism of effective schools' in Westoby, A. (ed.) *Culture and Power in Educational Organisations*, Buckingham: Open University Press.

Foskett, N.H. (1995) 'Marketing, management and schools: a study of a developing marketing culture in schools', unpublished PhD thesis, University of Southampton.

Foskett, N.H. (1998) 'Schools and marketization: cultural challenges and responses', *Educational Management and Administration*, 26 (2), pp. 197–210.

Foskett, N.H and Lumby, J. (2002) *Educational Leadership and Management – The International Dimension*, London: Sage.

Handy, C. (1986) *Understanding Organizations*, 3rd edn, Harmondsworth: Penguin Books.

Hargreaves, D. (1999) 'Helping practitioners explore their school's culture' in Prosser, J. (ed.) *School Culture*, London: Falmer Press.

O'Neill, J. (1994) 'Organizational structure and culture' in Bush, T. and West-Burnham, J. (eds) *The Principles of Educational Management*, Harlow: Longman.

Prosser, J. (ed.) (1999) *School Culture*, London: Falmer Press.

2

– CHAPTER 15 –

A strategic approach to finance and budgeting

BRENT DAVIES

Finance and other resources are allocated to a school in order to run its operations; this function is achieved through a budgetary process, which has often been considered an administrative or management function. This chapter takes a strategic view of the budgetary process so as to examine the broad underlying principles that affect the strategic and operational processes in the organization. School finance and budgeting are not just about spending money: they are also about a large number of leadership and management processes and functions that help relate educational objectives and the resources that facilitate them. The place of budgeting can be seen in Figure 15.1.

The key concept here is that budgeting should be seen as a facilitating process. It facilitates the translation of the values and core purposes of the organization through the organizational analysis and planning stage to the implementation stage. It should not be seen as the driving part or the starting point.

In order to take a strategic management view of the finance and budgetary system in a school, the following four elements are key to understanding the broader strategic leadership and management dimensions that are necessary to manage resources effectively in schools:

- the nature and functions of budgets
- the budgetary process
- approaches to decision making in budgetary systems
- a leadership and management overview.

Figure 15.1 Budgeting as a facilitating part of an organizational cycle

The nature and functions of budgets

Budgeting is a means of relating expenditure to the achievement of objectives. However, in breaking the budgetary process down, it can be seen that it also enables the organization to plan, coordinate, control and evaluate its activities. How budgeting is managed in terms of the decision-making process and the participation of individuals will have an effect on the people involved and, therefore, on their commitment to outcomes. For example, budgeting can be seen to have not only planning and coordinating components but also communicating and motivating aspects. So it is important to consider not only what is done but also how it is done. This dual approach is demonstrated in Figure 15.2 which considers the budgetary 'what' and 'how'.

The budgetary process can be seen to have four key sets of components. The first is planning: budgets are financial expressions in a quantified form of an organization's activities. They will lay down that 'x' amount of money is to be spent on an activity in a specific time period. A budget can demonstrate that the organization plans to spend a certain amount on staffing or spend another amount on an extension to its buildings. It is therefore a quantified plan for action. The parallel action to this is the 'how' of communication. If planning is to achieve anything, then it has to be communicated and understood by all members of the organization. Written plans that lie on the headteacher's office shelf will have little impact. To affect practice they have to be communicated and understood by all staff.

The second component of budgeting is that of coordination: budgets bring together a series of activities so that the amounts to be spent are organized in such a way that they contribute to meeting the organization's objectives. Organizations will fail unless the diverse set of expenditure activities dealing with staffing, materials, equipment, etc. is brought into focus by operationalizing the plan so that it is managed to achieve its objectives. This management activity can and should be a major motivational tool. It is a means of involving staff in bringing together the school's activities so they have both the bigger picture and an understanding of how the parts fit together and their role in the activities.

Figure 15.2 The budgetary 'what' and 'how'

A third component of the budgetary process is that of control. By approving expenditure on one particular activity, and not on another, an organization regulates and governs the activities of its employees to the achievement of specific objectives. How the control is exercised through a monitoring process is crucial. It can end up a demotivational activity or it can be a means of setting frameworks that are seen as clear and fair. As such, how this process is handled can significantly contribute to the success or otherwise of the budgetary process.

The fourth component of budgeting, that of evaluation, is the process of checking whether the expenditure has been undertaken as planned, whether the outcomes have been achieved and whether the best alternatives were utilized. How this is fed back is vital if the information is to be used not only to frame the following year's process but also to gain commitment to that process.

Leadership and management clearly involve getting things done through people. This approach highlights the 'how' dimension of budgeting. How the people in the organization are involved in the process is a crucial factor in the success of that process. Thus, focusing on how the budget is operationalized, by effective communication and motivation strategies, together with the monitoring of the activity and the provision of feedback, contribute as much to the success as the functional activities of planning, coordination, control and evaluation.

The budgetary process

If budgets are the means of relating expenditure to needs, it is necessary to consider how that process operates. The budgetary elements in Figure 15.3 can themselves be seen as a cycle of activity comprising four stages: budgetary review, budgetary forecasting, budgetary implementation and budgetary evaluation.

Budgetary review

This first stage of the budgetary cycle involves an assessment of the current financial position of the institution and the underlying causal factors. This review has two elements to it. One is a check of current levels of income and expenditure in key categories such as:

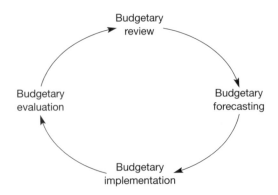

Figure 15.3 The budgetary cycle

- Income:
  - funds from funding formula linked to student numbers
  - funds from student charges
  - funds from specific bidding projects/categories
  - community-based financial support
  - income from investments
  - income from lettings.

- Expenditure:
  - Staffing
  - Premises-related expenses
  - curriculum-related expenses
  - organization-related expenses.

Once current levels of income and expenditure have been checked, the managers in the institution should move on to the second elements of the audit and ask some fundamental management questions:

- Is the school balancing its income and expenditure?
- Are there significant levels of over or under-spending in particular areas?
- Can financial resources be reallocated from one area to another to increase educational outputs or organizational efficiency?

Budgetary forecasting

Having assessed the current position, it is important that the impact of likely future financial trends is assessed to set any budgetary decisions in context. This is a significant activity that is new to many educational managers, since budgeting within the educational sector has traditionally taken place on an annual basis. It is now necessary to examine the impact of financial decisions and the general resource environment over a longer period to establish a multi-year time-horizon.

In a resource-constrained environment, educational organizations struggle to achieve their objectives while keeping their educational income and expenditure in balance. It is a mistake to view budgetary decisions within a one-year time-frame. There are several examples that illustrate this. One would be the adoption of learning schemes that use a workbook approach and thus incur considerable future material costs. Another would be the planned replacement of computers over time. In the staffing field, an example is provided by choosing between two new members of staff where an initial difference in salary (owing to the point on the salary spine) of £7000 can, over a five-year period, cost in the region of £35 000, depending on progress up the salary spine.

Another key management factor in the budgetary forecasting context is whether the institution has an increasing or decreasing resource base, and the relationship of that to the budget balance. If the student population is increasing, then, on for-mula-based funding, a positive financial framework will be created. This bonus can overcome any marginal over-spending in the current budget. This longer-term per-spective is necessary before the manager takes action to adjust the current budget, otherwise unnecessary cutbacks may be made. Conversely, if the institution is facing declining numbers, owing to either increased competition or demographic factors or both, then remedial action on the budget needs to be taken promptly or the deficit will get out of hand. A useful checklist of factors that should be included in a financial forecasting exercise might include:

- pupil/student roll;
- changes in the make-up of the overall roll – more older/younger students with their different formula weightings would affect the budget;
- changes in the formula-funding mechanism, either by the local education authority or the central government funding agency;
- projections of extra support funds, i.e. gifts, donation (parent–teacher associations etc.), income from lettings;
- projections of success in bidding for specific central government or private sector grants;
- costs of staffing changes, retirements, movement up the pay spine and their subsequent financial implementations;
- costs of new curricula or predictable replacement costs for learning schemes;
- costs of essential maintenance cycle;
- planned expansion/contraction costs re capital and revenue;
- new sources of income identified or additional areas of necessary expenditure.

When this context has been set, then the next stage, budgetary implementation, can be undertaken.

Budgetary implementation

When drawing up the annual budget, it is important to refer back to the previous two stages in order to set current decisions in the context of both the audit and future projections. A useful staged implementation process could be:

- set out headings and sub-headings of the budget;
- allocate fixed costs to headings;
- allocate recurrent costs;
- bring forward items from the audit and forecast stages to establish a priority list for available expenditure;
- decide between alternative projects and courses of action;
- put budget forward for approval by the institution's governors;
- set check points during the year for possible virement opportunities.

Even at this stage, as with all financial statements, this is a snapshot at a particular moment in time and adjustments will have to take place as events unfold. Finally, the cycle moves on to the evaluation stage.

Budgetary evaluation

It is important that institutions do not ignore this vital stage of the budgetary process, which can be split into two parts: *outcomes* and *process*. The evaluation of outcomes must involve a consideration of the extent to which the resource allocation decisions have enabled the institution to meet its objectives in an effective but also efficient way. There are a number of questions to be asked. Did we achieve what we wanted? Was the money well spent? Would alternatives have given us a better use of resources? Are we in surplus or deficit?

As well as the evaluation of the output of the budgetary processes, it is necessary to evaluate the process itself and the role of the people involved. For example:

- Who is involved in the budgetary process and did they make a positive contribution?
- Were the relevant data and information collected?
- Did the time-frame allow full and comprehensive analysis of issues?
- Was the process understood and were the outcomes adequately communicated?

A useful framework for performance outcomes is the 'best-value' approach as advocated by the Office for Standards in Education (Ofsted, 2000). In relationship to budgets it suggests that as part of the evaluation of the budgetary process schools should:

- compare their expenditure with similar schools;
- challenge their use of resources by examining what they provide and the different ways they can make that provision;
- use fair competition to ensure resources are secured at the lowest cost;
- consult stakeholders on major changes to the use of resources.

Approaches to decision-making in budgetary systems

The organizational culture, 'the way we do things around here', is an important factor in influencing the effectiveness of the budgetary process. It important that school leaders understand not only the mechanical or numerical dimensions of the process but the culture within the school that influences how resource decisions are to be made if they are to successfully lead and manage the process.

Organizational culture defines the framework in which resource decisions are made. The culture is reflected in the way that resource decision-making frameworks operate. Two broad decision-making frameworks or approaches, into which differing budgetary processes can be located, are examined here. These are the rational and the political approaches.

The rational approach

Rational approaches are based on the hypothesis that organizations directly relate resource expenditure to the achievement of organizational objectives. They assume that organizations have clear objectives and that resource allocation is organized in a systematic way to facilitate the achievement of those objectives. This approach means that, after assessing the alternative expenditure options, the finance spent and the resources acquired should maximize those outputs that contribute to fulfilling organizational objectives. It is possible to isolate three key elements that underpin a rational budgetary approach: output budgeting, zero-based resource decisions and multi-year time-horizon.

Output budgeting

In a rational framework, budgets should focus on outputs rather than on inputs. Expenditure patterns should relate to outputs rather than being characterized by a list of resource inputs. In that way they relate directly to fulfilling the objectives of the organization. The use of an output budgeting approach, it is claimed, facilitates more effective management processes. First, by definition, it necessitates the formulation of clear outputs and objectives. Second, organizations must engage in systematic planning because resources must be clearly related in advance to objectives. Third, priorities are established because assessing – and opting between – alternatives is necessary. Finally, performance indicators can be defined in terms of how far objectives have been met, utilizing the current mix of resources.

There has been a significant shift in planning and budgeting on a global basis over the last decade. The trend has been to put considerable emphasis on the outcomes to be achieved from differing resource inputs. Both in the UK and internationally, governments have focused more and more on target setting and learning outcomes for students. This focus has in turn increased the emphasis on relating outcomes to resources spent. One example of this can be seen in school plans, where instead of a list of input areas like curriculum, staffing, premises and so forth, it is now common to see 'target area 1', ' target area 2', etc. Another example is the number of 'specific grants' that central government has tied to detailed output and performance criteria.

Zero-based resource decisions

A fundamental part of a rational approach to budgeting is the adoption of a zero-based perspective to resource allocation, which involves taking a fresh look at expenditure by starting with a 'clean slate' rather than by basing decisions on previous practice. This involves not only taking a fresh look at additional expenditure but also examining existing core expenditure patterns or allocations. There is a need to justify all expenditure: by assuming no given expenditure for a particular area, a justification must be given for each item.

Giving schools control over their own budgets in decentralized systems aims to develop this perspective. However, governments often cannot resist the temptation to introduce special bidding for additional funding, thus undermining the principal of allowing schools to determine the most appropriate expenditure patterns to meet their particular objectives.

Multi-year time-horizon

This third element in a rational approach concerns the abandonment of simplistic one-year financial planning in favour of multi-year financial planning. Most head-teachers/principals have previously been faced with the dilemma of having to spend money by the end of the financial year instead of doing what, in many cases, would yield better outcomes – spreading the expenditure over a longer time period.

Traditional budgets have been on a one-year time scale. The weakness of this approach is that it fails to view education as an ongoing process with long-term resource needs that cannot be easily packaged into 12-month spending bouts.

Pupils are in schools for five years or more and students are in higher education for three or four years. What is needed is longer-term financial planning that makes some attempt to match the nature of education with resource expenditure that must, of necessity, be of the same time duration. This responsibility is particularly significant with premises-related costs that require longer-term financial planning. Thus, consideration of a multi-year-time-horizon budget is necessary if longer-term financial planning and budgeting is to take place.

The political approach

However logical the key elements in the rational framework discussed above appear, it is nevertheless true that political budgetary approaches show a remarkable capacity to persist. There are three key factors that influence the persistence of traditional budgeting processes: incrementalism, micro-political forces and the organizational process approach.

Incrementalism

The incremental process bases its decisions on what to spend this year on the previous year's budget and level of expenditure. Attention is given to minor adjustments in the spending pattern or the justification of additional spending. There is no significant attempt to reassess existing spending patterns; the existing budget is not challenged – there is general acceptance that it is valid. This approach provides a predictable and stable organizational climate. It also needs very little in terms of information and time requirements compared with zero-based approaches. Discussions focus around the 5 per cent increase or decrease in the budget, not about its fundamental composition. Marginal shifts in the budget occur, so that a fluctuating or disjointed pattern of change occurs around an unchanging central core. This has become known as 'disjointed incrementalism' or 'the science of muddling through'.

Micro-political forces

Resource decisions may not depend so much on what is clearly correct for the organization as on a number of other 'people-dependent' factors. For example, it is important to consider who is making the decisions because his/her value system may be a critical factor. Similarly, individuals may coalesce into groups that have power that rivals the power ascribed to the formal organizational structure. Everyone is familiar with the saying 'It's not what you know but who you know that is important'. Thus, who is making the decision, influenced by what group in what organizational setting, may be a more critical factor in determining the decision taken rather than the apparently rational alternative considerations. These sorts of influences and factors underlie the micro-political dimension of budgeting. A micro-political analysis therefore, is based on the view that budgetary decisions are not necessarily made on rational economic grounds but that the deciding factors may be other influences such as the power base of individuals or groups and their value systems.

The way in which the people involved manage the budgetary process may be as important as what is being managed, as far as outcomes are concerned. If resource patterns are to be understood, asking questions about the political forces at work may be as important as asking rational questions. It is useful to consider the following questions:

- Which individuals or groups are competing for resources?
- Are there different values and interests among the different parties who compete for resources?
- Which individuals or groups have more power?
- What political strategies or 'games' are being used?
- Who gains or loses funds?

The organizational process approach

The organizational process approach is based on the idea that, in addition to corporate objectives, organizations also pursue a number of other objectives. Organizations try to balance these factors with the achievement of set objectives in order to ensure harmony. For example, in the business sector, it is often assumed that profit maximization is the main goal. However, managers may prefer to safeguard their position by reducing competition through takeovers instead of maximizing profits by competition. They may also aim to produce satisfactory levels of profit to keep shareholders happy and may grant over-generous wage increases to avoid labour conflicts. The aim is to provide a series of acceptable solutions that meet the needs of the various constituencies that make up the organization.

In educational budgetary terms it may be preferable to produce a budget that keeps the main interest groups and constituencies of the organization happy rather than presenting radical solutions that dissatisfy key stakeholders. Allocating time and money for a school's Christmas production may have educational value, but it is also done because 'the parents expect it' and it is important to please this key group of stakeholders. Thus the organizational process approach would suggest that an acceptable solution that satisfies the different goals and objectives in an organization may be chosen rather than the most efficient and rational solution.

A leadership and management overview

In conclusion, it is important to recognize that while getting the details of the budget right is vital, it is also crucial to consider the broader leadership and management issues. As part of a senior team discussion or strategic conversation it is important to fit the budgetary process within a strategic leadership framework. What follows are some pointers for that conversation.

First and foremost, the budgetary process should link into the overall management planning cycle and not be seen as a bolt-on activity that is the sole responsibility of the financial manager or bursar. It is only the integration of the budgetary process into the general leadership and management cycle that will enable priorities to be taken into account in an educational context and, subsequently, facilitate the achievement of organizational objectives.

Second, budgetary activity should not be seen solely as an annual activity but should facilitate long-term planning by the development of a multi-year time-horizon. Thus short-term policies should always be considered with their longer-term implications, if effective and efficient decision-making is to take place.

Third, the 'how' of budgetary decision-making needs careful consideration and management in terms of the people involved. It is necessary, at the initial stage of the budgetary process, to determine the level of participation and consultation to be employed.

This links into a fourth point, a consideration of whether the institution employs centralized or decentralized decision-making structures. Just as decentralization in decision making has profound consequences when applied to allocations to organizations, it also has these consequences when applied to allocations within organizations. Institutions that operate in a decentralized environment must therefore examine their internal management philosophies to consider whether the decentralization concept should also apply to resource allocations within the school or college.

The fifth and final point is that the budgetary process itself should have positive characteristics. It should be a flexible process that encourages innovation and not have an enterprise-choking system of internal controls. The process should be easily understood and should not incur substantial costs in operation.

All these five factors will contribute to the process being widely accepted within the organization and thus reinforce its organizational effectiveness.

NOTE

This section is based on an earlier version by Brent Davies in Bush, T. and West-Burnham, J. (1994) *Principles of Education Management*, London: Longman.

REFERENCE

OFSTED (2000) *Getting the Best from Your Budget – A guide to the Effective Management of School Resources*, London: Office for Standards in Education.

PART THREE

The Policy Context for School Leadership and Management

MIKE BOTTERY

Introduction

As the title of Part Three indicates, the chapters within it contextualize school leadership and management within larger policy questions, while making this context constantly relevant to the work of leaders and managers. They do so in part by directly addressing the issues of leadership and management within a policy context, but also by addressing wider issues that impinge upon the work of leaders and managers and schools and that therefore affect how they conceptualize and practise their job. Mike Bottery's opening chapter takes an overview of global issues, looking deliberately beyond the educational policy arena, in an attempt to examine how such events frame current debates about the nature and function of educational systems. He suggests that 'globalization' is a complex term, not only because there are different kinds of global pressures, but also because while some are largely descriptive, others are normative – end states that those of a particular political disposition would like to see occur. He suggests that economic globalization is probably the most potent form at the present time, but argues that there is nothing inevitable about any of the forms described. Ben Levin's chapter integrates this debate into national policy contexts – primarily those of English-speaking industrialized countries – and similarly argues that while there are globalization pressures, and there are commonalities in many kinds of educational policies, these are nevertheless mediated at the national level by factors such as those of history, politics and national culture. He provides valuable and specific examples of such commonalities and their differential mediation.

Nick Foskett writes on the effects of one of the global orthodoxies of the present time – that of market policies – and suggests that their development has led to a fundamental shift in the relationship between government, educational professionals and the constituencies that schools serve. He argues that they have challenged schools and school leaders to be both responsive and innovative, but that they have also introduced significant new tasks for leaders and managers, as well as changing educational culture and ethos. Critically, suggests Foskett, we should beware of markets being seen and utilized as simplistic solutions to complex problems. Christopher Day extends this warning of over-simplification: his research on the reality of effective leaders is an uplifting one, which suggests that many current models of leadership are inadequate in their conceptualization of the role. Leadership, he argues, is a role of both complexity and value-centredness; furthermore, if leaders and managers are to be effective, they need to acquire a more complex blend of knowledge, qualities and skills than is at present provided by the hybrid business-education models that often dominate training and that seem so popular to many policy makers.

Peter Gilroy picks up this training theme in his own case-study examination of education policy and the initial education of teachers. He suggests that a combination of two factors in England – a centralist policy paradigm and the under-recruitment of teachers to the profession – has led to a situation where teacher educators are effectively omitted from policy-making mechanisms, and that they should accept that there is little prospect of consultation in the near future. His arguments, although context-specific, provide a wider cautionary policy story, because there are sufficient similarities of teacher under-supply and government centralization elsewhere.

The final chapter in this section, by Jenny Ozga, on researching education policy, draws together many of the threads of the previous contributions. It suggests that policy research needs to be aware of global movements and the pressures these place upon nation states, that policy creation is therefore constrained and directed at these levels, but also that because of this, government policies frame the commission, funding, agenda-setting and problem-defining aspects of research at 'lower' levels. Ozga argues that it is therefore critical that policy research be informed by an awareness of the developments that are setting such governmental agendas. A critical, independent, and evidence-based approach to policy research by educationalists generally is therefore essential.

CHAPTER 16

Globalization and the educational policy context

MIKE BOTTERY

The other chapters in Part Three devote their energies to issues within education. This chapter deliberately looks beyond the educational policy arena, to examine whether and how events occurring at a global level frame debates about the nature and function of educational systems. It is, however, recognized that the subject of this chapter – the effects of 'globalization' – is highly contentious. Part of this is due to the fact that there is no one agreed meaning to globalization. Part is due to a similar lack of agreement on the extent of the effect of such globalizations on national policies. Finally, there is also considerable debate as to whether such globalization is descriptive or prescriptive. With descriptive globalization, such movements are taken to be natural outcomes of other changes like industrialization or technological sophistication, and are therefore forces that, whatever one thinks about them, are inevitabilities to which one needs to accommodate. In the case of prescriptive globalization, however, some global changes, such as the move to global free markets, are seen, not as inevitabilities but as end states that those of a particular political disposition would like to see occur, and are suggested as being inevitable because they aid a particular political movement by convincing others that there is nothing that can be done to resist such change.

This chapter then will examine some of the meanings of globalization, and single out economic globalisation as a key force on national educational policies at the present time. It will assess to what extent such influences are desirable and suggest that such forces are not inevitable, for there remain a variety of strategies that nation states can use to mediate such influences.

Meanings of globalization

When in the twentieth century, the Earth was seen from space for the first time, the image led to the realization that here was 'a small and fragile ball dominated, not by human activity and edifice, but a pattern of clouds, oceans, greenery and soils' (World Commission on Environment and Development, 1987, p. 2). Undoubtedly this image acted as a catalyst to a wider understanding of globalization effects and movements. Yet, while 'globalization' is a much-used word, it has yet to have one precise meaning. At its most embracing, it can simply mean those forces or issues that transcend particular geographical areas or nation states, and influence the behaviours of a wide variety of peoples, cultures and beliefs. Waters (1995, p. 3) suggested that a more precise meaning might be that globalization is 'a social process in which the constraints of geography on social and cultural arrangements recede and in which people become increasingly aware that they are receding'. This definition neatly captures the fact that not only is this a physical process, but a psychological one as well – that as people become aware of the diminishing of physical constraints, they alter the manner in which they behave. Waters also argues that there are at least three different forms of globalization – economic, political and cultural – and that they are able to act as global forces largely because they are mediated by symbols; the more symbolic they are, the more easily they are diffused around the world.

Political globalization is probably the least 'global' precisely because much of its force rests with particular localities and it gains its strength from particular cultural beliefs and practices that do not transfer well. Yet even if incomplete, it would be foolish to ignore the drive towards political organization above that of the nation state (such as through the European Union or the North American Free Trade Agreement), since this is a movement that leaches from the nation state part of its authority and its legitimacy, and may be part of the reason for the decline in interest in nation state politics over the last few years. It would similarly be foolish to ignore the opposite trend – the move towards finding meaning at the local level. Naisbett and Aburdene (1988, p. 133) argue that as globalization effects increase, so people will 'treasure the traditions that spring from within' and seek for ontological and political identity at levels below that of the nation state. As Daniel Bell once said, it may be that the nation state is becoming too small for the big things of life, but too big for the small things.

So while there is clearly a trend towards political globalization, there are issues of extent and definition. There are similar problems with cultural globalization. Is cultural globalization, for instance, to be seen in the fact that I can buy a MacDonald's virtually anywhere in the world, or in the fact that in my own small-ish city (population one-third of a million) all of the major world religions are represented, most cuisines from around the world are available, and I have absolutely no problem in listening to any kind of music I wish? Is cultural globalization, then, the build-up of one particular movement or force around the globe, or the access by an individual at any place on the globe to all of its variety?

Furthermore, is globalization necessarily mediated by symbols? Environmental issues – such as global warming – are increasingly appreciated as global in their implications – and such issues do not rely upon the symbolic. Similarly, issues of demography are increasingly global in nature. Thus, while it used to be the case that the rich West was alone in experiencing a significant slowdown in its birthrate, and an increase in its elderly populations (with all the financial and social consequences these entail: see Bottery, 2000), Japan and a number of other Asian tigers are also now affected, and this is a long-term global trend in many other countries as well. So to the list of globalizations we may wish to add issues of demography as touching individuals irrespective of their national identity.

Yet if these examples of real or potential globalization – political, cultural, environmental and demographic – suggest that this issue is complex and that there is a lack of clarity and definition in certain areas, it is also clear that they all have enormous impact, and that it is precisely because their impact is beyond the reach or influence of any one particular nation state that no one state can handle them alone. This suggests that global thinking and a global response are required to deal with them, and that traditional handmaidens of the nation state – their education systems – designed primarily to bolster the power and legitimacy of the nation state (Green, 1997) – are likely to be ill-equipped to deal with these issues. They are likely to provide a myopic, parochial and partisan view of them because of their origins and present orientations, and are then likely to fail in providing students – the citizens of the future – with an appreciation of how to understand and come to terms with these supra-national issues. A first step, then, in such understanding is for those within an education system to step back from their national preoccupations and try to understand how such global forces contextualize and frame their work.

Economic globalization

While political, cultural, environmental, and demographic globalizations have all been mentioned, economic globalization has so far not been addressed. This is not because it is less important than the others, but because it is perhaps the most prevalent and influential at the present time, and therefore needs to be considered in rather greater detail. It is best characterized as the confluence of three different factors. First is the increasingly unrestrained movement of capital around the world, and, with the facilitation of such movement by information technology, the redirection of such money in and out of countries literally overnight. This can produce grave instabilities in a nation's currency, as well as prevent the development of national policies that do not fit into a free-market scenario. These, for instance, may be of a protectionist nature, designed to shield fledgling industries in developing countries, or may be ones aimed at the development of welfare schemes that attempt more than the merest safety net approach in the care of a nation's citizens. A second factor is the existence of supra-national bodies such as the World Trade Organization, the World Bank, and the International Monetary Fund, whose overriding preoccupations have been to help facilitate capital flows in a global free-market scenario, yet make virtually no attempt to regulate the flow of capital and prevent damage to national economies by speculative fiscal flows. They have also been keen to facilitate rapid transitions from state-dominated economies (such as in Russia) to more global ones, ignoring as they do the destruction of essential – if uneconomic – businesses, and the protection of the population from unemployment and widespread poverty.

A final factor is the increased influence of transnational companies (TNCs). Their power is impressive: Morgan (1997, p. 327), for instance, shows that the total value of Mitsubishi is larger than the gross national product of Indonesia, Denmark, Saudi Arabia or Turkey. Now, if one adds to this financial clout their ability, under present global market conditions, to move investment and plant from location to location, they then are able to play off nation states against each other. Nation states then have to compete against one another in terms of sweeteners, tax-breaks and financial inducements in order to persuade such TNCs to locate their factories on their soil. Some writers (e.g. Brecher, 1993) have described this as a 'race to the bottom', suggesting that the winner is the nation that is most willing to prostitute its natural assets, its citizens, and its values to the requirements of such companies.

Yet whilst some countries have taken this road, this is not necessarily the case. Palan, Abbott and Deans (1999) list a number of ways in which nation states mediate such forces, which may be summarized as:

- the use of abundant cheap labour to attract investors;
- joining a trading block to access a larger market and have more political power;
- the use of state power and money to engineer economic growth;
- attempts at selective integration into global markets while shielding particular social structures and values;
- attempts by large players at regional domination in order to set the rules in cooperative agreements;
- the development of parasitical tax havens to attract overseas finance.

It is by no means clear which strategy is likely to be the most successful. Indeed, it may well be that no particular strategy will be successful over the medium to long term, but must be adjusted to suit changing conditions. Thus Ashton and Sung (1997) describe the incrementalist strategy that Singapore adopted after gaining independence, which involved matching workers' skills (and the education system) to the requirements of particular TNCs, before ratcheting up such skill levels to meet the needs of different, more up-market companies. By such progressive reformation of the workforce and the education system, Singapore now has a workforce and a standard of living with enviable reputations. Yet even here a successful strategy is being radically re-examined, since the Singaporean government – and that of Japan as well – recognizes that in the information economy of the future the creative, independent-thinking worker will be at a premium, and the conformism that the education system has induced may now be counter-productive. The links between economic globalization and education systems are clear – global economic movements demand of countries that they prioritize the design of a competitive economy above all other issues; to this end, the education system is drawn into and is seen as a primary contributor to this competitiveness.

However, the effects of economic globalization do not stop at pressure to orient education systems to the production of globally competitive workforces. It has already been suggested that political globalization is having the effect of eroding the political legitimacy of the nation state by moving power both beyond and below its orbit. When combined with economic globalization, this has even greater effect. Ohmae (1995) argues that the global market is an inevitability and that the nation state has already forfeited its right to sovereignty, to be replaced by 'region states' – geographical areas overlapping existing nation states but sharing the same economic goals and imperatives. Davidson and Rees-Mogg's vision (1999) is again a largely economic one, but this time premised upon the belief that in an age of increased global movement, not only can money move easily around the world, but so can many of its inhabitants. In such a situation, citizenship becomes a matter of consumerism and choice over which nation state will provide the best return on the investment of taxes. Once again, the pressure on nation states comes from the rich and powerful, for it is they who can move the most easily, and they who will have the greatest financial effect by relocating. The nation state then finds itself in competition with others for the citizen-consumer's business. The nation state, rather than being a body concerned with a 'public good' – a concern for all – is increasingly concerned with selling to the highest bidder, and in the process its activity, its very language, is captured by the market.

Finally, Herz (2001) suggests that we live in a world where the politics of the nation state is ceasing to provoke interest, because populations are beginning to realize where the real power and influence lie – and it is with business. They then begin to vote with their feet, feeling that if they are going to change anything, then the people to access are not their politicians but the leaders of business. Herz (p. 116) quotes the Church of England prayer book, which advises its readers that 'Where we shop, how we shop, and what we buy is a living statement of what we believe … shopping which involves the shopper in making ethical and religious judgements may be nearer to the worship God requires than any number of pious prayers in church'. The message could not be clearer – business is the group to address, for it has the real power.

Global inevitability?

A fully fledged globalization would, Green (1999, p. 55) argues, result in three inter-related phenomena: first, the destruction of the nation state, second, the movement of power both upward to transnational bodies and downward to sub-regional assemblies, and third, the end of education systems with a distinctly national flavour. Yet it would be wrong to paint a picture of either present complete globalization or even of global inevitability. There are a number of reasons for thinking this. A first is, as Marginson (1999) argues, that the nation state still has a tremendous number of policy portfolios that it manages: it still retains considerable power to restructure economically, to differ its rates of taxation, to manage indus-trial relations, its transport system, its police, healthcare, and education and training systems. Granted that these may be constrained by global forces, they nev-ertheless remain nation-state decisions. A second reason is that if Clarke and Newman (1996) are right, the 'hollowing out' of the activities of the nation state that Rhodes (1994) described is not a hollowing out of its fundamental power base, but rather more of a 'dispersal' of assets that encumber its functioning, and the nation state continues to hold to itself the core functions – of which education is increasingly seen as critical. Third, it is important to reiterate that 'globalization' is both a descriptive and a prescriptive term, being used to describe not only what is the case, but also being used by those who cloak their prescriptivity in a false descriptivity. Last, and as we shall now see, nation states do mediate global changes rather than simply accepting and acquiescing to pressures, and there does remain considerable room for preferred change. It is to such mediations that we now turn.

National responses

As described above, Palan, Abbott and Deans (1999) suggest that there are at least six different strategies that nations currently use to mediate global pressures. Such strategies are partly determined by previous history, partly by culture, partly by political ideology. Thus the earlier example of Singapore (Ashton and Sung, 1997) shows how an impoverished island state, using a combination of such strategies, underpinned by continuous state intervention, was able to lever up its economy and education system to reach the economic position it has today. The history of western state mediation is very different from this. Nearly all, in a variety of ways, engaged with a social democratic framework after the Second World War, and some, particularly countries of continental Europe, have attempted to maintain such ethos and values up to the present day. Others, like the USA and the UK, have gone on to experiment with 'New Right' liberalism, moving from there in both cases to 'New Modernizer' approaches, though the USA, with the advent of George W. Bush, may be returning to New Right liberal policies again.

A first point then is that in the West there have been some similarities, but there has been no one coordinated response, only different approaches and different mediations. However, tracing these different responses is helpful for locating where commonalities do exist and why differences do occur. The first of these approaches, the social democratic approach, laid the foundations from which subsequent debates would spring, and was characterized by a belief in both a moral and economic basis for welfare states, the need for strong legislative frameworks, for public suppliers of services, and by a commitment to advancing equality of opportunity and enhanced social mobility through government legislation and structures. It was also, crucially, a system that did not fully engage with the global pressures faced today, for nation states were much more able to 'fire-wall' their domestic economies and policies against external intrusion (Brown and Lauder, 2001). It was also the golden age of professional autonomy and public regard, when governments legislated an educational framework and teachers filled in the details and supplied their own 'product'.

Yet as western states in the 1970s suffered escalating oil prices and stagflation, and national economies became increasingly susceptible to transnational and global forces, Keynesian economic solutions seemed inadequate in handling these problems. Welfare state agendas came under increasing attack, as did their principal servants – and beneficiaries – the professionals. Market forces in an increasing number of countries replaced the interventionist state as the major determinant of life chances. In education and other welfare state institutions, professionals were made to compete with other 'suppliers' of the educational 'product'; market standards were used to determine their success or failure, even if in the UK there was a blend of radical New Right individualism with strong centralizing tendencies.

However, by the end of the 1980s there were increasing suspicions in countries that had adopted New Right policies that many of these policies, rather than solving problems, were not only making them worse but causing new ones as well. As global trends led to more insecurity and less stability in social life, nation-state libertarian policies seemed to exacerbate them, as well as eroding wider social and ethical norms. This threat of societal breakdown – the problem that New Right governments were elected to solve – led to a necessary but ironic expansion of the public sector. Thus as the 1990s proceeded, there was a rethinking of some aspects of the political agenda. Clinton in the USA and then Blair in the UK largely accepted the inevitability of global markets, and sought to accommodate to them by devising policies that went with their free-market drift. New Right policies of deregulation and privatization, free trade, flexible labour markets, smaller safety nets and fiscal austerity were embraced, as Clinton attempted to position himself between Reagan and the Old Democrats, and Blair followed in attempting to position himself between Thatcher and Old Labour.

For Clinton, and other New Modernizers, government and the public sector generally had a key role to play: 'The market is a marvellous thing, but especially in a global environment, it won't give us safe streets, equal educational opportunities, a healthy start for poor babies, or a healthy and secure old age' (Clinton, 1996, p. 25). Further, in an age of globalized economic competition, when western states would need a high-skill, high-wage economy, leaving strategies for this to the vagaries of the market was considered dangerous, even irresponsible. Governments needed a more directive role than under a market system. Thus, if one part of this agenda meant accepting the reality of the market, another was the greater use of government direction. Such government involvement had two complementary strands. One of these involved devising policies that would ameliorate the position of the losers. This is one of the principal reasons that the phrase the 'inclusive society' came into fashion. It is also the reason why the 'Third Way' came to mean, as Reich (1999, p.14) suggested, the need for an agenda that sought 'to liberate market forces while easing the transition of those who'd otherwise fall behind'.

This easing of transition would, however, not be accomplished by old-fashioned state handouts, but as Clinton (1996, p. 22, 38) argued: 'The appropriate response is to *increase* investment in people power: by individuals themselves, by private industry in its employees and production technologies, and by government in the basic building blocks of economic opportunity – education, training, and technology'. In the UK, Giddens (1998, p. 117), close academic adviser to Tony Blair, described this as the development of a 'Social Investment State' to replace the old Welfare State; one that subscribed to 'investment in human capital wherever possible, rather than the direct provision of economic maintenance'.

Thus, in both the US and the UK, the commitment to social inclusion meant that government money and strategy were predicated on reducing unemployment and poverty through worker education and training, though without moving much further in terms of worker protection and social equity. In the light of the adoption of education by Clinton as a pivotal strategy in re-equipping an American workforce, Blair's announcement at the 1997 election that his major priority of 'Education, Education, Education' was also clearly a strategy to invest in education in order to produce the high-tech skills that would give the UK economy and its workers a competitive advantage. Reich's observation (1991, p. 1) that 'each nation's primary assets will be its citizens' skills and insights' was a view that was directly borrowed by David Blunkett in his introduction to *Excellence in Schools* (DfEE, 1997) when he said: 'We are talking about investing in human capital in the age of knowledge. To compete in the global economy, to live in a civilised society and to develop the talents of every one of us, we will have to unlock the potential of every young person'.

Finally, such a Third Way agenda needed more than a belief in the virtues of the market, and the development of a high-tech workforce: it also needed a workforce with the right kinds of attitudes and values for this dynamic, flexible, and unpredictable environment. American academics like Etzioni (1993) and Putnam (2000), and, in the UK, Leadbeater (1999) pointed to a decline in community and trust, which was linked to the argument that the most economically competitive societies were those that had social structures generating a high degree of trust beyond the level of the family (Fukuyama, 1996). It is then perhaps unsurprising that both the US and the UK governments sponsored an increased direction of educational agendas in the attempt to develop not only a more economically competitive workforce, but a more communal and cooperative social climate as well.

Some implications of Third Way policies

One important implication of such mediative policies is that, irrespective of the attempted amelioration of the losers, the combination of globalization, privatization and deregulation, might still lead to what Luttwak (1999) describes as 'turbocapitalism' – a possibility even more likely in the USA with the election of George W. Bush. Luttwak's analysis (*see* Table 16.1) suggests that under such a regime there is greater economic growth, less bureaucracy, more entrepreneurship, increased technological progress and less structural unemployment. Yet its downside is not insignificant, for under turbocapitalism societies essentially exist to serve the needs of their economies. Turbocapitalism, Luttwak claims, also leads to a widening of income differentials, a lower average wage, increased worker insecurity and decreased labour protection. These in turn lead to the creation of a permanent underclass, as the insecure worker in a restricted labour market is forced into taking on the jobs that those at the bottom end of the labour spectrum used to occupy, thus forcing the latter out of the market. The non-turbocapitalist society, of which many countries in continental Europe are seen as being representative, has the corresponding opposite upside and downside. Luttwak suggests that this is no 'good guy/bad guy' scenario, but a painful choice between alternatives.

A second implication of such mediative policies has led to the downplaying of public sector values. Both the Clinton and the Blair governments came to share

Table 16.1 *The turbocapitalist agenda*

Turbocapitalism	Non-turbocapitalism
Pros	
Rapid economic growth	Economies exist to serve their societies
Less bureaucracy	Wide range of societal values
Enhanced entrepreneurship	Reduced income differentials*
Increased technological progress	Increased worker security and protection*
Less structural employment	Increased average wages*
Greater rewards for innovation	Greater social cohesion
Cons	
Societies exist to serve their economies	Increased bureaucracy
Economics captures other discourses	Less entrepreneurship
Widening income differentials*	Depressed economic growth
Lower average wages*	More structural employment
Reduced worker security and protection*	Less flexibility
Increased social tensions and law-breaking	Fewer rewards for innovation

Source: based on Luttwak, 1999.

Note: it is clearly possible to dispute the location of items marked *. Thus a turbocapitalist economist would argue that the 'cons' of widening income differentials, lower average wages and reduced worker security and protection should actually be located in the 'pros', since it is precisely the creation of these items that furthers the development of a more flexible, adaptive and entrepreneurial economy. In the end, this comes down to an ideological position: how important one sees the creation of a vibrant economy in comparison with other societal aims.

the belief that it does not matter who supplies a service as long as it meets stringent criteria. Institutions within the public sector then find themselves competing in an increasingly aggressive market, which looks increasingly less like an internal market and more like the real thing. The use of Private Finance Initiatives (PFIs), where government uses private money to build and then lease institutions to the public sector, has also helped blur this public/private distinction; a distinction further obscured through the decade-long use of New Public Management techniques (Hood, 1991), a business-inspired creation from the USA, which aimed to create a business managerial revolution within the public sector, rather than simply moving entire projects out into the private.

A third implication follows from the belief that global economic and demographic pressures not only require a more highly directive state to ensure that monies are spent 'appropriately'; it also means that there can be no return to the golden days of professional autonomy. Money will have to be spent carefully, agendas clearly specified, and the assessment and surveillance of providers intensified. Educational agendas, then, need to be directed from the centre in terms of curriculum specification, assessment of results, and in the monitoring, surveillance and development of professionals.

Conclusion

This chapter has argued that there are considerable global influences present today that radically affect the ability of nation states to implement policy. It has acknowledged that there is a variety of intervening variables between the global and national level, and in the transference and borrowing of policy from country to country, which means that it would be far too simplistic to talk of such global pressures without taking particular mediative contexts into consideration. Nevertheless, the results for educators of such global influences are increasingly apparent – and particularly for those in the western world. Increasingly, the marketization of services, the state's use of the private sector and the popularity of business values dominate the thinking and policies of western governments; these values then intrude and 'capture the discourse' of both education and public policies in general. The result is likely to be a paradoxical combination. On the one hand, educators will be asked to function more and more as entrepreneurs, as players in a marketplace, and to think and use terms that some would argue are more suitable to business than to education. On the other hand, where the nation state can use assets in its struggle to mediate global forces and to maintain its own political legitimacy, it will do so. Education then becomes a prime object for governmental interest, control and direction, for it is seen as needing to perform the function of creating the globally competitive workforce of the future, as well as instilling in such individuals a continued loyalty to a nation state increasingly threatened and divested of its power from above and below. Thus the educator will not only feel fragmented by the demands of the market, but will also feel increasingly controlled by the demands of the state. The degrees of control and fragmentation will vary from nation state to nation state, but global demands are unlikely to diminish, and educators are likely to face this paradoxical combination in some form or another for some time to come.

REFERENCES

Ashton, D. and Sung, J. (1997) 'Education, skill formation and economic development: the Singaporean approach' in Halsey, A.H., Lauder, H., Brown P. and Wells, A. (eds) *Education, Economy, Society*, Oxford: Oxford University Press, pp. 207–18.

Blunkett, D. (1997) 'Preface' in *The Learning Age*, London: Department for Education and Employment.

Bottery, M. (2000) *Education, Policy and Ethics*, London: Continuum.

Brecher, J. (1993) 'Global village or global pillage?' *The Nation*, December, pp. 658–88.

Brown, P. and Lauder, H. (2001) *Capitalism and Social Progress*, Basingstoke: Palgrave.

Clarke, J. and Newman, J. (1996) *The Managerial State*, London: Sage.

Davidson, J. and Rees-Mogg, W. (1999) *The Sovereign Individual*, New York: Touchstone.

DfEE (1997) *Excellence in Schools*, Cm 3681, London: The Stationery Office.

Etzioni, A. (1993) *The Spirit of Community*, London: Fontana.

Fukuyama, F. (1996) *Trust: the Social Virtues and the Creation of Prosperity*, London: Penguin.

Giddens, A. (1998) *The Third Way*, Cambridge: Polity Press.

Green, A. (1997) *Education, Globalisation and the Nation State*, London: Macmillan.

Green, A. (1999) 'Education and globalization in Europe and East Asia: convergent and divergent trends', *Journal of Education Policy*, 14 (1), pp. 55–72.

Herz, N. (2001) *The Silent Takeover: Global Capitalism and the Death of Democracy*, London: William Heinemann.

Hood, C. (1991) 'A public management for all seasons?' *Public Administration*, 69 (Spring), pp. 3–19.

Leadbeater, C. (1999) *Living on Thin Air*, London: Viking.

Luttwak, E. (1999) *Turbocapitalism*, London: Orion Business Books.

Marginson, S. (1999) 'After globalisation: emerging politics of education', *Journal of Education Policy*, 14 (1), pp. 19–32.

Morgan, G. (1997) *Images of Organisation*, 2nd edn, London: Sage.

Naisbett, J. and Aburdene, P. (1988) *Mega-Trends 2000*. London: Sidgwick and Jackson.

Ohmae, K. (1995) *The End of the Nation State*, New York: McKinsey & Co.

Palan, R., Abbott J. and Deans, P. (1999) *State Strategies in the Global Political Economy*, London: Pinter.

Putnam, R. (2000) *Bowling Alone: the Collapse and Revival of American Community*, New York: Simon & Schuster.

Reich, R. (1991) *The Work of Nations*, New York: Vintage

Reich, R. (1999) 'We must still tax and spend', *New Statesman*, 1 May, pp. 3–14.

Rhodes, R. (1994) 'The hollowing out of the state – the changing nature of the public service in Britain', *Political Quarterly*, 65 (2), pp. 138-51.

Waters, M. (1995) *Globalization*, London: Routledge.

World Commission on Environment and Development (1987) *Our Common Future*, Oxford: Oxford University Press.

CHAPTER 17

Educational policy: commonalities and differences

....

BEN LEVIN

Educational leaders are living in a world where changes in policy are frequent, rapid and dramatic. As the importance of education is increasingly trumpeted for social and economic success, governments become more and more interested in what they can do to improve educational outcomes. As a result of the trends described in the pervious chapter, their decisions on this matter are increasingly made in the shadow of what other states are doing around the world.

This chapter, drawn from a study of education reform in several countries (Levin, 2001), looks at commonalities and differences in education policy in various countries. It takes as a starting point the importance both of international developments and of national or local context in shaping policy choices and implementation. As Barber (1996) put it, our world is subject simultaneously to homogenizing and differentiating influences. International developments influence, sometimes to a considerable degree, the kinds of policy choices that get serious consideration. However 'the facts on the ground' in each place – its history, culture, politics and institutions – remain very important in determining the actual policy choices governments make and the ways in which those choices are put into effect.

An important caveat is that this examination draws primarily on the experience of the English-speaking industrialized countries. Because these countries, and especially the USA, exercise a disproportionate influence on the world's 'climate of ideas', policy choices in many other parts of the world are also influenced by them. At the same time, there is evidence (Kallen, 1996) that some countries, such as those in western Europe or in Asia, have been able to move in rather different directions. Since even popular policies are rarely universally adopted, even within a country such as the USA (Mintrom, 2000), they are far less likely to be uniform on a world scale.

Background – history and scope

It is vitally important to remember that the current moment in education reform is shaped both by the history of education policy and by larger debates about the role of the state generally. Education reform has to be seen as a part of a larger fabric, both through time and across areas of service.

The present moment in education policy stands in sharp contrast to the decades after the Second World War in which a huge educational expansion took place around the world. The education system grew in almost every way. More people stayed in school for more years. The range of institutions, programmes and services at all levels was expanded and all kinds of supports were enriched. What was in 1945 in most countries still a relatively modest and selective system, grew into a very large and sophisticated system, with participation rates at all levels that were much higher than had ever been seen before.

This expansion was fuelled by factors such as the rapidly growing numbers of young people, the expansion of government generally, and economic prosperity that provided the additional resources to finance expansion. Widely held ideas about the importance of education for individual and social progress both supported and helped to create this climate. People were optimistic about the ability of the schools to improve equality, reduce social problems and create prosperity. In all these respects education was typical of state services in general. The same expansion of public activity also took place in other sectors such as health care, transportation or culture, and the same ideas about the importance and value of government were also dominant.

In the 1970s, however, the atmosphere began to change. All the drivers of the expansion of education, such as demographics, public finance and optimism, altered. Economic growth slowed, government deficits grew, resistance to taxation increased and confidence in public institutions declined, although schools continued to enjoy quite substantial levels of public support (Livingstone and Hart, 1998; Loveless, 1997). There was disenchantment – probably inevitable given such high expectations – with the outcomes of earlier expansion. The consensus on the vital role of the public sector vanished. Ideas about the importance of markets and about the need to control the power of professionals gained support at the expense of earlier beliefs in the powerful state. Some argue that these shifts were deliberately engineered by the powerful to preserve privilege, while others see the changes as a matter of the inevitable tides of historical fortune and belief.

The results were dramatic. Rapid expansion of education ended, as public funds were limited or reduced. The education system was increasingly subject to sharp changes in direction and to much greater scrutiny. The credibility of outside groups such as business or parents grew (Borman, Castenell and Gallagher, 1993; Manzer, 1994; Dehli, 1996), while the influence of educators was curtailed. Education politics built largely on consensus was replaced by a much greater degree of overt conflict.

Once again, the same kinds of shifts in discourse and policy that are seen in education can also be found more broadly. As Hart and Livingstone (1998) illustrate, confidence in many institutions has declined in the past 20 years, and governments have adopted similar policies directions in other sectors (Bottery, 1998). Ball (1997, p. 258) argues that

> During the last fifteen years we have witnessed in the UK, and indeed in most other Western and many developing societies, a major transformation in the organising principles of social provision right across the public sector. That is to say, the forms of employment, organisational structures, cultures and values, systems of funding, management roles and styles, social relationships and pay and conditions of public welfare organisations, have been subject to generic changes.

While all of this was happening, however, the perceived importance of education did not decline. If anything, the vital role of education in promoting human and social well-being gained increasing prominence, which led governments to look at new policies and strategies.

The internationalization of policy

One of the claimed impacts of recent social and economic change is the growing extent to which public policies are copied across national boundaries – often referred to as 'policy borrowing'. The claim for increased transfer has not been subject to much empirical investigation. The change may be exaggerated; there has always been considerable policy borrowing across boundaries (Fowler, 1994). For example, many public policy innovations, such as pensions, labour laws and compulsory education, also moved across national boundaries quite rapidly in the nineteenth and early twentieth centuries.

Just how policy borrowing takes place is still a largely unexplored question, although there is a developing literature in the area (Finegold, McFarland and Richardson, 1993; Rose, 1993; and Halpin and Troyna, 1995). Some see these policy movements as deliberately orchestrated by particular social and economic interests – what is usually referred to as the 'New Right'. Conservative governments and big business are seen to be working together to reverse some of the changes of the 1960s that redistributed wealth and attempted to reduce inequality (e.g. Apple, 1996; Dale, 1989; Barlow and Robertson, 1994; Berliner and Biddle, 1995). These commonalities are often linked to the larger economic and social phenomenon termed 'globalization'. Globalization is itself a disputed concept, used to refer to such disparate phenomena as the increasing impact of international organizations, the increasing movement of ideas across political jurisdictions, or, most frequently, changing economic production and finance structures that are seen to have diminished the power of the nation state (Davies and Guppy, 1997). Governments have certainly invoked globalization as a rationale for particular policies, sometimes arguing that they have no choice in the face of international developments but to follow particular policies such as reduced public spending. In any given situation, concerns about globalization, whether valid or not, may be a real motivation for policy or they may act as an excuse for policies that are desired on other grounds, such as ideological conviction.

Other explanations have also been advanced for policy movement across settings. Howlett and Ramesh (1995) propose what they call a 'convergence thesis' – that as countries move towards similar levels of industrialization they also tend to face similar issues and consider similar policy responses, but that this similarity is a matter of convenience rather than inevitability. Such an hypothesis would explain why developing countries tend to imitate the practices of more industrialized countries rather than the opposite.

Another approach can be found in dissemination theory (Rogers, 1983), which looks at the ways in which technologies move across settings – a pattern that Rogers characterizes as autocatalytic, increasing rapidly over time but not necessarily ever achieving complete dissemination. In a historical application of the same general concept, Diamond (1997) looks at the ways in which practices such as writing and agriculture spread across civilizations, and argues that ideas were adopted over time where they were seen as holding advantages for influentials. Another approach (Levin, 1998) has compared the spread of education reform ideas to the movement of diseases as described in the epidemiological literature. The diffusion of disease is held to be dependent on the three elements of agent (the carrier of the disease), host and context. Diseases only spread where all three factors line up appropriately, and the same might be said of the movement of policies in education. The epidemic metaphor draws attention to the combination of factors that may be necessary for a policy to have impact in other settings.

Moving from theoretical conceptions to the everyday world, vehicles that promoted policy borrowing can easily be identified. Political parties and politicians do have international contacts, such as the links between the Thatcher and Reagan governments, or Clinton and Blair. In federal states such as Canada and the USA, national educational organizations such as the Council of Chief State School Officers or the Council of Ministers of Education provide venues for the exchange of policy ideas through meetings and publications. At the international level, organizations such as UNESCO (United Nations Educational, Scientific and Cultural Organization) and the OECD (Organization for Economic Co-operation and Development) play a similar role. The growing number of international organizations has led to more meetings of political and bureaucratic leaders from around the world, such as the World Economic Summit in Switzerland (Boyd, 1999).

The same kinds of linkages also exist among those who try to influence policy, such as think-tanks and lobby groups of various kinds. Academic research, too, has become increasingly international in its scope and organization. Changes in communications technology have also led to a more international media. Outlets such as CNN or *The Economist* have a growing international stature. Publishing is increasingly concentrated in large multinational forms and popular authors or experts are more likely to have international stature. The internet has made it much easier to know what is happening in other places, at least at a superficial level.

All this contact will only have impact, though, if people are actually looking for ideas elsewhere. As work on political agenda-setting indicates (Kingdon, 1994), relevant ideas for addressing issues are always in demand. Leaders and experts often cite the experience of other countries in promoting their own similar ideas, such as the popularity of so-called 'Japanese management' before Japan fell into its current economic difficulties.

At any given moment there tends to be a conventional wisdom about what is true in any policy area – what Schon (1971) refers to as 'ideas in good currency'. These fashions in thinking occur in all areas of social life. Although we know that ideas held to be true a few years or decades ago turned out to be wrong, we continue to behave as if today's ideas will turn out to be immutable. For example, Manzer (1994) traces changing ideas about the appropriate organization of education in Canada, showing how different conceptions of the purposes of education came to be dominant at different times. Livingstone and Hart (1998) have used years of polling data in Ontario to show how certain ideas about education policy, such as the merits of testing, have gradually become conventional wisdom. These ideas do tend to dominate across national boundaries.

Commonalities

Given all of the above, we should not be surprised to find similarities in education policy across countries. For example, Guthrie (1996) describes common reform elements in many countries. Gewirtz, Ball and Bowe (1995) note the extent to which policies advocating greater use of markets have been adopted, albeit in varying forms, in many countries. Whitty, Power and Halpin (1998), looking at the US, UK, New Zealand, Australia and Sweden, see policy convergence towards 'a marketized model in an evaluative state' (ibid., p. 11).

Seven common policy features are described here: four related to the background to or context for reform and three to the nature of the proposed remedies. In the former category are:

- the dominance of economic rationales for change
- the climate of criticism of schools
- the absence of additional funding to support change
- the growing importance of diversity in thinking about education policy.

In the latter group are three kinds of proposals that are a key part of many reform packages:

- decentralization of operating authority to schools and the creation of school or parent councils to share in that authority;
- increased achievement testing, with publication of results and its corollary, more centralized curriculum;
- various forms of choice or other market-like mechanisms.

Commonalities of context

The need for change in education is now everywhere cast largely in economic terms, and particularly in relation to preparation of a workforce and competition with other countries. Education is described as being a key component of countries' ability to improve, or often even to maintain their economic welfare by ensuring a highly skilled workforce to meet emerging economic imperatives.

Economic goals have always been important to the development of schooling, but the intense focus on economic competitiveness and the allegedly apocalyptic consequences of failure in education are new to the dialogue. The justifications for education reform 30 or 40 years ago had much more to do with social mobility and individual welfare. Now a sense of fear seems to have replaced the sense of possibility: a change in keeping with the increasing emphasis on individual responsibility for life outcomes – what Giddens (1994) has called 'the self as a reflexive project'.

Second, recent education change grows out of criticism of schools. Governments take the position that reform is needed because school systems have failed to deliver what is required. Various kinds of evidence are adduced to support the attack, including drop-out rates, results of national and international achievement tests and the expressed concerns of employers about the quality of the workforce. Blame may be placed variously on progressive teaching methods, lack of rigour or protectionism by educators, but the common allegation is that current approaches have not worked, or at least not worked well enough. Critics also argue that the shortcomings of schools are especially lamentable in view of the high level of spending on education. The efficiency of the system is seen to have declined greatly as per-pupil costs rose significantly, while outcomes are held to be unsatisfactory. In short, the general tone underlying much reform is negative – an effort to undo damage.

Third, large-scale change is no longer accompanied by substantially increased funding of schools by governments. During the era of expansion, changes in education included substantial increases in financing. The picture varies around the world, with some jurisdictions having made real cuts and others modest increases, but in many jurisdictions governments have decoupled reform from funding, and in some cases dramatic changes have been accompanied by budget reductions. Again, this is not necessarily reflective of public views, where support for stable levels of social services, including education, remains quite high even at the price of higher taxes (Livingstone and Hart, 1998). The riposte about not 'throwing money at problems' is now heard so often that it has become widely accepted, but that should not blind us to its novelty. It is hard to think of any other major reform in education that was not accompanied by injections of large quantities of money. The attempt to move the gears of education without the grease of financing has produced some very loud noises from the machinery.

Finally, nations everywhere have become increasingly sensitive to issues of diversity in managing public policy. Differences within nations in ethnicity, language and religion have become major policy issues in most countries. The significant gap in educational achievement in many countries between majority and some minority groups has made this issue vitally important. Minority groups, whether ethnic, religious or linguistic, have grown increasingly assertive about what they consider to be their rights, and education has been one of the main areas of conflict (Riffel, Levin and Young, 1996). Both legal and political systems have changed in response, with legal institutions in particular often delivering important support to the claims of minorities. Whether the focus is on indigenous peoples in North America or Australasia, immigrants and migrant workers in much of the world, or the legacies of slavery in the USA and elsewhere, concerns about the place of minorities are high on the policy agenda. Ideas vary greatly on how best to cope with issues of diversity and the disagreements are very sharp, but the importance of the issues is evident to all, including those who wish diversity would just go away.

Common strategies

One of the strongest trends in education reform across national boundaries has been the shift of authority to the level of the local school. The first steps in this direction in the USA and Canada involved largely an administrative decentralization (Brown, 1990), in which school administrators were given more authority over staffing and budgets to improve efficiency. Later, emphasis shifted to political decentralization, which gives an increased role in governing schools to parents, and in some cases to other community members. This movement has perhaps more to do with effectiveness – questions of purposes and strategies – than with efficiency. The logic of decentralization assumes that changes in governance are key to improved performance of schools; that local bodies are in the best position to define and make necessary changes; and that parents especially have important knowledge about how the educational enterprise should best be carried on for their children. Unhappiness with the perceived bureaucratic character of large school systems and what some see as the excessive influence of educators have been important rationales for decentralization. The case for parental governance of schools is also linked by some proponents to issues of rights, such that parents ought to be able to influence substantially, if not determine, the nature of the schooling of their children.

The degree of control shifted to local schools, usually at the expense of regional authorities such as school districts, has varied. In many cases the commitment appears to be as much rhetorical as real, so that parent bodies are created but their powers remain limited – and usually entirely advisory. However in England and New Zealand, as well as some places in the USA (such as Chicago and Kentucky), school governing bodies – which are made up of parents and other community members – have been given very substantial authority over the schools.

A second common strategic element involves more testing of students on a standard curriculum or set of learning objectives, with results being made public. Testing is seen by advocates as important in providing information to parents and the public about the outcomes of schooling. For many, testing is also vital in efforts to move education closer to a market-like system. Since test results are regarded as the main basis for choosing a school, achievement testing needs to have public results. In addition a logic of testing leads to a prescribed curriculum, so that all students can both have the opportunity to learn and be tested on the skills and knowledge that are regarded as most important. Jurisdictions have taken different approaches to both these issues, but in many countries state testing has increased and has been coupled with more state control of curriculum.

Increasing national assessment is complemented by more and more international assessment, and these results are also used more overtly for public comparisons. Countries now proudly hold up their rankings on the latest international achievement study as a badge of honour, just as schools may cite their examination results (published in the newspapers in the UK) or test scores and college-entrance rates (widely reported by media in the USA) as evidence of the quality of their work. The literature on themes of assessment and accountability is burgeoning (e.g. Leithwood *et al.*, 2000; Mehrens, 1998).

A third reform proposal being implemented in many settings involves increasing the influence of parents over schools by giving them the right to choose the schools their children attend. Advocates of choice policies work from one or both of two beliefs. Some proponents urge the creation of systems that embody the characteristics of economic markets based on the belief that markets are inevitably more effective and efficient than state systems and will lead to improvement in schooling through the rigours of competition. A second, more complex line of argument rests on the belief that parents can make the best choice of school for their children, and ought by right to be able to make such choices even if they are not popular ones. These proponents of choice may have no particular liking for the capitalist economic system. Some are quite conservative (such as those who defend choice as a way of recognizing religious beliefs in schools, e.g. Holmes, 1998). Others regard the existing system as highly stratified and see choice as a way for those with less economic or political clout to have more influence over schooling (e.g. Nathan, 1996). A less flattering picture of the tendency to favour market solutions is provided by Plank and Boyd (1994), who term it 'the flight from democracy'. They see in the advocacy of private sector models a deep-seated distrust of democratic politics and a wish that difficult political decisions can be avoided through mechanisms such as choice.

Measures to increase choice have varied across settings. Some countries, such as England, simply mandated open enrolment and made parental choice compulsory. In other settings, choice has been increased through tying school funding to enrolment changes, providing more funding to private schools, the creation of what are called 'charter schools' or through more circumscribed and targeted plans, such as the US schemes in Milwaukee and Cleveland. However, in every case schools resemble a market in only a limited sense. No jurisdiction has a system yet that involves a direct payment between family and school, except in the case of private schools – and there the trend has been to reduce direct costs to families through higher public subsidies or tax credits. In general, there has also been more attention to the demand side of the equation than to changing the supply side by providing a significantly more diverse range of schools. In fact, market mechanisms have been constrained by other simultaneous reforms, such as testing and inspection, which have tended to push schools to be more homogeneous.

Reforms advocating school choice have been among the most controversial of all in recent years. Promoters see choice as fundamental to better schooling and to parental rights. Critics see choice as a fundamental challenge to public education, with particular threats to equity (Lauder and Hughes, 1999; Thrupp, 1999). The case has been argued in law courts as well as the court of public opinion. At present it seems safe to say that advocates on both sides are disappointed. The number of choice schemes continues to increase, and where it has been established there seems little possibility of a return to the *status quo ante*. On the other hand, in no setting has the role of the public school in serving the vast majority of students been called into question.

Outside pressures

As a set, these reform agendas are driven by what may be called a managerialist focus – a belief that the central problems of education can be remedied through changing the organization and management of the system in accord with a set of theoretical principles that can be applied in almost any context. The reforms embody an important if sometimes unstated set of assumptions about how schools work and what will result in change. They have in common the belief that educators cannot be trusted to deliver appropriate education because of their self-interest. Reform must therefore come primarily from outside pressures. Schools tend to be seen in this model as production enterprises, with students as the objects, curriculum as the vehicle, and management structures as the key variables of change. The reform strategies seem to imply that if schools are threatened with public disclosure of poor results, if enrolment and financing are dependent on academic success, if different people have control over decision making, then the right decisions will be made and student achievement will improve.

These assumptions seem paradoxically out of step with the conventional wisdom about improving organizational outcomes in other sectors. There is little in these reform programmes, for example, that mirrors the popularity of such private sector trends as quality management, learning organizations, focus on customer service, or constant research and development. Whereas schooling reforms focus on outside pressures and less autonomy for educators, the business literature is full of calls for more autonomy for workers, a stronger focus on teams, and the importance of an internally directed search for improvement. The extent to which such developments are actually occurring in the private sector is another question entirely (Lowe, 2000). Still, it seems ironic that education changes supported by business executives and intended to improve economic performance are moving in a different direction than the most touted reforms in the business sector.

Differences

Despite these common elements, there are also good grounds for being cautious about claims that policy developments are being widely copied by one country from another. It is easy to pull out statements by politicians or examples of similar policies and claim a greater degree of commonality than actually exists. For the most part, those who have looked more carefully across jurisdictions have concluded that differences among countries are at least as important as the similarities (Halpin and Troyna, 1995; Whitty, 1997; Levin, 2001). Policy by definition tends to have a broad sweep, but practice occurs in concrete and particular settings.

Looking beyond the English-speaking industrialized countries also changes the picture considerably. An OECD report on education reform and evaluation, for example, stressed the degree to which continental European countries were far less drawn to reforms based on stricter assessment and accountability regimes (Kallen, 1996). At the same time as the USA, Canada, the UK and New Zealand were experiencing policies of retrenchment and privatization, other countries, such as Japan and much of continental Europe, were moving in quite different directions. And, as noted earlier, policies are rarely adopted by all Canadian provinces or US states, where one might expect the highest degree of uniformity.

When one looks more closely at national experiences, the differences across jurisdictions are also compelling (Levin, 2001). England and New Zealand are often compared, for example, but a close look shows that the reforms in the two countries were really very different. New Zealand never adopted a national testing regime and has only very recently moved towards a national curriculum. Its reforms were largely confined to matters of governance and enrolment, whereas those in England have been much wider ranging and truly transformative. In Canada, much of the reform of the 1980s and 1990s was really motivated by provincial governments' wish to reduce spending on education.

Even where similar reforms have been adopted, they can end up looking very different in practice. Cibulka (1991) shows clearly how assessment reforms took on very different characters in three US states because of differences in political processes, structures, and cultures. In the UK, as Glatter, Woods and Bagley (1997) note, the impact of decentralization and choice varies greatly from one part of the country to another. Choice plans in the USA also vary greatly from one place to another (Fuller, Elmore and Orfield, 1996).

The main factors that militate against any straightforward transfer of policies from one setting into another include political culture and practices, geography and demography, and institutional structures. Some brief illustrations of each of these will show how powerful they are in shaping policy and implementation.

In regard to political culture, a society with deep divisions between political parties, such as England, may end up with more radical shifts in policy than one in which politics is somewhat more consensual, such as the USA. Countries with federal systems or with strong traditions of local autonomy automatically have a set of checks and balances that do not exist where a strong central government is able to move forward, even with dramatic initiatives. Hence the difference between New Zealand, which made dramatic changes from 1987 to 1991, and Australia, where policy has swung back and forth from state to state and over time.

Geography and demography are also vitally important. For example, school choice is one thing in an urban environment where there are many nearby schools from which to choose, and quite another in a sparsely populated rural setting in which there is only one school available. The impact of ethnic composition on education policy is also clear – every education policy in the USA, for instance, will be seen at least in part through the lens of its effect on African-Americans and Hispanics. In England and New Zealand also, ethnic considerations have had an important impact on the way that school choice develops in particular settings (Lauder and Hughes, 1999; Woods, Bagley and Glatter, 1998).

Institutions also matter. Settings with a large and diverse set of educational institutions or with strong traditions of local autonomy have very different political dynamics than do countries where the central government is all-powerful. In the USA both state and local autonomy have powerful effects on policy, whereas in a country like France the national government can move forward with much less trepidation. The fact that Canada has no national ministry or office of education certainly affects the shape of education policy in the country.

These differences draw attention to the ways in which context mediates the flow of ideas across and within national boundaries. As Whitty and Edwards put it, (1998, p. 223), 'This process is perhaps less a matter of direct policy exchange than of mutually reinforcing versions of reality which reflect shared reference groups and assumptive worlds'. Perhaps more importantly, differences in jurisdictions make it clear that policy choices can be made, and that there is no inevitable adjustment that everyone must make to accommodate globalization or economic competitiveness. People can set their own directions through their own political systems if they wish to do so. The options may not be unlimited, but they do exist.

REFERENCES

Apple, M. (1996) *Cultural Politics and Education*, New York: Teachers' College Press,

Ball, S. (1997) 'Policy sociology and critical social research: a personal review of recent education policy and policy research', *British Educational Research Journal*, 23 (3), pp. 257–74.

Barber, B. (1996) *Jihad vs. McWorld: How Globalism and Tribalism Are Re-Shaping the World*, New York: Ballantine.

Barlow, M. and Robertson, H-J. (1994) *Class Warfare*, Toronto: Key Porter.

Berliner, D. and Biddle, B. (1995) *The Manufactured Crisis: Myth, Fraud, and the Attack on America's Public Schools*, New York: Addison Wesley.

Borman, K., Castenell, L. and Gallagher, K. (1993) 'Business involvement in school reform: the rise of the business roundtable' in Marshall, C. (ed.) *The New Politics of Race and Gender*, London: Falmer Press, pp. 69–83.

Bottery, M. (1998) *Professionals and Policy: Management Strategy in a Competitive World*, London: Cassell.

Boyd, W.L. (1999) 'Paradoxes of educational policy and productivity', *Educational Policy*, 13 (2), pp. 227–50.

Brown, D. (1990) *Decentralization and School Management*, London: Falmer Press.

Cibulka, J. (1991) 'Educational accountability reforms: performance information and political power' in Fuhrman, S. and Malen, B. (eds) *The Politics of Curriculum and Testing*, London: Falmer Press, pp. 181–201.

Dale, R. (1989) *The State and Education Policy*, Buckingham: Open University Press.

Davies, S. and Guppy, N. (1997) 'Globalization and educational reforms in Anglo-American democracies', *Comparative Education Review*, 41 (4), pp. 435–59.

Dehli, K. (1996) 'Travelling tales: education reform and parental "choice" in postmodern times', *Journal of Education Policy*, 11 (1), pp. 75–98.

Diamond, J. (1997) *Guns, Germs and Steel*, New York: W.W. Norton.

Finegold, D., McFarland, L. and Richardson, W. (eds) (1993) *Something Borrowed, Something Learned? The Transatlantic Market in Education and Training Reform*, Washington, DC: Brookings Institute Press.

Fowler, F. (1994) 'The international arena: the global village' in Scribner, J. and Layton, D. (eds) *The Study of Educational Politics*, London: Falmer Press, pp. 89–102.

Fuller, B., Elmore, R. and Orfield, G. (eds) (1996), *Who Chooses, Who Loses?* New York: Teachers' College Press.

Gewirtz, S., Ball, S. and Bowe, R. (1995) *Markets, Choice and Equity in Education*, Buckingham: Open University Press.

Giddens, A. (1994) *Beyond Left and Right*, Cambridge: Polity Press.

Glatter, R., Woods, P. and Bagley, C. (eds) (1997) *Choice and Diversity in Schooling: Perspectives and Prospects*. London: Routledge.

Guthrie, J. (1996) 'Evolving political economies and the implications for educational evaluation' in *Evaluating and Reforming Education Systems*, Paris: Organization for Economic Co-operation and Development, pp. 61–83.

Halpin, D. and Troyna, B. (1995) 'The politics of education policy borrowing,' *Comparative Education*, 31 (3), pp. 303–10.

Hart, D. and Livingstone, D. (1998) 'The crisis of confidence in schools and the neoconservative agenda', *Alberta Journal of Educational Research*, 44 (1), pp. 1–19.

Holmes, M. (1998) *The reformation of Canada's schools*, Montreal: McGill-Queen's University Press.

Howlett, M. and Ramesh, M. (1995) *Studying Public Policy: Policy Cycles and Policy Subsystems*, Toronto: Oxford University Press.

Kallen, D. (1996) 'New educational paradigms and new evaluation policies' in *Evaluating and Reforming Education Systems*, Paris: Organization for Economic Co-operation and Development, pp. 7–23..

Kingdon, J. (1994) *Agendas, Alternatives and Public Policies*, 2nd edn, New York: HarperCollins.

Lauder, H. and Hughes, D. (1999) *Trading in Futures: Why Markets in Education Don't Work*, Buckingham: Open University Press.

Leithwood, K. and Earl, L. (2000) 'Educational accountability effects: an international perspective', *Peabody Journal of Education*, 75 (4), 1–18.

Levin, B. (1998) 'An epidemic of education policy: (what) can we learn from each other?', *Comparative Education*, 34 (2), pp. 131–41.

Levin, B. (2001). *Reforming Education: From Origins to Outcomes*, London: Routledge/Falmer Press.

Livingstone, D. and Hart, D. (1998) 'Where the buck stops: class differences in support for education', *Journal of Education Policy*, 13 (3), pp. 351–77.

Loveless, T. (1997) 'The structure of public confidence in education', *American Journal of Education*, 105 (2), pp. 127–159.

Lowe, G. (2000) *The Quality of Work*, Toronto: Oxford University Press.

Manzer, R. (1994) *Public Schools and Political Ideas*, Toronto: University of Toronto Press.

Mehrens, W. (1998) 'Consequences of assessment: what is the evidence?', *Education Policy Analysis Archives*, 6 (13), http://olam.ed.asu.edu/epaa

Mintrom, M. (2000) *Policy Entrepreneurs and School Choice*, Washington: Georgetown University Press.

Nathan, J. (1996) *Charter Schools*, San Francisco: Jossey-Bass.

Plank, D. and Boyd, W.L. (1994) 'Antipolitics, education, and institutional choice: the flight from democracy', *American Educational Research Journal*, 31 (2), pp. 263–81.

Riffel, J., Levin, B. and Young, J. (1996) 'Diversity in Canadian education', *Journal of Education Policy*, 11 (1), pp. 113–23.

Rogers, E. (1983) *Diffusion of Innovations*, 3rd edn, New York: Free Press.

Rose, R. (1993) *Lesson Drawing in Public Policy*, Chatham, NJ: Chatham House.

Schon, D. (1971) *Beyond the Stable State*, New York: Norton.

Thrupp, M. (1999) *Schools Making a Difference: Let's be Realistic*, Buckingham and Philadelphia: Open University Press.

Whitty, G. (1997) 'Creating quasi-markets in education: a review of recent research on parental choice and school autonomy in three countries', *Review of Research in Education*, 22, pp. 3–47.

Whitty, G. and Edwards, T. (1998) 'School choice policies in England and the United States: an exploration of their origins and significance', *Comparative Education*, 34 (2), pp. 211–27.

Whitty, G., Power, S. and Halpin, D. (1998) *Devolution and Choice in Education*, Buckingham and Philadelphia: Open University Press.

Woods, P., Bagley, C. and Glatter, R. (1998) *School Choice and Competition: Markets in the Public Interest?*, London: Routledge.

CHAPTER 18

Market policies, management and leadership in schools

NICK FOSKETT

A glossary of key terms in the educational literature of the last two decades will highlight meta-phrases such as 'marketization', 'standards',' school effectiveness' and 'school improvement'. While sometimes shy of precise definition, such ideas have framed much of the policy development of recent years, particularly in OECD countries. These terms are not distinct and unconnected, though, for they represent dimensions of a political thesis with simple principles – we must raise levels of educational attainment to compete in the global economy; it is schools that must produce raised achievement; to ensure that they do so, we must empower them and make them accountable through processes such as resource delegation, parental choice and the application of market forces. This thesis has become one of the 'global orthodoxies' of education (Lauder and Hughes, 1999), with implications and impact for teachers and school leaders, and represents a fundamental shift in the relationship between government, education professionals and the constituencies that schools serve.

The recent emergence of 'markets' as a concept within education is a product of the conservative political administrations that appeared first in the Reagan and Thatcher governments of the USA and the UK in the late 1970s. Economic recession and social conflict had begun to undermine the 'post-war settlement' in which the professional providers of public sector services were largely left to determine their own agendas and accountabilities. The late 1970s and the decade of the 1980s were a formative period. During these years there was a steady accumulation of evidence to support the rhetoric that existing operational models for public sector services were not working. Such a perspective encouraged in parallel an exploration of alternative models based on the primacy of markets and of choice. In the USA, for example, concern about the achievement levels of the school system were raised in the *Nation at Risk* report of the National Commission on Excellence in Education (NCEE, 1983), which predicted economic decline as a result of low levels of school achievement in the USA. In the UK right-wing political writers, including Boyson (1973), Flew (1987) and the Hillgate Group (1987), provided strong criticism of the standards of education in comprehensive schools and of the inability of the education profession to resolve its own difficulties. Perhaps most influential on both sides of the Atlantic was the seminal writing of Chubb and Moe (1990), which gave strong 'authority' to the markets movement.

Two real concerns underpinned such analyses. First was the economic concern about future competitiveness in the global economy. This in itself had two strands, for there are the opposing forces of the recognition of the need to raise levels of education and training in the workforce, while at the same time restraining public sector expenditure. Expansion of the system was seen to be essential, but required a significant increase in the efficiency with which the resources for education and training were to be used. Second was the desire, based on an ideological commitment to the values of freedom, individual autonomy and democracy, to enhance choice for individuals within society. Inherent within this perspective was a belief that it is in the 'natural' environment of choice and competition that individuals are enabled to show initiative and take opportunity that is in the joint interest of both individuals and society. Hence the formative phase of marketization was no less than a political/ideological movement underpinned by a commitment to cultural renewal in the context of conservative values.

The view that markets are the solution emerged from such analysis. The promotion of the role of markets as resource allocation mechanisms dates from the ideas of Adam Smith in the eighteenth century, but these ideas were revived in the modern context through the work of Milton Friedman (Friedman and Friedman, 1980) and of Friedrich von Hayek (1976). Market theory suggests that competition between providers of goods and services to satisfy customer wants causes them to seek ways of minimizing costs and increasing efficiency in their operations to enable them to create a price advantage over their competitors. At the same time, suppliers will seek to innovate in the goods and services they offer in order to gain market advantage. Entrepreneurship amongst producers and freedom of choice for consumers, therefore, are the essence of the market, and within a free market external intervention, for example through government policy or statute, is regarded as reducing the efficiency of the system.

Free markets, of course, never exist. In the context of public services such as education, the need for government to create the elements of a market, and also to ensure that the wider social and political aims they have for education and training can be met, has meant that such social markets cannot be free of strong external intervention. The form of the market, and the processes that are encouraged or permitted within that market, are therefore unique in every national setting in which marketization has developed. Le Grand (1990) has described such markets as quasi markets.

In their most developed form, quasi markets have at their core the principle of parental choice of the school to which they will send their children. To provide a basis for parental choice, information must be made available to parents and some form of performance indicator system must be established to enable them to judge the relative merits of schools. Finally, there must be a resource allocation system that ensures that resources follow pupil numbers to those schools successful in the selection process. In New Zealand, for example, the market system established by the 1991 Education Amendment Act introduced open enrolment, with schools free to choose their admissions criteria within limits imposed only by equal opportunities and antiracist legislation. Government direction over information provision, the availability of performance indicators and the detail of the curriculum was less tightly defined. Similar models have been established in Australia, although the detail varies from state to state, and in some parts of the USA, notably Chicago. In England and Wales, the 1988 Education Reform Act introduced many similar features of open enrolment and large-scale delegation of funding to schools, calculated by formulae linked to pupil numbers. However, the information elements of the market were strongly prescribed through earlier statutory requirements on information provision by schools and by the establishment of a tightly defined National Curriculum, public examinations to measure achievements against that curriculum, and a strong regime of school inspection. Publication of league tables of school performance and of their inspection reports was seen to provide a strong basis for parental choice.

The examples we have considered so far represent some of the strongest cases of the establishment of education markets. Although marketization may be described as a global metatrend, such systems have by no means been adopted universally. In many cultural settings where the value systems underpinning education are not those of the market, utilitarianism, human capital and choice, and strongly centralized command systems of education still predominate. Japan, for example, retains such a system, which is so embedded in the national culture that the prospects of change are small (Thrupp, 1999), and in high power-distance countries, such as many of the states of South-East Asia (e.g. Thailand) and the Islamic states of the Middle East (e.g. Pakistan – see Memon *et al.*, 2000) marketization and decentralization have made little impression during the 1990s. Even in countries fundamentally restructuring their educational system, such as Namibia (Auala, 1998), adoption of a market system has not necessarily been prioritized.

Marketization, therefore, is a generic term for developments that have unique form in every case where they have been adopted. The only common characteristic, in fact, is the decentralization of some degree of decision making and resource management away from central government. Choice, for example, will always have been enhanced, but may not necessarily be present as parental choice – it may exist in the form of choices by managers or administrators at district or regional authority level rather than in individual schools. Resource delegation may relate to some but not all resources (teacher recruitment and salaries are frequently still managed through a direct command system by government), or apply only to some types of school. In Indonesia, for example, delegation to secondary schools has been established, but for primary schools delegation of resources has been only to the level of local authorities.

Marketization is not a unidirectional trend, even in those countries that have moved strongly to a commitment to market allocation mechanisms. As the impact of markets is seen in practice and as governments change so that political leadership has a different ideological base, adjustments to the role of markets can be observed. The 1990s saw two important developments. First, those market systems established in the 1980s were able to provide some evidence of their impact on schools, and on school management, to inform decision making. Second, the replacement of conservative administrations in many OECD (Organization for Economic Co-operation and Development) countries by governments with a more centre-left ideological perspective led to a review of the role of social markets. Rather than radical rejection of the policies of their predecessors, however, a continuation of the prioritization of choice and of some elements of market allocation models was the chosen direction of the new administrations.

The appearance of 'Third Way' policies emphasizing public–private partnership, with a mix of government directive and control, the involvement of private sector organizations and some market processes, characterized the late 1990s in many western countries. In some aspects of educational policy, this involved a moderation of the role of choice and market forces, while in other areas there was a continued expansion of private sector models. In the UK, for example, notions of parental choice were replaced by an emphasis on parental preference but with a retention of formula funding and a commitment to the extension of the use of comparative school performance data in the form of league tables. At the same time, the role of the private sector was enhanced with the promotion of the Private Finance Initiative (PFI) to fund school building and the engagement of private sector companies to take over the management of failing schools. It is clear that the landscape of marketization is extremely diverse.

The impact of marketization on schools has been significant, leading to changes in management processes and organization, institutional culture (at all levels), and in perspectives on a wide range of dimensions of education from teaching and learning, to resource management and managing external relations, including relationships with parents.

Institutional culture is a significant but complex dimension of schools, with both implicit and explicit expressions through systems, relationships, visual identity, individual behaviours and expressions of values and beliefs. Marketization may be regarded as a project of cultural change, and such change can be observed at all operational levels, from the individual teacher in his/her classroom, to teams, to whole schools and to system-level changes. Gewirtz, Balls and Bowe (1995) draw on evidence from schools in England and Wales to identify some of these changes, characterizing the cultural shifts in terms of dichotomies – for example, from comprehensive values to competitive values, from individual teacher autonomy to strong teacher accountability, from collegiality between schools to competition, from role culture to task culture. In relation to the management culture of schools, Clarke and Newman (1992) have identified some of the key characteristics of 'new managerialism' and contrast it with previously dominant models of bureau-professionalism, using the paradigm of cultural shift to describe the changes. They perceive a change from a culture based on the values of professional education to a culture based on the values of business and entrepreneurialism. Such a culture emphasizes private sector values rather than public sector ethos, individual relations with staff within schools rather than communal relations (perhaps through trade unions), a concern for external rather than internal influences, and a focus on visible and measurable dimensions of educational processes rather than those that are less visible.

The centrality of entrepreneurialism as a desired characteristic of schools and school leadership in such a context (Campbell and Crowther, 1991) has impacted, of course, on the nature of appointments to leadership roles. Anderson (2000, pp. 41–2) identifies how:

> *Since the early 1990s, the innovative management of change and external relations has become a vital activity for effective headteachers, principals and other managers and, for some of these people, the experiences have brought to light hitherto undiscovered or, possibly, frustrated abilities and skills of innovation and entrepreneurialism. Thus both a new term has been introduced into educational language – the entrepreneurial leader – and a new attribute associated with effective educational leaders.*

Entrepreneurship requires skills of creativity, innovation and risk-taking both within and outside the organization. The role of 'champion of internal cultural change' has been emphasized by Boisot (1995) in the concept of 'intrapreneurship', which is the promotion of initiative and individual innovation within the organization.

Internal cultural change is only part of the scene, however, for the empowerment of parents and students as choosers in education and training markets is an important dimension of marketization. For schools, responding to the adoption of a consumerist perspective by parents is challenging. The wide range of work on choice in education markets (see Foskett and Hemsley-Brown, 2001) stresses how a consumer perspective has been adopted by parents and students, although by no means universally. Consumerism in public sector markets is dominantly a middle-class characteristic, although this may be more a result of the middle-classes' ability to exploit their cultural capital more effectively than working-class parents can. The impact of active choosers in the marketplace though, may be substantial, for two reasons. First, those who are the active choosers are those with the highest socio-economic status who are most likely to exercise their rights in terms of selecting a school other than that which is closest to home, and of utilizing their options of 'voice' or 'exit' (Hirschmann, 1970). It is their children who make most impact on school performance and reputation, and their choices have a disproportionate impact on schools. Second, to attract such parents, schools may seek to change their ethos, character and organization to be explicitly seen in terms of the cultural expectations of high socio-economic status parents, creating the danger of a narrowing of the values supported and developed by schools across the community and a prioritization of academic achievement and middle-class forms of behaviour and values. Woods, Glatter and Bagley (1998), in the context of England, and Lauder and Hughes (1999) in the context of New Zealand, for example, have shown that competition between schools causes those least successful schools to seek to be more like the successful ones in terms of espoused values, rather than seeking to create their own market persona.

Markets have stimulated the introduction of a wide range of operational changes to the management and leadership of schools. These changes have resulted from the processes of decentralization and the delegation of accountability for resource management and performance; from the need to interact with the external environment to engage with marketing, external communication and accountability processes. There have also been changes to learning, teaching and the curriculum to emphasize the prioritization of learning outcomes and accountability measures.

Decentralization takes many forms and is highly context specific. While the process involves some degree of delegation of decision making and accountability to lower levels in the education system, there are only a few examples of states that have promoted largely autonomous, self-managing schools as described by Caldwell and Spinks (1992). Whatever the degree of delegation, though, school managers have been required to take on a new suite of management and leadership tasks, ranging from staff recruitment to financial decision making and income generation, marketing, and managing relationships with external groups and organizations.

Managing external relations is a central requirement of marketization and self-management, but plays only a small role in traditional centralized school systems. External relations is a broad term that has many facets. Foskett (1999) distinguishes three types of external relationship that schools must 'manage':

- Transactional-based: the school is a 'buyer' or 'seller'. This may include promoting the school, recruiting pupils, or buying supplies and services from external providers. It includes the traditional elements of marketing: identifying and providing the curriculum demanded by the school's customers (parents, pupils, government, society).
- Relationship-based: the school works in partnership with those beyond the school boundaries – parents of pupils, community organizations (churches, police etc.), special services providers (for example, educational psychologists). Here the relationship is based on mutual professional trust rather than competition, buying and selling.
- Public accountability: the statutory management of accountability processes such as inspection, the publication of examination results and accounting for the resources allocated to the school.

The priority of these processes has meant that school leaders must be increasingly focused on the external environment as well as the internal world of the school. Furthermore, understanding the interactions between the three sorts of external relations and between internal and external processes is an important task in the planning and strategic dimensions of leadership roles. Scanning the external environment to identify necessary and desirable responses within the school is a key task, but so is the monitoring of internal processes and the prioritization of internal marketing activities to ensure that the perceptions of the school by all external stakeholders are favourable.

Evidence of the prioritization of external relations management has emerged from a number of studies. In the context of England and Wales Gewirtz, Balls and Bowe (1995) show how senior managers in a wide range of schools in London have begun to consider the external relations dimensions of the tasks they lead. Foskett (1998) has shown, too, how a cultural shift has occurred in some schools in which external relations management has a higher status and role; a view echoed in the studies of Thrupp (1999) and of Lauder and Hughes (1999) in New Zealand. Such shifts are not confined to the highly marketized educational systems. In Pakistan (Memon *et al.*, 2000) show how the management of relations with parents is a significant challenge for headteachers, despite the maintenance of a strongly centralized system, and in Tanzania (Babyegyega, 2000) a key function for headteachers is the management of relations with village communities and parents to encourage support in terms of resources and also in the enrolment of pupils within the school.

Finally, we need to consider the impact of marketization on learning and teaching and on pupil performance, which is one of the key *raisons d'être* of the prioritization of markets and choice. How far has market policy changed leadership, such that there is a measurable impact on pupils rather than a simple cosmetic change to the external appearance of schools? Measuring the effects of specific policy actions in education is notoriously difficult, for three reasons. First, there needs to be the identification of appropriate indicators and measures, and agreement on their value and their application. What outcomes are we actually looking to identify as the intended effect of policy change? Second, system complexity means that linking specific outcomes to particular actions in policy or practice is rarely possible, for the effect of other factors cannot be isolated in the analysis. Third, the impact of change may take many years to emerge. Individual pupils spend 10–15 years in the education system, and the evidence of the impact of change can be clear only when cohorts of pupils have passed through the whole system under the new set of conditions. While earlier evidence may emerge, it is clear from our understanding of the ways in which innovations are taken up and implemented that patterns of change in the early phases of cycles of development may not indicate the overall impact, patterns or outcomes (Rogers, 1993). The time requirement for empirical evidence meant that much of the substantial litera- ture on the impact of marketization on pupil performance in the first half of the 1990s was entirely theoretical in nature, arguing the likely outcomes on the basis of assumed operational models in the context of distinct ideological standpoints.

However, evidence is now beginning to emerge, and Caldwell (2000) has identi- fied three generations of research studies examining the relationship between marketization, self-management in schools and pupil performance. The first gener- ation is the research undertaken principally in the context of the USA in the early 1990s, and summarized by Summers and Johnson (1996). Drawing on a large number of studies, they suggest that there is no demonstrable link between marke- tization and the enhancement of pupil performance in schools. They emphasize, however, that the nature of the data available through such studies does not make any testing of the markets–pupil achievement link easy. Furthermore, they stress that in the context of the USA there is little explicit intent in the development of self-managing schools to emphasize the enhancement of pupil achievement, and that most of the 'experiments' are rooted in aims that are primarily related to liber- tarian ideologies and school/teacher empowerment.

The second generation studies are those undertaken principally in the mid-1990s in the context of significant shifts towards self-managing schools in England and Wales, Australia and New Zealand. While such studies demonstrate increases in cost efficiency in such schools (e.g. Levačić, 1995, in the context of local manage- ment of schools in England), they are unable to show any significant impact of marketization on pupil standards. Drawing from a range of studies in differing national contexts, Whitty, Power and Halpin (1998) suggest that there is still insuf- ficient evidence to show that schools operating in a regime of self-management enhance pupil achievement.

Third-generation studies are those that have emerged since 1998, and are founded in a number of important characteristics. First, they draw on evidence from systems that have been in operation for periods of up to a decade and so have had time to begin to demonstrate impacts on outputs at a system level. Second, the operation of performance measurement and accountability systems such as public examination performances and inspection reports has provided a significant set of data to enable analysis to be undertaken. Third, the development of suitable tech- niques of data analysis has facilitated analysis in relation to the complex multifactorial processes at work in such educational markets. The increased sophis- tication that such studies provide, though, indicates that although the relationship between self-management and enhanced pupil performance may exist, it does so only in some circumstances. At best, such markets provide the circumstances for pupils across the social and achievement spectrum to enhance performance. At worst, marketization generates the heat of competition and the accrued losses from declining collegiality while simply exacerbating contrasts between schools and enhancing polarization on the basis of socio-economic status.

In the context of New Zealand, for example, Thrupp (1999) and Lauder and Hughes (1999) emphasize that parental choice means that advantaged schools enhance pupil performance while the disadvantaged schools have little impact on achievement. This they attribute to 'school mix effects', in which the curriculum and the institutional culture of schools that are rooted in middle-class values provide an environment in which those schools attracting middle-class children thrive while those attracting children from families with other cultural values struggle to raise standards of achievement. In England and Wales, research by Gorard and Fitz (2000) and by Gibson and Asthana (2000) identifies enhanced achievement by pupils in those schools that are particularly attractive to parents in the school-choice market-place. Gibson and Asthana, for example, suggest that improvements in examination results at 16 are rising three times faster in the most popular schools than in the least popular schools – and such achievement in turn attracts parents of higher achieving pupils to seek places in such schools, thereby accelerating such improvement.

While there may be evidence of improvement, though, understanding the detailed causes and processes is challenging, and there are many significant debates about the nature, validity and interpretation of the data in such studies. Furthermore, while there may be emerging evidence of enhanced pupil achievement, the clear evidence of increased polarization between successful and less successful schools raises concerns on grounds of equity about the impact of marketization. Thrupp (1999, p. 182) believes that in such a context policy makers must 're-emphasize the social limits of school reform' and recognize that it is in the differences between schools and their pupil intake that the main handicaps to enhancing school effectiveness at the system level are to be found. The promotion of markets and parental choice may deliver enhanced standards in some schools, but achieving it across the whole educational system requires much more attention to active leadership in relation to the practice and management of learning and teaching.

Caldwell (2000), drawing on evidence from studies in the state of Victoria, Australia, identifies these strategies and practices as:

- identifying the enhancement of pupil learning as the primary purpose of the self-managing school;
- developing explicit planned links between every activity in the school and enhanced pupil learning;
- incorporating staff selection and staff development programmes that place learning at the heart of their focus;
- establishing high-performing teams that are committed to a needs-based, data-driven approach;
- operating through 'backward mapping', in which learning goals drive the development of practice and strategy rather than the other way round.

Where these characteristics are present, the responsiveness and scope for innovation that self-management resulting from marketization can facilitate can enable significant progress in raising pupil achievement. In contrast to perspectives that equate marketing with 'selling', such an approach – with its core values of the centrality of a 'customer/client' focus and responsiveness – is actually the essence of a marketing-focused organization. Furthermore, there is little conflict between such a perspective and traditional educational values emphasizing pupil development, and, indeed, the schools that are most effective in raising standards are actually those that implicitly espouse marketing values, even though they are couched in the language of learning and teaching. Where such perspectives are adopted, the impact of market forces on leadership may be seen to generate real impact on pupil learning rather than simply promoting new types of operational processes remote from classroom practice.

Conclusion

Marketization, whether it be the strong implementation of parental choice and formula funding or merely the delegation of some levels of resource (and hence choice and decision making) away from central government, represents a fundamental readjustment to the modus operandi of education systems. It has challenged schools and school leaders to be responsive and innovative in the pursuit of higher standards of pupil achievement but has also introduced significant changes to the tasks of leadership and management in schools, and has reconfigured their culture and ethos. However, the market revolution still remains to be judged in terms of its impact on pupils' school lives and their educational attainment. In considering the long-term impact of marketization, we should note the analysis of Fiske and Ladd (2000, p. 313) in their review of market reforms in the context of New Zealand, when they assert that:

> New Zealand's experience ... demonstrates that reformers in other countries who are tempted to put their faith in simple governance solutions to complex questions of educational quality are likely to find them wanting. It also demonstrates that over-reliance on simplistic solutions can cause considerable harm to both individuals and schools unless policymakers are willing to anticipate from the outset the limitations of such solutions and to build in appropriate safeguards.

REFERENCES

Anderson, L. (2000) 'The move towards entrepreneurialism' in Coleman, M. and Anderson, L. (eds), *Managing Finance and Resources in Education*, London: PCP.

Auala, R. (1998) 'Secondary education reform in Namibia', *International Studies in Educational Administration*, 26 (1), pp. 57–62.

Babyegyega, E. (2000) 'Education reforms in Tanzania: from nationalisation to decentralisation of schools', in *International Studies in Educational Administration*, 28 (1), pp. 2–10.

Boisot, M. (1995) 'Preparing for turbulence; the changing relationship between strategy and management development in the learning organisation' in Garrett, B. (ed.) *Developing Strategic Thought: Rediscovering the Art of Direction-Giving*, London: McGraw-Hill.

Boyson, R. (1973) 'The school, equality and society' in Wilson, B.R. (ed.) *Education, Equality and Society*, London: Allen & Unwin.

Caldwell, B. (2000) 'Local management and learning outcomes. Mapping the links in three generations of international research' in Coleman, M. and Anderson, L. (eds) *Managing Finance and Resources in Education*, London: Paul Chapman Publishing.

Caldwell, B. and Spinks, J. (1992) *Leading the Self-Managing School*, London: Falmer Press.

Campbell, D. and Crowther, F. (1991) 'What is an entrepreneurial school ?' in Crowther, F. and Caldwell, B. (eds) *The Entrepreneurial School*, Sydney: Ashton Scholastic.

Chubb, J. and Moe, T. (1990) *Politics, Markets and America's Schools*, Washington, DC: Brookings Institution Press.

Clarke, J. and Newman, J. (1992) 'Managing to survive: dilemmas of changing organisational forms in the public sector', paper presented at the Sociology Association Conference, Nottingham.

Flew, A. (1987) *Power to the Parents*, London: Sherwood Press.

Fiske, E. and Ladd, H. (2000) *When Schools Compete: A Cautionary Tale*, Washington, DC: Brookings Institution Press.

Foskett, N.H. (1998) 'Schools and marketization: cultural challenges and responses', *Educational Management and Administration*, 26 (2), pp. 197–210.

Foskett, N.H. (1999) 'Strategy, external relations and marketing' in Lumby, J. and Foskett, N.H. (eds) *Strategy, External Relations and Marketing*, London: PCP.

Foskett, N.H. and Hemsley-Brown, J. (2001) *Choosing Futures: Young People's Decicion-making in Education, Training and Careers Markets*, London: Routledge/Falmer.

Friedman, M. and Friedman, R. (1980) *Free to Choose*, London: Penguin Books.

Gewirtz, S., Balls, S. and Bowe, R. (1995) *Markets, Choice and Equity in Education*, Buckingham: Open University Press.

Gorard, S. and Fitz, J. (2000) 'Investigating the determinants of segregation between schools', *Research Papers in Education*, 15 (2), pp. 115–32.

Gibson, A. and Asthana, S. (2000) 'What's in a number ? Commentary on Gorard and Fitz's "Investigating the determinants of segregation between schools"', *Research Papers in Education*, 15 (2) pp. 133–53.

Hayek, F. (1976) *Law, Legislation and Liberty; Vol. 2: Rules and Order*, London: Routledge.

Hillgate Group (1987) *The Reform of British Education*, London: Claridge Press.

Hirschmann, A. (1970) *Exit, Voice and Loyalty: Responses to Decline in Firms, Organisations and States*, Cambridge, MA: Harvard University Press.

Lauder, H. and Hughes, D. (1999) *Trading in Futures – Why Markets in Education Don't Work*, Buckingham: Open University Press.

Le Grand, J. (1990) *Quasi Markets and Social Policy*, Bristol: University of Bristol.

Levačić, R. (1995) *Local Management of Schools: Analysis and Practice*, Buckingham: Open University Press.

Memon, M., Ali, R.N., Simkins, T. and Garrett, V. (2000) 'Understanding the headteacher's role in Pakistan: emerging role demands, constraints and choices', *International Studies in Educational Administration* 28 (1), pp. 48–56.

NCEE (1983) *A Nation at Risk*, Washington, DC: National Commission on Excellence in Education.

Rogers, E.M. (1993) *Diffusion of Innovations*, New York: The Free Press.

Summers, A.A. and Johnson, A.W. (1996) 'The effect of school-based management plans' in Hanushek, E.A. and Jorgenson, D.W. (eds) *Improving America's Schools: the Role of Incentives*, Washington, DC: National Academy Press.

Thrupp, M. (1999) *Schools Making a Difference – Let's Be Realistic*, Buckingham: Open University Press.

Whitty, G., Power, S. and Halpin, D. (1998) *Devolution and Choice in Education: The School, the State and the Market*, Buckingham: Open University Press.

Woods, P., Glatter, R. and Bagley, C. (1998) *School Choice and Competition: Markets in the Public Interest?* London: Routledge.

CHAPTER 19

What successful leadership in schools looks like: implications for policy and practice

CHRISTOPHER DAY

School principals' work, like that of teachers, has intensified and become more complex in recent times as ideologically driven external interventions by government in the curriculum and management of schools have increased. There has been a greater focus in all countries upon raising standards of student achievement for social and economic purposes and, alongside this, assessing teacher and school performance through a range of formal accountability measures. As the emphasis upon rationalistic means-ends approaches to education has grown, school improvement policies have been accompanied by a focus upon a range of leadership and management competencies and standards that are representative of segmented rather than holistic understandings of successful leadership and whose origins in research on the realities of school leadership remain unclear.

This chapter will suggest that, as a group, school principals need a more complex portfolio of leadership and management knowledge, qualities and skills than is at present available through hybrid business-education models that often dominate training. Framing programmes that, for example, emphasize the identification and application of particular attitudinal and behavioural approaches of individuals and groups in businesses that are concerned primarily with product, profit and loss, do not always articulate well with the complex, values-driven, dilemma-laden, differentiated leadership of schools that are primarily concerned with service and individual welfare. While there are similarities between public service and commercial concerns, there are also differences in, for example, the missions of the organizations. MacBeath (1998) in research into schools across England, Denmark and Scotland, and the extensive studies of Leithwood, Jantzi and Steinbach (1999) in Canada and Sergiovanni (1992) in the USA, have shown that successful leaders deploy a leadership model based on values-driven, human-resources and social-systems models of management. Yet while programmes in Australia (Glatter, 1998) and Scotland (Morris and Reeves, 2000) acknowledge the importance of values, ethics and the importance of emotional leadership, those in other countries do not. For example, in the English context it has been argued that the particular view of leadership that the nature, direction and pace of reform implicitly endorses as effective has become increasingly managerialist (Gunter, 1997; Slee, Weiner and Tomlinson, 1998). It has been claimed that the emphasis upon the 'monitorial' role of 'managing directors' has given principals less time to perform the role of 'leading professional' (Pollard, *et al.*, 1994). This observation directly contradicts the popular academic research view that the principal's main role is to influence the quality of teaching and learning in the school through purposeful 'transformative leadership' (Leithwood and Jantzi, 1990; Fullan, 1992), articulating a vision and promoting shared ownership (Louis and Miles, 1990; Blase and Anderson, 1995; Starratt, 1991). In this literature the search continues for a model of effective leadership that is suited to a postmodern context.

Recently, leadership studies have focused upon values – the 'moral purposes' and moral craft of leadership (Sergiovanni, 1992; Tom, 1984), the roles of leaders in creating a 'community of learners' (Barth, 1990; Senge, 1990) and the capacities of leaders to 'make a difference' through their ability to 'transform' (Sergiovanni, 1995) or 'liberate' (Tampoe, 1998) rather than simply 'transact'. The most popular theories are located in the 'transactional' and 'transformational' models identified more than 20 years ago (Burns 1978) and lately reinvented through such terms as 'liberation' (Tampoe, 1998), 'educative' (Duignan and McPherson, 1992), 'invitational' (Stoll and Fink, 1996) and 'moral' leadership (Sergiovanni, 1992). What is clear from these, and the effective schools literature, is that successful leaders not only set direction, organize and monitor, build relationships with the school community, and are people-centred, but they also model values and practices consistent with those of the school so that 'purposes which may have initially seemed to be separate, become fused' (Sergiovanni, 1995, p. 119)

What follows draws initially upon detailed 'multiperspective' empirical research, which reveals how good leadership in successful schools is closely connected to a values-led contingency model of leadership and, within this, the commitment and capacity of principals to engage in reflective practice (Day *et al.*, 2000).[1] Two hundred interviews were conducted with parents, governors (board members), teachers, students, ancillaries and principals in 12 schools in different parts of England. Each of the principals (from eight primary, three secondary and one special school) were known by their peers to be effective leaders and each of the schools had been ranked 'good' or 'excellent' by independent external inspections by the office for Standards in Education (OFSTED). Data from these interviews suggest that successful leaders who are able to ensure that their schools provide the high quality learning opportunities necessary for all students in the twenty-first century are those who engage in a range of reflective practices throughout their careers. Through such engagement these principals develop and maintain their critical thinking and emotional intelligence, exercise people-centred management, and remain 'one step ahead of the game' in mediating between externally determined initiatives and internal autonomy.

Beyond transformational leadership

The data suggest that existing theories of leadership do not adequately reflect or explain the current practice of effective leaders. Rather, they identify a people-centred model of leadership we term 'values-led contingency leadership'. In this model, principals adhered to a 'person-centred' philosophy that placed emphasis upon improving teaching and learning via high expectations of others. For them, the primary task of leadership concerned building and monitoring the conditions for professional, institutional and broader community growth (Leithwood, Jantzi and Steinbach, 1999). They were constantly engaged with the daily business of simultaneously managing interpersonal relations and challenging others to give of their best in the context of policy-driven imperatives that were not always universally welcomed.

Values led, achievement oriented, people-centred

The data further demonstrated that effective leadership is defined and driven by individual value systems, rather than instrumental managerial concerns. Management and leadership were essential components of these principals' roles, and heads were able to do both successfully. They engaged in people-centred leadership, constantly creating, maintaining, reviewing and renewing the learning and achievement cultures for students, staff and the close communities of parents and governors whom they served; and they modelled this in the many thousands of daily interactions through which common visions, expectations, standards, relationships and definitions of effectiveness were formed, framed, supported and tested. Of equal importance was their ability to create and monitor organizational structures appropriate to the fulfilment of the legitimate interests and aspirations of both internal and external stakeholders.

It follows that effective heads have a major responsibility both for the ongoing, evolutionary development of the schools in which they work and, within this, the more formal accelerated learning opportunities and challenges collectively known as 'school improvement' and 'teacher development'. The principals communicated their vision and values through their leadership relationships. They raised the self-confidence, morale and sense of achievement of staff by using these relationships to develop a climate of collaboration and by applying within them high standards to themselves and others. Their focus was always upon the betterment of the children, young people and staff who worked in their schools. In this respect, they exercised 'educative leadership' (Duignan and McPherson, 1992). They were empathetic, warm, genuine in their love for children and concerned for their well-being and achievement (Mintzberg, 1994; Jackson, Boostrom and Hansen, 1993; Noddings, 1992). All valued and encouraged collegiality, a feature of 'moving' schools (Rosenholtz, 1989; Hargreaves, 1992), and all fostered climates of openness in their schools between students, staff and community, encouraging staff to participate in discussions about values and beliefs as well as in decision-making processes, emphasizing mutual respect and providing supportive leadership for all their staff.

The heads in the study operated on the basis of both internally and externally determined measures of quality control so that their quality assurance criteria had a broader agenda in keeping with a holistic broader moral vision of a good school and good teachers. It involved everyone in the organization seeking systematically, with evidence, to ensure that standards were constantly improving. It was contingent but within a framework of unshakeable core values. All the heads:

- were clear in their vision for the school and communicated it to all the school's constituents;
- focused upon care and achievement simultaneously;
- created, maintained and constantly monitored relationships, recognizing them as key to the cultures of learning;

- were reflective in a variety of internal and external social and organizational contexts, using a variety of problem-solving approaches;
- sought, synthesized, and evaluated internal and external data, applying these to the school within their values framework;
- persisted with apparently intractable issues in their drive for higher standards;
- were prepared to take risks in order to achieve these;
- were not afraid to ask difficult questions of themselves and others;
- were entrepreneurial;
- were 'networkers' inside and outside the school;
- were not afraid to acknowledge failure but did not give up and learnt from it;
- were aware of a range of sources to help solve problems;
- managed ongoing tensions and dilemmas through principled, values-led contingency leadership.

A number of writers (Shakeshaft, 1996; Blackmore, (1989) have argued for a paradigm shift in conceptions of leadership, which start not from the basis of power and control but from the ability to act with others and to enable others to act. The heads in the study rarely used their personal rather than positional power to obtain the results they wanted. Yet at the core of their personal power resided a particular vision for the school shaped by a particular set of values. These effective principals saw themselves as the source of a vision for their institutions, working through their relationships with members of the school community. Centrally important in this model of leadership is the co-operation and alignment of others to the leaders' values and vision. The heads in the study communicated their personal vision and belief systems by direction, words, deeds and through a variety of symbolic gestures.

In short, the principals led both the cognitive and the affective lives of the school, combining structural (developing clear goals), political (building alliances) and educational leadership (professional development and teaching improvement) with symbolic leadership (presence, inspiration) and human 'principle-centred' leadership (demonstrating care and support) (Bolman and Deal, 1984; Covey, 1990). It was the human resource management that occupied most of their daily time and that created the most tensions and celebration. In this respect, their leadership approaches were heavily people-centred. Principals were both transactional – ensuring that systems were maintained and developed, targets were formulated and met and that their schools ran smoothly – and transformative – building on esteem, competence, autonomy and achievement, raising 'the level of human conduct and ethical aspiration of both the leader and the led' (Sergiovanni, 1992) and bonding 'by inspiring extraordinary commitment and performance' (Sergiovanni, 1992, pp. 25).

Contingency driven: managing tensions and dilemmas

What seemed to make the difference for the stakeholders was not only the persistence of vision and values with the simultaneous focus of the principals upon process and achievement (product), but also the principals' ability to manage a number of tensions and dilemmas that characterized the human imperfections in school contexts, which, like classrooms, were by their nature, dynamic, complex and unpredictable.

Use was made of two linked concepts – tensions and dilemmas – which are grounded in the data as 'lenses' (Berlak and Berlak, 1981) through which to focus in on leadership. The main distinction between tensions and dilemmas concerns the possibilities of choice and influence. The tensions identified tended to be those over which principals had little choice or influence. In the case of the dilemmas, possibilities of choice and influence did exist, but the degree to which the heads exercised such possibilities varied considerably. A dilemma, in this sense, is a situation that presents at least two contradictory propositions. Whichever is chosen will not be entirely satisfactory. Together these constructs of tensions and dilemmas capture the immediacy of the continuing conflicts faced by many of the heads in the study. They underscore the continuing dynamic between their core personal values, management functions and leadership demands. They capture their past, present and future pressures, challenges, and concerns and aspirations with which they are daily faced and that reflect the multifaceted demands of the role. Heads are constantly juggling competing demands upon their time, energy and resources.

The data revealed seven key tensions and three dilemmas of 'effective' principals, which focus upon their roles not only in maintaining and consolidating what they have already achieved, but also in managing the challenges associated with moving their individual schools forward. The tensions focus broadly on issues of leadership, personal time and professional tasks, personal and institutional values, maintaining presence, improving quality, developing staff, internal and external change, autocracy and autonomy, and leadership in small schools. They reflect the concerns of a group of principals who are primarily concerned with achieving success for the teachers and pupils in their schools, for whom improvement is a permanent part of their personal and professional agendas.

Leadership v. management

Leadership is essentially the process of building and maintaining a sense of vision, culture and interpersonal relationships, whereas management is the coordination, support and monitoring of organizational activities. To enact both roles successfully requires a careful balancing act.

> *Leadership is about having vision and articulating, ordering priorities, getting others to go with you, constantly reviewing what you are doing and holding on to things you value. Management is about the functions, procedures and systems by which you realize the vision.* (Infant school deputy)

Development v. maintenance

> *If I don't develop others, the school won't develop. So that's my priority. Other jobs can be delegated but not this one.* (Primary head)

There was a tension between the amount of time and energy devoted to system maintenance and that devoted to ensuring that staff were always more than competent and were challenged and supported actively in seeking higher standards.

Internal v. external change

The pressure is from outside, but I have to manage the pressure inside. (Secondary head)

The growth in external scrutiny of schools creates its own tensions. Principals found themselves positioned uneasily between those forces outside schools that were instigating and promoting changes and their own staff who, ultimately, had to implement them. They demonstrated their leadership by the selection of which initiatives to take on, the relative support which they provide for their implementation, their knowledge of how others were tackling new initiatives and by the ways they adapted initiatives to their particular values and circumstances.

Autocracy v. autonomy

Although we can work closely, there has to be a time when decisions are taken and she has to say whether we can or cannot do this. (Primary deputy)

In school cultures of collaboration in which decision making is no longer the exclusive preserve of principals, heads still remained responsible and accountable for the schools' success (or otherwise). A key leadership skill that these heads displayed was their ability to manage the boundaries of autocratic and democratic decision making.

Personal time v. professional tasks

I work at least 60 hours a week ... it worries me because I don't know how long I can go on putting in the amount of energy. (Primary head)

Increasing external requirements upon schools had led many heads to commit more and more of their personal time to school-related business. Although most heads in the study had found ways of managing the demands of intensification, the personal opportunity costs were universally high and, long term, potentially damaging.

Personal values v. institutional imperatives

He holds traditional human values – care for people and community and giving back to society the benefits of what you have been given at school. You are a better person if you achieve academically, but that is only part of being a balanced person. (Primary teacher)

Whilst there was little evidence in the study of opposing sets of values within the schools, tensions did arise from externally generated pressures of rationalism, as well as definitions of efficiency and effectiveness that were perceived as challenging strongly held people-centred values.

Leadership in small v. large schools

It's all the stress of planning and preparing and coordinating as a class teacher that is too much. (Primary head)

Heads in small primary schools were disadvantaged on two main counts. Because they had regular, significant class-teaching responsibilities, they were unable to fulfil their strategic leadership roles satisfactorily. The breadth of the curriculum that needed to be addressed also provided additional demands upon the small number of staff.

Development or dismissal?

You can support somebody who is incompetent for as long as you like, but there comes a point where you know that it is not going to make any difference, particularly if they have been doing it for a long time. (Infant head)

For principals who have to make decisions about teaching standards, continuing poor teaching by a member of staff creates a leadership dilemma, cutting across the principals' personal framework of values and beliefs, their ideological and educative commitments to the development of everyone in the school community. Engaging in dismissal procedures touches upon the culture of the school, staff morale, and the nature of the relationship between leader and led. The principals in the study, however, had not shrunk from taking such 'tough decisions', illustrating the clear if painful boundary that must be drawn at key times between the personal and professional relationships that are at the heart of the educational health of school communities.

Power with or power over?

We are leaders in our own little domain and sometimes it's hard to accept the overall leadership ... because you think you have got a better way of doing it. (Primary teacher)

The basis of this dilemma is the extent to which similar and dissimilar values can be reconciled. The principals in this study sought to achieve a balance between consulting and involving staff in their decisions whilst still providing a clear direction forward, but were aware that such involvement might well lead to demands for a bigger say in the direction and that this might well challenge their right always to make the final decision.

Sub-contracting or mediation?

At the end of the day the head has to have integrity and to stick to core values and beliefs. It is important that the head can demonstrate integrity in the face of adversity. (Infant head)

This final dilemma reflects the position of most heads in the study as they found themselves legally responsible for the implementation of externally imposed change, some of which challenged their own moral purposes, sets of core values and practices, and analysis of the needs of their particular school. The heads had not become 'sub-contractors' – unthinking links in a chain leading from those who developed policy to those who received it. Nor were they subversives, attempting to undermine the authority of policy imperatives. Rather, they managed changes with integrity and skill, integrating them into the vision, values and practices of their schools.

Reflection

It is not by chance that some principals are more effective than others, even when all are faced with the same demands and constraints. Effective principals have a better understanding of how the world of schooling and school leadership works. (Sergiovanni, 1995, p. 29)

It has long been argued that reflection is a necessary condition for teachers' learning (Grimmett and Erickson, 1998; Calderhead and Gates, 1993; Zeichner and Liston, 1996; Day, 1993). One of the forces that help or hinder teachers in this respect is the school culture; and chief among those who are recognized as exerting a powerful influence upon this is the principal. Because principals, like teachers, pass through particular development phases (Day and Bakioglu, 1996; Reeves, Mahoney and Moos, 1997), as 'leading learners' in the school community (Barth, 1990; Sergiovanni, 1992), they too must engage in reflective practices and revisit and review their own commitments, qualities and skills if they are to encourage others to do so. While much lip service is given to the value of reflection and reflective practice in training and development programmes, there remains a lack of clarity about which purposes and processes might be appropriate to principals who work in different contexts – who will have different value positions, personal histories and professional growth needs – and which will contribute most to improving practice.

There are few studies, also, that examine the relationship between reflection, critical thinking and principal effectiveness. Various writers have coined the terms reflection-in-action, reflection-on-action, reflection-about-action and reflection-for-action, which involve forward planning (Schon, 1983; Zeichner, 1993). Recently there have been critiques about the notion of reflection-in-action, which, it is claimed, is impossible in practice because there is insufficient time at a conscious level (Eraut, 1995). Reflection-on-action takes place when reviewing the action from outside its setting; reflection-about-action and reflection-for-action take place when reviewing the broader personal, social, economic and political contexts in which the action occurs or is likely to occur. These are often accompanied by a desire to achieve social justice, emancipation or improvement. However, different kinds of reflection are indicative of different views of what behaving as a professional means. They represent different values regarding the purposes and roles of principals.

The research data revealed a number of key characteristics by which the stakeholders recognized their principals' effectiveness. Underpinning these, either implicitly or explicitly, was their capacity to be reflective in different ways about:

- their values, beliefs and practices;
- the values, beliefs and practices of their staff;
- the position and progress of their schools in relation to others in local and national contexts;
- current and emerging policy matters that affected management and the curriculum;
- conditions of service for teachers in their schools.

The capacity to reflect in, on and about a broad range of contexts, and through this to form, sustain, review and renew an holistic view of the school, its needs and its direction was central to the principals' leadership. The data suggest further that hierarchical notions of reflective purposes and processes (Van Manen 1977; Carr and Kemmis, 1986; Handal, 1990; Hatton and Smith 1995) are less helpful to enhancing understanding and improving practice than those that argue for its application across a range of contexts and practices experienced by all effective professionals.

Evidence from and about each of the 12 principals in the study suggests that all engaged in at least five kinds of reflection:

- Holistic: focusing on vision and culture building.
- Pedagogical (on and in action): focusing on staff acquiring, applying and monitoring teaching that achieves results allied to their vision (which includes but is greater than the demands made by policy implementation imperatives).
- Interpersonal: focusing on knowing and nurturing staff, children, parents and governors.
- Strategic: focusing on entrepreneurship, intelligence gathering and networking to secure some control of the future.
- Intrapersonal: focusing on self-knowledge and self-development and fulfilment.

Holistic reflection

This kind of reflection meant maintaining an overview of the key purposes for the school:

Leadership is about getting across to the staff where we are now and where we are going. (Secondary head)

I think it's important for a head to have vision, to see the whole game. You have to be ahead of the rest and see the overall picture, otherwise you won't be able to manage effectively. (Primary head)

Leadership is about vision, having some idea of what the establishment will look like in the future. (Primary teacher)

To principals, vision meant 'being clear about the direction in which you are going', and, 'translating your beliefs into actions'. It was about, 'keeping the overview, the big picture'. Integrity, always associated with vision, meant, 'sticking to core values and beliefs' and having, 'a steadiness of purpose' in the face of rapid change. School ancillary staff, especially secretaries, arguably involved most intimately in all the work of the principal, described the principals variously as forward thinkers who seek 'the best way from experts, and seeks opinions' (school keeper/janitor). Parents and governors also recognized in the principals their 'ability to look ahead', to have their fingers 'on the pulse' and to engage in continuous development: 'He has an overview of everything ... He gets everyone ... to work to the common goal of higher standards'. Students spoke of principals' wisdom, and their willingness to listen and seek the best ways forward: 'She likes listening to children ... There is a "suggestion box" outside her office for sorting our problems' and 'He is a wise, knowledgeable leader – he would know what to do in a crisis'.

Teachers recognized that being a good leader was not only about caring for students, staff and the community but also about vision, 'having some idea of what the establishment will look like in the future'. The voices of deputy principals, at the heart of the management and leadership of the school and among the most experienced of its teachers, echoed those of other stakeholders. Like them, they highlighted the need for vision, but recognized the elements essential to its maintenance:

> *Leadership is about ... constantly reviewing what you are doing and holding on to things you value. [Management is about the functions, procedures and systems by which you real-ize the vision. (Primary deputy)]*

> *The Head has to keep an overall view of what is happening in the school. He is always monitoring progress and keeping a check on things. He has to keep his finger on the pulse.* (Secondary deputy)

Pedagogical reflection

This kind of reflection related to the leaders' role as standard bearers for high-quality teaching and learning. The teachers articulated most clearly the key role played by the principals in their maintenance of high standards of teaching and learning as they 'look to the future, recognizing strengths and building on them ... identifying weaknesses and remedying them'. Principals themselves all spoke of the need to 'be the front person of the organization', 'motivate, support and appreciate' staff and others, 'provide feedback on a daily basis', 'patrol the bound-aries' (between school and the local and policy communities), 'make sure that every child gets a fair chance' and 'be true to oneself', indicating their commit-ment to a range of reflective practice, in order 'to be prepared continuously to think how to do the job better'. Standards meant 'good quality of life for all the people in the school, so that the people who work here are contented in what they are doing, feel valued and can meet expectations'.

Interpersonal reflection

Reflection was also about knowing, understanding and interacting empathetically with the staff and students: 'She seems to know all about us and is always there to talk if we need to .. She pushes staff forward and encourages them to go on to bigger and better things'. It was the values and actions that went alongside such knowledge which really made a difference to teachers: 'She wraps her arms around the school and ... is someone who knows how the lifeblood of the school ebbs and flows'.

This recognition of and caring for the emotional well-being of staff and students was a key characteristic of the principals:

> *To him everyone is valued because he believes that if all have a sense of their own self-worth they will do their best.* (Primary teacher)

> *The Head makes staff feel valued and worthwhile and trusted to get on with the job. He knows when to leave people alone and what they need.* (Primary teacher)

> *The door is always open. You can come and talk about anything in your life ... a concern with your family or ... a problem in the classroom or ... someone's parent ... He has time for you.* (Secondary teacher)

> *A shoulder to cry on and a sound friend and guide ... just a good human being.* (Secondary teacher)

Principals were constantly assessing their staff's strengths and weaknesses: 'You can only make the right decisions if you know your staff personally ... I talk to a lot of pupils individually ... I walk around the school ... still try to build up personal knowledge of staff.' As a result, principals recognized the importance to school effectiveness and improvement of educating the staff and maintaining morale: 'Teachers must sparkle, for the good of the children'. 'They need new knowledge ... a sense of direction and opportunities to do what they want to do ... it is important to maintain their own sense of self-worth.'

Strategic reflection

All the principals were clear about the need to 'run ahead of the game', to 'look at other schools' and 'listen to colleagues from across the county':

> *Outwards looking in is often better than sitting in and not looking out.* (Secondary head)

> *A head has to have the ability to analyse problems and work out solutions ... To do this he has to be intellectually capable of thinking and making judgements on his feet.* (Secondary head)

> *I'm somebody who will look at other schools ... and listen to colleagues from across the country ... There is a cross-fertilization all the time of ideas.* (Primary head)

> *I enjoy getting the bigger picture ... you pick up what's going on.* (Primary head)

> *I think part of the role of a head is ... to network, network, network.* (Primary head)

> *You're looking at government papers, you're reading, talking, listening to other people ... you're looking back into your own school and thinking, 'Will that work?' Or 'Isn't that a good idea?' Or 'Thank God I don't do it that way'.* (Primary head)

Deputy principals, like others, saw the 'networking' role as a means of reflection on current and future practice and direction: 'He uses the local network of head-teachers as a source of information and as a means of filtering out what should be brought into the schools'. A classroom assistant also recognized that the principal was 'good at pushing for things. ... he's kept the school on the right track'.

A knowledge of macro, meso, and micro-contexts and an ability to connect these into an holistic view was, then, clearly perceived as a keystone of good leadership: 'The Head is very good at seeing the school as a whole rather than as little bits of interaction. She has a good overview of the organization and knows how to get the most from everyone here.' Students also recognized their strategic capacities. They were, 'like detectives, always on the case, sniffing out trouble and finding out the evidence ... Always wants to get to the bottom to it'. Critical judgement, having 'the ability to analyse problems and work out solutions ... to be intellectually capable of thinking and making judgements' and 'knowing what I think is good for the school and being able to discard what I think is not' were all associated with the ability to be strategic.

Intrapersonal reflection

Here the focus was upon self as lifelong learner. Although they were at different stages of their careers, of different ages and experiences and in very different settings – ranging from small rural primary schools to suburban and large inner city primary and secondary schools – all the principals associated leading with learning: 'I like the idea of being the leader of learning – children now have a range of opportunities in the world and I have the chance to provide them with more … I want them to be excited by the possibilities open to them when they leave'. Some principals had enrolled for a higher degree, 'because I cannot persuade staff to invest in their own professional development unless I invest in mine'. Others were members of informal networks of peers who met regularly to exchange information, while others were part of more formal networks that organized their own professional development programmes. Such active involvement in their own development enabled them to maintain their integrity of purpose.

All those interviewed had observed the long hours that all the principals spent in fulfilling the range of roles, responsibilities and commitments of their work, and the inevitable tensions and personal and professional stress that were associated. Almost all the principals had confronted these difficulties and had found ways of maintaining their mental, emotional and physical health. Some were part of peer support groups: 'We take turns in discussing issues'. Some used stress management strategies learnt from in-service courses, and others had regular support from family and friends.

The principals in this study all belonged to peer partnerships and networks. The problems in pursuing reflective practice on one's own have been well documented in research on the 'busyness' of classrooms and schools, the pressures caused by increased bureaucracy associated with new forms of accountability, and the difficulties of self-confrontation that challenge beliefs and practices that have become valued routines and may lead to potentially uncomfortable and temporarily disruptive change processes (Day, 1993). These, and school cultures that often discourage disclosure, feedback and collaboration, act as potential barriers to the kinds of participation in all forms of reflective practice previously identified. The problem with reflecting alone is that there is a limit to what can be disclosed and what information can be collected and received by an individual with a 'vested' interest in avoiding uncomfortable change processes. Others are necessary at some points in the process. Peer partnerships and networks – discussions and dialogues between practitioners with common purposes – are needed to move from routine to reflective practice in schools. A comment from one of the principals serves to summarize the feelings expressed by all about their work:

> Over the years, enthusiasm seems to grow rather than wane. The pace of life within the school has increased 100 per cent, but you learn to live with the pace … Where we are now is in a position where we are striving to be better than yesterday.

Discussion

Critical thinking: central to the head and heart of leadership

Teachers' work in many countries is increasingly being directed by closely monitored government policy initiatives, suggesting that only 'technical' reflection – a relatively simple form of practice-evaluation – is necessary. The evidence from this research suggests, however, that effective principals are those who move beyond this limited notion and encourage their teachers to do the same. They exercise 'metacompetencies' such as self-management, self-evaluation, learning from experience and 'juggling' (Glatter, 1996). Successful principals in this research saw themselves and their teachers as having a responsibility for the education of students that went beyond the instrumental, encompassing responsibilities to educate for citizenship and to imbue in their students a positive disposition towards lifelong learning.

Although it is claimed that reflection is central to leadership training in England, this is so only in the general sense that there are tasks on which principals are asked to reflect, for example, their strategic approaches to management. Sadly, there are as yet few structured opportunities for them to engage in a critique of practice, the values that were implicit in that practice, the personal, social, institutional and broad policy contexts in which practice takes place, and the implications of these for improvement of that practice. It is about the past, in the present and for the future; it is about 'problem posing' as well as 'problem solving' (Mezirow, 1991, p. 105); and it is essential for building and maintaining principals' capacity to provide effective leadership for all in schools whose work is focused upon the care and development of all children, young people and adults in changing circumstances. In the research reported, reflective principals were able to distance themselves from the worlds in which they were everyday participants and open themselves to influence by others, while at the same time being present and proactive in those worlds. They engaged in reflection in, on, about and for the action in each context in which they worked. Reflection upon practice, then, was not related to hierarchical levels identified by Handal (1990), Van Manen (1977) and Carr and Kemmis (1986). Rather, the data from this research demonstrate that such technical, practical and emancipatory forms of reflection are interactive and that effective principals use each differentially according to circumstance and purpose.

Effective leadership is as much about developing the self as it is about capacity building in others. Such effective leadership requires an intelligent head and an intelligent heart. Effective principals are, in fact, critical thinkers who have developed an awareness of the assumptions under which they and others think and behave. They are sceptical of 'quick fix' solutions to problems:

> *When we think critically, we ... refuse to relinquish the responsibility for making the choices that determine our individual and collective futures ... We become actively engaged in creating our personal and social worlds ... We take the reality of democracy seriously.* (Brookfield, 1987, pp. ix–x)

However, such critical thinking is underpinned by a recognition of the power of the heart as well as the head in influencing beliefs and practices. The ability to recognize emotions in others, handling relationships, managing emotions and knowing one's own emotions has been defined as, 'emotional intelligence' (Goleman, 1995) which is fundamental to effective leadership.

Traditional leadership theory, while useful, cannot apply in 'non-linear' conditions in which 'every decision that is made in response to conditions at the base time (time 1) changes these conditions in such a way that successive decisions also made at time 1 no longer fit'. (Sergiovanni, 1995, p. 42). The data confirmed that these principals' responses to the increasing complexity and intensity of their lives caused by imposed reform had been to use their capacities for reflection in a variety of real and imagined circumstances. We found that these principals were reflective and reflexive in a range of contexts, and that:

- reflection was integral to their success;
- the core informing concepts for reflection were their personal and educative values, which were closely linked 'Christian, humanistic';
- they reflected simultaneously in, on, about and for their own work and that of their staff and students, in different contexts interactively;
- reflection was always also for the purpose of self-development (they were lifelong learners) as well as for the good of the school;
- reflection combined the cognitive and emotional.

Principals asserted their own agency and that of their staff through their core values of 'fairness', 'equity' and 'equality of opportunity' for students and staff – the kinds of 'dialectic' reflection associated by some with their broader educative responsibilities:

> If they are not to be mere agents of others, of the state, of the military, of the media, of the experts and bureaucrats, they need to determine their own agency through a critical and continual evaluation of the purposes, the consequences and the social context of their calling'.
> (Zeichner and Liston, 1996, p. 11)

Such agency requires both principals and teachers to be 'knowledgeable, experienced, thoughtful, committed and energetic workers' (Devaney and Sykes, 1988, p. 20). It follows that in order to maintain capacity, principals need regular opportunities to exercise discretionary judgement, reflect upon their moral and social purposes, work collaboratively with colleagues in and outside school, engage in a self-directed search, and struggle for continuous learning related to their own needs for growth of expertise and maintenance of standards of practice as well as those of the school. They need to move beyond experience and intuition:

> In the actual world of schooling, the task of the principal is to make sense of messy situations by increasing understanding and discovering and communicating meanings. Situations of practice are typically characterized by unique events; therefore, uniform answers to problems are not likely to be helpful ... Intuition becomes necessary to fill in the gaps of what can be specified as known and what cannot. Yet, ordinary intuition will not do. Intuition must be informed by theoretical knowledge on the one hand and adept understandings of the situation on the other. (Sergiovanni, 1995, pp. 31–2)

Many principals (and teachers) still rely mainly upon experience and intuition – with all the limitations to change which these contain – to guide them through their careers.

If they are to take the business of reflective practice seriously, then 'good' and 'effective' principals need to exercise informed choice concerning the kinds and purposes of reflection necessary to challenge and support their professionalism at different times in their career histories, and the processes that will enable them to engage in them most effectively. Inevitably that choice itself will be constrained by prejudice, perception, experience and the challenges of changing policy contexts. While the awareness of such constraints will itself enhance capacities for reflection and change, to be and behave as a professional over a career span requires principals to engage in a range of reflective practices and translate these into action.

Whether most principals engage in systematic reflection that contributes to their development and capacity to improve the quality of learning opportunities for students remains an open question. Processes of reflection that combine the deliberative with the emotional seem still to be the exception rather than the rule. Yet the evidence suggests that if principals are to become and remain effective they need to nurture their critical thinking and emotional health through reflection. To continue to practise successfully requires them constantly to test what they know against what is happening as they negotiate the 'permanent white water' of their leadership journeys (Vaill, 1989). Even within the intensity and busyness of working lives there are choices to be made.

There are no easy or perfect answers. The worlds of schools, like those of classrooms, hold too many variables and few neat solutions. The concepts are useful because they reveal that effective leaders are not always successful at all times with all people and that a key characteristic is their determination and ability to continue to try to reconcile the irreconcilable.

3

Training and development

The characteristics of successful leaders and their ability to be simultaneously people-centred whilst managing a number of tensions and dilemmas highlight the complexity of the kinds of values-led contingency leadership exercised by successful principals. The study illustrates that there are no neat solutions to situations that hold within them so many variables; rather, successful leadership is defined and driven by individual and collective value systems rather than instrumental, bureaucratic, managerial concerns. Leaders were identified as being reflective, caring and highly principled people who emphasized the human dimension of the management enterprise. They placed a high premium upon personal values and were concerned more with cultural than structural change. They had all moved beyond a narrow rational, managerial view of their role to a more holistic, values-led approach guided by personal experience and preference. What, then, are the implications for the leadership training and development of aspiring and serving school leaders? Nations across the world are extending their provision of training and development programmes. In England, the establishment of such programmes for aspiring and serving principals as HEADLAMP, NPQH and LPSH provide a testimony of the importance attached by government to effective leadership, and this has been further underlined by the establishment of a high profile, innovative National College for School Leadership.

However, even the most recent training programmes fail to address the key themes that have emerged from this and other school-focused empirical research. Since values, it seems, are central to successful leadership, reflection in, on and upon these must be central to training. Alongside this must be a focus upon critical thinking – emotional and cognitive (echoing Barth's wise dictum that heads must be the 'leading learners' in their schools), and intra as well as interpersonal skill development. Recognition of the intimate link in successful leadership between the personal and the professional, between the development of the individual and the context of the organization is paramount. Finally, problem solving and the management of 'competing forces' must be key components of leadership training for school improvement if schools are to become the high-achieving learning communities espoused by government. The seven tensions and three dilemmas presented earlier highlight the complex and fraught nature of headship. They illustrate that effective heads, like others, must manage these while engaging in the central tasks of building cultures and promoting learning and achievement. Indeed, they are an inherent part of the contexts in which these occur.

Within governments' overall strategic vision for education, in all countries the training, reskilling and certification of heads rightly occupies a central place. The problem is that many of the training models focus upon managerial rather than leadership functions. In doing so they fail to build capacities of heads to reflect upon their own values and those of the whole school community and do not provide sufficient emphasis upon building the range of interpersonal qualities and skills necessary and appropriate to effective leadership. For governments' rhetoric of lifelong learning, high teaching standards, pupil achievement and school improvement to become a reality, schools need to be led by principals who are not only knowledgeable and skilled in managerial techniques but also, like those in this study, people-centred leaders who are able to combine the management of internal and external change with a strong reflective development and achievement orientation.

If schools are to become 'knowledge creating' in which 'the knowledge of all the school's members and partners is recognised' and shared (Hargreaves, 1998, p. 29), and if teachers are to continue to be committed to making a difference in the learning lives of their students through skilful teaching combined with the ethics of 'care, justice and inclusiveness' (Hargreaves and Fullan, 1998, p. 35), then effective principals may themselves be justifiably expected to demonstrate these qualities through the kinds of leadership that they exercise.

Power and politics will continue to provide the context and daily realities for life in all schools. It is the management of the tensions and dilemmas created by these that, within a strong values framework, is a distinguishing feature of effective leaders whose persistent focus is upon the betterment of the young people and staff who work in their schools, and who themselves remain, often against all the odds, enthusiastic and committed to learning.

NOTE

1   The data used in this chapter are drawn from a research project on effective school leaders, commissioned by the National Association of Headteachers (NAHT).

REFERENCES

Barth, R. (1990) *Improving Schools from Within: Teachers, Parents and Principals Can Make a Difference*, San Francisco: Jossey-Bass.

Berlak, H. and Berlak, A. (1981) *Dilemmas of Schooling: Teaching and Social Change*, London: Methuen

Blackmore, J. (1989) 'Educational leadership : a feminist critique and reconstruction' in Smyth, J. (ed.) *Critical Perspectives on Educational Leadership*, London: Falmer Press.

Blase, J. and Anderson, G. (1995) *The Micropolitics of Educational Leadership*, London: Cassell.

Bolman, L.G. and Deal, T.E. (1984) *Modern Approaches to Understanding and Managing Organisations*, San Francisco: Jossey-Bass.

Brookfield, S. (1987) *Developing Critical Thinkers: Challenging Adults to Explore Alternative Ways of Thinking and Acting*. New York: Teachers' College Press.

Burns, J.M. (1978) *Leadership*, New York: Harper & Row.

Calderhead, J. and Gates P. (eds) (1993) *Conceptualizing Reflection in Teacher Development*, London: Falmer Press.

Carr, W. and Kemmis, S. (1986) *Becoming Critical: Knowing through Action Research*, London: Falmer Press.

Covey, S.R. (1990) *Principle-Centred Leadership*, New York: Summit Books.

Day, C. (1993) 'Reflection: a necessary but not sufficient condition for professional development', *British Educational Research Journal*, 19 (1) pp. 83–93.

Day, C. and Bakioglu, A. (1996) 'Development and disenchantment in the professional lives of headteachers' in Goodson, I. F. and Hargreaves, A. (eds) *Teachers' Professional Lives* London: Falmer Press.

Day, C., Hadfield, M., Harris, A., Tolley, H. and Beresford, J. (2000) *Leading Schools in Times of Change*, Buckingham: Open University Press.

Devaney, K. and Sykes, G. (1988) 'Making the case for professionalism' in Lieberman, A. (ed.) *Building a Professional Culture In Schools*, New York: Teachers' College Press.

Duignan, P. A. and Macpherson, R. J. S. (1992) *Educative Leadership: A Practical Theory for New Administrators and Managers*, London: Falmer Press

Eraut, M. (1995) 'Schon shock: a case for reframing reflection-in-action?', *Teachers and Teaching: Theory and Practice*, 1 (1), pp. 9–22.

Fullan, M.G. (1992) *Successful School Improvement*, Buckingham: Open University Press.

Glatter, R. (1996) 'The NPQH: where is juggling?', *Management in Education*, 10 (5) pp. 27–8.

Glatter, R. (1998) 'Clashing images from abroad,' *Education Journal*, 23 (May), pp. 34–5.

Goleman, D. (1995) *Emotional Intelligence*, New York: Bantam Books.

Grimmett, P.P. and Erickson, G.L. (eds) (1998) *Reflection in Teacher Education*, New York: Teachers' College Press.

Gunter, H. (1997) *Rethinking Education: The Consequences of Jurassic Management*, London: Cassell.

Guskey, T.R. and Huberman, M. (eds) (1995) *Professional Development in Education: New Paradigms and Practices*, New York: Teachers' College Press.

Handal, G. (1990) 'Promoting the articulation of tacit knowledge through the counselling of practitioners', keynote paper at Amsterdam Pedalogisch Centrum Conference, Amsterdam, Holland, 6–8 April.

Hargreaves, A. (1992) 'Cultures of teaching' in Fullan, M.G. and Hargreaves, A. *Understanding Teacher Development*, London: Cassell.

Hargreaves, A. and Fullan, M. (1998) *What's Worth Fighting for Out There*, New York: Teachers' College Press.

Hargreaves, A. and Goodson, I.F. (1996) 'Teachers' professional lives: aspirations and actualities' in Goodson, I. F. and Hargreaves, A. (eds) *Teachers' Professional Lives*, London: Falmer Press.

Hargreaves, D. (1998) *Creative Professionalism: The Role of Teachers in the Knowledge Society*, London: Demos

Hatton, N. and Smith, D. (1995) 'Facilitating reflection: issues and research', *Forum of Education*, 50 (1), April 1995, pp. 49–65.

Helsby, G., Knight, P., McCulloch, G., Saunders, M. and Warburton, T. (1997) 'Professionalism in crisis', a report to participants on the Professional Cultures of Teachers Research Project, Lancaster University, January.

Hoyle, E. (1980) 'Professionalization and de-professionalisation in education' in Hoyle, E. and Megarry, J. (eds) *World Yearbook of Education 1980: The Professional Development of Teachers*, London: Kogan Page.

Jackson, P.W., Boostrom, R.E. and Hansen, D.T. (1993) *The Moral Life of Schools*, San Francisco: Jossey-Bass.

Leithwood, K. and Jantzi, D. (1990) 'Transformational leadership: how principals can help reform cultures', *School Effectiveness and School Improvement*, 1 (4) pp. 249–80.

Leithwood, K., Jantzi, D. and Steinbach, R. (1999) *Changing Leadership for Changing Times*, Buckingham: Open University Press.

Lieberman, A. and Miller, L. (1992) *Teachers – Their World and Their Work: Implications for School Improvement*, New York: Teachers' College Press.

Louis, K. and Miles, M. B. (1990) *Improving the Urban High School: What Works and Why*, New York: Teachers' College Press.

MacBeath, J. (ed.) (1998) *Effective School Leadership*, London: Paul Chapman Publishing.

Mezirow, J. (1991). *Transformative Dimensions of Adult Learning*, San Francisco: Jossey-Bass.

Mintzberg, H. (1994) *The Rise and Fall of Strategic Planning*, New York: Free Press

Morris, B. and Reeves, J. (2000) 'Implementing a national qualification for headship in Scotland: (a) critical reflection', *Journal of In-Service Education*, 26 (3).

Noddings, N. (1992) *The Challenge to Care in Schools*, New York: Teachers' College Press.

Pollard, A., Broadfoot, P., Croll, P., Osborn, M. and Abbot, D. (1994) *Changing English Primary Schools? The Impact of the Educational Reform Act at Key Stage One*, London: Cassell.

3

Reeves, J., Mahoney, P. and Moos, L. (1997) 'Headship: issues of career', *Teacher Development*, 1 (1) pp. 43–56.

Rosenholtz, S. (1989) *Teachers' Workplace: The Social Organisation of Schools*, New York: Longman.

Sachs, J. (2000) 'Rethinking the practice of teacher professionalism' in Day, C., Moller, J., Hauge, T. and Fernandez, A. (eds) *The Life and Work of Teachers in Changing Times: International Perspectives*, London: Falmer Press.

Schon, D.A. (1983) *The Reflective Practitioner: How Professionals Think in Action*, New York: Basic Books.

Senge, P. (1990) *The Fifth Discipline*, New York: Doubleday.

Sergiovanni, T.J. (1992) *Moral Leadership: Getting to the Heart of School Improvement*, San Francisco: Jossey-Bass.

Sergiovanni, T.J. (1995) *The Principalship: a Reflective Practice Perspective*, Boston: Allyn & Bacon.

Shakeshaft, C. (1996) *Women in Educational Administration*, Newbury Park: Unwin.

Slee, R., Weiner, G. and Tomlinson, S. (1998) *School Effectiveness for Whom?* London: Falmer Press.

Starratt, R. (1991) 'Building an ethical school; a theory for practice in educational leadership', *Educational Administration Quarterly*, 27 (2), pp. 153–78.

Stoll, L. and Fink, D. (1996) *Changing Our Schools: Linking School Effectiveness and School Improvement*, Buckingham: Open University Press.

Tampoe, M. (1998) *Liberating Leadership: Releasing Leadership Potential throughout the Organisation*, London: The Industrial Society.

Tom, A. (1984) *Teaching as a Moral Craft*, New York: Longman.

Vaill, P.B. (1989) *Managing as a Performing Art*, San Francisco: Jossey-Bass.

Van Manen, M. (1977) 'Linking ways of knowing to ways of being practical', *Curriculum Inquiry*, 6 (3) pp. 205–28.

Zeichner, K.M. (1993). 'Action research: personal renewal and social reconstruction', *Educational Action Research*, 1 (2) pp. 199–220.

Zeichner, K.M. and Liston D.P. (1996) *Reflective Teaching: An Introduction*, New Jersey: Lawrence Erlbaum Associates.

CHAPTER 20

Education policy and the initial education of teachers

PETER GILROY

Publications on research methodology tend to have at least one part where a case study drawn from real life is presented to substantiate the more general points made in the volume. The approach here is similar: first, presenting a number of significant policy changes affecting initial teacher education in England[1] and, second, arguing that these have been implemented in such a way as to marginalize those who might have taken a leading role in managing such change. The chapter concludes by pointing up the managerialist dilemma that has neatly and effectively rendered impotent those who once thought they had some measure of control over their profession of teacher education.

As with any case study, the conclusions to be drawn tend to be specific to the context that gives that case study its life. Consequently, the specific English initial teacher education context requires some explanation so that the impact of specific policy issues can be better understood. It should also be noted that, given the difficulties in recruiting teachers into the profession in other countries, and because government policy is inevitably driven by such concerns, then those fortunate enough not to be part of the context described below should be prepared for similar radical policy changes in the context that they currently take for granted (see Edwards, Gilroy and Hartley, 2002).

In brief, prior to 1984 students wishing to qualify as school teachers had only two main routes into the profession: they had to undergo a three or four-year undergraduate course or, if they already possessed a degree, a one-year postgraduate course in an institute of higher education. These institutions organized and validated their own programmes and their quality was checked by external examiners. Through a process described below, the situation that currently exists is one where there are now numerous routes into the profession, including those that do not require any contact at all with institutions of higher education; these institutions do not have control of the teacher education curriculum and the quality of their delivery of that curriculum is checked by a central government body. A major policy shift has occurred – one that began when the Labour Party was in power, was accelerated when the Conservative Party came into office, and has continued under their successors, the government of New Labour. This policy shift is identified in more detail below, followed by an examination of how, if at all, those professionally involved with teacher education can contribute to these policy changes.

The policy background

For those fortunate enough not to have been involved in the blizzard of change that has swept through English teacher education over the last decade, the situation that England's university teacher educators now find themselves in requires a little explanation. Those who have experienced these changes will need no reminding of their nature or import and will probably be happy enough to pass over this section as speedily as possible.

Up until 1984 university departments of education (UDEs) had virtual autonomy over the processes of teacher education that they saw fit to adopt. Over a period of approximately 150 years they had been given the lead role in moving the training of teachers from a crude system of learning on the job (as identified by the 1861 Newcastle Commission) to one where new entrants to the profession were graduates and courses had been approved by UDEs. Indeed, between 1947 and 1984 universities were responsible for 'all aspects of courses for the initial training of teachers' (Gosden, 1989, p. 2), the responsibility for the accreditation of such courses having been devolved to individual universities.

1984 saw the creation of the Council for the Accreditation of Teacher Education (CATE). This body advised the Minister for Education regarding whether courses could be approved or not, and so marked one of the first steps in the road to central control of teacher education programmes. Two further markers of this shift in the locus of control can be seen in the fact that CATE would inspect what had been autonomous university education departments and that the members of CATE were appointed by the minister (unlike, for example, members of the Law Society who regulate their own profession).

In 1992 the then Conservative government Secretary of State for Education gave a speech to the North of England Education Conference in which he made it clear that he would use his new powers to locate the majority of initial teacher education in schools, with resources being shifted from UDEs to the schools. It was acknowledged that 'the new plan for teacher training was finalised in the teeth of opposition from civil servants' (*TES*, 1991).

1994 saw CATE being replaced by the Teacher Training Agency (TTA). Its then chief executive was violently opposed to UDEs' work, stating publicly that 'initial teacher education is not an academic study; and therefore (not) an intrinsic part of higher education' (*THES*, 1997). An equally aggressive head of the inspection body, the Office for Standards in Education (OFSTED), found his responsibilities for school inspection expanded to include the inspection of initial teacher education courses. This inspection process graded courses on a complex set of scales, which required universities to follow the standards for teacher education courses laid down by central government.

Thus within a decade UDEs had lost the autonomy they once exercised over courses of initial teacher education. Managers of UDEs found themselves caught up in a rigorously directed system of central control laid out by the Minister for Education through the TTA and policed by OFSTED. This represents a situation where 'managing' had been redefined to mean 'implementing government policy', passively and submissively, and where to step out of line (by refusing to implement that policy as it affected the teacher education curriculum) guaranteed a negative OFSTED result, a concomitant loss of income and even the closure of courses. To use OFSTED's own terminology, initial teacher educators had to be 'compliant'.

Policy and the professionals

One way in which policy can be changed, in a democracy at least, is to change the government that is devising and implementing policy. In May 1997 the general election ushered in New Labour as the party of government. Those concerned with teacher education saw this election victory as 'heralding a new era of recognition and partnership between the politicians who decree the policies and the professionals who have to implement them' (Mortimore and Mortimore, 1998, p. 205). However, it soon became clear that the previous government's policy of central control of teacher education would not merely continue as before, but would be extended beyond initial teacher education to in-service education and even educational research. Thus all three aspects of an education department's work could be taken out of the hands of professionals and given over to the policy makers (for details of these developments see Gilroy, 1998, and Furlong *et al.*, 2000, p. 162).

One common element in the development of initial teacher education policy over the last decade has been what Professor Pring of the University of Oxford referred to as a 'sense of powerlessness' felt by those in teacher education (Gilroy, 1992, p. 12), in that their professional opinions on these changes were neither asked for nor heard. The frustration was especially felt by the Universities Council for the Education of Teachers (UCET),[2] which describes itself as a body that 'acts as a national forum for the discussion of matters relating to the education of teachers and … contributes to the formulation of policy in these fields' (www.ucet.ac.uk). Given this remit it was particularly galling to have no apparent voice in any national forum, nor to be contributing to policy changes affecting teacher education. As the academic secretary of UCET pointed out:

> Our weakness has been, though, the assumption of everybody who is involved with UCET… that rational arguments will win the day and when they don't come off we've been a bit stymied. This has not been the way the government has worked even in the past, and probably less and less so now. (Gilroy, Russell and Stones, 1995, pp. 129–30)

Thus when UCET wrote in 1992 to the Conservative Minister for Education, pointing out the many practical difficulties inherent in his proposals for radical change to initial teacher education, 'there was no response' (ibid., p. 133).

However, UCET has come to acknowledge that it has to become more proactive in defending the interests of its members against many elements of what became the 1994 Education Act. It is clear that UCET has taken to heart much that it had experienced in the late 1980s and has learned to go beyond a reliance on pure rationality, so as to work at a 'political level' in producing briefing papers for all involved with teacher education, including the media and politicians (ibid., pp. 136–7). It is recognized that working at this level requires in particular UCET:

- to contribute to the TTA's policy and practice;
- to ensure that teacher associations are aware of the points the UCET wishes to make about developments in initial teacher education;
- to keep Universities UK (previously the committee of vice-chancellors and principals) aware of developments in teacher education and their impact on universities;
- to inform the government and media of UCET's position on policy developments on a regular basis;
- to brief individual politicians of all parties more deliberately than in the past.

In this way the relationship UCET once had with the government, where UCET was seen perhaps as 'something that could be just rolled over' (ibid., p. 139) might well change.

Policy, paradigms and problems

Let us jump forward to 2001. We will have set aside significant policy changes, such as the way in which the TTA took over the funding and organization of in-service education, creating chaos as it did so (Gilroy 1998, pp. 225ff), or the sudden introduction of skills tests into programmes of initial teacher education in England (Hextall, Mahoney and Mentor, 2001). The academic year 2001–2 saw a raft of policy developments in initial teacher education; three of the key changes affecting education departments were:

- the application of the results of the recent review of the OFSTED inspection framework for initial teacher education;
- the continued expansion of the graduate teacher programme (GTP) route into the profession, which allows the student to enter the profession with little or no contact with a university education department;
- the eventual results of the pilots of the programme whereby undergraduates reading for their degree might, at the same time as reading for their under-graduate degree, acquire 'teacher education' credits.

How can teacher education professionals contribute to the 'formulation of policy' in these three areas? The blunt answer to this is that, except in cosmetic ways, they cannot.

With regard to the first development, it has to be recognized that there has been a much more thorough canvassing of opinion as to how OFSTED inspections might be reformed so as properly to identify and nurture quality in initial teacher education, with those opinions often being reflected in subsequent documenta-tion. However, the fundamental problems with OFSTED inspections have not been addressed not least their seriously flawed nature (where a problem with one ele-ment of a course can create a situation whereby the whole course is penalized – see Furlong *et al.*, 2000, p. 148), and the way in which they impact almost immedi-ately on the funding education departments receive.

The second development allows schools to recruit and train graduates into the profession (for details see www.canteach.gov.uk/info/grtp/salary_grant.htm). This route is currently being expanded and, although there have been a number of problems identified with it by teacher educators – especially issues concerning quality – these points have been ignored. However, the Scottish General Teaching Council has so far refused to accept that graduates from the GTP have qualified teacher status, on the grounds that they do not have sufficient subject knowledge. The English General Teaching Council has yet to address this issue.

The third development is still at the pilot stage, with the results of the pilot yet to be reported on. There are of course obvious implications of such an alternative route into the profession for university education departments, perhaps the most significant being the effect on their one-year postgraduate certificate in education

(PGCE) courses' structure and funding. Students who have already acquired some elements of a PGCE will be less than pleased at repeating elements of a course that they already have covered, with the added complication that universities may perhaps have to reduce the fees they charge to such students.

Furlong *et al.* (2000, p. 7) cite Bowe and Ball's useful distinction between three policy contexts – influence, text production (such as policy documents) and practice – and they develop the third context in considerable detail. Yet if we examine policy developments in initial teacher education from 1984 until the present we are left with the bleak realization that teacher educators have had little or no substantive influence on any of these three policy contexts.

Despite significant changes of personnel in the government, the TTA, OFSTED and, indeed, university education departments themselves, which have made two-way communication between the centre and UDEs much easier, there remains the problem that considered and expert views on policy changes are still being ignored. The three developments outlined above show that, although there has been a 'social lubrication' of the channels of communication, it is still difficult for UDEs' considered and expert views on policy changes to impact significantly on those changes at either the level of policy or its practical implementation. The revision of OFSTED remains largely cosmetic and the GTP route (or for that matter any of the plethora of alternative employment-based routes that currently exist – see www.canteach.gov.uk/teaching/routes/index.htm) into the teaching profession has yet to be subject to any meaningful review. The third development remains at the pilot stage, and it will be interesting to see how a review of that pilot feeds through to policy.

Despite attempts to influence policy, as indicated in the strategy laid out by UCET, there are two overriding considerations that steamroller any pressure that teacher educators might try to exert on policy makers. The first is the obvious fact that English teacher educators, like educators in general, operate in a context where 'centralization' is extreme (Bottery, 2000, p. 55). Consequently, voices that oppose a policy of the centralization of initial teacher education are unlikely to be heard, because they represent and are based upon an alternative policy paradigm that is simply not recognized by policy makers. That is, the centralist paradigm that underpins and justifies the actions of policy makers filters out any alternative paradigm. What is required is a fundamental shift in the current dominant policy paradigm, one that is deeply rooted and unlikely easily to occur, if only because what counts as 'rational' policy is determined by the dominant paradigm. In effect, the very act of voicing a non-centralist policy alternative can result in destroying the arguments being put forward. There is a vicious relativity of rationality in operation, made the more effective because it is apparently unrecognized by both parties.

Second, there is the overriding practical imperative of teacher supply. It is one thing to criticize teacher educators and their departments on ideological grounds, as seemed to be the case in the early 1980s (e.g. O'Hear, 1988, p. 23). However, given the debilitating shortages in teacher supply, it became necessary to introduce a number of alternative routes into the profession to complement the undergraduate and postgraduate routes that exist and that currently produce more than 95 per cent of new teachers. To criticize such routes, on the grounds of their suspect quality and dubious value for money for example, appears to ignore the overriding necessity of resolving the growing crisis in teacher supply. It is this political and practical necessity that drives the policy makers to find alternative routes into the teaching profession and means that counter-arguments about the quality of such alternatives inevitably go unheard.

Conclusion

The combination of these two factors, the centralist policy paradigm and the under-recruitment of teachers to the profession, have in part created the situation in which teacher educators in England find themselves today. The possibility that the one might have had some effect on the other – that removing autonomy and trust from professionals might affect recruitment into that profession – does not seem to have occurred to those driving forward the government's teacher education policy. It is perhaps the continued failure of the dominant policy paradigm to resolve the issue of teacher supply (and subsequently of retention, which of course impacts on teacher supply) that offers some optimism in creating a shared arena of discourse between those who are opposed to the centralist agenda in initial teacher education and those who advocate it.

In relation to the three significant policy contexts identified above, it is likely that teacher educators will see a slight lessening of the burden of OFSTED inspections, but not the root and branch overhaul of that centralist control mechanism. There is likely to be an expansion of the GTP programme and other alternative routes into the profession. There may well be relatively insignificant changes at the margins of current policy affecting initial teacher education, and the relationship between teacher educators and policy makers is likely to continue to thaw, given the current personalities involved. That thaw, however, is almost irrelevant, given the stranglehold that the dominant policy paradigm holds over teacher educators.

NOTE

1   The other regions that make up the UK – Northern Ireland, Scotland and Wales – have, for various reasons, not been affected in the same way.

2   I am currently the chair of UCET, but the views expressed in this chapter are my own.

REFERENCES

Bottery, M. (2000) *Education, Policy and Ethics*, London: Continuum.

Edwards, A., Gilroy, D.P. and Hartley, D. (2002) *Re-thinking Teacher Education: An Interdisciplinary Analysis*, London: Routledge.

Furlong, J., Barton, L., Miles, S., Whiting, C. and Whitty, G. (2000) *Teacher Education in Transition: Reforming Professionalism?* Buckingham: Open University Press.

Gilroy, D.P. (1992) 'The political rape of initial teacher education in England and Wales: a JET rebuttal', *Journal of Education for Teaching*, 18 (1), pp. 5–22.

Gilroy, D.P. (1998) 'New Labour and teacher education in England and Wales: the first 500 days', *Journal of Education for Teaching*, 24 (3), pp. 221–30.

Gilroy, D.P., Russell, M. and Stones, E. (1995) 'The Universities Council for the Education of Teachers: the facilitator's tale', *Journal of Education for Teaching*, 21 (2) pp. 119–43.

Gosden, P.H.J.H (1989) 'Teaching quality and the accreditation of initial teacher-training courses' in McClelland, V.A. and Varma, V.P. (eds) *Advances In Teacher Education*, London: Routledge, pp. 1–18.

Hextall, I., Mahony, P. and Mentor, I. (2001) 'Just testing? An analysis of the implementation of "skills tests" for entry into the teaching profession in England', *Journal of Education for Teaching*, 27 (3), pp. 221–39.

Mortimore, P. and Mortimore, J. (1998) 'The political and the professional in education: an unnecessary conflict?', *Journal of Education for Teaching*, 24 (3), pp. 205–19.

O'Hear, A.(1988) *Who Teaches the Teachers?* Research Report 10, London: The Social Affairs Unit.

TES (1991) *The Times Education Supplement*, 27 December.

THES (1997) *The Times Higher Education Supplement*, 18 April.

www.canteach.gov.uk/info/grtp/salary_grant.htm (accessed 22 March 2002).

www.canteach.gov.uk/teaching/routes/index.htm (accessed 22 March 2002).

www.ucet.ac.uk/ (accessed 21 March 2002).

3

CHAPTER 21

Researching education policy: interpreting the evidence

JENNY OZGA

Policy and politics

In this chapter I will present a series of arguments about researching education policy. These arguments represent current and probable future central issues in researching educational policy, rather than a comprehensive treatment of research on policy, or, indeed, a methodological guide. A discussion such as this has to be selective, so will focus on the relationship between research and policy, some international trends in that relationship, and their consequences for research on policy. A central topic here is the change in the nature of politics that is linked to globalization, and the consequences that this has for state action. States are subject to sharply contradictory pressures in their attempts to act globally and locally, producing what Castells (1997) has called an informational politics and a crisis of democracy. That crisis is evidenced in the weakness of the state and its inability to guarantee security, which in turn undermines citizenship identities; as a consequence, the absence of a political space denies the possibility of solidarity. The legitimation crisis is particularly apparent in the welfare arm of the state, which can no longer deliver comprehensive support for the well-being of citizens, nor claim to represent their will.

This produces a shift in the nature of politics towards informational politics, which in turn links to the move towards 'evidence-based' policy, which will feature largely in this chapter. Part of the shift in the nature of politics is apparent in influential criticisms of current political institutions as being archaic and barriers to the necessary process of modernization that will enable nation states and their citizens to become successful players in new knowledge economies. Bentley (2001, p. 13), who was policy adviser to the then Secretary of State for Education in England, suggests that:

> We need a new era of grown up government, which treats people as intelligent adults and expects them to do the same. It must distribute power with responsibility. This is the only way to deliver a new political agenda based on well-being and quality of life. Better health, education and jobs, a higher quality of life and genuine social inclusion can only be changed [sic] by persuading people to change the way they behave – government cannot deliver on behalf of the people.

This means forging new systems of co-operation, innovation and learning in every sector. Democracy in practice means the chance to shape our own lives, through systems that allow us to meet collective goals in a more diverse, fluid and individualised society: 'the goal of democracy is not accountable or responsive government by representative leaders, but self-government'(ibid., p. 13). Self-government, rather than accountable or responsive government, is achieved through the provision of information that enables people to make informed and responsible choices – about healthy living, about investment in lifelong learning, and so on. Government provides a model of this intelligent and rational action: considering evidence and acting upon 'what works'. Its citizens are exhorted to do likewise.

These developments have consequences for the nature of research, and the nature of the research–policy relationship, and it is on that relationship that this argument focuses. It is particularly important to raise questions about the impact of the changing nature of that relationship for the capacity of the academic research community to do research on policy. This is not just an issue of concern to academic researchers, but to educational professionals in general, who need to be engaged with education research and education policy in an active and informed way. Recent developments – which are shared across continents – in the relationship between research and policy, and in the formation and management of the teaching profession, add urgency to the task of supporting informed, independent research in partnership between academics and practitioners (Lingard, 2000; Ozga, 2000). While a general revival of interest among policy makers in evidence about 'what works' in education may herald a closer relationship between research and policy, the emergent terms of engagement that govern that relationship are a cause for concern.

Before looking in detail at developments in the policy–research relationship, we need to examine the context in which it is developing and the ways in which policy makers are interpreting that context as creating imperatives for a particular version of research.

Globalization and its interpretation

The pressure from policy makers to make research more policy-relevant and useful is linked to the current context of policy and of research that is being shaped by globalization. Globalization is often used rather loosely to refer to a range of developments in the economic, political, cultural and social spheres that have been driven, to a degree, by changes in communication and information technologies. A well-known definition describes it as the 'intensification of world-wide social relations which link distant realities in such a way that local happenings are shaped by events occurring many miles away and vice-versa' (Giddens, 1990). This is not a new process, but an extension and acceleration of an established one; the acceleration is provided by information technologies that support the global extension of capital and sustain its global reach. Gray (2000, p. 32) argues that this large-scale, historically embedded process may be distinguished from the particular, specific and possibly transient form of organization of the world economy as a global free market that is often taken to define globalization; that is, as a form of economic organization in which capital flows freely without interference from the nation state.

The definition of globalization as a form of economic organization seems to be shaping the thinking of policy makers when seeking to redesign and modernize the form and operation of their national education systems – and, indeed, of public services in general. Modernization invokes a logic based on globalization – and the resultant need for enterprise and flexibility – and contrasts this unfavourably with the self-interested agendas of professionals or bureaucrats (doctors, teachers, educational researchers) whose concerns are both selfish and archaic:

> *Reform is a vital part of rediscovering a true national purpose, part of a bigger picture in which our country is a model of a 21st century developed nation: with sound, stable economic management; dynamism and enterprise in business; the best educated and creative nation in the world; and a welfare state that promotes our aims and achievements ... the system must change because the world has changed.* (Blair, 1998, pp. iii–iv)

That economic definition seems also to have a powerful influence on defining and recognizing the problems to be addressed by national governments, and on assumptions about what education may be expected to do in addressing these problems. The freedom of capital to cross national frontiers challenges the capacity of nation states to mediate economic pressures, and, indeed, may challenge fundamental tenets of nation-state formation and operation (Novoa, 2000), including principles of distribution (for example, equality of opportunity). The implications of this shift and its interpretation by policy makers are considerable; it challenges the pursuit of a social democratic project of redistribution within a national system (of welfare provision of all kinds, including education) (Lindblad and Popkewitz, 2002). Instead, education policy seeks to maximize the attractiveness of its local products in the global marketplace; attempting to tie roving capital into long-term relationships based on the satisfaction of the needs of the new knowledge economy. Those needs require that public institutions as well as business become attuned to continuous change:

> *The modern world is swept by change. New technologies emerge constantly, new markets are opening up. There are new competitors but also great new opportunities ... This world challenges business to be innovative and creative, to improve performance continuously, to build new alliances and ventures ... In government, in business, in our universities and throughout society we must do more to foster a new entrepreneurial spirit: equipping ourselves for the long-term, prepared to seize opportunities, committed to constant innovation and improved performance.* (Blair, 1998 p. 5)

To deliver improved performance, the new knowledge economy produces pressures on national systems to improve their investment and performance in research and development, in information and communication technologies, and to find ways of making education deliver enhanced capacity to innovate and to develop new technologies. As nation states are competing with one another to achieve these goals, they are simultaneously open to international trends and developments in these areas to an unprecedented degree. Thus across the European Union and within North America and Australia there are shared policy agendas and preoccupations – mediated, in different ways, with varying degrees of success by 'local' situations (OECD, 1995). There are also shared principles of institutional and system design, and for the management and continuous improvement of performance of systems and their workforces (Pollitt and Bouckaert, 2000).

Modernized policy

The argument set out above suggests that the nature of policy making in education has shifted profoundly in a globalized context, with policy makers responding to economic globalization by focusing almost exclusively on using education to improve competitiveness and economic performance. The 'new production rules' of public policy formulation (Soucek, 1995) provide the conduits through which corporate interests may exert direct influence on public policy formulation. They do this in the obvious interventions such as enhanced private funding or public–private partnerships in education that may be discerned in different national systems (Hatcher, 2001; Hirrt, 2000). Influence is also achieved through what Grace (1989) has called the 'ideological manoeuvre' through which the rules of policy discourse are set in such a way as to privilege corporate interests, while marginalizing others. The impact of this influence can be seen in the redefinition of education as an appropriate mix of skills, and a technical consensus is created around concepts such as efficiency, quality and accountability. These concepts are not debated: their meaning is taken to be self-evident. Soucek (1995, pp. 92–3) draws on Habermas to suggest that the push towards technical definitions of education is connected to a de-democratization of the state. The issues of de-democratization and the technical definition of meaning connect to the earlier argument about the transformation of politics to informational politics.

De-democratization and the stripping out of meaning

The issue of de-democratization is important to research on policy. This is because policy should be engaged with by as wide a constituency as possible, to contribute to the creation of an informed, active citizenry supported, as Dewey (1916) imagined, by an informed, active system of public education. In particular, teachers must engage in policy research, in partnership with, and supported by, higher education institutions. All teachers should be encouraged to feel themselves part of a research community, and should be encouraged to participate in research debates, and to develop an orientation to research and enquiry that carries over into their professional practice.

Research-based practice creates an obligation of enquiry into the nature of teaching itself, which leads into questions about the purposes of education and the teacher's role in achieving those purposes. This connects directly to research on policy, since policy contains implicit or explicit statements about educational purposes. The fostering of wide participation in policy research (itself broadly defined) would enable educational researchers to engage more actively with policy as it is theorized and understood in the research community, and as it is understood, theorized and practised by teachers. This double-sided engagement is essential to educational research in general, including research on policy (Young, 1998; Ozga, 2000).

This argument in turn connects to questions of politics that return to issues of collective good and social solidarity that are not addressed by self-governments. These relate to the implications for teachers and researchers of the choice identified by

Connell (1995, p. 110) between accepting the emergent world system as a structure of inequality or engaging with the opportunities that global citizenship offers:

> *The way these possibilities are taken up depends to a considerable degree on teachers' capacities for reflection and strategic thinking about their work. If we take seriously the familiar arguments about the growing weight of organised knowledge in modern economies and political systems, then teachers' capacities to operate as designers and producers of knowledge are important to the vitality of education. And, if it is true ... that school systems have a major though indirect role in social change through the transformation of capacities for practice, then the capacity of teachers to steer that transforming process depends on the growth of their capacity to reflect on their practice.*

Research on education policy enables reflection on the formal construction of practice – and indeed of the profession – by policy. It is therefore essential that teachers are involved in such research alongside educational researchers in universities. In this way the larger project of education democracy may be enabled, and the reduction of educational aims to conservative or economistic ends challenged.

Concerns about the stripping out of meaning and the technical definition of quality and accountability are relevant here. Modernized managerialism has created a vocabulary that uses 'hollowed out' terms – like client, consumer, stakeholder, excellence, leadership and entrepreneurship – as requiring no further elaboration. In promoting this discourse it removes concepts that were once central to the organization of public life – for example citizenship, equality, justice and professionalism. These are interpreted as ideological positions, while ideas of economy, efficiency and entrepreneurship are advocated as if they were values (Nixon, 1995). Once again, the argument connects to changing politics, for if citizens are redefined as consumers and clients, so their role is 'cleansed of political participation' (Offe, 1996). By extension, if educational researchers are redefined as clients, so too is their role cleansed of political participation. Indeed, political participation is juxtaposed with 'objective' evidence, and deprecated in the building of bland, decontextualized versions of capacity building that ignore inequalities in education and society and lack 'attention to power, conflict and directionality' (Seddon, 2000).

Strengthening the policy – research relationship

A number of developments have brought educational research into closer alignment with the needs of policy makers. In England, strengthening of the steering capacity of policy makers has been achieved through shifts in the funding regime and the pursuit of a bland version of capacity-building through the creation of a new National Educational Research Forum. The process was initiated by a phase of criticism of educational research conducted in terms that left little room for the academic community to acknowledge genuine weaknesses in a spirit of self-criticism and reflection, for fear of finding themselves pressed into service in the official 'discourse of derision' (Ball, 1997).

Two official inquiries into the state of education research were commissioned in 1998 by the Office for Standards in Education (OFSTED) and the Department for Education and Employment (DfEE). The criticisms that justified these inquiries alluded to 'frankly second-rate research' that 'does not make a serious contribution to fundamental theory or knowledge' (Hargreaves, 1996, p. 7). The then Chief Inspector of Schools, Chris Woodhead, in his foreword to the OFSTED-commissioned report claimed that: 'Educational research is not making the contribution it should. Much that is published is, on this analysis, no better than an irrelevance and a distraction' (Tooley and Derby, 1998, p. i).

The DfEE inquiry sought recommendations for 'the development and pursuit of excellence in research relating to schools' (Hillage *et al.*, 1998, p. ix) and set out objectives through which these ends were to be achieved. They included the following:

> To ensure the relevance and practical value of educational research to teachers, schools, LEAs, central government, parents, governors and ultimately pupils; to strengthen the links between research, policy and practice; to enhance the fitness for purpose, robustness, reliability and validity of research undertaken; to ensure value for money/quality assurance. (Ibid, p. 3)

The report made a number of recommendations, including the establishment of a National Forum. The recommendations imply a straightforward and rather technical definition of both policy and research, and a relatively unproblematic relationship between them. They include: 'improving the capacity of research to provide support to policy-makers and educational practitioners, through improving quality ... establishing a commitment to evidence-based policy and development and approaches to the delivery of education' (ibid, p. xii).

Evidence of parallel developments in the steerage of education research is also available in the Australian context, where state and federal governments demand more say in agenda-setting for research:

> In an educational policy context where governments want better outcomes from schooling for all students and better proof of outcomes, the pressure has been for educational researchers, wherever they are located in the institutional sense, to do research framed by the policy and practice concerns of the government of the day. Such agenda-setting also has implications in terms of research methodologies, with governments usually being more enamoured of quantitative methodologies that simultaneously complement and express the governmental technique of 'policy as numbers'. (Lingard, 2000, p. 3)

In the same way as in England the DfEE and OFSTED reports constitute researchers as operatives who produce unproblematic 'findings' to be transmitted to practitioner-recipients, so changes in the framing of Australian research policy to give equal weighting for research quantum measures to consultancy and traditional inquiry-driven research illustrate the shared policy agenda and its potential impact on research and research identities. Further evidence of these international trends comes from the Strategic Educational Research Program (SERP) of the National Research Council in the USA, which has outlined plans to improve the contribution of educational research to raising student achievement levels through the improvement of practitioner use of research findings (Lingard, 2000). Teachers are once more defined as recipients of knowledge generated elsewhere and findings are assumed to be context-free. The flow of knowledge is one-way – from policy to research to practice.

There are indicators of both the contested nature of these agendas and the capacity of the agencies charged with their delivery to 'consensualize' debate in the next instalment in the story of the establishment of the National Forum in England. (As an aside, and in the context of globalization's simultaneous 'global' effects, the Forum has yet to clarify its 'national' identity, and is unclear about whether it is a UK or an English institution). The Forum was established in 1999 and published a consultation document in November 2000, outlining the possible components of a national strategy under the headings of priorities, funding, capacity quality and impact. Responses to the consultation from the academic research community were quite critical, and led the Chair of the Forum, in the foreword to the strategy document, to emphasize that:

> The Forum sees its role as a listener and facilitator in the process of overseeing the development of a strategy and the shaping of a framework. The Forum does not seek to control research; its role is to serve as a catalyst and enabler. To do this and retain the confidence of the range of stakeholders, it is essential for the Forum to conduct its activities independently of government while retaining strong links with policy formation and practice in education. (NERF, 2001, p. 2)

Researchers' responses to the consultation indicate that they have concerns about the 'independent but linked' position of NERF:

> All responses were supportive about the need for greater dialogue and to build on current initiatives but beyond this differences emerged between the research community and other respondents. Much of the research community felt that the proposals are centralised, government-driven and a threat to academic freedom and diversity. (Ibid, p. i)

The analysis of responses goes on to indicate that although there was

> some support for the idea of some sort of framework for educational research … there is enormous reservation about the Forum and the strategy in terms of aims, scope and ability to deliver. The main concern is that the strategy is an attempt to centralise decisions about research (i.e. that research will become government-determined as a result) and that it will seriously restrict academic freedom. (Ibid., p. ii)

Despite these indications of concern, but rather claiming to be informed by them, NERF (2002) set out proposals and a timetable for their implementation. These proposals include (ibid., p. 9):

A Foresight Exercise for Education with the following aims:

- to identify areas for action by different sectors to increase national wealth and quality of life, opportunities and to reduce barriers to participation;
- to identify emerging capacity to meet future needs;
- to highlight areas where government and others' actions would deliver widespread benefits.

Other proposals include the establishment of a Standing Group on Educational Research and Development Priorities. Identification of priorities is necessary so that there are adequate 'concentrations of energy and resources on issues agreed to be significant through a transparent and democratic process'. Funding of research is to be addressed through a 'Funders' Forum' to enable 'greater coherence' and 'targeted deployment' of funding.

These are significant developments in the steering of educational research in England, and connect to other initiatives such as the ESRC UK Evidence-based Policy Centre that seeks to improve the quality of research and practice in the social sciences, and to the Evidence for Policy and Practice Information and Co-ordinating Centre that provides systematic reviews of what is known about a range of policy and practice issues. These initiatives in knowledge management self-consciously echo the Cochrane Collaboration, which was established in 1993 to provide systematic up-to-date international reviews that enable people to make well-informed decisions about healthcare through the use of evidence-based information.

While these initiatives are local to England, they are echoed elsewhere. Also echoed elsewhere is the overall reduction in funding and in opportunities to pursue independent research within higher education institutions. Lingard (2000) gives an account of the intensification of pressures on educational researchers in Australia as marketized approaches to funding are adopted. Australian Research Council (ARC) grants have become more competitive, there is less infrastructure support, and contracts are pursued with government Departments of Education and Training. These contracts are short-term, policy-driven and very targeted. There are considerable consequences not only for the content and direction of research, but for researcher identities and research practices, as Marginson (1993, p. 19) has pointed out:

> When economic conceptions of education become applied in education programmes, they start to produce the very behaviours that economists of education have imagined. To the extent that university research is commercialised, researchers begin to think like entrepreneurs, and the free exchange of knowledge begins to be replaced by the alienation of intellectual property.

In the competitive pursuit of research funds, and the increasing need to accept research as inquiry into a pre-specified problem, the 'entrepreneurial researcher' (Ozga, 2000) is formed. The pursuit of wide-ranging intellectual inquiry is replaced by pursuit and management of research effort. Research management becomes the paramount activity, and coordination of processes associated with contract winning and maintenance becomes the main concern of the research manager. Content and purpose are relegated to secondary issues. As Readings (1996, p. 53) puts in his scathing critique of the contemporary 'University of Excellence':

> The model of the academy rules with the process we know as 'professionalization', bringing about the increasing integration of functions so that research is non-referential. That is to say, the content of research comes to matter less and less as research is ever more indistinguishable from the mere reproduction of the system.

Managerialism in the universities invokes powerful measures of control, and operates a series of interconnected mechanisms that contain a powerful internal logic of competition linked to rewards of resource, time and status. Entrepreneurial practices, especially those associated with government funds, act to seduce the researcher. The public process of bidding, the negotiation with significant others, the pleasure of being 'chosen' all give researchers the feeling of being close to power. It is in this context that the research–policy relationship needs to be scrutinized, and the opportunities and threats to independent research on policy assessed.

The new knowledge users – the policy makers – seem to stand in a dominant relationship to knowledge production, in the emergent research–policy relationship. What is currently being constructed is not capacity for social scientists to scrutinize policy in the public interest. It is more a reconfiguration of educational researchers as a resource for policy makers – as producers of evidence for the use of policy makers. Topics, problems and resources are increasingly established, defined and regulated by policy makers, and the consequences of such a process must include a reduction in space, and capacity for independent research. Once again, the argument connects back to the earlier discussion of the transformation of politics into 'informational' politics.

It is also useful to look at the ways in which 'evidence' itself is framed in the discourse of evidence-based or evidence-informed policy making. There is a strong implication that evidence will guide policy without further translation; that 'findings' dictate or shape clear courses of action or policy choices. In this denial of complexity, there is a refusal to consider the experience of past decades of educational research, and the often uncomfortable relationship between evidence, policy and practice. The past is irrelevant because responsibility for lack of clarity lay with the research community and its inadequate or politicized practices: appropriately steered research will provide findings that users can use.

Conclusion

This critical appraisal of the emergent relationship between research and policy is intended to promote the project of research on policy as a task for educational researchers and for teachers. It emphasized the contextual pressures on research, and the government and policy frames that guide commissioning, funding, agenda setting and problem defining. It discussed the ways in which these may influence the research labour process and thus the identities of researchers. In so doing, the intention is to reinforce the need to make such developments the topic of research; that is, to do research on policy, informed by awareness of developments that are setting the policy makers' agenda, and alert to the limitations of these interpretations and responses. Critical, independent research on education policy can play a formative and challenging role in holding the state to account for its policies. Claims that policy is made on the basis of 'evidence' permit those assertions to be subjected to scrutiny, and enable the exercise of accountability through which the attempted de-politicization of politics might be challenged (Halsey *et al.*, 1997).

REFERENCES

Ball, S.J. (1997) 'Policy, Sociology and Critical Social Research: a personal review of recent education policy and policy research', *British Education Research Journal*, 18, pp. 5–14.

Bentley, T. (2001) *It's Democracy, Stupid: An Agenda for Self-government*, London: Demos.

Blair, T. (1998) *Leading the Way: A New Vision for Local Government*, London: Institute for Public Policy Research.

Castells, M. (1997) *End of Millennium: The Information Age*, Oxford: Blackwell.

Connell, R. (1995) 'Teaching as transformative labour' in Ginsburg, M. (ed.) *The Politics of Educators' Work and Lives*, New York: Garland Press.

Dewey, J. (1916) *Education and Democracy*, New York: Ann Arbor.

Giddens, A. (1990) *The Consequences of Modernity*, Cambridge: Polity.

Grace, G. (1989) 'Education: commodity of public good', *British Journal of Educational Studies*, 37 (3), pp. 207–21.

Gray, J. (2000) 'Inclusion: a radical critique' in Askonas, P. and Stewart, A. (eds) *Social Inclusion: Possibilities and Tensions*, London: Macmillan.

Halsey, A., Lauder, H., Brown, P. and Wells, A.S. (eds) (1997) *Education: Culture, Economy, Society*, Oxford: Oxford University Press.

Hargreaves, D. (1996) *Teaching as a Research-Based Profession: Possibilities and Prospects*, Teacher Training Agency Annual Lecture. London: Teacher Training Agency.

Hatcher, R. (2001) 'The Business of Education', paper to conference on 'Travelling policy/local spaces: globalisation, identities and education policy in Europe', Keele University, June.

Hillage, J., Pearson, R., Anderson, A. and Tomkin, P. (1998) *Excellence in Research in Schools*, London: The Stationery Office.

Hirrt, N. (2000) 'The millennium round and the liberalisation of the education market', *Education and Social Justice*, 2 (2).

Lindblad, S. and Popkewitz, T. (2002) *Education Governance and Social Integration and Exclusion: Studies in the Powers of Reason and the Reasons of Power*, Uppsala: Uppsala University Press.

Lingard, R. (2000) 'Some lessons for educational research: repositioning research in education and education in research', presidential address to the AARE Conference, Sydney, November.

Marginson, S. (1993) 'Education research and education policy', *Australian Review of Education*, 2, pp. 15–29.

NERF (2001) *A Strategy for Development*, London: National Education Research Forum.

NERF (2002) *Research and Development Strategy for Education: Developing Quality and Diversity*, London: National Education Research Forum.

Nixon, J. (1995) 'Teaching as a profession of values' in Smyth, J. (ed.) *Critical Discourses on Teacher Development*, London: Cassell.

Novoa, A. (2000) 'Europe and education: historical and comparative approaches' in Bouzakis, J. (ed.) *Historical-Comparative Perspective*, Festshrift for Andreas Kazamias Athens, Gütenberg.

OECD (1995) *Governance in Transition*, Paris: Organization for Economic Co-operation and Development.

Offe, C. (1996) *Modernity and the State*, Cambridge: Polity Press.

Ozga, J. (2000) *Policy research in Educational Settings: Contested Terrain*, Buckingham: Open University Press.

Pollitt, C. and Bouckaert, G. (2000) *Public Management Reform: A Comparative Analysis*, Oxford: Oxford University Press.

Readings, B. (1996) *The University in Ruins*, Harvard: Harvard University Press.

Seddon, T. (2000) 'Exploring capacity building; between neo liberal globalisation and national systems of education and training', paper to EERA Conference, Edinburgh, September.

Soucek, V. (1995) 'Flexible education and new standards of communicative competence' in Kenway, J. (ed.) *Economising Education: The Post-Fordist Directions*, Geelong: Deakin University Press.

Tooley, J. and Darby, D. (1998) *Educational Research: A Critique*, London: HMSO.

Young, M.F.D. (1998) *The Curriculum of the Future: From the New Sociology of Education to a Critical Theory of Learning*, London: Falmer Press.

3

PART FOUR

Leadership, Governance and Community

JANET OUSTON

Introduction

JANET OUSTON

It is an undesirable academic habit to start an essay by discussing definitions but this is where we must begin. 'Governance' is currently used in two very different ways, but both are concerned with external influences on schools, rather than internal management practices. The first definition is very broad and is discussed by Glatter (Chapter 22 and Glatter, 2001) and Arnott and Raab (2000). They see governance as a problematic concept that involves both formal and less formal controls and influences over schools, and which operate as a network of pressures influencing school practice.

The second use of the term 'governance' has been promoted in Department for Education and Employment (DfEE) and Department for Education and Skills (DfES) documents to denote the responsibilities and activities of school governing bodies. Indeed, in this collection, Peter Earley and Michael Creese (Chapter 24) use it frequently with this meaning. It would be possible to argue that the 'domestication' of the term limits its usefulness by reducing our understanding of how both formal education policy and other informal influences change practice. The narrower use of the term may make formal policy, either from the DfES or the local education authority (LEA), and formal decisions made by governors, appear to be the only external influences on schools.

Formal educational policy may have its intended effects, it may have little effect, or it may have unpredicted (and possibly undesirable) effects on schools. Taking an example from the contributions included here, Stephen Gorard and Chris Taylor show how increased school diversity has led to increased social segregation. Policies to increase school diversity were not explicitly introduced to increase segregation, but appear to have had this effect. Similarly the Office for Standards in Education (OFSTED) inspection framework is not explicitly part of the governance of schools but could be seen as a powerful contributor to the network of influence on school practice, as could the assessment of school performance using the 5+ A*–C passes at GCSE. Both of these have made a serious impact on school practice, which have had both positive and negative outcomes. Some years ago, Deming (1993; Greenwood and Gaunt, 1994; Sallis, 1996) warned about the negative impact of setting artificial targets on organizations, an issue that was also discussed in the context of the pressures for accountability by Ouston, Fidler and Earley (1998).

Formal changes in governance have, in the main, been part of a 'marketization' and 'devolution' agenda. Here, Suzanne Hood explores the new role of parents in education – as the customers of state schools. More recently 'diversity' has become a political focus, as has been the increasing privatization of public services. The current enthusiasm for diversity – the conversion of comprehensive schools into specialist schools and the proposed increase in the number of faith-based schools – has raised widespread political anxieties. These have led to such policies as Diversity Pathfinder to ameliorate their adverse effects by increasing collaboration between schools of different types – between Beacon and local community schools, between the selective and the non-selective, between specialist and 'bog standard' comprehensives, between public and private. The balance between diversity and collaboration, and its outcome for the education of young people, are difficult to predict. But it looks very likely that increasing diversity will lead to increasing selection and segregation.

Limiting the definition of governance to the work of governing bodies could leave us without a framework for examining – and challenging – these 'unintended outcomes' of policy. The broader definition allows us to see schools as part of an education system, in which decisions made by individual schools have an impact on the educational experience of other students living in the same community. The narrower definition may lead us to see schools as isolated institutions, each looking after their own needs but ignoring the wider community.

The privatization of school governance has been evident in two areas: the 'contracting out' of LEAs' responsibilities, and the management of individual schools by private companies. In general, private-sector education staff have been recruited from the maintained sector, rather than from non-educational commercial enterprises. These initiatives are too new for it to be possible to draw any conclusions at present, but privatized LEAs are inspected by OFSTED and by the Audit Commission, as are privatized school managements. The strengths of these arrangements appear to be twofold: the companies are able to attract excellent staff with much higher salaries than would be customary within the public sector; they are also able to create change merely by being different, and by being given psychological permission to be different. Employees of LEAs and schools know that 'things will change' when the service is privatized, and provided that positive outcomes can be ensured for employees very quickly, change can be 'kick-started' in a way that it would not be in the traditional management patterns of the public sector. But it is too early to draw conclusions about these initiatives, and also to assess their impact in the longer term. And will private companies, with the limited profits to be made from managing the public sector, want to continue working in education?

Recent changes in policy and governance

There have been many changes in policy and governance, but two stand out as interesting and as having very different outcomes. The grant-maintained (GM) schools initiative was set up to 'free' schools from local authority control. It was a successful initiative in that it was taken up by a minority of school governing bodies and is a model of how change can be introduced. While these GM schools have been brought back into their local authorities (in the main as 'foundation' schools), much of the independence they were given has subsequently been extended to all schools (Wise, Anderson and Bush, 2001). The contrasting initiative is that of Education Action Zones (EAZs), where governing bodies of the participating schools could cede their powers to the Zone Forum (Dickson and Power, 2001). While the success of EAZs in improving education for schools 'in challenging circumstances' is still being debated, no governing body has ceded its responsibilities. The reasons for this difference are not hard to find: when schools operate in a competitive marketplace, with teacher shortages and a perceived lack of resources, schools and their governing bodies will support initiatives that increase their income and their status. The Education Action Zone proposals did neither. It is difficult to see why governors – all volunteers – would vote to give up their responsibilities.

The chapters in Part Four cover a range of issues of governance. The section could have been much longer – including, for example, chapters on GM schools, the changing role and impact of OFSTED, and the impact of publishing examination results and the criteria used. There are also interesting very small-scale initiatives in governance that might inspire changes in the next few years. Home education (Education Otherwise: www.education-otherwise.org) and the Human Scale Education Initiative (www.hse.org.uk) may lead to an education system that is more open, diverse and liberal. But such initiatives will not thrive in the current climate of competition, testing and accountability assessed by simple numerical targets.

4

REFERENCES

Arnott, M.A. and Rabb, C.D. (eds) (2000) *The Governance of Schooling: Comparative Studies of School Management*, London: Routledge/Falmer. (pp. 1–76).

Deming, W.E. (1993) *The New Economics*, Cambridge MA: MIT.

Dickson, M. and Power, S. (2001) 'Education Action Zones: a new way of governing education?', *School Leadership and Management*, 21 (2), pp. 137–41.

Glatter, R. (2001) 'The governance of education: current challenges', *Management in Education*, 15 (2), pp. 6–9.

Greenwood, M.S. and Gaunt, H.J. (1994) *Total Quality Management for Schools*, London: Cassell.

Ouston, J., Fidler, B. and Earley, P. (1998) 'The educational accountability of schools in England and Wales', *Education Policy*, 12 (1–2), pp. 111–23.

Sallis, E.J. (1996) *Total Quality Management in Education*, London: Kogan Page.

Wise, C., Anderson, L. and Bush, T. (2001) 'Foundation schools and admissions: the local dimension', *School Leadership and Management*, 21 (4), pp. 383–95.

– CHAPTER 22 –

Governance and educational innovation

RON GLATTER

© Ron Glatter 2003, The Open University

Theories of management abound; those of governance are few.
(GRAYSTONE, 1999, P. 7)

Studies of educational leadership and management too often neglect the framework of governance as a significant element of the wider context within which school leaders operate (Glatter, 1997). The purposes of this chapter are to:

- briefly review some recent analytical work on the governance of education;
- ask how appropriate our current models of governance are for meeting the needs of education in a fast-changing society, and whether any more appropriate models can be suggested.

Governance: a brief review and a framework

The notion of 'governance' is contested. Rhodes (1997) has identified six distinct uses of the term. A simple, open definition, from the *Concise Oxford Dictionary*, is 'the act or manner of governing'. This avoids the strong implication in some definitions about how governance is, or should be, conducted. For example, some writers classify governance structures in terms of hierarchies, markets or networks (Thompson *et al.*, 1991; Rhodes, 1999) but tend to equate 'governance' with networks alone. They assume that the task of governing has now outrun the capacity of governments to perform it, and that it is increasingly undertaken by complex networks or 'partnerships' of groupings from the private and voluntary sectors, professional 'experts', lay people and others. This leads to difficulties of 'steering' and monitoring and to 'opaque accountability' (Rhodes, 1999, p. xxiii).

However, it is an open question whether these more indirect forms of system management, compared with the traditional ones based on command and direction, have really led to a dispersal of power. Perhaps there has simply been a shift from one form of control to another. Reviewing governance changes throughout the UK social welfare sector, Clarke and Newman (1997, p. 30) speak of 'a "rolling out" of state power, but in new, dispersed, forms'. From his analysis of educational governance in Norway and the Canadian province of British Columbia, Karlsen (2000, p. 530) concludes that there now exists a paradox of 'decentralized centralism', in which:

> Arguments for decentralization from the national level may function to prevent a threat to central legitimacy and thereby consolidate the central power platform. Given this background, it is not surprising ... that decentralization reforms have often led to new central legislation and regulations.

This aim of consolidating central power will not, however, necessarily be achieved, and we need to ask how successful are governments in the difficult task of 'steering at a distance' or what Jessup (2000, p. 23) calls 'metagovernance': 'the process of managing the complexity, plurality and tangled hierarchies characteristic of prevailing modes of co-ordination'. The changing governance of school systems displays a series of tensions, including tensions between:

- system coherence and fragmentation
- institutional autonomy and the wider community and public interest
- diversity and equity
- competition and collaboration
- central and local decision making.

The processes involved are delicate ones, and the balances struck at any point will have a significant impact on the nature of the schooling made available to students.

I have proposed elsewhere (Glatter, 2002) a framework for understanding and applying models of governance in education. This is summarized in Table 22.1. It is undoubtedly a crude and over-simplified analysis. Four models are distinguished: competitive market (CM), school empowerment (SE), local empowerment (LE) and quality control (QC). These models should be seen as ideal types, which are separated here purely for analytical purposes. In practice each governance system or jurisdiction will operate on some composite of these models. Sometimes they may complement or reinforce each other as they impact on localities and institutions, but their interaction is also likely to cause conflicts, which participants must seek to resolve. We shall return to these conflicts after briefly reviewing the models.

The major perspective underlying the CM model relates to the analogy with the commercial marketplace. The school is viewed as a small or medium-sized business with a high degree of autonomy and few formal links to the governance structure. The main focus within the system is placed not on the individual school but on the relevant 'competitive arena' (Woods, Bagley and Glatter, 1998), which will contain a group of (generally) adjacent schools in competition with each other for students and funds. The nature of this arena will vary widely from context to context, depending on such factors as the socio-economic character of the area, including access to private transport and the relative density of the population.

The perspective underlying the SE model might be either or both 'political' (in the broad sense of dispersing power and promoting freedom and choice) and 'managerial' (on the principle that decisions are best taken close to the point of action). Although this model is often combined with the CM model, it is analytically distinct and in some respects contrasting. The focus is more on the

Table 22.1 *Models of governance in education*

Models	Competitive market (CM)	School empowerment (SE)	Local empowerment (LE)	Quality control (QC)
Indicative policies	Pupil-number-led funding, e.g. by vouchers More open enrolment Published data on school performance Variety of school types	Authority devolved to school on finance, staffing, curriculum, student admissions Substantial powers for school council/ governing body	Authority devolved to locality on finance, staffing, curriculum, student admissions Substantial powers for local community council/ governing body	Regular, systematic inspections Detailed performance targets Mandatory curriculum and assessment requirements
Main perspective(s)	Commercial	Political and/ or managerial	Political and/ or managerial	Bureaucratic
How the individual school is viewed	As a small business	As a participatory community	One of a 'family' of local schools	As a point of delivery/local outlet
Main focus within the system	The relevant competitive arena	The individual school	The locality as a social and educational unit	Central or other state bodies

institution itself and the way it is run than on its competitive activities 'against' other institutions. It encompasses ideas of participation, identification and partnership – the school conceived of as an extended community. The unit within the system that provides its main focus or 'centre of gravity' is the school itself.

Although the LE model shares the term 'empowerment' with the SE model, and there are a number of commonalities, there are also significant differences between the two models. As with the SE model, the justification can be in either political or managerial terms. However, the school is here viewed explicitly as one of a 'family' of schools, as part of a local educational *system* and as a member of a broader community in which there are reciprocal rights and obligations. The contrast with the CM model is particularly evident here. The main focus is on the locality as a social and educational unit and its representative bodies.

Under pressure from global competition and growing demands on public expenditure, governments are increasingly seeking control over key school processes and products, even in highly devolved and/or market-like systems. The major underlying perspective in the QC model is bureaucratic, involving laid-down rules and requirements and operating through set procedures, controls and monitoring arrangements. The picture of the school implied here is a kind of 'point of delivery', with many of the 'goods' on offer and the targets established having been determined at either the centre or the state level, depending on the constitutional arrangements in the country concerned. Under this model the units within the system that provide the main focus or 'centre of gravity' tend to be located within, or closely connected to, central or regional government.

The four models are by no means comprehensive and the framework could well be formulated differently, but it provides a useful instrument through which to examine some key issues of structure and process. I have explored elsewhere differences between each of the models in the nature of schools' autonomy, the form of accountability, the purpose of performance measurement, the function of intermediate authorities and the key school leadership role (Glatter, 2002). For example, I have suggested that the key leadership role under the CM model is that of 'entrepreneur', under the SE model it is 'director and co-ordinator', under the LE model 'networker' and under the QC model 'production manager' (see Glatter, 2002 for a detailed discussion). Clearly this is over-simplified, since in practice school leaders will interpret and enact their role in a variety of ways depending on their individual personalities, the cultures of their schools and other factors. The purpose of the analysis is to suggest that the governance context is an important and often neglected influence on school leadership. Generalizations are often made about what constitutes effective school leadership without taking into account the specific and diverse frameworks of policy and governance within which it is exercised.

As indicated earlier, in practice jurisdictions operate on some composite of the models, so that elements of the CM model may be combined with the SE and QC models for example. The particular mix is also liable to frequent change. As Leithwood (2001) suggests, most reform initiatives are eclectic, bundling different approaches together in a single reform package and creating significant leadership dilemmas. In the face of this 'policy eclecticism', he argues, 'school leaders can be excused for feeling that they are being pulled in many different directions simultaneously. They *are* being pulled in many different directions simultaneously' (ibid., p. 228). Such eclecticism is to be expected: no single model would be adequate as a strategy for governance. However, significant issues emerge where they conflict with one another, as will be considered later.

Do the models facilitate innovation?

The need for educational institutions and systems to adapt more effectively to a fast-changing society is widely accepted. An array of economic, social and technological forces presses on governments and institutions. Change is 'constant, unpredictable and accelerating' (NCSL, 2001, p. 1). The OECD (Organization for Economic Co-operation and Development) has reviewed the major trends and proposed six possible scenarios for the future of schooling (OECD, 2001; see also Chapter 62). Yet it is often remarked that the forms and content of schooling appear to change very little (see for example Hargreaves, 1997; Levin and Riffel, 1997). This volume is much concerned with educational change and the leadership and management of schools of the future, so it is relevant to consider whether existing models of governance promote or hinder a culture of innovation.

There is limited research overall on this question in relation to the four models of governance, so much of what follows is necessarily speculative. However, in the case of the CM model a great deal of research has been carried out in a number of countries in recent years and the findings on innovation can only be briefly referred to here. A large-scale study of choice and competition in secondary education in England in which the present author was involved (Woods, Bagley and Glatter, 1998) found little evidence that the competitive arrangements established in the 1990s had encouraged innovation within the system. Where innovation did take place it was running counter to the centralizing trends of policy, and there were indications of it being curbed sometimes by a reluctance on the part of school leaders to step outside the dominant model of the high-status (academically orientated) school. Connected with this, there was a tendency for schools to appeal to a broad grouping of potential parents and pupils rather than differentiate themselves sharply in order to focus on a specific niche. This tendency towards homogenization arose both from central prescriptions such as the National Curriculum and also from market incentives promoted by per capita funding and more open enrolment.

This overall conclusion has been broadly confirmed by other studies both in England and elsewhere. For example, in a detailed review of relevant research in New Zealand, Chile, the UK and the USA, Lubienski (2001) concludes that there is no evidence of the direct relationship between competitive markets and innovation in education that is claimed by advocates of this model. He also refers to the standardizing tendencies of markets, both in education and other sectors.

Unlike the CM model, the rationale for the SE model does not focus on system improvement and innovation. Its emphasis is on the school as an individual unit and on the responsibility of institutional staff and/or governing board members to take as many decisions as possible close to the point of action, under the 'principle of subsidiarity' (McGinn and Welsh, 1999). There may be substantial innovation, but if so it is likely to be confined to the school itself rather than generalized to the wider system. Considerable variation in the extent of innovation is likely to result from this model. Whatever its strengths in terms of improving the quality of decision making – and evidence of its impact on pupil learning thus far is very thin (Levačić, 1998) – it reflects some of the weaknesses of the fragmentation of governance frequently found in contemporary society. Clarke and Newman (1997, p. 155) have described the effect of what they call 'the dispersal of public services' in the following way: 'Each organisation pursues its "core business" more or less single-mindedly, with wider conceptions of the public realm or public good disappearing into the spaces between them'.

Under the LE model the individual school's autonomy is qualified by its being a member of a 'family' of local schools. This raises the possibility of 'network' or 'partnership' arrangements that could under certain circumstances facilitate the spreading of innovation within the locality, but there is evidence that such arrangements can also create difficulties, as will be discussed later. There is also the potential under this model to create a local infrastructure to sustain and nourish school-based innovation. From his extensive studies of educational change and innovation around the world, Fullan (2000) concludes that 'the emphasis on school-based management over the past decade has led us down the garden path'. An infrastructure must be in place to provide pressure and support and to achieve 'synergy, connectedness and coherence'. The LE model may not, however, achieve these outcomes consistently across a nation and so, as with the SE model, innovation may be patchy and haphazard.

The QC model's rationale is not to promote innovation but to ensure that the existing system is operating effectively. To this end, a range of technical-rational, performance-based processes such as target setting, performance reviews, audit and inspection have been mandated by central or state bodies in recent years. However, given the much greater awareness of turbulence and complexity in the macro-environment, there is a question about how far these tightly coupled systems are likely to continue to be viable, and for how long (Glatter, 1999). As Ouston (1998) argues in her review of models of managing change, those that make 'rational' and 'linear' assumptions are most suitable for stable environments and conditions in which the outcome of management action are regarded as predictable. In the coming years it will be extremely difficult to meet these conditions. Bentley (2000, p. 357) expresses the problem graphically: 'A system for educating the young that resembles a programmed machine does not necessarily prepare them to thrive in less certain, more complex environments'.

So it appears that none of these models of governance is adequate, either singly or in combination, for reshaping educational systems through a process of continuous adaptation in contemporary conditions. It might be argued that central authorities have addressed the QC model's limitations by energetically pursuing 'reform' agendas. In many countries over the past decade or two governments have produced a continuous stream of initiatives to which institutions and their leaders and teachers have been required to respond. However, as Levin (2001) concludes from his detailed study of the process of reform in four countries, the evidence on their impact is scanty, particularly considering the importance attached to them and the enormous efforts that have been put into them. The link between the problems that are identified and the solutions proposed to tackle them – the so-called 'reforms' – is by no means clear-cut, and the policies are often driven by short-term political agendas. There is an ongoing problem of reform initiatives being seen as top-down impositions on an unwilling system:

> *The reality is that we do not know how to solve the educational and social problems we face. Success is not a matter of simply implementing someone's nostrum. The problems are deep-seated and multi-faceted. In such a situation the only way forward is to focus on experimenting and learning.* (Levin, 2001, p. 198)

This seems a key point. Many reform initiatives that are mandated for widespread adoption are actually experiments, which, at the time they are introduced have little evidence to support them, though they are not presented as such (Glatter, 2001). As politicians and their officials become identified with them, they fear the potential costs of loss of legitimacy and credibility: 'they have a "sunk investment" in what looked originally like "really good ideas" but in fact turn out on investigation to be poor ones' (Levačić and Glatter, 2001, p. 14). An alternative approach to governance for educational innovation is required that explicitly recognizes the tentative and experimental character of the great majority of educational changes, whether at institutional or system level.

A learning system model

The last few years have seen many calls for educational institutions to become 'learning organizations'. Rarely has this type of injunction been applied to educational systems and their governments. If we envisaged a learning system (LS) model of governance, what would some of its chief characteristics be? One formulation of a learning organization applied to schools includes the following features (Leithwood, Jantzi and Steinbach, 1999, p. 216):

- openness to new ideas
- tolerance for divergent points of view
- valuing strategic failure as a source of learning
- questioning of basic assumptions
- speculative thinking about future states
- interconnectedness: systems thinking; seeking coherence.

Such a formulation provides an indication of the type of culture that an LS model of educational governance would seek to generate. In Table 22.2 the framework of Table 22.1 is applied to this LS model in order to suggest some of its chief characteristics. The table posits a fifth model of governance and should be seen as an extension of Table 22.1. This model is presented as an ideal type; many existing systems already contain elements of it, alongside features of the other models.

Table 22.2 *Towards a learning system model of governance*

Indicative policies	Reform by small steps
	Focus on evidence-informed policy and practice (EIPP)
	Tolerance of divergent views – minimal blame/derision
	Creation of test-beds for innovation
	Genuine partnerships built on trust
	Reduction of conflicting incentives
Main perspective	Developmental
How the individual school is viewed	As a creative, linked unit within a wider system
Main focus within the system	The connections between stakeholder groups and between system levels

The following points expand this model:

- The model does not dispense with the need for system leadership. It is not a *laissez-faire* model. In spite of Levin's conclusion about the limited evidence of impact of reform initiatives, Lubienski's (2001) cross-national review found a number of cases where government intervention was more successful than market mechanisms in producing innovations.
- The model emphasizes evidence-informed policy and practice (EIPP) and especially independent evaluation through pilot studies. This would require a culture change among both politicians and researcher/evaluators (Levačić and Glatter, 2001). It would involve changing to a culture of 'reform by small steps' for, in words attributed to Soichiro Honda, founder of the Japanese car company, 'Success can only be achieved through repeated failure and introspection'.
- The model recognizes the value of partisanship and contending positions. It is not a recipe for bland consensus-seeking, since the contest of ideas

and solutions can play a vital role in the enhancement of learning (Lindblom, 1990).

- The model embraces the networking and partnership focus of LE, while recognizing the difficulties of implementing it successfully. For example, a number of UK studies have shown how policies based on partnership – including the business sector – and promoting the concept of a local 'family' of schools have been frustrated by existing power structures or incentive systems (Jones and Bird, 2000; OFSTED, 2001).

- The model requires trusting the various stakeholder groups, including teachers and intermediate authorities, and valuing their contributions. Such an approach is in line with recent research on effective policies for human resource management in the business sector (see Glatter, 1999). This indicates that fostering employee commitment, trust, participation and job satisfaction is more effective than any other development strategy in its impact on hard outcome measures such as productivity and profits.

- The model assumes that innovation and development must be balanced by maintenance. The hyperactivity of recent reform strategies and their transformational discourse have often generated 'innovation fatigue'. The imbalance between change and continuity, between dynamism and stability, may, as Lessem (2001) suggests, be a reflection of a dominance of western and eastern cultures and styles over northern and southern ones. As complexity theory indicates (Fullan, 2001), organizations have to operate on the boundary between stability and instability: the former presses towards ossification and the latter towards disintegration. This suggests that the QC model, with its emphasis on the smooth operation of the existing system, has an important contribution to make within an LS framework, both to ensure continuity and to generate evidence for system development.

- The model implies managing and reducing the conflicts that arise for stakeholders from policy eclecticism. These conflicts have been a feature of many recent reform programmes. How can government-initiated development projects produce the radical innovations expected of them when they are also required to demonstrate short-term success in narrow measures of standards (Hallgarten and Watling, 2001)? Or again, 'the growing emphasis on competitive positioning acts as an obvious barrier to collaboration. In addition, the focus on core business, linked to outputs and output-based funding, means that there are a number of "perverse incentives" which inhibit inter-organisational cooperation' (Clarke and Newman, 1997, p. 147). An LS model would seek some form of reconciliation between such conflicting incentives – or 'competing, countervailing movements' (OECD, 2001, p. 105) – rather than leave stakeholders at or near the 'front line' to wrestle with them.

There is an inevitable risk that such a formulation will appear sanitized and utopian, and imply that the tensions in educational governance referred to at the start can be wished away and, in particular, that the realities of power can be ignored (Fielding, 2001). This danger is recognized and hopefully has to some extent been addressed. However, the evident limitations of existing models of governance in promoting innovation in a turbulent world call for an attempt at something better. That is what is tentatively offered here.

REFERENCES

Bentley, T. (2000) 'Learning beyond the classroom', *Educational Management and Administration*, 28 (3), pp. 353–64.

Clarke, J. and Newman, J. (1997) *The Managerial State*, London: Sage.

Fielding, M. (2001) 'Learning organisation or learning community? A critique of Senge', *Reason in Practice*, 1 (2), pp. 17–29.

Fullan, M. (2000) 'Infrastructure is all', *The Times Educational Supplement*, 23 June.

Fullan, M. (2001) *Leading in a Culture of Change*, San Francisco: Jossey-Bass.

Glatter, R. (1997) 'Context and capability in educational management', *Educational Management and Administration*, 25 (2), pp. 181–92.

Glatter, R. (1999) 'From struggling to juggling: towards a redefinition of the field of educational leadership and management', *Educational Management and Administration*, 27 (3), pp. 253–66.

Glatter, R. (2001) 'The governance of education: current challenges', *Management in Education*, 15 (2), pp. 6–9.

Glatter, R. (2002) 'Governance, autonomy and accountability in education' in Bush, T. and Bell, L. A. (eds), *The Principles and Practice of Educational Management*, London: Paul Chapman Publishing.

Graystone, J. (1999) 'Developments in the governance of further education sector colleges', paper presented to the Third Annual Further Education Research Network Conference, Churchill College, Cambridge, December.

Hallgarten, J. and Watling, R. (2001) 'Buying power: the role of the private sector in Education Action Zones', *School Leadership and Management*, 21 (2), pp. 143–57.

Hargreaves, D. (1997) 'A road to the learning society', *School Leadership and Management*, 17 (1), pp. 9–21.

Jessop, B. (2000) 'Governance failure' in Stoker, G. (ed.) *The New Politics of British Local Governance*, London: Macmillan.

Jones, K. and Bird, K. (2000) ''Partnership' as strategy: public–private relations in Education Action Zones', *British Educational Research Journal*, 26 (4), pp. 491–506.

Karlsen, G. E. (2000) 'Decentralized centralism a framework for a better understanding of governance in the field of education', *Journal of Educational Policy*, 15 (50), pp. 525–38.

Leithwood, K. (2001) 'School leadership in the context of accountability policies', *International Journal of Leadership in Education*, 4 (3), pp. 217–35.

Leithwood, K., Jantzi, D. and Steinbach, R. (1999) *Changing Leadership for Changing Times*, Buckingham: Open University Press.

Lessem, R. (2001) 'Managing in four worlds: culture strategy and transformation', *Long Range Planning*, 34 (1), pp. 9–32.

Levačić, R. (1998) 'Local management of schools in England: results after six years', *Journal of Education Policy*, 13 (3), pp. 331–50.

Levačić, R. and Glatter, R. (2001) '"Really good ideas"? developing evidence-informed policy and practice in educational leadership and management', *Educational Management and Administration*, 29 (1), pp. 5–25.

Levin, B. (2001) *Reforming Education: from origins to outcomes*, London: Routledge/Falmer Press.

Levin, B. and Riffel, J. (1997) 'School system responses to external change: implications for parental choice of schools' in Glatter, R., Woods, P. A. and Bagley, C. (eds) *Choice and Diversity in Schooling: Perspectives and Prospects*, London: Routledge.

Lindblom, C. (1990) *Inquiry and Change*, New Haven: Yale University Press.

Lubienski, C. (2001) *The Relationship of Competition and Choice to Innovation in Education Markets: A Review of Research on Four Cases*, Occasional Paper No. 26, New York: National Center for the Study of Privatization in Education, Teachers' College, Columbia University.

McGinn, N. and Welsh, T. (1999) *Decentralisation in Education: Why, When, What and How?* Paris: UNESCO International Institute for Educational Planning.

NCSL (2001) *Leadership Development Framework*, Nottingham: National College for School Leadership.

OECD (2001) *What Schools for the Future?* Paris: Centre for Educational Research and Innovation, Organization for Economic Co-operation and Development.

OFSTED (2001) *Specialist Schools: An Evaluation of Progress*, London: Office for Standards in Education.

Ouston, J. (1998) 'Managing in turbulent times' in Gold, A. and Evans, J. (eds) *Reflecting on School Management*, London: Falmer Press.

Rhodes, R.A.W. (1997) *Understanding Governance*, Buckingham: Open University Press.

Rhodes, R.A.W. (1999) 'Foreword: governance and networks' in Stoker, G. (ed.) *The New Management of British Local Governance*, London: Macmillan.

Thompson, G., Frances, J., Levačić, R. and Mitchell, J. (1991) (eds), *Markets, Hierarchies and Networks: the Co-ordination of Social Life*, London: Sage Publications in association with the Open University.

Woods, P. A., Bagley, C. and Glatter, R. (1998) *School Choice and Competition: Markets in the Public Interest?* London: Routledge.

4

Diversity or hierarchy? The role of secondary school allocation procedures in maintaining equity

STEPHEN GORARD AND CHRIS TAYLOR

This chapter uses findings from a study of the changing social composition of secondary schools in England and Wales from 1988 to 2001 (ESRC, grant number R000238031). It argues that local levels of segregation of disadvantaged students (chiefly those from families living in poverty) are largely determined by non-educational factors, such as the geography of each area. Once these wider factors are accounted for, then areas in which there is little diversity in the nature of local schooling – where all schools are local education authority (LEA) controlled comprehensives for example – have generally lower levels of segregation, and have until recently tended to reduce those levels further. Areas with considerable diversity on the other hand (where school allocation by selection, faith, fees or specialism appears) have higher levels of segregation, and have tended to maintain these levels over time. Where diversity increases, so too does segregation (in the main).

The implications of, and dangers for, the current expansion of specialist and faith-based schools are obvious. Whatever merits these schemes have (and the evidence for these merits is far from conclusive), they also present a real danger of creating greater socio-economic division in the education system. The authors argue that we should, on the other hand, be aiming for less division, since school compositions are related to their performance (Gorard 2000a, 2001). However, the same argument applies to areas with relatively high proportions of foundation (opted out) schools (and to Welsh-medium schools in Wales), even where these schools are not specialist, faith-based or selective. What all of these minority school types have in common is the ability to act as their own admission authorities, and perhaps it is this, rather than their 'marketing' identities, that is the chief determinant of increased segregation in their local areas.

Methods

There is insufficient space here to describe fully the methods used in this complex project, and interested readers are invited to follow up the references given below (or visit www.cf.ac.uk/socsi/markets). The database used contains a record of each secondary school in England and Wales from 1989 to 2000. Each year details (subject to availability) the data from the annual census of schools, including the number of students in total, those eligible for and taking free meals, and ethnic, first language and special needs. It also contains information on school organization, including type, age range, finance and admission procedures (where known). To these have been added public examination results, and contextual information for the local authority area, including school allocation procedures, population density, school closures, political control, levels of deprivation, and information on local levels of residential segregation by poverty and unemployment. For 41 LEAs we have added semi-structured interviews with one or more LEA officers involved in allocating school places, and in nine of these LEAs we added interviews with one or more school officers handling the admission process.

Our statistical analysis uses the census figures on school composition as 'dependent' variables. For each we calculate a variety of indices of segregation, based at national, regional, local, district and school level. The best such index uses poverty as measured by free school meals (FSM). These have the advantage of having the same meaning and method of collection over the entire period (Gorard and Fitz, 2000). The index itself is our own segregation index, which has been shown to be able to distinguish between simple changes in the level of poverty and its distribution between schools (Gorard and Taylor, 2002a). The most appropriate calculation is of segregation at the LEA level (Taylor, Gorard and Fitz, 2001a). The remaining variables have been used here as the 'independent' variables in forward stepwise regressions to explain variations both between localities and within each authority over time (Taylor, Gorard and Fitz, 2001b). We explain the resulting patterns in terms of our subsequent documentary and interview analyses (White, *et al.*, 2001; Fitz *et al.*, 2002).

Findings

From January 1989, the last annual census before the introduction of parental choice as defined by the Education Reform Act 1998, to 1996 there was an annual decline in segregation of pupils in poverty. This took place in both England and Wales, and in all economic regions of England, and represents a powerful social 'movement' (Gorard, 2000b). From 1997 to 2001 segregation by poverty had begun to rise again, and the rate of this rise appears to be increasing annually (although it remains well below 1989 levels). Where other indicators are available (and we were able to use ethnic group, first language, and statements of additional educational need), segregation in terms of these has also declined over this period, and continues to decline (Gorard, Fitz and Taylor, 2001). Levels of, and changes in, segregation are far from uniform across England and Wales however. Not all local education authorities have experienced desegregation, and a few have even experienced increased segregation throughout. In general, Wales has less segregation than England, and urban areas have less segregation than rural ones. Urban areas have also shown the greatest change over time, and some inner-London LEAs (ILEAs) now have almost no segregation by poverty for a variety of reasons (Taylor and Gorard, 2002). The scale of these geographical variations is not always clear to commentators and policy-makers based in London (see below).

We attempted to explain these differences in socio-economic segregation between different areas, and the changes in these patterns over time, and have developed an explanation of both phenomena that accounts for 100 per cent of the statistical variation. In general terms our model has three elements – local geography, school organization and admission arrangements – and these are presented in descending order of importance, and in temporal order as determinants of segregation.

Geography

The largest single factor determining the level of segregation in schools is the pattern of local housing, since even in a system of choice most children attend a school near their home. As one of our rural LEA respondents puts it, whatever system of allocation is used, 'it has always been preferable to live closer rather than further, even before the 1988 Education Reform Act'. Some of these rural LEAs only have a part-time school admissions officer, who can tidy up the few cases to be decided in an afternoon, and many would probably agree with one who says: 'We haven't really got a problem with admissions'.

What was clear from our rural respondents was that the whole issue of choice in the 1988 Act and the subsequent School Standards and Framework Act was not intended for them. It was seen as a London-based solution to a perceived London problem. One LEA officer comments: 'It does seem a lot of it is aimed at solving problems in London that don't exist in other parts of Britain'. Rural LEAs have always cooperated. Now, because of the need for admissions this officer has to formally consult with 13 authorities and all of them simply say 'no comment, no comment, no comment'. This leads to frustration: 'Just because there is a problem with four London boroughs with different types of schools ... why impose nationally a system to deal with that? It has been a total and utter waste of money.'

Where richer and poorer families live 'cheek by jowl', usually in densely populated areas, then residential segregation is low, meaning that school segregation in also low. In urban areas, residential segregation is the single most important explanation for school segregation (a factor that is overlooked by many educational commentators).

Other indicators of relevance at this level are population density and the actual levels of local poverty and unemployment. As would be expected, areas with more similarity among inhabitants (where there are no 'rich' or 'poor', for example) have less segregation by schools. When these geographical factors change, through the provision of new housing estates or the closure of local industry, the levels of segregation in local schools are affected. An officer from a London LEA near Heathrow explains:

> We've had a huge influx of refugees over the last five or more years from Somalia, Kosovo, Albania, and also way back this was a huge area for new Commonwealth settlements ... We had a huge rising population in [LEA] and we are looking at having to build another school in the north.

Owing to population changes, this LEA has ended up with parts where there are plenty of nearby school places but not enough residents to use them, and other areas where there are enough nearby residents but the local schools are seen by some as undesirable. All these geographical factors are unrelated to markets and are non-educational in nature, and between them they explain the vast majority of variance in levels of local segregation. Hammersmith and Fulham in inner-London, for example, had 16 per cent segregation in 1989 (i.e. 16 per cent of children with free school meals would have to change schools for there to be no segregation). This compared to 12 per cent in urban Knowsley, and 26 per cent in the county of Shropshire.

School organization

The next most important factor affecting segregation is the nature of local school-ing. A key indicator here is a change in the number of schools (Gorard, Taylor and Fitz, 2002a). When schools are closed or merged then local segregation tends to decrease (as happened in several areas in the early 1990s), and when new schools are opened then segregation tends to rise, at least temporarily (as has happened in the later 1990s). Another important indicator is the diversity of schooling. Areas with elements of selection have higher levels of segregation and show less change over time. The same is true of areas with higher proportions of voluntary-aided, voluntary controlled, foundation, Welsh-medium and independent schools (and more recently specialist schools appear to have a similar impact). In Shropshire, for example, a large proportion of the schools were foundation or fee-paying and the county has retained its initial level of segregation over time (actually rising from 26 per cent in 1989 to 27 per cent in 1996). Hammersmith and Fulham contained one very famous and popular foundation and many fee-paying schools, and increased its segregation from 16 per cent to 24 per cent over the same period. It is now almost as segregated as a typical rural area. Knowsley contained one founda-tion but no fee-paying schools, and its segregation decreased from 12 per cent to 6 per cent. Trafford, with one of the highest proportion of selective schools, had a massive 35 per cent segregation in 1989.

One inner-London LEA officer complains:

> All bar two of our secondary schools became grant-maintained ... which meant that for admission purposes we had no control whatsoever and still don't ... I forgot to mention that there is quite an outflow into the grammar schools [in adjacent LEA] which is really upset-ting for schools.

A rural LEA officer explained how foundation schools using apparently the same admissions criteria as the community schools can lead to segregation:

> I picked three or four at random and they're all remarkably similar to [county admissions procedures]. I think where the problems arise is that they can, for example, annexe a larger bit of catchment that didn't belong to them before and we have no power to say they can't do that.

The same thing happens with faith-based schools, according to the officer at another London LEA: 'Because we've got predominantly voluntary-aided schools' so they take from the diocese rather than locally ... across Central London'.

Thus, only around 50 per cent of local children attend a state school in this bor-ough. The remainder go to nearby LEAs (usually faith-based schools) or to fee-paying schools, meaning that this wealthy borough has a very high proportion of children in poverty (and, of course, little LEA-level segregation). As with many LEAs, having multiple admission authorities within one LEA makes it almost impossible for officers to be certain about first preferences. This was seen in an adjacent LEA as a problem for particular schools:

I think it [growth of faith-based schools] will polarize more if we're not very careful ... That was the issue with most of the other heads that the church schools were interviewing because they're looking at religious affiliation ... but seem to be interviewing for other criteria as well.

And on specialist schools:

One is a language college and therefore highly sought after because if you're doing languages you're going to be bright and if you're bright it's going to be a good school and if it's a good school you're going to go there.

Similar impacts on local levels of segregation, for different reasons, seem to occur when families have a choice of medium of instruction. The head of a rural English-medium community school in Wales pointed out how the traditionally 'privileged' Welsh speakers go to Welsh-medium schools, or *ysgolion Cymraeg*, in adjacent LEAs (and these schools, like foundation and faith-based ones, do not have local catchments), and that even the English speaking 'incomers' cannot compensate for the relative poverty of those remaining:

The Welsh families from this area go to [school] and you can imagine the converse, you have the English-medium kids from [LEA] coming here ... They are basically very English people who have moved to the area and don't like the Welsh element ... and you know the medium of communication here is mostly English ... The parents perhaps are a little bit more alternative than the usual ... more towards the hippie end. It is not always professionals, some come down from [English city] and claim dole here basically.

Areas with only LEA-controlled comprehensives have less segregation, and tend to reduce that segregation over time. We separate the school organization factors from the impact of admissions arrangements because factors such as diversity of schooling pre-date 1988. Limited 'choice' has always been available, but was previously dependent only on income, aptitude or family religion. Perhaps the problem is not so much to do with diversity of schools, as with the different forms of intake they are allowed to attract – for example, Welsh LEAs will only pay for travel to the nearest school or a more distant Welsh-medium school.

Admission arrangements

The vast proportion of variation in levels of segregation and changes over time is accounted for by the kind of factors already outlined (Gorard, Taylor and Fitz, 2002b). Given that geography and school organization precede school allocation procedures in historical terms, this means that the impact of increased market forces, if there is any, is likely to be confined to the margins of change. Policy changes at the Westminster Parliament, the action of the adjudicator, and even the growing number of appeals are not related to substantial changes in socio-economic segregation in schools. Most families still get their first preference school, and most of these use a nearby traditional or catchment school. Most of the remaining families would probably not have used these schools even if the national policy had been different. Increasing parental choice has not reduced the proportion of pupils in fee-paying or faith-based schools, which have never used their LEA school allocation procedures, and over-subscription criteria are anyway only relevant to schools with more applicants than places. It is important to recall that some schools are 'just taking what we can get. We are fighting for as many as we can.'

Even where schools are over-subscribed, most schools and LEA get around the problem of making difficult decisions by simply expanding. The planned admission numbers (PAN) are usually somewhat artificial. In Wales the Popular Schools Initiative has allowed schools to expand owing to popularity, but even in England the same thing happens, but less publicly and less formally. Whether they agreed with this 'policy' or not, most LEAs and all school interviews reported popular schools expanding to meet demand. One rural LEA has a school with a PAN of 370 but is now taking 490 per year. A popular community school in a new unitary authority regularly negotiates an increase every year:

> With [pre-unitary authority] the phone call would have been: 'This is the number and can you take an extra 30?' 'No, we need two new classrooms' – and it would be done ... With [new unitary authority] we applied to increase our number and the LEA opposed it. After that we went to the Secretary of State and ... they caved in at the end. We then changed our admission number to 227 ... Because we were continually increasing our standard number, I would say that ... everyone who applied got in.

A foundation school says: 'We have been expanding a lot ... we have just had a basic need bid that is extra funding from the DfEE to expand the school still further', while a rural county LEA admits:

> It is very difficult if you have got a 1233 school to say you can't take 1234 or 1235, so unless we have a strong case, i.e. health and safety ... we don't go to appeal because the school down the road has got places ... We don't necessarily publish admission numbers at the standard number. We consult with the governors each year ... if we have exceeded it we have exceeded it. We are now trying to get a PAN that reflects reality.

The same kind of thing happens in London LEAs: 'The members wanted to respond to this public feeling ... and what they wanted for their children ... and they expanded [school] just like that – 25 extra places'. The local level of appeals has no clear relation to segregation, but is naturally inversely related to the number of surplus places. It is not clear whether appeals are a natural and expected outcome of market forces, or whether they are a symptom of the failure of the market (Taylor, Gorard and Fitz, 2002). What is clear is that any area can elect to spend local tax income on funding surplus places, or on holding an increasing number of appeals.

However, both the LEA and school-level admission procedures do play a small part in producing our 100 per cent model. For example, LEAs that have retained some element of banding (mostly ex-ILEA) have levels of segregation in their schools running at half what would be expected *ceteris paribus*. LEAs that use catchment areas as their main method of allocating places have levels of segregation around 20 per cent higher than would be expected otherwise, and, as explained above, LEAs where a large proportion of schools are their own admissions authorities also have above-average segregation.

Choice policies do not appear to have either the clear benefits their advocates had hoped or the dangers of segregation their opponents feared. In many areas there is considerable doubt that they have made any difference – except symbolically – at all. A rural LEA officer believes that choice has been minimal because of travel limitations, that nearly everyone gets their *expressed* preference, and that it has become increasingly used by families from a wider range of socio-economic backgrounds:

> *Unless you live in an urban area, maybe with two or three schools in your general community, you don't particularly have a choice ... because we haven't extended our transport policy ... I come at that from the opposite end, which is the number of parents who don't win an appeal is probably 1 per cent and by definition 99 per cent are not totally unhappy about it. A majority of parents certainly get their first choice ... I think parental preference initially was something that was taken advantage of by relatively few people, more informed maybe. There is greater awareness now I would say.*

An officer from another rural LEA agrees with all of these points. Families do not have much choice in reality, and since 95 per cent or more choose their traditional catchment schools it is relatively easy to accommodate everyone, but the remaining 5 per cent represent a range of backgrounds:

> *When the government started talking about parental choice ... I think parents got misled into thinking they'd got choice when in fact there's very little ... This only led to more appeals, with no chance of them winning unless we have made a mistake ... I would have to say that a lot of our appeals are from people who are not particularly articulate. We get terribly scrappy notes with bad punctuation, not very well written, so it's not necessarily the most articulate middle class who are submitting appeals.*

Her counterpart in a London LEA has been in post for a long time and also sees no real change since 1988:

> *I am not sure if there was any difference in the admittance to schools. I think the schools that are popular have always been popular and vice versa ... [On the other hand] when it changed in 1976 ... those schools remained over-subscribed because they were ex-grammar schools and that's continued [and had an effect on local house prices].*

Diversity of hierarchy?

In terms of children from families in poverty, England and Wales has a socially divided secondary education system. These divisions are lowest in urban areas with good transport, low residential segregation, and mostly LEA-controlled comprehensives (and banding). Divisions are highest in mixed rural/urban authorities with poor public transport, high residential segregation, and a large number of schools that are their own admission authorities (and control their own selection). The first type has tended to decrease segregation still further since the 1988 Education Reform Act, while the second has tended to remain static. We have argued that it is important to reduce school segregation still further. Therefore, *if* a policy of increased diversity is deemed desirable, then our analysis argues that it should be organized fairly. Specialist (and the anachronistic faith-based schools) should not receive preferential funding. Nor should they be allowed to select, or to use a different admissions process to the schools with which they are in competition. Then we will be able to see the strength of their advocates' arguments. Two LEAs in our sub-sample have specialist schools that are based on catchment areas just like the remaining schools in the LEA (Gorard and Taylor, 2002b). These specialist schools take approximately their 'fair share' of disadvantaged students, but they do not have superior public examination results.

REFERENCES

Fitz, J., Taylor, C., Gorard, S. and White, P. (2002) 'Local education authorities and the regulation of educational markets: four case studies', *Research Papers in Education*, 17 (2), pp. 125–146.

Gorard, S. (2000a) '"Underachievement" is still an ugly word: reconsidering the relative effectiveness of schools in England and Wales', *Journal of Education Policy*, 15 (5), pp. 559–73.

Gorard, S. (2000b) *Education and Social Justice*, Cardiff: University of Wales Press.

Gorard, S. (2001) 'In defence of local comprehensive schools: Part II', *Forum*, 43 (1), pp. 34–6.

Gorard, S. and Fitz, J. (2000) Investigating the determinants of segregation between schools. *Research Papers in Education*, 15 (2), pp. 115–32.

Gorard, S., Fitz, J. and Taylor, C. (2001) 'School choice impacts: what do we know?', *Educational Researcher*, 30 (7), pp. 18–23.

Gorard, S. and Taylor, C. (2002a) 'What is segregation? A comparison of measures in terms of strong and weak compositional invariance', *Sociology*, 36 (4), pp. 875–895.

Gorard, S. and Taylor, C. (2002b) 'Specialist schools in England: track record and future prospect', *School Leadership and Management*, 21 (4), pp. 365–381.

Gorard, S., Taylor, C. and Fitz, J. (2002a) 'Does school choice lead to "spirals of decline"?', *Journal of Education Policy*, 17 (3), pp. 367–384.

Gorard, S., Taylor, C. and Fitz, J. (2002b) 'Variations on a theme: the relationship between local school admission arrangements and segregation by poverty', *International Journal of Sociology and Social Policy*, 21 (4, 5, 6), pp. 10–36.

Taylor, C. and Gorard, S. (2002) '"Local schools for local children" and the role of residence in segregation', *Environment and Planning*, 30 (10), pp. 1829–1852.

Taylor, C., Gorard, S. and Fitz, J. (2001a) 'The modifiable a real unit problem: segregation between school and levels of analysis', *International Journal of Social Research Methods*, 16 (forthcoming January).

Taylor, C., Gorard, S., and Fitz, J. (2001b) 'Explaining segregation', presentation at BERA annual conference, Leeds, September (available on Education-line).

Taylor, C., Gorard, S. and Fitz, J. (2002) 'Market frustration: admission appeals in the UK education market', *Education Management and Administration*, 30 (3), pp. 243–260.

White, P., Gorard, S., Fitz, J. and Taylor, C. (2001) 'Regional and local differences in admission arrangements for schools', *Oxford Review of Education*, 27 (3), pp. 317–37.

4

CHAPTER 24

Lay or professional?
Re-examining the role of school
governors in England

PETER EARLEY AND MICHAEL CREESE

Following the 1986 Education Act, the 1988 Education Reform Act and subsequent legislation, governing bodies of schools in England have had more and more responsibilities placed upon them, most recently for whole-school target setting, headteacher appraisal and senior staffs' salaries linked to performance objectives. The increased responsibilities given to governing bodies (for a list of their current responsibilities, see DfEE, 2000a) are a part of the process that has been taking place over the last 15 years and that has seen the gradual transfer of power from local education authorities (LEAs) in two directions; downwards to schools and upwards to central government. The balance of power between central and local government envisaged in the 1944 Education Act has been drastically altered and much of the role previously played by paid professionals in county and town halls is now in the hands of governing bodies. As governors are given more responsibilities and their role enhanced, the question arises of just how much it is reasonable to expect unpaid volunteers, often with minimal administrative support and training, to accept. Indeed, if governors are unable or unwilling to take on or accept such responsibilities, to what extent are headteachers stepping into the 'power vacuum' that has been created? There is some evidence to suggest that the change in the balance of responsibilities between LEAs and school governing bodies has led to some headteachers being in possession of considerable power and potentially in a very strong position (Shearn *et al.*, 1995).

Schools and their governing bodies depend very heavily upon the time and commitment given by individual governors; already some schools, particularly those located in socially and economically disadvantaged areas, experience difficulties in recruiting and retaining governors, and in attracting governors of sufficient quality (Scanlon, Earley and Evans, 1999). Has the time come when the unpaid, lay volunteer must give way to the properly trained and remunerated quasi-professional? Should governors lose their 'lay' epithet or label in recognition of the responsibilities they currently hold?

The role of the governing body

In the mid-1990s, the broadsheet *Governing Bodies and Effective Schools* (DFE/BIS/OFSTED, 1995) was distributed to every serving governor. It posited that governing bodies had three main roles; to provide a strategic overview, to act as a critical friend and to ensure accountability. More recently, the revised school inspection framework, which came into effect from January 2000, stipulates in clear terms that inspectors should examine 'how well the governing body fulfils its statutory responsibilities and is able to account for the performance and improvement of the school' (OFSTED, 1999). It goes on to state (ibid., p. 92) that the main tasks of the governing body are:

- *to provide a sense of direction for the work of the school;*
- *to support the work of the school as a critical friend; and*
- *to hold the school to account for the standards and quality of education it achieves.*

Governors' involvement in monitoring the standards of education provided in their school is an important link in the chain of accountability between the school and the community that, after all, is funding the school through taxation. In the words of the House of Commons Select Committee's report (1999, p, xi) on the role of school governors:

> It is important for the governing body to exercise 'governance skills' by which we mean asking the right questions, so that the school's line of accountability is clear ensuring that the particular interests of the local community are understood by the school, supporting the headteacher by acting as a critical friend, etc.

One source of strength for a governing body is the degree that the governors are representative of the communities served by their schools and feel themselves accountable to those communities. A recent large-scale Department for Education and Employment (DfEE) funded project found that while most headteachers and chairs (about three-quarters) felt that their governing bodies were representative of the community, schools in inner-city locations serving disadvantaged catchment areas were more likely to report that their governing body was not representative, particularly in terms of social class and ethnic background (Scanlon, Earley and Evans, 1999).

There are, however, potential difficulties for governors in fulfilling the roles first set out in *Governing Bodies and Effective Schools* (1995) and now enshrined in the Office for Standards in Education (OFSTED) framework (1999). They may lack the necessary skills, confidence and knowledge that would enable them to give a clear sense of direction to the school while also acting a critical friend (Corrick, 1996). The nature of the relationship between them and the staff, especially the headteacher, may be called into question if the governors offer too high a level challenge without, at the same time, offering a high level of support. The level of governors' awareness with regard to the effectiveness of their school may be problematic, and therefore an important link in the chain of accountability is weakened. Headteachers will, almost inevitably, fill the vacuum created when governing bodies fail to fulfil their obligations. This can lead to too much power being concentrated in the hands of the headteacher and the governing body becoming merely a rubber-stamp for his/her decisions.

The teachers' perspective

The views of teachers, and especially of headteachers, are important because it is they who have to work most closely with the governing body. Both staff and governors recognize that the governors' role has changed in the past decade. However, both groups are also aware that there is a fine line between helpful comment and interference. In the 23 case-study schools involved in a study of the role of governors in school improvement (Creese and Earley, 1999) and the nine case studies of effective governing bodies undertaken as part of the DfEE research (Scanlon, Earley and Evans, 1999), the headteachers and senior staff interviewed all agreed that there were many benefits in having an effective governing body. One of the most important attributes of a governing body was said to be that it is largely composed of individuals who bring different (lay) perspectives to the headteacher and the school, which helps to prevent the school from becoming insular. Having a group of people with a variety of skills and experience was an added resource for headteachers, which was said to enhance their role and make their jobs easier. Governors were seen as 'adding value' by calling heads to account, by questioning where necessary, and helping with important decisions that had to be made. The case-study heads found that their governing bodies gave them opportunities to learn from different people from diverse backgrounds, since sometimes the professionals were too close to the issues or had trammelled vision.

Headteachers and senior staff valued the contribution that governors made to their schools and stated that they would regret their disappearance. Governors were seen as an important resource for the school, offering in particular the following (Scanlon, Earley and Evans, 1999, p. 37):

- *a critical and informed sounding board for the headteacher*
- *support for the school*
- *help in breaking down the isolation of the head*
- *a link with parents and the community*
- *in partnership with the staff, direction and a vision for the school*
- *a forum within which the teachers could explain their work*
- *a range of non-educational expertise and experience.*

However, there is another side to the coin. In a recent survey of teacher governors carried out in 500 schools (Earley and Creese, 2001), just over half of the teachers in those schools were reported as not being particularly interested in the work of the governing body. While the majority of teachers welcomed the involvement of governors in their schools and were prepared to work closely with them, about one-fifth of the teacher governor respondents agreed with the statement that 'on the whole my teaching colleagues resent what they see as interference by the governing body'. This figure agrees closely with that found earlier in a detailed study of the relationships between governors and teachers in eight schools. Creese (1994) found that one-fifth of the staff in those schools were opposed to any greater involvement by the governors in the life and work of their institutions. They resented what they perceived as interference by untrained non-professionals; as one primary school teacher said: 'After all, it is *our* school!'.

The selection of and training of governors

Following the introduction of Local Management of Schools (LMS), there was some anecdotal evidence that suggested that the ideal governing body would include an accountant, a lawyer, a builder and so on. In fact, research shows that many heads were of the view that it was less important that governors should bring individual specialist skills to the governing body, useful though these may be, than that they display a genuine commitment to their schools and a readiness to work as part of a team (Earley, 1994). The House of Commons Select Committee (1999, p. xii) also agreed that:

> relying too heavily on the professional skills of individual governors may run the danger of distorting the proper role of the governing body. Being a school governor should not be seen as a job that only professionals could do.

Some governors may already possess appropriate skills and experience upon appointment, though they are likely to lack a detailed knowledge of the education system in general and their school in particular. Other governors may seek to develop their skills in areas such as teamwork. For all governors, therefore, training is an important issue, although becoming a school governor is one of the very few roles in the voluntary sector for which no training is essential. Survey findings from the DfEE research (Scanlon, Earley and Evans, 1999) show that although most governors (about three-quarters) reported having received some form of induction for the role, almost half had received no further training since induction. Furthermore the statement 'the governing body gives high priority to governor training and development' was one of only five statements (from 31) that elicited greater levels of disagreement than agreement by all three sets of respondents involved in the DfEE research – heads, governors and chairs of governing bodies. Governors often commented on the need for an increase in the training, both in range and quality of the courses offered, but also the uptake by governors of those courses. The government has so far refused to accept the suggestion of the House of Commons Select Committee (1999) that newly appointed governors should be required to undertake some training, although the Department for Education and Skills (DfES) has recently developed induction training materials, focusing on the earlier mentioned three key roles, available for use by LEA trainers (and others) from September 2001.

The characteristics of governors

Drawing on evidence from a long-term study of ten governing bodies in two LEAs, Deem, Brehony and Heath (1995) drew attention to the division between the lay governors and the education professionals in terms of their differing interests, location relative to the school and especially knowledge. In a governing body, the headteacher and teacher governor(s) possess professional knowledge that might be expected to far outweigh that of the other members of the governing body. However, the DfEE national survey (Scanlon, Earley and Evans, 1999) found that nearly four out of every ten 'lay' governors have, or have had, experience of an occupation related to the educational sector (see below). Deem, Brehony and Heath, (1995, p. 73) suggest that such governors play a particularly significant role because of their ability to ask pertinent questions and offer constructive advice.

To what extent do the lay governors need to acquire professional knowledge? Some commentators (e.g. Sallis, 1988) have argued that governors need no more professional knowledge than might be reasonably expected of any literate person. Lay governors gain their knowledge of schools and education in general first through their own experience as pupils and subsequently from the media, through their membership of various community organizations and through governor training. Class, gender and ethnicity may have a considerable effect on the way in which that knowledge is used (Deem, Brehony and Heath, (1995, p. 77). Governors who are unused to the relatively formal setting of a governors' meeting may find such a situation intimidating. There is a need to ensure that every governor, whatever their status or background, has an opportunity to contribute as fully as they wish. It is especially important that newly appointed governors are properly introduced to their colleagues and made to feel welcome.

A very detailed picture of governors was drawn up by the DfEE research (Scanlon, Earley and Evans, 1999) and as response rates to this large-scale national survey were exceptionally high it seems reasonable to assume it presents a reasonably accurate picture. The 'typical' governor that emerges is interesting in the light of the comments of Deem and her colleagues. Most governors were employed (26 per cent of chairs and 13 per cent of governors were retired) and the vast majority (83 per cent) were in professional or managerial occupations. Governors were found to have relatively high levels of education and professional qualifications: over one-third were graduates, about one-in-eight possessed a higher degree and just over one-quarter of chairs of governing bodies held a qualification from a professional institute. Interestingly, many governors reported having experience of working in education. In fact 40 per cent of chairs of governing bodies indicated that their current or previous occupation was related in some way to education. The figure was even higher for governors (50 per cent) and when teacher governors were removed from the analysis, the figure was 38.5 per cent. In other words, with teacher governors included, over four out of every ten governors and chairs of governing bodies reported having some connection in their current or previous occupation with the education sector. This would suggest, to some extent at least, that the boundary in terms of knowledge between the lay governors and the educational professionals as envisaged by Deem and her colleagues is disappearing.

The DfEE research showed that governors exhibited high levels of commitment and brought valuable experience to the role. The majority of governing bodies were reported to have a good balance of skills and interests among their governors. Thus the basic composition of school governing bodies indicated that in many there was a sound foundation for the creation of an effective team. But the question as to whether they are being asked to do an 'impossible job' or act increasingly as 'professionals' must be addressed. Currently, governors devote, on average, some 20 hours a term to their schools, with chairs of governing bodies spending about twice that amount of time (Scanlon, Earley and Evans, 1999). In the view of nine out of ten governors this was a reasonable workload (the proportion falls to just over three-quarters in the case of chairs of governing bodies). The DfEE research also found that 27 per cent of chairs and 13 per cent of governors were currently governors of another school. It is therefore hard to argue, at least in terms of time, that governors are over-burdened by their duties.

Lay or professional?

As the responsibilities of governing bodies continue to be extended (e.g. into monitoring, target setting, performance management and headteacher appraisal) one possible danger is that lay governors will be perceived as 'mini-inspectors' and that their role will increasingly be seen by teachers (the professionals) as one of surveillance and 'checking up'. This is especially likely in relation to the monitoring role of the governing body (Earley, 2000). Governors value the OFSTED inspection process but have no desire to operate as 'inspectors' or to be perceived as inspectorial (Ferguson *et al.*, 2000). Governing bodies are being asked to take over activities, many of them operational or managerial in nature (e.g. headteacher appraisal), that were once seen as being the province of the paid professionals of the LEA. It may be appropriate to ask, for instance, to what extent lay governors should become actively and directly involved in the monitoring process (Creese and Earley, 1999). Is such involvement comparable to that of the lay inspector in an OFSTED inspection?

The comparison with lay inspectors is an interesting one. The original idea behind the notion of the lay inspector was that they would be 'untainted' by not having worked in education and their job was to ensure that judgements about good practice were not just left to the professionals. Is it the case, as Millett and Johnson (1999, p. 75) suggest, that lay inspectors have now learned so much about 'schooling' that they can perform the management and overview role of the registered inspector? (Indeed a few lay inspectors have trained and become registered inspectors.) Is the same true for school governors? Are some sufficiently experienced and immersed in educational matters to be able to shed the lay title? Have some governors become professionalized and is the tendency to involve governors increasingly in matters 'managerial' (e.g. headteacher appraisal) rather than 'gubernatorial' (e.g. setting policies and acting strategically) encouraging such a process?

Towards a new model of governance?

Is it time for the lay perspective of the governing body – bringing a 'fresh pair of eyes', offering differing viewpoints, asking naïve or alternative questions – always seen as its fundamental strength, to be re-emphasized to avoid any possible misunderstandings or confusion? A redefinition of the role of the governing body might enable governors to focus more clearly upon 'making a difference', i.e. helping their schools to improve. The DfEE research (Scanlon, Earley and Evans, 1999, p. 7) concluded that where governing bodies were working well and making a difference they were characterized by commitment, cooperation and 'professionalism'. It noted that 'although governors are volunteers, their work is of such importance in the life of the schools, that it is essential that they bring rigour and a professional attitude to their tasks'. This 'professionalism' meant that governors were able to work together as an effective team having efficient working arrangements, they offered support and commitment to their schools and enjoyed a good relationship with the professional staff. They did not waste time discussing trivia and were concerned to ensure that they 'added value' to their schools.

However, the question of what reasonably can be expected from a group of unpaid, lay volunteers has still to be addressed. Governors themselves do not 'wish to trespass on the job of the professionals' (see, e.g. Scanlon, Earley and Evans, 1999, p. 25) but for many there still exists some confusion about their precise role and a lack of clarity regarding the exact nature and importance of lay and professional perspectives. A greater focus and concentration on governance[1] rather than management would assist in a number of ways. The earlier mentioned DfES induction training materials, which help to clarify the three key roles, are helpful in this regard.

One model of governance is that the role of the board of governors is first and foremost to monitor school policies (Carver, 1990). This model makes an important distinction between the setting of broad principles (expressed through policies) and inappropriate interference in operational matters. Carver refers to this as 'controlling the inside by staying on the outside'. Several LEAs in England have promulgated this model and it is most clearly articulated by Walters and Richardson (1997). If the policy sets out clearly what the governors want the school to achieve, the governing body can then focus its efforts on checking whether specific policy statements (with success criteria) are being achieved. The governing body itself is not seen as needing to monitor school progress; this is regarded as the proper function of the school's management, not its governance. The headteacher, as the senior professional, is seen as having the responsibility to ensure that the governing body is kept informed and provided with the information it has identified in the manner in which it wants it.

A related view has been put forward in a report from the Better Regulation Task Force (2000). It suggests that the government's agenda for raising standards in schools is accompanied by too much 'red tape' and that the lines of accountability between headteachers, governing bodies, LEAs and the DfEE have become too blurred. It argues that a governing body can create a considerable burden for the headteacher while providing little in the way of overall direction or real accountability. The report suggests that the present prescribed size of governing bodies and their over-detailed responsibilities, together with difficulties in recruiting suitable persons to become governors, contribute to the ineffectiveness of some governing bodies. Reducing the size of governing bodies and simplifying their responsibilities so that they are less involved in detailed operational matters and more able to concentrate upon what they and the school need to achieve would, it is suggested, lead to an increase in both effectiveness and efficiency. The Task Force report recommends that the governing body should be seen as a board of non-executive directors responsible for approving the appointment of the headteacher, monitoring his/her performance and endorsing the school's broad strategies and policies.

Such changes, along with appropriate induction, might ensure that governing bodies focus more closely on the three key areas of responsibility envisaged initially in *Governing Bodies and Effective Schools* (DFE/BIS/OFSTED, 1995) and specifically on the performance of the school's headteacher (or chief executive) and its staff. The availability of external advisers to the governing body to assist with the formulation and monitoring of headteacher performance objectives (introduced from September 2000) along with governing bodies' new responsibilities for performance management policies and practices, may offer a positive way forward. Research has consistently, and unsurprisingly, found that the role of the head is crucially important to school effectiveness and school improvement. Perhaps governing bodies should focus their attentions specifically on ensuring the professional staff are enabled to do as good a job as they can; after all that is what they are paid to do. School policies, necessarily shaped and constrained by national government, and the direction in which the school wishes to develop are the proper subject of governing body deliberations, albeit in close partnership with the paid professionals. The model of the non-executive board of directors, advocated by the Task Force and others, that does not involve itself to a great extent in day-to-day operations merits closer examination and the time is right for further discussion of the respective (and complementary) roles of lay governors and paid professionals.

Conclusion

The recent consultative documents on the work of governing bodies (DfEE, 2000b; DfES, 2001) argue for a more strategic and less operational role. In particular, it is suggested that governing bodies should be less involved in staffing issues, restricting their involvement to appointments to the leadership group for example. The appearance of these consultation documents will provide an opportunity for public debate as to the future role of governing bodies and whether or not the role is best fulfilled by the present pattern of untrained, volunteer, lay school governors or whether the time has come to adopt a more professional approach to school governance.

However, to adapt a well known aphorism, 'education is too important to be left to the professionals!' The view that 'we're the professionals – we know best' has a long, and sometimes ignoble, history. Yet a number of recent high-profile cases, for instance within the health service, social services and the police force, has shown that the latter view can be very dangerous and blinkered. The public, quite rightly, demands that the professionals that it indirectly employs, whether as doctors, social workers, police officers or teachers, should be held accountable, not only to their fellow-professionals, but also to the wider community. As Sallis (2000) has noted 'no important service in society is run without professional accountability to a lay body'. For this accountability to remain as clear and as open as it needs to be, school governors should continue to be drawn predominantly from within their local communities and from as many different strata and strands of that community as possible.

Though there may be some scope for reducing the size of the largest governing bodies, as suggested in the consultation documents (DfEE, 2000b; DfES, 2001), governors should continue to be drawn from lay members of the school's local community and continue to bring to their schools what Sallis (1988) has called 'the blessed light of ordinariness'. Teachers, who educate the community's children on its behalf, should remain directly accountable through a governing body that is truly representative of that community. Efforts to recruit governors from every part of society should be continued and, indeed, increased, and every governing body should have properly trained clerks. There also needs to be a greater public recognition of the key role the governing body plays in our educational system. Allowing five days absence a year from work *with pay* for all governors would be a step in the right direction. There is a need for a greater acceptance among teachers, and especially some headteachers, of the significance of accountability and of the value that a representative and effective governing body can add to a school (Sallis, 2000). In addition, there should be greater emphasis on the role of the governing body in initial teacher training and particularly in preparation for headship.

Less effective governing bodies need to be helped to become more effective. The importance of developing the governing body as an effective team and of having sound committee structures that reflect the key areas of the work of the school and governing body cannot be underestimated, nor can the importance of a good relationship between governors and staff. There may need to be a continued shift in emphasis in governor training and development in order to reflect these ideas; certainly whole-governing-body training has been shown to be helpful in enhancing effectiveness (Scanlon, Earley and Evans, 1999; Creese, 2000). Appropriate induction and further training for governors is crucial if they are to develop the skills, knowledge and confidence that they undoubtedly need.

For governing bodies to become more effective – more 'professional' in the way they work – the role needs to give greater emphasis to strategy and accountability. Training is needed, preferably but not exclusively school-based, that helps governing bodies to operate in this way and ask 'the right questions' about the school and its performance. The induction materials for newly appointed governors produced by the DfES should prove most helpful in this respect.

One thing is certain – change will continue and the role of the governing body will continue to evolve. This evolution is closely linked to changes in local government and local education authorities in England. The government is seeking 'best value' and a more sharply defined focus for accountability, with a much smaller number of elected members than in the past being responsible for all major decisions. Such a system translated to governing bodies might mean a smaller governing body concentrating upon headteacher performance, strategy and policy, with even greater management delegation to the headteacher. An open debate on the proper role and responsibilities of governing bodies is still needed. It is hoped that this chapter has contributed in a small way to such a discussion.

NOTE

1 The word 'governance' is used here to mean the activities of governing bodies.

REFERENCES

Better Regulation Task Force (2000) *Red Tape Affecting Head Teachers*, London: Cabinet Office.

Carver, J. (1990) *Boards that Make a Difference*, San Fransisco: Jossey-Bass.

Corrick, M. (1996) 'Effective governing bodies, effective schools?' in Earley, P., Fidler, B. and Ouston, J. (eds) *Improvement through Inspection*? London: David Fulton Publishers.

Creese, M. (1994) *Governor-teacher relationships following the 1986 and 1988 Education Acts*, unpublished PhD thesis.

Creese, M. (2000) 'Enhancing the effectiveness of governing bodies', *Professional Development Today*, 3 (3), pp. 49–58.

Creese, M. and Earley, P. (1999) *Improving Schools and Governing Bodies: Making a Difference*, London: Routledge.

Deem, R., Brehony, K. and Heath, S. (1995) *Active Citizenship and the Governing of Schools*, Buckingham: Open University Press.

DFE/BIS/OFSTED (1995) *Governing Bodies and Effective Schools*, London: Department for Education.

DfEE (2000a) *Roles of Governing Bodies and Headteachers*, London: Department for Education and Employment.

DfEE (2000b) *Consultation on School Governing Bodies*, London: Department for Education and Employment.

DfES (2001) *The Way Forward – A Modernised Framework for School Governance*, London: Department for Education and Skills.

Earley, P. (1994) *School Governing Bodies: Making Progress?* Slough: NFER.

Earley, P. (2000) 'Monitoring, managing or meddling? Governing bodies and the evaluation of school performance', *Educational Management and Administration*, 28 (2) pp. 199–210.

Earley, P. and Creese, M. (2001) 'The uncertain teacher governors: seeking a role?' *Research Papers in Education*, 16 (4) pp. 323–35.

Ferguson, N., Earley, P., Fidler, B. and Ouston, J. (2000) *Improving Schools and Inspection: The Self-inspecting School*, London: PCP/Sage.

House of Commons, Education and Employment Committee (1999) *The Role of School Governors*, Vol. 1, London: HMSO.

Millett, A. and Johnson, J. (1999) 'Odd one out? Some views of lay inspection', *Cambridge Journal of Education*, 29 (1) pp. 63–76.

OFSTED (1999) *Inspecting Schools: Handbook for Inspecting Secondary Schools*, London: HMSO.

Sallis, J. (1988) *Schools, Parents and Governors: A New Approach to Accountability*, London: Routledge.

Sallis, J. (2000) 'Learn to love your governors', *The Times Educational Supplement*, 9 June.

Scanlon, M., Earley, P. and Evans, J. (1999) *Improving the Effectiveness of School Governing Bodies*, London: Department for Education and Employment.

Shearn, D., Broadbent, J., Laughlin, R. and Willig-Atherton, H. (1995) 'The changing face of school governor responsibilities: a mismatch between government intention and actuality?', *School Organisation*, 15 (2), pp. 175–88.

Walters, J. and Richardson, C. (1997) *Governing Schools through Policy*, London: Lemos & Crane.

4

The role of parents in schools and education: current debates and future visions

SUZANNE HOOD

In recent decades, in Europe and elsewhere, there has been a widespread increase in policies that promote the involvement of parents, families and communities in schools and education. Governments are responding to the need to provide the levels of education that are required in a competitive and global market, and parental involvement in schools is widely assumed to play a key and critical role in raising pupil achievement.

Parental involvement can, however, take on both a variety of meanings and a range of forms (Ouston and Hood, 2000). The relationship between parental involvement in schools and pupil achievement is by no means as well or as clearly supported by the international evidence as might be supposed (Hallgarten, 2000; de Carvalho, 2001). Moreover, ideas about the kinds of relationships that should be fostered between parents and schools are constructed within a broader social and economic context. The rationale that governments use to involve parents in education is influenced by the particular values of national political culture: as a means towards school accountability, as a right that accompanies democratic values, or – as is increasingly the case in England and Wales – as a consumer-based right (OECD, 1997).

This chapter draws on current debates on the role of parents in schools and education and it aims to raise some key questions and concerns for future policy with regard to parental involvement. In particular, it examines how far parents can and should influence the processes of decision making within education and schools; and it asks whether and how this can be achieved without risk to what is another professed government goal: the promotion of equity. The content is based primarily on policy and practice in England and Wales, but the issues that are raised are of wider international relevance.

The transformation of education since the 1980s

Educational provision in England and Wales has undergone a major transformation since the 1980s. A key driving force in this transformation has been the concern of government to improve standards by increasing the power of parents, who are seen as consumers of education. Also important, however, is the view that parental involvement in learning and schools has a key role to play in promoting the achievement of children who are socially and economically disadvantaged.

This educational transformation has been evidenced in a legislative revolution that allows parents to express a preference for one school over another, and (in the recent past) to vote for their schools to 'opt out' of local authority control. Parental representation on school governing bodies has increased and more recently parents have obtained places on local government education committees. Schools are required to provide parents with information on the National Curriculum and on their children's progress at school under the Education Acts of 1980 and 1986 and the 1988 Education Reform Act (DfEE 1980, 1986, 1988). Additionally, recent government rhetoric has prioritized the notion of 'partnership' between home and school, as embodied, for example, in the rationale for written home–school agreements (DfEE, 1998a, p. 3):

> *Parents are a child's first enduring teachers. They play a crucial role in helping their children learn. Children achieve more when schools and parents work together ... home–school agreements will provide a framework for the development of such a partnership.*

This new model of parental involvement sets the conditions for greater levels of involvement and participation by all parents (Crozier, 1997). It gives parents considerable prominence within education and it represents a marked 'sea-change' from the policy of the post-war years, when parents were frequently positioned as the cause of educational problems with little role to play in relation to schools beyond ensuring their child's attendance.

It might be reasonable to assume that this new 'parentocracy' would go hand in hand with higher levels of parental involvement and with increased parental influence on decision making and governance within schools. However, more than a decade after the educational revolution, the truth appears to be far from this. Indeed, the research evidence suggests that the field of home–school relations in England and Wales is characterized by unchanging power relations between parents and schools, and that current education policy displays a fundamental lack of clarity about what role parents should play and about what the end-goal for home–school policies should be.

Parental roles in school and education in the new millennium

School choice

Governments that are aiming to promote parental involvement in schools commonly legislate for forms of collective action by parents (OECD, 1997). However, unlike in many other European countries, parents in England and Wales have no rights to form a collective body to represent their views, at national, local or school levels. As Vincent (2000, p. 6) notes, the legislation of the late 1980s, predicated on an individual market model, is 'clearly at odds with collective action'.

Parental choice of school does not, of itself, lead to higher levels of parental involvement with the chosen school (Whitty, Power and Halpin, 1998). Further, school choice researchers, who have studied the longer-term impacts of the market reforms on education, have suggested that the consumer power of parents derives from their capacity to withdraw their custom from schools – 'the power of exit' – rather than to participate in their running – 'the power of voice' (Hirschman, 1970). Importantly, it is the parents with greater social, cultural and material resources who are more at liberty to make school choices (Hughes, Wikeley and Nash, 1994; Gerwitz, Ball and Bowe, 1995; David *et al.*, 1997).

While it seems that the market system may be leading to greater socio-economic heterogeneity in schools, it is also clear that the stratifying process that is promoted by the market gives greater advantage to some parents than others (Gorard, 1999; Gorard and Taylor, Ch. 23 of this Handbook). The problems of choice are occurring at the extremes, particularly in urban areas. Thus, popular and over-subscribed schools in many of our cities continue to choose their children by overt or more covert means, while at the other extreme we see the creation of 'failing' sink schools (Hallgarten, 2000).

School governance

Individual school governing bodies in England and Wales are empowered to make almost all the significant organizational-level decisions for their school and they have greater powers than similar bodies in most other countries (OECD, 1997). They are accountable, for example, for the performance of the school, they plan the school's future direction and they select the head teacher. They are also required to make decisions on the budget, the teaching of the National Curriculum, and the approaches to be taken to ensure that the school provides for all its pupils and for their spiritual, moral and cultural development.

However, since the introduction of Local Management of Schools (LMS), governing bodies have increasingly had to emphasize their managerial role at the expense of their role in developing the school ethos (Hallgarten, 2000). It seems that increased parental representation on powerful governing bodies has done little to enhance the collective power of parents in school decision making. Indeed, the role of governing bodies in relation to the wider parent body appears to be characterized by 'top-down' information giving. Parent governors in England and Wales are required to see themselves as integral parts of the governing body, rather than as representatives of parents as a group (Vincent, 2000). Parent governors also constitute only a tiny minority of parents as a whole, and ethnic minority and working class parents are under-represented amongst them (Deem, Brehony and Heath, 1995). Finally, although governing bodies must allow parents to vote on resolutions at annual parents' meetings, and the governing body is required to consider any resolution that is passed where the number of parents attending is at least 20 per cent of the number of pupils at the school, such meetings are often poorly attended and inhibitive of parents' voices (Martin, Ransom and Rutherford, 1995).

Class, ethnicity and gender

The Parents' Charter urges all parents to become active partners with the school and its teachers in order to get the best education for their child (DfEE, 1994, p. 25). But parents are not a homogeneous group and recent research has demonstrated the key role of class, and also of ethnicity and gender, in determining parental willingness and opportunities to be 'involved'.

It is commonly mothers – not fathers – who are most engaged in day-to-day work in support of their children's education (David, 1993). Working-class mothers, although equally involved with and interested in their children's learning, may lack the cultural resources or the 'cultural capital' of their more middle-class counterparts (Bourdieu,1977). These resource-based distinctions between the social classes have been shown to be critical in determining the kinds of consumer role that mothers actually play (Crozier, 1997; Reay, 1998). Thus while middle-class parents tend to be more active consumers who are able and willing to engage and negotiate with the school and teachers, working-class parents appear to be more reluctant to question teachers' professional knowledge. These parents are also less likely to hold a specific view of their children's future that would cause them to intervene should the school be seen to be failing the child in that particular endeavour.

Research has also documented some of the cultural barriers to the involvement of parents from non-white ethnic minority groups, particularly the processes by which parents from these groups have been stereotyped and identified as 'problems' by teaching staff (e.g. Tomlinson, 1993). More recent studies have also focused, importantly, on the perspectives of ethnic minority parents themselves, and have argued that current parental involvement policies fail to recognize ethnic diversity amongst parents and institutional racism within the education system (Crozier, 2001).

School-based resistance

While the majority of teachers clearly recognize and endorse the importance of involving parents in schools and education, school-based resistance to parental involvement in school decision making remains remarkably entrenched. In a survey of 2000 primary and secondary teachers (Hallgarten, 2000), there was widespread disapproval, for example, of all the suggested areas in which parents could become more involved in decision making. Nearly three-quarters of the respondents (74 per cent) rejected the government assertion that parents should have 'a greater say in the way schools are run' (DfEE, 1997).

The parental roles that are acceptable to and encouraged by schools appear to be principally those that effectively serve to support and uphold the values and interests of the school as an institution. Thus parents are welcomed in 'supporter/ learner' roles in support of their and other children's education (e.g. home-reading schemes; volunteers in the classroom), and as active fundraisers and events' organizers in Parent–Teacher Associations. Parental involvement appears to be less acceptable when it may lead to parents having greater influence over what is taught in their child's school; when it means that parents, in general, might have a greater say in how school budgets are spent; and especially when parents might be accorded a role in the appraisal of teachers. In essence, parental involvement is unpopular where it is seen to threaten teacher autonomy and professionalism (Hallgarten, 2000).

Parental involvement: a problematic concept?

There are, as this brief overview suggests, many conceptual problems and inherent contradictions in the idea of parental involvement and in the notion of partnership that underpins the policy framework for home–school relations. We move on briefly to summarize these before focusing on the future prospects for parental involvement in school decision making.

First, the use of the term 'partnership' in 'home–school partnership' implies an equal and reciprocal relationship; but we have shown that the school remains a powerful institution in relation to parents, and an institution in which any efforts to affect the operation of the school or to influence the practices of teachers will be fiercely resisted. Schools need parents to be involved but the relationship is likely to be one of unequal partners in which the parameters for approved involvement will be determined and regulated by school staff.

Second, recent participatory initiatives ignore this fundamental inequality between professionals and parents, but they also ignore the inequalities and differences between parents themselves. Participation levels in all forms of civic or political activity tend to be skewed in favour of the middle classes, and the same is true in schools. This is a critical factor because initiatives that seek to promote parental participation may serve, in effect, to increase rather than reduce existing inequalities in education. There may be an inherent contradiction, therefore, between the policy goals of promoting partnership and promoting equity.

Third, the equality and reciprocity that is implied by partnership is far removed from the notion of a binding or compulsory relationship. Yet, in England and Wales, we see a strong policy impetus towards parental involvement for all. Parents, it seems, are both expected and required to 'be involved'. This uncomfortable alliance between partnership and a more formal contractual arrangement is evidenced in recent legislation to introduce written and signed home–school agreements between parents, pupils and schools (DfEE,1998b). These agreements set out the school's aims and responsibilities, the parental responsibilities and the school's expectations of its pupils. Their explicit policy aim is the enhancement of parents' consumer rights and the promotion of improved partnership between parents and schools. However, agreements may also implicitly serve as a monitoring tool for those 'problem' parents who fail to comply with school expectations (Ouston and Hood, 2000). Thus the concept of home–school agreements embodies more recent models of parents as 'consumers' and 'partners' with the more long-standing model of parents as 'problems': a complex, and perhaps incompatible, mix of agendas.

Fourth, and perhaps most significantly, the policy impetus and call for generalized parental involvement entails an assumption that its benefits are somehow applicable to all, but as de Carvalho (2001, p.5) notes (in relation to the USA) there may be significant problems with the theoretical sustainability of this assumption:

> The benefits of parental involvement have been concretely and ultimately related to its exclusivity – that is, student success (a quantitatively limited phenomenon) has been constructed on the basis of parental involvement as a rare resource, as involvement pays off against non-involvement, becoming a positive marker for teachers and influencing student evaluation.

There are also practical barriers to school-based involvement for all – indeed, schools do not have the capacity or the wherewithal to engage in partnerships where this means that *all* parents are playing an active role as classroom volunteers, or as participants in the whole range of school decision-making processes (de Carvalho, 2001, p. 6).

Future visions for parental involvement

So what then are the future possibilities for parental involvement in general – and in school and education decision making, in particular? Do the considerable theoretical problems with the concept render it as totally unviable?

Certainly, the evidence here does not leave a great deal of room for optimism for any significant and meaningful extension of parental roles beyond that of helper/supporter. Schools clearly appear to be institutions that need and wish to maintain autonomy and discretion in defining education and in prescribing the appropriate boundaries for partnership with parents. Schools, as institutions, do not offer very positive models of participation in relation to children – who are arguably their principal customers (Jeffs, 1995; Rudduck and Flutter, 2000).

It is perhaps unsurprising that teachers in England and Wales resent any additional threats that may be posed to their autonomy by parental involvement. For many school staff the new centralized curriculum and the highly regulated and inspected education system has meant 'initiative overload' and a reduction in professional autonomy. Any policies or practices that are seen to compound this are, understandably, unwelcome. This remains problematic if government is truly committed to improving parents' involvement in school decision making (DfEE, 1997).

Nevertheless, problems of viability do not render the concept valueless, and there continue to be many good reasons to continue to promote parental involvement in schools and education. For example, parents who have local knowledge are well placed to know the strengths and weaknesses of their children's school and to suggest improvements. Moreover, granting parents (and pupils) a greater voice in school decision making, is, as Hallgarten notes (2000, p. 93), a critical element in respecting and recognizing local diversity, and in the building of trust and social capital. The challenge is, of course, to think afresh – to recognize and confront the inherent contradictions and confusion within public policy making to date.

Current education policy emphasizes parental involvement for all (with an implicit agenda of targeting the 'problem' parents) but at the same time it provides little opportunity for parents to influence school decision making. We need, we believe, to see a shift in policy emphasis in both these areas: away from the mandatory involvement for all and towards the empowerment of parents' collective voice. The most difficult – and possibly most intractable – challenge will, of course, be to develop strategies for parental involvement that include, rather than exclude, those parents who are traditionally under-represented.

A good starting point, we believe, is to learn from international policy and practice, and to use this learning to develop new and innovative forms of parental participation at national, local and school levels (see also Hallgarten, 2000; OECD, 1997). For example, we could begin by following the example of Ireland (and many other countries) in introducing a National Parents' Forum or Council, which would be consulted on all education initiatives. We could go on to legislate for school and class-based parents' forums in every school. These are currently the rare exception in England and Wales, but the rule in nearly every European and OECD (Organization for Economic Co-operation and Development) country. These forums could input directly into school policy decisions and they could be given decision-making as well as advisory powers. We could also use the opportunity provided by the inclusion of citizenship education in the National Curriculum to involve both children and parents in contributing to the development of this part of the curriculum. This process could provide exciting and innovative models for improved pupil and parent participation in other aspects of school decision making.

While we may never be able to achieve full equity in the processes of participation, we could also experiment with ways of improving the representation of traditionally underrepresented groups in all mechanisms for promoting parental involvement (perhaps with the use of quotas perhaps or payments for governors). Such approaches would require imaginative and creative thinking, and a change of attitude amongst many teaching staff.

Last, but by no means least, we could make use of our newly developed mechanisms to enhance parental voice to consult with parents themselves about whether – and how – they wish to be involved in the governance of education.

REFERENCES

Bourdieu, P. (1977) *'Cultural Reproduction and Social Reproduction'* in Karabel, J. and Halsey, A.H. (eds) *Power and Ideology in Education*, New York: Oxford University Press.

Crozier, G. (1997) 'Empowering the powerful: a discussion of the interrelation of government policies and consumerism with social class factors and the impact of this upon parent interventions in their children's schooling', *British Journal of Sociology of Education*, 8 (2), pp. 187–200.

Crozier, G. (2001) 'Excluded parents: the deracialisation of parental involvement', *Race, Ethnicity and Education*, 4 (4) pp. 329–41.

David, M. (1993) *Parents, Gender and Education Reform*, Cambridge: Polity Press.

David, M., Davies, J., Edwards, R., Reay, D. and Standing, K. (1997) 'Choice within constraints: mothers and schooling', *Gender and Education*, 9 (4) pp. 397–410.

de Carvalho, M. (2001) *Rethinking Family–School Relations: A Critique of Parental Involvement in Schooling*, Mabwah, NJ: Lawrence Erlbaum Associates.

Deem, R., Brehony, K. and Heath, S. (1995) *Active Citizenship and the Governing of Schools*, Buckingham: Open University Press.

DfEE (1980) *Education Act*, London: Department for Education and Employment.

DfEE (1986) *Education Act*, London: Department for Education and Employment.

DfEE(1988) *Education Reform Act*, London: Department for Education and Employment.

DfEE (1994) *The Parents' Charter*, London: HMSO.

DfEE (1997) *Excellence in Schools*, London: HMSO.

DfEE (1998a) *Home–School Agreements: Guidance for Schools*, London: Department for Education and Employment.

DfEE (1998b) *The School Standards and Framework Act*, London: Department for Education and Employment.

Gerwitz, S., Ball, S. and Bowe, R. (1995) *Markets, Choice and Equity in Education*, Buckingham: Open University Press.

Gorard, S. (1999) 'Well. That about wraps it up for school choice research: a state of the art review', *School Leadership and Management*, 19 (1).

Hallgarten, J. (2000) *Parents Exist, OK!? Issues and Visions for Parent-School Relationships*, London: Institute for Public Policy Research.

Hirschman, A.O. (1970) *Exit, Voice and Loyalty: Responses to Decline in Firms, Organizations, and States*, Cambridge, MA: Harvard University Press.

Hughes, M. Wikeley, F. and Nash, T. (1994) *Parents and their Children's Schools*, Oxford: Blackwell Press.

Jeffs, T. (1995) 'Children's Educational Rights in a New Era' in Franklin, B. (ed.) *The Handbook of Children's Rights: Comparative Policy and Practice*, London: Routledge.

Martin, J., Ransom, S. and Rutherford, D. (1995) 'The annual parents' meeting: potential for partnership', *Research Papers in Education*, 10 (1), pp. 19–49.

OECD (1997) *Parents as Partners in Schooling*, Paris: Organization for Economic Co-operation and Development.

Ouston, J. and Hood, S. (2000) *Home–School Agreements: A True Partnership?*, a research project for the Research and Development in State Education Trust (RISE), London: RISE Publications.

Reay, D. (1998) 'Engendering social reproduction: mothers in the educational marketplace', *British Journal of Sociology of Education*, 19 (2), pp. 195–209.

Rudduck, J. and Flutter, J. (2000) 'Pupil participation and pupil perspective: "Carving a new order of experience"', *Cambridge Journal of Education*, 30 (1), pp. 75–89.

Tomlinson, S. (1993) 'Ethnic minorities: involved partners or problem parents' in Munn, P. (ed.) *Parents And Schools: Customers, Managers or Partners*, London: Routledge.

Vincent, C. (2000) *Including Parents? Education, Citizenship and Parental Agency*, Buckingham: Open University Press.

Whitty, G., Power, S. and Halpin, D. (1998) *Devolution and Choice*, Buckingham: Open University Press.

4

CHAPTER 26

Governance of Japanese schools

KEIKO WATANABE

Until recently, Japanese primary and secondary schools have been greatly influenced by central and local government. This system, and the peoples' commitment to the education of their children, has led to Japan achieving high educational standards. This restored the country's industrial and cultural status in the world after the Second World War had disastrously destroyed the Japanese social system and its industry.

In spite of the success of the Japanese educational system, violence and bullying in schools increased rapidly in the 1980s. This phenomenon led to widespread concern, and agreement that schools needed to have sufficient power and discretion to tackle these problems. At the same time concepts of deregulation and decentralization became part of Japanese government reform. The government cautiously introduced these reforms in the early 1990s and accelerated them in late 1990s. Initiatives are also being planned for the future.

This chapter will describe:

- the current partnership in school management and governance between central government, local government and individual primary and secondary schools;
- recent reforms, together with their background;
- likely future developments.

First, I would like to describe the basic functions of central government, local government and individual schools. The major roles of central government in educational administration are:

- To establish the basic framework for the school education system regulated by School Education Law: including qualifications for enrolment (children enter primary school in the April after their sixth birthday, secondary schools accept only those who have graduated from primary school); the number of years of compulsory education.
- To create and/or review national standards: including standards for the establishment of new schools; courses of study and curriculum standards; qualification standards for teachers; standards of class size, etc.
- To support local government to improve educational services: including financial support such as salaries of teachers and other staff, and the construction of school buildings.

- To support effective educational administration in individual schools: including guidance, advice and assistance concerning educational content, school management and other relevant issues.

Local Boards of Education act on behalf of their respective local governments. They establish, administer and operate public schools under the School Education Law. The regulations of Boards of Education prescribe the administration and operation of schools. Although details of the regulations may differ between Boards of Education, their major responsibilities are:

- curriculum administration
- the enrolment of students
- personnel administration of teachers and other staff
- administration of school buildings and other facilities.

The regulations of Boards of Education assign the daily management of individual schools to principals. Other issues, such as details of the curriculum and students' health check-ups, are conducted under the direct jurisdiction of the principals guided by the law. The Boards of Education also give guidance and assistance, if necessary. Principals have the authority and responsibility to manage administrative school issues and to monitor the performance of teachers and other staffs. Administrative mechanisms in schools, as mentioned above, are delegated to schools and are under the authority and responsibility of the principal. The ultimate responsibility, however, for school administration lies with the respective Board of Education.

This fundamental division of responsibilities and functions between central government, Local Boards of Education and individual schools, remained unchanged until now. The Central Council for Education,[1] however, proposed reform of these functions in its report issued in 1998. Its 1998 Report examined the relationship between central government and Local Boards of Education at that time and concluded:

- central government's excessive control over the Local Boards of Education discourages them from their independent operations;
- as changes in the social environment such as globalization and the knowledge-based society become more pervasive, central government must strengthen its planning functions, supplying information and research findings about the implications of such changes;
- Local Boards of Education should have discretion over class sizes.

Taking these points into consideration, central government has changed the laws accordingly so that each Local Board of Education has sufficient discretion to implement its own policy independently – such as lowering the number of students in a class compared with national standards, based on their own local circumstances.

The 1998 Report also described the relation between Local Board of Education and individual schools at that time:

- Local Boards of Education have excessive power over schools ,which deters them from developing their own individuality;
- on the whole schools lack originality and diversity because they have a long established tendency not to compete with other schools. This does not encourage them to develop their individuality and originality;
- schools should have better communication and cooperation with their students' families and the local community.

The Central Council for Education then recommended the following changes:

- Revision of the regulations: Local Boards of Education should revise their regulations to transfer more discretion to individual schools than before. These revisions should also explain to the local community, including students' families, how administrative responsibilities are shared between Local Boards of Education and schools.
- Strengthening principals' leadership: Local Boards of Education should transfer more responsibility and authority to individual schools so that their principals' decisions have more influence on the work of teachers and other staff. Local Boards of Education should give schools more discretion in budget planning so that they have more flexibility in their expenditure and can take account of their particular needs. Principals should have sole discretion in spending a certain amount of the budget.
- Introduction of a school adviser system:[2] schools should be open to their community, so parents and the community should be involved in school management. For this purpose, Local Boards of Education are permitted to appoint school advisers for each school, based on principals' recommendations. School advisers advise on school management issues such as educational activities and cooperation with the local community. Ideally they are appointed from a wide range of backgrounds outside education, for example parents, representatives of youth organizations and knowledgeable and well-informed persons in the community.
- Self-evaluation of schools: schools should be open to the local community and ensure that their management enhances the quality of education provided and that they cooperate with students' families and local community. For this purpose, schools should publish their educational goals, the details of their educational plan and their self-evaluation reports to students' families and the local community.

Following these recommendations from the Central Council, central government and Local Boards of Education have introduced the necessary legislation to implement these reforms quickly. The school adviser system is an example. The central government changed its regulations in April 2000, enabling each school to have a school adviser as part of its formal structure. By April 2001, 20 per cent of Local Boards of Education had decided to have school advisers, and 15 per cent of Local Boards have established school advisers in all their schools. An additional 7 per cent of Boards have School Advisers in some of their schools.

About one year before the Central Council for Education's 1998 Report, central government changed its policy about school zoning in response to a recommendation of the government's Deregulation Council. Local Boards of Education were allowed to be more flexible in school zoning so that schools can accept students who live outside their area. Before this change, it was only the case for those who needed special treatment, for example, if they had suffered violence and bullying in their nearest school. Now Boards are required to respect parents' wishes and give them a greater choice of schools, including those located outside their local catchment area. This is just one more example of recent reforms.

These reforms aim to ensure that individual schools have more flexibility and responsibility in their own administration, so that they can offer an education with more individuality. Prior to this, the Japanese central government and Local

Boards of Education could not solve the problems of individual schools, and enforced a very similar education programme in all schools. At the same time, these reforms also provide schools with support from outside, including the local community, so that schools can operate with less direct support of Local Boards of Education. It is the central government's intention that the local community will learn to support their schools by themselves.

In spite of these movements and reforms, fundamental role-sharing between central government, local government and individual schools is resistant to change, and consequently central and local governments' influence over individual schools is still very powerful. On the other hand, the increasing delegation to schools and the increased influence of parents and the community is an accelerating trend. From April 2002, central government started to fund a feasibility study of devolved school administration on the model of the English 'community school' under the LMS system. Furthermore, the government's Deregulation and Decentralization Councils are centrally involved in discussions of change in public services, and are expanding their interests in primary and secondary school education. Much still remains to be done in the field of school management and governance.

4

NOTES

1 'Twelve advisory councils are attached to the Ministry of Education, Culture, Sports, Science and Technology (MEXT). They deliberate on specific matters and conduct inquiries with the aims of democratizing administration, introducing specialized knowledge, maintaining fairness in administration and keeping a balance between various interests. The MEXT attaches great importance to the reports and propositions presented by the councils and considers them carefully with regard to administration' (from the MEXT website: www.mext.go.jp/english/index.htm). The Advisory Councils are funded by central government.

2 In Japan these advisers are called school counsellors. The terminology has been changed here to avoid confusion.

PART FIVE

The Business of Education: Social Purposes, Market Forces and the Changing Organization of Schools

GUILBERT HENTSCHKE

Introduction

GUILBERT HENTSCHKE

Until recently, the industrialized fields of education and business were framed as antithetical, pursuing contradictory goals as 'partners on behalf of children'. The subtext in all cases was that education and business are distinct entities, and for good reason. Throughout most of world in the twentieth century, the responsibility for providing education (especially the compulsory schooling of young people) had become the province of governments, and businesses were associated largely with private, for-profit enterprises. Private schooling, where it existed, was the province of non-profit organizations (also referred to as charities and societies in different parts of the world).

Coincident with the world's steady emergence from the industrial age to the information age, the value of education (and the cost of lack of education) has fuelled a great increase in demand for schooling. Now the consequences of a 'good' or 'bad' education to an individual's well-being are much, much greater, as they also are for societies, regionally, nationally, and internationally. This increase in demand for education has outstripped governments' ability to be education's sole financier and provider, requiring, instead, more comprehensive and complex relationships among public and private education providers and between providers and students or households.

As a consequence, new issues and old policies in education are in contest, and many are reflective of forces far beyond education. Performance competes with compliance as a means for oversight. Private choice competes with public assignment in the allocation of services. Household demand competes with provider supply in debates on equity. Access to private capital competes with appropriation of public resources to fuel organizations. The private benefits of education compete with the public good elements of education as a means for regional development. Comprehensive reach competes with focused niche in mission development. Minimal but broadly spread equity competes with maximal but selective excellence in public policy. 'Competition' itself competes with 'cooperation' as institutional strategy. And the distinctive and separate character of each of the three major economic sectors in education is dissolving.

Each of the nine chapters in Part Five on the business of education reflects some of these tensions. As a group they also fall into two broad categories, the first five dealing with the overall evolution of education as a three-sector business, and the last four addressing schooling practices in different contexts and across boarders. All the chapters address central issues associated with this metamorphosis and what it implies for educational leadership and management.

James Guthrie and Jason Walton provide a framework for understanding this evolution from the perspective of 'education reform' in the US context. Moving from early thinking about new forms of contracting to early, often problematic initiatives involving private educational providers working with public school districts, the authors describe why the problems and benefits of multisector provision of education services will be neither as 'bad' or as 'good' as most current educational advocates and critics have argued.

The 'flip side' of the coin described by Guthrie and Walton, is provided by Michael Sandler. Instead of addressing the recent developments from the perspective of school reform, Sandler addresses them from the perspective of the 'education industry', i.e. private (largely for-profit) education businesses that have coalesced into a moderately coherent and reasonably recognized sector of state, national, and global economies. Though still embryonic in many respects, the education industry has evolved into significant measurable sub-sectors of firms based on differentiation by major market segment (for example compulsory age schooling) and by core business mission (for example whole-school operation). Rapid advances in information technologies and pressures to innovate have accelerated growth across most of these sub-sectors.

As educators and communities increasingly confront issues and choices of for-profit schooling provision, inordinate attention is focused on the nature and appropriateness of profits (as distinct from the much more familiar financial elements of public appropriations and charitable grants). Arguments about profits in education (pro and con) often mask underlying understanding of the role of profits in accessing capital investments, how those investments are used to finance innovative services, and how the prospect of profits (including risks and rewards) fuels investments in businesses. Jeffrey Fromm, Todd Kern and Guilbert Hentschke provide an analysis of the entreprenurial dimension across three economic sectors in education.

Education organizations that are operated as private, non-profits (sometimes also referred to as non-governmental organizations or NGOs, charities, societies, or philanthropies) are undergoing their own form of transformation. As portrayed by Dean Millot, Keith Collar, and Renée Jacob, contextual forces surrounding education are forcing educationally-oriented non-profits to concern themselves more with issues of quality, scale, and sustainability not traditional priorities for non-profits. Consequently, these organizations are struggling to fill what the authors call a 'social capital gap' in the system of school services and improvement.

Kim Smith underscores the importance of access to capital, the new realities of knowledge work and the special role of non-profit enterprises in education – themes introduced in the previous two chapters. She then builds on these frameworks to highlight three interrelated themes that increasingly impact educational leaders everywhere: the growing importance of entrepreneurial activity by educational leaders, increasing attention to the 'consumer' as a factor in decision making, and growing recognition of not-easily-reconciled tensions inherent in the missions of public, non-profit, and for-profit educational organizations.

Beneath the sea changes affecting the provision of education as a whole, and regardless of sector location and primary funding source, schools and school-based leaders continue to operate the engine that most directly converts educational services to students into valued learning by students. Perhaps no more concrete perspective on the mutual interdependency of education and business can be provided than that presented by Allan Odden. The fundamental premise underlying his work is that schools achieve (only) those goals to which they allocate resources (financial, physical and human), and he analyses schools that have not waited to be allocated more money, having instead taken dramatic steps to reallocate available resources toward significantly higher priorities.

When schools are resistant to such transformations and continue to deliver unacceptably low performance, more dramatic measures are required. Arguably no more problematic issue confronts education today than chronically low performing schools, and it is here that governments are forging partnerships with newly emerging for-profit education providers to provide fresh approaches to improving failing schools. David Crossley provides a first-hand perspective on school leadership within the context of state takeover and company responsibility for improving a failing school. The case study involving 3Es Enterprises in England bears a strong resemblance to the experience of similar corporations in the USA, like Edison Schools.

'School failure' must be, of course, very context specific, in that the same school (and schooling practices) can be seen as 'failing' or 'fully acceptable' depending on the other schools with which it is compared. So too must the oft-held perception that private-pay private schools arise only to serve the well-to-do. The study of 'private unaided' schools by James Tooley and Pauline Dixon challenges the assumptions of many educators whose professional work has been limited to one or more highly industrialized countries. With growing income polarization around the world, the 'poor' in this case study of the educational services for the poor is of growing importance, regardless of locale. The global middle class, made up of individuals with incomes between $3470 and $8000 according to the World Bank, constitute just 11 per cent of the world's population, with the rich (above $8000) making up another 11 per cent. This leaves the poor of the world (less than $3470) constituting 78 per cent of its population, or 3.58 of them for every one of us who is not poor.

The growing value of human capital raises to new levels the importance of means for valuing human capital through degrees, credentials, certificates, test scores and other measures of academic achievement. These indicia of educational accomplishment have inherent value to individuals who claim and hold them, and different kinds of credentials will increasingly have differing market values in both local and global markets. Stephen Heyneman not only maps the rapidly globalizing trade in education but raises the moral and ethical dilemmas facing governments in promoting or prohibiting citizen access to education services across their borders.

Taken together, these chapters both capture paradigms of educating organizations as business enterprises and, at the same time, provoke new enquiries of three continually asked questions of education: who should pay for it, who should provide it, and who should benefit from it? How do the answers to these questions change when: (i) what one learns determines more than ever what one earns, and (ii) the polarization between those who earn a lot and those who earn very little is greater than ever? Educational leaders cannot avoid facing these issues in their professional work.

CHAPTER 27

Market-based reform of education: a critique

JAMES GUTHRIE AND JASON WALTON

Few people would question that formal education is a colossal enterprise. To equip students with a prescribed set of knowledge, skills and values through conventional means requires, among other things, teachers who have appropriate credentials and training, skilled support staff, administrators, adequate facilities, up-to-date technology, reliable transportation and food services. In the USA in 2002, federal, state, local and private sources will funnel approximately $390 billion into American public schools at the elementary and secondary education levels. According to the US Department of Education, this is a figure that is approximately one-fifth the size of the entire $1.9 trillion US federal budget.

Given the sum of money that is channelled towards public education in the USA, there has been no shortage of criticism and political rancour. Over the course of the past two decades, diverse and competing lines of philosophical inquiry in education have driven efforts aimed at reforming schools and positively shaping teaching and learning. Throughout this time, choruses of education critics and reformers alike assembled and went forth in waves to caterwaul one undeniably disturbing truth after another, all the while touting the solution of the moment. These reforms fan outward to the left and right from a common centre in successive wakes of discarded government and market-based reform alternatives. This chapter seeks to move inward from those ever-widening wakes of reform alternatives to a common centre by isolating the core of education that is so often targeted, yet so often missed – instruction.

The reform landscape

The oft-committed fallacy of reform alternatives has been addressed by Wolf (1993), who asserts that reform-minded individuals, whether they are in education, politics, business or financial communities, invariably and inaccurately frame their efforts as a cardinal choice between relatively perfect government-based (i.e. public) solutions and relatively perfect market-based (i.e. private) solutions. Wolf states: 'The actual choice is between imperfect markets, imperfect governments, and various combinations of the two' (ibid., p. 7).

For the purpose of providing context, it is useful to array the more contemporary reform proposals of American education. Wolf's divergent dichotomy of government-based and market-based initiatives is reflected in Table 27.1, which displays

Table 27.1 *Education reform efforts of the 1980s and 1990s*

Reform setting	Management responsibility	
	Government-based reforms	*Market-based reforms*
School system	Traditional public schools Systemic reforms National Standards Movement	Contract management of entire district
Individual school	University-based school reforms Magnet schools University laboratory schools	Charter schools Private schools for the handicapped Charter schools hiring private operators
	School-based management	School boards hiring private groups to operate schools

Source: adapted from Hill, Pierce and Guthrie, 1997, p. 55, © RAND Corporation.

and categorizes school reform efforts of the 1980s and 1990s. The table arranges reforms according to their locus and management responsibility. Unregulated vouchers are excluded from the table because their insertion would not allow for public oversight of schools' performance.

The 'government-based reforms' column in this table illustrates the manifestations of reform that emerged during the 1980s. These reforms were rooted in 'loosely coupled systems' literature – one of the major theoretical advances in the study of schools as organizations of the 1970s. Advocates of this line of scholarly research noted the virtual absence of organizational mechanisms for control and co-ordination within schools (Rowan, 1990). The lessons taken from the loosely coupled systems literature dovetailed solidly with the newly emerging effective schools movement of the post-*A Nation at Risk* 1980s (NCEE, 1983). These separate, yet complementary, bodies of research could be seen in the early to mid 1980s focus on tighter bureaucratic, organizational and professional controls (Rowan, 1990). Systemic reform, the National Standards Movement, and efforts to promote faculty and staff buy-in through school-based decision making could also be seen during this decade (Hill, Pierce and Guthrie, 1997, p. 55)

The 'market-based reforms' column on the right-hand side of the table captures the pendulous swing of the reform debate of the 1990s away from traditional tinkering within the existing system (ibid., p. 55). One of the principal underpinnings of this debate was the notion that traditional American public education had evolved, to the detriment of the public, into a near monopoly that was shielded from competition. Although there existed alternatives to traditional public education, it so dominated the existing market that true competition was negligible. Criticisms also surfaced over public school unresponsiveness to parental concerns, bureaucratic inertia, regulatory excess, preoccupation with compliance, rising costs, and diminishing results – all fuelling a willingness within the education establishment to consider alternatives that allowed for reform solutions that ranged from privatization schemes to passage of charter school laws in several states (ibid., 1997 p. 73).

These shifting winds of acceptance within the public and political arena were a remarkable departure from the more traditional reform approaches of the past. Until this time, the dominant lens through which most viewed education was one that presumed public education to mean government-operated education (ibid., p. vii). These reforms of the 1990s, when considered as a collective, spurred innovation and altered the public consciousness in terms of what a public education was supposed to look like. Public education was slowly undergoing a redefinition. The American public was lessening its collective white-knuckle grip on the traditional government-funded, government-operated understanding of public education and beginning to see private provision through government funding as an acceptable alternative. Chester Finn (1996), President of the Thomas B. Fordham Foundation, stated that the contract school, in contrast to the traditional American public school, should be thought of, 'as a [private] school that serves the public, is open to the public, financed by the public and accountable to public authorities for its results'.

Early private provision in K–12

Early forays into the K–12 (kindergarten through to grade 12: roughly ages 5–8) marketplace, however, met with considerable difficulty. One of the earlier examples was that of Education Alternatives Inc. (EAI). EAI, later known as TesseracT Group Inc., contracted to operate both individual schools (12 in Baltimore, Maryland) and an entire district (Hartford, Connecticut). Beginning in 1992, EAI not only introduced its own instructional programme in its Baltimore schools, but also took over custodial and food services. This met with a full-frontal offensive from both local and national members of the American Federation of Teachers (AFT) (Hill, Pierce and Guthrie, pp. 5–6). The union filed an unsuccessful lawsuit against the city of Baltimore and the school system asserting that the school board was bound by the Dillon Rule[1] and lacked the authority to contract with private school operators, just as it lacked the authority to contract with teacher unions (Plano and Greenberg, 1993, pp. 595–6).

Evaluations of the EAI initiative were also problematic. Predicated in the EAI arrangement with Baltimore was a set of programme evaluations based on a range of factors including student test scores, attendance and parental support. Ambiguity over how these indicators would be calibrated, and who would judge relative progress, significantly tipped the scales of perceived success in favour of the entrenched unionized interests. Under financial strain, Baltimore terminated its arrangement with EAI in November of 1995 when the company would not accept a $7 million cut in its annual contract (Hill, Pierce and Guthrie, 1997, p. 122).

In early 1996, EAI also lost its more ambitious contract to manage the entire public school district of Hartford, Connecticut. Plagued with contention from the outset, the EAI experiment in Hartford was scuttled before reaching the midway point of its contract period for managing the district's 32 schools. Ultimately, disagreements between the school board and the company over many of the fundamental provisions of the contract related to money and funding could not be resolved (ibid., 1997 p. 122).

While opposition litigation proved unsuccessful in Maryland, a Pennsylvania lawsuit forced the termination of a smaller for-profit school-management company based in Nashville, Tennessee named Alternative Public Schools (APS). APS received its first contract, to operate a single 375-student elementary school in Wilkinsburg, Pennsylvania. Antiprofiteering forces fanned the political flames that flared when APS replaced all the school's teachers with its own employees. Now known as Beacon Management, APS operated the Pennsylvania School for three years until a state court ruled that state law did not permit school districts to contract with for-profit organizations (Hill, *et al.*, 1997, p. 131).

New contracting strategies emerge

The hard lessons learned from these early attempts at private provision of public education, along with numerous others, were added to the growing discussion concerning the appropriate role of government in American public education. Revised contracting strategy proposals, which built on these lessons, began to emerge. One such strategy advanced in a RAND research study by Hill, Pierce and Guthrie (1997) offered interested groups a field manual for navigating the veritable minefield of the K–12 marketplace. The authors maintained that while contracting was just one form of privatization, it was the most common form and preserved the strongest governmental control over provision of services (ibid., p. 57).

Under this proposal, public education authorities would, through the issuance of open requests for proposals, gather propositions that catered for the district's special needs from any number of groups, including independent groups of teachers, administrators, parents, non-profit groups, universities, private firms and social service organizations (ibid., p. 53). Ideally, districts would manage diverse portfolios of contract schools, each with their own specific missions and instructional programmes that catered for the district's various needs and constituencies. The authors offer the example of a district with a significant Spanish-speaking population inviting groups to submit proposals for running a bilingual elementary school (ibid., p. x).

Specific to this proposal is that contract schools would need to be individual legal entities (in most scenarios non-profit 501(C) (3) organizations). This would give them the legal authority to negotiate contracts for products and services, as well as defend their interests in court – a legal recourse not currently available to public schools or charter schools. Just as with other publicly funded entities, contract schools would be financially accountable, through the audit process, to public authorities. Standard to these contracts would be many of the requirements met by traditional public schools, including basic requirements for student graduation, state licensing, civil rights guarantees and health standards (ibid., p. 54). With an eye towards the lessons learned from the earlier contract schools' ambiguous terms of assessment, every contract would explicitly outline each school's instructional programme, performance benchmarks and methods of assessment. Contracts could also be linked to established state curricula and standards. Schools would be allowed to pursue their mission as long as they could do right by the children they served and maintain the terms of their contracts.

What do we know now?

In retrospect, it would seem that the American education community is enraptured with models of reform. The evidence of this phenomenon that litters the twentieth century would seem enough to discourage anyone from offering up new constructs.

Still, new and recycled patterns for imitation and emulation continue to surface. Schools regularly gather at this wellspring to drink in new reforms and wash themselves of the finely powdered residue of abandoned reforms. These residues, as described by Tyak, Kirst and Hansot (1980) are the remnants of reform that are retained or left behind once the larger effort has been abandoned. For all the many reform models that have gone before, there is none that has been wholly successful. Even among the government and market-based approaches sketched in the discussion above, there are no advocates in either encampment resolved or comfortable enough in their own convictions to point to an unfailingly successful model.

At present, it would seem that the burden of proof rests squarely on the shoulders of those advocates who would propose market-based solutions to education's mounting woes. Virtually all the solutions touted by market proponents are in place as alternatives to more traditional methods of reform. Many would argue, though, that in contrast to the approximate 150-year time span that has been allotted to conventional approaches to education, to try and render a definitive judgement on the empirical effects of an approach to schooling that is still very much in its infancy would be both premature and speculative.

This is not to say that there have not been empirical evaluations of market-based solutions. As one might expect, anything that represents such a fundamental conceptual shift relative to education is certainly due its share of inquiry. What is known at this early stage about market-driven initiatives was recently the focus of another book by RAND by Gill *et al.* (2001). Areas of empirical convergence in academic achievement, choice, access, integration and civic socialization were all examined. Admittedly the authors state that even the strongest evidence of success or failure is based on programmes that have been in place for a short period of time with a small number of participants. An abridged version of the findings is summarized in Table 27.2. The table arranges, in two columns, market-based reform areas of inquiry and the corresponding empirical evidence associated with those reform areas. As was the case with Table 27.1, unregulated vouchers are excluded because their insertion would not allow for public oversight of schools' performance. The authors understandably conclude that serious doubt looms over any attempt to make generalizations about market-based initiatives, given the paucity of evidence currently available (ibid., p. xiv).

Looking to the horizon

In the coming years it is unlikely that the apocalyptic predictions coming from those who line up on opposite extremes of the school choice ledger will actually come to fruition. The prognostications of the fanatical government-based reform advocates who feel that public education as we know it will be unalterably changed by evil, conservative-minded profiteers are as likely as predictions by the over-zealous market-based reform advocates who feel the demise of public education is just within sight. In all likelihood, we will probably see a pluralist public policy model emerge.

Among countervailing theoretical efforts that posit how public policy comes into being in the American system of government, it is the pluralist model that holds that policy is the product of conflict. The public interest emerges from the welter of

Table 27.2 *Empirical evidence of market-based approaches to reform*

Area of inquiry	Empircal evidence
Academic achievement	'Achievement results in charter schools are mixed, but they suggest that charter-school performance improves after the first year of operation. None of the studies suggests that charter-school achievement outcomes are dramatically better or worse on average than those of conventional public schools.'
Choice	'Parental satisfaction levels are high in virtually ... all charter programs studied, indicating that parents are happy with [their school choices].'
Access	'Students with disabilities and students with poorly educated parents are somewhat underrepresented.'
Integration	'Limited evidence suggests that, across the nation, most charter schools have racial/ethnic distributions that probably fall within the range of distributions of local public schools. In some states, however, many charter schools serve racially homogeneous populations ... Large scale unregulated choice programs are likely to lead to some increase in stratification.'
Civic socialization	'Virtually nothing is yet known empirically about the civic socialization effects of charter schools.'

Source: Gill *et al.*, 1997, pp. 203–4, © RAND Corporation 2001.

competing groups' agendas. The truth is that modern society is not made up of homogeneous institutions and organizations. Rather, the institutions and organizations are heterogeneous, with an exponentially more complex set of interests. These institutions and organizations all share in the exercise of power (Plano and Greenberg, 1993, p. 101). In an education system that is moving toward a healthier pluralism where power increasingly becomes balanced against power, it is unlikely that any organization or interest group will maintain continued dominance.

It is, however, the conflict inherent in the domain of a pluralistic policy model that disperses the collective public attention along education's grand periphery. In the clash of opposing ideals and personalities, education's core function – instruction – often finds itself in the dimly lit wings of the American school-choice production. Education's core function should be restored to its rightful centre stage. After all, children are most profoundly affected, for good or bad, through those methods utilized to convey a school's curricula. Further, principals, district administrators and school boards are frequently overheard lamenting the burdens of how rife with administrative detail (i.e. hiring personnel, managing activities, maintaining facilities, operating transportation systems, etc.) schools have become. The import of instructional leadership, while preached from the pulpits of education schools and touted in the mission statements of countless schools, matches poorly with the sad reality of practice where instruction is habitually undermined by the very nature of the work schools require.

This is not to say that all functions outside instruction are superfluous. On the contrary, they are indispensable. Their importance should not be marginalized or understated. These are what might be termed as the enabling functions of schools, radiating outward from that core function like spokes in a wheel. The wheel of American education in the absence of these critical support mechanisms would quickly find itself unrounded and worthless to those who sought to avail themselves of its usefulness.

It is not necessary to look hard, though, to notice the burgeoning education industry that seeks to offer its own products and services to American schools for many of these enabling functions. Outside those companies marketing the private provision of instruction, there is a plethora of market-based alternatives for most of the crucial enabling functions that today's schools require. Many districts already have a considerable history of contracting out for non-instructional services such as construction, repair, transportation, accounting, legal representation, food preparation and staffing (Hill, Peirce and Guthrie, 1997, p. 52). Similarly, schools have long relied on private companies when purchasing those materials that supplement instruction, such as textbooks, hardware, software, multimedia, e-services and professional training for teachers and administrators. Instructional evaluation and measurement through testing is almost exclusively private. Some districts even successfully contract out their at-risk services, rehabilitative services, correctional services and counselling services. A number of companies are in the early stages of contracting to provide schools fully digital library solutions. In sum, few objects, services or functions in any school are not currently provided for in some way through today's education industry.

In this age where accountability is education's watch word, it is the public to whom an account is owed for schools' performance (Leithwood and Earl, 2000, p. 6). Schools are most often expected to give an account for meeting the goals of their core function – instruction. However, when it comes to the enabling functions of schools, the public seems much more tolerant of inefficiencies because of the pervading feeling that there is an end product of some intangible public good that outweighs ineffective means by which instruction is enabled. Seemingly, there is in the public consciousness a disconnect in how these enabling functions, while essential, seriously dilute the amount of attention that can be allotted by school personnel to the core function of instruction. Private provision of education's essential enabling functions not only offers schools cost savings but also creates a resource vacuum that can be filled with efforts pointed toward instructional improvement.

This is not a call to privatize all enabling functions within schools. Just as education itself is a highly localized endeavour, so too would be the implementation of such a strategy to contract out the enabling functions of schools. This would be done in varying degrees according to the needs of a school or district, as well as the availability of venders in an area. The education industry that provides these products and services, while growing, is certainly not where it should be currently in order to offer solutions on a scale commensurate with what would be required across the nation. School boards and school administrators should, however, seek out those available areas of the industry that might offer cost savings and opportunities for expansion of instructional focus.

There are, of course, possible costs associated with contracting out for these services, which school officials would be wise to note. Politically, board members need to know that in contracting out for products and services the responsibility for answering public concerns is not contracted out. School board members must continue to monitor provision, just as under more traditional circumstances. They must serve as liaisons between citizens and providers. Other costs, which are more economic in nature, might arise when local businesses lose out on contracts as school providers. Social costs might also be incurred when local service providers lose contracts because local jobs occupied by local people might be in jeopardy. Such consequences are the nature of the market. As the layers of enabling functions in education are peeled back in schools across the nation, in order to serve education's core function of instruction, those in the education community must be ready to withstand the associated pressures in the more pluralistic approach to education.

NOTE

1   Local education agencies, such as school boards, are considered instruments of the state and are therefore defined in terms of their power and structure by state law. States that observe and are limited by the Dillon Rule forbid local public entities from redelegating functions assigned to them by the state (Plano and Greenberg, 1993, pp. 595–6).

REFERENCES

Finn, C. (1996) 'Hartford schools boot out EAI – and return to the status quo', www.edexcellence.net/issue-spl/subject/contract/finneai.html (accessed 5 March 2002).

Gill, B.P., Timpane, M., Ross, K.E. and Brewer, D.J. (2001) *Rhetoric Versus Reality: What We Know and What We Need to Know about Vouchers and Charter Schools*, Santa Monica, CA: RAND.

Hill, P.T., Pierce, L.C. and Guthrie, J.W. (1997) *Reinventing Public Education: How Contracting Can Transform America's Schools*, Chicago: University of Chicago Press.

Leithwood, K.L. and Earl, L. (2001) 'Educational accountability effects: an international perspective', *Peabody Journal of Education*, 75 (4), pp. 1–18.

National Center for Educational Statistics (2001) 'Elementary and Secondary Education', *Digest of Educational Statistics*, 2001, http://nces.ed.gov/pubs2002/200213ob.pdf(accessed 5 March 2002).

NCEE (1983) *A Nation at Risk*, Washington, DC: National Commission on Excellence in Education.

Plano, J.C., and Greenberg, M. (1993) *The American Political Dictionary*, 9th edn, San Antonio, TX: Harcourt Brace Jovanovich.

Rowan, B. (1990) 'Commitment and control: alternative strategies for the organizational design of schools', *Review of Research in Education*, 16, pp. 353–89.

Tyack, D.B., Kirst, M.W. and Hansot, E. (1980) 'Education reform: retrospect and prospect', *Teachers' College Record*, 8 (3), pp. 253–69.

US Department of Education, 'The federal role in education', www.ed.gov/offices/OUS/fedrole.html (accessed 5 March 2002).

Wolf Jr., C. (1993) *Markets or Governments: Choosing between Imperfect Alternatives*, 2nd edn, Cambridge, MA: MIT Press.

5

CHAPTER 28

The emerging education industry

MICHAEL SANDLER

The education industry takes form

The twentieth century witnessed dramatic economic growth that transformed every sector of the American economy except education. A visitor from the 1880s to a classroom in the 1980s would find a remarkably familiar setting. While the fashions and furnishings of the modern classroom would have changed, the overall design of the classroom would seem quite the same, with students receiving instruction from a teacher standing in front of the classroom. While schools have largely maintained the same fundamental structure over the past two centuries, parents and policy makers, recognizing the need for education to adapt to the needs of a changing world, have increasingly brought education to the forefront of political platforms and legislative agendas. Alongside the growing political clamour, education industry pioneers have been arduously blazing a trail to demonstrate that for-profit education providers can complement, supplement and improve the existing structure of education.

In the USA, with public demands for education alternatives just beginning to rumble in the early 1990s, John Golle, CEO of Education Alternatives Inc., and Chris Whittle, CEO of the Edison Project (now known as Edison Schools), appeared on the scene to introduce the concept of for-profit school management and outsourcing school operations. The concept of mixing profits with schools was not initially well received; John Golle had taken over Baltimore's public schools (an experiment that ultimately failed), and the Edison Project faced persistent roadblocks from teachers unions and city governments as it sought to create a chain of for-profit public schools.

Clearly, as the last sector of the American economy untapped by the private sector, education – at 10 per cent of the GDP – presented ripe opportunities. The foremost business leaders in the USA identified education as the country's top priority. David Kearns, former chairman of Xerox and founder of New American Schools, said, 'Business can solve any problem in America – except education; it is our biggest challenge'. Fortune 100 CEOs responded to Kearns' challenge with over $150 million in corporate contributions to support New American Schools. However, there was little connection in the USA between public perception of the need for education reform and action to accomplish it. Although education would consistently show up on opinion polls as the number-one problem of American society, significant public engagement around education initiatives had yet to

emerge. Public concern about the state of education consistently reflected that parents were dissatisfied with education in general but were usually satisfied with
their own neighbourhood schools.

As long as problems with schools remained 'not in my back yard', there was no
impetus for large-scale changes in education. While consistently poor test scores,
when compared with international counterparts, were not enough to mobilize the
public to demand changes in education, technology eventually served as a catalyst
to create widespread concern about schools. When Whittle announced that each
student in fourth grade and above in Edison Schools' traditionally underserved
student population would receive a laptop computer, parents in schools around
the country began to demand technology for their schools. With technology and
entrepreneurial leaders serving as catalysts, the public became engaged in reform
efforts. This served to create more linkages for businesses and education; in this
light, for-profit education businesses were seen as change agents instead of as a
threat. Major barriers and obstacles remain for the seamless integration of for-
profit involvement in schools, but important steps in advocacy and investment are
paving the way for increased acceptance of education businesses in schools.

More than $10 billion in private equity has poured into the American educa-
tion industry since the initial efforts of Golle and Whittle in the early 1990s, and
Eduventures has tracked the industry's movements each step of the way.
Eduventures has seen that the private sector can improve a person's lot in life and
that instead of seeking to supplant public school education, the efforts of entrepreneurial educators in the USA enrich and support the existing infrastructure.
Despite the fact that public education remains a highly political and emotional
topic, and there persists a steady level of public scepticism about private sector
involvement in education, education markets have heated up. In 1999 and 2000
alone, more than $5 billion was invested in education businesses (Evans, 2001).
Unfortunately, in 2001–2, investors who sought to make short-term profits in the
sector lost half of that $5 billion. The weeding out of speculators has been posi-
tive, however, as now top investors in education businesses include such major
industry players as Pearson and Vivendi/Houghton-Mifflin, Reed Elsevier, Sylvan,
Kaplan, Knowledge Universe and McGraw-Hill, which are clearly committed to
the marketplace for the long haul.

An early challenge to investors in education businesses was the absence of a
common language and market definition. In an effort to create such a shared language for the nascent industry, in 1993 Eduventures began to publish *The
Education Industry Report* and *The Education Industry Directory*. Since then, annual
industry revenues also climbed from $24 billion to $115 billion in 2001 (Evans,
2001). By 1994, this consistent growth attracted the attention of Wall Street,
which had previously covered education companies through its splintered interests in publishing, educational software, childcare and school supplies, instead of
looking at these investment opportunities as part of a single industry with multiple sectors. However, Lehman Brothers, Salomon Smith Barney, Montgomery
Securities, CSFirst Boston and Bank of America soon began covering the education
sector, providing knowledgeable and well-respected analysts such as Michael Moe,
Greg Cappelli and Howard Block. Middle-size firms such as Todd Parchman's and
Lara Vaughan's Parchman & Vaughan and Bill Bavin's Education Capital Markets
emerged to provide investment banking services to the industry. 'The lure of the

education industry' hit the front page of *The New York Times* by January 1996, and other investment banks followed suit by adding education and training as a separate practice within their firms. By 1999, *Business Week* presented the education industry as a distinct sector in its annual report on the American economy.

The early players: 1990–8

Critical to any emerging market are the entrepreneurs, innovators and visionaries who lead the way. Far from engaging in cut-throat competition, such early adapters usually find that cooperation and association are vital to their survival and success. In the spring of 1990, the Association of Educators in Private Practice began its journey with a meeting of the board of directors that wanted to provide teachers the same option open to all other professions: the ability to extend their skills and knowledge to create a business. These founders – including Jim Boyle (Ombudsman Educational Services), Senn Brown (Wisconsin Association of School Boards), Wayne Jennings (Designs for Learning) and Chris Yelich (Science Capsule) – shared their experiences, frustrations and dreams at a time when no one had ever heard of educators going into business for themselves. Ted Kolderie and Ruth Anne Olson had introduced the idea in the mid-1980s, but it was otherwise foreign to the mainstream of American education.

By 2002, this fledging group, known as the Association of Education Practitioners and Providers (AEPP), had grown to 800 members and now holds an annual conference attended by representatives from all segments of the educational marketplace, including:

- at-risk service providers
- charter schools
- charter school service providers
- education and learning clinics
- educational consultants
- education investment companies
- education management companies
- education policy specialists
- educational publishing companies
- educators in private practice
- higher education faculty
- internet education companies
- learning centre operators
- proprietary schools and universities
- special education providers
- suppliers of educational products
- tutors/tutoring service operators
- other educational entrepreneurs.

As the industry association, the AEPP is a valuable resource for networking and professional development. Through its members, AEPP provides professional contacts, technical support, business advice, operating models, and encouragement for entrepreneurs. The AEPP has also established a sister foundation, the Educators in

Private Practice Foundation (EPPF), which provides a funding vehicle for industry research and education and also coordinates activities of the Education Industry Leadership Board.

The Education Industry Leadership Board (EILB) comprises the most prominent gathering of education industry leaders in The USA. Established in 1999, the EILB includes educational entrepreneurs, business executives, industry investors and education policy experts, all representing the cutting-edge of the educational marketplace. As an advocacy organization for the industry, the EILB promotes public understanding of the education industry and its commitment to advancing opportunities for lifelong learning in the global education economy. From its beginning, the membership of AEPP attracted entrepreneurs and innovators committed to the improvement of education. Some of those early visionaries were operators of alternative schools. This market – which often provided correctional, educational and rehabilitative services to at-risk and adjudicated youth – represented a business opportunity, since many public schools were unwilling to assume the additional expenses associated with these services.

The opportunity to provide drop-out recovery and at-risk services in independent settings also emerged as one of the earliest bridges for educators into 'private practice'. The US Department of Health and Human Services estimates that at least one in ten children (approximately six million young people) may have serious emotional disturbance – a common factor in the at-risk population. The desire to serve these students created opportunities for entrepreneurial innovators such as Ellen Lerner and Dave Winikur at Kids 1, John and Joan Hall at Options for Youth, Jim Boyle and Lori Sweeney at Ombudsman Educational Services, Robert Crosby at Richard Milburn Academy, and Elliot Sainer at Aspen Youth Services (now Aspen Education Group). These early pioneers in the at-risk market created private alternative programmes or contracted with schools to provide specialized services for children who could not succeed in mainstream classrooms.

Education management services also appeared early on the scene. William DeLoache and John Eason began Alternative Public Schools (APS), an education management company, in 1992. They encountered powerful opposition when the teachers union in Wilkinsburg, Pennsylvania, opposed their contract with the school district to manage an elementary school in 1994. The ultimate victory for private contracting in this case revealed one of the earliest examples of underlying public support for outside management of schools: the school board election that took place during the controversy returned a 7–2 majority of members supporting the school management company.

By the mid-1990s, alternative (at-risk) public schools, public schools managed under contract, and traditional proprietary schools were joined by a new phenomenon – the charter school – which widely expanded market opportunities for industry entrants. Ted Kolderie, an early leader in the AEPP, was one of the key architects of legislation in Minnesota that created the nation's first charter school law in 1991. Minnesota was followed closely by Michigan, Massachusetts and Arizona. By 1995–6, 25 states and the District of Columbia had enabled charter school legislation and 450 charter schools were in operation.

The charter school movement provided an important stimulus to market growth by creating a more favourable environment in which schools could contract with private providers. Prior to charter school legislation, most state law did not prohibit contracting by schools, but school boards typically did not want to face the inevitable grievances from local teachers unions, which would entail costly litigation. Under charter school legislation, charter schools were able to contract with private providers without facing union barriers. This provided a critical driver for education companies seeking to work with public schools.

As opportunities in the education market increased in the mid-1990s on the wings of the charter school movement, many existing educational entrepreneurs discovered new opportunities in the charter field. Lavelle and Hall launched new companies (Total Education Solutions and Education Management Systems), while others such as Ombudsman expanded their existing offerings to the charter field. Smaller companies such as Lynne Master's Learning Disabilities Clinic and Sue Fino's Learning Styles began doing business with charters as providers of special education services.

The rapid expansion of the charter school market also created a more promising opportunity for educational management companies as well. Today, for-profit companies operate about 10 per cent of the 2400 charter schools in operation. Early industry pioneers such as Education Alternatives Inc., the Edison Project, and Alternative Public Schools (later to become Beacon Education Management, which merged with Chancellor Academies to become Chancellor Beacon) quickly focused attention on the charter school market. New companies such as Advantage Schools, Educational Development Corporation (now National Heritage Academies), Mosaica Education and Chancellor Academies quickly appeared. The entrepreneurs behind these companies – including J.C. Huizenga, Michael Connelly, Gene Eidelman and John J-H Kim – were passionate about improving education, and each company implemented its own philosophy and unique curriculum and content.

While the K–12 (kindergarten through to grade 12, roughly ages 5–8) schools market was emerging, the public demand for high quality, educational day-care centres presented business opportunities for innovators in the childcare market such as Marguerite Sallee and Lamar Alexander of Corporate Family Solutions, and Roger Brown and Linda Mason of Bright Horizons. Jack Clegg, CEO of Nobel Learning Communities, built his substantial childcare and K–12 proprietary school business from the earlier acquisition of Rocking Horse School.

Traditional school supply companies such as J.L. Hammett Company (founded in 1863) and School Specialty Company took active roles in serving not only school districts but also the newly emerging school chains. Hammett, a technology leader and innovator, developed its e-Zone, where schools can purchase materials online through an interface that streamlines the procurement process. Such efficiencies are the result of new value-added services that have helped reduce procurement costs at the school level.

The state and national standards and assessment movements created significant opportunities for another sector of the educational market: supplemental services. Shortfalls in public education expanded the need for tutorial and test preparation, immigration generated increased need for English-as-a-Second-language (ESL) instruction, and the baby-boom echo increased college admissions competition. Supplemental services opportunities gave rise to entrepreneurial companies such as Lisa Jacobson's Inspirica (founded as Stanford Coaching) and Success Lab. Doug Becker and Chris Hoehn-Saric established the market leader in the tutoring and test preparation market – Sylvan Learning Systems – in the early 1990s. Today, the company's market capitalization stands in excess of $1 billion.

The technology age: 1998–2002

While the promise of technology was an early driver for the emerging education industry, the impact of technology on education has only just begun. Technology integration into schools has ushered in a new era of innovation for the education industry. The last decade of the twentieth century saw internet access at the classroom level soar from almost no connections to 64 per cent of public school classrooms; internet access at the school level became ubiquitous. After four years and nearly $6 billion committed, the governmental e-Rate programme, in spite of some setbacks caused by its lengthy application process, has been highly successful in wiring schools and individual classrooms for connectivity.

As a result, the education industry and educators alike have been experimenting with and developing new technology-enabled products and services that are being implemented in schools across the USA. In 2001, revenues for technology-based education companies exceeded $8 billion (Evans, 2001). While sales of technology applications and content are far outweighed by sales of computer hardware and net-working equipment in this market sector, the efficiencies offered by new technology applications are turning the heads of administrators, educators and students. Coined by Eduventures as the 'e-education framework', technology innovations have the potential to impact on everything from the way in which schools purchase pencils to the way education itself is delivered. Figure 28.1 illustrates the overlapping tools and services being used in schools that make up the e-education offering.

While software applications for both classroom and back-office use have been the mainstay of education technology for more than a dozen years, the internet has brought a wealth of new opportunities for online products and services. Initially, platform and portal providers emerged to bring a wealth of resources to children, parents and educators. Originally, companies in this space such as Family Education Network (acquired by Pearson in 2000 for $129 million) offered a collection of online resources and content-related links for parents, students and educators. Later, platforms evolved that offered classroom calendars and homework help to link homes and schools together. These platforms often included

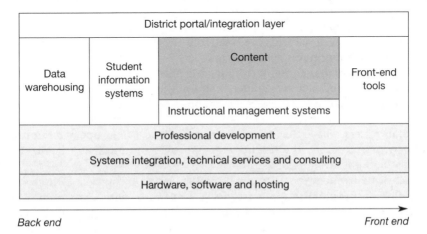

Back end   Front end

Figure 28.1 K–12 e-education framework

tools such as e-mail or chat functions, and parents and teachers had access to grading and reporting tools that later spawned more sophisticated student information systems with web-based interfaces. Originally conceived as advertising-sponsored sites in the late 1990s, many portal and platform providers were acquired by larger publishing companies seeking to build an end-to-end solution for schools.

An important component of the end-to-end school solution will be testing and assessment tools. The Bush Administration has set the stage for an era of increased and widespread testing initiatives that will compel states to develop standards-based state-wide tests in reading and mathematics for elementary, middle and high-school students. These high-stakes tests will be linked to funding for schools and graduation for students. Consequently, the demand for test development, delivery and administration, as well as tutoring and test preparation services, is soaring. Revenues in the tutoring and test preparation market alone have reached $3 billion annually (Evans, 2001). The market remains somewhat fragmented, as tutoring chain providers such as Sylvan and Kaplan make up just a quarter of the tutoring market, while the majority of services continue to be provided by independent tutors and single-centre operators.

Technology is now changing the ways in which students are assessed and data are reported and used by educators and parents. Web-based tests by NCS Pearson and CTB McGraw-Hill automatically store results and are replacing their paper-and-pencil-based counterparts. Data about student performance no longer sit in filing cabinets – instead, teachers and administrators have access to simple web-based tools that allow them to track individual student performance and pinpoint areas of strength and weakness as well as look at aggregate classroom, school or district data. These systems can be used to bring focus to school improvement plans and district strategic goals.

As more classrooms are wired with high-speed internet access, teachers will be limited only by their imaginations in terms of the volumes of resources that are available within the classroom walls. While traditional textbooks remain the norm in classrooms, digital content providers have emerged to supplement and sometimes replace textbooks. Publishing giants such as Pearson, McGraw-Hill, Vivendi/Houghton-Mifflin and Reed Elsevier/Harcourt have all created web-based supplements for traditional textbooks. Because these companies are not inhibited by the long adoption cycles and slow integration process that is inherent in bringing new technology applications into schools, these established publishers are able to make a broad imprint on digital content.

Supplemental digital content providers such as Bigchalk offer age-appropriate materials, including reference guides, web links, dictionaries and online libraries for students. Primarily marketed as a subscription-based service for which parents, teachers, schools or districts pay a monthly or per-student fee to access, supplemental providers believe that the ability to provide real-time, updated information that can be tailored by the teacher will improve content delivery and student access to relevant information.

Other digital content providers are using the web to encourage new types of collaboration and exploration by students. For example, with Classroom Connect (owned by Reed Elsevier), students can participate in a multidisciplinary curriculum that follows a group of educators as they travel down the Amazon River. In addition, content is being organized so that it can be aligned with state and district standards, and each student can have a personalized education plan using systems created by companies such as Classwell, SchoolNet and Lightspan. These companies have created instructional management systems (IMS) or student information systems (SIS) that combine classroom curriculum tools, assessments and data-reporting features that are tied directly to back office student information systems. This streamlines the education process so that, for example, if a student assessment indicates that a child cannot differentiate consonant blends, the system will suggest appropriate lessons to build those skills.

With the range and depth of education technology projects growing rapidly, professional development is a key area of interest for education constituents and companies. Lack of computer equipment or internet connections in classrooms was cited as the biggest inhibitor of technology integration. Recently, the blame has shifted to teachers and their lack of training in how to use technology as a teaching tool. Consequently, federal (more than $3 billion) and state monies are being allocated to professional development programmes that help teachers build technology skills. For-profit professional development operators generated more than $1.5 billion in revenues in 2001 (Evans, 2001).

Online professional development is emerging as a viable option for teacher training. However, providers such as Riverdeep's Teacher Universe and Classroom Connect find that a blend of online and in-person training is most effective. Online professional development providers typically deliver either text-based or streaming video to describe or show teaching best practices. Offerings include a wide range of courses, from university-based credit courses that can be applied to a graduate degree to non-credit informational pieces and chat sessions. Operators such as TeachScape are banking on the idea that their professional development offerings will see high demands as teacher turnover and new teacher recruitment take centre stage on the national education agenda.

With such rapid changes in technology, pedagogy, skills and product offerings, the road for teachers, administrators and technology coordinators is often a confusing jumble. Schools are now juggling a range of solutions – systems for everything from procurement, reporting, assessment, curriculum, attendance and accounting can all be found in schools. Logically, there is a movement to build interoperability so that procurement activities can be directly linked with financing systems, and student information systems can incorporate data from assessments. The standard for interoperability has yet to be defined, and consequently schools do not yet have the ability to streamline operations when, for example, the system that is used to operate the school cafeteria cannot be used with the system for attendance, or when the testing and reporting systems cannot be joined. As a result, firms that specialize in systems integration have emerged to assist schools. For example, Co-nect, a New American Schools comprehensive school reform design, helps a school through each step of the process of technology implementation – from strategic planning to implementation and integration.

Because technology integration necessitates significant changes in teaching and delivery practices, most schools are far from truly integrating technology into the curriculum. Revolutionary ideas such as virtual schools and online nationwide teacher colloquies are now a reality, but both students and educators have miles to go before they tap the potential that technology has for reshaping education.

Emerging as an education industry: 2002 and beyond

Technology has generated significant growth in education markets, and acceptance of for-profit involvement in the improvement of education is a mainstream concept. However, the education markets, technically, have yet to emerge as a true industry. Today, there are approximately 80 publicly held education companies with a market value of nearly $70 billion. To be considered a genuine industry, however, there must be dozens more public companies, and the market capitalization of publicly held education companies needs to be at least twice the size of revenues, or in excess of $200 billion.

Despite impatient calls for more rapid expansion, current industry figures represent a remarkable rate of growth. More than half of the current $70-billion market capitalization is from companies that were created since the early 1990s. These companies, fuelled by the ability to leverage public demands for improvements in education, a federal platform in support of innovation in schools and an environment that is more willing to experiment with for-profit involvement in schools, will serve as the engines of the education industry. In another ten years, these businesses will have matured, much like the established publishing giants of today, and the shift from an emerging industry to a true industry will take place. The acceleration of the education industry has only just begun. Fasten your seat belts.

NOTE

This chapter was originally published as a White Paper for the Education Industry Leadership Board, April 2002.

REFERENCE

Evans, T. (2001) 'Education industry revenues top the $100 billion mark', *Markets and Opportunities*, an Eduventures, Inc., annual report.

CHAPTER 29

Education leader as educational entrepreneur: managing the educational mission within and across the economic sectors

JEFFREY FROMM, GUILBERT HENTSCHKE
AND TODD KERN

Over the last several decades and for several overlapping reasons the role of educational leader has evolved in emphasis from spokesperson for the public-good elements of education on behalf of the public sector, to architect for innovations in the public-good elements of education on behalf of multisector constituencies. Although the changes fostering this evolution in schooling have been discussed at length elsewhere (e.g. Davies and Hentschke, 2002), less well examined are the implications of these trends for what educational leaders will increasingly need to know and be able to do. Principal among these – and the focus of this chapter – are the knowledge and skills associated within (and across) non-profit and for-profit as well as public organizations, especially as those skills are required to raise financial resources.

Stated simply, to the traditional role of educational leader as principal lobbyist for (and steward of) public appropriations has been added: pursuer and steward of gifts and grants (plus sales) from and within the voluntary non-profit sector and pursuer of venture capital (plus sales) from and within the for-profit sector. After acknowledging the forces that have fostered the growth of these new roles, we outline the primary differences in incentives, mechanisms and expected outcomes that educational leaders face when seeking financial resources from differing sources across the three sectors, emphasizing the motivation of the (for-profit) investor, in contrast to the (public) appropriator and (non-profit) donor. Because business development and cross-sector alliance building is now more important, we label this new reality 'incorporating the skills of educational entrepreneur onto the skill sets of educational leader'. We conclude by suggesting that the resulting new set of skill demands provide the educational leader with both greater challenges and greater opportunities than has been the case heretofore.

Reversing the trend towards solely public financing and public schooling

For a variety of reasons educational entrepreneurs and educational entrepreneurship are beginning to compete with educational leaders and educational leadership as the paradigm of what has historically been referred to as educational administration. The characteristics most highly valued in educational leaders at a particular point in history are, by definition, shaped by the context of the time. Today's valued qualities are attributable to social, political and economic conditions in education that fostered them. Those changes over the last half century have increasingly valued attributes of a government employee responsible for judicious spending of public appropriations (despite significant rhetoric about 'risk-taking').

Since about the time of the American Civil War (1861–5), public education has been considered a right and 'public' requirement for all American citizens up until age 18 (Tyack, 1974). Before that period, most American schools were privately run institutions that were accessible primarily to the children of those privileged either socially or by religious affiliation. The political goal of assimilating large numbers of new immigrants ran parallel to the growing belief that schools should teach people the necessary job skills to become effective and productive members of society. The advent of the 'common school' brought with it acceptance of the notion that every citizen (not just parents) should be taxed to support schooling and the taxing authority should be the school provider. Proponents brought about a widespread system of public education that formed the basis of what has evolved into today's public educational system in the USA.

Over the last century this K–12 schooling system of federal agencies, 50 separate state governments, nearly 15 000 school districts, and over 90 000 individual public schools has traditionally been a governmental function, with the educational leader defined as 'public official' – until recently. What factors , then, are spurring today's departure from this historical trajectory?[1]

Increasing publicly expressed dissatisfaction.

The public is increasingly dissatisfied with the public sector performance in general. Results of national polls indicate that only three in ten US citizens think the government operates for the benefit of everyone. National surveys further reveal public perceptions of government planning as inadequate and of government programme outcomes as problematic (Nye, Zelikow, and King, 1997).

In addition, surveys over the past few decades have highlighted the trend toward declining public confidence in their public schools, in part owing to increases in the individual, personal consequences of a 'good' or 'bad' education.[2] The proportion of people who expressed a 'great deal' or 'quite a lot' of confidence in public schools dropped from 58 per cent to 36 per cent from 1973 to 1999. Over that same time period the percentage of respondents who said they had 'very little confidence or none' grew from 11 per cent to 26 per cent.[3] A further marker for the public's lack of apparent confidence in public schooling is the steady increase in home schooling recorded during the last two decades,[4] as well as general over-subscription of newly created schooling options.

Increasing reliance on multiple sources of revenue

Inherent limits to funding of public educational institutions have encouraged educational leaders to pursue a variety of non-traditional revenue streams, including revenue sources not directly linked to the public school system (e.g. educational partnerships in the juvenile justice and health areas), non-profit educational philanthropy, commercial advertising in schools, and for-profit education businesses. Examples include business support of private schools, public school foundations, employer funding of adult retraining and developer fees for new school construction. The pursuit of these alternative revenue streams has in turn fostered the creation and growth of new ventures in the non-profit and for-profit segments of the private sector.

Changing organizational frameworks: from centralized public models to decentralized market models

Just as exclusively public financing has given way to mixed financing from a variety of sources, exclusively public provision of publicly financed education services is giving way to educators employed through new blends of public, non-profit and for-profit organizations. These new organizations, which in part reflect the 'market' seeking to address perceived shortfalls in both the productivity and the quality of public education, provide direct services to students via contracts with public educational organizations – or charge private fees directly to students. The new firms also are providing desired services to existing schools, colleges and universities through various forms of alliances and vendor contracts.

Increasing interpenetration by education service providers of historically protected markets

Geographic segmentation for purposes of organization, control and delivery of educational services is evolving into a market blend that crosses traditional geographic boundaries of educational services. Charter schools, magnet schools, public/private voucher programmes, interdistrict transfers and open enrolment policies exist alongside and interpenetrate across the fixed attendance boundaries of neighbourhood public schools. Distance-delivered programmes at universities are crossing state boundaries in which they are chartered, as well as boundaries of regional accrediting agencies. As political barriers to entry fall, new 'virtual' education businesses, providing web-enhanced education, are increasingly able to serve students across attendance area, district, state and national boundaries.

Changing relationships between the 'policy end' and the 'operation end': from compliance to performance

Direction from the 'top' of traditional (largely public sector) education organizations has shifted from enforcing compliance in providing uniform educational services to creating incentives for improving student performance. Especially in K–12 and community college systems, the federal and state governments are seeking increasingly to tie government funding to student academic performance while ostensibly increasing the flexibility of laws and regulations that require compliance with uniform procedures. The same is true for state licensing programmes in teacher education, in which local providers have increased 'accountability' for the performance levels of graduates in tandem with greater flexibility in programme design. Similarly, as they are being held more accountable for improved student performance, educators providing direct services to students are also gaining more latitude in determining how they will provide services. As a consequence, new education ventures (and new programmes created by existing education enterprises) that promise increased student performance are gaining more acceptance as viable alternatives for public school 'customers' than in the past.

Increasing reliance on technology for service delivery, organization and operation

Rapid developments in technology are driving down dramatically the cost of handling information in existing organizations, but they also are influencing significantly the form and creation of newer education ventures. Communication technology platform advances and interactive learning paradigm enhancements are enabling the evolution of new types of education enterprises and fundamentally altering the organization and service mix of many existing education institutions and firms. A number of education firms have emerged in recent decades whose core mission entails some form of e-learning.

Growing number and variety of education organizations

Partly in response to some of the factors described above, a large and growing variety of education organizations have come into existence (and, on occasion, gone out of business, been acquired or merged) within the last several decades. Most of these firms are located in the private for-profit sector – the natural location for educational entrepreneurs. Although one of several factors fostering the growth of educational entrepreneurship, the scope and scale of these firms is sufficiently large – and their growth as an industry is sufficiently robust – to warrant separate examination here, if only to support the concept of K–12 education becoming a three-sector enterprise.

Multisectoral leadership

These and other broad forces and trends have had the effect of blurring the traditional distinctions associated with operating within a specific economic sector. Many firms are now pursuing missions and revenues once considered 'outside the walls' of their traditional sector location – not only in K–12 education but throughout a wide variety of human service policy areas:

> Privatization of government and nonprofit functions are forcing nonprofits into new fundraising strategies at a time when there is more demand for their services. For government, public demands for efficiency, lower taxes, and less regulation are coupled with a gradual retrenchment from areas of historical social involvement. Businesses have been seeking new markets in social arenas once thought the exclusive purview of government and nonprofit organizations. More global companies are turning to nonprofit networks as partners to

address social questions affecting their business and to influence their reputation in the marketplace. Nonprofits have been the beneficiaries of government privatization and contracting initiatives, but they have also faced growing competition from the for-profit sector. (Conference Board *et al.*, 2000, p. iii)

The net effect of these trends for school leadership is that it is become 'multisectoral', wherein the school may be structured and governed in one of a variety of possible ways. Although the modal school remains (and will for some time) the traditional organization, structured as a 'branch office' of a school district with politically determined attendance boundaries, the trend is away from this towards other forms, as in Table 29.1.

Table 29.1 *Dispersion of governance and primary revenue source of K–12 schooling (from A to Bs)* The proportion of traditionally financed and governed schools (A) is declining relative to emerging alternatives (B).

Sector of schooling provider

		Public sector	Private non-profit sector	Private for-profit sector	Households
Primary operating revenue source		Traditional schools	Charter schools Voucher-funded	Contract schools Charter schools Teacher co-ops	Virtual charters
		A	B	B	B
		Voucher-funded	Voucher-funded	Proprietary schools	Home schools
		B	B	B	B

Providing education services – differences among the sectors

In contrast to the model role of educational leaders in the recent past, today's (certainly tomorrow's) educational leaders will increasingly:

- find and assume positions during their careers in private non-profit and for-profit firms as well as public agencies;
- develop alliances (partnerships, contracts, etc.) with educating organizations in all three sectors in order to enhance effectiveness and impact in their current positions.

Because of these two factors, educational leaders will also be required critically to appraise both the educational and the business models of a multitude of firms across all sectors, including the degree to which those models are reflective of the firm's principal mission and senior management's motivation.

The net effect of these and perhaps other factors is altering the role of the typical educational administrator, from one emphasizing 'leadership' to one with greater emphasis on 'entrepreneurship'. The characteristics of the educational entrepreneur and (to a lesser degree) distinction between leadership and entrepreneurship in K–12 administration has been described in similar, but not identical, ways by a number of writers, for example Leisey and Lavaroni (2000), Brown and Cornwall (2000), and Kourilsky and Hentschke (2002). Without restating the details among these and similar works, the general distinction is between the skill sets required for business development (entrepreneurship) and those required for managing a public sector agency (leadership). Despite significant overlap of skill sets (for example the ability to execute mission), we seek to focus attention on the features of entrepreneurship that represent a new addition to the skill set of educational leaders.

There are fundamental structural features associated with each economic sector that shape not only the overall incentives (rights and responsibilities) faced by educators in that sector. In addition, these incentives characterize the overall behaviour of the organizations within which they work. For a number of reasons, the alignment of incentives with organizational behaviour is not perfect, but taken as a group, patterns emerge and have been reported by others both generally and with reference to specific policy areas (e.g. Osborne and Gaebler, 1992). The principal structural distinctions among sectors in K–12 schooling are portrayed in Table 29.2.

Table 29.2 *Sector differences among K–12 education organizations*

Economic sector location of education providers

		Public	Private non-profit	Private for-profit
Features	'Profit' (Can earn excess revenues?)	No	Yes	Yes
	Buy and sell shares	Yes	No	No
	Tax revenue claims?	Yes	Few	None
	Bearing tax costs?	No	No	Yes
	Direct access to K–12 markets?	Yes	Yes	No
	Public-good responsibility?	Yes	Yes (self-imposed)	No
	Pricing services?	Free	Subsidy	Market
	Access to financial resources?[5]	Taxes	Donations/sales	Investments/sales
	Rules of the market?	Makes/follows/lobbies	Follows/lobbies	Follows/lobbies

Comparing principal missions: public-good equity, public-good niche and private good niche

Through contracting and other forms of strategic alliances, the lines between the sectors are blurring in K–12 education. Nonetheless, the primary features of organizations associated with economic sector location remain. With the growing presence of the three sectors in education, the sector-specific features of organizations take on increasing importance for the educational leader – including the organization's primary interests, emphases and structures. Intersector comparisons of organizations have been reported by numerous authors, but much more often when reporting on fields other than education.

In one comparison, for example, the primary interests of public sector organizations, include legislation, regulations and authorities; political opinion and political influence; democratic decision-making processes; the minimization of risks; and the realization of social goals. These interests stand in contrast to private sector firms' orientation towards achieving returns on the invested funds; daring to take business risks; having to anticipate market and competitive developments; and realizing a corporate goal (Reijniers, 1994, pp. 139 ff). K–12 education is similar to other fields and industries with respect to its evolution from largely public to increasing three-sector composition of the organizations providing services and goods.[6] Kourilsky and Hentschke (2002) and others have described these differences as 'comparative advantages', a term that captures not only the distinctions but the potential synergies among firms across the sectors.

Public sector

The public sector tends to be better ... at policy management, regulation, ensuring equity, preventing discrimination or exploitation, ensuring continuity and stability of services, and ensuring social cohesion (through the mixing of races and classes, for example in the public schools). (Osborne and Gaebler, 1992, pp. 45–6)

The public sector has the advantage of access to tax revenues, has the responsibility (and greatest capacity) for assuring minimally acceptable levels of schooling to all eligible children regardless of social, demographic or economic background, and makes and modifies rules of commerce that govern education firms in all three sectors. Equality for all is perhaps its core value. The comparative advantages of the K–12 organizations in the public sector include core basic learning, basic socialization and equity initiatives. The public schools manifest a comparative advantage with respect to their historical responsibilities for the delivery of K–12 core learning – the foundational knowledge and skills in areas that include reading, language arts, mathematics and basic science. As creative and innovative as private non-profit and private for-profit suppliers might be with respect to K–12 core learning, they in the end still constitute a 'market' with all that implies – free to come and go, free to change what they teach and to whom they teach with the vagaries of philanthropic funding and missions and the oscillations of supply, demand and the general economic health of the economy.

Because of the potential for damage to students as a result of supply variations or interruptions, K–12 core services represent a class of functions for which public sector responsibility can be argued to be preferable (Hirsch, 1991). Public schools thus have the structural advantage (and responsibility) with respect to reliable delivery to all students over the long-term of K–12 core learning and – with that advantage – an argument for retaining that responsibility to assure delivery of services.

Government-operated public schools also exhibit an advantage with respect to the pursuit of the 'public-good' elements of K–12 education. Public schools are in a better position to have relationships with and understand the unmet needs and inequitable access profiles of their community constituencies that are underserved. Additionally, their scale, public monopoly powers and their close linkage to government funding position them more strategically to be the delivery agents for broad government reform initiatives in public-good areas where widespread equity and coverage are valued. Private non-profit and for-profit enterprises certainly can and do engage in both minor and major initiatives for the enhancement of equity initiatives, especially in partnership with governments, for example taking over responsibility for operating heretofore failing schools. However, it is the public school systems that have the advantages of structure, reach and knowledge of their surrounding communities.[7]

Finally – particularly for the underserved – the public schools are in the best position to act as an anchor point for the student as a whole, as each student makes her/his way through K–12 schooling. Private schools are capable of performing such functions for limited populations of students (often students at the unusually high and low ends of the socio-economic spectrum), but only subsets resulting from market forces. For the majority of students, the public schools retain the responsibility for being the learner's homebase – their primary physical point of contact for learning as well as the nexus of information and functions that track the student's entire academic profile and provide equitable guidance and career counselling.

Private non-profit sector

The [non-profit] sector tends to be best at performing tasks that generate little or no profit, demand compassion and commitment to individuals, require extensive trust on the part of customers or clients, need hands-on, personal attention (such as day care, counseling, and services to the handicapped or ill), and involve the enforcement of moral codes and individual responsibility for behavior. (Osborne and Gaebler, 1992, p. 46)

The non-profit sector has access to the 'hearts' of individuals who greatly value specific elements of K–12 education, and provides a means and incentives for them to give land, labour, and capital (human, social, fiscal and physical) to K–12 education causes. This is the sector that first fills in the gaps left by government provision. Just as governments respond to 'private market failure', non-profits respond to 'public market failure'. Literally tens of thousands of voluntary, 'cause-oriented' K–12-related organizations provide a very wide range of public goods 'needs' not being provided by the public sector (see Weisbrod, 1977). Filling unmet social needs is perhaps the core value of firms in this sector. While the government and the public are often sceptical about the motivations and role of the for-profit sector in serving the public good, that is often less so with regard to the non-profit sector. Thus many of the charter school laws throughout the country provide that only non-profit organizations may be granted charters.

For-profit sector

Business tends to be better at performing economic tasks, innovating, replicating successful experiments, adapting to rapid change, abandoning unsuccessful or obsolete activities, and performing complex or technical tasks. (Osborne and Gaebler, 1992, p. 46)

The ability of the for-profit segment of the private sector to identify market opportunities, access investment capital, build compelling and innovative business models and successfully sell goods and services lies at the heart of its comparative advantage. Examples of goods and services from for-profit providers can be found across the full range of the K–12 enterprise, but their existence is based very largely on their value as determined in the marketplace. Achieving profitability through effective demand at scale is perhaps its core value.

That 'market test' is reflected in goods and services sold to households (for example encyclopedias) as well as to other educating businesses (for example school buses). The business-to-customer (B2C) v. business-to-business (B2B) – sometimes called business-to-government or business-to-education (B2G or B2E) – distinction is important here, because such a large proportion of educational enterprises are public. In many B2B instances, for-profit firms concentrate on serving niches and customers where the firm's cost/value proposition and scale economies yield a product or service which is more competitive than that which could be provided within the average size school district (six schools, $23 million annual operating budget).

Private for-profit sector firms provide a wide variety of goods and services both to public education agencies and to households, including vocational education, substitute teacher bureaus, and services for at-risk children, testing, drivers' education, instructional technology, professional development, pre-school and after-school programmes, instructional camps and supplementary curricular areas such as foreign languages and science.

Comparative sector advangages

To the extent that the generalizations about comparative advantages of firms in different sectors reflect reality, the subsequent issue is raised about the relative merits of these different advantages for K–12 schooling services, for example universal access to minimal services, innovation, efficiency and so on. It might be tempting to respond that all 'advantages are good', but that would fail to recognize that leaders must choose to operate in a specific sector and that each sector has associated 'disadvantages' (discernable above as the implicit or 'flip-side' of the advantages).

Instead, we presume for purposes of discussion that various combinations of comparative advantages are valued by the educational leader in a particular context. Further, that the educational leader will increasingly seek cross-sectoral relationships and alliances with people (and their organizations) that reflect that leader's sense of highest and best use.

Comparing primary sectoral motivations: appropriator v. donor v. investor

Few forces define the valued qualities of the educational leader more than the context of that leader's organization and its environment, and there is arguably no greater contextual influence than the sources (direct or indirect) of the capital and operating revenue to the organization. Therefore we seek here to identify the principal differences in sources of capital and revenue in order to ascertain the impact on the educational enterprise. One of the principal features that distinguish educational organizations is whether their services are sold to households or provided free of charge. Much attention has already been devoted to the growing importance of the consumer and the role that markets play in 'allocative efficiency.' The second principal difference – and the one we discuss here – entails the motivation and control of those who provide capital to the organization other than through sales. To reflect the principal motivations and roles of resource providers across sectors, we have relied on three terms: appropriator, donor and investor.

The appropriator

Public sector appropriators are (usually) public officials who lobby government agencies in order to shape the amount and targets of financial appropriations for K–12 schooling. They constitute a wide variety of specific roles included, but by no means limited to, district administrators and boards, elected officials at multiple levels of government, and interest group representatives who actively participate in legislative activity. The appropriator provides resources to the public agency to provide a promised set of services.

The appropriator is virtually compelled to provide some level of resources to specific agencies, but the conditions (strings) attached to the appropriations can vary greatly. Usually, the less confidence the appropriator has in the agency, the greater the conditions attached to the appropriation. Because of the public-good component of public funding to public agencies, both the appropriator and the agency are in virtually constant negotiation of funding (and funding levels) for basic and special projects.

The educator whose organization is funded primarily by appropriations is often involved in lobbying for more resources from the appropriator, but also is virtually guaranteed some minimum level of annual appropriation. That is not the case with the educator whose organization is funded primarily, or even largely, by donors or investors.

The donor

The non-profit donor shares the motivation of the public sector appropriator (to provide promised services to a specified population), but, unlike the appropriator, is not compelled to fund a specific organization or even to serve a specified population continuously. Non-profit donors operate in a market environment, picking and changing the organizations and projects that they will fund, and attaching conditions to funding in order to increase the likelihood that donor preferences will be carried out. Indeed, non-profit donors often require, explicitly or implicitly, that the recipient organization become self-sustaining by finding other, stable long-term sources of funding or revenue to replace the donor's capital. At the same time, the educator is also free to pursue multiple sources of donations (and revenue) and to negotiate grant conditions to suit his or her preferences to the extent possible.

Both donors and appropriators are paying for services to targeted populations and also doing what they can to improve the likelihood of efficiency and effectiveness in service delivery as they view it.

The investor

The for-profit investor is unlike the appropriator and the donor, seeking return on investment primarily, and relying on similar incentives of senior management (the educator in our analysis) to pursue returns on investment through efficiency and effectiveness. Like the non-profit donor, the for-profit investor picks and chooses among the organizations in which to invest. Relative to the other two sectors, the for-profit form of education and investor motivations have gained increased visibility in K–12 education recently, and, for that reason we devote more attention here to investor motivation and for-profit organization.

Investors tend to like large, growing markets undergoing rapid transformation, because these markets offer myriad opportunities to earn a significant return on investment. The American education industry fits this description. Total US spending (both government and private) on education and training is approximately $815 billion, second only to healthcare as a percentage of US gross domestic product (GDP). Similarly, K–12-related spending is about $375 billion. Even the for-profit sectors of the education industry are large, estimated at $105 billion for the entire industry and $33 billion for K–12 schools, products and services (of which $3 billion is spent just on schools). In addition, the growth in both total K–12 spending and for-profit K–12 spending has significantly outpaced the growth rate of the overall US economy (Eduventures.com, 2001a).

These factors have not been lost on the investment community. In the ten-year period from 1991 to 2000, private equity investors invested nearly $9 billion in education and training companies, with roughly $5.5 billion of that invested in 1999 and 2000 alone. Specifically in the K–12 sector, investment increased steadily and dramatically from $98 million in 1997 to $723 million in 2000 (Eduventures.com, 2001b). Each of these dollars is 'profit-seeking'. (While investment has slowed dramatically in 2001 and 2002, this reflects the broader economic environment without implying a targeted move away from the education sector.)

Unlike non-profit organizations, for-profit businesses typically cannot rely on government funding or private grant sources to meet their cash requirements. Yet there are a number of reasons why businesses need access to cash. They must incur start-up expenses, such as for research and development, to make their product or service ready for sale to customers. Operating expenses typically must be paid before the cash income from sale of the product or service will be received. As the business grows, the need for cash is often the greatest, because the investment necessary to achieve growth usually occurs before the generation of sufficient revenue from new sales.

Unlike the sponsor and the donor, the investor faces decisions involving trade-offs between assumed risks and expected rewards – that is, investors or lenders expect to earn a higher return on their investment when the risk of losing their money is high, and are willing to accept lower returns when the risk of losing their money is low. The risk of losing money in a start-up business is generally greater than the risk of losing money in an established business. The risk of losing money that is not secured or backed by assets of the business (such as inventory, receivables from customers, equipment or real estate) is greater than the risk of losing money that is secured by such assets.

Education businesses are often thought to be riskier than their non-education counterparts, owing to the perceived combination of government regulation, uncertain funding streams, non-economic decision making, union opposition and traditionally long sales cycles.[8] While this factor clearly reduces investor interest in this segment, a small number of pioneering investors have made substantial bets on K–12 schools. It appears that the sheer magnitude of the K–12 market, together with its perceived need for change, has attracted these investors. At the time of writing, several of the prominent for-profit K–12 enterprises (for example Edision Schools, Nobel Learning Communities) are experiencing the downside impact of the aforementioned risks, which (whether or not justified) serves both to hamper the enterprises' function and deter future investment.

Investors seek to achieve significant financial returns on investment, without regard to social mission. This is just as true for education-industry investors as it is for investors in semi-conductors or oil refineries. While the psychic benefit that results from investing in an education-related company may be welcome, investors generally do not reduce their investment expectations just because the underlying business has a positive social purpose. Over the last decade or so, there has been an emerging trend (of which TIAA-CREF is a part) towards socially responsible investments (SRI). A growing number of institutional investors (for example mutual funds and private equity funds) now apply either or both negative screens (for example anti-guns, anti-tobacco) or positive screens (for example pro-education, pro-health) to their investment decisions. Generally, these screens only supplement the financial criteria rather than eliminate or reduce them.

It is very significant in the context of for-profit enterprises that, in order to earn any return on investment, investors must have an 'exit' for their investment. That is, at some point of time in the foreseeable future, investors must be able to sell their shares in the enterprise, sell the enterprise itself to new purchaser (company or investor) or, less frequently, collect a stream of ongoing dividend payments. Undoubtedly (indeed, by design), managers of these for-profit enterprises feel pressure to devote part of their operational attention to enabling the enterprise to help investors achieve their financial objectives. This pressure is itself a double-edged sword, in that it fosters the management behaviour that results in innovation, operational efficiency and organizational effectiveness, while risking the negative impact of 'cutting corners', focusing on short-term rather than long-term goals, and potentially emphasizing the needs of investors over the needs of educational consumers or, more so, the public at large. This dual-sided impact forms part of the reason for our belief that for-profit enterprises have an important role, but not one that should ever be exclusive, in K–12 education.

Leading the educational mission beyond one sector and one source of financial capital

The comparative advantages of educational organizations in different sectors are closely associated with the principal motivations of those who provide capital to such organizations. Increasingly the ability of the educator to 'improve the scope, reach, and quality of K–12 education services' will require increasing sophistication in understanding the motivation of providers of capital in all three sectors. Most fundamentally, increased sophistication will be defined as understanding of the 'business model' as well as the 'education model' of any organization or programme. The motivation and perspective of the investor complements those of the appropriator and donor. Although individual schools are spreading across and located in individual economic sectors (the either/or circumstance), they (and the educators who manage them) are operating in a blended multisector industry. Educational leadership remains a valued paradigm, but its component parts increasingly include those of educational entrepreneur.

NOTES

1 See Davies and Hentschke (2002) for a more detailed discussion of most of the elements mentioned below.

2 Increasingly, what individuals know and can do ('human capital') is a key determinant of their personal 'socio-economic horizons' and their capacity for social and economic impact – as well as the overall economic and social well-being of the regions, states or countries in which they live. This fact has fuelled significant increases in aggregate and per capita demand for schooling to levels that are very difficult to supply and/or finance through traditional models of provision and funding.

3 Figures supplied by Public Agenda, a not-for-profit organization, which has polled Americans on education related issues for decades.

4 The National Home Education Institute estimates that between 1.5 and 1.9 million K–12 students were homeschooled during the 2000–1 school year, and those numbers are growing between 7 and 15 per cent per year (www.nheri.org).

5 The fact that much if not most of the financial resources flowing to and through the government and non-profit organizations originated in the wealth-creating process of the for-profit sector indicates the fundamental interdependence of the sectors and leading decision makers across sectors in a region. However, because it occurs in sometimes very different periods (years, decades), it is not considered material in this discussion.

6 A number of studies have been conducted that address the interplay of the characteristics of firms in different economic sectors in particular policy areas as well as intersector collaboration in those policy areas. See for example Conference Board *et al.* (2000), Rosenau (2000) and Weisbrod (1977, pp. 51–71).

7 Voucher plans are outside the scope of this chapter's discussion. Voucher plans might of course impact the choice of educational organization or institution within segments or sectors. However, such plans would not affect materially the intrinsic comparative advantages of the private not-for-profit segment, the private for-profit segment, and the public sector. Similarly, home schooling is also outside the scope of this chapter.

8 In the 1999 Venture Economics/KnowledgeQuest Ventures Survey of Education Venture Capital, over 40 venture capital firms reported their perceptions of opportunity and risk for each of 15 industry segments. The survey found that investments in the K–12 school market were percieved to contain much greater risk than opportunity. Undoubtedly, the lower perceived opportunity is due in part to concerns about whether and when K–12 companies can in fact be profitable (most profit-seeking schools are not actually profitable at the time of writing).

5

REFERENCES

Brown, R.J. and Cornwall, J.R. (2000) *The Entrepreneurial Educator*, Lanham, MD: Scarecrow Press.

Conference Board, Council on Foundations, Independent Sector, National Academy of Public Administration, National Alliance of Business and National Governors Association (2000) *Changing Roles, Changing Relationships: The New Challenge for Business, Non-profit Organizations, and Government.* http://www.independentsector.org/programs/leadership/changeroles.pdf.

Davies, B. and Hentschke, G. (2002) 'Changing resource and organisation patterns: the challenge of rescourcing education in the 21st century', *Journal of Educational Change*, 3 (4).

Eduventures.com (2001a) *Markets and Opportunities*. www.eduventures.com.

Eduventures.com (2001b) *Education Quarterly Investment Report*, March. www.eduventures.com.

Hirsch, W.Z. (1991) *Privatizing Government Services: An Economic Analysis of Contracting out by Local Governments*. Los Angeles: Institute of Industrial Relations, University of California.

Kourilsky, M. and Hentschke, H. (2002) 'Educational entrepreneurship and covisionary multisectorism', Paper presented at the ISEE Think Tank on Educational Entrepreneurship, UCLA, Los Angeles, CA, 6–7 June.

Leisey, D. E and Lavaroni, C. (2000) *The Educational Entrepreneur: Making a Difference*, San Rafael, CA: Edupreneur Press.

Nye, J.S., Zelikow, P.D. and King D.C. (eds)(1997) *Why People Don't Trust Government*, Cambridge, MA, Harvard University Press.

Osborne, D.E. and Gaebler, T. (1992) *Reinventing Government: How the Entrepreneurial Spirit Is Transforming the Public Sector*, Reading, MA: Addison-Wesley.

Reijniers, J.J.A.M. (1994) Organization of public–private partnership projects, *International Journal of Project Management*, 12, pp. 137–42.

Rosenau, P.V. (ed.) (2000) *Public–Private Partnerships*, Cambridge, MA: MIT Press.

Tyack, D.B. (1974) *The One Best System: A History of American Urban Education*, Cambridge, MA: Harvard University Press.

Weisbrod, B.A. (1977) *Toward a Theory of the Voluntary Non-profit Sector in a Three-Sector Economy*, Lexington, MA: Lexington Books.

CHAPTER 30

Social investing for our children's future

DEAN MILLOT, KEITH COLLAR AND RENÉE JACOB

From 'command and control' to competition

Public schooling in the USA is in the midst of important changes that hold great promise for America's students but are highly disruptive to the institutions that dominate the system today. Over the last decade, political demands to improve public school performance have been translated into state and federal legislation that sets standards for performance, holds schools and districts accountable for results, expands flexibility in the use of funding streams, develops the supply of effective educational programmes, and opens the system up to market forces and competition. These changes have begun to erode an all-too-comfortable set of exclusive relationships that typified public education in the past: school districts that offered a 'one-size-fits-all' education to a captive audience of students; non-profits who provided their 'good works' to schools as the third-party beneficiaries of foundation funds; and foundations who gave away hundreds of millions promoting programmes for schools without a significant base of objective evidence to aid them in their decision making.

Today, the exclusive franchise of school districts is under challenge. Increasingly, legislatures are giving state education agencies the right to take over failing districts and change the delivery of public school services. In response to these threats, school districts show signs of evolving away from the one-size-fits-all approach. In a growing number of districts, the school system's core functions – built around the processes of teaching and learning – are being contracted-out, based on expectations of what will most likely improve student performance. Decision makers at the district level are more open to having outside service providers, both for-profit and non-profit, work in the classroom to support instruction. In most cases, districts are deliberately engaging in multiple contracts to increase choice and optimize performance.

The implications for providers of school reform services are tremendous. Until recently, external support to help school systems improve teaching and learning was provided almost exclusively by non-profit entities, generally financed by philanthropy for school reform. In a growing number of districts, however, responsibility for curriculum, pedagogy and professional development is moving to for-profit providers such as Sylvan Learning Systems, Lightspan and Open Court, as well as contracts with such non-profit providers as Success For All, Accelerated Schools Project and Different Ways of Knowing. Districts are increasingly prepared to pay for results and, as a consequence, they are demanding more from the providers they pay than they demanded from those willing to offer intervention programmes for free.

The Education Entrepreneurs Fund, the non-profit financing arm of New American Schools, meets a growing need for intermediary institutions to support socially motivated enterprises in a marketplace that is fast making the traditional paradigm of school intervention by grant-maintained non-profits obsolete. As a social investor in the rapidly growing market for public school reform, the Fund helps non-profit and other social enterprises that have developed promising educational programmes to achieve national scale and financial sustainability. The Fund exists to meet the need of foundations and non-profits that recognize the demise of the old paradigm, see an important role for social enterprise in the growing market, and feel confident in their ability to learn how to harness business discipline in pursuit of their missions.

The fact that the rapid emergence and growth of the market for school improvement services disrupts the traditional paradigm of foundation and non-profit engagement with school districts does not mean that either is irrelevant – far from it. The old system, based on the command and control values of central planning, failed because of inflexibility. The new system, based on market forces, is highly flexible, but markets are not perfect instruments of public policy. Markets are based on the value of profit. If quality will yield a profit, the market will value quality. But no profit-seeking entity will value quality in and of itself. And without a battle over quality, competition will focus on price. If viable high-quality offerings are available to enough schools, other providers will always be forced to compete on quality as well as price.

Non-profits and the emerging school improvement industry

In an area as important as the education of the nation's children, it is imperative that a sufficient share of the market be held by organizations that will always favour improving the quality of their products and services over the distribution of profit to shareholders. A substantial market share for non-profits is the best market mechanism to influence the quality of for-profit offerings. But if non-profits are to become the standard-bearers of quality, they cannot be completely non-competitive on price.

In this respect, the USA's experience with health care is instructive. As part of an effort to control soaring costs, much of the nation's health care system transitioned from non-profit to for-profit status. In a decade, non-profits went from the dominant force in the market to its margins. While this resulted in greater efficiency and affordability, many Americans would contend that the quality of care has diminished considerably. The USA faces an analogous situation today in public education. Although the school improvement market remains dominated by non-profits, for-profits have made incredibly rapid advances. Unless something is done to help the non-profit sector remain a vibrant force in education, quality will be sacrificed and the nation's children will pay the price.

As critical as the non-profit sector is, however, there are some formidable obstacles to assuring its survival in the school improvement market. The primary operational challenge facing non-profits that seek to enter the school improvement market is capacity. The starting point for most is a management structure built around research, an administrative structure for overseeing projects, and a revenue stream based on grants. This level of infrastructure is insufficient for organizations operating in a market. This type of non-profit might be rich in 'raw materials' – it generally has a wealth of intellectual capital, a broad base of experience in schools and districts, pervasive contacts throughout the system, and the good will of at least some foundations – yet it is generally asset poor – it has done little to create intellectual property, has no formal repository of knowledge, and relationships are more likely to be owned by individuals than the institution.

Turning these latent assets into goods and services that can be disseminated at scale is an ambitious undertaking. It requires:

- bringing finance to the decision table and giving it a say equal to research and field work;
- developing routines and standard processes, and reducing expert knowledge to written manuals and guides;
- hiring outsiders and accelerating staff training that historically took two to three years;
- replacing the conference table with formal systems of quality control;
- paying close attention to the costs incurred in the process of achieving the same result in multiple schools;
- focusing on cash management, because fees are paid in small amounts and generally late, while the expenses incurred in working with schools stay on track.

In most cases, non-profit organizations need considerable technical assistance if they are to become competitive. And making this transition cannot simply be a matter of becoming a business. If the non-profit's social purpose is to be realized, it must learn to harness business discipline in pursuit of its mission. For this reason, the Education Entrepreneurs Fund provides a wide array of assistance to the social enterprises it serves, including:

- investment in the form of loans and equity;
- technical assistance in business planning, finance, marketing and operations;
- facilitated networking in support of business development and marketing opportunities.

Forging a path to quality, scale and sustainability

The collective experience of New American Schools and the Education Entrepreneurs Fund over the past ten years has created a path to quality, as measured by student achievement; scale, as measured by the number of schools served; and sustainability, as measured by a viable business model that can serve schools over a long period of engagement. This path required a new way of thinking about bringing high-quality education programmes to large numbers of schools and students. Today the market for school improvement is so much larger than foundations' direct funding for the same purpose, and growing so much faster that the traditional role of foundations must be questioned. While grants were – and will continue to be – a critical component of building social enterprises, education organizations also need to address the challenges of generating fees for their work and financing their growth with sources of financing other than grants. Experience indicates that both supply and demand around education reform are well served by a fee-for-service approach, as outlined in Table 30.1.

While he was superintendent in Houston, the current US Secretary of Education, Rod Paige, pioneered the movement of districts becoming informed and paying consumers. The strength of Paige's efforts lay in his ability to leverage changes in federal policy that increased the flexibility with which schools could use Title I funding streams, and promoted the development and dissemination of promising school improvement services that schools could purchase through initiatives like the Comprehensive School Reform Demonstration Program. The recently reauthorized Elementary and Secondary Education Act will accelerate this trend, with more money earmarked for schools to purchase privately provided for-profit and non-profit educational programmes and greater flexibility to use other federal funds for the same purpose. As a consequence, the value of many free programmes is being called into question and more non-profits are finding it necessary to move towards an approach based on fee-for-service dissemination of their services.

Table 30.1 *Advantages of a fee-for-service model in educational reform*

	Supply	Demand
Quality	A fee-for-service model more acutely focuses the provider on the needs of the purchaser. Accountability is becoming more and more prevalent, with greater attention to performance measures; unconditional grant-making is likely to decline as accountability continues to gain momentum.	Users attach more value to products and services for which they pay; real change requires a new spending pattern. Commitment to a programme is reflected in paying for it; a budget is the manifestation of priorities.
Scale	Not enough grant money exists to bring these activities to scale. Raising the academic achievement of all students and all schools is beyond the scope of a grant-based business model.	Local leaders need external support for new ideas. Potential purchasers value the solutions but need the credibility of a national research base to garner local support.
Sustainability	A fee-for-service model enables the provider to control its own destiny and to create a business that is built to last. The long-term viability of the business is founded in the activity itself, not in the reliance on third-party grants.	Users implementing education programmes need assurance that their providers will be operative for the long term and can be depended upon to deliver on a continuous improvement strategy over a number of years.

Barriers to levelling the playing field

As education organizations move to a fee-for-service dissemination strategy, they begin to encounter the challenges faced by most businesses. One of these challenges is the need for adequate capital. Developing organizations need capital for several vital purposes, including:

- hiring staff in advance of collecting revenue to cover those costs;
- investment in infrastructure, such as quality assurance systems that will form the foundation of future programmatic success;
- managing the cash-flow gaps that are an inherent part of providing services to schools and districts, which are reliable but sometimes painfully slow payers.

While millions of dollars of grants are extended to education organizations every year, not enough grant dollars exist to bring high-quality education programmes to schools that need them the most. Social enterprises serving education must find alternatives to grant financing if they are to reach their programmatic and financial potential. For the most part, however, education organizations are limited in their options to access this type of financial support. Few early-stage education organizations have the wherewithal to access financing from traditional sources such as private investors or commercial lenders. Traditional lenders, such as commercial banks, are seeking longer track records, larger capital bases and perhaps outside credit enhancement.

The question then becomes, how can traditional non-profits seeking to enter the school improvement market make the transition to becoming fee-for-service operations and realize the goals of quality, scale and sustainability if they lack a counterpart to the business and financial infrastructure available to for-profits?

In for-profit markets, there exists a 'transmission belt' for taking good ideas to scale. Individuals and firms, commonly known as angel investors, motivated by the potential for profit, create funds to provide seed capital to inventors and entrepreneurs and lend them their experience and contacts. When the idea has become a product or service, these angels have relationships with venture capital firms that specialize in growing companies – providing another level of funding, expertise and contacts. As the new firm begins to achieve scale, the venture capitalists may work with investment bankers to raise 'mezzanine' financing. Eventually, the firm may go to Wall Street for an initial public offering (IPO) of shares to the public, be acquired by a larger company to fill a strategic need, or gain access to bank financing. In so doing, these organizations reach a stage of maturity. Surrounding this growth process is an army of professionals providing specialized strategic, research, legal, financing, marketing and accounting expertise.

Social enterprises, particularly non-profit organizations, lack this transmission belt. Foundations and government agencies have made hundreds of millions of dollars available for research, development and pilot projects in the area of school improvement – they are the 'angels' in this equivalent of the seed-capital stage in for-profit parlance. At the other end of the growth process, mature non-profits like the Boys' Club, the Girl Scouts and the American Red Cross regularly access private financing. In between, some funds might be available from foundations and government for refinement of school improvement models, but for the most part, there is simply no way to get from the 'here' of research to the 'there' of maturity.

There is little in the way of a process by which non-profits move from grant to fee, little capital to do so, a scant body of expertise to bring business disciplines to bear on nonprofit challenges, and no mechanism for convening non-profits to surmount these challenges collectively. The Education Entrepreneurs Fund terms this lack of a transmission belt for these enterprises the 'social capital gap'.

Foundation/ government grants	Social venture capital	Social capital loans	Private debt/ equity markets
	Capital gap		
Start-up organizations	Early-growth organizations	Late-growth organizations	Mature organizations

Figure 30.1 The social capital gap

Figure 30.1 depicts the lack of social venture capital and social capital loans for these growing education enterprises. Until and unless these parts of the transmission belt are put into place, non-profits will struggle to move their reform models beyond a few pockets of excellence and numerous schools and students will be deprived of the high-quality programmes that could have a major impact on student achievement. Interestingly enough, the social capital gap adversely affects some high-quality for-profit enterprises as well. While for-profit education companies have the option of raising equity, the projected returns are not always attractive enough for venture capital-type investment. Investors tend to view such enterprises as service companies that command lower multiples and have limited long-term potential.

Closing the gap

The Education Entrepreneurs Fund stepped in to close the social capital gap by developing a transmission belt for social enterprises in public education (*see* Figure 30.2). As a community, the non-profits working in school reform and the foundations that fund such work still look more to the old paradigm than the new, but a growing number have embraced the market. The Education Entrepreneurs Fund exists for them. It provides financing and support to social entrepreneurs committed to taking high-quality educational programmes to scale and focused on becoming sustainable through business models based on fee-for-service dissemination.

First, the Education Entrepreneurs Fund provides financing. The Fund itself represents a true public–private partnership, since it is capitalized with grants from the US Department of Education and foundations as well as a low-interest social capital loan from the Prudential Insurance Company of America. The Fund's capital is invested in social enterprises, particularly non-profits, in the form of loans, equity and joint venture financing. The Fund will make investments in quality for-

Foundation/ government grants	Social venture capital	Social capital loans	Private debt/ equity markets
	Education Entrepreneurs Fund		
Start-up organizations	Early-growth organizations	Late-growth organizations	Mature organizations

Figure 30.2 Closing the gap

profit programmes under special conditions, but its primary focus is in supporting non-profit organizations. Fund investments are tailored to the unique needs of the invested organization, on terms that would not be available in traditional capital markets and at rates that are discounted for mission. Fund financing is available to help manage cash flow, build staff capacity in anticipation of new business, and develop the managerial and technological infrastructure necessary to assure quality at scale.

Second, the Education Entrepreneurs Fund provides a broad range of technical support. Like the classic venture capitalist, the support and expertise of the Fund's staff is at least as important to the success of these enterprises as the financing. The Fund has developed a broad network of consultants and strong ties to other segments of the school improvement industry. Drawing on over ten years of experience that New American Schools has had with a diverse set of school reform organizations, the Fund has experience in every stage of non-profit growth, many different service delivery models, the full range of problems facing non-profit organizations as they shift from relying on grants to earning income from fees, and a large selection of related educational products and services. Along with investment, this mix of expertise, experience and relationships works to ensure the success of invested organizations.

A new type of social agent for education reform

Social investors, such as the Education Entrepreneurs Fund, are attractive partners for foundations, government agencies and private investors. While grants are critical to the development of education organizations, financial intermediaries provide an approach and capabilities designed to take social enterprises beyond the research and development phase. It is in investment underwriting, and accompanying due diligence and loan monitoring activities, that financial intermediaries provide their greatest service to education organizations as they transition to strategies based on fee-for-service dissemination. Such credit principles are not a part of traditional grant-making activities, but are required in order to accelerate the process by which social enterprises build viable business models. Without the financial discipline inherent in repaying investments, education organizations might be less focused on business plans, financial benchmarks and other critical success factors.

Financial intermediaries can also bring a dimension of flexibility for which grants are not suited. An education organization needing to hire staff, invest in quality-assurance systems, or manage the gaps in cash flow caused by slow-paying schools and districts can have widely fluctuating financial requirements. Quarterly adjustments are not unusual for intermediaries that invest in developing organizations, particularly in the early stages of an investment. The timing of these needs can be acute, and grant makers are not always equipped for making these short-term, but critical decisions. This is not a shortcoming of grant-making entities. It simply points to a need for a different financing vehicle with a different set of capabilities.

While the ability to instil credit principles and financial discipline in education organizations is essential for social investors, investment expertise is not sufficient in and of itself for financial intermediaries in the school improvement space. To be of real service to the education organizations they serve, social investors also need to bring to the table a keen understanding of how the market for school improvement services works. As a result of having this knowledge and background, these investors will have more realistic expectations of the financial returns and exit strategies of their investments. For education, in which the quality of a product or service is paramount, financial return cannot be the sole motivator. Acceptance of a below-market return is a reality for social investors. A social enterprise cannot always pay a market rate on its debt, or be expected to generate a market return on an equity investment. Instead, social investors must factor in the educational benefit of the programmes delivered by their invested organizations.

Social investors also need to have different considerations of the exit strategies available in their investments. The concept of exit strategy as applied to for-profit businesses, often in the form of IPO or the sale of companies, may not necessarily hold true for school improvement organizations. In this context, exit strategy is better defined as the critical transition for a grant-reliant organization to a viable business that can deliver products and services to schools at scale, with quality, over a long period of time. These differing expectations of financial return and plausible exit strategies lead non-profit intermediaries like the Fund to be especially well suited to engaging in this type of investing.

Just as financial intermediaries carry the expectation that the social enterprises in which they invest will become financially sustainable over time, they also need to set that expectation for themselves. In the case of the Education Entrepreneurs Fund, fees and interest generated from investment activities cover the costs of underwriting operations. The Fund operates as a revolving fund, reinvesting the repayments it receives from investments; that portion of the Fund's investment capital that it has borrowed is repaid. The Fund's reliance on interest and fee revenue to cover operating expenses and the fact that it is required to repay money it has borrowed provide a strong incentive for the Fund to invest in organizations most likely to succeed, and to work with them to make sure that they do succeed. In this way, the Fund's credibility to its foundation, government and corporate partners is enhanced.

Financial intermediaries have the potential to become effective coaches for social enterprises by virtue of the investment and industry expertise they possess. They serve as that all-important gateway as education organizations grow eventually to gain access to traditional capital markets, having built a track record in repaying social investments. Filling the social capital gap effectively takes these organizations along the transmission belt from development to maturity. The ability to nurture these social enterprises as they become mature organizations delivers the social good that foundations, government and the private sector all seek – quality suppliers of school improvement services that are sustainable over the long term and able to maximize the impact of the funds that financed their initial research and development.

Outcomes

Filling the void in the transmission belt of social investment in school improvement remains both a daunting challenge and an evolving practice. In recent years, many foundations in the USA have withdrawn from the education arena because of their despair over the politics of reform and the apparent intractability of the nation's most troubled school districts. In addition, many foundations are extraordinarily frustrated by their inability to measure the social return on their grant investments: whether the programmes actually improve student performance, whether they can be taken to all the students who might benefit, and whether the programme and the organization that provides it can have any staying power.

Quality school improvement models that are widespread and long lasting are sought not only by the philanthropic sector, but business and government as well. The challenges seem enormous, but solutions are within grasp. The three values of quality, scale and sustainability have been the foundation upon which New American Schools and the Education Entrepreneurs Fund have collectively supported 11 comprehensive school improvement organizations, providing $100 million in services to over 4000 schools across the USA.

Increasing the achievement of more students in a growing number of schools remains the Education Entrepreneurs Fund's key benchmark for measuring its success. The impact of its social investments is also realized as business methods are adapted to non-profit operations, research is translated into widespread practice, competence is developed in service delivery, access to traditional sources of capital is increased, and business expertise is integrated into the senior management of the social enterprises working in school improvement.

As social investors like the Education Entrepreneurs Fund demonstrate more precisely how these outcomes can be achieved, it is likely that more foundations will begin to redefine their traditional role in nationwide school improvement and that more capital will become available for cutting-edge social investment. Such a shift would hardly be inconsequential considering that foundations in the USA already spend over $250 million on school reform annually. In the meantime, more research remains to be done on the types of support social enterprises require in order to become 'good invested organizations' and the capacity within the market to provide this support and foster the implementation of high-quality school improvement programmes at scale.

Conclusion

Learning about the innovative approaches that education entrepreneurs throughout the USA are developing is one of the most encouraging aspects of the Education Entrepreneurs Fund's social investment practice. The high-quality products and services being developed can lay the foundation for significant increases in student achievement in the future. At the same time, the failure of these promising products and services to reach the schools and students who need them most is one of the biggest challenges facing social investors. The good work of many education entrepreneurs fails to move beyond pockets of excellence, impacting the lives of only a small number of students. Some promising programmes might disappear altogether without business models that ensure their viability over the long term.

Social investors can help more of these promising programmes address the challenges of quality, scale and sustainability. Social enterprises need the discipline that investment underwriting and monitoring bring, but they also need the flexibility and patience of investors who understand that quality needs to be the primary focus. Social investors can also be good examples for invested organizations by building their own sustainable business models and by encouraging partnerships among social enterprises. Greater collaboration among high-quality providers is a critical success factor in attracting capital and achieving national scale. By working in concert, social enterprises can leverage each other's strengths, mitigate each other's weaknesses and share the benefit of lessons learned both separately and collectively.

By filling the social capital gap, with financing, networking opportunities and much-needed technical assistance, investors like the Education Entrepreneurs Fund can provide the resources that will enable social enterprises to have a long-term impact on the lives of millions of students.

5

CHAPTER 31

Educational entrepreneurs and the capital gap

KIM SMITH

Recent historical trends

In the 1980s in the USA, on the heels of the Carnegie Foundation report, *A Nation At Risk*, concerned business leaders wanted to help improve low performing public schools and so brought a newly discovered sense of enlightened self-interest to the table. They saw that the USA's public schools, particularly in high poverty urban and rural areas, were simply not preparing students to participate in the knowledge economy. Recognizing both the inherent inequity, and the large expense of providing remedial training, business leaders wanted to find a better way. Adopt-a-school, compacts, career academies, comprehensive school design and other business-informed models emerged during this period. Educators, for the most part, were wary, sceptical about motives and also about whether business people had anything to offer to remedy the bureaucratic, financial and political problems facing urban and rural public schools.

Following this, the amazingly fast-paced growth of the information technology industries, which drove 40 per cent of the growth in US GDP during the 1990s, created an almost insatiable need not only for people with advanced technology and symbolic reasoning skills, but also for people with complex thinking and problem-solving capabilities and advanced communication skills. With unemployment among skilled workers at a record low, and knowledge workers being imported from other countries through special visas in order to fill openings in the technology industries, even more pressure was created for a public education system to prepare all American children to participate in the knowledge economy.

This economic boom also led to other related trends. Business schools replaced law schools as the preferred graduate school. A large and growing portion of the economy was made up of companies whose businesses fundamentally depended on mastering the process of constant learning. As one technology executive put it: 'In the knowledge economy, the fastest learner wins' – at the corporate level, the product level and the individual level. And, seemingly everyone in the USA became an investor in the stock market, whether through his or her new retirement fund or directly. These phenomena together led to a significant increase in leaders who look at the world through a business lens, an increased similarity between successful education and business processes, and a huge increase in available investment capital.

Alongside this, three intersecting social trends led to what is being called the 'convergence of the sectors' – public, private, and non-profit looking more and more alike. First, decades of 're-inventing government' meant an increase in privatization[1] – private providers contracted for what had previously been public services, for example rubbish collection, city maintenance, public transportation, prison management and a host of diverse social services. Initially these services were either low-skilled or serving populations that were small or not vocally organized about the issue of privatization. Second, the public sector needed to be more customer-focused to compete with emerging private competitors – witness the US Postal Service response to Federal Express. And third, private-sector companies discovered a strong emerging concern among consumers for social causes. The private sector responded to this social concern with cause-related marketing like 'Rain Forest Crunch' to benefit the Amazon basin, Paul Newman's 'Newman's Own' brands (which have donated over $100 million to designated charities), and also the development of socially responsible businesses like the Calvert Socially Responsible Mutual Funds.

Focus on education

While these exogenous trends were happening, policy shifts took place within American public education as well. Partly owing to the increased coordination between business leaders and policy makers, an intensified focus on standards and accountability shifted the conversation towards outcomes rather than just inputs, and popularized the concept of creating an education system designed for the knowledge economy, to replace a long-outdated system designed to serve the industrial age. Politically, extreme frustration with the apparent lack of progress in low-performing schools created a tolerance for riskier innovations in order to get around bureaucratic constraints, and innovative programmes like Minnesota's charter school legislation began to grow and spread. Even though it led to very few actual vouchers, the State of Florida's A+ Plan, which incorporated vouchers for students in repeatedly underperforming schools, represented a major shift in what appeared possible in American education policy and politics. Hugh Price, CEO of the National Urban League, summed up one view of this shift towards more of a customer-orientation: 'We care about our public schools, but we care about our children more'.

A new hybrid culture

As a side-effect of these factors, there began to develop a critical mass of what can be called 'hybrid' leadership – that is, leaders who have a deep appreciation for the different sectors, often bred from personal experience. These hybrid leaders create a new kind of opportunity. In the 1980s, business and education leaders did make some progress, but stepped gingerly around a clash of cultures in order to develop partnerships where each had their own separate domain knowledge, and argued about different priorities in policy debates. The new hybrid leaders have an opportunity to define a new culture – one that integrates the best of the different sectors, instead of accepting a watered-down lowest common denominator, or a politically polarized winner-takes-all approach. This means acknowledging that neither traditional educators, nor business leaders, nor policy makers, have the entire solution. It also means engaging in conversations about delivering high-quality public education that include not only instructional strategies and theories of psychological development, but also the more business-minded concepts of customer satisfaction, customer segmentation, efficient operations, management specialization, as well as questions about policy shifts and the appropriate role for the public sector and privatization in this new context.

Attention to instruction and human development should not be replaced by these other issues; rather, it should be integrated into a systems analysis, as an expert technology, with a rigorous attention to how they all interrelate. In management terms, technology companies typically have a chief technology officer as well as a chief executive officer, and often a chief operating officer too. Education is a highly complex knowledge business, further complicated by the political and social context and expectations within which it operates. Truly hybrid leaders have a deep appreciation for the need to combine expertise from each of these different areas. To build this hybrid culture requires funding the capacity of educational institutions to include leaders with specialized expertise, and developing a leaders who are prepared to manage in this complex environment.

Another shift has happened with respect to culture – the 'silicon valley way' has spread far and wide. This young and energetic culture, with an emphasis on entrepreneurship, meritocracy and a more informal work style emphasizing outcomes rather then bureaucratic processes, has shaped a generation's expectations about what a professional knowledge-based work environment is like. This new business culture increases the frustration with what appear to be process-oriented rules in the public education system, rules that do not seem to lead to quality outcomes and in fact seem to inhibit outcomes in high-poverty, low-performing schools. This has, in turn, put even more pressure on a public education system seen by many as designed for an industrial age gone by – too process-oriented, too rules-based, and not flexible or outcomes-oriented enough.

Further, the silicon valley way heavily emphasizes competition as the means to inspire constant improvement and growth, and this leads to a push to increase the competitive and market forces at work in public education. Technology business leaders understand the way competition forces them to be constantly vigilant about customer satisfaction and product quality, and they see no reason why public educators should not also benefit from these forces. In addition, these technology leaders have seen employee ownership motivate high performance, and they tend to believe in providing incentives for performance and rewarding success. The blunt instrument created for this in the private sector is employee stock ownership. No widely useful programme has yet emerged in public education, in part because of the culture clash surrounding the issue of personal motivation versus group process for teachers and principals, and in part because of severe disagreements about what kind of performance metrics would make sense and actually motivate improved short- and long-term student achievement.[2]

In spite of the progress in defining a new hybrid culture, there remain some strong differences, on average, between the sectors with respect to culture, priorities and ways of seeing the world. High-quality leadership requires the constant balance of three things – process, results and relationships. According to research by Interaction and Associates, most individuals fall on one side of the triangle in Figure 31.1, overemphasizing two of these at the expense of the other. With apologies for an

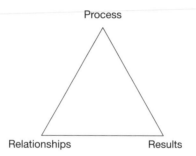

Figure 31.1 Achieving a balance in leadership

overly simplified generalization – educators typically emphasize relationships and then process; business people typically overemphasize results (particularly a desire to quantifying results) regardless of their secondary focus; and, because of their role in the political process, policy makers often overemphasize process and relationships at the expense of results. The key to this evolving cultural shift is to get the balance right: not to over-correct too far towards results at the cost of the necessary attentiveness to relationships and process that is required for good education, but to integrate a strategy for demanding and rewarding results as well.

The emergence of entrepreneurs

Entrepreneurs have risen in prominence over the past two decades in the USA. Among admired business leaders, more often than ever before, it is entrepreneurs who come to mind – Jeff Bezos of Amazon.com, Bill Gates of Microsoft, Steve Case from AOL. The story of Hewlett and Packard creating HP in their garage has reached mythic proportions, and builds on the traditional American mythology of rising to great heights on the wings of hard work, personal tenacity and a meritocracy, which, coincidentally, is generally based on skills gathered through education rather than inherited wealth.

Entrepreneurs are important to shifts in public education as well. Entrepreneurs are, by definition, change agents. Entrepreneurs have a vision that inspires others to follow. They see an opportunity for a better way, and, refusing to be bound by tradition, strike out to make it happen. They are action-oriented and act with a sense of urgency that motivates energy and confidence in others, thus leading teams to surmount rather than be stopped by bureaucratic obstacles. They have what is sometimes referred to as 'learned optimism', that is, the opposite of 'learned helplessness'. In other words, their internal locus of control leads them to believe they can make a difference and that when things go wrong it is most often circumstantial, and thus not a reason to lose faith and give up, but rather a cause for renewed creativity in problem solving to change the circumstances that stand in their way. When asked if a disabled paraplegic *can* drive, most people will say no. When asked *how* a paraplegic can drive, most people begin to create strategies for how – foot pedals, mouth controls, voice-activated technology. True entrepreneurs are wired to ask 'how' instead of 'can'.

A point of clarification about what it means to be an entrepreneur. There are many, many, clever innovators out there. But to be a true entrepreneur, one must strike out to create an institution. 'Intrapreneurship', or the development of innovative programmes within larger institutions, is an important contribution to organizational evolution and learning, but is fundamentally different from entrepreneurship. While they share characteristics of innovation and tenacity, they require a different risk profile in their leadership and are different in their ability to put pressure on systems and institutions to change. It is precisely by striking out to create a new institution that entrepreneurs distinguish themselves, allying with their customers and their vision of the future rather than with current institutions. Intrapreneurs, who must rely on current institutional stakeholders for their funding and existence, operate within inherent constraints.

A special kind of entrepreneur – the social entrepreneur – is important to note. Another product of the 1980s and 1990s, social entrepreneurs are motivated by the desire to solve a social problem. They assess their success in terms of positive social outcomes or a 'social return'. They may choose to be structured either as a non-profit or for-profit or enterprise, but what makes them a social entrepreneur is their laser-like focus on their social purpose. First and foremost, they want to improve a social condition, and thus they make social outcomes their top priority. Wendy Kopp, founder of Teach For America, which recruits new teachers for under-resourced urban and rural schools, is a classic non-profit social entrepreneur. Inspired by Kopp's model, and seeing the emerging need to develop leaders better prepared to manage in this new hybrid environment, Jon Schnur has created a new organization called New Leaders for New Schools, which will recruit, train and support a cadre of new hybrid school leaders using a combination of best practices from business and education fields. Most social entrepreneurs create non-profits, because those who create a for-profit business must create a profitable business, and thus face more complicated pressures if they attempt to prioritize social outcomes. This can lead to a conflict if investors and entrepreneurs are not aligned on this issue of prioritization and appropriate expectations about timing of financial return.

Virtually all private sector investors, and the public market by legal definition, expect for-profit entrepreneurs to maximize return to shareholders as their first priority. For example, as a public company, Edison Schools has a fiduciary responsibility to prioritize financial returns. That does not mean it will not have social returns in the form of improved student achievement, nor that individual employees do not personally believe in the need to prioritize educational outcomes, but it means that, as a institution, Edison has promised its investors to prioritize a return to shareholders before everything else. In many situations where social return and financial returns are both maximized by the same choice, there is no conflict. But with a public capital market used to quarterly reporting, there is intense pressure for short-term growth. Many believe that 'good education is good business', meaning that getting good educational outcomes is precisely what building a good and profitable education business over the long term requires. I happen to agree. However, the key question is – do the specific investors in a given company agree? And can the public market, as it is now structured, possibly allow this long-term approach? What are the appropriate time horizons in this kind of environment?

This leads to another important emerging concept – the 'double bottom line'. Originally coming from the environmental and sustainable development fields, double bottom line means paying attention to both the financial and social returns. Jed Emerson's recent work (2002) on the 'blended value proposition' artic-ulates in more detail the emerging capital market in which there is a continuum of investors who value various combinations of financial and social returns, depend-ing on their motivations and type of institution.

The role of the capital markets

As Figure 31.2 indicates, traditional financial investors are motivated solely by finan-cial return on investment (ROI). Traditional grant-making foundations, at the other end of the capital spectrum, care only about social returns (SROI). Over the past few decades what has emerged is a larger community in the middle – for-profit 'socially responsible investors' who put an emphasis on increased social returns in at least some portion of their portfolio, and an increase in programme related investments among foundations. These trends are related to the significant increase in invest-ment funds generated by the economic boom, and the increasing focus on social purpose businesses and the increasing desire to 'give back'. This blended capital market is not limited to education, but it did create an environment where ambi-tious education entrepreneurs faced a more diverse capital market than ever before.

Investing in the middle range of this spectrum is complicated. Typically, founda-tion programme-related investments have been limited to loans, because of legal IRS (Internal Revenue Service) restrictions, and because it is easier to assess risk for loans, while private equity investments are difficult and require deep domain knowledge and expensive and specialized staff and legal support. And, on the other side, because deal flow was limited, socially motivated investors often did not develop the specialized pattern recognition required to master a given domain or industry, and thus were not able to make truly informed decisions and to pro-vide 'value-added' investments. This created what can be called the 'capital gap'.

The New Schools Venture Fund

In response to this capital gap, a novel kind of funding institution was created. Motivated by the belief that it is important and possible to give all children access to a high-quality public education, the New Schools Venture Fund is a non-profit venture philanthropy fund harnessing the power of entrepreneurs to improve dra-matically public education in the USA. The New Schools Venture Fund applies the principles of venture capital to the work of supporting exceptional education entrepreneurs who are tackling difficult systems problems in public education. New Schools is a true value-added investor, providing intellectual, human and financial capital to the most promising ventures. As a non-profit funder explicitly prioritizing social educational returns, yet with openness to both non-profit and for profit structure, New Schools sits squarely in this capital gap.

As a non-profit venture philanthropy fund, New Schools is more than just ven-ture production. New Schools is an 'action-tank' combining the intellectual power of a think-tank with the action orientation of a venture fund, and the catalytic force of a nationwide network of business, education, non-profit and policy lead-

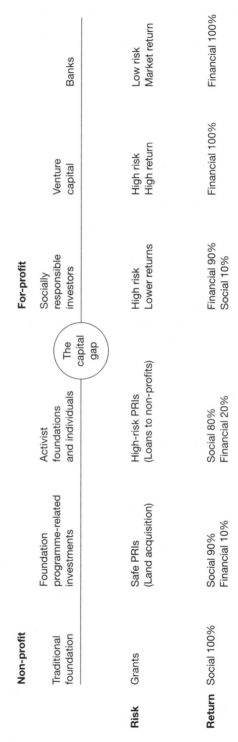

Figure 31.2 The capital gap

ers. Because we believe in the power of entrepreneurs to change large systems and in the importance of investing in scale and the institutional capacity to deliver at scale, we designed the New Schools Venture Fund to invest in both non-profit and for-profit businesses, as appropriate, given their intended goals. Our initial hypothesis was that for-profits would be better able to raise follow-on funding in order to grow to serve large markets of under-served students. Where possible, we hoped to have non-profit and for-profit analogues, the better to learn about the convergence of the sectors and to analyse and learn about the different structures and what impact if any they have on social returns in the form of outcomes for children.

With the recent severe constrictions in the American private sector capital markets, and growth in 'venture philanthropy' funders, it is not clear whether, in the short term, our initial hypothesis was correct about for-profits having an easier time accessing growth capital. One thing that is clear is that funding requirements drive what is prioritized (whether for-profit investors or foundation grant makers), so it is crucial that investors and entrepreneurs are aligned in their intentions.

How the new schools venture fund operates

As a non-profit fund, New Schools explicitly prioritizes social educational returns. The Fund's investment criteria include:

- scaleable, with the potential to impact thousands of students;
- sustainable, with sound revenue models or clear alternative funding plans;
- hybrid leadership, combining education and business expertise;
- high leverage opportunity to improve public K–12 education:
  - targets a vulnerability in the system, meets a real need;
  - measurable progress towards educational outcomes can be assessed;
  - catalytic – designed to overcome systemic inertia and to have an impact far beyond its own operations.

Nonetheless, once we satisfy our first priority – that a venture stands a chance to make a dramatic improvement in low-performing schools – if it is a for-profit business, we do extensive business due diligence on the investment, exactly as any financial investor would. This is because if the venture does not grow as a business, it will not have any educational outcomes at all. Our approach can be confusing to some co-investors, who are surprised by the combination of our intense focus on educational outcomes, as well as on financial planning, business model and strategy. Any returns generated by our investments are re-invested into the fund and recycled into additional education investments. Nothing is ever disbursed back to our donors.

Conclusion

For years, and with little resistance, private companies have been contracting with public schools for a variety of goods and services including buildings, furniture, food services, transportation and other services not central to educational instruction. Indeed, because of the required specialization and high up-front investment required, there is a virtual publisher oligopoly that has evolved to hold a great deal of power over distribution of content and assessment, and many growing businesses focusing on specialized services like technology. For the past few decades, the number and type of businesses supplying public education with goods and services have been expanding.

After a few false starts like Education Alternatives, the survival and growth of Edison Schools and a handful of other private providers of school management services heralds a new phase of this 'business of education' – one in which private institutions play a role in the core activities of providing schools to the public. As an investor in both for-profit businesses and non-profit institutions, New Schools sees this phase as a very important opportunity to harness the energy of entrepreneurs to improve fundamentally the quality of public education in the USA. Unlike other investors, we prioritize first the social return, and thus our vision of where the greatest opportunity and risk lie may be somewhat different from other purely financial investors.

Two key opportunities for the next decade

All these forces have created an opportunity for dramatic improvement, particularly where public schools have historically underprepared their students for the knowledge economy. In addition to continuing to support ways to bring more human capital to the field as a whole (Teach for America and New Leaders for New Schools), one very important opportunity we see is to create more branded systems of charter and charter-like schools that demonstrate what can happen when parents and students are treated as customers. By allowing parents, teachers, leaders and even board members to self-select according to their own educational and philosophical priorities, these public schools of choice can reduce the friction that currently holds back improvement in some of the most troubled geographically defined districts. By creating these scaleable systems from the ground up, they can be designed to be aligned in goals and processes from governance through management and operating systems and all the way to instructional content and assessment tools. This alignment prevents having to pull against the inertia of the system's status quo, or trying to manage a system made up of hundreds of individual microturfs. While we support quality for-profit providers in this business, and in fact heavily invested in creating LearnNow, which is now a part of Edison Schools, because of the constriction of the private capital markets, and the current political backlash against for-profit school management organizations, we believe these new brands need to be created as scaling non-profits, at least in the short run. We need to create more non-profits like Aspire Public Schools, created by social entrepreneur and 35-year public school veteran Don Shalvey, as a non-profit brand of charter schools to serve high-poverty students in California.

Another important opportunity, both for social and financial return, is to create better tools to use the power of technology to improve student assessment. Techology gives us the resources to create cost-effective tools for interim assessment of where students are in the learning process, and to assess better a richer skill set beyond simple knowledge capture and retention of facts. Early efforts like Carnegie Learning's 'cognitive tutor', which combines expert systems and artificial intelligence technology to increase students' mastery of algebra problem-solving skills, indicate progress, but there is a wide open opportunity here to have a dramatic impact. And in this context of increased accountability and high-stakes testing, tools like these will be crucial to making sure the system does not create a catch-22 for students and teachers who are trying to master an increasingly complex system of knowledge and skills – thus there will also be an increasing financial opportunity here as well.

Risks

The primary caution in this emerging business of education is to articulate clearly the competing priorities of social and financial returns. It is important to make sure investors and entrepreneurs and customers agree on what each venture prioritizes, in both the short and long term. There is nothing wrong with building a strong business that prioritizes return to shareholders and employs talented people interested in serving education. And it is admirable to attempt to make a positive social impact through such a company. Conversely, even non-profits attempting to build scaleable institutions must wrestle with difficult decisions about balancing efficiency with social effectiveness; for example, should a non-profit created to serve high-needs children open a school in a high-income community because they are willing to provide the building? Or, how does a non-profit balance the desire to create small schools to support social intimacy and caring adult–student relationships, while also generating enough economies of scale to support the special services and resources they want? Each enterprise, for-profit or non-profit alike, should be clear with investors and customers and the public on how it will balance the competing pressures of financial and social priorities. And, in turn, policy makers are responsible for building into this private provision of public goods reasonable safeguards for quality and safety accountability, while also attempting to create an atmosphere that produces the greatest social good for the greatest number of citizens. And lastly, parents and students are responsible for becoming educated consumers who know what a quality education is – through programmes like Greatschools.net – and must use this information to vote with their feet.

The good news is that we are at an exceptional moment in time, one ripe with opportunity to make a real difference in improving public education. Exceptional education entrepreneurs are out there – tenacious, dedicated leaders ready to devote their lives and careers to tackling the most pressing problems in our beleaguered public school system. And, by bringing together leaders from all three sectors who appreciate the incredible complexity of the art of human learning and development, and the necessity to be attentive to customers, operations, systems and management practices and the need to focus on real outcomes as well as collegial processes, we have an important opportunity to create a new kind of lasting high-impact public school system.

NOTES

1 There is an important distinction between privatization and commercialism: an increasing trend towards advertising to students while they are in public schools has often been incorrectly connected to contracting with non-profit or for-profit managers for school services. Private providers can, and in my opinion should, be restricted from advertising to students (commercialization), but that is a separate issue from whether they can be trusted to manage services and products for students (privatization).

2 Typically, performance-based pay proposals rely heavily on standardized test scores, which often do not resonate as good success metrics with those being compensated, thus further complicating the situation.

REFERENCES

A Nation at Risk (1983) report from the US Department of Education's National Commission on Excellence in Education, April.

Emerson, J. (2002) *Total Foundation Asset Management and Unified Investment Strategy*, Center for Social Innovation, Graduate School of Business, Stanford University, January.

CHAPTER 32

Using public education money to produce increased educational performance

ALLAN ODDEN

Across the globe, schools are being asked to produce higher levels of student performance. In the USA the reform goal has been to 'teach all students to high standards'. Taken seriously, this goal is ambitious. According to the National Assessment of Educational Progress, the USA currently educates about 25–30 per cent of students to or above a rigorous national proficiency standard (National Center for Education Statistics, 2000). The reform goal is to double if not triple this performance over the next several years. Since no one expects education revenues to double or triple, the reform goal implies that current and any new education resources need to be used more productively. This fiscal education reform message is much the same across the world. Largely because of economic globalization and the spread of information technologies, nearly all countries know their children must be educated to much higher levels without commensurate increases in educational resources.

It is reasonable to question whether the USA or any country could double or triple the level of student academic achievement over the next decade or so, with or without more money. On the other hand, at least some schools should be expected to produce quantum improvements, especially given advances in cognitive psychology about how people learn complex materials (Bransford, Brown and Cocking, 1999; Richardson, 2001). Further, efforts across the globe to create more effective 'whole-school designs' have begun to show that schools can educate students to much higher levels, even students who come from families with low incomes or who must struggle to learn English while also learning academic content (Slavin and Madden, 2001; Slavin and Calderon, 2001; Stringfield, Ross and Smith, 1996). In addition, these and other school-wide educational strategies (for example, overall class size reduction) deploy educational resources differently than 'typical' schools (Odden and Picus, 2000) and are financed by schools reallocating extant resources (Odden and Archibald, 2000). Finally, these restructured schools take on more of the characteristics of 'high-performance organizations', with more resources devoted to front-line workers (teachers), professional development and training, and less to support staff and administration (see, for example, Lawler, Mohrman and Benson, 2001; Odden and Busch, 1998).

The remainder of this chapter develops the above arguments in more detail, primarily with examples from the USA. The next two sections comment on how education resources are used in 'typical' American schools, and summarize various research studies on how the substantial increases in education resources provided for the USA's schools over the past 40 years have been spent. This is followed by discussions of how educational resources are used in what are called whole-school designs and how schools across the country engage in resource reallocation to support these new educational strategies. The chapter concludes with a short summary and comments on next steps toward more effective use of education dollars.

How education dollars are spent

A series of empirical studies conducted with national, state, district and school databases in the first part of the 1990s produced a somewhat surprising profile of the 'typical' *use of the education dollar (Monk, Roelke and Brent, 1996; Odden et al.,* 1995; Picus and Wattenberger, 1995; Picus and Fizal, 1995; Picus, Tetrealt and Murphy, 1996). Across states and districts with widely varying characteristics and spending levels, functional resource-use patterns were quite consistent. Educational expenditures per pupil were allocated across functional categories in the following approximate proportions:

- 60 per cent for instruction;
- 8–10 per cent for instructional support;
- 8 per cent for administration, with the bulk of administrative costs at the site and not central office level;
- 8–10 per cent for operation and maintenance;
- 5–7 per cent for transportation;
- 5 per cent for debt service, food and miscellaneous.

Though there was variation on all of these patterns, the central tendencies for these functional allocations of the education dollar were remarkably similar for high, low and average-spending districts, both within and across states, and held true across other geographic, size and demographic variables.

Moreover, the studies showed that administrative expenditures were not large by any comparative standards, and even more surprisingly that central office administrative expenditures per pupil in the large urban districts of Chicago, Los Angeles, Miami and New York were below their respective state averages – there was no 'administrative blob.' While these districts' central office administrative staffs were large in an absolute sense, the districts spent less per pupil on such administration than many other districts and were consistently below the state average.

Finally, the studies showed that these expenditure patterns had not changed much over time: these functional uses of the education dollar at the end of the century were quite close to what they had been during the middle of the century, despite large real (inflation-adjusted) increases in education dollars per pupil, dramatic changes in student socio-demographic characteristics and the proliferation of categorical programmes focused on a variety of special needs of students (Odden and Picus, 2000).

Stability of spending patterns while spending levels rose

The stability of education resource-use patterns across functional categories remained during a time of rapid rise in the level of per-pupil education spending. It is well known that from about 1960 to 1990 real dollars per pupil grew by about 300 per cent in inflation-adjusted dollars (Odden and Picus, 2000). Although general education revenues comprised part of this significant dollar increase, during the 1960s and 1970s dozens of categorical programmes were enacted at the federal, state and district levels to ensure that students with special needs received extra services focused on those needs. Indeed, a significant portion of the new education dollars provided to schools was used to fund the extra services required by these programmes (Odden, 1991).

Initially, the funds for special needs programmes were infused into general school budgets and spent on hiring more regular classroom teachers. But programme designers wanted the funds to be used only for services for the students identified by the various programmes. Thus regulations were developed to ensure that the funds 'supplemented' and did not just enhance the regular programme. Over time, this led to the development of a series of specially trained teachers, with expertise for teaching students with disabilities, students for whom English was not the primary language, and students from low-income backgrounds with reading and other learning problems (Kirst and Jung, 1991; Odden, 1991; Peterson, Rabe and Wong, 1986). Moreover, most of these teachers taught the special needs students in settings outside the regular classroom, usually in 'resource rooms' with much smaller class sizes, and often with a less rigorous or 'remedial' curriculum. Sometimes students were exposed to the 'regular' instructional programme and then were pulled-out to be served in a resource room, and sometimes they simply received instruction in the resource room, missing regular instruction all together. These were the common practices that ensured that the supplement regulations and programme requirements to serve the special-need students were met. Equity goals were behind these practices.

Given these fiscal and programmatic phenomena – increases in dollars overall and increases in categorical dollars and programmes – the stability of allocation practice patterns across functions still begged the question of how the large real-dollar increases in educational appropriations were spent and whether there had been changes in the use of education dollars within functional categories. An additional series of studies then pushed beyond analysing expenditure patterns across functions and investigated how the above educational practices impacted expenditures within the instructional function (Lankford and Wyckoff, 1995; Miles, 1995; Rothstein and Miles, 1995; Schwartz, 1999). These studies came to a relatively common set of conclusions.

First, the largest portion of new dollars that was injected into the school system was used to hire specialist teachers and instructional aides catering to a wide variety of special student needs; the bulk of these teachers served students with disabilities, students who were learning English as well as academic content, and students from low income backgrounds. Second, and relatedly, the composition of instructional expenditures changed dramatically from 1960 to 1995. In the mid-part of the century, most instructional expenditures were for classroom teachers – licensed teachers who taught a classroom of students the regular curriculum for most of the day, for example the typical elementary school teacher at the primary level and subject-matter teachers in mathematics, science, social studies and English at the secondary level. By the close of the century, the portion of classroom teachers as a percentage of the instructional budget had declined significantly and the portion of specialist teachers instructing students with special needs, largely in resource rooms separate from the regular classroom, had increased.

Thus although expenditures for instruction remained the same approximate percentage of overall expenditures, the pattern of spending within instruction changed. By the late 1980s instructional expenditures were comprised of a smaller percentage of front-line workers, or regular classroom teachers, and a larger percentage of specialist staff – both teachers and instructional aides – working outside the regular classroom and providing extra help for students with special needs. Though some of the increase in education funding from 1960 to 1990 was used to raise teacher salaries and modestly reduce actual class sizes (Hanushek, 1996; Miles, 1997), the bulk was used for services outside the classroom provided by individuals addressing a range of special-student needs. In some cases, the vast bulk of extra teachers provided services just for students with disabilities or handicapping conditions (Lankford and Wyckoff, 1995), a pattern that was especially prominent for large city school districts.

Two problems emerged with these practices. The first was that schools began to look like bureaucracies, with rising numbers of specialized staff working outside the regular classroom to help accomplish overall organizational goals – and the more student achievement goals were not met, the greater the demand for more teacher and other staff resources outside the regular classroom. The second was that while the correct students received the extra services, they tended not to learn much more from the extra help – the additional educational strategies were not very effective (see, for example, Borman, Stringfield and Slavin, 2001; Odden, 1991).

These realities lead in part to the education excellence reforms of the 1980s (Murphy, 1990) which evolved into the standards-based education reform movement of the 1990s (Fuhrman, 1993; Odden, 1995), which had a two-part goal: (i) to make the regular curriculum programme more rigorous for all students, and (ii) to ensure that special needs students were taught this regular curriculum initially in the regular classroom and then, if needed, in a more powerful and effective extra help strategy to help them master the standards of the core instructional programme.

How restructured schools use education resources differently

As the 1980s closed and the 1990s began, it became clear that accomplishing the above goals of education reform required restructured schools (Elmore, 1991). The primary goal was to teach many more students to higher achievement standards. The concept of restructuring entered the education lexicon as teachers, education leaders and policy makers realized that schools as they had come to know them were not sufficiently effective, either to teach a more rigorous curriculum to 'regular' students or to teach it successfully to special needs students who, for a variety of reasons, had to struggle to learn to new, higher standards.

Some argued that the only way to restructure the system was to break up the old educational bureaucracy by injecting choice into the public school system (see, for example, Chubb and Moe, 1990). But others supported an initiative, first called the New American Schools Development Corporation and now just New American Schools (NAS), to commission several teams of experts around the country to create higher performance, 'break the mould' schools. These schools would be designed around a 'high standards' curriculum programme, with changes in both school and classroom organization and instructional strategies, all targeted on teaching students to rigorous performance levels for the evolving standards-based education reforms adopted by nearly all states in the country (Stringfield, Ross and Smith, 1996). The goal was to create a number of different 'whole-school' designs that would cost about the national average expenditure per pupil.

What emerged were several new school designs that actually met that fiscal constraint (Odden and Busch, 1998; Odden and Picus, 2000). More importantly, the schools used numbers and types of staff very differently from typical schools (Odden, 1997) and thus restructured their instructional budgets. Table 32.1 provides a typical example of those changes.

First, class sizes in the typical school before restructuring were 25 and there were three 'extra' teachers providing some type of extra instruction – not for special needs students – in small classes outside the regular classroom. Second, the typical school

Table 32.1 *Staffing in a typical v. New American School (500 students, 50 per cent poverty)*

Typical school before restructuring	Restructured school
Principal: 1	Principal: 1
Assistant Principal: 0	Instructional facilitators, focused on professional development: 2
Teachers with class sizes of 25 students: 20	Teachers with class sizes of 20 students: 25
Extra teachers: 3	Extra teachers: 0
Art, music and PE teachers, who teach content and provide planning and preparation time for teachers: 6 plus 1 librarian	Art, music, PE teachers who teach content and provide planning and preparation time for teachers: 5 plus 1 librarian
Teachers in categorical programmes for low income students, gifted and talented and mild disabilities (mainly learning disabilities): 7	Teacher tutors offering one-to-one help to struggling students, whatever the specific reason for the struggle: 4
Instructional aides: 4	Instructional aides: 0
Pupil support (guidance counsellor, social worker, nurse, etc.) working independently: 4	Personal pupil support/family outreach team: 4
Money for professional development: almost none	Money for ongoing professional development provided by external experts: $100 000

had one category of specialist teachers (art, music, etc.) who taught non-academic subjects and during that time provided planning and preparation time for classroom teachers. Third, this typical school had another and larger number of specialized staff focused on various specialized student needs, 'supporting' teachers outside of the regular classroom. These included seven teachers in categorical programmes, mainly working in resource rooms, four instructional aides providing some version of the same service, and four professionals working independently and providing various types of non-academic student support and family outreach. The school had no funds for ongoing professional development. The school also had staff for severely disabled students, but these staff and their services were not changed.

The restructured version used school and staffing resources quite differently. First, there were now 25 regular classroom teachers with smaller classes of 20 students (not all schools have sufficient staff to reduce class sizes, but some do). Second, there was a large investment in ongoing training and professional development, including two full-time instructional facilitators who worked as within-school coaches, and an additional $100,000 for purchasing ongoing professional development from outside experts. Third, students struggling to learn to high standards – whatever the particular reason for the struggle – received one-to-one tutoring from licensed teachers trained to be tutors, rather than remedial help in resource rooms with a less rigorous curriculum. Fourth, the pupil support and family outreach professionals were organized into a team that provided co-ordinated supports for these functions. The art, music, etc. teachers remained and continued to provide planning and preparation time for teachers. Not shown is that when reading was provided for 90 minutes each day, nearly all licensed professionals taught a class, so reading class sizes were below 15 students. Thus students were taught in smaller classes generally and in very small classes for reading. And all these changes were implemented without any additional funding, i.e. via resource reallocation.

Though the specific staffing configurations varied across many of the whole-school designs (see Odden, 1997; Stringfield, Ross and Smith, 1996) and school designs that were not part of New American Schools emerged over time, the restructured schools all had more of the features on the right-hand side of Table 32.1 than on the left-hand side. Instructional expenditures were the same for both sides, but the details of those expenditures were quite different, as were the use of staff during the day to implement the programme. Not only did some programmes provide smaller classes for targeted subjects like reading (see also Miles and Darling-Hammond, 1998), but also some school strategies grouped students with the same teacher over the course of two years and scheduled common planning time for teams of teachers inside the school. This joint scheduling allowed teachers to work collaboratively on curriculum and instructional issues.

The restructured school provided a high-standards curriculum to all students (except the severely disabled). The restructured schools shifted specialist staff into regular teachers so they had more front-line workers – regular classroom teachers. The restructured school created more cohesive, effective and integrated support programmes – tutoring for academic needs and student/family health teams for non-academic needs. And the restructured schools took ongoing professional development seriously, with a large investment in both within school coaches and outside expert trainers. All such differences are characteristic of higher performing organizations in general (see Lawler, Mohrman and Benson, 2001).

The resource reallocation process in education

Shifting from a school that reflected the left-hand side of Table 32.1 to a version that reflected the right-hand side entailed two large-scale organizational change efforts: one that restructured the entire school's educational strategy and a complementary one that reallocated large amounts of school resources to support fiscally that educational strategy. Odden and Archibald (2001) studied several schools that had engaged in the restructuring and resource reallocation processes and found a number of common features of them.

First, the stimulus for change was faculty dissatisfaction with its old educational strategies. Faculties concluded that the old strategies were both ineffective for their old goals and not strong enough to accomplish their new goals – particularly for educating their students with special needs to high standards. Second, the faculties then engaged in various versions of self-study by analyzing both student achievement and other socio-economic school data; the purpose was to determine the performance position of the school and to identify other problems that related to performance deficiencies. This step usually included one or two weekend retreats with parents, which resulted in joint faculty and parent understanding of the condition of the school. This 'needs-assessment' process also produced teacher 'ownership' of the problems that emerged from the joint analysis.

The third step entailed identifying, adapting or creating a new, cohesive educational strategy, usually one quite different from the previous strategy. Often, this search and adoption process resulted in the school adopting a 'whole-school design'. Because this adoption process was faculty-led, it represented strong faculty commitment to the new educational strategy; the faculty believed that the new strategy would allow it to boost student performance, including the performance of special needs students.

The fourth step entailed a parallel implementation and resource reallocation process that sometimes took two to three years to complete. Each school had to implement some type of shift of resources from the left-hand side of Table 32.1 to the right-hand side as it put its new educational strategy into place. Since these shifts entailed eliminating certain staff positions in the school and creating others, and sometimes 'cashing out' staff positions for professional development contracts, schools had to phase in the new programme and reallocate resources as personnel changes could be made. In some cases, staff were shifted to new roles, but in many cases staff were released and new staff for new roles had to be hired. The new educational strategy 'drove' the resource reallocation process, both by identifying new types of staff that were needed and, by implication, old types of staff that were not.

Because nearly all schools restructured how they served special needs students, all student individual education programmes (IEPs) that were provided for disabled students had to be written, so that the new service strategy was legally prescribed.

Finally, during the process of resource reallocation, each school encountered various problems – regulatory constraints, personal connections to individuals whose jobs were eliminated, appeals to local teacher unions to block the changes, etc. And in each instance faculties were able to overcome the problems because of the ownership of the schools' performance problems that emerged from the needs assessments and because of faculty commitment to the new educational strategies.

Rather than glitches halting progress, glitches became something that joint faculty action overcame in order for the faculty as a whole to realize the new educational vision for the school.

In this process there was usually a shift from specialist staff to more regular teachers and to more professional development and training. This shift was the strongest for schools that reduced class sizes to 15 for the entire day (see, for example, Odden and Archibald, 2001). In terms of specifics, schools generally have the following types of staffing resources that form the pool of resources that can be reallocated:

- regular classroom teachers;
- specialist teachers, such as art, music, physical education and library teachers; who teach a non-academic subject and provide teachers with planning and preparation time;
- specialist teachers, who usually work in resource rooms catering to the special needs of disabled students, students from low income backgrounds or students struggling to learn English;
- instructional aides;
- pupil-support professionals, such a guidance counsellors, psychologists, social workers and nurses;
- custodial workers and secretaries;
- small amounts of discretionary dollars;
- administrators, such as assistant principals.

In the resource reallocation process, the number of regular teachers was either maintained or increased; the latter occurred when the primary new educational strategy was lower class size during the entire school day. The art, music, etc. teachers remained, thus retaining planning and preparation time. Specialist teachers and instructional aides working in resource rooms were usually eliminated or dramatically reduced, and the funds were used for training for the entire faculty and for a more powerful strategy to help those students master the regular curriculum, such as individual tutoring. Assistant principals, usually found only in larger schools, were often eliminated, as schools first divided themselves into smaller, relatively independent units of no larger than 500 students, each headed by one or two instructional facilitators who provided ongoing training and coaching for these schools within schools. Finally, the professional development pot was enlarged to engage outside expert trainers – often individuals associated with the whole-school design adopted. Only small changes were made with classified staff; and the numbers of student support staff usually remained, though they were reorganized into more cohesive teams.

Next steps

The research has found schools in very different locations all around the USA that have reduced class sizes to 15 for the entire day, other schools that quintupled expenditures for professional development, other schools that implemented a more powerful extra-help strategy such as one-to-one tutoring for students struggling to learn a harder curriculum, and some implementing two or more of these new strategies. These schools have adopted these expensive strategies by taking the resources from programmes that were not working and deploying them to the above strategies, which teachers as a faculty had decided would work better. Through that resource reallocation process, schools shifted how they used their instructional budgets, reducing outside-the-regular classroom staff positions and increasing the number of regular teachers and investments in professional development and training. What the research has shown is that at least some schools in the USA can implement new and more powerful educational strategies without spending more money, and in doing so they spend their extant money very differently.

Odden and Archibald (2000) and Archibald (2001) show that each of the schools engaging in resource reallocation produced improvements in student performance during the first and second years of implementation. In the future, the hope is that such improvements will be maintained and enhanced. Over a longer time period, there need to be examples of schools increasing student academic achievement in quantum amounts – perhaps even doubling achievement results. But the examples researched so far show that many schools in the USA are able to boost student performance by implementing very different and more powerful educational strategies without needing new resources. And in the process, such schools alter how resources are used in schools.

More examples of such better use of resources are needed in the future, as are more examples of ways schools can double or triple student achievement results, so even more dramatic resource reallocation possibilities can be identified. In these future examples, it could happen that schools begin to replace some school 'labour' with 'technology', a practice that has characterized private-sector restructuring and re-engineering processes (Lawler, Mohrman and Benson, 2001). More powerful technology applications need to emerge to allow this phenomenon to happen in education, but it could represent the next stage of resource reallocation. When this happens, education resource reallocation could also take the freed-up resources and boost teacher salaries, a phenomenon that has not yet occurred in education, but again has been successful in the private sector (Lawler, Mohrman and Benson, 2001).

American schools, and perhaps schools in many other countries, are at a crossroads. They are being asked to produce much higher levels of student learning, without commensurate increases in dollars. Research shows that movement forward on this challenge is possible, both by adopting new and more effective educational strategies and by funding them via the resource reallocation process, thus changing the patterns of resource use that have evolved over the past 50 years. But whether these fledgling beginnings are sufficient to accomplish the ambitious education reform goals most countries have set will be determined in the future. It could be that even more powerful educational strategies, which use computer technologies to a greater degree, and require even more radical resource-use patterns, will be required. It also could be that more money will ultimately be needed.

REFERENCES

Archibald, S. (2001) *A Case Study of Dramatic Resource Reallocation to Improve Student Achievement: Harrison Place High School*, Madison: University of Wisconsin, Wisconsin Center for Education Research, Consortium for Policy Research in Education.

Borman, G., Stringfield, S. and Slavin, R. (eds) (2001) *Compensatory Education at the Crossroads*, Mahwah, NJ: Lawrence Erlbaum Associates.

Bransford, J., Brown, A. and Cocking, R. (1999) *How People Learn*, Washington, DC: National Academy of Education.

Chubb, J. and Moe, T. (1990) *Politics, Markets and America's Schools*, Washington, DC: Brookings Institution Press.

Elmore, R. & Associates (1991) *Restructuring: The Next Generation of School Reform*, San Francisco: Jossey-Bass.

Fuhrman, S. (ed.) (1993) *Designing Coherent Education Policy*, San Francisco: Jossey-Bass.

Hanushek, E. (1996) 'Understanding the 20th-century growth in US school spending', paper presented to the annual meeting of the American Educational Finance Association.

Kirst, M. and Jung, R. (1991) 'The utility of a longitudinal approach in assessing implementation: a thirteen-year view' in Odden, A. (ed.) *Education Policy Implementation*, Albany: State University of New York Press, pp. 39–54.

Lankford, H. and Wyckoff, J. (1995). 'Where has the money gone? An analysis of school district spending in New York', *Educational Evaluation and Policy Analysis*, 17 (2), pp.179–94.

Lawler, E.E., Mohrman, S.A. and Benson, G. (2001) *Organizing for High Performance*, San Francisco: Jossey-Bass.

Miles, K.H. (1995) 'Freeing resources for improving schools: a case study of teacher allocation in Boston public schools', *Educational Evaluation and Policy Analysis*, 17 (4), pp. 476–93.

Miles, K.H. (1997) 'Spending more at the edges: understanding the growth in public school spending from 1967 to 1991', unpublished doctoral dissertation, Ann Arbor: University of Michigan Press.

Miles, K.H. and Darling-Hammond, L. (1998) 'Re-thinking the allocation of teaching resources: some lessons from high performing schools', *Educational Evaluation and Policy Analysis*, 20 (1), pp. 9–29.

Monk, D.H., Roelke, C.F. and Brent, B.O. (1996). *What Education Dollars Buy: An Examination of Resource Allocation Patterns in New York State Public School Systems*, Madison, WI: University of Wisconsin, Wisconsin Center for Education Research, Consortium for Policy Research in Education.

Murphy, J. (ed.) (1990) *The Educational Reform Movement of the 1980s*, Berkeley, CA: McCutchan.

National Center for Education Statistics. (2000) *Trends in Academic Progress: Three Decades of Student Performance*, Washington, DC: US Department of Education.

Odden, A., (ed.) (1991) *Education Policy Implementation*, Albany: State University of New York Press.

Odden, A. (1995) *Educational Leadership for America's Schools*, New York: McGraw-Hill.

Odden, A. (1997) 'How to rethink school budgets to support school transformation', *Getting Better by Design Series*, Vol. 3, Arlington, VA: New American Schools.

Odden, A. and Archibald, S. (2000) *Reallocating Resources. How to Boost Student Achievement without Asking for More*, Thousand Oaks, CA: Corwin Press.

Odden, A. and Archibald, S. (2001) *A Reallocation Case for Small Class Size*, Madison, WI: University of Wisconsin, Wisconsin Center for Education Research, Consortium for Policy Research in Education.

Odden, A. and Busch, C. (1998) *Financing Schools for High Performance*, San Francisco: Jossey-Bass.

Odden, A. and Picus, L.O. (2000) *School Finance: A Policy Perspective*, 2nd edn, New York: McGraw-Hill.

Odden, A., Monk, D., Nakib, Y. and Picus, L.O. (1995) 'The story of the education dollar: no academy awards and no fiscal smoking guns', *Phi Delta Kappan*, 77 (2), pp. 161–8.

Peterson, P., Rabe, B. and Wong, K. (1986) *When Federalism Works*, Washington, DC: Brookings Institution Press.

Picus, L. O. and M. Fizal. (1995) 'Why do we need to know what money buys? Research on resource allocation patterns in elementary and secondary schools' in Picus, L.O. and Wattenbarger, J.L. (eds) *Where Does the Money Go? Resource Allocation in Elementary and Secondary Schools* (*1995 Yearbook of the American Education Finance Association*), Newbury Park, CA: Corwin Press, pp. 1–9.

Picus, L., Tetreault, D. and Murphy, J. (1996) *What Money Buys: Understanding the Allocation and Use of Educational Resources in California*, Madison, WI: University of Wisconsin, Wisconsin Center for Education Research, Consortium for Policy Research in Education.

Picus, L.O., and Wattenberger, J.L. (eds) (1995) *Where Does the Money Go? Resource Allocation in Elementary and Secondary Schools* (*1995 Yearbook of the American Education Finance Association*), Newbury Park, CA: Corwin Press pp. 1–9.

Richardson, V. (ed.) (2001) *Handbook of Research on Teaching*, 4th edn, Washington, DC: American Educational Research Association.

5

Rothstein, R. and Miles, K.H. (1995) *Where's the Money Gone?*, Washington, DC: Economic Policy Institute.

Schwartz, A. (1999) 'School districts and spending in the schools' in Fowler Jr., W. (ed.) *Selected Papers in School Finance 1997–1999*, Washington, DC: National Center for Education Statistics.

Slavin, R. and Calderon, M. (eds) (2001) *Effective Programs for Latino Students*, Mahwah, NJ: Lawrence Earlbaum Associates.

Slavin, R. and Madden, N. (2001) *Success for All: Research and Reform in Elementary Education*, Mahwah, NJ: Lawrence Earlbaum Associates.

Stringfield, S., Ross, S. and Smith, L. (1996) *Bold Plans for School Restructuring: The New American Schools Designs*, Mahwah, NJ: Lawrence Erlbaum Associates.

CHAPTER 33

The role of the private sector in the UK in turning around failing schools: a case example

DAVID CROSSLEY

Kings College in Guildford, Surrey, UK, is a new 11–18 school. It is the first state school in the UK to be privately managed. 3Es Enterprises has a contract to run the school for ten years. 3Es believes that it has a replicable model that can be applied to other schools. The second 3Es school opened in September 2001 and the third in September 2002. What was initially a local government initiative under existing legislation has become a significant influence on national government, with the model being extended and embedded in the Labour government's Green Paper *Schools – Building on Success* and its subsequent Education Bill. This will allow external partners, including successful schools, other public sector, private sector or voluntary sector bodies, to work with a failing school in order to turn it around. This chapter explores the background to the creation of the new school and explains what private involvement in state schooling has been able to contribute.

Background

The previous school on the site, King's Manor, was closed in late July 2000 and Kings College opened on 1 September. King's Manor had been in long-term decline, culminating in a virtual collapse in student roll, with just over 40 first preferences for Year 7 entry in September 1999. It was also put in 'special measures'; in other words it was judged as failing by the national inspection body the Office for Standards in Education (OFSTED). Parental pressure led to a reprieve and Surrey Local Education Authority decided on the innovative solution of inviting private contractors to run the school. What had been billed as the first 'privatized state school' attracted massive media attention. Bids were received initially from nine organizations or companies. The contract was finally awarded to 3Es Enterprises, a wholly-owned subsidiary of the CTC Kingshurst in Birmingham, with ex-Berkshire County Council Chief Executive, Stanley Goodchild, as the managing consultant for the project. Here is a clear example of innovation leading to innovation. Kingshurst was the first City Technology College in the UK, set up as part of a radical scheme in the late 1980s by the then Conservative government to encourage business to invest in and help create schools in disadvantaged areas.

A management contract between Surrey and 3Es sets out clear targets for attainment, attendance and other areas for the years ahead. The new college was created under existing legislation. This is interesting in that it demonstrates that where there is a will there can be a way of achieving things. This is a lesson that can be used to empower schools: too often public education is disempowered and a 'can't do' culture prevails. The new college operates as a voluntary-aided school, with the trust that owns and controls 3Es making up the majority on the governing body, alongside the usual elected parents, teachers and other staff. This is the way most state church schools are operated in the UK. The Department for Education and Skills (DfES) formally approved the creation of the new college. During the last year of King's Manor's operation, an ex-assistant principal of Kingshurst was temporary principal and 3Es had an office based on the site. A key element of the success of the endeavour to date was preparation over an extended period of time.

What is the contribution of private involvement?

So what is it that 3Es has brought to the school? First, a focus, a clear vision and expertise. 3Es put some considerable effort into communicating its plans and ideas to the community. A school's reputation is a most precious flower and it takes a great deal to convince parents that a school with a bad name is going to change. In the case of the previous school it had had a name change and a change of head in 1993, but that was not enough. Certainly the private involvement in the project did convince parents that, this time, the change would be dramatic. The result of this was very directly seen in a considerable increase in potential Year 7 roll to 120 for September 2000, even before the college opened and in spite of the fact that the college did not even exist at the time. This was in no small part due to the successful and innovative school that was already being run in Birmingham. Parents wanted a similar school for their children. One parent remarked that in Birmingham they saw children who were from a more deprived area but were being given a proper chance – one that was being denied to their own children. This success in attracting students has continued and the College was oversubscribed for its entry in September 2002. So track record was important – but what is the essential difference between a local authority promising to regenerate a school and 3Es as a private company?

Clear ideas of what schools could be like

3Es first brought expertise not so much in administering a number of schools but in terms of clear ideas of what schools could be like. It also brought proficiency in governance, since the core members of the new school's governing body were from the sister school in Birmingham. They in turn attracted key local people to join the board, including, in this case, the University of Surrey's Vice-Chancellor. This, in combination with community members, elected parents, teachers and staff, provides a powerful synergy. From the beginning, the major focus was on creating a new ethos of trust and a culture of achievement. In transforming a failing school, a major challenge is to build self-esteem. Students understand the importance of this and articulate the impact well. One commented on the praise they now get: 'I think you get more confident when you are treated with respect', Another feels that he is working at a much higher level now, because: 'We have a better relationship with our teachers'. Yet another describes the depth of the change when she remarks: 'There is a whole atmosphere about the school; you feel that you can learn without other students saying you're a boffin. Everyone just wants to do well – that is what is really good about the school.'

The development of accommodation was less about space and needs than about the curriculum design and ethos that the developments would help foster. A capital project was planned to provide a new foyer reception area. This has been described as being more like a hotel reception than a school. One of the main corridors is directly adjacent to it, but its design helps communicate a purposeful and calm atmosphere. It is far from utilitarian, but it is also integrated into the whole school. Its style is seamless with the rest of the areas that flow from it. It adjoins a new Learning Resource Centre developed from three classrooms and adjacent office/corridor areas. This is open from early morning until evening and is a light, airy and welcoming place to work and learn. Inspectors noted with surprise the way students arrive and use the facility in an adult way, more akin to a university library than a school.

Why does everyone need to go to lunch at the same time?

A lot of what we do echoes the world of business. We seek to move on from the conventional 'factory school' and to create a modern working and learning environment. Thus the cyber café/restaurant, whilst impressive to visit, is also part of a fundamental reappraisal of the conventional school day, as part of the new ethos 3Es sought to establish.

We take so much about the routines of schools for granted and, though at one level we all complain about constant change, the core routines of our schools have changed little from those of a very different age. Mass education was originally developed to meet the needs of the factory age. Scenes of large numbers of people emerging from factory gates at the same time have all but disappeared, but schools are still organized on factory lines, with students treated as class or year entities ruled by the bell, with a rigid timetable and short lessons adding to the need for mass movement. Lunchtimes often combine the worst aspects of this model. Large numbers descend on inadequate dining facilities, which are then left unused for most of the day. Teachers retreat to staff rooms and many senior staff dread the wet lunchtime and the number of behavioural or other incidents that can follow. Lunchtimes often model styles of eating and personal and social interaction in direct contrast to what is put forward in a school's aims. Yet it is self-inflicted and there are other ways.

From the beginning, Kings decided to operate longer lessons and a continuous school day. Students have two breaks in the day, one for brunch and another for lunch. They visit the cyber café/restaurant where there is a seat for everyone and there is a scheduled time for everyone. There is no need to queue for more than a few minutes. Food quality is enhanced and teachers join students in an atmosphere that bears more resemblance to a shopping centre food court on a quiet day than a conventional school dining room. Breaks are organized by class, with no more than

180 students going for a break at any one time. Breaks often take place within lessons and students leave their work on their desks and return after the break.

The significance of this new approach to breaks is dramatic and all-pervading. It is a fundamental element of our ethos of trust and culture of achievement. Its impact extends well beyond the basics of breaks and catering organization. It enables almost constant unobtrusive adult supervision and turns on its head many of the usual truisms of schools. Of course, students must show consideration, moving about the college whilst lessons are going on, but this is well understood and appreciated as reasonable and logical. The break is of an appropriate length too: 20 minutes for brunch and 30 for lunch. Visitors feel comfortable and welcome in the restaurant, where a calm and pleasant atmosphere prevails.

In the old days the students formed long queues outside the dining room and were let into the servery a few at a time. The pressure on catering staff to provide for so many at once only detracted from food quality and created the need to do the equivalent of 'putting on the sprouts in October for Christmas' each day. Conditions have, almost by definition, had to be somewhat squalid and few canteens can guarantee a seat for all. Even if they do, it can result in tremendous waste of a major resource. Reengineering on this scale is possible without private or business involvement, but the injection of new ways of thinking makes it more likely to happen. This involvement encourages radical thinking and a 'can do' culture.

A school for the future and the value of developing strategic partners

The development of an information technology (IT) infrastructure is also directly linked to the college ethos, with a computer on every teacher's desk. These are for administration, presentation and communication. The old 'eye in the back of the teacher's head' now has technological assistance! Ease of access and communication enables work to be published online, worksheets to be e-mailed to students and, of course, an online reference library with links to the whole world at every teacher's fingertips.

The use of IT for learning was a key objective of the college. It links to our aims of encouraging lifelong and independent learning. Yet IT in schools has had a very different impact overall to the one it has had in business and on other organizations. In far too many cases it remains a peripheral add-on that is far from mission-critical. Contrast this with so many other organizations that could no longer operate without IT. In addition, IT in schools has usually created a demand for more labour rather than less. From the beginning, we sought to maximize the benefits of IT for learning and to develop a virtual school alongside our real school. This would build on the multimedia academy that had been established in our sister school. In addition, 3Es attracted a number of major investor partners to support its schools in their work.

IT and its use for learning is a major priority of the college. We have only just begun, but we have started to see the beginnings of numerous leading-edge developments. We are working with one of the strategic investors, a major e-learning partner, putting a significant proportion of our curriculum online and also developing an online homework centre. Access is supported by our Learning Resource Centre, already open from 7.30 am to 6 pm each day. In partnership with one of our strategic investors, we have installed high-quality videoconferencing links to work with our partner schools, particularly in the delivery of our post-16 curriculum and joint staff training. We have fast internet access and a full site network. We are piloting leading-edge 'anytime, anywhere' wireless technology, and this will soon enable any room to be a computer room. We have installed our first six interactive whiteboards.

The real yield in terms of raising achievement will take time as the hardware and software developments are embedded, but they are already having an impact. Private involvement again has fostered a 'can do' rather than a 'done to' culture. Companies are keen to work with us and support these leading-edge developments. Their staff time, expertise and support are as important as any investment they may or may not make. They in return learn from our expertise about what works in schools.

Drawing on the approach of business

Staff structure and training

In addition to expertise in school design and ethos, 3Es brought a radical approach to staff structure. Conventional hierarchies in UK schools were replaced by a flatter structure with real flexibility; you are what you do rather than what you are called. Instead of conventional heads of department and pastoral team leaders, we have an assistant principal team with each member responsible for a broad curriculum and pastoral area, as well as whole-school responsibilities. Staff in their teams are empowered and take on a range of responsibilities that are reviewed each year. The development of a portfolio of experiences will serve them well in terms of their future career progression and development. This approach to staff extends to support staff too. Staff development is a priority and is integral, rather than something that you are sent away on a course to experience. Again the theme is empowerment. Each academic year begins with a residential conference that reflects on achievements and prepares all for the priorities of the year ahead.

Delighting the customer

Writings on quality management stress the importance of delighting the customer. These sorts of notions can provoke at best wry smiles from teachers. Yet the college from the beginning put considerable effort into treating students and their parents as individuals. This brought a more business-focused approach to customer service, care and marketing. The principal and senior staff were recruited and took up post on 1 May 2000, some five months before the college opened. Every student was seen at least once individually with their parents before the college opened in September. Every student and their parents committed themselves to the ethos and expectations of our new college.

Media attention required particular skills. 3Es has attracted wide-ranging and extensive media coverage, and has embedded a clearly focused approach to this challenge. While at one level the media interest is because a private company is involved, schools in challenging circumstances – and even schools more generally

– now attract more media focus than ever before. So expertise in dealing with the media is perhaps more important than ever. Beyond this, the involvement of 3Es was even more important. Its very existence convinced a sceptical community that something quite different was going to happen. Techniques like meeting parents in the local supermarket, arranging press conferences and other events all had an impact. Expectations were raised and communicated. Teachers were attracted to the challenge and were then inspired to implement the new culture.

The emergence of the 3Es brand

3Es and Surrey worked together on issues such as staffing and site development. However, 3Es also brought clarity of vision, expertise and determination. As the organization takes on further schools, the emergence of a brand becomes important. Certainly a number of essential characteristics begin to emerge. These take the form of ethos, the way young people are treated, staff and curriculum structure and building development. This leads to some interesting conclusions. An empowered school that is clear about its aims and purpose could take on the regeneration of other schools. In many ways it has the most expertise to carry out this task, yet this has been done relatively rarely in the state sector. Self-management and development of more autonomous state schools do encourage these sorts of developments that empower and enable. However, for a school to reengineer another, it would need both the excess capacity and the expertise. In addition, the school would need skills beyond its professional areas of proficiency.

The 3Es model combines and extends both requirements. A school could perhaps develop or support another. This model is of wider significance as it is designed to be extended to a number of schools. To date, 3Es has taken on two further schools, one in Surrey and one in Kent, the latter a new City Academy. It has also formed a Federation of schools, which amongst other aims fosters collaboration between 3Es schools and some impressive curriculum collaboration initiatives.

The business of education

3Es is a not-for-profit company that invests any income it earns back into its endeavours. Its strengths clearly emerge from its enthusiasm and expertise. Writing in the *Guardian*, (24 July 2001) a journalist remarked that the most striking characteristic of the key players was 'how steeped they are in the ethos of public service and egalitarianism'. Yet the business involvement does bring advantages, since it challenges the fundamental weakness that can detract from the provision of excellent public services. Too often they can be dominated by a 'can't do', 'done to' disempowered culture, where 'playing safe and sticking to the status quo' is the hallmark. By their nature, organizations like 3Es are able to question and challenge established ways of doing things. Further, all public service organizations need to be run as efficiently as possible and here best practice ideas from business can surely help.

In the final analysis most schools are required to operate within their budget and should deliver the best value for money that they can. Education is too important and public funds are too limited for anything less to be acceptable. Steve Clarke, Surrey's Deputy Director of Education, takes this further and gives his views about those who object in principle to business involvement in schools: 'You can't just stick to your principles and say everyone should have the same, because then the poorest get the worst public services'. In the UK the private sector has always provided education for the country's most prosperous families. The business of education is a mainstay for many companies who provide it with supplies and services. Transforming underperforming schools, often in disadvantaged areas, is perhaps the most vital task facing the UK's educators. If business involvement can provide a better service for the same cost, it is certainly worth it. Furthermore, it would surely be wrong to preclude it.

Kings College has been heralded as a success by inspectors, but the best validation comes from both teachers and students. One teacher, who also taught in the old school, claims she has never had so much fun in the job in her 20 years of teaching. She talks of 'a miraculous upturn in behaviour and expectations'. Even more fundamental are the words of one parent: 'I think the best thing is the sense of hope and purpose and pride, which seemed almost impossible a year ago. I love the enthusiasm of staff and the atmosphere. I am very proud to be part of it.'

5

Providing education to the world's poor: a case study of the private sector in India

JAMES TOOLEY AND PAULINE DIXON

A little appreciated area of the business of education is the 'budget private school' sector, particularly in developing countries. That is, little attention has been given to the private schools that serve poor and low-income families. Indeed, it is a frequently-made assumption about private education in developing countries that it caters only for the élite, and that its promotion would only serve to exacerbate inequality. On the contrary, recent research points to the important ways in which private schools can provide opportunities where government schools fail to deliver. The argument of this chapter is that any moves towards promoting 'education for all' should take seriously the opportunities provided by this private entrepreneurial sector. There may even be business opportunities for discerning investors.

Given the paucity of information on this sector, this chapter serves as a 'primer' on budget private schools, by outlining a case study from India. We describe aspects of our recent research in Hyderabad, Andhra Pradesh, India, setting out answer to questions such as: What are the schools like? Why do parents send their children to these schools? Who are the parents? How many such schools are there? How are they financed? And what does government think of them? Before embarking on this, however, the chapter puts findings about these schools into the context of earlier research on how public education serves the needs of low-income families in India. First, we need to clarify the sector investigated. In India, there are public, private aided and private unaided schools. The private aided schools have teacher salaries fully paid by government, and teacher contracts, terms and conditions identical to those in the public schools. Such schools are, as with the public schools, heavily unionized, and research has shown the two sectors to be more or less identical, in terms of costs and achievement outcomes (Kingdon, 1996). The subject of this part, then, is the private un-aided schools, that receive no funding at all from government and which are, in substantial ways, quite different from public and aided schools.

How does public education serve the needs of the poor?

How do government schools serve low-income families in the slums and villages of India? The recent PROBE report – the *Public Report on Basic Education in India* (Probe Team, 1999) – gives a useful picture of the relative merits of public and private schools for such families in states that are likely to be similar in some respects to Andhra Pradesh, that is, Bihar, Madhya Pradesh, Uttar Pradesh and Rajasthan.

The picture that the report paints of the government schools is bleak. It describes the 'malfunctioning' in these schools for the poor. The schools suffered from poor physical facilities and high pupil–teacher ratios, but what is most disturbing is the low level of teaching activity taking place in them. When researchers called unannounced on their random sample, only in 53 per cent of the schools was there any 'teaching activity' going on (ibid., p. 47). In fully 33 per cent, the headteacher was absent. The deterioration of teaching standards is not just to do with disempowered teachers:

> The PROBE survey came across many instances where an element of plain negligence was ... involved. These include several cases of irresponsible teachers keeping a school closed or non-functional for months at a time; a school where the teacher was drunk, while only one-sixth of the children enrolled were present; other drunk teachers, some of whom expect pupils to bring them daru [drink]; a headteacher who asks the children to do domestic chores, including looking after the baby; several cases of teachers sleeping at school; ... a headteacher who comes to school once a week; another headteacher who did not know the name of a single child in the school. (Ibid., p. 63)

Significantly, the low level of teaching activity occurred even in those schools with relatively good infrastructure, teaching aids and pupil-teacher ratio. In such schools, 'generally, teaching activity has been reduced to a minimum, in terms of both time and effort. And this pattern is not confined to a minority of irresponsible teachers – it has become a way of life in the profession.' (p. 63).

But all of these highlight, for the PROBE researchers, the underlying problem in the government schools: the 'deep lack of accountability in the schooling system' (p. 54).

Interestingly, the PROBE report itself points to the existence of many private schools serving the poor and low-income families, and concedes – perhaps rather reluctantly – that the problems that were found to exist in the government schools were not apparent in the private alternative. In the great majority of private schools – again visited unannounced and at random – there 'was feverish classroom activity' (ibid., p. 102). Private schools were successful because they were more accountable:

> In a private school, the teachers are accountable to the manager (who can fire them), and, through him or her, to the parents (who can withdraw their children). In a government school, the chain of accountability is much weaker, as teachers have a permanent job with salaries and promotions unrelated to performance. This contrast is perceived with crystal clarity by the vast majority of parents. (Ibid., p. 64)

So much so, that the majority of parents reported that 'if the costs of sending a child to a government and private school were the *same*, they would rather send their children to a private school' (ibid., p. 102).

The case of budget private schools in Andhra Pradesh

To many readers, the existence of such private schools for the poor will be a surprise. One of us first came across such schools by chance, while conducting other fieldwork for the International Finance Corporation, the private finance arm of the World Bank, in Andhra Pradesh in January 2000. Since then we have been working closely with a range of these schools based in the twin cities of Hyderabad and Secunderabad (henceforth referred to in the usual way as 'Hyderabad'). Part of our work from September 2001 to May 2002 has involved gathering data from 15 'budget' private schools, as well as interviewing government officials on the sector.

The 15 private schools that were researched have fees of between Rs. 35 – Rs. 350 per month (about 70c to $7.00 per month), with most in the lower range. All of these private schools are located in 'slum areas'. (The term is the one commonly used in India, and is certainly not meant to be disparaging.) Fourteen of the school 'correspondents' – the official name for the school manager, usually the entrepreneur who set up the school – also gave information relating to business issues, one of the 15 declining to provide details of income and expenditure. From the 15 schools, 315 parents and 315 students (in both cases, 21 randomly selected from each school) and 244 teachers (all the teachers in the schools on the days that the researchers called, with the exception of those related to the correspondent) were also interviewed using detailed questionnaire protocols. Much of the information asked of the teachers, parents and students was used to triangulate that given by the correspondent (hence the exclusion of teachers related to the correspondent).

The 15 schools were taken from a list of some 50 schools, drawn up by three researchers employed in Hyderabad, selected opportunistically during visits to areas of the city where it was known there was a significant number of such schools. The 15 schools chosen were those whose managers agreed to have a researcher in their school for significant amounts of time to talk to parents, teachers and students, to observe classes and to divulge all financial information to the researchers (although in one case this did not happen, as mentioned above). In return, schools were promised to be included in phase two of the project (not reported here), where they could take part in various school improvement programmes. Given the schools' understandable reluctance about having data made public, we have made all data anonymous, coding schools from A to N. Details of the schools are given in Table 34.1.

There are two education districts in the twin cities: Ranga Reddy and Hyderabad Districts. Both District Education Officers (DEOs) were interviewed to gauge their views on the private sector, as well as the (political) Minister for Education for Andhra Pradesh, and the Director of School Education, the leading education civil servant in the state.

Who are the parents?

The first significant point to note about the budget private schools is that they are patronized by parents who recognize the inadequacy of the public schools, and want better opportunities for their children. But such parents cannot be described as élite or middle class – the common assumption about parents who send their children to private school. The parents are poorly educated, generally in manual labour on daily wages, with family incomes near or below the minimum wage in India.

Table 34.1 Case study schools: student numbers, fees, free places, profits and recognition status

School	Boys	Girls	Total	Monthly fees (Rs. 45 = $1)	Number of free seats	Concessionary monthly fees (Rs. 45 = $1)	Number of students with concessions	Annual surplus (2000–1) (Rs. 45 = $1)	Recognition status; date obtained recognition
School A	210 (53%)	190 (47%)	400 (100%)	Rs. 75–150 ($1.66–3.33)	21 (5% of total)	Rs. 50–120 ($1.11–2.67)	175 (44% of total)	Rs. 517 146 ($11 492)	Class VII (1994)
School B	154 (53%)	139 (47%)	293 (100%)	Rs. 35–130 ($0.78–2.89)	0	Rs. 25–85 ($0.56–1.89)	63 (22% of total)	Rs. 129 520 ($2878)	Not recognized
School C	206 (55%)	170 (45%)	376 (100%)	Rs. 60–140 ($1.33–3.12)	15 (4% of total)	0	0	Rs. 348 180 ($7737)	Class X (2002)
School D	441 (56%)	353 (44%)	794 (100%)	Rs. 150–200 ($3.33–4.44)	23 (3% of total)	Rs. 10–25 ($0.22–0.56)	141 (18% of total)	Rs. 1 070 617 ($23 791)	Class X (1985)
School E	271 (60%)	183 (40%)	454 (100%)	Rs. 100–200 ($2.22–$4.44)	6 (1% of total)	Rs. 50–135 ($1.11–3.00)	37 (8% of total)	Rs. 195 164 ($4336)	Class X (2000)
School F	255 (53%)	228 (47%)	483 (100%)	Rs. 100–175 ($2.22 – 3.89)	0	0	0	Rs. 52 550 ($1167)	Class X (2000)
School G	484 (53%)	431 (47%)	915 (100%)	Rs. 70–150 ($1.56–3.33)	98 (10.7% of total)	Rs. 15–30 ($0.33–0.67)	99 (11% of total)	Rs. 403 868 ($8974)	Class X (2000)
School H	420 (55%)	338 (45%)	758 (100%)	Rs. 130–350 ($2.89–7.78)	2 (0.3% of total)	Rs. 10–75 ($0.22–1.66)	4 (0.5%)	RS 879 995 ($19 555)	Class X (1998)
School I	337 (56%)	264 (44%)	601 (100%)	Rs. 90–150 ($2.00–3.33)	8 (1% of total)	Rs. 10 ($0.22)	8 (1% of total)	RS 330 338 ($7340)	Class X (1993)

Table 34.1 *Continued*

School	Boys	Girls	Total	Monthly fees (Rs. 45 = $1)	Number of free seats	Concessionary monthly fees (Rs. 45 = $1)	Number of students with concessions	Annual surplus (2000–1) (Rs. 45 = $1)	Recognition status; date obtained recognition
School J	408 (50%)	410 (50%)	818 (100%)	Rs. 60–120 ($1.33–2.67)	46 (6% of total)	Rs. 15–30 ($0.33–0.67)	50 (6% of total)	Rs. 112 425 ($2498)	Class X (1994)
School K	193 (51%)	187 (49%)	380 (100%)	Rs. 100–180 ($2.22–4.00)	28 (7% of total)	Rs. 20 ($0.44)	91 (24% of total)	Rs. 343 770 ($7639)	Class VII (1992)
School L	188 (53%)	169 (47%)	357 (100%)	Rs. 85–160 ($1.89–3.56)	0	Rs. 10 ($0.22)	2 (0.5% of total)	Rs. 151 404 ($3364)	Class VII (1991)
School M	207 (57%)	155 (43%)	362 (100%)	Rs. 100–200 ($2.22–4.44)	48 (13% of total)	Rs. 25–60 ($0.56–1.33)	24 (7% of total)	RS 355 636 ($7903)	Class VII (2000)
School N	281 (59%)	199 (41%)	480 (100%)	Rs. 100–150 ($2.22–$3.33)	14 (3% of total)	Rs. 70–100 ($1.56 – 2.22)	84 (17.5% of total)	Rs. 636 680 ($14 148)	Class VII (1994)

Regarding the parents' educational background, 15 per cent of fathers have had no schooling at all, rising to 30 per cent for the mothers. Indeed the great majority of the mothers (63 per cent) either have had no schooling, or are educated at Grade VII or below (*see* Table 34.2).

Parents' employment also gives some indication of the background of the children who attend these private schools. About 60 per cent of fathers are manual workers, undertake jobs that would be considered as 'manual' work, including market traders, daily hired porters and rickshaw drivers. Only about 15 per cent are in low-level clerical jobs (*see* Table 34.3). As would be expected in India, the majority of mothers are housewives.

The minimum wage currently in India is recognized as between Rs. 1500 and Rs. 2,000 per month, depending on sector. More than half the parents indicated that their income is paid on a daily basis, and although some households have two or three breadwinners (around 20 per cent of those sampled) around 33 per cent receive an income that is either below or very close to the minimum wage.

Table 34.2 *Budget private schools: educational standards of parents*

Educational standard	Percentage of fathers	Percentage of mothers
No schooling	15	30
Up to grade III	2	3
Up to grade V	5	11
Up to grade VII	17	19
Up to grade X	33	27
Up to grade XII	17	6
Degree	10	2
Post-grad/professional	1	0
Missing data	0	2
Total	100	100

Table 34.3 *Budget private schools: occupation of fathers*

Employment status	Percentage
Unemployed	1.0
Irregular employment	9.0
Domestic or personal	9.3
Service worker	14.5
Market trader	11.4
Rickshaw driver	5.9
Hired porter ('coolie')	6.9
Clerical worker	15.2
Manager	2.8
Other	24.1
Total	100.0

Finally, it is worth noting that these parents have high aspirations for their children. More than 70 per cent of the parents want their children either to take a degree or become a professional, as shown in Table 34.4.

Table 34.4 *Highest aspirations of parent for child*

	Percentage
I want my child to be able to read and write	0.3
I want my child to complete up to Grade VII	0.3
I want my child to complete up to Grade X	17.3
I want my child to complete Inter	11.2
I want my child to take a degree	36.4
I want my child to become a professional engineer/doctor/lawyer	34.4
Total	100.0

Why do parents choose private schools?

Why do parents, given the availability of free state education, send their children to these private schools, when this means paying fees, and, as we have seen, parents are largely poor? First, 96 per cent of parents said that the fact that the schools were English medium – something not allowed in public schools until Grade VI – was a very important factor. Some critics claimed to us that these budget schools simply called themselves 'English medium' in order to hoodwink parents. In fact, in our schools we found a variety of innovations to ensure that children did receive a thorough grounding in English, including the use of language cassettes and the avoidance of the official curriculum from Nursery to Grade 5 to ensure that a large amount of time could be spent on English tuition.

Second, our research showed that the parents know that the government schools are not up to scratch and vote with their feet, sending their children to the schools that they perceive will provide a better education. 98 per cent of the parents indicated that this was an important criterion when they chose their child's school. The government officials were remarkably candid about this. One senior official commented: 'The teachers in the private unaided schools are accountable to the parents. The parents insist on quality. The teachers in the private unaided schools are faced with the sack if they do not perform. They can easily be removed.' Another commented: 'In the private schools the manager watches the teachers all the time. In turn therefore the teachers watch the children.' Such accountability is not present in the government schools, the officials agreed, where teachers and staff are guaranteed a 'job for life' owing to the strength of the teachers' unions and employment contracts. The government officials indicated that it is rare that a teacher from the government sector loses his or her job owing to incompetence.

But this accountability also impacts on the competition between the private schools. There is considerable choice and parents are free to move their children to different schools that are only a few yards apart if they deem their child's school to be failing. For instance, one illiterate father from School A remarked that if the standard did not improve at his child's school, he would place him somewhere else. Interestingly, he felt that the teaching of English was not up to standard. He had been comparing the standard and ability of his child with his neighbour's children who went to another school in the same street, and felt that his child was not doing so well – even though, of course, he understood and spoke no English himself.

What are conditions like in the schools?

Schools are operating in very close proximity to one another – a thriving market of private schools often only streets apart. Many types of buildings are used to house these schools, from rented buildings, family homes, buildings that once housed chicken farms, and rooms situated above shops. Within the schools, the general impression is of concerted teaching activity, with well-behaved children in a strict environment, in usually small classrooms furnished with desks and chairs, blackboards, chalk and dusters. Most children have textbooks, workbook and pencils, although those in the nursery often have chalkboards for their writing and drawing. Most of the classrooms have neither window panes nor doors. Many of the schools provide separate toilets for boys and girls. All the children wear school uniform. All the private unaided schools in the study – and the great majority in general – are English medium schools, although they often teach one or two other languages from the choice of Hindi, Urdu or Telegu. The schools cater for all religious faiths, including Moslem, Hindu and Christian.

How many schools are there?

It came as a surprise to us how candid senior government figures were about the extent of the private unaided schools. Official figures obtained from Hyderabad District showed that almost two-thirds of total students are enrolled in the private unaided sector (67 per cent at upper primary and 61 per cent at high school). There are also three times as many teachers in the private unaided sector as in the government sector. Altogether, the official figures show almost 1000 private schools in the Hyderabad district, or 46 per cent of the total number of schools.

However, these government figures are subject to some interpretation, which makes the picture even more favourable to the private unaided sector. The figures are likely to overestimate the proportion of children in government schools, in part because of corrupt over-reporting (something about which, again, the officials were surprisingly candid). They are also likely to underestimate the number of private unaided schools, because they report only those that are recognized. But many private unaided schools will be unrecognized, particularly at the primary school level – in part because there is no need to be recognized at this level in order for children to take state examinations. And it is at this lower level that there is the smallest official percentage of private schools (15 per cent of all schools, compared to 65 per cent at the upper primary and 61 per cent at the high school level). Observations from the streets suggest that the figure for private unaided primary schools should be considerably higher than this.

Table 34.5 *Hyderabad: public and private school pupils, 2000–1*

SL. No	Type/management	Primary schools	Upper primary schools	High schools	Higher secondary schools	Total
1	State/central government	35 472 (58%)	34 563 (22%)	63 945 (13%)	3464 (24%)	137 444 (19%)
2	Private aided	6 558 (11%)	18 109 (11%)	120 388 (25%)	–	145 055 (20%)
3	Private unaided	19 206 (31%)	105 597 (67%)	301 792 (62%)	11 100 (76%)	437 695 (61%)
Total		61 236	158 269	486 125	14564	720 194

Table 34.6 *Hyderabad: number of institutions, 2001–2*

Type	Primary school	Upper primary school	High school	Total
Government	528 (80%)	120 (24%)	132 (18%)	780 (41%)
Private aided	33 (5%)	51 (10%)	153 (21%)	237 (13%)
Private unaided (15%)	100 (15%)	322 (65%)	447 (46%)	869
Total	661	493	732	1886

Table 34.7 *Hyderabad: public and private school teachers, 2000–1*

SL. No	Type/management	Primary schools	Upper primary schools	High schools	Higher secondary schools	Total
1	State/central government	695 (46%)	889 (18%)	2541 (17%)	179 (28%)	4 304 (20%)
2	Private aided	164 (11%)	518 (10%)	3127 (21%)	–	3 809 (17%)
3	Private unaided	660 (43%)	3596 (72%)	9187 (62%)	463 (72%)	13 906 (63%)
Total		1519	5003	14855	642	22019

How does government impact on the private schools?

In theory, the private unaided schools are strictly controlled by government, with a huge range of regulations for them to meet, from teacher salaries and qualifications, class size, playground size, school facilities, advertising of positions, composition of governing bodies, etc., etc. (see Tooley, 2000). However, in practice, these regulations are widely ignored, subject to the payment of bribes. Indeed, the surprising picture emerges of a highly liberalized market for private unaided education, subject to these unofficial payments. Of course, this is far from ideal for the entrepreneurs, especially given the uncertainty that it brings, but it is nonetheless not as highly regulated a business environment as it appears on paper.

Again, the government officials were quite candid about this. According to one, in practice private unaided schools needed to comply with only four regulatory requirements (*see* Table 34.8) in order to become recognized:

- a playground of a certain size;
- a Rs. 50 000 ($1200) fund in a joint school–government bank account to pay teachers' wages if the school goes bankrupt);
- teacher training; and
- a library.

However, 'there is no way of enforcing the regulations' the official said:

Bribes are offered by the school owners in order for them to become recognized. They also will lie in order to become recognized initially and then there is no way of checking up on the schools ... We can't go into every individual case: we have three inspectors for 600–700 private recognized schools.

The school correspondents also made it clear that this is the way the system worked on the ground: School C put it this way:

In order to get recognition we would have to abide by many regulatory requirements. It is just not possible for us to be able to do this ... Therefore when the government inspectors come we pay them ... We have to pay initially Rs. 50 000 and then we have to pay Rs. 4000 inspection charges. After bribes, this fee will add up to around Rs. 80 000. You see we don't have everything we need here in order to get recognized. If we did, it would cost us a lot of money ... Therefore it is cheaper to bribe the inspector and give him what he is looking for and then we don't have to abide by the regulations.

When the schools were investigated, it was clear that both correspondents and officials gave an accurate picture. Fourteen of our schools were recognized to some level or other. Of the four 'minimal' requirements mentioned by the senior official, none of the schools complied with all of them. Indeed, there was only one school (School H) that reached three of these requirements. Yet, all these schools are recognized!

Interestingly, around 40% of parents said that they did not know whether their child's school was recognized or not.

Table 34.8 *Regulatory requirements and adherence*

School	Minimum regulatory requirements			
	Library	Playground	All qualified teachers	Do they make a profit?
School A	No	No	No	Yes
School B	Yes	No	No	Yes
School C	No	Yes	No	Yes
School D	No	No	No	Yes
School E	No	No	No	Yes
School F	No	Yes	No	Yes
School G	No	Yes	No	Yes
School H	No	Yes	Yes	Yes
School I	Yes	No	Yes	Yes
School J	No	No	No	Yes
School K	No	No	No	Yes
School L	No	No	No	Yes
School M	Yes	No	No	Yes
School N	No	No	No	Yes

Are the schools profitable?

One of the particularly fraught areas of regulation and of concern in national policy terms is the issue of profit. All the schools must be set up, by law, as education societies. Across India there is a prohibition of the 'commercialization' of education, under the Unni Krishnan Supreme Court judgement of 1992, which stated:

> *Education has never been commerce in this country. Making it one is opposed to the ethos, tradition and sensibilities of this nation ... commercialisation is positively harmful, it is opposed to public policy.*

However, in practice, this does not seem to impinge upon the actual behaviour of schools, except in terms of their reporting of accounts, and, of course, in the associated payment of bribes. One senior education officer put it this way: 'all institutions make a profit.... We do not stick to the laws and rules, we are very flexible, and all institutions make a profit, we just let them do it.'

All the schools that participated in the research do make a profit, according to the figures they gave the researchers – and they were more likely to err on the side of caution with these figures, given the illegality of what they do. Profits ranged from just over $1000 (School F) to nearly $25 000 (School D) per year (*see* Table 34.1). Because it is illegal to make a profit, many of the schools kept two record books – one for the government inspectors, and the other for their own use.

Conclusions: objections to budget private education and ways forward

Private unaided schools are thriving in India – as in many other developing countries (Tooley, 2001). They are meeting the needs of parents – many poor, many illiterate – who want something better for their children than is provided in the public schools. And parents are willing to vote with their feet to take children to schools that seem to be offering something better. Such schools are set up by entrepreneurs who, while recognizing their social duty to these poor communities, also wish to run their schools as businesses, and make some profit. Government regulations are heavy on these schools, in theory. But in practice, the regulatory environment is extremely liberal – a liberalization bought with the aid of bribes. All this leads to a vibrant market. In Hyderabad, the city of our case study, the official figures – which are likely to underestimate the private sector's contribution – show over 60 per cent of all students in private unaided schools, and the number is growing each year.

However, it turns out that not everyone is in favour of these schools. Perhaps most surprisingly, given the positive picture painted of private schools *vis-à-vis* the government sector, the PROBE report (Probe, 1999) balked at recommending a greater role for the private sector. The team admits that its report has painted a 'relatively rosy' picture of the private sector, where 'accountability to the parents' leads to 'a high level of classroom activity ... better utilisation of facilities, greater attention to young children, responsiveness of teachers to parental complaints' (ibid., p. 105). But there are four reasons why such findings do not convince them that a greater role for the private sector is desirable or required:

5

- Private schools 'often take advantage of the vulnerability of parents', as many 'parents have little idea of what goes on in the classroom' (p. 105).
- Private teachers teach to the test: They have 'little reason to promote the personal development of the children, to treat them with sensitivity, or to impart a sense of values. Their overwhelming objective is to cram the heads of the pupils, so that they may pass the relevant tests and examinations' (p. 105).
- The expansion of private schools will undermine state education: 'this carries a real danger of undermining the government schooling system' (ibid., p. 106).
- Private schools are out of reach of the vast majority of poor parents (ibid., p. 105).

The first two criticisms are of the quality of private education. They are not based on the evidence in the PROBE report. Certainly our research, (yet to be published), which has investigated the quality of what is offered in the private schools, would not concur with these conclusions, nor does other research that looked at selected achievement outcomes (Kingdon, 1996). Of course, there are many shortcomings in terms of quality in these schools, as might be expected in schools that charge perhaps $20 per year. But if there is a genuine concern for helping the poor, then ways need to be explored that can help these schools to improve, rather than damning them for failing to reach desired standards. Indeed, the opportunity is there for outside agencies to help these schools in capacity building, in finding investment and reaching certain quality conditions, such as providing teacher and management training, and improved curriculum and pedagogy. Most poignantly, because the schools do make a profit, such improvements could be arrived at through investment in the schools, or associations of schools, rather than only in philanthropic handouts, leading to the long-term sustainability of any intervention.

The third objection is not an objection to private education *per se*, but to the impact that private education will have on the state system. But if state education for the poor is as bad as it is described in the PROBE report, and private schools do significantly better, then why worry about the demise of state education, *provided that* this doesn't mean that poor parents are deprived of educational opportunities for their children?

Which brings us to the fourth objection: and it is true that not all parents can afford private education. Fees even as low as the ones we found in our schools are out of the reach of many – they amount to perhaps 6 per cent of a rickshaw puller's annual expected income, and with many families having five or more children, such sums will be out of reach to many. But two points must be made about this. First, in all but two of our case study schools, free places for the poorest in the community were provided – sometimes as many as 13 per cent of all total places. And all but one of the schools offered concessionary fee rates, for those unable to pay full fees. Indeed, in the schools with some of the largest profits (Schools D and N), free and concessionary places amounted to about 20 per cent of all places offered. So the schools themselves are aware of the need to serve the poorest.

Second, if the state sector provides schools that seem so indifferent to the needs of children, then this suggests that reformer efforts would best be served by helping to set up scholarship schemes (public or private) to enable the poorest to access this kind of education. Indeed, such a scholarship scheme could relieve some of this burden from the schools themselves, and help them to pour more resources into investment.

REFERENCES

Kingdon, G. (1996) 'The quality and efficiency of private and public education: a case study of urban India', *Oxford Bulletin of Economics and Statistics*, 58 (1) pp. 57–81.

Probe Team (1999) *Public Report on Basic Education in India*, Oxford: Oxford University Press.

Tooley, J. (2000) *Investment Opportunities in Private Education in Andhra Pradesh: A Survey of the Regulatory and Investment Climate*, Washington, DC. International Finance Corporation.

Tooley, J. (2001) *The Global Education Industry: Lessons from Private Education in Developing Countries*, 2nd edn, London: Institute of Economic Affairs, in association with the International Finance Corporation.

CHAPTER 35

The knowledge economy and the commerce of knowledge

STEPHEN HEYNEMAN

Education goods and services

Demand

The sources for manufacturing have dramatically shifted. Economies in North America and western Europe, which had depended on manufacturing prior to the Second World War, have now shifted to service industries. In the 1940s, manufacturing drove 40 per cent of the American economy while only 14 per cent was driven by services. By the late 1990s, the relative positions had shifted: 35 per cent of the economy was driven by services and less than 18 per cent by manufacturing.

But even manufacturing has changed its requirements for efficiency. Efficiency requires as much human and social capital as physical capital. For instance, expenditures on technology now dominate capital expenditures. In 1970 the proportion of capital expenditures allocated to technology was less than 5 per cent, but by the late 1990s it had risen to 45 per cent. These shifts have had profound influences on the nature of work itself. Under the older corporate structures, it was common for decision making to be made within a hierarchical corporate structure; under newer commercial models, the structures are more 'flat' and decisions are most often made on the 'front lines'. The impact of electronic communications over the last few years is one illustration. Beginning with faxing in the era of library card catalogues and video rental, in just a few years it has progressed through the digitalization of information to one-on-one marketing by e-mail, with search engines and online website catalogues. Provision of these new services has in themselves become a major industry. E-Bay for instance has 10 million users with a market capitalization of $1673 per user. Yahoo! has over 120 million users with a market capitalization of $5513 per user.

These shifts to a knowledge economy have heavily influenced education standards, and the spread of those standards around the world. These include:

- universal school attendance, with a broad range of subjects to be mastered by the full gamut of the population and specialization delayed until increasingly older ages;
- broad access to higher education, making higher education institutions cater to a mass population rather than an elite clientele;

- significant demand from commercial firms to upgrade and repurpose, with the consequent demand for retraining;
- longer lives and better health extending productivity well into what used to be old age.

This is what defines the knowledge economy today and what helps determine the economics of knowledge provision.

Educational programmes

In every country educational programmes are provided in elementary, secondary, undergraduate, postgraduate, vocational and technical education. They are also provided through early childhood education and childcare, special education, adult and continuing education, corporate training, distributed learning, and technology-based training.[1] Programmes are defined as an organized set of curricular activities, which can lead to a certificate or to a degree. They can be owned and operated privately or by public agencies and they can be local or international.

Educational goods

Educational programmes cannot operate without educational materials and equipment. These constitute the industry in educational goods. Commercial activities include the design, manufacture and sales of textbooks, teaching materials, vocational and scientific equipment, educational software, videos, multimedia and school furniture, as well as school supplies.

Educational services

No matter how well manufactured, educational materials and equipment cannot be used efficiently unless there is a supply of high-quality education services. These services are necessary in any complex sector that has to manage fairly the needs of millions of individuals, hundreds of millions in pieces of equipment, and significant political visibility associated with the results. Commercial activities in educational services include the design, marketing and sales of testing, certification, test preparation, tutoring and other enhancement programmes, management consulting, administrative and human resources – accounting, pension, health care and in-service training.[2]

Educational consumers

Educational programmes, goods, and services are provided for consumers of divergent types. These include individual schools and colleges as well as systems of schools and colleges, both public and private, NGOs (non-governmental organizations), commercial corporations, and private individuals.

Market size and trends

North America (Kearns, 1999)

The education and training sector

Education companies have raised $3.4 billion in equity capital since 1994 through 38 initial public offerings (IPOs).[3] The education and training industry is now North America's second largest, accounting for nearly 10 per cent of GDP. Education services constitute the fifth largest service export ($US 8.5 billion in 1997). The industry is generally divided into different 'sectors', with segmented market prospects. There is a K–12 sector, a higher education sector, and an adult education sector. These may be differentiated from corporate training and human capital management services (for school systems and universities).

While the ratio of students per computer has fallen, the proportion of classroom and schools with internet connections has risen. In 1992 the ratio of students/computer was 16:1, by 2000 it had fallen to 6:1. Similarly, the portion of schools and classrooms with internet connections in 1994 was only 3 per cent and 35 per cent. By 2000 these had risen to 65 per cent and 96 per cent. By 2003 internet connection is expected to be universal in schools, about 90 per cent in classrooms, about 67 per cent in homes. Of students themselves, by 2003 about 60 per cent of the teens and about 55 per cent of the pre-teens will have access to the internet. This has helped to define the commercial opportunity. For internet portals and hubs, by 2003 the market is expected to be about $800 million; for e-commerce, the market is expected to be about $4billion. The total K–12 learning market in 2003 is expected to be about $6.9 billion .

Goods and services sub-sectors

$26 billion were spent on education-related goods and services in 1997. These included $11.6 billion on textbooks and supplementary materials, $4.8 billion on technology and $3 billion on testing and test preparation. Within the government and corporate sector, $9.6 billion was spent on goods and services and $6.1 billion on information technology (IT) training. How large is the market in the private provision of education in comparison to the private market for education goods and services? In the USA the three are approximately equal in terms of their proportion of overall revenues (services, 30 per cent; products, 24 per cent; education programmes, 28 per cent).

The education services sub-sector consists of three major components: training (81 per cent), supplementary services (15 per cent), and 'at-risk' services (4 per cent). Training consists of a combination of instructor-led, internet-based, computer-based or video-based training to professionals, with a certificate awarded on successful completion (revenues in 1998: US$24 billion). The at-risk market consists of services for children and youth experiencing difficulties. It includes rehabilitation as well as correctional services (revenues in 1998: $1.3 billion). Supplementary services include educational consulting, test preparation, after-school and summer programmes, language services, psychological and skill assessments (revenues in 1998: $4.4 billion).

The market for educational products in the USA consists of publishing (35 per cent), school supplies (29 per cent), hardware (27 per cent), and electronic media (9 per cent). Hardware consists of companies that provide computers, networking, VCRs, televisions and other audiovisual systems to schools. School supplies consist of learning tools and equipment (maps, blackboards, chalk, laboratory equipment marketed to schools, teachers or individual consumers). Publishing consists of textbooks and other print-based materials, but also electronic media curriculum materials designed either for students or instructors. Electronic media consists of software and internet-delivered products and services to home and school markets. These may include CD-ROMs, videos and laser disks. Internet products include tools for online student publishing. Web services include school-home based connections, education and tutoring web-based sites, and network systems (revenues in 1998: $2.1 billion).

OECD countries

The amount of non-salary educational expenditures varies widely from one OECD country to another, from a high of $2394 per student in Sweden to $57 per student in Greece. However, many of the economic influences that pertain within the USA, also pertain to OECD (Organization for Economic Co-operation and Development) countries in general. Published materials and textbooks account for much of the non-salary expenditures.[4] The objective of individualized instruction, and the tendency for teachers to be the 'managers' instead of the 'providers' of information, is a general phenomenon across OECD countries. This in turn can be expected to drive choices of educational technologies.[5]

There is an increasing emphasis on educational software, and internet use is growing rapidly. Throughout the world, internet use has grown from 61 million users in 1996 to 147 million in 1998, and is expected to grow to 320 million in 2000 and to 720 million in 2005. The USA led the list of internet-using countries, followed by Japan, the UK, Germany, Canada, Australia, France, Sweden, Italy, Spain, The Netherlands, Taiwan, the People's Republic of China, Finland and Norway. These top 15 countries account for 89 per cent of internet use worldwide (Nua Ltd, 1999).

The outlook for sales of educational hardware and software is strong. Between 1995 and 1998 the number of computers in homes rose from 13 to 31 million in the USA, from 7.5 to 32 million in Europe and from 9.5 to 28 million in the rest of the world (see Table 35.1). The market for educational software is rising in parallel fashion, from $775 million in 1996 to $2.5 billion in the USA in the year 2000, from $130 to $460 in Europe, and from $200 million to $1.1 billion in the rest of the world . The worldwide market in educational software, worth US$ 4.1 billion in the year 2000 in schools, is augmented by an additional $2.1 billion in educational software sales to the consumer market outside schools, with a total market for educational software worth $6.2 billion in the year 2000 (Heller Reports, 1999).

Table 35.1 *Consumer market home multimedia computers (in 000s of units)*

	1995	1996	1997	1998
USA	13 000	16 000	22 000	31 000
Europe	7 500	11 000	19 000	32 000
Rest of world	9 500	13 000	19 000	28 000
Total	30 000	40 000	60 000	91 000

Low and middle-income countries

It is clear that in low and middle-income countries the spending per student on teaching materials and other non-salary expenditures is significantly less than in OECD countries. While the Seychelles spent $95 per student in 1998, China spent $4.71, Benin spent $3.54 and India spent, $0.68. The question is whether this is sufficient information to suggest that the market in educational goods and services is insufficient to justify commercial interest. It would be unwise to assume that low expenditures per student implied small markets, for two reasons. First, some low-spending countries have a large number of students. In Benin the low expenditures per student is exacerbated by the small number of students, thus suggesting a market size of about $3 million per year. In India, however, even low expenditures combined with the number of students would suggest a market size of $123 million, and China a market size of just under $1 billion.

Second, these markets are not stagnant. Public education expenditures have doubled around the world between 1980 and 1994. In North America they grew by 103 per cent, and in Europe by 135 per cent. But in East Asia public expenditures grew by over 200 per cent in the same time period.[6] If economies grow, more is spent on educational goods and services per student. This will significantly raise the size of the education markets in large countries with healthy rates of economic growth. This trend suggests that by the year 2009 the education market in India will grow to $200 million, in South Africa to $580 million and in China to $1.7 billion.

The overall growth in education goods and services in OECD countries may also mask the considerable local opportunity in developing countries. One example is the demand for school science equipment in Thailand, where the estimated growth is expected to be 25 per cent between 1997 and 2000. Another illustration is that of textbook demand in Ethiopia, where the demand is expected to grow from 11.4 million in 1997 to 17.9 million in 2002.

5

Determinants of change

Technology

Highly capitalized educational publishers have shifted from marketing individual titles to marketing publishing services – for high-end graphics for instance – to local publishers. High-quality, low-cost books are now feasible in many parts of the world, and in countries at different income levels. Just as many automobiles are manufactured by using parts and materials from many places, so too are textbooks no longer exclusively a local product. The story may be from Uganda; the photograph of the stars may be from a company in Paris; the paper, ink and binding may have been put together in Singapore. Local publishing no longer has the same meaning: if the story is relevant and effective, it no longer matters as much as it once did whence the binding and ink come. What matters is that children in rural Uganda have an adequate supply of effective books – of less concern is whether efficient procurement and management practices require a change in the sources of supply.

Modern testing agencies are also undergoing a similar shift. Instead of every agency trying to design tests autonomously from one another, many agencies are 'renting' the use of items to local test agencies. These items come with the psychometrics already validated on international samples.[7] These agencies may also supply test security or technologies of online scoring, item response or sampling frames. It may be the case, as with automobiles and textbooks, that it will soon be difficult to say exactly what is a 'local' test. Parallel processes of sharing materials and technologies and drawing upon widely disbursed sources of expertise can be found in international education management consulting, the provision of inter- net education services and the design of curriculum materials. Common problems tend to generate international markets, and the international markets tend to help generate more participants in the marketplace. In turn, having more participants in the supply of education goods and services might be expected to reduce costs, expand international trade and allow rapid local product customization.

Internationalization

Standards for educational performance are drawing on experience outside the local community. For example, with respect to individualized instruction, schools are expected to provide emphases for students with different learning needs, multiple options in curriculum and higher general performance. The psychometric standards for student evaluation may no longer be decided by each school independently, but instead are subject to review by more central authorities. Moreover, these in turn may be informed by international psychometric standards. Test items, sampling procedures and administrative efficiency are subject to quality controls. Skill stan- dards, the certification procedures for nursing, medicine, food process handlers, pilots and airline mechanics, and the English language quality of air traffic con- trollers and telephone operators are now subject to global standards. This can be expected to affect the provision of educational goods and services in three ways.

First, multinational corporations, such as General Motors, Shell Oil and Hyatt Hotels, infuse job standards irrespective of national borders. Second, international associations, nurses, architects and international regulatory agencies for example, (the ICC and IATA), propose rigorous standards on the grounds that they are rele- vant internationally. Third, in economies with high volumes of foreign trade, the standards of the trading partners often determine the local application. Certification of food process handlers in Mexico and Chile using US certification methods is rele- vant because of the importance of health standards to the agricultural trade. Where there are economic demands for this certification of standards, there will be a demand for commercial suppliers of certification tests and assessments.

International trade

With the end of the cold war the ideology in education was replaced with demands for efficiency and quality. This has generated a trade in ideas for educa- tion reform as well as goods and services to help make them effective (Heyneman, 1997). Trade patterns are not confined to 'north–south' routes. Textbooks used in British schools may be manufactured in Singapore or Hong Kong; Indian publish- ers may export to Latin America; educational software may be designed in Cincinnati or St Petersburg.

The trade in educational goods and services is not free from restriction. Barriers to free trade have recently caught the attention of the US Department of Commerce as well as other trade ministries. Among the principal concerns are:

- monopolization of educational goods and services by public agencies;[8]
- closed systems of educational accreditation and professional licensure;[9]
- copyright infringement of educational brand names and protected items;
- significant difference in tariffs on educational goods.

Political trends

With the trend toward more democracy have come demands for greater accountability, higher levels of equity, access for larger portions of the population, and greater participation in decision making. Each of these helps drive the demand for modern educational goods and services. Accountability helps increase the use of examinations and assessments open to public scrutiny and international standards. Greater equity and access raise the demands for less expensive and a wider divergence of educational materials appropriate to multiple interest and ability groups. Open debate helps raise the demand for consultant services for ideas on education reform.

Consolidation of industry

The rising costs of technology and capital investment imply that some companies will be better positioned than others for the global marketplace. Competition from higher-quality and lower-cost producers will put new pressures on other providers. Consolidation is evident already in the test and publishing industries. Five years ago there were ten autonomous examinations agencies in the UK; today there are four. The largest examination agency in western Europe (CITO in The Netherlands) has been privatized recently. The proportion of its budget received from the Ministry of Education has dropped from 100 per cent to 20 per cent in 2001–2. Pressures on testing and assessment agencies are similar across the world: diversify sources of revenue, develop alternative product lines, raise standards and deliver technologies.

Privatization and outsourcing

Education was once assumed to be a public good, financed and provided by public agencies. In the former USSR, the education sector, like health, agriculture and industry, was organized on the basis of self-sufficiency. Ministries of Education produced all programmes, trained all staff, designed all textual curriculum materials and manufactured all goods and services (pencils, desks and even student meals). Some of these same assumptions about the need for public provision of educational goods and services are common to developing countries in Africa, Asia and the Middle East and elsewhere.

However, just as it is true that the state is not necessarily the best manufacturer of pharmaceuticals, neither is it necessarily the most cost-effective manufacturer of textbooks, tests and school furniture. Just as hospitals may contract out for accounting and human resource services, schools and school systems may contract out for services they need not necessarily manage. Today, the education sector is subject to the same questions as other sectors. This has greatly increased the speed by which the sector has opened up the processes of privatization of state-owned industries, as well as the process of outsourcing. However, neither trend necessarily challenges the essential public good nature of the education purposes and objectives.

Demographics

Many developing countries are characterized by higher population growth rates and by large student age populations in comparison to OECD countries. In instances of economic growth, such as in Malaysia, Thailand or Brazil, the growth in markets for education goods and services may be rising faster than in OECD countries. This is evident by the growth in education spending per student, for which the highest rates (200 per cent between 1980 and 1994) have emerged from Asia.

Issues for private investors

The growth in the markets for educational goods and services appears significant and this should attract new investment. However, no international strategy to guide these investments is currently feasible. Data on gross sales, trends and trade are inadequate. Some essential data simply are not measured. This includes data on current private education investments. Other data are categorized in a manner that prevents analysis: textbook trade figures, for example, are merged with other categories of 'cultural' trade – films, novels, scientific research materials and the like. Some data are badly measured (Heyneman, 1999a). Lastly, in many instances, current data are poorly analysed.

More importantly, financial institutions, necessary for any growing industry, have little experience in making investments in educational goods and services. Because of the regulatory distortions and the lingering traditions of state monopolization, markets open to private investment can be radically segmented. In one country commercial publishers may be invited to compete for the higher education market, but not the secondary school market. In another country it may be the opposite. There is no available 'road map' to discern where these lines of market segmentation may lead – andhence no simple manner to predict them.

Are these trends good?

It is evident that the private sector in education includes non-governmental institutions, which provide education and training programmes on a not-for-profit basis, but also private institutions that supply education goods and services on a commercial basis.[10] It is also true that every country in the world, rich and poor, already has a commercial sector supplying local education goods and services.[11] And it is true that every commercial provider hopes to expand the business, including perhaps to other countries. It is also evident that the private provision of education goods and services is changing and growing rapidly, but unexplored in terms of financial-sector lending or analysis from the academic community.

But is growth in education commerce good or a bad? Answers to this question sometimes fail to distinguish among sub-sectors. Some may feel that international private education is harmful because it may squeeze out local providers. But these answers may not include whether it is equally harmful when the trade is in science laboratory equipment, pedagogical software or supplemental tutoring, as it is, for example, in higher education programmes.

Whether these trends are bad or good may vary within countries as between countries. For example, in the USA there is wide support for publicly assisting private (including religious) providers of pre-school and post-secondary education, but not for providers of K–12 education. In the Philippines, non-governmental provision of higher education is the norm; in Greece it is illegal. Clearly the meaning of 'good' and 'bad' differs from one sub-sector to another, and may depend as much on the example given as the principle.

On the other hand, a number of concerns seem to be arising from the academic community (IJED, 2000). For instance, Shumar (1997, p. 94) points out that 'the logic of the market is rapidly becoming the only logic on the university campus'. But Shumar seems less concerned about the busy commuter who may want to buy higher education at home through the Internet. Should s/he be prevented from seeking a private solution?[12]

Currie and Vidovich (2000, p. 138) observe that public financing in Australia has now dipped to less than half of the university's total budget. Yet financing of universities out of the regular state budgets, such as to the University of Arizona, long ago dipped to the 50 per cent level, and is now about 25 per cent of recurrent expenditures.[13] Does this imply that the quality of the University of Arizona has declined in parallel fashion with the proportion of its regular budget from traditional state sources?

Education, trade and the World Trade Organization

While there are some who argue against trade, most experts are convinced that, for the most part, more trade is a good thing. Over the last 50 years for example, over eight rounds of negotiations, tariffs have been reduced by 75 per cent and world trade has expanded by 15-fold (Ascher, 2001). But education services have never been a part of these discussions. This has now changed.

The US Department of Commerce treats education as one of many services. Informally, services are defined as 'something which, if dropped, won't break your foot'. In other words, it is not easily categorized, and as technology develops the lines become more blurred. Are textbooks a product? What if they are delivered as part of a curriculum within an education programme and delivered electronically? What about testing? Items are physical products that can be bought, sold rented or leased. Like many other products they have a copyright. But testing itself is categorized as a service.

Ascher (2001) gives three examples of how these products and services are becoming global:

July 5, 2000: Pensare, Inc., a global provider of e-learning solutions announced a strategic alliance with Duke Corporate Education, Inc. (DCE), a private corporation to be formed by Duke University's Fuqua School of Business to provide corporate clients with tailored business education and distributed-learning consulting services. Under terms of the agreement, Pensare will provide its leading Internet-based technology platform, tools and content to support DCE's programs. Initial clients will include Deutsche Bank, Ford, Siemens, and Ericsson. Pensare also is a partner with Duke in the Duke MBA-Cross Continent program, which offers a blend of classroom-based and online MBA education to students around the world.

September 11, 2000: Carnegie Mellon University announced that it will offer computer-programming courses in India via the Internet. University officials said it would be the first Internet-based, teacher-led certification in computer programming available throughout the Indian subcontinent ... Software-development courses will be available through a partnership between Carnegie Technology Education and the Indian-based technology company Sterling Infotech Ltd. A subsidiary of Sterling, DishnetDSL, has 90 computer centers across India and plans to add 100 more centers, with 20 to 120 computers in each location ... India cannot train IT professionals fast enough to meet demand. The problem is exacerbated because India's best programmers are lured abroad.

April 4, 2001: General Motors and UNext announced that they have formed an innovative e-Learning alliance. As part of the four-year alliance, GM's 88,000 executive, management, professional and technical employees will have access to UNext's Cardean University, which offers courses developed with Columbia Business School, Stanford University, the University of Chicago Graduate School of Business, Carnegie Mellon University, and the London School of Economics and Political Science. GM's courses are conducted in classrooms and learning laboratories throughout the world and are also available electronically via GM's Intra and Interactive Distance Learning satellite network. UNext is a privately held company, which brings world-class education to the global marketplace through its online academic institution, Cardean University, which is accredited by the Accrediting Commission of the Distance Education and Training Council of Washington, D.C. and is authorized to grant degrees by the Illinois Board of Higher Education.

The US government has become concerned that restrictions may constrain the development of the education services. Is it possible that countries could achieve a consensus about the trade in education services as they have in the trade over telecommunications, tourism, or pharmaceuticals? What kinds of restrictions might be considered? Examples might include:

- the prohibition of education services offered by foreign entities;
- the lack of opportunity for foreign suppliers of education services to obtain authorization to establish facilities;
- the non-recognition of degrees or credits for quality education;
- the inappropriate restriction of electronic transmission of course materials.

At recent meetings of the World Trade Organization (WTO) the US government joined 21 other countries in committing itself in some way to reducing the restriction on trade in education services. The US position limited itself entirely to the post-secondary education market. Hence, proposals from the USA are designed, perhaps unsuccessfully, to allay worries over privatizing K–12 education, the interference of education's tax status, or education policies governing curriculum, admissions, or scholarships. The consequences of the US proposals may not yet have been fully appreciated. For example, one important constraint on the non-recognition of degrees is from within the USA itself in terms of its medical schools. Doctors from overseas, even with impeccable training and long experience, are required to begin their medical training again, if they want to practice medicine in the USA. Many would regard this as a restriction in trade – and so it is.

It is often suggested that using management practices, which have proved successful in business and commerce, could prove helpful to public sector activities, such as education. But is the management of education really analogous to the management of the financial sector? And are the issues surrounding its trade treated as analogous to the financial sector? Many countries and interest groups feel ambivalent about including education among the international topics for trade negotiations. The source of this ambivalence is not economic in nature, but ethical. It concerns the degree to which nations and communities are able to 'protect' themselves for legitimate reasons. Cultural protection, even among those who favour lowering trade barriers, usually constitutes a legitimate concern (Friedman, 1999; Giddens, 2000). But how should the ethical questions be managed?

What should countries do?

There seem to be several lessons about how to manage questions of whether education commerce is good or bad. First, when objections are made against education trade, it might be useful to ask those who make them to distinguish between programmes, goods or services. The perceived problem may pertain to one, but not all equally. If objections are raised to private pre-school and primary education, it is useful to ask whether they also apply to Montessori or Steiner elementary schools. And when objections are raised the private provision of services such as testing and assessment services, it might be useful to know whether those objections include the private provision of textbooks, furniture and school chemistry laboratories. The problems sometimes stem from the simplicity of the perception about education. The lack of understanding of how complex education already is as an industry creates many needless misunderstandings.

Second, concerns over the 'commercialization' of higher education are often raised by scholars based in public universities and financed by public tax resources. It is not unfair to point out that their objections may be biased. They may be as concerned about the need to preserve their personal positions and programmes as they are about the public good. This is not to suggest that one set of critics is more appropriate than another. But scholars based in public universities are more likely to raise concerns about private education than are scholars based in private universities or private educational businesses.

Third, at least as important as the providers of education, such as professors in universities, are the consumers of higher education themselves. They have rights too. What right has the government to deny access to the education that a consumer wishes to procure? If the internet provider of higher education is shut out of a market, it will mean that some consumers will be denied an essential service. In this instance, the client may not be the traditional student already in a university, but a potential student who may not have an opportunity otherwise to attend at all.[14] A citizen of Greece may wish to take a course at the British Open University. Does the state in a democracy have the right to prevent a citizen from privately financing what s/he may wish to learn? If individuals have been 'protected', not on grounds of health or safety or on grounds of likely damage to the environment, but on grounds that private or foreign education represents a danger to the culture, then one might ask whether a human right has been abrogated.

What about cultures said to be threatened by the private provision of education? There are many with strong views on this. Lional Jospin (1999, pp. 8–9), the Prime Minister of France, has pointed out that:

> *Its suppleness and adaptability make capitalism a dynamic force. But it is a force that of itself has no sense of direction, no ideals or meaning – none of the elements vital to a society. Capitalism is a force that moves but does not know where it is going ... The financial crisis of 1997 and 1998 in Asia and Russia ... shattered the claims of neo-liberalism ... so we must seek to create a regulatory system for the world capitalist economy.*

It is true that some cultures find it difficult to combat influences from elsewhere. But this is certainly not limited to education. It is also true with fashionable clothing, medical practice, religious belief, language, technologies, transportation, music, film, art, literature and many other fields. And while many countries find it difficult to 'control' these influences through traditional mechanisms of regulation,[15] it is also true that some influences on hindsight have been positive and welcome. One can think of examples in the fields of medicine, music and literature. How can one know ahead of time if the influence will have constructive or adverse consequences? And what about recipient cultures? What future is there for a 'protected culture'? Will it exist like an endangered species in a nature preserve?

It is worth considering whether capitalism (or international trade in education) has any 'direction' (i.e. moral value). In fact it may have a direction in the sense that the rights of individuals are regarded as being very important. If individuals wish to eat rice rather than pasta, learn Italian rather than Russian, study at home through the internet rather than at a traditional university, it is taken as axiomatic that the market should determine their right to do so. International trade in education may also have direction (i.e. moral value) in that it assumes efficiency to be a public good. If a public monopoly provides an inefficient service, the market may provide an opportunity to improve it. It may not always be true, but when it is then it may represent a significant improvement. And when significant improvements happen, they are highly appreciated by the public. In essence, the moral question of international trade in education may not be solely focused on whether international companies will upset local culture and tradition. It may also include the opposite: by what right may local authorities deny individuals access to education that they want, or deny individuals the right to efficient service?

Some have suggested that traditional public universities might import some of the efficiency-raising practices of the private sector. Others have responded by suggesting that '[neo-liberal] policy-makers seem to have little concern for the potential damaging effects of business practices in universities' (Currie and Vidovich, 2000). It is true that business practices may mean many changes. They may imply that budgets will have to be justified more carefully and scholarship mode more accountable to public demand (after all, the public may argue 'we pay for it'). They may imply that special skills and teaching performance should be rewarded differentially, that property and services should be utilized efficiently, or that new revenues be reallocated in accordance with the university's strategic objectives. They may also mean that universities exhibiting these elements may be seen as providing a higher quality education and hence be in higher demand. All these characteristics may be an outgrowth of importing business practices into the university environment, but it is not clear whether they are a problem or an asset.

Responding to change

These trends in the education and knowledge industry may provide a rare opportunity for schools of education to expand into new endeavours, forge new public and private alliances, and develop new areas of academic scholarship (Heyneman, 1999b). Examples of these areas include joint degree programmes between education and business administration, between education, international finance and trade, and (with respect to education's influence on social cohesion) joint degree programmes between education and fields of foreign policy and national security (Heyneman, forthcoming). It may also include research and development combining new education technologies and special education, pioneering forms of international teacher assessment, and many others.

Perhaps schools of education may have to make more of an adjustment to the changes in education and knowledge than other parts of the university. After rapid expansion in the 1960s, schools of education sometimes became handicapped by an ageing faculty whose professional training was out of date, whose international experience was limited and whose ideologies, in some instances, reflected issues long ago put to rest.

Comparative education programmes, too, have to make an adjustment (Heyneman, 1977, 1993a, 1993b, 1995, 1997, 1999). In a sense, comparative education has won the disciplinary principle on which the war was fought. Local priorities and local relevance – in school administration, pedagogy and curriculum development – now depend on understanding universal issues and international experience. All educational disciplines must now be comparative or risk being second rate.

Education has greatly benefited from the study of the private provision of education and training in developing countries, and would similarly benefit from a new emphasis to monitor and assess the ramifications of the growing commercial trade in educational goods and services. There is sometimes a perception that commerce and education are incompatible. In fact the opposite may be true. No public education system can be effective without a vibrant and competitive commercial sector to provide education goods and services, because the two are interdependent.[16]

It is sometimes believed that developing countries will be exploited by commercial enterprises in education. Some commercial suppliers will have a comparative advantage: some will be quicker to supply higher quality, less expensive, even more relevant products. And it is true these products could derive from regional or even transregional suppliers. This is no less the case in education than with other service sectors such as health, agriculture, transport, banking and telecommunications. Those who are convinced that competition in these other sectors is against the interests of developing countries will not believe it is in their interest in the case of education. But the reverse is also true. If one appreciates the virtues of fast and inexpensive service, and the growing participation and competition from 'developing' countries with open economies that export their own products, then one is more likely to appreciate the utility of an open economy with respect to education services.

The debate, however, is more than of academic interest. For much of the twentieth century in many parts of the world the quality of education provided to children has been adversely affected by a public policy that constrains the private provision of goods and services (Heyneman, 1998). The key element is not solely whether the state has a right to restrict the importation of foreign services, including education services. The key is whether individuals have a right to choose freely the education services they want.

NOTES

1 Corporate training is provided for internal staff members of commercial enterprises. The Saturn Program of Corporate Training is one illustration. Distributed learning is education and training from a central provider, but delivered to widely disperse locations. One example is the University of Phoenix that has campuses in many parts of the USA and around the world. Technology-based training means learning a specific technology. Microsoft for instance offers certificates, at different levels of mastery, of Microsoft programs.

2   The key distinction between an educational programme and an educational service is the presence of a degree or a certificate. Technology-based training is a programme if it leads to a certificate and a service if it does not. Similarly, the teaching of reading is a service if it is after-school tutoring, and part of an education programme if it is not.

3   Public-traded education stocks do not rise uniformly. In 1999, education industry (EI) index figures show that the average EI stock lost almost 20 per cent. This compares unfavourably with a gain of about 8 per cent in the Russel 2000, 18 per cent in the Dow Jones, and 53 per cent for the NASDQ. Some sub-sectors seem more problematic than others. Among the largest losers were post-secondary education, at risk-youth and adult training. On the other hand, stocks in educational product companies gained fairly consistently (EIG, 1999, p.7).

4   OECD countries neither design nor manufacture textbooks within the Ministry of Education but instead encourage private competition among commercial publishers to respond to publicly set curriculum objectives and standards.

5   Statisitcs on non-salary expenditures are often unreliable because there has yet to be a common agreement on their definition; some countries include only national expenditures, while others include local and even private expenditures. Considerable progress has been made in solving these problems with the OECD INES project, and for non-OECD countries through the World Education Indicators Project. Because of the problems on non-comparability, non-salary statistics should be high on the agenda of the new UNESCO Institute of Statistics.

6   These growth figures are offset, however, by stagnation in some of the Arab States and sub-Saharan Africa. The average growth of OECD countries (149 per cent) is significantly higher than for developing countries in general (55 per cent) and contrasts starkly with the average for the least developed countires (0 per cent).

7   In fact there are several drivers for the demand in copyrighted test items. In addition to having them validated on larger samples, modern testing agencies may provide test items already calibrated to a rapidly changing profession. For example, the Philippine Regulatory Commission offers certification for candidates in more than 40 fields ranging from electrical engineering to architecture. Requirements in many of these fields are rapidly shifting in OECD countries as new regulations governing the environment, technology and health standards take effect. As demand increases to upgrade local certificates, a company may find it less expensive and more efficient to 'rent' the right to use and validate items on local samples rather than to design and validate items from scratch. The same principle applies to pedagogical software, educational MIS systems, standards of education statistics and the like.

8   This prevents not only international trade, but restricts the participation of local commercial enterprise as well.

9   In some countries any university may apply for accreditation, but in other countries accreditation is reserved for established, public institutions. In some countries anyone who passes an open examination may practise his/her profession; in other countries no one, regardless of proven competence, may enter a particular profession without training from a local provider. These situations are now referred to as 'open' or 'closed' systems of accreditation and licensure.

10 A distinction is usually made between not-for-profit and for-profit institutions. A for-profit will distribute profits among shareholders; a not-for profit will distribute profits among its business units. In terms of lending, the key issue is not how the surplus is distributed, but whether the institution is sufficiently well organized to generate a surplus at all. And no not-for-profit institution wants to be a 'for-loss' institution.

11 Even improverished countries, such as Uganda, may have a thriving commercial sector of education furniture makers, copybook printers and school supply stores serving the needs of public schools. See Heyneman (1975).

12 Fifty per cent of all students enrolled in higher education in the USA are working adults.

13 Public sources finance a considerable portion of an overall budget of a public university, but these other sources are gained on a competitive basis, with results shifiting up or down over time. Washington, DC: May 10, 2001.

14 The nature of the client's concerns may differ from one kind of country to another. Bray (1996, p. 1) points out that the drivers of private education differ between low and high-income countries. In high-income countries they tend to reflect the movement toward accountability, choice and efficiency. In low-income countires they reflect concerns over shortages of public resources and inefficiency.

15 It is curious, too, that dominant world actors are not always prominent in terms of curriculum. Frank *et. al.* (2000, p. 43) point out that both western Europe and classical western civilization have declined in importance over the same time as western capitalism expanded.

16 The same cannot be said of education programmes, where there are many example of public school-ing having an adequate performance. It is relevant however, that in no OECD country, whether decentralized or centralized, are educational services and goods supplied exclusively by the public sector. For illustrations of the argument see: Smith (1975); Altbach (1983, 1989); Breyer (1970); Heyneman (1990); BRQ (1990).

REFERENCES

Altbach, P.G. (1983) 'Key issues of textbook provision in the third world', *Prospects*, 13 (3).

Altbach, P.G. (1989) 'Copyright in the developing world' in Farrel, J.P. and Heyneman, S.P. (eds) *Textbooks in the Developing World: Economic and Educational Choices*, Washington, DC: World Bank, EDI Seminar Series, pp. 88–102.

Ascher, B. (2001) *Education and Training Services in International Trade Agreements*, US Trade Representative, Washington, DC, 10 May.

Bray, M. (1996) *Privatization of Secondary Education: Issues and Policy Implications*, Paris: UNESCO, International Commission for Education in the Twenty–First Century.

Breyer, S. (1970) 'The uneasy case for copyright: a study of copyright in books, photocopies and computer programs', *Harvard Law Review*, 45, December.

BRQ (1990) 'Stephen P. Heyneman: "Protection of the textbook industry in developing countries: in the national interest?", *Book Research Quarterly*, Winter, pp. 3–11.

Currie, J. and Vidovich, L. (2000) 'Privatization and competition policies for Australian Universities', *International Journal of Educational Development*, 20 (2), March.

EIG (1999) *The EI Index*, Sioux Falls, ND: Education Industry Group.

Frank, D.J., Wong, Suk-Ying, Meyer, J.W. and Ramirez, F.O. (2000) 'What counts as history: a cross-national and longitudinal study of university curricula', *Comparative Education Review*, 44 (1), February.

Friedman, T.L. (1999) *The Lexus and the Olive Tree: Understanding Globalization*, New York: Farrar, Straus & Giroux.

Giddens, A. (2000) *Runaway World: How Globalization is Reshaping Our Lives*, New York: Routledge.

Heller Reports (1999) *International Markets for Educational Technology: EduSoft, and Isreali-based International Educational Software Developer*.

Heyneman, S.P. (1975) 'Changes in equity and efficiency accruing from government involvement in Ugandan primary education', *African Studies Review*, April, pp. 51–60.

Heyneman, S.P. (1977) 'Educational cooperation in the next century' in Kondon, C., von Kopp, B., Lauterbach, U. and Schmidt, G. (eds) *Comparative education: Challenges, Intermediation and Practice*, Bohlau: Verlag, pp. 219–33.

Heyneman, S.P. (1990) 'The textbook industry in developing countries', *Finance and Development*, March, pp. 28–9.

Heyneman, S.P. (1993a) 'Educational quality and the crisis of Educational Research', *International Review of Education*, 39 (6), pp. 511–17.

Heyneman, S.P. (1993b) 'Comparative education: issues of quantity, quality and source', *Comparative Education Review*, 37 (4), November, pp. 372–8.

Hyeneman, S.P. (1995) 'Economics of education: disappointments and potential', *Prospects*, 15 (4), pp. 559–83.

Heyneman, S.P. (1997) 'Economic growth and the international trade in education reform', *Prospects*, 27 (4), December, pp. 501–31.

Heyneman, S.P. (1997) 'Transition from party/state to open democracy: the role of education', *International Journal of Educational Development*, 18 (1), pp. 21–40.

Heyneman, S.P. (1999a) 'The sad story of UNESCO's education statistics', In *International Journal of Educational Development*, 19, January, pp. 65–74.

Heyneman, S.P. (1999b) 'Changes in the education and knowledge industry: effects on the university', paper presented to the David M. Kennedy Center for International Studies, Bigham Young University, February.

Heyneman, S.P. (1999c) 'Development aid in education: a personal view' in King, K. and Buchert, L. (eds) *Changing Aid to Education: Global Patterns and National Contexts*, Paris: UNESCO, pp. 132–46.

Heyneman, S.P. (2000) 'From party/state to multi-ethnic democracy: education and social cohesion in Europe and Central Asia', *Educational evaluation and Policy Analysis*, 22 (2), Summer, pp. 173–91.

IJED (2000) *International Journal of Educational Development*, 20(2), March.

5

Jospin, L. (1999) *Modern Socialism*, London: Fabian Society.

Kearns, D. T. (1999) 'The Education Industry: Markets and Opportunities', Boston, MA: EduVentures, Spring.

Nua Ltd (1999) *Computer Almanac Industry Inc Report Ranks World's Most Wired Countries*.

Shumar, W. (1997) *College for Sale: A Critique of the Commodification of Higher Education*, London: Falmer Press.

Smith Jr., Datus (1975) 'The bright promise of publishing in developing countries', *Annals of the American Academy of Political and Social Science*, 421, September, pp. 130–9.

PART SIX

Learning, Teaching and the Curriculum

BARBARA MACGILCHRIST

Introduction

BARBARA MacGILCHRIST
© Barbara MacGilchrist 2003

Part six explores leadership and management issues concerned with learning, teaching and the curriculum.

The first three chapters focus on the school as a learning community – why this is important and ways of promoting student and adult learning. Patricia Collarbone argues that the future of schools is bound up with the concept of a learning community in which all young people and adults have a shared interest in the desire to learn. To achieve this, teachers need to transform classrooms into collaborative learning laboratories that, through the use of information communication technologies, can form part of a global learning network. Collarbone argues that such a transformation requires a rethinking of the traditional information-led curriculum.

Frank Hartle and Russell Hobby focus on the motivational role of leaders in the promotion of independent learning for pupils and teachers. They argue that to raise standards for the long term, teachers must become leaders and leaders must become teachers. They offer a new curriculum for learning that reflects the complex skills demanded by a knowledge economy.

Peter Hill and Carmel Crévola offer a model of organizational learning predicated on a systems view of schooling. The core focus of the model is student learning and building the capacity of staff to enhance that learning through changing and improving their practice in the classroom. Hill and Crévola present a six-tier model for promoting professional learning in schools.

In the next two chapters the authors take a close look at the relationship between pedagogy, the curriculum and learning. Dennis Lawton focuses on pedagogy and the professional autonomy of teachers. He argues for a radical rethink about the processes of schooling to enable pupils to have shared ownership of learning, teaching and the curriculum.

Paul Black and Dylan Wiliam provide an example of how the changes in pedagogy argued for by Lawton can be achieved. They describe the outcomes of a research project focused on supporting teachers in the development of assessment for learning in the classroom. They consider the implications both for pedagogy and for leadership and management. The research provides insights into ways of bringing about significant changes in pedagogy that also change the pupils' views about, and approaches to, learning.

In the last two chapters the authors take a step back and look at schools as human communities. The emphasis is on the importance of learning to live with one another and recognizing our common humanity. Barbara MacGilchrist identifies nine intelligences at work in schools that create a sense of community in which the rights and responsibilities and the needs of learners are at the heart of the enterprise. She argues that school leaders can and need to foster and develop these intelligences. She focuses in particular on emotional, spiritual and ethical intelligence and concludes that the development of these intelligences is of central importance if schools are to become human communities.

Finally, Len Barton argues for the need to reflect critically on the beliefs and values that underpin education. He does this against the backdrop of the events of 11 September 2001 in New York and the context in which educational policy making, implementation and change took place during the last two decades of the twentieth century. Barton explores the meaning and importance of inclusive education and the implications of this for pedagogy and leadership, raising some questions and issues for future reflection and engagement.

Leadership for the future

Leadership for learning is at the heart of Part Six. An underlying theme is the need for a radical rethink about the nature of schools and schooling and the core values that underpin what it means to be an educated person. The chapters challenge received views about learning, teaching and the curriculum. The authors urge a redefinition of the aims and purposes of leadership away from traditional views of schools and schooling towards a focus on the learning, both of pupils and adults and the kinds of teaching and the content of that teaching that can best support this focus.

Throughout Part Six, there is an exploration of the interrelationship between learning, teaching and the curriculum. The main message is that the relationship between these three is changing, which in turn is having and will continue to have a profound impact on leadership and management in the future.

CHAPTER 36

Leading the learning community

PATRICIA COLLARBONE

Is the universe actually infinite or just very large? And is it everlasting or just long-lived? Is it presumptuous of us even to make the attempt? Do we risk the fate of Prometheus, who in classical mythology stole fire from Zeus for human beings to use, and was punished for his temerity?

(HAWKING, 2001, P. 69)

At the turn of the twentieth century physicists were unlocking mysteries we mere mortals did not want to hear about. By 1925 250 years of carefully thought through and proven explanations of the Universe had been overturned by theory of relativity and quantum theory. Yet a paradox remained. The theory of relativity and quantum theory were not easy bedfellows. They could not coexist. The search for the theory of everything had begun in earnest.

At the start of the twenty-first century those of us in education are faced with a similar, if less all-encompassing, paradox. What exactly are our schools for? What is it we expect them to achieve? Why do we have them in the first place? And in an era when information is available so abundantly why do we cling on to organizations that have been described as 'the generative institution for machine-age thinking' (Senge *et al.*, 2000, p. 34)? Yet the same sentence suggests 'so too could it be a pivot for creating more learning-oriented societies'.

Several of the contributions in Part Six examine the question of the school as a learning community. This contribution acknowledges that schools do have a future. This future is bound up with the concept of learning communities. Exactly what this might mean is not within my remit. What this chapter does consider, however, is what leadership will be like within such a context – and whether there is any one particular model, which will embrace the theory of everything.

Fullan (2001, p. 136) argues that we live in a culture of complexity and that the role of leadership is 'to mobilize the *collective capacity* to challenge difficult circumstances'. It is this notion of collective capacity that underpins the justification for the continuing existence of organizations such as schools. Collarbone (1999, p. 71) suggests that schools are:

> *not necessarily a structure within the current conceptual understanding of the schoolhouse. In a community there is a shared interest for all stakeholders. In a learning community the shared interest is the desire to learn. Everyone becomes a learner and because it is a community there is a desire to share knowledge for the benefit of everyone.*

Barth (2001, p. 31) believes 'much rides on the adults becoming insatiable learners in our schools'. He defines a community of learners as 'a collection of youngsters and grown-ups working together to provide and sustain their own and one another's learning'. But both these definitions retain the same essential flaw. They are both inward looking. They view the school as a self-supporting entity, rather than embracing a more all-encompassing role that 'thinks locally but acts globally' (Naisbitt, 1996, p. 218). Hargreaves and Fullan (1998) suggest the real challenge for schools is the need to open their gates and 'get out there'. Certainly one of the challenges facing schools is recognizing the learning environments within which they operate and developing the culture through promoting learning for all. This requires more than tinkering with structures. In this sense leaders within this community are 'designers, stewards and teachers ... responsible for learning' (Senge, 1990, p. 341).

Leadership models for leading within such communities are plentiful, many of them developed by contributors to this book. Fullan (2001) has honed his model to five basic dimensions:

- moral purpose
- understanding change
- building relationships
- knowledge creation and sharing
- coherence making.

This model is underpinned by three attributes – hope, enthusiasm and energy. In 1997, Hay McBer developed their Models of Excellence for the UK government, based on research into what effective headteachers actually did. The research identified 15 characteristics, which when combined in different ways can lead to highly effective performance. Hay McBer have clustered these characteristics into five groups:

- personal values and passionate conviction
- creating the vision
- getting people on board
- planning for delivery
- monitoring and evaluation by gathering information and gaining understanding.

Both the Fullan model and the Hay McBer model bear many similarities, including an emphasis on the same six leadership styles and the importance of emotional intelligence. However, there is more emphasis in the Fullan model on understanding change, sharing knowledge and coherence-making to suggest that this model is more suited to leading a learning community. Moreover, the Fullan model is more distributive and can be applied at any level within the organization.

Barth (2001) suggests that in order to transform the culture of a school into a learning community, leaders must first and foremost be learners themselves; and Senge *et al.* (2000, p. 58) are adamant that pupils hold the key:

> *I have come to believe that the real hope for deep and enduring processes of evolution in schools lies with students. They have a deep passion for making schools work. They are connected to the future in the ways no adult is.*

Hill (2000) argues that school-based leadership should be instructional in nature and depends on the school leader undertaking three key roles:

- leading and managing change
- motivating and managing people
- designing and aligning systems, processes and resources.

Leaving aside Fullan's (2001, p. 33) argument that you cannot manage change, 'it can be understood and perhaps led, but it cannot be controlled', much of what Hill has to say about leadership relates more to the role of principal or headteacher than to the concept of distributive leadership. Hill is arguing for the building of capacity across the organization and places emphasis on leaders as coaches and mentors. The building capacity notion is a strong one and absolutely essential for the learning community.

So what are some of the conclusions we can draw from the gurus cited above? If we are to develop as leaders then we need to dispel the myths – the mental models – that often surround the concept of leadership. The first one, leaders are born and not made, contradicts what we know from biology. What makes us living beings is a combination of our genes, our environment and our learning. The major competencies of leadership can be learned, even if the task is not easy. Everyone has leadership potential, and although everyone may not be a great leader, we often display that potential in our actions. Leaders may be charismatic, but it is not a necessary requirement. It may in fact work the other way round. Charisma arises out of leadership, particularly in the eyes of followers. Leadership permeates our organizations. It is recognizing that leadership quality and enabling it to blossom that is key to the role of headteacher or principal. Leaders do not control or direct or prod or manipulate; rather they empower through enablement, through pulling rather than pushing, and by encouraging initiative.

We need efficiency, of course, and good management is about achieving it. However, learning organizations also need effectiveness, and that quality is achieved through leadership. One of the essential qualities of leadership is to create a culture in which people do not fear making mistakes because they know that we, adults and children, can learn from making mistakes. Such a culture does not avoid accountability, as that would be an unethical stances on the part of leadership; it does avoid a culture of blame.

At the 2001 London Leadership Centre Annual Lecture, the Chief Education Officer of Birmingham, Tim Brighouse (2001), suggested that the leadership role, at whatever level, required four dispositions and six tasks. The dispositions he cited were:

- unwarranted optimism
- the ability to regard crisis as the norm and complexity as fun
- an endless supply of intellectual curiosity
- a complete absence of paranoia and self-pity.

The tasks required, he suggested, were to:

- create energy
- build capacity
- constantly seek and chart improvement
- secure the environment
- meet and minimize crisis
- extend the vision.

Bowring-Carr and West-Burnham (1997) contend that we need to address urgently the fact that schools and schooling in many respects survive residually in a post-modernist age. Gone is the linear world for which they were designed and in its place moves a non-linear chaotic world. Schools, 'because of societal and governmental pressures and because there is a great inertia in so large a system' (ibid., p. 33), are failing to realign themselves to meet the needs of the new age. Schools tend to continue to organize themselves around a bureaucracy, which has little or nothing to do with meeting the needs of either pupils or staff, as learners. The pragmatic demands of the organization override the individual learning needs of the various stakeholders. Since the traditional concept of schooling is still widely prevalent, apparently successful schools continue to be able to operate in this manner. Although some will argue that schools are a product of an industrial age and in a post-industrial context no longer have a place, I am not one of those. I do agree that the current model is past its sell-by date, but accept that it may continue for many years to come.

Papert (1996) has suggested how three particular change forces exert influences on schools. First, there is a powerful industrial sector associated with the new technologies that views education as a marketplace. This sector is creating a new digital world: curriculum material, assessment for learning opportunities and whole courses are freely available on the worldwide web. However, without sharing that information there is no new knowledge. Papert discerns a wonderful opportunity for schools to exploit this situation and to develop true partnerships that marry the best practice inside schools with the learning opportunities presented by these very same technologies.

Second, there is a growing recognition of the need for new approaches and particularly an acknowledgement of different learning styles and possibly intelligences in learning. The importance of emotional intelligence is now being recognized, and there is growing realization that in the long term the only genuinely marketable skill is that of learning itself. Consequently, knowing 'what' is not as important as knowing 'where', 'how' and 'why'. Learning, and learning how to learn, are recognized increasingly as essential life skills and the keys to the future.

Third, Papert suggests that child-power is the most powerful change force of all. It is becoming more and more apparent that children have less and less regard for school as it lags behind the society it serves. Surveys in the UK, for example, find that approximately a quarter of all students are dissatisfied with their schooling (McCall *et al.*, 2001). Some are wholly disaffected with schooling and others may have 'disappeared' from the formal system (Barber, 1996). Yet, according to Papert, becoming a change agent in school offers pupils great rewards and new opportunities for learning. Teachers, Papert argues, need not fear the changes, provided they take on the role of learners themselves and transform their classrooms into collaborative learning laboratories where all are engaged in the learning process.

Recently, I was privileged to facilitate in an online discussion on the website of the National College for School Leadership (NCSL), designed for aspiring school leaders who are currently studying for the National Professional Qualification for Headship (NPQH). The questions I asked initially were:

- What are the actions and behaviours of school leaders in the role of leaders of learning and lead learners?
- How do they create a creative learning community?

- What are the levers that help to develop a domain of enduring change?
- What are the barriers that prevent school leaders taking up the role of lead learners?

The responses were illuminating, as the sample below demonstrates:

As a teacher with pastoral responsibility for a group of Y6 girls who are approaching senior school entrance examinations, I have found it very useful to share my experiences of learning with them ... This is showing children that learning is something enjoyable, something life-long: 'adult' as opposed to 'childish', an accomplishment to be proud of and something that does not always come easily. How much easier is it, then, for the pupils themselves to feel proud of their efforts and determined not only to succeed but also to support all members of their community in the pursuit of a common goal?

The dimension that we, as a school, chose to pursue was that of 'Developing a Learning Community'. We felt that this was a necessary stage at which to begin. Initially our project seemed diverse and encompassed many areas in need of development. We began by 'listening' to our community and taking a real interest in what each stakeholder perceived to be a 'learning community'.

We have just begun to work in self-managing teams. Staff have elected to work in each team and to contribute to the learning in each team through an inquiry-based approach to professional development. Each team has time for professional reading and we have actively encouraged an action research approach to implementing improvements. This has led to staff discussing the changes that are to be implemented and relating the changes to improvements in the progress of children.

It seems to me that real learning is all about change and for a school to be really effective, it needs to embrace change and be prepared constantly to re-evaluate itself. However, wouldn't you agree that this is a frightening prospect for most people?

So, are we able to surmise a role for schools, school leaders and learning in the future?

6

- Schools need to be a part of a learning community in which all members of the community 'continually expand their capacity to create the results they truly desire, where new and expansive patterns of thinking are nurtured, where collective aspiration is set free, and where people are continually learning how to learn together' (Senge, 1990, p. 3).
- Pupils and adults as learners characteristically start from different points in the learning cycle. Cognitive science has explained much about how the brain functions and begun to suggest some key implications for learning. Applying this science and releasing the individual and collective brain-power within the organization, while developing an understanding of metacognition in all learners, involves activities of a higher order than those required to deliver an essentially subject-based, taught curriculum.
- For the foreseeable future the headteacher will need to continue to be a lead-learner in a learning community. The development of leadership learning is, and will continue to be, an area of crucial importance.
- As our understanding of cognitive science develops over the next few years, the emphasis will shift away from teaching knowledge towards learning. This learning will be facilitated through a developing competence/competencies-led rather than information-led curricula. Learners will be enabled to acquire the knowledge, skills, abilities, intelligences and understandings required to equip them to lead successful lives and to contribute to and lead society.

- The concept of organizational learning will provide a key. A greater appreciation of the importance of sharing information to create new knowledge will become the focus of school CPD (continuing professional development) programmes. The closed classroom will become an issue of past generations.
- The needs of the individual learner will become paramount and organizational changes will be made that will enable the needs of the learner to take precedence over the logistical requirements of managing the organization, rather than vice versa.
- Information and communications technologies will be developed to become a central, integrative and interactive part of the learning cycle. The school will become the hub of a learning community involving parents, pupils, teachers and other stakeholders, linked through virtual and real-time access. This learning community will not be confined to the immediate neighbourhood but will constitute part of a global learning network.

REFERENCES

Barber, M. (1996) *The Learning Game: Arguments for an Education Revolution*, London: Victor Gollancz.

Barth, R. (2001) *Learning by Heart*, San Francisco: Jossey-Bass.

Bowring-Carr, C. and West-Burnham, J. (1997) *Effective Learning in Schools*, London: FT Pitman Publishing.

Brighouse, T. (2001) 'Doomed to succeed: the Eldorado of school leadership', *Leading Edge*, 5 (2), London: London Leadership Centre, Institute of Education, pp. 196–208.

Collarbone, P. (1999) 'Schools of the future and their leadership: a blueprint for success', *Leading Edge*, 3 (1), London: London Leadership Centre, Institute of Education. pp. 65–76.

Fullan, M. (2001) *Leading in a Culture of Change*, San Francisco: Jossey-Bass.

Hargreaves, A. and Fullan, M. (1998) *What's Worth Fighting for in Education*, Buckingham: Open University Press.

Hawking, S. (2001) *The Universe in a Nutshell*, London: Bantam Press.

Hill, P. (2000). 'What principals need to know about teaching and learning', paper commissioned for the National Center on Education and the Economy, Washington, DC.

McCall, J., Smith, I., Stoll, L., Thomas, S., Sammons, P., MacBeath, J., Boyd, B. and MacGilchrist, B. (2001) 'Views of pupils, teachers and parents: vital indicators of effectiveness and improvement' in (MacBeath, J. and Mortimore, P. (eds) *Improving School Effectiveness*, Buckingham: Open University Press.

Naisbitt, J. (1996). 'From nation states to networks' in Gibson, R. (ed.) *Rethinking the Future*, London: Nicholas Brealey Publishing, pp. 212–27.

Papert, S. (1996) *The Connected Family: Bridging the Digital Generation Gap*, Atlanta: Longstreet Press.

Senge, P. (1990) *The Fifth Discipline: The Art and Practice of the Learning Organisation*, New York: Currency/Doubleday.

Senge. P., Cambron-McCabe. N., Lucas, T., Smith, B., Dutton, J. and Kleiner, A. (2000) *Schools that Learn*, London: Nicholas Brealey Publishing.

CHAPTER 37

Leadership in a learning community: your job will never be the same again

FRANK HARTLE AND RUSSELL HOBBY

In the world of the independent learner, where do teaching and leadership fit in? If we encourage children to take control of their own learning, if we persuade adults to manage their own professional development – as the new orthodoxy contends – surely there is little left for the role of direction and organization, for strategy and vision? In this world, schools would be little more than a useful location for learning to take place – ripe for virtualization and disintegration across the internet.

But here is a curious phenomenon: the more independent we become, the greater our need for outstanding leadership – not management, not organization, not order, but rather inspiration. For with independent learning, the role of our values, beliefs and self-confidence come to the fore; ahead of the framework or the plan. Great leaders help to shape our values and bolster our confidence. They do their most important work in the world of motivation.

Part of our work at the Hay Group is to investigate what makes someone a top performer. What are the hallmarks of an outstanding headteacher? What are the defining characteristics of a highly effective teacher? We have long noted that the two roles seem very similar – that much of what makes a good teacher, makes a good leader; that our models can often work interchangeably for both. This finding goes far beyond the observation that we need leaders at every level of education. We are suggesting that, to raise standards for the long term, teachers must become leaders and leaders must become teachers. The two roles meet in their impact on performance through motivation, and in their ability to provide a structure (a curriculum) for change.

The force and urgency of this perspective is clear. Teachers can best meet their challenges – engaging all children, of all backgrounds, on demanding and individualized courses of learning that fit them for life as well as work – by taking on the role of a leader and by thinking about teaching in terms of leadership. Leaders can best meet their challenges – of creating the capacity for meeting and embedding almost constant change – by becoming teachers, by not only caring about the development of their staff but supplying a curriculum to promote this development.

When the two roles of teaching and leadership meet on the common ground of motivation, they hold the power to transform schools into a vibrant and essential force in the community. Schools, at their best, are never mere locations. They are cultures. They are characterized by an ethos created from the interactions and relationships of everyone who works and learns there. It is this ethos that drives standards and creates independent learners. This emphasis on relationships holds a stark message for the internet. In so far as distance diminishes relationships and weakens interactions, 'distance learning' is diminished learning.

Let us start by examining the demand for changes in the way we educate children and, consequently, lead our schools.

An era of profound change

Numerous commentators on trends in society have stressed that we are about to enter a period of profound change in our society. The Demos report (Jupp, Fairly and Bentley, 2001, p. 4) says that:

> We are witnessing a fundamental transition in the underlying structure of the economy ... away from an industrial model ... Knowledge is now the primary source of economic productivity ... This transition represents a longer wave of change in the evolution and structure of all industries, the nature of work and the definition of economic value.

The report also states that over the next two decades society will become more diverse, open and fluid. The range of lifestyles and occupations available to most people will be far wider than a generation ago.

At the same time, our understanding of how people learn has been enhanced by developments in educational and developmental psychology and neuroscience. Old assumptions about how learning takes place – what some commentators (Senge, 2000) call our 'Industrial Age assumptions about schooling' – are being challenged. The new science of learning emphasizes the existence of multiple intelligences and recognizes wide variation in the cognitive style and intellectual profile of learners.

The impact of new technologies on information and communications is hugely significant for the future of education. Network-based technologies offer the prospect of a radical structural shift in what we need to learn and how education can be organized. Technology is beginning to empower individuals to take charge of the pace and direction of their own learning (for example, the Transforming Learning Initiative). In contrast to this positive note, the wholesale application of network technologies raises serious concerns about the relationships that sustain communities and cultures.

Implications for the education system

The growing importance of knowledge puts a new premium on learning and suggests a revaluation of the respective roles of teacher and learner. The changes discussed above challenge our received views of the curriculum, assessment and the role of teachers. In particular they challenge the organizational principles of schools – the structures through which education is institutionalized; even ones as dear to us as the 'class', the 'lesson', perhaps even the 'teacher'.

In the UK there has been considerable debate about how current education systems can meet the longer-term challenges of the knowledge society. The consensus view seems to suggest that greater attainment against current standards is not enough: different kinds of learning and new ways of providing education may be necessary. Schools face unprecedented pressures and a one-size-fits-all education system that owes itself to the industrial age may not be the appropriate vehicle to enable schools to cope with these pressures. Whilst educational institutions have grown to accommodate ever-increased demand for places, the internal organizational characteristics have changed very little. The Demos report suggests that schools remain hierarchical, vertically organized 'institutions', which operate for about one-third of a day on five days each week. The ability of this kind of organization to sustain motivation and engagement for each individual learner and employee – fundamental demands for the acquisition of the complex skills demanded by the knowledge economy – is increasingly doubtful.

These changes and their implications suggest some straightforward criteria for the evaluations of any educational reforms:

- A wider range of intelligence and capability need to be developed for education to provide a preparation for life. We also need to think not only about what emotional intelligence and citizenship mean but how they are best fostered. Traditional courses of study rarely capture the necessary ingredients or the very personal nature of the ambitions and needs that drive this learning.
- Therefore, we need an education system that is focused on individual learning needs and geared towards unlocking the ability of people to manage their own learning throughout their lives (not just their childhood).
- If we are to promote the skills and values for this 'lifelong learning', the context of learning is as important as the content. How we learn is as important as what we learn, because we will always be required to repeat the process in ever more complex and demanding situations.
- There will be few roles in society to which this rule applies more than that of teachers themselves. Schools will be asked to absorb ever more far-reaching changes – not only to the ways they teach, but the ways they organize themselves. This will demand a deep capacity for change on the part of adults in the education system; school leaders must develop their ability to outline, promote and sustain personal development for adults as well as pupils.

'Smarter not harder' means people not process

For decades the teaching profession has been bombarded by initiative after initiative in a struggle to raise standards to match the demands of modern society. And as old targets are reached, entirely new standards evolve around us to move the goalposts. At the same time, like other public services, the amount of investment in people and resources for education has remained tightly constrained. The end result is a feeling on the part of heads and their staffs of having to do more and more with less and less.

The implication is that we will not be able to raise standards simply through greater investment – through more teachers, more development, more classrooms. We will have to make our existing resources more effective – better teachers, better development, better classrooms.

But we also need to think carefully about exactly which 'resources' have the greatest impact on educational outcomes – about where the capacity of a school is embodied. The most significant influence (within our control) on standards is the quality of teaching itself. So when we speak of raising standards, we are also talking about helping teachers improve themselves. When we talk of new standards, of new ways of learning and new things to be learned, we are again requiring change and development of teachers. This is not, therefore, some clinical analysis of how inanimate resources can be used efficiently – the only really critical resource in schools is the people who work there. These 'resources' can say no, they resist being moved around and reassigned, and maintain a troublesome tendency to have ambitions of their own.

The implication, then, is that the most significant role of leaders within schools seeking to respond to the demands of modern society, is to work with their staff to help them improve themselves. Looking at the history of professional development (across the economy rather than specifically in schools) this is a prospect that fills us with gloom. It is unfortunately clear that the vast majority of professional development activities have failed to make a meaningful difference in anyone's performance at work.

There are three main reasons for this failure:

- The development fails to address the characteristics, skills or knowledge that are important for success in a specific role and which that individual lacks. This failure derives, for example, from ignoring the true causes of success (for example, assuming that analytical intelligence is a prerequisite of any leader); the generic application of standards (for example, everybody must have a degree before they embark on this role); and from a lack of measurement (for example, sending someone on a course to learn something they already know). In general in any role, but especially in teaching, the characteristics that are important for success tend to lie at a deeper level than skills or qualifications. Outstanding teachers have the skills and subject knowledge but it is their attitude, behaviour, values and characteristics that make the difference. This brings us to the second major cause of failure:
- The development is done *to* someone rather than *by* someone. Deep and lasting change in someone's professional characteristics will never occur without their explicit and enthusiastic commitment to the goals of change. You can not send someone on a course to acquire self-confidence in front of pupils, a passion for learning or respect for individuals. These attributes grow slowly, often painfully, over time. Lasting professional development occurs when the individual and the organization jointly agree on the importance of the goal. Many leaders are quite aware of the first two reasons for faliure; the third is less obvious:
- We rarely offer adults a model of success, or a curriculum that charts a manageable route to that model. So you want to be an effective subject leader? Well go on then, what are you waiting for? It is not quite that easy, of course. The first step is a clear definition of what we mean by an effective subject leader – not in terms of outputs and results but rather the inputs, the things that lead to success. Let us say that we are clear that one of the causal factors of success in middle-management roles is the ability to offer sensitive but challenging feedback to team members. Once someone is aware of this, what stops them from just doing it? Well, there are a few people who can change as soon as a lack is identified. For most of us, however, the reason we are not doing it now is because we do not know how.

The aim of a curriculum for professional development, therefore, is to break apart and abstract the model of success into manageable chunks. So that, for example, someone can practise a behaviour in a less challenging environment, gradually increasing the challenge over time; or that someone can start on one part of a skill set, hone that to perfection, and add other parts over time. We do not expect children to become expert mathematicians in one go. We break maths apart into its components. Children acquire these components one step at a time, hone them against more and more complex problems and eventually integrate them into a consistent whole. Quite often, when we set professional development targets, we are asking for the equivalent of moving from innumeracy to mathematical expertise in one gulp. Failure and disaffection is a frequent consequence.

It is in this sense that we mean that leaders must take on the attributes of the best teachers. For the creation, delivery of, and assessment against, a curriculum is clearly at the heart of the teaching role. It is possible to translate this into language that sits more comfortably with the adult world. It just so happens that 'what must succeed' in schools is the development of teachers – it is the most important part of a vision or strategy for change that will result in a real difference for children.

And, behind the management jargon, is not this just what outstanding teachers do with their pupils every day?

Role reversal – teachers and leaders

What do we mean by proposing that 'teachers must behave like leaders' and 'leaders must behave like teachers'? In our studies of successful organizations (inside and outside education) we find that they usually possess leaders who are concerned with the motivation and engagement of their staff.

The literature on teaching and instruction – from developmental psychology to practical experience – presents the role of the teacher as the provider of 'guided participation' (Rogoff, 1990) or 'scaffolding' (Wood, 1998). The teacher sees the big picture (the learning goal), breaks apart the goal into tasks of manageable complexity, then guides the individual through these tasks until they reach *and* comprehend the big picture. We are therefore suggesting that successful teachers manage academic performance through attention to the motivation and engagement of their pupils. Successful leaders deconstruct the goals of the school into practical programmes of development.

There is, of course, an infinite regress to this perspective. If pupils can learn most successfully when teachers behave as leaders in the classroom, then leaders in the school need to be able to break apart what it means to be a leader as the foundation of a programme of development for every member of staff.

Teaching

The body of evidence on the impact of motivation on learning is convincing. Indeed, when we reflect upon our own experience as learners it is clear that, for example, we need to believe that a course of study is important; we need to value our task above all the other demands on our time and attention; and, as Claxton (1999) particularly notes, we need the emotional resilience to commit to and sustain a programme of learning.

In acknowledging the importance of active and independent commitment to learning on the part of the learner themselves, we also acknowledge the importance of the role that teachers and instructors can play in building and supporting this commitment. With a clearer vision of why any aspect of learning might be important, with an outsider's view of an individual's strengths, weaknesses and needs, a teacher can sustain motivation and channel it more appropriately than the individual alone.

In one of the largest studies of highly effective teachers (DfEE, 2000) the Hay Group refined a list of those aspects of a pupil's classroom experience that were most influential on their motivation. These were:

- Clarity: the transparency and explicit relevance of what goes on in class.
- Environment: the comfort and attractiveness of the physical environment.
- Fairness: justice and equality within the classroom.
- Interest: stimulation and fascination in class.
- Order: discipline and structure in the classroom.
- Participation: pupil involvement and influence in the running of the class.
- Safety: absence of threat or fear.
- Standards: expectations of achievement and encouragement to improve.
- Support: encouragement to try new things and learn from mistakes.

Collectively, we call these items 'classroom climate'. They are the aggregate of the perceptions of pupils about what it feels like to be a member of a class. Through correlations with value-added data, each of these items has been shown to be a significant force for learning. The 'transmission mechanism' between climate and learning outcomes is through the motivation (engagement, commitment, excitement) of the pupils themselves. In our study of highly effective teachers there was also a strong correlation between measures of classroom climate and value-added measures of pupil progress.

Many things can affect climate within the classroom or the whole school. The pupils themselves contribute to it, as does school culture, parental attitudes and national initiatives. The single most powerful force, however, is the teacher. And, fundamentally, teachers build climate through their behaviours, characteristics, values and attitudes as much as (or more than) their skills, knowledge or experience (*see* Figure 37.1).

The implications for the professional development of teachers are crucial. It is the development of the characteristics of effective teaching that will have the biggest impact on standards. We have already argued that most developmental activity either ignores characteristics and behaviour or entirely fails to make an impact upon them.

Leadership

This definition of outstanding teaching requires us to reassess the role of leadership itself. The most important goal of leadership is the development and support of the characteristics of highly effective teachers yet this activity repeatedly fails. How can we address this challenge?

First, school leaders will obviously continue to manage performance through motivation. The Leadership Programme for Serving Headteachers (LPSH), for example, explores the impact of school climate and leadership styles on the moti-

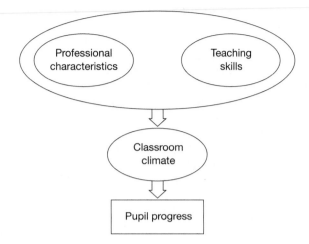

Figure 37.1 A causal model of effective teaching
Source: DfEE, 2000.

vation and performance of adults. It is interesting to note the similarity of the components of the whole-school climate (perceived by adults) to those discovered as relevant to the classroom (perceived by pupils):

- Flexibility: 'There are no unnecessary rules here'.
- Reward: 'If I do well, it gets noticed and recognized'.
- Clarity: 'I know our goals and how I contribute'.
- Standards: 'We are expected to do well and improve'.
- Responsibility:'I can get on with my job, make decisions'.
- Team Commitment:'People are proud to work here'.

There is strong evidence linking school climate not only to standards of academic achievement but also to broader measures of success like teacher retention. Recent investigations also suggest that school leaders can actively change the climate for the better in their schools and can change it relatively quickly. A study by the University of Newcastle of the LPSH (Smith, 2002) shows a significant increase across all dimensions of school climate, with the greatest gains being made by the previously lowest achieving quartile (showing that this is a viable strategy for schools in challenging circumstances, not just the more favoured).

The need to build and sustain an effective climate across the whole school is relatively uncontroversial. It is one of the prerequisites for effective development but, in order to counteract the common failures of adult learning, we also need a new perspective on professional development – one that actually draws upon the existing expertise of the teaching profession. There are three elements to this view of professional development:

- *Theory*. There needs to be a clear model of how success is achieved – not the expected outcomes but a theory of the causal relationships between actions and outcomes. Pedagogic skill lies in the translation of this theory into abstracted or simplified tasks. In conjunction with individualized, formative assessment, the performance of these tasks builds up into achievement of the overall goal.

- *Values*. For almost all learning, and certainly for far-reaching personal change, learners need to be able to commit to and sustain a course of action in the face of challenges and conflicts. They need to prioritize the goals of learning above the other distractions they face. Shared values and beliefs sustain the learner in this process. This motivation is sustained both through the learner's own emotional intelligence and also through the climate of the organization.

- *Action*. Learning does not really occur until learners perform the tasks, perfecting their attainment against feedback. Unless there is a theory then the tasks are just shots in the dark – they may or may not help them achieve their goals. Unless there is individual assessment, the tasks may be out of reach or fail to stretch the learner.

It is the interplay between each of these elements (*see* Figure 37.2) that offers the maximum opportunity for leadership to support the independent learner:

- theory connects with action through curriculum and assessment;
- values connects with theory through goals and strategy;
- action connects with values through climate and emotional intelligence.

As well as its application to individual development, the model can be applied at the level of whole-school improvement and the promotion of a learning community.

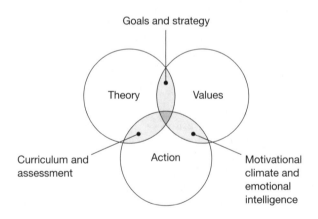

Figure 37.2 The three elements of effective development

Thinking in circles: the learning community

The idea of a school that can learn, as well as being a place for learning, has become increasingly prominent in the last few years. In a school that learns, parents and teachers, educators and local businesses, students and adults – people inside and outside the school walls – work together to build a learning community. A learning school is:

Not so much … a separate place (for it may not stay in one place) as a meeting ground for learning – dedicated to the idea that all those involved with it will be continually enhancing and expanding their awareness and capabilities: a learning school puts the pupil at the centre and connects up pupils, teachers, leaders, schools and communities. (Senge, 1999)

The 2001 government White Paper, *Schools Achieving Success* (DfEE, 2001), extends the UK government's focus on setting targets into secondary education. There are clear goals in terms of Key Stage 3 achievement and minimum acceptable rates of GCSE passes. But the communication of targets is only one half, and the least important half, of raising standards. Merely by setting targets we do not influence someone's ability to reach those targets.

It is essential to analyse schools as a 'system' – as a series of inputs, throughputs and outputs, causally connected to each other. It is only by understanding what inputs (for example, teaching techniques, investment, strategies, etc.) cause the desired outcomes (for example, higher rate of exam passes, greater emotional intelligence, etc.) that we can start to influence change. As our previous discussion of the nature of successful teaching and leadership makes clear, the most important system within a school is that which describes the relationships between the people who work and learn in the school. These relationships are both formal – in terms of managerial duties, statutory accountabilities, hierarchies, etc. – and informal – in terms of climate, friendships and culture. Although hard to measure, the informal side is frequently the more powerful.

We have suggested that motivation is the connecting factor within these informal relationships. It is a straightforward step to connect the models of successful teaching and successful leadership together into a whole-school system. In this system the motivational climate created by leaders enables the adults within the school to learn and develop their ability to create a motivational climate for children (see Figure 37.3).

This is very much an interpersonal theory of the workplace. In focusing on the most important factors it does ignore other additionally important organizational

6

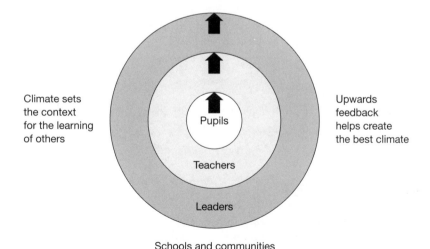

Climate sets the context for the learning of others

Pupils

Teachers

Leaders

Upwards feedback helps create the best climate

Schools and communities

Figure 37.3 The relationship between classroom, school and community climate

issues such as strategy, management processes and job design. As Burke and Litwin (1992) remind us, when thinking about the school as a system we must be aware of these issues – ultimately changes in one area will be amplified or frustrated by events in another. Thus, for example, attempts by leadership to promote a feeling of greater responsibility through the promotion of accountability and effective delegation could be frustrated if the way jobs are designed does not leave people freedom to act.

The picture of the school as a system (*see* Figure 37.4) suggests the content of the curriculum that leaders must provide. The three elements of effective professional development highlight the potential pitfalls in implementation.

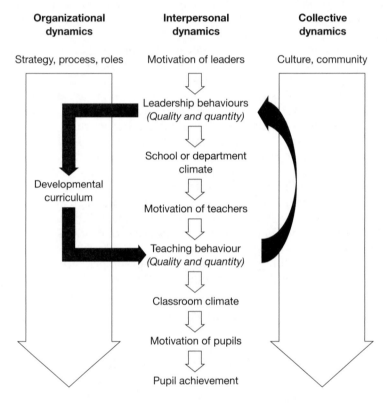

Figure 37.4 The school system, with emphasis on interpersonal dynamics
Source: adapted from Burke and Litwin, 1992.

Sustaining leadership

In UK schools the headteacher traditionally exercises great authority and control over school life. Much power is vested in the position and consequently much is expected from the holder. Arguably, over the last decade, these expectations have increased to an intolerable level for some headteachers. Although a recent study has revealed that headteachers compare strongly with their counterparts in private industry in terms of their ability to build a motivational climate and in the flexibility of their styles of leadership (Forde, Lees and Hobby, 2000), even outstanding individual performance may not be sufficient in the face of exceptional pressure.

So what can sustain school leaders through the challenges identified? Below we highlight those factors that can sustain and support effective leadership.

Creating a learning organization

The need for continuous innovation and adaptation means that schools themselves need to learn – to develop the structures, cultures and systems of communication that enable them to improve their effectiveness and respond to new challenges. Schools need to become more supple, more confident about risk-taking and better able to draw on knowledge and intelligence from their external environment. It is essential for all schools not only to be 'places of learning'; they must also develop a genuine 'culture of learning' that reinforces the message that all members of the educational community are learners. In genuine learning organizations there is a recognition that learning is a continuous process and that managing change is a permanent part of a school's role.

A community of leaders

In the learning school everyone can contribute to its leadership. The myth of the 'hero' CEO – exemplified by statements such as 'significant change only occurs when it is driven from the top' – is damaging to both institutional effectiveness and individual happiness. A wider view of the nature and sources of leadership could help relieve some pressure. We have already seen how teachers are called upon to exercise leadership in the classroom – they can also extend this role across the whole school.

Senge *et al.* (2000, pp. 43–9) view leadership as the capacity of a community to shape its future, and specifically to sustain the significant processes of change required to do so. In the old industrial-age model, leaders are synonymous with the top managers; in the new model there is a community of leaders. As Senge *et al.* say: 'Leadership actually grows from the capacity to hold creative tension, the energy generated when people articulate a vision and tell the truth about their current reality'. By this definition, every organization has many leaders because there are people at each level in the hierarchy who play critical roles in generating and sustaining creative tension.

The task of the 'top leader' is to cultivate leadership in others – the ultimate leadership contribution is to develop leaders in the organization who can move the organization even further after you have left. It is a question of building strong, forward-looking and adaptable institutions, not creating heroic leaders.

Role modelling

One way to extend leadership is consciously to model the role for others. Effective leaders model the values and behaviour associated with best practice. Harris (2001), for example, found that in schools in difficulty, the best leaders modelled what they expected of others and demonstrated the highest standards of professional practice.

Of crucial importance is championing the collection and acceptance of feedback. There are few surer ways to shore up less confident staff or demonstrate the value of feedback than for leaders to seek it and act upon it.

Emotionally intelligent leaders

The research of Goleman (1998) into what makes effective leaders concluded that they are alike in one crucial way – they have a high degree of 'emotional intelligence'. It is not that IQ and technical skills are unimportant. They do matter, but mainly as 'threshold capabilities', that is, the baseline requirements for leaders. When Goleman compared star performers with average ones in senior leadership positions, nearly 90 per cent of the difference in their profiles was attributable to emotional intelligence factors rather than cognitive abilities. Goleman identified five components of emotional intelligence:

- Self-awareness: the ability to recognize and understand your moods, emotions and drives, as well as their effect on others.
- Self-regulation: the ability to control or redirect disruptive impulses and moods.
- Motivation: a passion to work for reasons that go beyond money or status.
- Empathy: the ability to understand the emotional make-up of people.
- Social Skills: proficiency in managing relationships and building networks.

Interestingly for its application in schools, later research (Goleman, 2000) linked emotional intelligence to the 'leadership styles' underpinning the Leadership Programme for Serving Headteachers (LPSH). Behind the four styles that are most effective in influencing culture and performance – the authoritative, affiliative, democratic and coaching styles – lies high emotional intelligence. The LPSH connected leadership styles with school climate; emotional intelligence goes one step further up the ladder of causality and shows how we can develop and extend our leadership styles.

Lead learners

In promoting the learning of adults and children in school, leaders must become the most active learners of all. To lead learning means to favour a 'learner-centred' as opposed to an 'authority-centred' approach to problem solving. A key dimension of school improvement is the creation of an environment in which adult learning (as well as pupil learning) is acceptable and is the norm.

It is no longer important to appear 'learned'. Instead, in the words of Senge (1999, pp. 10–21), leaders can allow themselves to be 'uncertain' because this attitude is also 'inspiring, expectant of surprise, and perhaps ... joyful about confronting the unknown'.

REFERENCES

Burke, W. and Litwin, G. (1992) 'A causal model of organisational performance and change', *Journal of Management*, 18, p. 3.

Claxton, G. (1999) *Wise Up: The Challenge of Lifelong Learning*, London: Bloomsbury.

DfEE (2000) *Research into Teacher Effectiveness*, London: HMSO.

DfEE (2001) *Schools Achieving Success*, London: HMSO.

Forde, R., Lees, A. and Hobby, R. (2000) *The Lessons of Leadership*, London: Hay Group.

Goleman, D. (1998) 'What makes a leader', *Harvard Business Review*, (Nov/Dec), pp. 93–102.

Goleman, D. (2000) 'Leadership that gets results', *Harvard Business Review*, (March/April), pp. 79–90.

Harris, A. (2001) 'Holding the fort?', *Management in Education*, 15 (3).

Jupp, R., Fairly, C. and Bentley, T. (2001) *What Learning Needs. The Challenge for a Creative Nation*, London: Demos/Design Council.

Rogoff, B. (1990) *Apprenticeship in Thinking: Cognitive Development in Social Context*, Oxford: Oxford University Press.

Senge, P. (1999) *The Dance of Change*, London: Nicholas Brealey Publishing.

Senge, P. (2000) *Schools That Learn*, London: Nicholas Brealey Publishing.

Smith, F. (2002) *Leadership Programme for Serving Headteachers: Analysis of Context for School Improvement Data*, Department of Education, University of Newcastle.

Wood, D. (1998): *How Children Think and Learn: The Social Contexts of Cognitive Development*, London: Blackwell.

6

CHAPTER 38

Organizational learning

PETER HILL AND CARMEL CRÉVOLA

*Over the past four decades it has become increasingly clear that economic
globalisation and technology have changed forever the nature of the economy and
of the world in which we live. Our lives are dominated by the increasingly rapid
flow of information and ideas and by constant pressure for change and
improvement. Survival in the Knowledge Society and in a world of constant
change is highly dependent upon the capacity to learn, to adapt to new
circumstances, to solve problems and create new solutions.*

(LEADBEATER, 1999)

Almost simultaneously with the awareness of the emergence of the knowledge
society and the demise of the old industrial economy, the concept of 'organizational learning' was born. After some two decades, the concept remains elusive,
but powerful, and has captured the imaginations of many, particularly since popularized by Senge (1990) more than a decade ago. A recent search of the catalogue
of a well-known on-line bookseller threw up 341 books for sale on the topic, ranging from highly academic works, to detailed 'how-to' guides to transforming
organizations and short paperback summaries for the general reader. They bear testimony to a new truth: change is constant, therefore organizations do not have the
option of standing still; they either go backwards or forwards, and going forwards
involves organizational learning.

Indeed, the challenge for the corporate world has often been expressed more
forcibly as one of becoming a 'learning organization', which can be regarded as a
corporate 'ideal' (Argyris and Schön, 1996) that inspires as a vision of a preferred
future, but is seldom, if ever, achieved. The concept of the learning organization
typically includes the notion of a group of individuals committed to a collective
purpose who engage in systematic, collaborative problem solving, resulting in continuous improvement and transformation in order to adapt to external change.

In one sense, organizational learning could be said to occur with or without conscious encouragement or nurturing, prompted by the need to respond to external
pressures. But it is more useful to regard such automatic responses as 'organizational adaptation' and to reserve the term 'organizational learning' for the
higher-level learning that arises as a result of conscious and deliberate processes
(Fiol and Lyles, 1985). The notion of 'triple-loop' learning is helpful in this context. If organizational adaptation, or making a short-term response to an emergent

problem, is single-loop, then double-loop learning involves developing a deeper appreciation of and alternative perspectives on the problem (Argyris, 1976). Triple-loop learning investigates the context and nature of learning itself and focuses on the nature and appropriateness of the customs, ethos and behaviour of the organization (Isaacs, 1993). The effective learning organization is one that can engage in all three forms of learning, as appropriate.

Organizational learning in schools

The emergence of the Knowledge Society can be seen to have generated ambivalent attitudes to schools. There is now a keener appreciation of the critical role of schooling in educating future generations. This awareness is evident in the rhetoric of political leaders everywhere. At the same time, there has been considerable scepticism regarding the capacity of schools to adapt to the new realities of the Knowledge Society, let alone take a leading role in defining the shaping educational provision in the community at large. (Beare, 2001)

Despite successive waves of reform, schools have until recently struggled to accommodate externally imposed change, and attempts to improve them have typically resulted in sporadic and short-lived improvements in standards of academic performance (Elmore, 1996; Sarason, 1990; Zywine *et al.*, 1995). In a curious twist of irony, schools have often been places that fall far short of the ideal of the learning organization. Indeed, many schools could only be described as 'learning disabled' in terms of their capacity for organizational learning. In our experience, this is not because they resist the notion, but because those who control them have not allowed them to become learning organizations.

This situation appears to be changing, however, as improvement by design becomes entrenched as the prevailing paradigm (West-Burnham, 2001) and as devolution of authority to the school level becomes more widespread (Caldwell and Spinks, 1998). Much has been learnt about the characteristics of effective professional development programmes for improving teaching and learning (Hargreaves and Fullan, 1991). As identified in Crévola and Hill (2001), such programmes need to:

- be theoretically based yet emphasize practically situated learning;
- be well researched and draw upon the latest relevant professional literature;
- be purposeful and in support of specific and important outcomes that have the backing and commitment of the whole school;
- involve the whole staff or a significant proportion of the staff within a school, rather than individual teachers;
- value the knowledge and experiential base of teachers;
- involve the establishment of professional learning teams with a team co-ordinator who acts as a lead learner, coach and mentor;
- mix both input from outside experts and opportunities for participants to work through issues and engage in professional learning activities;
- be structured, well-planned and well-presented;
- encourage the contribution of teachers to the learning process by providing opportunities for them to help shape key components of their professional learning;

- introduce teachers to new and challenging understandings that are directly relevant to achieving agreed outcomes;
- be ongoing, with opportunities to try out new ideas and approaches and then to come back and reflect upon the impact of implementing change in the classroom;
- allow time for teachers to reflect upon their practice and be involved in visiting, observing and discussing practice with other colleagues in their own school and in other schools;
- provide opportunities to try out new practices with the support of a peer coach or mentor;
- involve systematic processes for providing feedback on the extent to which change has resulted in the achievement of the intended outcomes;
- involve systematic processes for ongoing support and assistance between sessions;
- be conducted in a pleasant environment that puts participants at ease, respects them as professionals and is attentive to their personal requirements.

Needless to say, designing programmes that have all these characteristics presents a great challenge. All too often, professional development is under-resourced and without sufficient regard to what is known about the characteristics of effective professional development programmes. In other cases, the resources are available, but they are used in ineffective and inefficient ways that leave teachers overwhelmed and confused. As a consequence, teachers experience many professional development activities that in themselves are informative and stimulating, but which result in little real impact on their practice.

The systems view of learning – learning by design

Teachers have always shown a strong commitment to learning as professionals, but all too often this has been pursued outside the context of whole-school change. In recent years there has been a growing awareness that improving schools cannot be achieved through the combined endeavours of teachers acting individually, but through a systematic, whole-school approach to improvement. Sergiovanni (2000, p. 73) describes this as a 'change away from a pretentious objective science preoccupied with effective and efficient means to change schools, teachers and others ... to a design field'. He quotes the systems theorist, Herbert Simon (1996, p. 111), in support of the notion that education, like health, law, engineering and architecture, is centrally concerned with the process of design.

Design is about the application of systems thinking, or thinking holistically. Senge (1990, pp. 12–13) refers to systems thinking as the 'fifth discipline' and the discipline that prevents new ideas from becoming gimmicks or fads:

> Systems thinking makes understandable the subtlest aspect of the learning organization – the new way individuals perceive themselves and their world. At the heart of the learning organization is a shift of mind – from seeing ourselves as separate from the world to connected to the world, from seeing problems as caused by someone or something 'out there' to seeing how our own actions create the problems we experience.

Design as applied to schools means identifying all the critical elements of schools and school systems, working out what needs to change in order for them to operate effectively and in alignment with all the other elements, and then redesigning them accordingly (Hill and Crévola, 1999; Wilson and Daviss, 1994). Design involves 'a coherent mix of vision, intuition and research-driven knowledge' (Dimmock, 2000, p. 5). When done well, its effect is to bring clarity of purpose and intentionality to actions, and alignment of structures, processes and programmes. It should be research-based and data-driven. And at its best, it is able to generate high levels of synergy and that sense of being part of something larger than oneself, which leads to extraordinary levels of organizational commitment, capacity and performance.

Systems thinking is critical to promoting professional learning in schools directed at improving student learning outcomes and the capacity of the school to respond to change. Organizational learning is learning by design. It is about:

- the integration of theory and practice and of beliefs and actions;
- the alignment of purpose and means;
- developing an intuitive understanding or gestalt of the whole, which illuminates detailed knowledge of the parts;
- developing shared beliefs and understandings and a common language with which to discuss them.

As Fullan and Hargreaves (1992, p. 11) comment:

As individuals, ...[teachers] must therefore take responsibility for improving the whole school, or it will not improve. If they don't, their individual classroom will not improve either, because forces outside their classroom heavily influence the quality of classroom life: forces like access to ideas and resources, timetabling arrangements, and sense of purpose and direction.

A model of organizational learning for schools

In the remaining sections we present and illustrate a six-tier model for promoting professional learning in schools, in which training and development are not so much 'events' as ongoing processes driven by data on and understanding of student learning needs. The model, which was first presented by Crévola (2000), is based on the following premises:

- Design-based learning: embedding the professional learning within a whole-school design for improving student learning outcomes.
- Data-driven improvement: the use of data on student learning outcomes to drive teaching and learning.
- Teachers as learners: a focus on change and development in the beliefs and understandings of teachers as the key to effective teaching and learning.
- Systemic scale-up: achieving systemic change through a six-tiered model of professional learning and school improvement:
    - the student as the beginning and end point of professional learning;
    - the classroom teacher as the person with the greatest capacity to impact on student progress;

- the professional learning team, including the role of the coordinator as an 'internal' change agent;
- the school, including the role of the principal as the instructional leader;
- the 'project', including role of the facilitator as an 'outside' agent of change;
- the system, including support structures, funding arrangements and accountability systems.

This model has been used as a framework by the authors in three separate school improvement initiatives aimed at improving early literacy. The largest of these has been the Children's Literacy Success Strategy (CLaSS), which we use here to exemplify the model in action. CLaSS was initiated by the Catholic Education Office of the Education Commission of Victoria, which serves Catholic schools in the Archdiocese of Melbourne, Australia. The project, which is ongoing, began in 1998 with an intake of 39 schools. In 1999, a further 86 schools joined the project, in 2000 a further 82 schools, and in 2001 a further 42 schools, with a further 32 schools expected to join in 2002, making a total of 281 elementary schools, or more than three-quarters of all Catholic elementary schools in Victoria.

Design-based learning

For the reasons canvassed earlier, the model is premised on the notion of organizational learning within schools as occurring within the context of a design approach to school improvement. To reiterate, organizational learning is learning by design.

Schools involved in the CLaSS initiative have undertaken to implement a single design for improving literacy outcomes in the first three years of schooling. While the main elements of the design had previously been specified in detail, and certain non-negotiables had been identified as preconditions of participation (Crévola and Hill, 2001; Hill and Crévola, 1999), schools have nonetheless been expected to function as co-researchers in further refining the design through their participation. The design is based on nine elements, as summarized in Figure 38.1.

Over a period of four years, schools have progressively implemented the design so that all the key elements that comprise the learning environment of the school are functioning effectively and in alignment with all other elements. As a consequence, the professional learning of all within the school has been design-based and directed at a single goal, namely improving student learning by adopting a systems approach to improving the effectiveness of the school.

Data-driven improvement

A second premise of the model of professional learning is an insistence on starting and ending professional learning with information on and an understanding of students and what they know and can do. This is in line with Elmore's notion (1979–80) of backward mapping, or beginning with the end in mind and mapping backwards to identify what should be done, with the end being student learning. Curiously, as Joyce and Calhoun (1996) note, schools are 'both information-rich and information-impoverished'. School personnel collect a prodigious amount of

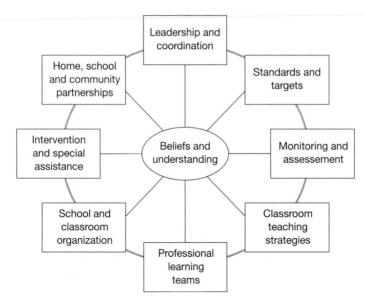

Figure 38.1 School improvement design elements

information, from test scores to attendance figures, yet rarely link this wealth of data to school-improvement efforts.

Within CLaSS, an initial resistance to an emphasis on data was encountered, which could be attributed in the main to a general unfamiliarity with their use and interpretation. During the course of professional development sessions, teachers have been presented with comprehensive pre-test data on their students' starting points. These data have been used to set overall learning targets for the school and individual targets for each student, against an objective set of standards. Teachers have been encouraged during the year to collect a range of semi-formal data, including weekly running records of students' text levels, analyses of students' writing and spelling, notes on difficulties experienced by students taken at the end of small-group instruction, word knowledge in terms of high frequency word lists, and so on. At the end of the year, students have been retested and the cycle has repeated in following years.

The data obtained from these sources have formed the starting point for weekly team meetings of teachers. Teachers have been required to come to the meetings with data on their students and these data have provided the basis for exploring ways of improving teaching and learning. In this way, teachers' instruction has become data-driven.

Teachers as learners

A third premise of the model is that ongoing improvement in teachers' practice involves the development and consolidation of their core beliefs about and understandings of teaching and learning. The model thus places a premium on teachers being able to articulate what they do and why.

Within CLaSS, teachers and administrators have been challenged to reflect upon their attitudes to core propositions about teaching and learning. For example, two such propositions that have been the subject of repeated consideration are:

- all students can perform at a high standard, given sufficient time and support;
- all teachers can teach to high standards, given the right conditions and support.

What these reflections have revealed has been a pre-existing culture of low expectations that has had to be challenged and progressively replaced by a culture of high expectations, both for students and staff.

Teachers have also been invited to deepen their understandings of how students become literate and of effective strategies for teaching students to read and write. The emphasis has not been on pre-packaged solutions, but rather on thinking through the issues. At times this has generated some frustrations. A teacher would say: 'Just tell me what to do, and I will do it', to which the response has invariably been: 'Let's think it through so that you can tell me what to do'. The end result has invariably been teachers who have acquired a greater confidence in their professional judgements and who make intelligent decisions in response to the unique needs of individual students. As Rowe (1995) has demonstrated, increased teacher confidence in their professional judgements leads to positive effects on their professional self-perceptions and levels of energy and enthusiasm, which, in turn, have a positive influence on student learning.

Professional learning has not been confined to classroom teaching, but has encompassed all aspects of the school's operation that impinge on student performance. The intention has been that teachers will have a big-picture, systems view of schooling and will thus be aware of broader issues beyond the classroom that affect what they do in the classroom. Indeed, the aim has been to promote triple-loop learning in which participants reflect on the very culture of the school and fundamental assumptions underlying its operation.

Systemic scale-up

One of the reasons for the dismal track record of efforts to achieve scale-up of best practice in schools is the failure to develop professionally all participants involved in bringing about change. A fourth premise of the model is that there will be a multitiered approach to professional learning to ensure that there is understanding at all levels regarding the intended changes, and that learning is systemic, rather than individual or confined to a particular school.

The first of the six tiers is the student, since it is student learning that should provide the beginning and end point for all professional learning. Other tiers include:

- the classroom teacher;
- the senior teacher who coordinates professional learning and who acts as lead learner, mentor and coach for teams of teachers;
- the principal and other school administrators;
- the external facilitator or design team;
- the system itself, be it a district, a local education authority, or some other grouping of schools.

In CLaSS, there has been a strong and long-term commitment from the Director of the Catholic Education Commission of Victoria to sustained reform using a whole-school, design approach, and to a multitiered model of professional learning. Professional learning has been planned as a combination of off-site and on-site learning. The off-site component has involved teams of teachers attending four spaced professional development days in which the focus has been on big-picture thinking aimed at challenging and extending participants' beliefs and understandings and sharing experiences across schools. An additional eight professional development days per year have been provided for the literacy coordinator from each school (a senior teacher with significant release from classroom teaching to perform the role). The off-site professional development for the coordinators (the third tier in the model) has included a strong focus on leadership and mentoring skills, in addition to going into greater detail on professional issues covered in the off-site professional development for classroom teachers.

The on-site learning has been delivered primarily through professional learning teams that have met weekly and that have been chaired by the literacy coordinator, who has organized classroom visits, classroom observations and acted as lead learner, co-researcher, mentor and peer coach. Team members have increasingly assumed joint responsibility for the literacy outcomes of all the students they teach, so that successful learning has become a shared responsibility, not just a responsibility of the individual classroom teacher. They have also assumed shared responsibility for each other's professional growth and development, so that successful teaching is also a shared responsibility, in which the team provides individual members with both the pressure and the support to improve.

Within CLaSS, the fourth tier of professional learning has been addressed through six planned professional development days that principals have attended with their literacy coordinators. These sessions have focused on giving principals the 'big picture' with respect to early literacy, on joint problem solving in areas such as staffing, resources and school organization, and on understanding what it means to be an instructional leader. A significant innovation was the introduction of the 'Principal's Walk', which is a strategy for an effective and visible presence of the principal on a daily basis in classrooms. Another accompanying feature has been the formalization of weekly meetings of the leadership team to review progress and set the focus for the Principal's Walk.

The fifth tier of the model comprises the role of the facilitator as an external agent of change. Within CLaSS, a number of facilitators has been progressively trained for this role and given responsibility for interacting with approximately 25–30 schools. The facilitators have met on a bi-weekly basis to deepen their own understandings and to plan for training sessions. This training has been provided by the CLaSS director and trainer coordinator, who for the first three years of CLaSS was the second author of this part.

The sixth tier of the model is the system itself. Within CLaSS it has been important that senior administrators of the Catholic Education Office understand in some detail the rationale behind the design and are a part of planned professional learning activities. Given the nature of their responsibilities and the types of decisions they have to make, this could not be addressed through the kinds of professional development activities provided to teachers or principals. Instead, quarterly meetings have been organized, as well as more informal breakfast and dinner meetings. Annual reports and data-rich reports of evaluation studies have also played an important role in ensuring the commitment and the understanding of senior administrators.

The impact of the model

The model of organizational learning outlined here is an all-encompassing model that is predicated on a systems view of schooling. It is a model in which organizational learning is evaluated in terms of the extent to which it results in an improvement in student learning and in the building up of the capacity of staff for further change and improvement. It is also a resource-intensive model, but one that can be expected to pay both short- and long-term dividends.

The experience of the CLaSS initiative has been that the model is associated with dramatic improvements in student learning outcomes, which have been maintained over four years. Students in CLaSS schools have consistently outperformed students in non-CLaSS schools and the effects have been large (in excess of 0.6 of a standard deviation in scores on outcome measures). The evidence of effectiveness has been critical in justifying and maintaining expenditure on establishing and implementing the professional learning model.

The evidence regarding teacher capacity is unfortunately only anecdotal at this stage and comes from teacher journal entries. They include comments such as: 'I have worked in a "team" for as long as I have been a teacher, but I have never known a team like this!' (CLaSS, 2704); 'We are always talking about our successes. What a change, we used to blame the kids!' (CLaSS, 901); 'The talk that is happening in our building now is so different to anything that I have ever heard, and I have been there for 14 years' (CLaSS, 99).

Perhaps the greatest indicator of the success of the model is that it has led to institutionalized change in which the new ways of doing things have become standard operating procedures. It has also led to the development of multitiered capacity that ensures reinforcement of the changes and sustained improvement.

REFERENCES

Argyris, C. (1976) *Increasing Leadership Effectiveness*, New York: Wiley.

Argyris, C. and Schön, D. (1996) *Organisational Learning: A Theory of Action Perspective*, Reading, MA: Addison-Wesley.

Beare, H. (2001) *Creating the Future School*, New York, NY: Routledge/Falmer Press.

Caldwell, B.J. and Spinks, J.M. (1998) *Beyond the Self-managing School*, London: Falmer Press.

Crévola, C.A. (2000) 'Conceptualising and facilitating the professional learning of teachers as part of a systemic, whole-school design approach to improving early literacy outcomes', paper presented at the International Congress for School Effectiveness and Improvement, Hong Kong, 7 January.

Crévola, C.A. and Hill, P.W. (2001) *Children's Literacy Success Strategy: An Overview*, 2nd edn, Melbourne: Catholic Education Office.

Dimmock, C. (2000) *Designing the Learning-centred School: A Cross-cultural Perspective*, New York: Falmer Press.

Elmore, R.F. (1979–80) 'Backward mapping: implementation research and policy decisions', *Political Science Quarterly*, 94 (4), pp. 601–6.

Elmore, R.F. (1996) 'Getting to scale with good educational practice', *Harvard Educational Review*, 66 (1), pp. 1–26.

Fiol, C.M. and Lyles, M.A. (1985) 'Organisational learning', *Academy of Management Review*, 10 (4), pp. 803–13.

Fullan, M.G. and Hargreaves, A. (1992) *What's Worth Fighting For? Working Together for Your School*, Buckingham: Open University Press.

Hargreaves, A. and Fullan, M. (1991) *Understanding Teacher Development*, London: Cassell.

Hill, P.W. and Crévola, C.A. (1999) 'The role of standards in educational reform for the 21st century' in Marsh, D.D. (ed.) *ASCD Yearbook 1999: Preparing our Schools for the 21st Century*, Alexandria, VA: Association for Supervision and Curriculum Development, pp. 117–42.

Isaacs, W.N. (1993) 'Taking flight: dialogue, collective thinking, and organizational learning', *Organizational Dynamics*, 22 (3), pp. 24–39.

Joyce, B. and Calhoun, E. (1996) 'School renewal: Not a prescription' in Joyce, B. and Calhoun, E. (eds) *Learning Exeriences in School Renewal; An Exploration of Five Successful Programs* Eugene, OR: ERIC Clearinghouse on Educational Management, ED 401 600.

Leadbeater, C. (1999) *Living on Thin Air*, London: Viking.

Rowe, K. J. (1995) 'Factors affecting students' progress in reading: key findings from a longitudinal study', *Literacy Teaching and Learning*, 1, pp. 57–110.

Sarason, S. (1990) *The Predictable Failure of Educational Reform*, San Francisco: Jossey-Bass.

Sergiovanni, T. J. (2000) 'Changing change: towards a design science and art', *Journal of Educational Change*, 1 (1), pp. 57–75.

Senge, P. (1990) *The Fifth Discipline: The Art and Practice of the Learning Organization*, New York: Doubleday.

Simon, H. (1996) *The Sciences of the Artificial*, 3rd edn, Cambridge, MA: MIT Press.

West-Burnham, J. (2001) *Leadership for Transformation*, Seminar Series 108, Jolimont, Victoria, Australia: IARTV.

Wilson, K.G. and Daviss, B. (1994) *Redesigning Education*, New York: Henry Holt & Company, p. 22.

Zywine, J., Stoll, L., Adam, E., Fullan, M. and Bennett, B. (1995) 'Leadership effectiveness and school development. Putting reform in perspective', *School Effectiveness and Improvement*, 6, pp. 223–46.

6

CHAPTER 39

Pedagogy reborn: opportunities and dangers?

DENIS LAWTON

Pedagogy: a neglected area

For many years pedagogy was a neglected area of educational studies. Back in the 1980s Simon (1981) asked the interesting question 'Why no pedagogy in England?' Despite a tradition of pedagogy stretching from Comenius to Dewey and Montessori, amongst many others, pedagogy seemed to have been driven out by a narrow psychology that emphasized intelligence and testing rather than teaching and learning. Before the end of the twentieth century, however, the revival of pedagogy was already in progress, and several books had been produced on the subject. But there may be problems as well as opportunities in this development, as Millett (1996) indicated when she was asked to lecture on the subject: 'Pedagogy – the last corner of the secret garden'.

One of the problems facing a reforming administration, whether at school or national level, is the delicate balance between having a clear vision of what needs to be done and respecting the professional autonomy of those who must implement the reform. There is often a tension between zealous central direction and acknowledging the validity of professional experience. In the past, mistakes have been made in the UK at national level in curriculum planning: too much detailed top-down prescription in the early versions of the National Curriculum, which had to be removed later. Professional teachers jealously guard their right to exercise judgement. What was true of the curriculum is equally a problem in specifying pedagogical methods, even when it may seem obvious that changes are essential. We shall return to that point later.

First, however, we look at the nature of the present situation in schools, especially secondary schools, where there would seem to be a set of difficulties concerning the motivation of large numbers of young people, despite the probability that academic standards, narrowly defined, have never been higher. The White Paper (DFES, 2001), optimistically entitled *Schools – Achieving Success*, acknowledges a number of problems facing schools:

- there is a poor record in retaining young people at school beyond age 16;
- classroom behaviour is tending to deteriorate;
- violence and the need to exclude pupils is increasing;
- working-class boys are seriously under-achieving;
- too many secondary pupils aged 11–13 actually regress from their primary school achievements.

The White Paper is in some respects a good document, but it fails to analyse a fundamental problem of school organization and leadership: should we not be asking what lies behind the five kinds of problem specified above? Instead, a complex theoretical issue is simply buried beneath a list of practical difficulties with which heads and teachers are expected to deal – presumably by trying harder. Although there is an attempt to theorize in the White Paper (for example, paragraphs 2.19 and 2.20), the analysis is superficial, being content with asserting that some schools are better than others in dealing with all these problems. And the implication is that better computer skills and more teachers learning from others in effective schools is the solution.

Maybe. But what if the problem is more deep-rooted? Is it possible that in the twenty-first century the schools, curricula and pedagogical methods developed in the nineteenth century now need complete rethinking? What follows is not a prescription for deschooling, but some radical suggestions about the ways in which the processes of schooling, especially curriculum and pedagogy, need to be carefully re-examined. (I will not explore any of the other defects of the White Paper, such as the folly of reintroducing selection.)

School: a nineteenth century institution

The school in the nineteenth century was one of a number of institutions, including workhouses, prisons and factories, that were 'invented' to solve some of the consequences of industrialization and urbanization. These institutions shared several common features: the need for a large number of inmates to be controlled by a small number of supervisors; the need for strict discipline and hard labour. Several procedures were developed to ensure control over inmates' time, space and movement. For example, punctuality, assisted by bells, sirens or hooters; sitting still in rows (or, in prisons, Bentham's Panopticon); and marching in lock-step and in silence. Control was the dominant factor in the treatment of inmates, prisoners and pupils. Schools in the UK in the twenty-first century are different, but are the Victorian vestiges still too strong?

Reforms

For various reasons schools have been slower to change than other institutions such as factories. Schools now tend to be out of step with the rest of society. How should they now change? Hargreaves (1994), for example, has advocated that schools should move away from the factory model to institutions that are less bureaucratic, probably smaller, with an emphasis on more enlightened teacher–student relationships with modern teaching and learning methods. Other reformers go further: Elliott (2000) has drawn attention to the Labour government's 'Healthy Schools Standard', which relates particularly to school ethos but has clear implications for teacher–student relationships in the classroom, especially in encouraging young people to discuss their experience as learners. Elliott also refers to the work of Posch (1994), in Austria, who connects social and economic change to consequential reforms of curriculum and pedagogy. The following changes are discussed:

- attitudes to authority make it necessary for schools to move the curriculum away from 'a culture of pre-defined demands' to programmes that are open to negotiation;
- other social changes result in students ceasing to see teachers as guides for their futures: teachers are increasingly seen as old-fashioned and irrelevant as role models for secondary pupils; schools need to develop forms of collaborative learning that foster mutual respect and a sense of community;
- teachers need to be able to encourage students to develop techniques of coping with the unstructured situations of everyday life, making sense of practical problems and also taking responsibility for their own actions;
- teachers need to be able to help students to understand and evaluate 'risks' in their own society, using scientific and technical knowledge.

All this will demand changes in both pedagogy and the curriculum: Posch advocates moving away from traditional subjects to a curriculum based on the environment that would have clear relevance to modern life.

These ideas suggest that we need to rethink the functions of the school in the twenty-first century, to change the organization of schooling into a caring community where pupils take more responsibility for their own learning and teachers are seen as relevant to the students' needs. What is required is not a programme of total individualized self-instruction (because some kinds of social learning are also important), but a shift in the balance away from teacher direction to individual responsibility for and ownership of the teaching–learning process and the curriculum. The Organization for Economic Co-operation and Development (OECD) has published the findings of a conference that discussed such problems in schools in advanced industrial societies (OECD, 2001). The OECD educationists recommended that negotiation and consensus-seeking should replace compulsion (ibid., p. 19); they comment on the decline of 'mystique' in schools and the need for professionals to be transparently accountable (ibid., p. 37). This discussion is also connected with the decline in the authority of expert knowledge (ibid., pp. 38 and 114). Schools, they recommend, need to be revitalized (ibid., p. 66). At the same time, there have been tremendous advances in information and communication technology, which do not make teachers redundant – far from it – but make it essential for teachers to see their role and their pedagogy differently.

Some schools have already moved in that direction: they are less hierarchical and less authoritarian; more concerned with individual needs rather than age group norms; concerned with learning more than teaching; and concerned with the kind of learning that is both experiential and, where possible, self-directed, with students who are more autonomous and self-evaluating. Targets and tests, as officially perceived at present, are an obstacle to the new vision of schooling. They need not be abandoned completely, but their purpose and usage need to be rethought.

This reform of secondary education has a number of specific implications for teacher education. We need teachers with the ability to 'learn' with the students (even if teachers do not know all the answers, they should be good at finding out). Teachers must also become more knowlegeable about learning styles as well as teaching methods; they should be experts in curriculum design rather than lesson planning – knowing how to help plan individualized learning programmes as well as how to instruct a whole class.

Part of the professional expertise of the teacher should be the ability to plan carefully what kind of learning needs to be individual, what should be learned in a group, and when it would be better to have a whole-class presentation by the teacher, always bearing in mind that pupils benefit from oral interaction with a good teacher. Teachers also need to cater for different levels of ability, however, it is not enough to have classes set or streamed for ability – what is needed is a much more complex pattern of school organization to cater for a range of individual differences. As long ago as 1993 the National Commission on Education recognized this and devoted a whole part of its report to 'innovation in learning'. It found the evidence about 'flexible learning' impressive. The report recommended that by the age of about 14, pupils should have acquired the ability to work independently in a flexible learning environment, taking responsibility for their own learning programmes.

The above suggestions are not simply responses to a less compliant student body. For many years educationists and other writers have advocated rethinking the process of teaching and learning for purely educational reasons. For example, Bruner (1960) argued convincingly about process, structure and the need for children learning science to begin to think like scientists; other writers have advocated that students should spend less time memorizing and recalling facts and more on acquiring fundamental understandings (Higginson, 1988). More recently, Reich (1993) has discussed the need for much higher levels of thinking skills in the computerized world of symbolic analysts who need greater powers of 'abstraction, system thinking, experimentation and collaboration'. And Handy (1997) has suggested that he would 'have more faith in a national curriculum if it were to be more concerned with process than with content'.

I began by pointing out the tension between the need for change and avoiding top-down reforms that ignore professional experience. There is another danger: the inability to persuade professionals to undertake more and more innovations. This is part of educational planning too. It may also be necessary to point out to those responsible for planning and organizing schools that there are now not many problems that can be solved by teachers being told to work harder. In many respects teachers need to learn to do less but to teach students to do more for themselves.

6

Conclusion

Many of the educationists referred to here have made similar observations about curriculum and pedagogy, albeit from different points of view. First, some have expressed disappointment that at the beginning of the twenty-first century so much educational discourse is put in the context of greater economic efficiency, when the purpose of education should be seen much more widely. Second, the world is, especially for young people in secondary schools, complex and confusing. The school does not do enough to make the world more meaningful. The solution should be seen more in terms of curriculum, pedagogy and school organization. Third, the curriculum is seriously out of date; teaching methods even more so. Reform should mean not simply greater use of information technology, but changes in attitude and organization. Much greater flexibility is needed, moving away from the standard situation of one teacher and about 30 students doing more or less the same thing, in the same way, at the same pace. Finally, much has been written about schools and citizenship, or education for democracy. Above all, schools must become better models of cooperation and community as well as teaching and learning.

The need to change pedagogy is central to all the above issues. There is still a place for some didactic teaching, but good teachers know that today it is essential to be expert in a variety of pedagogic methods – especially those that encourage students to think for themselves, to be responsible for organizing their own work and to develop techniques of self-evaluation and self-criticism. That view of the teaching profession means greater autommony for teachers as well as for students.

REFERENCES

Bruner, J. (1960) *The Process of Education*, Cambridge, MA: Harvard University Press.

DFES (2001) *Schools – Achieving Success*, London: HMSO.

Elliott, J. (2000) 'Revising the National Curriculum', *Journal of Educational Policy*, 15 (2), pp. 247–55.

Handy, C. (1997) 'Schools for life and work' in Mortimore, P. and Little, V. (eds) *Living Education*, London: PCP.

Hargreaves, A. (1994) *Changing Teachers: Changing Times*, London: Falmer Press.

Higginson, A. (1988) *Advancing A Levels*, London: HMSO.

Millett, A. (1996) *Pedagogy – The Last Corner of the Secret Garden*, London: King's College.

Mortimore, P. and Little, V. (eds) (1997) *Living Education*, London: PCP.

National Commission on Education (1993), *Learning to Succeed*, London: Heinemann

OECD (2001) *What Schools for the Future?* Paris: Organization for Economic Co-operation and Development/Center for Educational Research and Development.

Posch, P. (1994) 'Changes in the Culture of Teaching and Learning', *Educational Action Research*, 2 (2), pp. 153–61.

Reich, R. (1993) *The Work of Nations: Preparing Ourselves for 21st Capitalism*, New York: Simon & Schuster.

Simon, B. (1981) 'Why no pedagogy in England?' in Simon, B. and Taylor, W. (eds) *Education in the Eighties*, London: Batsford.

CHAPTER 40

The development of formative assessment

PAUL BLACK AND DYLAN WILIAM

Permission granted: © Paul Black and Dylan Wiliam 2003,

Kings College London

The value of formative assessment (or assessment for learning as it is now some-times called) for enhancing students' attainment in science has been attested by a variety of research studies (see Black and Wiliam 1998a for a review of these). In suggesting how this work might be taken forward (Black and Wiliam 1998b), we argued for development work in partnership between researchers and teachers, and since then we have been able to carry out such a project. The main result of this work has been that the teachers involved have made very significant changes in their classroom practices, while also improving the performance of their students (Wiliam and Lee, 2001). These changes turned out to be more radical in character than the simple addition of some formative assessment routines to pre-existing practice. In this chapter we draw on teachers' written reflections on their involvement with the project (made near the end of the project) in order to review the main outcomes of this work, and we then consider the implications, both for pedagogy and for the task of leadership and management in schools.

Developing formative assessment: experience and evidence

Twenty-four science and mathematics teachers, drawn from six comprehensive schools in two local education authorities (LEAs), Medway and Oxfordshire, were invited to take part in a collaborative project with us – the King's Medway Oxford Formative Assessment Project (KMOFAP).

The project was based on the understanding that if assessment is to function formatively, the teacher must:

- set up a task or situation to elicit information about the student's understanding;
- interpret that information in terms of that student's learning needs (and not just his/her attainment);
- ensure that appropriate action (either by the teacher, the student, or both) follows.

Our stance with the teachers was that, while many features essential to fruitful development had been documented, there was no magic recipe that teachers could take up and follow. The project's aim was to invite the teachers to explore how the broad strategies associated with formative assessment might be implemented in their own classrooms. This was done by proposing three main aspects of teachers' work that could be changed to make teachers' classroom practice more formative in nature: (i) questioning, (ii) marking and comments, and (iii) self-assessment and peer-assessment.

Questioning

One of the most interesting findings in the research literature – and one that was most surprising to our teachers – was the research on 'wait time'. Rowe (1986) and others have found that the period of silence that teachers allow after asking a question before, if no answer was forthcoming, asking another question, or answering their own question, is often less than one second. In such a short time, all that a student might do would be to give a factual answer from memory, and in consequence the only questions that 'worked' would be questions that called for memorized facts. In an early meeting of the project, the wait-time research was discussed and the teachers took away and worked on a suggestion that they might try to allow longer times. As they tried this, teachers realized some of the limitations of their current practice. Most teachers found it hard to break their long-standing habits in the classroom, not least because it meant that the expectations of their students would also have to be confronted.

The overall effects of their efforts to improve the use of question-and-answer dialogue in the classroom were summarized by one teacher as follows:

> *My whole teaching style has become more interactive. Instead of showing how to find solutions, a question is asked and pupils given time to explore answers together. My Year 8 target class [the class with which the teacher was developing formative assessment] is now well-used to this way of working. I find myself using this method more and more with other groups ... Unless specifically asked, pupils know not to put their hands up if they know the answer to a question. All pupils are expected to be able to answer at any time, even if it is an 'I don't know' ... Pupils are comfortable with giving a wrong answer. They know that these can be as useful as correct ones. They are happy for other pupils to help explore their wrong answers further.* (Nancy, Riverside School)

As the routine of limited factual questions was abandoned, the quality and the different functions of classroom questions became the focus of attention. One function was the use of a 'big question' as an opening question that would evoke a discussion involving many students and would serve to set the scene for a whole lesson. However, if such procedures were to be productive, both the actual content of the questions and ways of following up the responses became important. As the changes have become established, the teachers have come to value collaboration with their peers in sharing and discussing possible questions to explore and enhance their exploration of critical features of students' understanding. The overall change is that questions have become a more significant part of teaching, and the teachers' main concern now is to think harder about how they can be constructed and used to develop students' learning:

> *Not until you analyse your own questioning do you realise how poor it can be. I found myself using questions to fill time and asking questions which required little thought from the students. When talking to students, particularly those who are experiencing difficulties, it is important to ask questions that get them thinking about the topic and will allow them to make the next step in the learning process. Simply directing them to the 'correct answer' is not useful.* (Derek, Century Island School)

Overall the developments can be summarized as follows:

- teachers have shifted in their role, from presenting ideas to the students to one in which they are exploring the ideas of their students, and involving all students in such exploration;
- students have become more active as participants, and have come to realize that learning may depend less on their capacity to spot the right answer but more on their readiness to express and discuss their own understanding;
- teachers have had to spend more effort on framing questions to explore issues that are critical to the students' development of understanding of the subject matter.

Marking and comments

The main starting point for our work on this aspect was the results of research experiments that established that, while students' learning can be advanced by feedback through comments, the giving of marks does not usually help and, moreover, has a negative effect in that students ignore comments when marks are also given (see, for example, Butler, 1988). Many of the project teachers found, through working with this idea, that their experience confirmed the research findings, and so were led to abandon their practice of giving of marks or grades for every piece of work they marked. As one described her experience:

My marking has developed from comments with targets and grades, which is the school policy, to comments and targets only. Pupils do work on targets and corrections more productively if no grades are given. CL (a researcher) observed on several occasions how little time pupils spent reading my comments if grades are given as well. My routine is now, in my target class, to not give grades, only comments. The comments highlight what has been done well and what needs further work, and the minimum follow-up work expected to be completed next time I mark the books. (Nancy, Riverside School)

Putting into practice a policy of attention to comments required some initial work, since teachers had to attend to the quality of their comments as they marked homework. Over time, experience led to more efficient fluency. However, there is more to this than just writing better comments because the comments become useful feedback only if students use them to guide further work: this new requirement called for new procedures:

I was keen to try and have a more easy method of monitoring pupils' response to my comments without having to trawl through their books each time to find out if they'd addressed my comments. I implemented a comment sheet at the back of my Year 8 class's books. It was A4 in size and the left-hand side is for my comments and the right-hand side is for the pupils to demonstrate by a reference to the page in their books where I can find the evidence to say whether they have done the work. The comments have become more meaningful as the time has gone on and the books still only take me one hour to mark. (Sian, Cornbury Estate School)

In retrospect, it has become clear that the previous efforts of many teachers in marking homework may have been misdirected. A numerical mark or grade does not tell you what to do, and if students do not have feedback about how to improve their work, the opportunity to enhance their learning has been lost.

6

Significant features of the changes in practice involved here were:

- teachers have changed their view of the role of written work in promoting students' learning;
- teachers have felt challenged to compose comments on written work, which are framed in the light of clear thinking – about the subject matter and about the learning needs of each individual student;
- teachers have had to pay more attention to differentiation in the feedback given to students;
- students have changed in their perception of the role of their written work as part of their learning.

Self-assessment and peer-assessment

In this third aspect, drawing on the work of Sadler (1989) we emphasized with the project teachers the importance of helping students to develop self-assessment skills. In developing self-assessment skills the most difficult task is to get students to think of their work in terms of a set of goals, and of the criteria for the quality implied. Once they do so they begin to develop an overview of their work so that it becomes possible for them to manage and control it for themselves. One teacher reported on the use of both self and peer-assessment of homework:

> We regularly do peer marking – I find this very helpful indeed. A lot of misconceptions come to the fore and we then discuss these as we are going over the homework. I then go over the peer marking and talk to pupils individually as I go round the room. Pupils regularly read their own work or another pupil's as a matter of course. This has made them realise how important it is to write clearly. Previously I would have said that I could not read their work – their peers saying they cannot read the writing has more of an impact. (Rose, Brownfields School)

Peer work appears to have three principle benefits. First, the interchange can be in the language that students themselves would naturally use. Second, students appear to gain greater insight into the topic by taking the role of teachers and examiners of others. Third, students will often pretend they have understood an explanation from a teacher when they have not. Sometimes this will be because they do not wish to appear stupid, while at other times this will be because the students do not want to monopolize the teacher's limited time. In contrast, with their peers they keep on asking for explanation until they have understood. Peer-assessment is therefore not just a 'work-around' for busy teachers – it can lead to higher quality learning than would be possible with one teacher for every student.

Many of the teachers have implemented self and peer-assessment in devising new ways of helping students to prepare for examinations. The problem being tackled was described as follows (the term 'revision' here denotes the activity of reviewing one's work as a preparation for a test):

> They did not mention any of the reviewing strategies we had discussed in class. When questioned more closely it was clear that many spent their time using very passive revision techniques. They would read over their work, doing very little in the way of active revision or reviewing of their work. (Tom, Riverside School)

Another teacher describes how he started to change this situation:

> One technique has been to put the students into small groups and give each student a small part of the unit to explain to their colleagues. They are given a few minutes preparation time, a few hints, and use of their exercise books. Then each student explains their chosen subject to the rest of their group. Following the explanation, each of the other students then gives the speaker a 'traffic light' mark – green means it was explained better than they could have done so themselves. Amber means it was explained at about the level they would have been able to do, and red means that they feel it was not explained as well as they feel they could have explained it. (Philip, Century Island School)

The idea of using the 'traffic lights' icons, which serve as a simple means of communication of students' judgements about their understanding, spread rapidly to the other teachers and schools in the project. One advantage of traffic lighting is that a teacher can identify at a glance the main learning difficulties that have arisen, without lengthy interrogation of each student individually. However, it should be noted that the students' responses are not comparable – boys often gave themselves a green, while girls with a similar level of understanding gave themselves an amber. The major impact of the traffic lighting was to help students see that they were learning something and making progress, thus contributing to a view of ability as incremental rather than fixed (Dweck, 1986). Traffic lighting also facilitated communication between students.

The aftermath of tests can also be an occasion for formative work. Several teachers initiated peer marking of test papers. Some found this particularly useful if the students were required first to formulate a mark scheme – an exercise that focuses attention on criteria of quality relevant to their productions. Another idea that arose from the research literature was to ask students to set test questions (Foos, Mora and Tkacz, 1994; King, 1995). This idea was taken up by several KMOFAP teachers, and several found it helpful because they could see that pupils had to think about what makes a good question for a test and in doing so had to clarify their understanding of the subject material.

Thus these teachers have been involving students in the setting of test questions, in learning how to manage their own systematic preparation for a summative test, and in the marking of test productions. Such initiatives have shown that in place of the usual separation of summative from formative work, there can be a more positive relationship – of synergy rather than tension.

The changes initiated by the focus on self and peer-assessment may be summarized as follows:

- students have been learning to assess their own and one another's work in the light of the purposes, and in so doing have developed criteria for judging its quality;
- students have started to develop the habits and skills of collaboration in learning;
- both teachers and students have come to see that tests can play a positive part in reviewing learning ;
- students have become participants, rather than victims, in the testing process.

Implications for pedagogy

Developing formative assessment was not just a process of bolting on some techniques to teachers' classroom practice, but instead involved substantial changes of the 'standard operating procedure' of classrooms. These changes were most marked in the teacher's role, the student's role, the teacher's pedagogical content knowledge, and theories of learning and the nature of the subject. Each of these is discussed below in turn.

The teacher's role

At the beginning of the project, many of the teachers were convinced of the desirability of the changes we were suggesting, but saw involving the students in their learning as entailing a loss of control for the teacher. However, over the course of the project, these same changes came to be viewed by the teachers not as a loss of control, but as a sharing of responsibility for learning with the learners. Many of the teachers realized that they had been trying to do the learners' learning for them.

> *What formative assessment has done for me is made me focus less on myself but more on the children. I have had the confidence to empower the students to take it forward.* (Robert, Two Bishops' School)

The student's role

The perception of our teachers, as reported above, is that their students have changed role, from being passive recipients of knowledge to being active learners who can take responsibility for, and manage, their own learning. One teacher reported:

> *They feel that the pressure to succeed in tests is being replaced by the need to understand the work that has been covered and the test is just an assessment along the way of what needs more work and what seems to be fine. They have commented on the fact that they think I am more interested in the general way to get to an answer than a specific solution, and when Clare [a researcher] interviewed them they decided this was so that they could apply their understanding in a wider sense.* (Belinda, Cornbury Estate School)

Pedagogical content knowledge

Although many of the strategies we have described above are generic, and would have some role in almost any classroom at one time or another, it became apparent that generic pedagogical skills could only go so far. As teachers became more thoughtful about the questions they asked and how they responded to students' answers, it was clear that effective classroom questioning depended crucially on the quality of the questions used, and that selecting or devising good questions required a very high level of understanding of the subject matter. A high level of subject knowledge was also important in interpreting the students' responses to questions in terms of learning needs (rather than just whether the answer was correct or not).

In this context, it should be noted that this kind of knowledge (called pedagogical content knowledge by Shulman, 1986) is not the same as traditional views of subject knowledge. In fact, a study of primary school teachers (Askew *et al.*, 1997) found no relationship between learners' progress in mathematics and their teachers' level of qualification in mathematics, but a strong positive correlation with their pedagogical content knowledge. This suggests that it is important to think of the relationship between the teacher and the subject matter as a two-way relationship, in that the teacher's capacity to explore and reinterpret the subject matter is important for effective pedagogy.

Theories of learning and the nature of the subject

A year after starting our work with mathematics and science teachers, we extended the project to include teachers of English, which has strengthened our view that the subject disciplines create strong differences between both the identities of teachers and the conduct of learning work in their classes. One clear difference between the teaching of English and the teaching of mathematics and science is that in the latter there is a body of subject matter that teachers tend to regard as giving the subject unique and objectively defined aims. It is possible to 'deliver' the subject matter rather than to help students to learn it with understanding, and even where help with understanding is given priority, it is help that is designed to ensure that every student achieve the 'correct' conceptual goal.

In contrast, in the teaching of writing, there is very little to 'deliver' (except in the case of those teachers who focus only on the mechanics of grammar, spelling and punctuation), and there is no single goal appropriate for all. Thus most teachers of English are naturally more accustomed to giving individual feedback to help all students to improve the quality of their individual efforts at written communication. There is a vast range of types of quality writing – the goal can be any point in a whole horizon rather than one particular point. These inter-subject differences might be less sharp if the aims of the teaching were to shift: for example, open-ended investigations in mathematics or science, or critical study of the social and ethical consequences of scientific discoveries are activities that have more in common with the production of personal writing or critical appreciation in English.

It is also relevant that many teachers of English, at least at high-school level, are themselves writers, and students themselves have more direct interaction with the 'subject', through their own reading and writing, than they do with, say, science. Nevertheless, while teachers might naturally use more feedback than many of their science colleagues, the quality of the feedback that they provide still needs careful, often radical, development.

One of the key outcomes of this project has thus been that teachers of very different subjects (i.e. mathematics and science on the one hand, and English on the other) have come to understand that they have much to learn from practices that are common in other subjects.

Implications for leadership and management

While most of the teachers in the project made substantial changes in their practice, the reasons for wanting to change varied widely. For some teachers it was the promise of improved test and examination results that was most important, while for others the possibility of teaching in a style more aligned with their personal beliefs about learning was paramount. Teachers also followed very different trajectories of change. Some teachers put most effort into changing their own performance as teachers, concentrating on improving their questioning and the way they gave feedback to learners. Others focused on student peer and self-assessment, partly to help the students become independent learners, but also to provide the students with the skills of self-diagnosis that mean that they could ask for the teacher's help in a more specific way.

Given this, we have been strengthened in our belief that there can be no magic recipe for improving classroom practice. Each teacher does have to find for her or himself ways in which the broad strategies described here can be put into practice. However, there are several themes that we think were important in the success of the KMOFAP (Lee, 2001).

- *Evidence*. While all schools are under pressure to improve the achievement of their students, not all the ways that have been suggested as routes to school improvement have such compelling research evidence in their support as does formative assessment. In the early stages, this was important because many of the teachers were more concerned with improving test and examination results than with improving the quality of learning. We are not, of course, suggesting that members of senior management teams need to become familiar with all the research evidence on school improvement. However, it is important that staff are aware that the development of formative assessment is much more than 'this year's new idea'.
- *Ideas*. Although we began by telling the teachers that there was no 'package' that we wanted them to implement, the use of some simple techniques (such as traffic lighting) that could be implemented in a straightforward way seemed to be important in getting teachers started. Once teachers get beyond a view that their own subject faces unique difficulties, they can pick up ideas from other subjects that can be adapted for their own subject (the idea of traffic lights was introduced to the project by a history teacher). There are many ways this could be done. One of the most effective is to create an assessment working group of teachers with differing subject-specific expertise. Each member of the group introduces a technique they have tried out for promoting formative assessment, and then each member of the group has to find a way that the technique could be used in their specialism. This process quickly generates a large number of techniques that can then be tried out.
- *Support*. Having 'put a toe in the water', the opportunity to discuss their own experiences with other teachers, and the opportunity to hear of other teachers' experiences with similar ideas, was a crucial part of the stimulus for continuing change. The meetings of the teachers, originally organized by us, were increasingly taken over by them, both in terms of what was discussed, and, later, even in the running of the meetings. School leaders and managers can support this procedure by ensuring that such exchanging of ideas, which can often seem little more than sharing of anecdotes, is not only an acceptable use of teachers' time, but is actually encouraged.

- *Reflection.* As well as general support, the creation of more structured opportunities for reflection on their practice, including writing journals, was an important aspect of the project's work. These journals allowed the teachers to weave together the various techniques into more coherent strategies, but also provided vivid accounts of the work that could be used to encourage other teachers to develop their practice along the same lines. While writing journals will not be appropriate for all settings, it will be important to structure teachers' reflections in some way – after all, simply asking teachers to reflect on their experience is unlikely to be productive. One useful technique is for groups of teachers to 'unpack' actions that are normally undertaken without time for thinking. For example, a group of teachers can profitably spend an hour discussing how to mark half-a-dozen students' books, exploring the assumptions that need to be made about where the student has reached, and what would be appropriate next steps.
- *Time.* Although the classrooms of most of the teachers involved in the project were changed radically, this change was gradual and slow. By halfway through the project, many of the teachers had changed only small details in their practice and although these changes were significant changes for the teachers, the outward appearance was that little had changed. For those wanting a quick fix, it would be tempting to conclude at that point that the intervention was not working, and that something else needed to be done. However, in the second half of the project, the changes were much more radical, and for many of the teachers the various techniques that they had adopted cohered to form a unified approach to formative assessment. If schools are serious about developing formative assessment, it must not be squeezed out by other initiatives, and school leadership teams need to send clear messages that this will be a priority for the long term.
- *Freedom.* In framing their 'action plans' for what they wanted to change in their practice, many of the teachers felt constrained by school policies on assessment. For example, while reducing the salience of grades and marks (or abandoning their use completely for classwork and homework) was felt to be desirable by most teachers, they believed that such a step would not be allowed by the senior management of their schools. Only a quarter of the teachers (6 out of 24) included comment-only marking in their action plans, and although half the teachers (12 out of 24) had moved towards comment-only marking of classwork and homework by the end of the project, it is clear that school policies acted to constrain innovation. School leaders have a role in not only allowing such innovations, but also in creating an environment where teachers' ideas about how to improve things are actively encouraged – if not actually required.

Conclusion

The changes in practice we have described here go well beyond what is generally connoted by the term 'assessment' – it could well be argued that the kinds of changes involved are really much more to do with pedagogy than with assessment. However, we believe that the most important kinds of assessment are those that happen not just day-to-day or week-to-week but minute-to-minute in classrooms. In this sense, our use of the term 'assessment' to describe these activities represents an attempt to re-appropriate the meaning of the term and to place assessment firmly at the heart of good teaching. Our development work with teachers described above shows that, despite the widespread belief to the contrary, good teaching is not incompatible with securing higher attainment, even when this attainment is measured in the narrow terms of success at public tests and examinations. Students have become more engaged with their learning, and the teachers involved have become more fulfilled professionally. Perhaps it *is* possible to have it all!

REFERENCES

Askew, M., Brown, M.L., Rhodes, V., Johnson, D.C. and Wiliam, D. (1997) *Effective Teachers of Numeracy: Final Report*, London: King's College, School of Education.

Black, P.J. and Wiliam, D. (1998a) 'Assessment and classroom learning', *Assessment in Education: Principles Policy and Practice*, 5 (1), pp. 7–73.

Black, P.J. and Wiliam, D. (1998b) *Inside the Black Box: Raising Standards through Classroom Assessment*, London: King's College, School of Education.

Butler, R. (1988) 'Enhancing and undermining intrinsic motivation: the effects of task-involving and ego-involving evaluation on interest and performance', *British Journal of Educational Psychology*, 58, pp. 1–14.

Dweck, C.S. (1986) 'Motivational processes affecting learning', *American Psychologist*, (Special Issue: *Psychological Science and Education*), 41 (10), pp. 1040–8.

Foos, P.W., Mora, J.J. and Tkacz, S. (1994) 'Student study techniques and the generation effect', *Journal of Educational Psychology*, 86 (4), pp. 567–76.

King, A. (1995) 'Inquiring minds really do want to know – using questioning to teach critical thinking', *Teaching of Psychology*, 22 (1), pp. 13–17.

Lee, C. (2001) 'The KMOFAP project: studying changes in the practice of two teachers', paper presented at the British Educational Research Association 27th annual conference, University of Leeds, September.

Rowe, M.B. (1986) 'Wait-time: slowing down may be a way of speeding up!', *Journal of Teacher Education*, 37 (January–February), pp. 43–50.

Sadler, D.R. (1989) 'Formative assessment and the design of instructional systems', *Instructional Science*, 18, pp. 145–65.

Shulman, L. (1986) 'Those who understand: knowledge growth in teaching', *Educational Researcher*, 15 (1), pp. 4–14.

Wiliam, D. and Lee, C. (2001) 'Teachers developing assessment for learning: impact on student achievement', paper presented at the British Educational Research Association 27th annual conference, University of Leeds, September.

CHAPTER 41

Learning and teaching in the intelligent school

BARBARA MacGILCHRIST

© Barbara MacGilchrist 2003

If I had one wish for all our institutions, and the institution called school in particular, it is that we dedicate ourselves to allowing them to be what they would naturally become, which is human communities, not machines. Living beings who continually ask the questions: Why am I here? What is going on in my world? How might I and we best contribute?

(SENGE, 2000A, P. 58)

Senge's wish is premised on his argument (Senge, 2000b) that there is an urgent need for schools, and therefore the education system as a whole, to move from a nineteenth-century industrial model of learning and teaching to an organic model that reflects what we know about living systems. Unlike the industrial assembly-line model, which is exemplified by conformity, control, a fragmented curriculum and a standardized product, living systems evolve of their own accord and are 'composed fundamentally of relationships and the interrelatedness of subject matter' (ibid., p. 44). Senge argues that 'By continuing to prop up the industrial-age concept of schools through teacher-centred instruction, learning as memorizing, and extrinsic control, we are preparing students for a world that is ceasing to exist' (ibid., p. 51).

Senge believes that the way to combat this is to organize schools around an appreciation of living systems. He argues (ibid., p. 56) that in such schools: The learning process would come alive. It would:

- *become learner-centred learning rather than teacher-centred learning;*
- *encourage variety, not homogeneity – embracing multiple intelligences and diverse learning styles; and*
- *understand a world of interdependency and change, rather than memorizing facts and striving for right answers* (p. 55).

Underpinning Senge's argument is an emphasis on the need for schools to lay the essential foundations of lifelong learning to enable the next generation to embrace the challenges, opportunities and uncertainties of the twenty-first century. The exponential pace of change in information communication technologies and the related explosion in the growth of and accessibility to knowledge add much weight to Senge's argument. The events of 11 September 2001 in the USA provide an even greater sense of urgency for schools to become the kind of human communities that Senge envisages.

How can this be achieved? What are the implications for learning and teaching? In turn, what are the implications for school leaders? The purpose of this chapter is to attempt to answer these questions. It takes a fresh look at schools as organizations that reflects their dynamic and their organic nature. It draws on Gardner's notion (1983) of multiple intelligence and on recent thinking about the nature of institutions to offer a new way of looking at schools as living systems.[1]

The intelligent school

Schools that create a sense of community in which the rights, responsibilities and the needs of learners are at the heart of the enterprise appear to be using, in combination, at least nine intelligences. The way in which the term 'intelligence' is used is not straightforward because it is not easily observable and is even harder to measure. It concerns a range of collective capacities that school leaders can foster and develop to maximize the effectiveness of the organization. It involves the use of wisdom, insight, intuition and experience, as well as knowledge, skills and understanding. These intelligences provide something analogous to the fuel, water and oil in a car. They all have discreet functions but, for their success, need to work together. In this way the collective or 'corporate intelligence' of a school becomes greater that the sum of the parts. Table 41.1 identifies the nine intelligences and provides a summary of their characteristics.

For the purpose of this chapter, I intend to focus in particular on the last three intelligences in Table 41.1 The reason for this is that in the literature on school leadership, management and improvement much has been written about the first six kinds of intelligence. Much less has been written about the last three. Yet I would argue that these three are of central importance if schools are to become human communities.

Emotional intelligence

Emotional intelligence is concerned with a school's capacity to allow the feelings of both pupils and staff to be owned, expressed and respected. Goleman (1999. p. 317) describes emotional intelligence, or EQ as it has come to be known, as 'the capacity for recognising our own feelings and those of others, for motivating ourselves, and for managing emotions well in ourselves and in our relationships'. This definition is not dissimilar to Gardner's notion (1983) of intrapersonal and interpersonal intelligence. Goleman argues that EQ is distinct from, but complementary to, academic intelligence (IQ) and that EQ is a basic requirement for the effective use of IQ and for the education of young people in the future. He argues that we need to 'rethink the notion of the "basics" in education: Emotional Intelligence is now as crucial to our children's future as the standard academic fare' (Goleman, 1999, p. 313).

Table 41.1 *The corporate intelligence of the intelligent school*

1	Contextual intelligence	<ul><li>understands the relationship between the school and the wider community</li><li>able to read internal and external context</li><li>is flexible and adaptable</li><li>knows no 'quick fixes'</li></ul>
2	Strategic intelligence	<ul><li>uses contextual intelligence to establish clear goals</li><li>establishes shared aims and purposes</li><li>puts vision into practice through planned improvements</li></ul>
3	Academic intelligence	<ul><li>emphasizes achievement and scholarship</li><li>values pupils' engagement in and contribution to learning</li><li>values and promotes teachers' learning</li><li>encourages the 'can do' factor</li></ul>
4	Reflective intelligence	<ul><li>monitors and evaluates the work of the school</li><li>uses data to judge effectiveness and plan improvement</li><li>uses data to reflect, in particular, on pupils' progress and achievement</li></ul>
5	Pedagogical intelligence	<ul><li>emphasizes learning about pupils' learning</li><li>ensures learning and teaching are regularly examined and developed</li><li>challenges orthodoxies</li></ul>
6	Collegial intelligence	<ul><li>views the staff as learners</li><li>improves practice in the classroom through teachers working together</li></ul>
7	Emotional intelligence	<ul><li>values expression of feelings</li><li>understands others and how to work cooperatively</li><li>enables individuals to understand themselves</li><li>encourages motivation, persistence and understands failure</li></ul>
8	Spiritual intelligence	<ul><li>has compassion</li><li>values the development and contribution of all members of the school and its community</li><li>creates space to reflect on ultimate issues</li></ul>
9	Ethical intelligence	<ul><li>has clear values and beliefs</li><li>has a sense of moral purpose and principle</li><li>is committed to access and entitlement for all</li><li>has high but not complacent self-esteem</li></ul>

Source: MacGilchrist, Myers and Reed, 1997.

Drawing on Salovey and Mayer's theory (1990) of emotional intelligence, Goleman (1999, p. 318) has adapted their model to help understand how the characteristics of EQ impact on the effectiveness of organization. His adaptation includes these five basic emotional and social competencies:

> *Self-awareness: Knowing what we are feeling in the moment, and using those preferences to guide our decision-making; having a realistic assessment of our own abilities and a well-grounded sense of self-confidence.*

Self-regulation: Handling our emotions so that they facilitate rather than interfere with the task at hand; being conscientious and delaying gratification to pursue goals; recovering well from emotional distress.

Motivation: Using our deepest preferences to move and guide us towards our goals, to help us take initiative and strive to improve, and to persevere in the face of setbacks and frustrations.

Empathy: Sensing what people are feeling, being able to take their perspective, and cultivating rapport and attunement with a broad diversity of people.

Social skills: Handling emotions in relationships well and accurately reading social situations and networks; interacting smoothly; using these skills to persuade and lead, negotiate and settle disputes, for cooperation and teamwork.

All these aspects have significant implications for the content and processes of learning and teaching. Goleman (1996) has defined them as 'emotional literacy' which can be taught and must not be left to chance. He argues (1998) that EQ is a vital capacity for learning and a key characteristic of effective leadership. This means that the model provided by teachers and leaders is important: 'An emotionally intelligent organization needs to come to terms with any disparities between the values it proclaims and those it lives' (Goleman, 1999, p. 281).

Spiritual intelligence

Spiritual intelligence is ephemeral in nature. Burns and Lamont (1995, p. xiii) describe spirituality as:

a source of creativity open to us all. It brings that quality of aliveness which sparks inquiry, ideas, observations, insights, empathy, artistic expression, earnest endeavour and playfulness. It opens us to life and to each other. Spirituality is a thread that runs through our life, bringing hope, compassion, thankfulness, courage, peace and a sense of purpose and meaning to the everyday, while reaching beyond the immediate world of the visible and tangible. It drives us to seek and stay true to values not ruled by material success.

Zohar and Marshall (2001, pp. 3–4) argue that there is emerging scientific data to indicate that as well as IQ and EQ, there is a third kind of intelligence in the form of spiritual intelligence (SQ):

SQ is the intelligence with which we address and solve problems of meaning and value, the intelligence in which we can place our actions and our lives in a wider, richer, meaning-giving context, the intelligence with which we can assess that one course of action or one life-path is more meaningful than another.

Zohar and Marshall go on to say that in their view 'SQ is the necessary foundation for the effective function of both IQ and EQ. It is our ultimate intelligence' (ibid., p. 4); 'it is a third kind of thinking that places actions and experiences in a larger context of meaning and value' (ibid., p. 87). Schools with a developed sense of spiritual intelligence seek to know themselves at a deep level. They are the kind of schools that ask the sorts of questions Senge identified in the opening quotation in their exploration of fundamental issues. SQ require schools to be deeply honest and aware of themselves and – as Zohar and Marshall argue – 'to stand up to what they believe in'.

Spiritual intelligence is characterized by a fundamental valuing of the lives and development of all members of a school community. Everyone is seen to matter and to have something to contribute. The children in particular are helped to 'develop a deeper understanding of their place in the world' (Jubis, 2001, p. 14). This intelligence also recognizes the need to balance the busy life of a school community with times of peace and an opportunity to be in touch with ultimate issues. Fisher (1999, p. 65) argues for the need for schools to create a community of philosophical enquiry. Such enquiry leads to:

> *a focus on the underlying concepts of daily experience such as time, space, truth and beauty. As children probe these concepts they learn how to ask relevant questions, detect assumptions, recognise faulty reasoning and gain a sense of competency in their ability to make sense of the world.*

SQ values that in our experience which is neither tangible nor measurable. It concerns the capacity to enable profound learning to occur.

Ethical intelligence

Ethical intelligence recognizes the importance of pupils' rights and of the pupil voice and therefore the need to involve pupils in decisions about their own learning.

Rudduck, Chaplain and Wallace (1996, pp. 177–8) found that 'pupils are urging us to review some of the assumptions and expectations that serve to hold habitual ways of teaching in place – we have to take seriously young pupils' accounts, and evaluations of teachers and learning and schooling'. Cambron-McCabe (2000, p. 276) reminds us that 'teaching is a moral undertaking'. It is important therefore for teachers to think about how they teach and the aims, purposes and underlying values and moral principles of their teaching:

> *Through reflective questioning the teacher can conscientiously engage with moral dimensions of schooling connected to his or her relationship with the students and their access to knowledge ... Our choice of teaching methods and school designs is an ethical decision.*
> (Ibid., pp. 277–8)

This intelligence incorporates the clear statement of values and beliefs covered in a school's aims statement. It concerns the way a school conveys its moral purpose and principles such as justice, equity and inclusivity. It is characterized by a concern to ensure access for all pupils to a broad and balanced curriculum and a concern about the distribution and use of resources. The concept of entitlement underpins this intelligence. This means that support for learning is highly valued and there is an understanding about the nature of learners and what learners need and want.

Schools with ethical intelligence have high self-esteem as an organization – which is not the same as complacency. They rarely feel totally satisfied about what they are doing and usually have ideas about how they can do even better next time. Lightfoot (1983, p. 130) found that: 'This more modest orientation towards goodness does not rest on absolute or discrete qualities of excellence and perfection, but on views of institutions that anticipate change, conflict and imperfection'.

Leading the intelligent school

All nine intelligences have at least three important implications for school leaders: (i) they are interdependent, (ii) they have maximum impact when used in combination, and (iii) they each have the potential to be developed and improved. The challenge for school leaders therefore is to establish a collective understanding of the range of intelligences being used and identify those that need to be developed further.

The three intelligences that have been the particular focus here have specific implications for school leadership and, indeed, the way schools are managed. McMaster (1995) suggests that, as a species, we are still bound up in a world view that is mechanistic, reductionist and essentially rational. Many writers, particularly in the fields of organizational transformation and the new sciences (Wheatley, 1992; Senge, 1993; Capra, 1996) suggest that the views that have been held of how the world works since Descartes and Newton are changing. This shift is referred to variously as the postmodern view, postindustrialism, the age of information, the ecological paradigm. What these writers suggest is that a renewed sense and understanding of the interconnections of all life is developing. The global impact of the events of 11 September 2001 is a classic example of the interconnectedness of the world in which we live.

Providing the kind of leadership that recognizes the concept of interdependence and fosters and develops learning and teaching in the context of emotional, spiritual and ethical intelligence requires a move away from currently held views about the characteristics of effective leadership. It requires a view and an exercise of leadership that is far removed from a technicist, competency-based model of school leadership. It is the kind of leadership that, through the development of these three intelligences and their application through learning and teaching, creates a human community.

NOTE

1 This chapter draws on the last part of MacGilchrist, Myers and Reed (1997), with kind permission of Paul Chapman Publishing.

REFERENCES

Burns, S. and Lamont, G. (1995) *Values and Visions, Handbook for Spiritual Development and Global Awareness*, London: Hodder & Stoughton.

Cambron-McCabe, N. (2000) 'Schooling as an ethical endeavour' in Senge, P. (ed.) *Schools That Learn*, London: Nicholas Brealey Publishing.

Capra, F. (1996) *The Web of Life*, London: Harper Collins.

Fisher, R. (1999) 'Philosophy for children: how philosophical enquiry can foster values education in schools' in Leach, J. and Moon, B. (eds) *Learners and Pedagogy*, London: Paul Chapman Publishing/Open University.

Gardner, H. (1983) *Frames of Mind: the Theory of Multiple Intelligences*, New York: Basic Books.

Goleman, D. (1996) *Emotional Intelligence*, London: Bloomsbury.

Goleman, D. (1998) 'What makes a leader', *Harvard Business Review*, Nov./Dec., pp. 93–102.

Goleman, D. (1999) *Working with Emotional Intelligence*, London: Bloomsbury.

Jubis, R. (2001) 'A crisis of meaning', *The 21st Century Learning Initiative Journal*, May, pp. 13–14.

Lightfoot, S.L. (1983) *The Good High School: Portraits of Character and Culture*, New York: Basic Books.

MacGilchrist, B., Myers, K. and Reed, J. (1997) *The Intelligent School*, London: Paul Chapman Publishing.

McMaster, M. (1995) *The Intelligent Advantage: Organising for Complexity*, Knowledge Based Development Co. Ltd.

Rudduck, J., Chaplain , R. and Wallace, G. (1996) *School Improvement. What Can Pupils Tell Us?* London: David Fulton Publishing.

Salovey, P. and Mayer, J.D. (1990) 'Emotional Intelligences', *Imagination, Cognition and Personality*, 9, pp. 185–211.

Senge, P.M. (1993) *The Fifth Discipline: The Art and Practice of the Learning Organisation*, London: Century Business.

Senge, P.M. (2000a) 'Systems change in education', *Reflections*, 1 (3), p. 58.

Senge, P.M. (2000b) *Schools that Learn*, London: Nicholas Brealey Publishing.

Wheatley, M.J. (1992) *Leadership and the New Science: Learning About Organisations from an Orderly Universe*, San Francisco: Berrett-Koehler.

Zohar, D. and Marshall, I. (2001) *Spiritual Intelligence – The Ultimate Intelligence*, London: Bloomsbury.

6

CHAPTER 42

Is there impact beyond the commercial breaks?

LEN BARTON

The shocking events in New York in September 2001 have certainly had an effect on my thinking concerning both my personal and professional values, priorities and vision. At a meeting with primary head teachers we shared some of our feelings and it was quite clear that the impact had affected people in a variety of ways. This chapter presents some of the key features of the context within which we work in education and then raises some questions and issues as a stimulus for further reflection and engagement. The focus is on the events in New York, the question of inclusive education and the position of headteachers in terms of their leadership.

The context

It is important to remind ourselves and more thoroughly understand the context in which educational policy making, implementation and change has been taking place during the past two decades. It has been one in which extensive and explicit forms of government intervention have been focused on changing the governance, funding, process and outcomes of educational provision and practice. This intervention has left no aspect of education untouched, even though the impact on particular schools and teachers has been experienced in different ways (Tomlinson, 2001a; Coffey, 2001; Furlong *et al.*, 2000).

In an analysis of the role of the impact of market principles on schools, which are increasingly viewed as functioning as small businesses, Gewirtz and Ball (2000, p. 256) argue that a new managerialism has emerged:

> *The new management discourse in education emphasises the instrumental purposes of schooling – raising standards and performance measured by examination results, level of attendance and school leaver destination – and is frequently articulated within a lexicon of enterprise, excellence, quality and effectiveness.*

The public government discourse has been centred on encouraging schools to be more effective, efficient and accountable, especially in relation to the raising of standards and quality performance within and between schools. Increasing competition, selection and specialization, supported by new forms of inspection, publishing of league tables and performance-related pay for senior managers, combine to legitimate such developments. In this climate the extent to which staff have a sense of the ownership of change – of being proactive rather than fundamentally reactive – is a crucial issue.

One of the difficulties headteachers and teachers face is the number, speed and cumulative impact of policy changes. Another is the contradictory nature of government policies which, for example, simultaneously advocate inclusive education and increasing competition, league tables and assessment-led learning.

Inclusion

Inclusive education is concerned with the quest for equity, social justice, participation and the realization of citizenship. It is about the removal of barriers of discrimination and oppression and it is about the well being of all learners, including disabled individuals. It is based on a positive view of difference in which pupil diversity is viewed as a resource. Priority is given to the pursuit of change, with a strong emphasis on the importance of learning to live with one another and recognize our common humanity.

Inclusive education is not about containment, assimilation or accommodation. It is not about placing particular pupils in unchanged, under-resourced and unplanned circumstances. It is about the well-being of all learners and providing a culture and practice in which all barriers to participation can be identified and ultimately removed (Booth *et al.*, 2001). This is why Tomlinson (2001b, p. 192) is critical of those aspects of policy making and implementation that contradict inclusive values and practices:

> *In my view, it seems clear that creating competitive markets in education based on parental 'choice' of schools and fuelled by league tables and competition for resources, is totally incompatible with developing an inclusive education system. In England there is now a divided and divisive school system.*

Part of this divisiveness relates to the extent to which pressures of league tables and performance are making it increasingly difficult for some schools to view particular pupils in a favourable light in the context of admissions to the school.

Globalization

Globalization, its development and impact has been the outcome of massive technological changes and political decision making. These capital-led innovations, with an increasing prominence of transnational corporations, have involved national economies being 'turned into an unregulated global market where private speculators and corporations have freeplay. A number of international agreements and organisations have paved the way for this globalisation process' (Brock-Utne, 2001, p. 164). Thus, the ways in which these developments contribute to the legitimation of significant forms of inequalities between societies is a very serious issue.

One of the significant features of globalization is the interdependency of societies in terms of economic and social conditions and relations. Nor is this a relation of equals. In this context schools and educational systems are open to the real pressure of external forces. This includes the repercussions of events taking place in other parts of the world.

Conclusion

In a speech on the events in New York, the British Prime Minister, Tony Blair, contended that: 'One illusion was shattered on September 11: that we can have a good life irrespective of the state of the rest of the world' (O'Mally, 2001). For Brown and Lauder (2001) the events in New York provided them with an opportunity to reflect critically on their own beliefs and values. They powerfully advocated the necessity of recognizing what is important in life but in such a way that goes beyond the period of the commercial breaks following such events. Part of their concern was over the way in which a 'creed of greed' has weakened our appreciation of our common humanity and cooperative interests. The terrible events in New York paradoxically involved some wonderful reactions:

> It was the human traits of friendship, bravery, sorrow, fear and dignity that filled the airwaves and television screens in the aftermath of the attacks. People were not distraught because they had lost a breadwinner, but because they had lost people they loved. Colleagues lost friends, not career rivals.

Hopefully, the belief of Brown and Lauder that such events have led people to reassess the dominant values of society and the way they live their lives will also be a feature of those of us who work in the field of education. Such critical incidents provide an added impetus for exploring the meaning and importance of inclusive education and the sorts of leadership that such an alternative policy and practice requires.

Teacher unions are aware of the challenges that 'terror and war' can have on schools, highlighting issues of prejudice, stereotyping, ignorance and fear (*The Teacher*, 2001). Part of the task of inclusive pedagogy is contributing to the building of citizenship and the promotion of social justice. This process includes removing exclusionary barriers and learning to value positive, respectful forms of interaction and social relationships. In this context leadership excels in a culture of trust, empathy and encouragement. Given, for example, the sheer increase in administrative responsibilities, then the extent to which headteachers have been able to spend time and thought on contributing to the provision of a collegial and supportive ethos within schools is a crucially important issue.

This tension is of particular significance at times in which critical episodes such as the events in New York and their aftermath occur. The following questions highlight some of the leadership issues that can be explored:

- How far have the issues relating to the events in New York raised questions about your vision and priorities?
- How has attention been given to the emotional and psychological needs of staff, including your own?
- In what ways have pupil fears, anxieties and prejudices been addressed?

- To what extent have the events strengthened the importance of a commitment to whole-school policies?
- What are the implications for reconsidering teaching and the content of the curriculum?

Certainly, one of the worrying concerns as a leader is that, as Brown and Lauder (2001) imply, there have been too many commercial breaks since those terrible events.

REFERENCES

Booth, T., Ainscow, M., Black-Hawkins, K., Vaughan, M. and Shaw, L. (2000) *Index For Inclusion*, London: DFES.

Brock-Utne, B. (2001) 'Introduction' in Brock-Utne, B. (ed.) 'Globalisation, language and education', *International Review of Education*, 47 (3 & 4), pp. 163–84 (special issue).

Brown, P. and Lauder, H. (2001) 'Time to end creed of greed', the *Guardian*, 29 October, p. 23.

Coffey, A. (2001) *Education and Social Change*, Buckingham: Open University Press.

Furlong, J., Barton, L., Miles, S., Whiting, C. and Whitty, G. (2000) *Teacher Education in Transition: Refining Professionalism?* Buckingham: Open University Press.

Gerwirtz, S. and Ball, S. (2000) 'From "welfareism" to "new managerialism": shifting discourses of school headship in the education market place', *Discourse* 21 (3), pp. 253–68.

O'Mally, B. (2001) 'Comfort zone and wars', *The Times Education Supplement*, 3 November, pp. 28–9.

The Teacher (2001) 'Children, terror and war', November, pp. 26–7.

Tomlinson, S. (2001a) *Education in a Post-Welfare Society!* Buckingham: Open University Press.

Tomlinson, S. (2001b) 'Sociological perspectives on special and inclusive education', *Support For Learning*, 16 (4), pp. 191–2.

6

PART SEVEN

Achieving and Sustaining Change in Schools

DEAN FINK AND ANDY HARGREAVES

Introduction

DEAN FINK AND ANDY HARGREAVES

Educational change must be easy because virtually every educational jurisdiction in the western world has initiated some form of change. Schools are busily attending to such changes as revised standards for student achievement, mandated testing and accountability measures, altered role descriptions and new forms of school governance. Educational changes that enhance and enrich students' learning however, have proven more problematic (McNeil, 2000; Hargreaves *et al.*, 2001; Fielding, 2001; Sirotnik, 2002). Sustaining such consequential changes over time has presented even greater challenges for educational reformers. Books and articles with titles such as *The Predictable Failure of Educational Reform* (Sarason, 1990), 'Reforming Again and Again and Again' (Cuban, 1990) and *Good Schools/ Real Schools: Why School Reform Doesn't Last* (Fink, 2000) address the difficulty and frustration of sustainability. Part Seven examines these challenges and in particular the role of school leaders in addressing issues of sustainability. The chapters offer change agents an insight into issues of sustainability and put forward strategies to sustain educational changes that enhance students' learning.

First, Andy Hargreaves and Dean Fink look at sustainability through a wide lens. A definition of sustainability is given that is compatible with its origins in ecological thinking and that connects to emerging issues of the knowledge society and the shifting demographics of western societies. This introductory chapter relates leadership to sustainability in terms of leadership of learning, distributive leadership and succession planning.

Michael Fullan advances these themes by exploring the role of principals in a climate of 'large-scale' change. He contends that the concept of the principal as 'instructional leader' has been a valuable, but too narrow a solution. Instead, he argues, the instructional focus must be embedded in a more comprehensive and fundamental set of characteristics, which he calls 'the principal as leader in a culture of change' with the ultimate goal of transformation of the teaching profession. To this end he calls for system-wide efforts at the level of schools, communities and districts, as well as radically more enlightened policies and incentives at the level of the state.

Hugh Mehan, Amanda Datnow and Lea Hubbard look at models for school improvement that are developed by organizations external to the school or district and purchased by these educational jurisdictions and introduced into settings that are quite different from the contexts in which the reforms were developed. When these models fail, blame is often directed at the school – its leaders and teachers. Mehan and colleagues conclude that sustainable educational changes do not rise or fall at the school level exclusively, but rather that forces at the state level, in districts, design teams, the school and classrooms all interact to shape the longevity of reform. They maintain that educators in schools, policy makers in districts and states, and personnel in design teams 'co-construct' reform success or failure.

Ann Lieberman and Diane Wood provide an alternative to top-down mandated large-scale reform with its focus on formal leadership. They argue that networks, such as the highly successful Bay Area Writing Project, provide sufficient evidence that building professional communities that are flexible, open to new learning and sensitive to local contexts can sustain significant change in students' learning over time. While candidly addressing the difficulties of developing and sustaining large-scale networks they conclude, that the democratic and inclusive ways of working, together with a network-like way of organizing, appears to provide teachers not only with opportunities to learn and to lead, but also to gain a professional community. This has made a difference to how teachers think of themselves and how they go about their work.

While the first four chapters in Part Seven examine sustainability of educational change at a macro level, in the concluding chapter, Louise Stoll and Lorna Earl bring the issue of sustainability into the individual school. They suggest that the key to sustainability at the school level is 'internal capacity'. This they define as a quality of people or organizations that allows them routinely to learn from the world around them and apply their learning to new and sometimes novel situations so that they continue on a path towards their goals, even though the context is ever-changing. The authors show that sustaining change in a school is the result of a complex combination of many internal and external factors that requires a judicious mix of formal and informal leadership.

The chapters collectively represent an approach to sustainability that closely parallels ecologists' understanding of the concept and that takes the meaning of sustainability far beyond the simple idea of maintainability of educational change over time – good or bad, right or wrong. For Capra (1997), sustainable natural and human communities are open to new influences and learning – flexible, diverse, non-linear, adaptable to changing contexts, and dependent on partnerships. Each community therefore must be looked at holistically rather than in terms of its parts. These chapters therefore demonstrate how the principle of sustainability is an antidote to superficial, simplistic reform, not a way of perpetuating it.

REFERENCES

Capra, F. (1997) *The Web of Life: A New Synthesis of Mind and Matter*, London: Harper Collins.

Cuban, L. (1990) 'Reforming again and again and again', *Educational Researcher*, 19 (1), pp. 2–13.

Fielding, M. (ed.) (2001) *Taking Education Really Seriously: Three Years of Hard Labour*, London: Routledge/Falmer Press.

Fink, D. (2000) *Good Schools/Real Schools: Why School Reform Doesn't Last*, New York: Teachers' College Press.

Hargreaves, A., Earl, L., Moore, S. and Manning S. (2001) *Learning to Change: Teaching Beyond Subjects and Standard*, San Francisco: Jossey-Bass.

McNeil, L. (2000) 'Creating new inequalities', *Phi Delta Kappan*, 81 (10), pp. 729–34.

Sarason, S. (1990) *The Predictable Failure of Educational Reform*, San Francisco: Jossey-Bass.

Sirotnik, K. (2002) 'Promoting responsible accountability in schools and education', *Phi Delta Kappan*, 83 (9), pp. 662–73.

CHAPTER 43

Sustaining leadership

ANDY HARGREAVES AND DEAN FINK

In a survey of his research and writing on educational change over the past 25 years, Fullan (1998) described three eras of emphasis in educational change. The literature of the 1970s addressed the few successes and many failures of large-scale reform in the 1960s and attempted to understand why change does or does not occur in practice (Sarason, 1971; Fullan, 1982; Fullan, 1991; McLaughlin, 1990; Louis and Miles, 1990). This 'implementation decade' evolved into the 'meaning decade' in which scholars pursued a deeper comprehension of the change process from the perspective of 'every day participants' (Fullan, 1998, p. 219). By the 1990s, large-scale radical reform throughout the western world had motivated academics to develop insights into the 'change capacity' of schools and school systems (Fullan, 1993, 1999; Hargreaves, 1994; Hopkins, Aincow and West, 1994; Stoll and Fink, 1996; Stoll, 1999). Inspired by literatures from other fields, scholars have looked at educational issues using different lenses, such as chaos theory (Fullan, 1993; Wallace and Pocklington, 2002), the 'emotions' of educational change (Hargreaves, 1998), micro-politics (Blasé, 1998), culture (Deal and Kennedy, 1983; Hargreaves, 1994; Stoll and Fink, 1996) and moral purpose (Sergiovanni, 1992, 2000). By the middle and late 1990s, change researchers began to focus their energies on how to get small-scale examples of successful improvement to spread around wider systems (Elmore, 1995), and how to make large-scale reform endure, once the initial impetus for change and pressure to comply has passed. In this respect, researchers have begun to examine the sustainability of educational change over time. To continue Fullan's pattern, the first decade of the twenty-first century therefore might well be called the 'decade of sustainability'.

This chapter discusses the deeper meaning of sustainability and how contemporary efforts to sustain change over time in policy and practice do or do not relate to and express the ecological origins and ideas of the concept. We contend that the demands of the emerging knowledge society, along with dramatic demographic changes in society and also in teaching and leadership, require different ways of thinking about human and natural systems than conventional approaches to planned change have allowed. We connect this discussion of sustainability to the leadership literature in education and outline different interrelated principles that underpin the ideas and practices of 'sustaining leadership'. Our chapter draws on a five-year programme of school improvement involving six secondary schools in Ontario, Canada. We will illustrate our analysis of sustainability, leadership and improvement by drawing on three sets of positive and negative examples in our research on leadership – leadership of learning, distributed leadership, and leadership succession.

For many years, educational change theorists and change agents have been concerned with the problem of how to move beyond the implementation phase of change – when new ideas and practices are tried for the first time – to the institutionalization phase – when new practices are integrated effortlessly into teachers' repertoires, and affect many teachers, not just a few (Stiegelbauer and Anderson, 1992). 'Institutionalization means a change is taken as a normal, taken for granted part of organizational life; and has unquestioned resources of time, personnel and money available' (Miles, 1998, p. 59). Many long-standing practices, such as the graded school, the compartmentalized, hierarchical, bureaucratized secondary school, tracking or streaming according to students' abilities, and didactic, teacher-centred teaching, are examples of policies and practices that have been institutionalized over long periods of time and that have become part of the 'grammar' of schooling (Tyack and Tobin, 1994). The persistence of this grammar and of everyone's ideas of how schools should really work as institutions has repeatedly made it exceptionally difficult to institutionalize other changes, innovations and reforms that challenge the grammar or that imply a different and deviant institutional appearance and way of operating for schooling (Meyer and Rowan, 1977).

Innovations that challenge the traditional grammar of schooling often arouse intense enthusiasm. They prosper and flourish in well-supported pilot projects, in specially staffed and charismatically led schools, or among an atypical minority of teachers and schools whose teaching careers and identities are characterized by risk and change (Fletcher, Caron and Williams, 1985; Smith *et al.*, 1987; Riley, 1998; Fink, 2000a). But, typically, innovations fade, lighthouse schools lose their lustre and attempts to spread initiatives across a wider more sceptical system – to scale them up – meet with little success (Elmore, 1995). Even those few innovative settings that survive often serve as outlier exceptions – giving the system a safety valve where all its most critical and questioning educators and their clients can be congregated together in one site (Sarason, 1990; Lortie, 1975).

In the face of the traditional grammar of schooling, and those whose interests its abstract academic orientations repeatedly serve, the vast majority of educational change that deepens learning, and allows everyone to benefit, neither spreads nor lasts. The traditional and long-standing problem of institutionalization is now coming to be understood as an even more complex problem of sustainability. Couching the problem of securing improvement over time in the language of sustainability elevates our understanding of the obstacles to long-lasting change beyond problems of convention, routine, misunderstanding or poor support that are encompassed by the idea of institutionalization, to more complex questions about the priorities and practices of policy makers and administrators who instigate change and reform. Sustainability, in the deeper sense, raises questions about the preoccupation of policy makers with short-term success over long-term improvement, statistical appearances that make policy makers look good and ignore sustained changes that ensure students learn well, and change timelines that address electoral cycles of popularity rather than change cycles of durability

Contemporary discussions of sustainability in educational change in some ways repeat these traditional preoccupations with how to keep change going over time. In doing so, however, they often trivialize the idea of sustainability (Barber, 2001). They reduce it to maintainability – to the question of how to make change last – and add little to the traditional analysis of institutionalization.

The meaning of sustainability

Sustainability is more than a temporal matter. It concerns more than a change's life and death. In line with its origins in the Brundtland Commission on the environment, sustainability is also a spatial issue. As we have argued elsewhere: 'Sustainability does not simply mean whether something can last. It addresses how particular initiatives can be developed without compromising the development of others in the surrounding environment, now and in the future' (Hargreaves and Fink, 2000, p. 32).

Specifically, this implies several things. First, sustainable improvement is enduring, not evanescent. It does not put its investment dollars in the high-profile launch of an initiative, then withdraw them when the glamour has gone. Sustainable improvement demands committed relationships, not fleeting infatuations. It is change for keeps, and change for good. Sustainable improvement contributes to the growth and the good of everyone, instead of fostering the fortunes of the few at the expense of the rest. It does not channel water to prosperous villages while their poorer neighbours die of thirst. Neither does it promote model schools, magnet schools, or schools with special emphases that raid scarce resources from the rest.

Second, sustainable improvement develops and draws on resources and support at a rate than can match the pace of change. It does not let change outrun its resource base and deplete the reserves that are needed by others. Sustainable policies do not lavish resources on computer hardware when long-term spending commitments cannot support continuing maintenance or updates in software. Supporters of sustainability do not make Easter Islands of educational change, where wanton years of plenty and beliefs that the trees will last for ever suddenly lead to barren plains of famine and drought. As Machiavelli (1532, p. 88) warned in *The Prince*, 'it is a common defect in men not to consider in good weather the possibility of a tempest'. In this respect, sustainable educational policies do not squander all the resources on pilot projects, leaving little for everybody else; or invest improvement funds in coordinators who disappear once the money has dried up. Sustainable improvement requires investment in building long-term capacity for improvement, such as the development of teachers' skills, which will stay with them for ever, long after the project money has gone (Stoll, 1999).

Last, promoters of sustainability cultivate and recreate an educational environment or ecosystem that possesses the capacity to stimulate ongoing improvement on a broad front. They enable people to adapt to and prosper in their increasingly complex environment. Rational, standardized scientific efficiency is the enemy of healthy and creative diversity. It produces overly simple systems that are too specialized to allow the learning and cross-fertilization that is necessary for healthy development. Excessive specialization also makes species exceptionally vulnerable to parasites and predators – an attack on one member of the species eventually becomes an assault against all.

Standardized reform strategies make school systems less like rich, biodiverse rainforests of cross-fertilizing influence that can achieve sustainable improvement over time, than like regimented coniferous plantations, whose super-efficient ugliness is exceeded only by their limited capacity for mutual influence and their lack of contribution to wider environmental sustainability. The evidence of research that we

7

have undertaken with our colleagues on the long-term impact of educational reform in Ontario is that standardized reform is destroying diversity and seriously endangering the lives and futures of the weakest members of the school system – the poor, the marginalized, those who are learning through a new language and those with special educational needs. Standardization is endangering these students to the point of educational extinction where failure to meet the regimented standards is denying severely disadvantaged students the right to graduate (Hargreaves *et al.*, 2001). Similarly, high-pressure improvements in test results in the short run are being bought at the expense of a long-term recruitment and retention crisis in teaching – since teaching driven by short-term results is not the kind of teaching that teachers want to do (Hargreaves, 2003).

In education, one important addition to this definition of sustainability is that not anything or everything is worth keeping. In education, it matters that what is sustained is what, in terms of teaching and learning, is itself sustaining. To sustain is to keep alive in every sense. Sustenance is nourishment. Sound education, good teaching and learning are inherently sustaining processes. Supporting and maintaining those aspects of teaching and learning that are deep and that endure, that foster sophisticated understanding and lifelong learning for all defines the core of sustainable education. This includes not just knowing what, but knowing why (deep understanding), knowing how (application) and knowing who (building social networks and social capital) (OECD, 2001). Merely maintaining practices that raise test scores or produce easily measurable results does not sustain these deeper aspects of teaching and learning.

To sum up, sustainability in educational change comprises five key and interrelated characteristics:

- improvement that sustains learning, not merely change that alters schooling;
- improvement that endures over time;
- improvement that can be supported by available or achievable resources;
- improvement that does not impact negatively on the surrounding environment of other schools and systems;
- improvement that promotes ecological diversity and capacity throughout the educational and community environment.

Clearly, this means that sustainability raises questions not only about the endurance of educational and organizational change over time, but also about its arrangement and articulation through space. Sustainable improvement, in other words, is a matter of social geography as well as social history.

Sustainability in the knowledge society

At its heart, sustainability is a way of thinking that is at once integrative, holistic and ecological; it is an intellectual paradigm about the complex nature of human and natural systems that is particularly crucial to addressing the complexities of a 'knowledge society' (Drucker, 1993; Castells, 1996; OECD, 2001). Today's knowledge society has three dimensions. First, it comprises an expanded scientific, technical and educational sphere. Second, it involves complex ways of processing and circulating knowledge and information in a service-based economy. Third, it entails basic changes in how corporate organizations function so that they enhance continuous innovation in products and services, by creating systems, teams and cultures that maximize the opportunities for mutual, spontaneous learning. The second and third aspects of the knowledge society depend on having a sophisticated infrastructure of information and communication technology that makes all this learning faster and easier (Hargreaves, 2003). The knowledge society creates enormous economic opportunities, since knowledge goes to the heart of more and more of what we produce and how we produce it. But the 'runaway world' (Giddens, 2000) of the knowledge economy also creates immense social and systemic problems.

Homer-Dixon (2000) argues that our increasingly complex, interdependent and fast-paced world generates a profusion of urgent and unpredictable problems that demand instant and effective responses. Instantaneous and endless stock-market trading and speculation across the globe means that currency crises in Thailand or Argentina can immediately undermine confidence in economies elsewhere. Global warming produced by carbon dioxide on one part of the planet, and the disappearance of rainforests in another, create floods and gales in a third. The frog population is disappearing everywhere and we have no idea why. The world is more interdependent. So are its problems. In the computer age, there are more and more information and data to help people address and respond to these problems, but this information glut, or 'data smog' (Shank, 1997) can itself become part of the problem as it assails us in ever greater quantities with increasing rapidity. In organizations critical to society's economic well-being, their key workers may be smarter and able to work faster, but are less wise and less capable of drawing on experience and institutional memory to influence their judgement.

What the knowledge society needs, says Homer-Dixon (2000, p. 21) is lots of ingenuity, which defines as:

> *Ideas that can be applied to solve practical, technical and social problems, such as the problems that arise from water pollution, cropland erosion and the like. Ingenuity includes not only truly new ideas – often called 'innovation' – but also ideas that though not fundamentally novel are nevertheless useful.*

The shortfall between the 'rapidly rising need for ingenuity' and its 'inadequate supply' is what Homer-Dixon means by the 'ingenuity gap'.

The ingenuity gap is, in large measure, the by-product of society's continuing commitment to a rationalist style of thought that has influenced western societies for the past 400 years. When combined with the Newtonian mechanical school of physics, which contended that we live in an orderly universe that is knowable through rational scientific methods, the Descartian dictum – I think therefore I am – has bequeathed us an intellectual paradigm that has led people to believe and act as if the world is knowable through logical, linear, rational strategies. This paradigm remains especially dominant in the hierarchies and bureaucracies of governments who seem to respond to increasing complexity with ever more frantic efforts to impose control and certainty. Since the early 1970s, proponents of the newer sciences such as quantum physics, molecular biology, Gestalt psychology and ecology have challenged the conventional, rational paradigm. Its advocates have argued that rationality must be balanced by an ecological approach that looks at human and natural systems holistically. Systems should be known not only in terms of their parts but also in terms of their interrelationships and connections within larger systems. Everything is connected to everything else. Unlike the mechanical universe of Newton, the universe of the systems-thinker is like a bubbling bowl of porridge that is chaotic yet still produces patterns of activity that are knowable.

Within this emerging intellectual paradigm, Capra (1997, pp. 289–90) explains that ecosystems and human communities 'are networks that are organizationally closed, but open to the flows of energy and resources; their structures are determined by their histories of structural changes; they are intelligent' (p. 289). While admitting that we cannot learn much about human values and their shortcomings from ecosystems, he suggests that 'what we can learn is how to live sustainably'. From the study of ecosystems, he states, we can determine a set of organizational principles that we can use as 'guidelines to build sustainable human communities'. These guidelines are:

- Ecological and human communities are interdependent. To understand both, one must understand relationships. It requires 'a shift of perceptions to look at the whole as opposed to the parts ... from the parts to the whole, from objects to relationships, from content to patterns' (ibid., p. 290).
- Ecological communities are non-linear and involve multiple feedback loops. 'Linear chains of cause and effect exist very rarely in ecosystems', so that a disturbance in one part of the system spreads out in 'ever-widening patterns' (ibid., p. 290).
- Ecosystems maintain the flexibility necessary to adapt to changing conditions.
- Ecosystems respond to contradictions and conflict by maintaining a dynamic balance between and among competing forces. 'Diversity means different relationships, many different approaches to the same problem. A diverse community is a resilient community, capable of adapting to changing situations' (ibid., p. 295).
- Partnerships are an essential feature of ecosystems. 'The cyclical exchanges of energy and resources in an ecosystem are sustained by pervasive cooperation' (ibid., p. 293).

Method

What contribution can leaders make to sustainable improvement according to the sense of sustainability we have outlined? In our view, leaders develop sustainability by how they approach, commit to and protect deep learning in their schools; by how they sustain others around them to promote and support that learning; by how they sustain themselves in doing so, so that they can persist with their vision and avoid burning out; and by how they try to ensure the improvements they bring about last over time, especially after they themselves have gone. We now look at three particular aspects of what we call sustainable leadership that illustrate the different components of sustainability (and non-sustainability) that we have outlined – leading learning, distributed leadership and leadership succession.

The examples are drawn from our research and experience of working with four and then six secondary schools over five years (1997–2002) to help them implement a major set of legislated changes in secondary school reform in ways that were consistent with principles of successful school improvement and their own professional values as educators. All schools were located in a large urban and sub-urban school district in Ontario, Canada which funded the project in partnership with the Ontario Ministry of Education and Training. The first four schools that joined the project sent large and inclusive school teams to a two-day long work-shop that introduced the key ideas and principles of the project and invited school participation if there was strong evidence of a critical mass of staff support. The four schools out of ten that subsequently volunteered were varied in nature and type. With increased funding, two further schools joined the project in its last two years, their new principals having previously served as administrators in the initial group of four.

In the first three years, our project team worked closely with all four schools – helping them identify school-wide improvement priorities, building cultures of commitment and support in the schools, providing staff development input when required, and bringing lead teachers together across the schools to share ideas and practices and discuss difficulties together. Detailed case studies were produced for each school and fed back as a basis for reflection and further improvement efforts (Hargreaves *et al.*, 2000). All the schools' administrators were drawn together on a monthly basis in half-day meetings to discuss recent initiatives, share their experi-ences and concerns about the implementation of the mandated reforms, and engage with relevant research and literature introduced by the project team. Two remaining schools joined the project in the final two years, during which the administrators' support meetings were maintained, while the remainder of the project concentrated on developing and administering school-wide surveys of all staff to elicit their responses to and perceptions of secondary school reform in their schools, and identify particular areas where support was most needed (Hargreaves *et al.*, 2000).

The project design generated relationships of trust and candid disclosure among the schools, between the schools and the project team, and accordingly built an authentic understanding of how teachers and leaders were experiencing and coping with reforms over a relatively long five-year period when other major changes were also affecting their schools.

7

Examples of sustainability and non-sustainability

Let us look now at the three paired examples of sustainability and failed sustain-ability in our project schools.

Leading learning

The prime responsibility of all school leaders is to sustain learning. Leaders of learning put learning at the centre of everything they do: students' learning first, then everyone else's learning in support of it (Stoll, Fink and Earl 2002; Glickman, 2002). The leader's role as a leader of learning is put to the strongest test when his or her school faces demanding measures or policies that seem to undermine true learning or distract people's energies and attention away from it. High-stakes test-ing can push teachers to deliver improved results, but not necessarily to produce better learning. What educators do in this situation depends on their commitment to student learning and on their attitudes to their own learning. In 2001 the Canadian province of Ontario introduced a high-stakes literacy test in Grade 10. It was applied to virtually all students who were required to pass in order to graduate. High stakes, high pressure!

Ivor Megson was the new principal[1] at Talisman Park secondary school. Promoted from being assistant principal at the school, Ivor was dedicated to his work as a leader but did not like to rock the boat too much. Most of his staff had been at the school a long time. They liked being innovative in their own academic subjects but were sceptical and often cynical about larger-scale reform agendas. A coffee circle of embittered staff met every morning before school to complain about the government's latest, almost daily initiatives and announcements. Like many principals, Ivor saw his responsibility as being to protect or buffer his staff from the deluge of reforms that descended on the school. This, he felt, was the best way he could help them.

With his staff, Ivor therefore worked out the most minimal and least disruptive school response to the Grade 10 test: one that would produce the best results with the least amount of effort. Quickly, Ivor and his staff began identifying a group of students who, on pre-tests, indicated they would fall just below the pass mark. The school then coached or 'prepped' these students intensively in literacy learning, so they would perform acceptably when the real test came around. Technically, the strategy worked. The school's results looked good. But teachers' energies are finite, and as staff concentrated on those students near the cut-off point, the students who really needed help with literacy and had little chance of making the pass threshold were cast by the wayside. In Talisman Park, authentic literacy – learning for all, and especially for the most needy – was sacrificed to appearances and results.

Charmaine Williams was the principal of Wayvern High school, just up the road from Talisman Park. Wayvern was a culturally and ethnically diverse school and had a high number of students for whom English was their second language. Wayvern had a lot to lose on the literacy test. Yet Charmaine's school made literacy, not the literacy test, one of its key improvement goals. Charmaine engaged her staff in inquiry about how to improve literacy so it would benefit all students in the long term, instead of focusing on how to manipulate the short-term scores on the test. Working with large staff teams, across disciplines and with workshop training support, Charmaine's school undertook an audit of existing literacy practices in classrooms, researched effective literacy strategies that might be helpful, and undertook a 'gap' analysis to see what improvements would be necessary. Teachers shared their literacy strategies across subjects, and then dedicated a whole month to a high-profile focus on literacy learning in the school and with the community. They also continued a successful literacy initiative they had already started, in which everyone in the school read together for 15 minutes a day. Charmaine harnessed her staff's learning in support of student learning. The immediate results were not spectacular (as is usual with more sustainable change), but together, the staff and parents were confident that long-term improvement mattered the most. Wayvern teachers were convinced that, in future years, scores would increase as genuine reflections of learning and achievement, rather than because of cynical manipulations of the testing process (Talbert and MacLaughlin, 1994).

One reform, two principals, two schools: different outcomes! Especially in the most adverse circumstances, it is those principals who are leaders of learning who make the most lasting and inclusive improvements for their students in their schools.

Distributed leadership

Outstanding leadership is not just the province of individual icons and heroes (Saul, 1993). In a complex, fast-paced world, leadership cannot rest on the shoulders of the few. The burden is too great. In highly complex, knowledge-based organizations, everyone's intelligence is needed to help the organization to flex, respond, regroup and retool in the face of unpredictable and sometimes overwhelming demands. Locking intelligence up in the individual leader creates inflexibility and increases the likelihood of mistakes and errors. But when we call on what Brown and Lauder (2001) call 'collective intelligence' – intelligence that is infinite rather than fixed, multifaceted rather than singular, and that belongs to everyone, not just a few – the capacity for learning improvement is magnified many times over. For these reasons, more and more efforts are being made to replace individual leaders with more distributed or distributive leadership (Spillane, Halverson and Drummond, 2001; IEL, 2000, 2001). Distributed leadership sees leadership as a network of relationships among people, structures and cultures (both within and across organizational boundaries), not just as a role-based function assigned to, or acquired by, a person in an organization, who then uses his or her power to influence the actions of others. Leadership is seen as an organic activity, dependent on interrelationships and connections (Riley, 2000, pp. 46–7).

Mark Warne was the principal of North Ridge High School. Three years from retirement, Mark has a keen intellect and a deep knowledge about imposed change and its effects. Mark valued and was skilled at seeing the 'big picture' of reform. When legislated reforms were announced, Mark produced detailed and thoughtful written and projected timelines for implementation that he circulated to staff for comment. However, the response was disappointing, and Mark confided from time to time that his staff was generally apathetic about getting involved with change. Mark's strength was that he possessed great intellectual clarity, but he could not develop the capacity among his staff to share it with him. The big-picture change belonged to Mark, not to everyone. His office was packed with policy statements, resources and materials, which might better have been distributed around the school.

Mark controlled the school's directions through the line management of the department heads. The department heads were quite autonomous in their areas, and staff involvement, therefore, depended on the leadership style of each head. One of the assistant principals, also close to retirement, performed traditional discipline and administrative roles. The other was battling with what sadly turned out to be a terminal illness.

Mark delegated to his subordinate department heads and accepted their advice in areas where they were more expert than he. The heads of department generally described him as 'supportive', 'compassionate' and 'well-intentioned'. Yet the wider staff was excluded from decisions and ill-informed on important issues. They considered him to be 'indecisive', 'inconsistent' and 'lacking a personal vision'. At a school improvement workshop we ran with the whole staff, it was the only school of the six to identify itself as 'cruising' (Fink and Stoll, 1998) – its mainly affluent students were getting good results but the school lacked purpose and direction. The chief problem the staff chose to address at the workshop was 'communications with the administration'.

Soon after this the school began to change dramatically, but not through a change of principal. In 1998 two new assistant principals were appointed, and together they infused the school's administration with renewed enthusiasm, optimism and focus. Diane Grant, with an athletic bearing and infectiously ener-getic style, brought sophisticated knowledge of curriculum and classroom assessment to the problem of reform. Before long she was skilfully leading the staff in curriculum gap analysis, or having them share successful experiences in class-room assessment by seating them in cross-disciplinary tables at the staff picnic where they scribbled their ideas as graffitti on paper table cloths. Meanwhile, Bill Johnson, the other assistant principal, drew on his counselling skills to develop effective communications and relationships with and among the staff. Diane aroused teachers' passion and Bill calmed them, and as a team they were able to set a common vision for the school and a more open style of communication. In this new style, staff focused on collaborative learning, inquiry and problem solv-ing. Mark's strength was in having the good sense to 'distribute' the leadership of important classroom-related changes to his assistant principals, who in turn redis-tributed much of the leadership among the staff, who learned to be critical filters for government mandates rather than mere pipelines for implementing them.

Leadership succession

Sustainable leadership outlives particular individuals. It does not disappear when particular leaders leave. There is evidence that the departure of the initiating prin-cipal or the critical mass of early leaders from model or beacon schools is the first symptom of decline (Sarason, 1972; Fink, 2000b). Macmillan (1996, 2000) has observed that the practice in some school districts of regularly rotating leaders between schools can harden teachers against change because they come to see the school's principalship as little more than a revolving door in a building where they are the permanent residents. Whether principal rotation is formalized or not, leadership succession events always pose a threat to sustainable improvement.

Bill Mathews was a tall, commanding figure who brought vision, energy and intel-lectual rigour to his role. The son of a policeman, he believed strongly that students came first and pursued this belief with a sense of clear expectation and relentless deter-mination. Some staff respected his commitment to children and his willingness to take action and put himself on the line for their sake. Prior experience of principalship buttressed his self-confidence, and in a teacher culture that revelled in argument and debate, his somewhat adversarial style (Blasé and Anderson, 1995), which encouraged and entertained well-reasoned and supported opposition to his ideas, suited a sizeable number of staff very well. It also stimulated some extremely lively staff meetings, not least one in which student recommendations for improving school climate occasioned teacher protests about maladroitly expressed student opinions! Bill led Stewart Heights School with firm expectations and clear example, accompanied by lively argument and considerable humour. The most outstanding instance of leading by example was when he personally solved the scheduling problems of 80 students to demonstrate to staff that better service for students was possible.

In the wake of his example and expectations, Bill was quick to move to action by getting staff to analyse data consciously and make action plans on the basis of what they learned. He integrated several improvement teams to permit far greater voice and participation for teachers in the work of the school, compared to the previous dominance of the department heads' council. In this culturally diverse school, Bill encouraged the staff to initiate a range of changes that made students feel more included and parents feel more welcome. Structures, planning and initiation, backed up by his own personal interactions with people and his visibility around the school, were the ways that Bill brought about change. Many staff, including most of those on the School Success team, warmed to this decisiveness and sense of direction. Staff referred to him as a 'visionary', 'change agent' and 'efficient manager'. Others however, especially women, indicated they had respect for him, but questioned what they construed as being a somewhat authoritarian style.

The assistant principals offered complementary, indeed dramatically contrasting approaches within the administrative team. One presented a quieter, more restrained and more procedural version of masculinity in leadership than his more 'up-front' principal. The other took a more relationship-centred approach to students, curriculum and staff development, in which caring coupled with hard work and high expectations played an important role. With their contrasting styles, they too fostered greater teacher participation in the work of the school.

Bill Matthews felt it had been a struggle to change the school culture to provide 'a service to kids and the community'. Yet, when he presented the staff with survey data showing that 95 per cent of staff were satisfied with the school and only 35 per cent of students and 25 per cent of parents were, this created a common problem that staff then had to solve together.

With more time to help staff work through their doubts and difficulties, Bill Matthews and his team may well have been able to convert the temporary success of short-term innovation into sustainable improvement. But by the end of his third year, changing circumstances within the school system resulted in Bill moving to a superintendency,[2] one of the assistant principals to his first principalship, and the other to her second assistant principalship. Stewart Heights' leadership successor was new to the school and to the role and had to feel his way carefully into both of them. Meanwhile, the mandated reform agenda was quickly gathering pace. The result of these converging forces was that staff and the new principal turned their attention to implementation more than improvement. Observations at the school climate meetings indicated that with the previous principal's departure, student-centred policies now gave way to more conventional behaviour-code initiatives. The early achievements of school improvement at Stewart Heights quickly began to fade. If school improvement is to be sustainable, continuity of or longer tenure for the initial principal, or consistency in relation to those who follow him or her, is essential.

By comparison, Blue Mountain School, an innovative model school established in 1994, planned its own leadership succession from the outset. The fate of most innovative schools is to fade once their first principals have left. Blue Mountain's principal anticipated his own departure, although he worked hard to create a school structure that would survive his departure and 'perpetuate what we are doing'. He was especially alert to the threats posed by leadership succession (Fink, 2000b: Hargreaves and Fink, 2000; Macmillan, 2000) where an ensuing principal might import a different philosophy. He therefore 'negotiated very strongly (with the district) to have my deputy principal appointed principal'. After four years the system moved the principal who founded the school to a large high-profile school in the system and promoted his assistant principal in his place. In her words:

> *We talked about [this move] and we talked about how we could preserve the direction that the school is moving in and we were afraid that if a new administrator came in as principal that if he or she had a different philosophy, a different set of beliefs, then it would be quite easy simply to move things in that particular direction and we didn't want that to happen.*

Blue Mountain is a rarity. In general, planned succession is one of the most neglected aspects of leadership theory and practice in our schools and one of the most persistently missing pieces in the efforts to secure sustainability of school improvement.

Discussion

Our definition and dimensions of sustainability in education and our ensuing case illustrations carry a number of implications for what it might mean to develop sustainable leadership.

Leadership must be embedded in the hearts and minds of the many, and not rest on the shoulders of an heroic few

We want dedicated and committed professionals in school leadership, not martyrs to management – severed heads whose all-consuming devotion to their work comes at the cost of their families, their lives, their health and themselves.

School leadership is not the sum of its individual leaders, still less, its separate heads. School leadership is a system, a culture. Schools are places where headteachers/principals, teachers, students and parents all lead. To sustain quality leadership, school systems must apply systems thinking to their mandate of leadership quality, qualifications and development – not just by setting common standards and criteria, but by applying systems thinking to all initiatives: seeing leadership as a culture of integrated qualities rather than merely an aggregate of common characteristics.

School jurisdictions should see leadership as a horizontal system across space, where leaders can learn from each other within and across their schools through peer-support groups, online dialogue, pairing of schools and their heads such as in Birmingham in England or the Halton Board in Ontario (Stoll and Fink, 1996), joint research and development projects, etc. As we experienced in our school improvement project, one of the components most consistently valued by school leaders is the regular opportunity to meet and converse with each other to talk openly about shared professional and sometimes personal concerns (Beattie, 2002).

Educational systems should see leadership as a vertical system over time

The efforts of all leaders are influenced by the impact of their predecessors and have implications for their successors. No leader is an island in time. Principals and their systems tend to put all their energy into what is called inbound knowledge – the knowledge needed to change a school, improve it, make one's mark on it, turn it around. Little or no attention is devoted to outbound knowledge – the knowledge needed to preserve past successes or keep initiatives going once the originating leader has left. The moment headteachers/principals get new appointments, they immediately start to focus on their new school, their next challenge, or on how to ensure their present achievements live on after their departure. Few things in education succeed less than leadership succession. Heroic heads do not plan for their own obsolescence. The emphasis on change has obliterated the importance of continuity. In inner-city schools, teachers see their principals come and go like revolving doors – and quickly learn how to resist and ignore their leader's efforts (Macmillan, 2000). The result is that school improvement becomes like a set of bobbing corks – with many schools rising under one set of leaders, only to sink under the next. If we want sustainable as well as successful leadership, we must pay serious attention to leadership succession (Fink, 2000b). Leaders must be asked and must ask themselves – what will be their legacy and how will their influence live on after their professional departure or death? The time to think about this is when they start their leadership, not when they draw it to a close.

Sustainable success in education lies in cultures of distributed leadership throughout the school community, not in a tiny leadership elite

In the contextual realities of high expectations, rapid change and a youthful profession in the first decades of the twenty-first century, teachers cannot be the mere targets of other people's leadership, but must see themselves as being – and be encouraged to be – leaders of classrooms and of colleagues from the moment they commence their careers. Distributed leadership means more than delegation. Delegation involves passing across lesser and often unwanted tasks to others. The individual leader decides what will be delegated and to whom. Distributed leadership means creating a culture of initiative and opportunity, where teachers of all kinds propose new directions, start innovations, perhaps sometimes even challenging and creating difficulties for their heads in the overall interests of the pupils and the school. In its fullest development, distributed leadership extends beyond the staff to the pupils and the parents. Distributed leadership gives depth and breadth to the idea and practice of leadership.

Recruiting and developing educational leaders will require focusing on their potential rather than recycling their existing proficiencies

7

The recruitment and development of leaders in the public service in most western countries has become a major concern as the 'baby boom' generation moves on (NAPA, 1997; Langford, Vakii and Lindquist, 2000; Jackson, 2000; Government of Western Australia, 2001). For example, by 2005, 70 per cent of the senior managers in the US public service will be eligible for retirement, 'causing unique challenges for numerous agencies in maintaining leadership continuity, institutional memory and workforce experience' (FEI, 2001). In education, after years of top-down, market-driven reforms, many existing leaders are retiring at their first opportunity, so creating a crisis of 'recruitment and retention' (Earley et al., 2002).

Education has much to learn from the private sector about succession planning. The 'best' private sector organizations consider investing in the development of leaders as an asset to the organization not a cost. These forward-looking organizations look at the long term to determine the kinds of leadership skills and aptitudes that will be needed in the future (Jackson, 2000). Rather than focusing on existing competencies based on existing roles, they recruit and develop people who have 'learned how to learn' and are sufficiently flexible to adjust to changing circumstances (Stoll, Fink and Earl, 2002). We need to prepare leaders for their future, rather than 'polishing yesterday's leadership paradigm' (Peters, 1997).

Conclusion

Schools that sustain 'deep' learning experiences for all pupils should address the breadth of school leadership in supporting and promoting the learning of present and future leaders themselves. They should address the length and sustainability of school leadership over time, helping leaders to plan for their own professional obsolescence, and to think about the school's needs for continuity as well as change. School systems will have to acknowledge and create conditions that distribute leadership far beyond the headteacher's office to the entire culture of the school, and even to the larger community. And then they will need to concentrate on the leadership skills and qualities that will sustain leaders into the future rather than merely help them manage and survive in the present. Successful leadership is sustainable leadership; nothing simpler, nothing less.

NOTES

1 For convenience we have used 'principals' to refer to 'headteachers' and 'assistant principals' to refer to 'deputy heads' or 'vice-principals'.

2 In an Ontario context, superintendents report to the Director of Education (the Chief Executive Officer). The role is similar to a local education authority inspector in the UK.

REFERENCES

Barber, M. (2001) 'High expectations and standards for all, no matter what: creating a world class educational service in England' in Fielding, M. (ed.) *Taking Education Really Seriously: Three Years of Hard Labour*, London: Routledge/Falmer Press.

Beattie, B. (2002) 'Emotion matters in educational leadership', unpublished PhD thesis, Ontario Institute for Studies in Education, University of Toronto.

Blasé, J. (1998) 'The micropolitics of educational change' in Hargreaves, A., Lieberman, A., Fullan, M. and Hopkins, D. (1998) *International Handbook of Educational Change*, Dordrecht, The Netherlands: Kluwer Academic Publisher pp. 544–57.

Blasé J. and Anderson, G. (1995) *The Micropolitics of Educational Leadership: From Control to Empowerment*, New York: Teachers' College Press.

Brown, P. and Lauder, H. (2001) *Capitalism and Social Progress: The Future of Society in a Global Economy*, New York: Palgrave.

Capra, F. (1997) *The Web of Life: A New Synthesis of Mind and Matter*, London: Harper Collins.

Castells, M. (1996) *The Rise of the Network Society*, Oxford: Blackwell.

Castells, M. (1997) *The Power of Identity*, Oxford: Blackwell.

Castells, M. (1998) *End of Millennium*, Oxford: Blackwell.

Deal, T.E. and Kennedy, A. (1983). 'Culture and school performance', *Educational Leadership*, 40 (5), pp. 140–41.

Drucker, P. (1993) *Post-capitalist Society*, New York: Harper Collins.

Earley, P., Evans, J., Collarbone, P., Gold, A. and Halpin, D. (2002) *Establishing the Current State of Leadership in England*, London: Department for Education and Skills.

Elmore, R. (1995) 'Structural reform in educational practice', *Educational Researcher*, 24 (9), pp. 23–6.

FEI (2001) *Building Human Capital: The Public Sector's 21st Century Challenge*, Financial Executive International.

Fink, D. (2000a) 'The attrition of educational change over time: the case of an "innovative", "model", "lighthouse" school' in Bascia, N. and Hargreaves, A. (eds) *The Sharp Edge of Educational Change*, London: Routledge/Falmer Press.

Fink, D. (2000b) *Good Schools/Real Schools: Why School Reform Doesn't Last*, New York: Teachers' College Press.

Fletcher, C., Caron, M. and Williams, W. (1985) *Schools on Trial*, Buckingham: Open University Press.

Fullan, M. (1982) *The Meaning of Educational Change*, Toronto: OISE Press.

Fullan, M. (1993) *Change Forces: Probing the Depths of Educational Reform*, London: Falmer Press.

Fullan, M. (1998) 'The meaning of educational change: a quarter of a century of learning' in Hargreaves, A., Lieberman, A., Fullan, M. and Hopkins, D. *International Handbook of Educational Change*, Dordrecht, The Netherlands: Kluwer Academic Publishers, pp. 214–28.

Fullan, M. (1999) *Change Forces: The Sequel*, London: Falmer Press.

Fullan, M. with Stiegelbauer, S. (1991) *The New Meaning of Educational Change*, New York: Teachers' College Press.

Giddens, A. (2000) *Runaway World: How Globalization is Reshaping our Lives*, London: Profile Books, pp. 4–5.

Glickman, C. (2002) *Leadership for Learning: How to Help Teachers Succeed*, Alexandria VA: Association for Supervision and Curriculum Development.

Government of Western Australia (2001) 'Managing succession in the Western Australia public sector', www. mpc.wa.gov.au.

Hargreaves, A. (1994) *Changing Teachers, Changing Times*, London: Cassell.

Hargreaves, A. (1998) 'The emotional politics of teaching and teacher development: implications for leadership', *International Journal of Leadership in Education*, 1 (4), pp. 315–36.

Hargreaves, A. (2003). *Teaching in the Knowledge Society*, New York: Teachers' College Press.

Hargreaves, A., Earl, L., Moore, S. and Manning S. (2001) *Learning to Change: Teaching Beyond Subjects and Standards*, San Francisco: Jossey-Bass.

Hargreaves, A. and Fink, D. (2000) 'The three dimensions of reform', *Educational Leadership*, 57 (7), pp. 30–4.

Hargreaves, A., Shaw, P., Fink, D., Retallick, J., Giles, C., Moore, S., Schmidt, M. and James-Wilson, S. (2000) *Change Frames: Supporting Secondary Teachers in Interpreting and Integrating Secondary School Reform*, Toronto: Ontario Institute for Studies in Education/University of Toronto.

Homer-Dixon, T. (2000) *The Ingenuity Gap: Can we Solve the Problems of the Future?*, Toronto: Alfred A. Knopf.

Hopkins, D., Aincow, M. and West, M. (1994) *School Improvement in an Era of Change*, London: Cassell.

IEL (2000) *Leadership for Student Learning: Reinventing the Principalship*, Washington, DC: Institute for Educational Leadership.

IEL (2001) *Leadership for Student Learning: Redefining the Teacher as Leader*, Washington, DC: Institute for Educational Leadership.

Jackson, K. (2000) 'Building new teams: the next generation', presentation at the 'Future of Work in the Public Sector' conference, organized by the School of Public Administration, University of Victoria, Victoria, BC (www.futurework.telus.com/proceedings.pdf).

Langford, J., Vakii, T. and Lindquist, E.A. (2000). 'Tough challenges and practical solutions', Report on conference proceedings, School of Public Administration, University of Victoria, Victoria, BC (www.futurework.telus.com/proceedings.pdf).

Lortie, D.C. (1975) *School Teacher: A Sociological Study*, Chicago: University of Chicago Press.

Louis, K.S. and Miles, M.B. (1990) *Improving the Urban High School: What Works and Why*, New York: Teachers' College Press.

Machiavelli, N. (1532) *The Prince*, trans. Bull, G., 1999, London/New York: Penguin Books.

Macmillan, R. (1996) 'The relationship between school culture and principals' practices during succession', unpublished PhD thesis, University of Toronto (OISE), Toronto, Ontario.

Macmillan, R. (2000) 'Leadership succession, culture of teaching, and educational change' in Bascia, N. and Hargreaves, A. (eds), *The Sharp Edge of Educational Change*, London: Falmer Press.

McLaughlin, M. (1990). 'The RAND Change Agent Study: macro perspectives and micro realities', *Educational Researcher*, 19 (9), pp. 11–15.

Meyer, J.W. and Rowan, B. (1977) 'Institutional organizations: formal structures as myth and ceremony', *American Journal of Sociology*, 83, pp. 340–63.

Miles, M. (1998) 'Finding keys to school change' in Hargreaves, A., Lieberman, A., Fullan, M. and Hopkins, D. (1998) *International Handbook of Educational Change*, Dordrecht, The Netherlands: Kluwer Academic Publishers, pp. 37–69.

7

NAPA (1997) *Managing Succession and Developing Leadership: Growing the Next Generation of Public Service Leaders*, Washington, DC: National Academy of Public Administration.

OECD (2001) *Schooling for Tomorrow: What Schools for the Future?*, Paris: Organization for Economic Co-operation and Development.

Peters, T. (1997) *The Circle of Innovation: You Can't Shrink Your Way to Greatness*, New York: Alfred A. Knopf.

Riley, K. (1998) *Whose School is it Anyway?*, London: Falmer Press.

Riley, K. (2000) 'Leadership, learning and systemic change', *Journal of Educational Change*, 1 (1), pp. 57–75.

Saul, J.R. (1993) *Voltaire's Bastards*, Toronto: Penguin Books.

Sarason, S. (1971) *The Culture of the School and the Problem of Change*, Boston: Allyn & Bacon.

Sarason, S. (1972) *The Creation of Settings and the Future Societies*, San Francisco: Jossey-Bass.

Sarason, S. (1990) *The Predictable Failure of Educational Reform*, San Francisco: Jossey-Bass.

Sergiovanni, T. (1992) *Moral Leadership*, San Francisco: Jossey-Bass.

Sergiovanni, T. (2000) 'Changing change: toward a design and art', *Journal of Educational Change*, 1 (1), pp. 57–75.

Shank, D. (1997) *Data Smog: Surviving the Information Glut*, New York: Harper Collins.

Smith, L.M., Dwyer, D.C., Prunty, J.J. and Kleine, P.F. (1987) *The Fate of an Innovative School*, London: Falmer Press.

Spillane, J.P., Halverson, R. and Drummond, J.B. (2001) 'Investigating school leadership practice: a distributed perspective', *Educational Researcher*, 30 (3), pp. 23–8.

Stoll, L. (1999) 'Raising our potential: understanding and developing capacity for lasting improvement', *School Effectiveness and School Improvement*, 10 (4), pp. 503–32.

Stoll L. and Fink, D. (1996) *Changing Our Schools: Linking School Effectiveness and School Improvement*, Buckingham: Open University Press.

Stoll, L. and Fink, D. (1998) 'The cruising school: the unidentified ineffective school' in Stoll, L. and Myers, K. (eds) *Schools in Difficulty: No Quick Fixes*, London: Falmer Press.

Stoll, L., Fink, D. and Earl, L., (2002) *It's About Learning (and It's About Time)*, London: Routledge/Falmer Press.

Stiegelbauer, S.M. and Anderson, S. (1992) 'Seven years later: revisiting a restructured school in northern Ontario', Paper presented at the American Educational Research Association Meetings, San Francisco.

Talbert, J. and MacLaughlin, M. (1994) 'Teacher professionalism in local school contexts', *American Journal of Education*, 102, pp. 123–53.

Tyack, D. and Tobin, W. (1994) 'The grammar of schooling: why has it been so hard to change?' *American Educational Research Journal*, 31 (3), pp. 453–80.

Wallace, M. and Pocklington, K. (2002) *Managing Complex Educational Change: Large Scale Reorganization of Schools*, London: Routledge/Falmer Press.

CHAPTER 44

Principals in a culture of change

MICHAEL FULLAN

The more that large-scale, sustainable educational reform becomes the agenda, the more that leadership becomes the key. In this chapter I will argue that 'the principal as instructional leader' has been a valuable, but too narrow a solution. Instead, the instructional focus must be embedded in a more comprehensive and fundamental set of characteristics, which I call 'the principal as leader in a culture of change'. I will also argue that to achieve the latter we must address the even deeper matter of 'leadership and sustainability'.

The emphasis on the principal as instructional leader has been a valuable first step in increasing student learning. For example, Newmann, King and Youngs (2000) found that 'school capacity' is the critical variable in affecting instructional quality and corresponding student achievement. At the heart of school capacity was principal leadership that focused on the development of teachers' knowledge and skills, professional community, programme coherence and technical resources.

This same model has been extended to the work of entire districts in achieving large-scale turnaround in literacy and numeracy. Some of the core strategies for developing the role of the principal as instructional leader are well described by Fink and Resnick (2001). They discuss five mutually reinforcing sets of strategic activities that they have used, including nested learning communities, principal institutes, leadership for instruction, peer learning and individual coaching. The effect is to develop large numbers of principals as instructional leaders, which, in turn, serve to increase literacy and numeracy.

Despite these impressive results, they do not represent deep or lasting reforms. Indeed, one can improve literacy and numeracy scores in the short run, while the moral and working conditions of teachers deteriorate over the mid to long run. To accomplish lasting reform we need fundamental transformation in the learning cultures of schools and of the teaching profession itself. In brief, the role of the principal as instructional leader is too narrow a concept to carry the freight of the kinds of reforms that will create the schools we need for the future.

Principal as leader in a culture of change

We are now beginning to discover that leaders who have deeper and more lasting impact provide more comprehensive leadership than a simple focus on higher standards. Collins (2001) examined 11 businesses that had a minimum of 15 years of sustained economic performance. Collins identified the Level 5 Executive Leader who 'builds enduring greatness' in comparison to the Level 4 Effective Leader 'who catalyses commitment to a compelling vision and higher performance standards'.

The Hay Group has been analysing leadership, including the characteristics of highly effective principals. In Australia, for example, they identified 13 characteristics across four domains: driving school improvement, delivering through people, building commitment and creating an educational vision (the latter included analytical thinking and 'big-picture' thinking) (Hay Group, 1999). In the UK, Hay Management Consultants (2000) compared 200 highly effective principals, with 200 senior executives in business. They found that both groups were equally impressive and that 'the role of headteacher is stretching, by comparison, to business'. The five domains of leadership they identified were: teamwork and developing others, drive and confidence, vision and accountability, influencing tactics and politics, and thinking styles (conceptual and analytical).

Similarly, Goleman, Boyatzis and Mckee, (2002) claim that emotionally intelligent leaders and emotionally intelligent organizations are essential in complex times. They identify 18 competencies around four domains: self-awareness, self-management, social awareness and relationship management. Such leaders are aware of their own emotional make-up, are sensitive and inspiring to others, and are able to deal with day-to-day problems as they work on more fundamental changes in the culture of the organization.

My point is that the principal of the future has to be much more attuned to the big picture, and much more sophisticated at conceptual thinking and transforming the organization through people and teams. This, too, was my conclusion when I examined successful leadership for businesses and in school systems (Fullan, 2001). If the goal is sustainable change in the knowledge society, business and education leaders have increasingly more in common. This convergence requires a new mindset and action for leading complex change. Figure 44.1 depicts this framework. It consists of personal characteristics of energy, enthusiasm and hope, and five core components of leadership: moral purpose, understanding change, relationship building, knowledge creation and sharing and coherence making. In the following paragraphs I describe the five components, illustrating each component in action with a reference to a hypothetical principal whom I will call 'culture change principal' or CCP.

Moral purpose

Moral purpose, defined broadly as we will see, is one of the five hallmarks of leading in a culture of change. In addition to the direct goal of making a difference in the lives of students, moral purpose plays a larger role in transforming and sustaining system change. Within the organization, how leaders treat all others is also a component of moral purpose. At a larger level, moral purpose means acting with the intention of making a positive difference in the (social) environment. The goal here is system improvement (all schools in the district). This means that school principals have to be almost as concerned about the success of other schools in the district as they are about their own school. This is so because sustained improvement of schools is not possible unless the whole system is moving forward. This commitment to the social environment is precisely what the best principals must

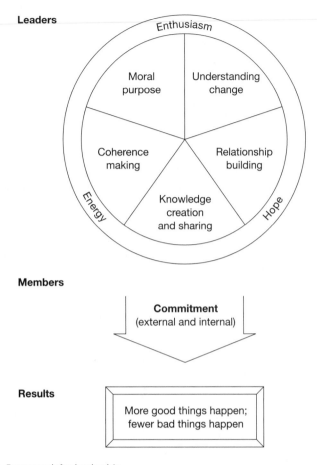

Figure 44.1 Framework for leadership

Source: Fullan, 2001.

have. (Incidentally, the strategies discussed by Fink and Resnick (2001) do indeed foster shared commitment among principals across the district.)

Moral purpose means closing the gap between high performing schools and lower performing schools – and between high performing and lower performing students – by raising the level of achievement of all, while closing the gap. This is the only way for large-scale, sustainable reform to occur – and it is moral purpose of the highest order.

Our hypothetical cultural change principal would behave differently than most principals, even instructionally focused ones. Yes, a CCP would make it clear that student learning was paramount, and would monitor it explicitly with all teachers. But a CCP would also be concerned with the bigger picture – how well are other schools in the district doing; what is the role of public schools in a democracy; is the gap between high performing and low performing students being reduced: (i) in my school, (ii) in our district, (iii) in the state and nation? The CCP's moral purpose would also permeate how he/she treats others, whether they be students, teachers, parents and others. The CCP would also be concerned about the development of other leaders in the school with a view to how prepared the school would be to go even further after the CCP's tenure as leader. In short, a CCP would have explicit, deep and comprehensive moral purpose.

Understanding change

It is essential for leaders to understand the change process. Moral purpose without an understanding of the change process is moral martyrdom. Having innovative ideas and being good at the change process are not the same thing. Indeed, the case can be made that those firmly committed to their own ideas are not necessarily good change agents because the latter involves developing commitment with others who may not be so enamoured by the ideas. Previously (Fullan, 2001), I suggested six guidelines for understanding the process of change:

- The goal is not to innovate the most, but rather to innovate selectively with coherence.
- It is not enough to have the best ideas; you must work through a process where others assess and come to find collective meaning and commitment to new ways.
- Appreciate early difficulties of trying something new – 'the implementation dip'. It is important to know, for example, that no matter how much pre-implementation preparation there has been, the first six months or so of implementation will be bumpy.
- Redefine resistance as a potential positive force. Naysayers sometimes have good points, and they are crucial concerning the politics of implementation, but this does not mean that you listen to naysayers endlessly. Look for ways to address their concerns.
- Reculturing is the name of the game. Much change is structural, and superficial; the change required is in the culture of what people value and how they work together to accomplish it.
- Never a checklist, always complexity. There is no step-by-step shortcut to transformation; it involves the hard day-to-day work of reculturing.

Our CCP has learned the difference between being an expert in a given content innovation and being an expert in managing the process of change. A CCP would not make the mistake of assuming the best ideas would carry the day. A CCP would provide opportunities for people to visit other sites using new ideas, would invite questions (even dissent), and would not expect the change process to go smoothly in the first few months of implementation. Such a principal would also push ahead, expecting progress within a year having created the conditions for the process of change to yield results sooner than later.

Relationship building

The single factor common to successful change is that relationships improve. If relationships improve, things get better. If they remain the same or get worse, ground is lost. Thus leaders must be consummate relationship builders with diverse people and groups – especially with people different from themselves. This is why emotional intelligence is equal to or more important than having the best ideas. In complex times, emotional intelligence is a must.

The CCP knows, as the Hay Management Consultants (2000) found, that developing relationships and team building is the most difficult skill set of all for both business and educational leaders. The CCP works on the full range of emotional intelligence domains, especially self-management of emotions and empathy toward diverse others (Goleman, Boyatzis and Mckee, 2002). This is not just a matter of boosting achievement scores for next year, but rather laying the foundation for years two and beyond. Motivating and energizing a disaffected teacher and forging relationships across otherwise disconnected teachers can have a profound multiplying effect on the overall climate of the organization. Building relationships is the resource that keeps on giving.

Knowledge creation and sharing

The new work on knowledge creation and sharing is central to effective leadership. There are several deep insights here. One is that information (of which we have a glut) only becomes knowledge through a social process. This is why relationships and professional learning communities are essential. Another is that organizations must foster knowledge giving as well as knowledge seeking. We all endorse continuous learning when we say that individuals should add constantly to their knowledge base, but there will be little to add if people are not sharing. A norm of contributing one's knowledge to others is the key to continuous growth for all.

This is a good place to take up the relationships between the knowledge society and moral purpose. Hargreaves (2003) argues forcefully that the knowledge society can easily become amoral where selfishly seeking new ideas becomes the draw. For the knowledge society to thrive on a deep and continuous basis, it must have a moral compass. The knowledge society and moral purpose (social responsibility to others and the environment) need each other. It is easy to see why moral purpose will not go very far without knowledge, but the knowledge society literally will not sustain itself without moral qualities. This is not just a value statement; substantively, the technical quality of knowledge and its usability will be superficial unless it is accompanied by social and moral depth.

The CCP exquisitely appreciates that teaching is both an intellectual and moral profession. This principal constantly reminds teachers that they are engaged in practising, studying and refining the craft of teaching. Through the sharing of latest readings, action research and inquiry groups, the CCP models being the lead learner. Teachers working with a CCP know that they are engaged in the scientific discovery and refinement of the knowledge base of teaching. Knowledge creation and sharing fuel moral purpose in schools led by CCPs.

Coherence making

Finally, since complex societies inherently generate overload, fragmentation and non-linearity – in complexity theory terms, that is what they are perennially good at – effective leaders must always work on connectedness or coherence making (Fullan, 1999, 2001). Coherence making is a complex and somewhat elusive concept. Principals not attuned to leading in a culture of change make the mistake of seeking external innovations and taking on too many projects. CCPs on the other hands, focus on student learning as an integrator, and look for external ideas that can further the thinking and vision of the school. They realize that overload and fragmentation are natural tendencies of complex systems. They appreciate the creative potential of diverse ideas, but they strive to focus energy and achieve greater alignment. They also look to the future, preferring to create a culture that has the capacity not to settle on the solution of the day.

The previous four capacities help forge coherence through the checks and balances embedded in their interaction. Leaders with deep moral purpose provide guidance, but they can also have blinders if their ideas are not challenged through the dynamics of change, the give and take of relationships, and the ideas generated by new knowledge. Coherence is part and parcel of complexity and can never be completely achieved. Leaders in a culture of change value and almost enjoy the tensions inherent in addressing hard-to-solve problems because that is where the greatest accomplishments lie. This clearly places the principal well beyond the role of instructional leader.

Leadership and sustainability

Those of us working on the development of leadership have increasingly turned our attention to sustainability – the likelihood that the overall system can regenerate itself continuously in an ever-improving direction. Because little attention has been paid to sustainability and because the 1990s represented a decade of neglect of supporting, developing and nurturing new leaders, the dearth of leadership has reached crisis proportions. Many states, foundations and other agencies have made leadership development their number-one priority.

My colleague, Andy Hargreaves, and I have been focusing particularly on the relationship between leadership and sustainability, which we see as the way to large scale reform. Here I discuss four components of sustainability:

- leadership and the (social) environment;
- learning in context;
- leaders at many levels and leadership succession;
- the development of the teaching profession.

Here, in other words, I turn to the conditions – policies, programmes, infrastructures – under which principals as leaders in a culture of change can be produced and sustained in large numbers.

Leadership and the (social) environment

The concept of sustainability was originally applied to concerns about the depletion of resources in the physical environment. Our concern is the depletion of resources in the social and moral environment (see also Hargreaves, 2003). This is an abstract concept, so I want to be as practical as possible here. By the social/moral environment I include questions of 'closing the gap' of achievement between high and low performers; the development of all schools in the system; and ultimately, the link to the strength of democracy in society. Put directly, if individual leadership does not concern itself with the development of the social/moral environment (as well as the internal development of the school), not only will the system deteriorate but so will the individual organization over time. There are strategies for cultivating such leadership, which essentially involve focusing on the moral purpose of all leaders, while reinforcing it with interaction across leaders – interaction that monitors performance (including closing the gap of achievement) and engages in problem-solving activities therein.

Learning in context

Attempting to recruit and reward good performance is helpful to the organization, but is not the main focus. Providing good training is useful but that, too, is a limited strategy. Elmore (2000, p. 25) makes a similar observation: 'What's missing in this view [focusing on talented individuals] is any recognition that improvement is more a function of learning to do the right thing *in the setting where you work*' (my emphasis). Learning in context, for example, occurs when principals are members of intervisitation study teams in a district in which they examine real problems and their solutions as they evolve in their own systems. Learning out of context takes place when principals go to a workshop or conference. The latter can be valuable as an input to further development but it is not the kind of applied learning that really makes a difference.

Learning in the setting where you work, or learning in context, is the learning with the greatest pay-off because it is more specific (literally applied to the situation) and because it is social (thereby developing shared and collective knowledge and commitments). Learning in context is developing leadership and improving the system as you go. This kind of learning is designed to simultaneously improve the organization and the (social/moral) context. Learning in context is related to sustainability because it improves the system in a way that establishes conditions conducive to continuous development. These conditions include opportunities to learn from others on-the-job, the daily fostering of current and future leaders, the selective retention of good ideas and best practices, the explicit monitoring of performance, and the like.

Leaders at many levels/leadership succession

The organization cannot flourish (or at least not for long) by the actions of the top leader alone. The commitment necessary for sustainable improvement must be nurtured up close in daily organizational behaviour, and for that to happen there needs to be many leaders around us. There needs to be leaders at many levels. Learning in context helps to produce such leaders. Furthermore, for leaders to be able to deal with complex problems (what Heifetz (1994) calls 'leadership without easy answers') they need at least ten years of cumulative development on the job. Leadership for many, over time, accomplishes just that in a built-in way. In this sense, ultimately your leadership in a culture of sustained change will be judged as effective not by who you are as a leader but by what leadership you leave behind.

This brings us to leadership succession. As Hargreaves says, 'Nothing fails to succeed like succession' – or, 'Nothing fails like succession'. There have been massive numbers of studies of leadership, but little attention to succession. Succession is more likely if there are many leaders at many levels, but also must be addressed in its own right. Organizations at all levels must set their sights on continuous improvement, and for that they must nurture, cultivate and appoint successive leaders who are moving in a sustained direction.

The good news for most of us is that charismatic leaders are a liability for sustained improvement. In Collins' study (2001) of 11 companies with long-term financial performance profiles (a minimum of 15 continuous years), he compared them with other companies that made short-term shifts from good to great, but failed to sustain their gains:

> *Larger-than-life, celebrity leaders who ride in from the outside are* negatively *correlated with taking a company from good to great. Ten of eleven good-to-great-CEOs came from inside the company, whereas the comparison companies tried outside CEOs six times more often.* (Ibid., p. 10, emphasis in original)

Leaders who built enduring greatness were not high profile, flashy performers, but rather were 'individuals who blend extreme personal humility with intense professional will' (ibid., p. 21). Sustainability depends on many leaders, and thus the qualities of leadership must be attainable by many, not just a few.

The teaching profession

There is a growing shortage of teachers around the world, and the sustainability worry is not the massive exodus associated with demographics, but whether or not we can attract and retain a high-quality teaching force. Heroic principals can help compensate for limits in the profession, but by definition such principals will be in the minority. More fundamentally, we will not have quality principals on any scale until we have quality teachers on a large scale, both for reasons of getting the job done, and because quality teachers (on a large scale) form the pool for appointing quality principals (on a large scale).

Once again, individualistic strategies (signing bonuses, pay hikes, etc.) will not work, unless the conditions of work are conducive to continuous development and prideful accomplishment. This is decidedly not the case now, and until improving the working conditions of teachers is addressed we have no chance of accomplishing large-scale, let alone sustainable, improvement.

In England and Wales, PricewaterhouseCoopers (2001) completed a study on teacher workload for the government. Among other things, they found that principals and teachers work more intensive weeks (but not necessarily more intensive years) than other comparable managers and professionals. In any case, they conclude that if the government is to transform the teaching force, then: 'an essential strand will be to reduce teacher workload, foster increased teacher ownership, and create the capacity to manage change in a sustainable way that can lay the foundation for improved school and pupil performance in the future' (ibid., p. 2).

It is beyond the scope of this chapter to discuss what this will entail (there is a pilot project in England and Wales about to get underway to address these issues). The main point is that principal leadership is an instrument of this transformation (of the working conditions of teachers), and – in the contect of sustainability – the 'principalship' is a beneficiary because we will only get quality principals across the board when we have quality teachers across the board.

Conclusion

The principal as instructional leader has taken us only so far in the quest for continuous improvement. We now must raise our sights and focus on principals as leaders in a culture of change and the associated conditions that will make this possible on a large-scale, sustainable basis, including the transformation of the teaching profession. This will require system-wide efforts at the level of schools, communities and districts, as well as radically more enlightened policies and incentives at the level of the state. Sustainability depends on it. Never has there been a more precious time to tackle this agenda than the next five years.

REFERENCES

Collins, J. (2001) *Good to Great:Why Some Companies Make the Leap ... and Others Don't*, New York: Harper Collins.

Elmore, R. (2000) *Building a New Structure for School Leadership*, Washington, DC: Albert Shanker Institute.

Fink, E. and Resnick, L. (2001) 'Developing principals as instructional leaders', *Phi Delta Kappan*, V (82), pp. 598–606.

Fullan, M. (1999) *Change Forces: The Sequel*, London: Taylor & Francis/Falmer Press.

Fullan, M. (2001) *Leading in a Culture of Change*, San Francisco: Jossey-Bass.

Goleman, D. Boyatzis, R. and McKee, A. (2002) *Primal Leadership*, Boston, MA: Harvard Business School Press.

Hargreaves, A. (2003) *Teaching in the Knowledge Society*, New York: Teachers' College Press.

Hay Group (1999) *Excellence in School Leadership*, Victoria, Australia: Department of Education, Employment and Training.

Hay Management Consultants (2000) *The Lessons of Leadership*, London: Hay Management Consultants.

Heifetz, R. (1994) *Leadership Without Easy Answers*, Cambridge, MA: Harvard University Press.

Newmann, F., King, B. and Youngs, P. (2000) 'Professional development that addresses school capacity', paper presented at the annual meeting of the American Educational Research Association.

PricewaterhouseCoopers (2001) *Teacher Workload Study*, London: Department for Education and Skills.

7

CHAPTER 45

Why educational reforms sustain or fail: lessons for educational leaders

HUGH MEHAN, AMANDA DATNOW AND LEA HUBBARD

In this chapter we take up the issues of sustainability and expiration – the ability of educational reforms to endure (or not) over time. Our particular interest is externally developed reforms – models for school improvement that are developed by organizations external to the school or district. Schools and districts purchase these reforms and/or reform assistance from vendors, or what are called reform design teams. The scale-up of these reforms is happening at an unprecedented rate, as evidenced by the fact that there are dozens of school reform designs (for example Coalition of Essential Schools, Success for All, AVID, Comer School Development Program) being implemented in thousands of schools in the USA. Their increased scale-up has been bolstered by recent federal Comprehensive School Reform Demonstration Program legislation providing $150 million for the adoption of such models, and by changes in federal Title I legislation allowing for the use of funds to support schoolwide programmes. Some of the models are also being implemented outside the USA, including the UK, Israel, South Africa, Canada and Mexico, but not to the same degree.

While the growth in the use of these models is perhaps an indicator of their success, effectively transferring an innovation across school contexts is said to be difficult at best, and perhaps impossible (Elmore, 1996; Fullan, 1999; Hargreaves and Fink, 2000; Stringfield and Datnow, 1998). Meanwhile, some argue that the current generation of externally developed reform models provides the best hope for school improvement on the grand scale that has existed in the past several decades (Slavin and Madden, 1998). What factors, then, enable externally developed reform designs to last and what factors lead to their expiration?

Very few studies have actually examined the sustainability of reform or school improvement over long periods of time, in part because few fundamental reforms actually institutionalize (Tyack and Cuban, 1995; Cuban, 1986, 1992; Anderson and Stiegelbauer, 1994; Kirst and Meister, 1985). Additionally, such studies are costly and labour-intensive, and the reward structures of universities can be antithetical to longitudinal research efforts (Sarason, 1996; Yonezawa and Stringfield, 2000).

In their *Special Strategies* follow-up study, Yonezawa and Stringfield (2000) took advantage of the unusual opportunity to document the sustainability of reform over an extended period. This study included eight schools that had implemented either an externally or internally developed reform model with at least moderate success in the early 1990s. Eight years later, Yonezawa and Stringfield found that three schools had moved toward institutionalizing their reforms. In these schools, educators and design teams successfully maintained reform through:

- the alignment of the 'cultural logic' of the reform design and that of the local reformers;
- securing political support (or, at least not acquiring powerful political enemies);
- integrating reform structures into the daily lives of the school community.

Schools that simultaneously attended to these change processes – and, more importantly, the interaction between them – were able to sustain reforms.

Also presenting a 'multiple-processes' perspective on reform sustainability, Hargreaves and Fink (2000, p. 1) argue that only three issues matter in educational reform:

- depth: can a reform improve the important rather than superficial aspects of students' learning?
- length or duration: can a reform be sustained over long periods of time?
- breadth: can a reform be extended beyond a few schools?

All too often large-scale reform projects fail to achieve depth, length and breadth.

Researchers have pointed to a number of reasons why sustainability is so problematic. While the authors we review consider a wide range of variables when analysing the reasons innovations are not sustained, they emphasize certain points more than others. We find it useful to group these explanations according to their point of emphasis – agency, culture or structure. Some explanations of the failure to sustain reforms emphasize the actions of educators, that is, their agency. Notable here are those explanations that blame educators in schools for not implementing the reform as designed and those explanations that blame the design team for not being sensitive to local circumstances. Other explanations focus on cultural considerations, suggesting that reforms fail because they do not touch or challenge cultural beliefs or core values – the 'culture of the school'. A third set of explanations emphasizes structural considerations, suggesting that the social organization of the school and district, the actions of the state and the features of the reform itself enhance or inhibit attempts to sustain reform.

In the following sections we intersperse our findings and observations with those of earlier commentators. We examine how reform sustainability or expiration is a joint accomplishment of multiple actors in the classroom, school, district, design team, and state government offices. These are not outcomes that result from individuals or institutions acting in isolation from one another; instead, forces in all these settings shape the longevity of reform. We end with a discussion of lessons for educational leaders on what can be done to support sustainable school reform.

Methodology

This chapter draws upon data gathered in three different studies of externally developed reforms. First, we present data from the Scaling Up School Restructuring in Multicultural, Multilingual Contexts Study, which involved 13 elementary schools in one culturally and linguistically diverse urban district (Sunland County) over a four-year period (for a description of the methodology, see Stringfield *et al.*, 1998). Each of the schools was implementing an externally developed school reform design. The reform designs include three of the New American Schools (NAS) models (Success for All, Modern Red Schoolhouse and the Audrey Cohen College System of Education) and three independently developed reform designs (not part of NAS). including the Core Knowledge Sequence, the Coalition of Essential Schools and the Comer School Development Program.

The second major data source for this part is the Tracking Untracking Study, in which we studied the scale-up of the Advancement Via Individual Determination (AVID) untracking programme in 12 high schools in four US states (Virginia, California, Kentucky and North Carolina) over a three-year period (Hubbard and Mehan, 1999a; Mehan *et al.*, 1996). The third source of data is an in-depth two-year qualitative study of implementation and teaching in three Success for All (SFA) schools (Datnow and Castellano, 2000, 2001). This study took place from 1998 to 1999 and involved three elementary schools implementing Success for All in three different California school districts. All the schools served a majority of low-income students, many of whom spoke English as a second language.

Together, these research projects involved case study (Yin, 1989) data collection at a total of 28 schools during the period of 1995–9, though we draw on only a limited number of examples here. We analysed transcripts and notes from all the aforementioned interviews, coding for specific references to sustainability and expiration and then conducting cross-site and within-site pattern matching. In some cases we also drew upon background information from the case reports our research teams had written on each school. For the purposes of confidentiality, pseudonyms are used for all school names. Table 45.1 includes a description of each of the reform designs we refer to in this part.

The study of diverse reforms in Sunland County provides an interesting opportunity to investigate reform sustainability or expiration. After four years of our study, only seven of the 13 schools were still continuing to implement their chosen reform designs (and two of the seven were only minimally implementing reforms). Reforms expired in six schools. AVID, in contrast, was sustained in all of the 12 schools we studied over the three-year period of our study, but the reform's depth and breadth varied across contexts. We provide some explanations for why these varied outcomes occurred.

Agency-based explanations of the failure to sustain reforms

According to some commentators, the movement of innovative reforms to scale can be thwarted by actions taken in one of two domains, 'on the street' or in the design team. In the first case, the design team encounters resistance and the like in classrooms. We will call this 'failure by subversion'.

Reforms fail because 'street level bureaucrats' subvert reform

One reason given for the failure of innovations is that the design team has good ideas but actors at the local level undermine them. This subversion explanation of the failure to sustain reform treats educators in schools as culprits; they circumvent well-intended reforms, either because they are irrational, or they are selfish, or they are protecting their own interests, or they do not understand the intentions of the design team.

Table 45.1 *Externally developed reform designs*

Design	Major characteristics
New American Schools	
Audrey Cohen College System of Education	*Developer:* Audrey Cohen College, New York. *Primary goal:* Development of scholarship and leadership abilities using knowledge and skills to benefit students' community and larger world. *Main features:* • Student learning focused on complex and meaningful purposes. • Students use what they learn to reach specific goals. • Curriculum focused on Constructive Actions (individual or group projects that serve the community). • Classes structured around five dimensions (e.g. self and others, values, etc.) that incorporate core subjects. For grades K–12. Materials and training provided.
Modern Red Schoolhouse	*Developer:* Modern Red Schoolhouse Institute, Nashville. *Primary goal:* To combine the rigour and values of a little red schoolhouse with latest classroom innovations. *Main features:* • Challenging curriculum (Core Knowledge recommended in K–6). • High standards for all students. • Emphasis on character. • Integral role of technology. • Individual education compact for each student. For grades K–12. Some materials and training provided.
Success for All/Roots and Wings	*Developer:* Robert Slavin, Nancy Madden, and a team of developers from Johns Hopkins University. Now based at the Success for All Foundation in Baltimore. *Primary goal:* To guarantee that every child will learn to read. *Main features:* • Research-based, prescribed curriculum in the areas of reading, writing, and language arts. • One-to-one tutoring, family support team, cooperative learning, on-site facilitator and building advisory team. For grades K–6. Mostly all materials provided. Training required.
Independent	
AVID (Achievement Via Individual Determination)	*Developer:* Mary Catherine Swanson, San Diego County Office of Education *Primary goal:* To ensure that all students, but especially disadvantaged students in the middle with academic potential, will succeed in rigorous curriculum and increase their enrolment in four-year colleges. *Main features:* • Elective programme of academic and social supports to facilitate student success in a rigorous curriculum. • Methodologies are writing, inquiry and collaboration. • Strong emphasis on study skills and college awareness. • AVID Site Team (school-wide support team for AVID students) composed of teachers, administrators and counsellors. • AVID Essentials detail compliance to the AVID philosophy and ensure permission to use the AVID trade name. For grades 7–12. Curriculum guidelines and materials provided. Training required.

7

Table 45.1 *Continued*

Design	Major characteristics
Core Knowledge Sequence	*Developer*: E.D. Hirsch, Jr. (University of Virginia) and the Core Knowledge Foundation, Charlottesville, VA. *Primary goal*: To help students establish a strong foundation of core knowledge for higher levels of learning. *Main features*: ● Sequential programme of specific grade-by-grade topics for core subjects; the rest of curriculum (approximately half) is left for schools to design. ● Instructional methods (to teach core topics) are designed by individual teachers/schools. For grades K–8. Curriculum guidelines provided. Training available but not required.
Coalition of Essential Schools	*Developer*: Ted Sizer, Brown University, Providence, RI. Now based in Oakland, CA. *Primary goal*: To help create schools where students learn to use their minds well. *Main features*: ● Set of Ten Common Principles upon which schools base their practice. ● Personalized learning. ● Mastery of a few essential subjects and skills. ● Graduation by exhibition. ● Sense of community. ● Instruction and organization depend on how each school interprets the Common Principles (may involve interdisciplinary instruction, authentic projects, etc.). For grades K–12. No materials. Range of training options, mostly provided by regional centres.
Comer School Development Program	*Developer*: James Comer, Yale University, New Haven, CT. *Primary goal*: To mobilize entire community of adult caretakers to support students' holistic development to bring about academic success. *Main features*: ● Three teams (school planning and management team, student and staff support team, parent team). ● Three operations (comprehensive school plan, staff development plan, monitoring and assessment). ● Three guiding principles (no-fault, consensus, collaboration). For grades K–12. Training and manual with materials.

Sources: Catalog of School Reform Models; AVID, 1996.

According to Lighthall (1973), Smith and Keith's narrative (1971) of a school district's failed attempt to implement progressive reform is one of the earliest studies that identifies subversion as the reason why change is not sustained. The school district Smith and Keith studied hired a new superintendent and an architectural firm to develop a unique, novel and ultra-contemporary educational programme. The new superintendent, in turn, hired high-level curriculum specialists to implement the new plan; thus, all the ideas for the innovation came from the top of the school organization.

While Smith and Keith, like all the other authors we consult, consider a wide range of variables when analysing the reasons innovations are not sustained, they emphasize the actions of recalcitrant actors at the school site. The superintendent and the principal had tried to isolate the school from undue interference and out-side pressure ('establish a protected subculture' was the expression that they used), and to build a school to facilitate progressive education, but, within a couple of years, the plan unravelled. According to Lighthall (1973), Smith and Keith's emphasis (1971, p. 366) upon teachers circumventing reform is evident when they describe their purpose in writing their book:

> We want our monograph to be useful to the educational administrator who is contemplating the possibility of innovation in his school. The theory we have been developing is one that will enable him to analyse his situation clearly, to anticipate hazards, and to create mecha-nisms and solutions to the problems that arise.

This statement of intentions clearly adopts the perspective of the school's leader-ship. Schools belong to administrators. If administrators act rationally, then they can anticipate barriers to innovation that may arise down the chain of implemen-tation. Smith and Keith more explicitly blame the teachers for the failure of the school to sustain the innovation when they analyse the reasons why teachers expressed concerns about disciplinary issues in team teaching situations:

> My own guess is that this group will not go back to any systematic team teaching, except for the minimal kinds of things like music and maybe occasionally PE, because of the difficulty in implementing the curricular areas ... As it stands now, the total shift has been overwhelm-ing and the people have retreated. (Ibid., p. 367, emphasis added by Lighthall, 1973)

The teachers' 'retreat' is presumably from progressive to traditional methods of instruction, that is, the authors' phrasing represents reform failure as the result of uninformed or recalcitrant teachers subverting the good intentions of a design team.

In the California study of three Success for All (SFA) schools, we found that there were numerous examples of teachers who were seen as subverting the intentions of the SFA reform and the leaders who promoted it. For example, at one school the SFA facilitator believed that the SFA would work better 'if the teachers modified it less'. As this comment implies, she trusted that the SFA curriculum was 'correct' as written and believed that some teachers were errant for not complying with it. A principal in another school contrasted the new teachers who were in favour of SFA – described as 'just great' – with the veteran teachers who were openly hostile towards SFA – described as 'reactive'. These resistant teachers constituted a barrier to sustaining the reform, one that the principal would try to overcome: 'The bottom line is that the program is not going away'.

Reforms fail because reformers do not understand local circumstances

The subversion explanation of the failure to sustain reforms expresses sympathy for the change agents, and blames street-level bureaucrats for any failure. A second agency-based set of explanations criticizes the reformers who work in design teams, state or federal offices for being removed from and not understanding or adapting to local circumstances (Sarason, 1982; Lipsky, 1980; Fullan, 1991). From this point of view, reforms are not sustained because reformers in distant locations are not sensitive to the culture of the school or the perplexities of the daily life of educators, not because educators in schools openly subvert innovations out of hostility, indifference, slough or resistance. We call this 'failure due to insensitivity'.

The great curricular reform movement of the 1960s is often cited as a case in point (Silberman, 1970; Sarason, 1982; Fullan, 1991; Muncey and McQuillan, 1996). This effort emerged from a combination of university professors interested in upgrading the quality of discipline-based teaching, and government officials preoccupied with the importance of producing better scientists and mathematicians after the Soviet Union launched Sputnik. Silberman (1970) argues that the curriculum reform movement failed, however, because the well-intentioned, intelligent university professors and experts on education had abstract theories that did not relate to practice, had limited or no contact or understanding with schools, and failed to consider explicitly the relationship between the nature of the proposed innovations and the purposes of the schools.

Fullan (1991, pp. 22–3) says that 'hyperrationalization' – the assumption that reformers initiating reforms in state or federal offices know everything there is to know about educational goals, the means to achieve them and the consequences of actions – has plagued many innovations initiated from outside the school system. The core belief supporting educational reform is that an external group (state, district or design team) is best suited to be the engine driving reform. But instead of facilitating reform, the top-down vector of change sometimes actually contributes to its very difficulties.

Similarly, in some of the schools we studied, some educators were resentful of the design teams' role as the creator of the innovation. When this occurred, the demise of the reform was not far behind. For example, in one school the design team representative was described as 'alienating' instead of open and 'inflexible' instead of willing to adapt the reform to the school. At one school in Sunland, almost all teachers complained that the whole-school reform they had bought into did not provide the curriculum, pedagogy or resources for students' initial acquisition of skills. This 'major deficit' in the model, as the teachers saw it, was articulated by many of the teachers we interviewed. The model was strong on higher-order thinking skills and authentic pedagogy, which, while important, were not the areas of most pressing need, according to the teachers.

Cultural explanations of the failure to sustain reforms

In the agency-based set of explanations, reforms are not sustained because of the misdeeds of social actors. Either educators at the school sites did not implement the reform as designed, or the design team or district did not develop sufficient sympathy for the lived experiences and practical circumstances of the people asked to implement reforms. While these accounts are helpful in calling attention to the importance of individuals' actions, they tend to overlook cultural considerations that become practical and political constraints. With those concerns in mind, we now turn our attention to a set of explanations that focuses more on social context than actors' intentions.

In these culturally based explanations, observers recognize that replication is rendered complicated because the conditions under which an innovation is implemented are always different from the conditions in the replication setting (Healey and De Stefano, 1997; Fullan, 1999). These conditions are influenced by the culture of the school and the political climate surrounding it. The difficulties of transferring innovations have been associated with the fact that design teams have not always recognized that the transfer of products is very difficult. Reformers assume that their model can be replicated, because from their perspective the reform is explicit. But, according to Schorr (1997, p. 29), 'what is essential is invisible to the eye'. In other words, the transfer of knowledge about reforms is not straightforward and is not always complete because it is dependent on the ability to impart the complexity, essence and context-specific dimensions of the reform.

Practical circumstances constrain reform

A case study of special education implementation emphasizes the power of local conditions to modify reform. Mehan, Hertweck and Meihls (1985) do not blame the failure to sustain educational reform on misguided designers or recalcitrant educators. Instead, they say educators' actions are constrained by 'practical circumstances' in local schools. According to these authors, reform efforts are not implemented exactly as they were planned because educators adapt mandates to pre-existing norms, routines and standard operating procedures. These adaptations occur because schools are sites of pragmatic accommodation in which educators try to achieve multiple goals simultaneously (Cuban, 1992; Berman and McLaughlin, 1978). The innovations are absorbed into the culture of the organization and are adapted to fit accordingly.

When new reforms, such as special education mandates, place new demands on local educators, they work hard to maintain previous routines while conforming to the new demands. In the act of trying to balance new demands and established routines, educators cause educational innovations to undergo changes as they become institutionalized. Educators at the local level inevitably modify attempts to reform or change organizations, especially those introduced from above or from outside. The innovations are absorbed into the culture of the organization and adapted to fit pre-existing routines or standard operating procedures.

The history of the junior high school is another example of a reform absorbed into previously established routines due to practical circumstances. Although designed to be a fundamental change in schooling, over time it has been revised to become only a modest addition to the high school (Cuban, 1992). Machine technologies (radios, film, instructional television and computers) have also been blended into the existing social architecture of the school, traversing a cycle of exhilaration, scientific credibility, disappointment and blame (Cuban, 1986). These results were then used by supporters of technological innovation to criticize both teachers and administrators for blocking the advance of technology and classroom improvement.

Similarly, in a school we studied in Virginia, the success of the AVID reform was undermined when the district implemented AVID solely as a programme, for grades 9 and 10 rather than offering it for four years; this was because of conflicts with another reform designed to help minority and low-income students that was well-entrenched in the district. This College Partnerships programme was perceived as 'the gifted and talented education program for African-American kids'.

Apparently the two programmes could only coexist at different grade levels because of the competition for students and prior agreements that protected the College Partnership 'territory'. Their turf battle resulted in minimizing the support available to AVID students.

Cultural and political changes that accompany leadership shifts

Problems of sustainability also occur in part because of leadership and teacher turnover (Hargreaves and Fink, 2000). District administrations impact the pace, quality and form of school reform through their stability or instability of leadership (Bodilly, 1998; Bryk, 1998; Desimone, *et al.*, 2000). It takes three to five years to bring real change, yet we know that the average tenure of an urban school superintendent (in the USA) is often only a few years. Principals and faculty move and along with them goes the commitment to reform.

Nowhere was this more true than in Sunland County. In 1995–6, Sunland's then-superintendent was very much in favour of promoting the use of externally developed reforms. As one teacher explained, he was 'very supportive'. Under his tenure, the district created an Office of Instructional Improvement to support the designs' implementation. This office had six regional directors who were responsible for providing the various restructuring schools within their regions with training and support. The purpose of these regional directors was to provide information, practical assistance and encouragement to the restructuring schools.

The following year, however, the district leadership changed dramatically. First, the district, which had elected its school board members at-large, moved to a sub-district-specific election format, dramatically altering the make-up of the board. Second, industry leaders in the district and surrounding areas began to make their voices heard, publishing a high visibility report. A culture and value shift had occurred. The focus on student employability intensified with the arrival of a new superintendent whose background was in vocational and secondary education. This superintendent's reform agenda matched the concerns of the new board and local businesses and shifted the district's focus away from externally developed reform models.

The new district administration eliminated the Office of Instructional Improvement in early 1997. District officials reasoned that the dismantling was a response to fiscal belt-tightening at the district level, however, many educators in the restructuring schools and other local observers saw the move as a priority shift. The director of the office was transferred to another division. Three of the six district regional directors were also transferred to other district offices and two retired. The last regional director was given a new position in which she was responsible for doing the same job that six directors had done the year prior. Not surprisingly, district support for many of the restructuring schools decreased dramatically, and several schools dropped their reforms shortly thereafter.

Reforms that neglect the culture of the school are difficult to sustain

Every school has its own culture that is socially constructed by the members within it (Sarason, 1982, 1996). As a result, Hargreaves (1994) claims that educational reform requires more than restructuring. It requires the 'reculturing' of a school. This is a significant challenge because, as Tyack and Tobin (1994) point out, reforms often challenge the 'grammar of schooling'. Educational reform efforts often challenge the most fundamental beliefs about education and force educators to wrestle with age-old cultural beliefs. When reformers call for new practices that diverge too far from educators' common understandings about schooling, they do not sustain.

In our study we found that AVID teachers overwhelmingly held positive views of their students' ability to succeed in school and attend university. The AVID co-ordinator at one high school explained that AVID students have the potential to do well, but many of them could fall through the cracks unless they received the kind of academic support that AVID could provide:

> *AVID works, whether it's the label and making the kids feel like they can do it or that they [feel that they are] special. Because at this school there are not a lot of positive programs and so all of a sudden, here's one that says, hey, we believe in you, we know you can do it, and we're going to help you.*

AVID teachers repeatedly articulated these beliefs to their students. As a result, students came to believe in their own efficacy (Mehan *et al.*, 1996). The success and longevity of the programme hinged on these convictions.

However, the positive attitudes and support of AVID teachers were often in conflict with the ideologies held by other faculty members at their schools. For example, when AVID was implemented in a district in North Carolina, the reform confronted educators' entrenched beliefs about African-American students' inability to achieve. In some cases, teachers resisted the placement of African-American AVID students in their Advanced Placement classes, arguing they were not qualified. An English department chairperson said she was afraid that placing 'underqualified' black students in advanced courses 'will cripple them'. She stated, 'I'm afraid I'm just one of those old-fashioned people who believes self-esteem follows a job well done; it doesn't always precede it' (*Oakwood Times*, 15 December 1996).

To be sure, reform efforts that call for social justice, the blurring of hierarchies and the dismantling of centralized control of knowledge challenge traditional conceptions of education. When reforms threaten individuals' fundamental beliefs about education, the reforms are diminished or become unable to be sustained. However, when innovations do not fundamentally challenge the beliefs and values of the school or threaten the practices of a school or politics of a district, they can be more easily accommodated in the existing school culture.

The expansion policy of the AVID programme illustrates this point well. AVID, which began as the idea of one high-school English teacher in San Diego, has grown to become a nationwide programme. From an activity in a single classroom in one school, it now serves students in more than 700 schools in 13 states and 11 foreign countries, enrolling more than 20 000 students. Viewed in terms of Hargreaves and Fink's criteria (2000) of breadth, AVID has expanded considerably since its inception in 1980. And AVID has sustained its implementation in all 12 of the schools in our study. When we view AVID expansion in terms of Hargreaves and Fink's criteria of depth however, we get a different picture. There are, on the average, 3.2 sections of AVID students with 30 students per section at each of its schools. When viewed as a proportion of the average secondary school population, AVID has not penetrated deeply into the schools it has entered. Yet AVID encounters resistance when it challenges preconceived notions concerning race and intelligence and challenges schools to untrack all of their classes. As long as AVID is relegated to a safe niche, it offers hope and opportunity to a small number of low-achieving students and their families, but does not seriously challenge the special privileges accruing to students and their families in high-track classes (Hubbard and Mehan, 1999b).

Structural explanations of the failure to sustain reforms

To this point, we have considered the actions of design teams and educators and the cultural conditions of schools and districts as possible reasons for the difficulties associated with sustaining reforms deeply and over long periods of time. In this section, we shift our focus to structural issues. We acknowledge that structural issues at the school level influence reform sustainability, as our section on culture-based explanations makes clear. Many of the cultural issues we discussed were framed within structures, such as track systems, board arrangements, etc. Typical school-level structural reasons for or barriers to reform sustainability, such as the use of time, were evident in the schools we studied. Here, we examine the role of the district and the state as structural enablers or constraints to reform. Again, as we will show, these structures were intertwined with culture and agency. Studies of school change seldom document how actions at the school level interact with actions taken in a broader policy context – the district or state – to sustain or spell the demise of reform. Recently, however, researchers have begun to argue for treating the policy context as integral to school and district reform efforts, rather than simply as an 'irritant' to local school change efforts (Hargreaves and Fink, 2000).

The role of the district in sustaining reform

District support for reform, at least a commitment that the district will enable rather than hinder long-term implementation, is critical to sustaining reform at the school level. As we explained, a significant issue in the sustainability of reforms in Sunland was the dramatic change in district leadership and the change in beliefs and values that accompanied it. New mandates and priorities were introduced by the district administration, some of which did not mesh with the schools' chosen reforms. In general, educators felt that they had so many demands on their time that sustaining externally developed reforms was difficult, and thus often not a priority.

Marking a significant shift away from external reform models, in 1998 the district developed its own reading programme. The district gave schools the option to vote for the new Comprehensive Reading Plan developed by the district language arts department, the SRA reading programme, or to stay with Success for All (if they were already implementing it). Educators in most schools told us that the writing was on the wall – in other words, the district reading programme was the best supported option by principals largely because it had the district endorsements.

Two of the three Success for All schools in our sample dropped the reform at this time in favour of the district's new plan. Two of the 13 other sites we studied elected SRA, and the remaining schools went with the Comprehensive Reading

Plan. The new reading programme occupied two hours per day, which meant that schools had to restructure the organization of time and the curriculum to accommodate it. This often meant less time devoted to reform-related activities.

As one principal in a Coalition of Essential Schools site explained:

> *This year, with the district-mandated Comprehensive Reading Plan, we've kind of been swamped ... and we really haven't looked at our Coalition work as closely ... Our directions have been to deal more with the administrative changes and initiatives that are politically supported by the school board ... Once we get through this initial change, we plan to go back to some of our Coalition activities.*

Despite the best of intentions, this did not occur. Teachers in a Core Knowledge school voiced similar statements about having to put Core Knowledge 'on the back burner' while they learned the new reading programme.

Educators in Sunland reacted to the lesser emphasis or expiration of reforms in their schools with a mix of glee and disappointment. Some teachers and principals who heartily embraced the changes reform had brought to their schools felt a profound sense of loss. They also complained that this was yet another example of where support for change received no follow-through from the system. On the other hand, some teachers and principals were relieved that they no longer had to implement reforms that they felt were ill matched to their schools from the beginning.

The power of the state in sustaining reform

Like districts, states play an active role in and sustaining reforms (Furhman and Fry, 1989; Lusi, 1997; Ross, Alberg and Nunnery, 1999). Comparing the circumstances in California with those in Kentucky offers us an example of the power of the state in providing structural support for the AVID reform. Efforts to implement AVID in California are helped considerably by permanent state funding. In 1980, under the auspices of the Tanner Bill, AVID received $50 000 from the Department of Education to develop programmes that supported under-represented students' participation in post-secondary education. Between 1996 and 1997, AVID was awarded $1,000,000 to establish eight regional centres in California and to establish the position of AVID state director. This state fiscal support has been key to the sustainability of AVID in California. While schools do not directly receive money from the state for implementing AVID, they receive assistance from their regional directors and co-ordinators, whose salaries, or at least a portion of them, are paid by the state.

Whereas AVID in California is a budgetary line item, AVID in Kentucky never achieved that status. The former Kentucky state commissioner explained the importance of a programme being part of the state budget, to avoid it being subject to the fragility of leadership:

> *It was never viewed as a state grant [in Kentucky]. One of the differences in having it be a legislative line item v. an administrative priority is that the administrator changes more often than the legislator. And as soon as you get something in there as a line item you have a constituency and it's hard to get it out.*

The director of a Kentucky education advocacy group reinforced his observation about the importance of permanent state funding: 'AVID in general doesn't have any champions ... I don't think it is on anybody's radar screen politically'.

The Kentucky State Department of Education reduced funding for AVID to $7000 per school for the 1998–9 school year, and $3000 for the 1999–2000 school year – the last year of state support. From that point on, if districts and schools want to continue AVID, they must do so with their funds. Without state directors to provide professional assistance to school sites, local schools and districts must contract directly to the AVID Center for services. Some AVID programmes are limping along without tutors, field trips, guest speakers and curriculum, which raises the specter of decertification by the AVID Center. AVID's longevity is precarious when state funds dry up and local sites must scurry for money.

Reform sustainability was impacted by a different set of structural issues at the state level in Sunland. In particular, the state's new high stakes accountability system – a powerful external structure – had the unintended consequence of destabilizing reform efforts in most of the schools. Beginning in 1999, schools received ratings based on student performance on norm-referenced and criterion-referenced tests. The schools in our study received grades ratings depending on their ability to meet minimum criteria for performance. The state's new rating system proved demoralizing to teachers in the schools that received poor marks, particularly given the extensive effort they had expended on reform in the past several years. Often, teachers admitted to putting reform-related activities aside in order to prepare students for 'the test'. Educators lamented that test scores were not the proper measure of success for their reform efforts, but they realized the constraints under which they operated.

The situation in Sunland is not unique. Prior studies of externally developed reforms have documented that in schools where state accountability demands were high, reform strategies were abandoned in favor of test preparation (Bodilly and Berends, 1999; Datnow, Borman and Stringfield, 2000). District and school administrators are increasingly making decisions about whether to continue reforms – and their contracts with design teams – on the basis of this single, rather narrow reform 'effectiveness' standard (Cuban, 1998). Meanwhile, teachers, like reformers, seek improvement in student performance, but what counts as success or results are seldom test scores, but rather attitudes, values and actual behaviour on academic and non-academic tasks in and out of the classroom. Moreover, what 'becomes especially important for teachers is how they can put their personal signature on the mandated reform and make it work for their students and themselves' (ibid., p. 459). This debate illustrates the differences of perspective of teachers and policy makers and the differing values about what sustains a reform.

Conclusion and implications

This chapter has discussed reform sustainability and expiration in terms of the agency, cultural and structural forces that shape it. Studies of school change that focus on the school as the unit of change either praise or blame local educators for the outcome of reform efforts. But school-level factors do not tell the complete story. Our research shows that reform sustainability or expiration does not result from individuals or institutions acting in isolation from one another. Forces at the state, in districts, design teams, the school and classrooms all interact to shape the longevity of reform. Structures and cultures do not exist 'out there' but rather are the contingent outcomes of practical activities of individuals. As we have shown, real people – confronting real problems in classrooms, school board meetings and reform design teams – interact together and produce the texts, the rules and the guidelines that are part and parcel of the school-change process. In sum educators in schools, policy makers in districts and states, and personnel in design teams 'co-construct' reform success.

In our other work, we discuss how the process by which schools adopt reforms (Datnow, 2000), the influence of the local context (Datnow, Hubbard and Mehan, 1998; Hubbard and Mehan, 1999b), the importance of leadership (Datnow and Castellano, 2001) and the relationship between the school and the design team (Datnow, Hubbard, and Mehan, 2002) all profoundly affect reform sustainability as well. The collective wisdom we have gathered results in the following implications for educational leaders.

Reforms that have an inauthentic beginning almost surely will not be sustained

The schools that dropped their reforms almost always exhibited an absence of staff buy-in initially. Staff in these schools were often hurried to make decisions or coerced to go along with the choice of reform, regardless of their true wishes. In contrast, in some of the sustaining schools, educators were more likely to have chosen a reform with which they could engage with integrity and for which there was substantial teacher and principal support.

Reform sustainability requires building ideological commitment and ownership among teachers

No doubt teachers need to have substantial interest in attempting reform at the outset. However, establishing ownership over the long term requires that teachers understand and commit to the theory behind the reform. Just as we have concluded that students have to construct their own meaning for learning to occur, people in all change situations must construct their own meaning as they go about reform. Teachers need to wrestle with what the reform model means for them and their students (Yonezawa, 1998). Some level of local development or adaptation seems necessary to create this ownership, particularly when teachers are implementing a highly structured model (Datnow and Castellano, 2000).

Reform models with more flexibility are more sustainable in the face of changing district and state constraints

Flexible reforms more easily mould to local circumstances, but they can potentially have less of an impact in the short term. The reforms that lasted in Sunland were those that helped educators meet local district and state demands, or at least did not come into conflict with them. These tended to be less structured reforms, whereas reforms that included more demands on the system and its resources faced greater difficulty. So, too, successful AVID programmes were those that adapted to local circumstances. In addition to the discontinuation of district support and the changing political climate at both the state and district levels, frustration with the lack of workability of some reform models caused them to expire. Some reform designs appeared more naturally suited or better equipped to work in particular contexts than others. Their ability to adapt to local circumstances impacted on their longevity in the schools.

A stable resource base is essential to reform sustainability

Some school reforms require substantial funding to implement and to sustain over time. In the face of budget cuts, reform models that require a continual financial outlay might find themselves at risk of expiration or at least instability. Yet the reforms that are the most comprehensive are often the most expensive. As we well know, school change is resource hungry (Fullan, 1991). Enabling legislation may provide some level of start-up funding, but because local sites often do not have the resources to sustain government-sponsored programmes, they often do not last more than a year or 18 months. Worse, they are abandoned entirely when other similar programmes become available. The net result of the opportunistic search for reforms that work and the funds that accompany them is often a hodge-podge of uncoordinated, disconnected programmes at school sites.

High-stakes accountability systems may inhibit dramatic, sustainable change in schools

Prevailing measures of reform effectiveness run counter to school change, serve to hold in place existing structures and practices, and do not fit with teachers' realities. Reform success needs to be more broadly measured. Few would argue with the fact that students should benefit academically, but this should not only be in terms of the narrow measure of standardized achievement tests. Understanding the value of school, the development of civic virtue and critical thinking are other possible valuable goals for students. Moreover, the interests of those responsible for implementing the reform – teachers – and whether the change serves their interests are also of utmost importance in measuring success. Finally, measures of reform success should address whether the implementation of a reform design leads to long-term school improvement and the development of a school culture that is ripe for change, or whether it hinders such efforts.

Policy systems need to be aligned to support school reform efforts

Already over 1800 schools have received federal funding for reform through the US federal Comprehensive School Reform Demonstration (CSRD) programme. Meanwhile, many states are simultaneously implementing high-stakes accountability systems. Districts are also promoting their own change efforts. In other words, change vectors are coming at schools from several directions. Districts promoting the use of externally developed reforms (and the seeking of federal CSRD funds) often believe that the reforms will produce better outcomes on state-mandated assessments. Meanwhile, many reform models are not necessarily aligned towards these outcomes, nor can they produce desired results in short periods of time.

Reform strategies that seek a 'safe niche' may have limited impact on school improvement

Although programmes that do not seek to change the whole school improve their chances of sustainability, the goal of offering an excellent education to all students will not be achieved by limited reform efforts that impact on only part of the school. As long as such programmes only occupy a safe niche, inequities will remain in place and low income and minority students will continue to be disadvantaged because they are not placed in rigorous and demanding courses. Educators must actively confront deep-seated values and cultural beliefs as well as modify institutional practices to achieve educational equity and excellence. This transformation will not happen automatically or naturally. A concerted effort must exist on the part of design teams and school-site educators to accomplish social justice goals.

ACKNOWLEDGEMENTS

This chapter derives from Datnow, Hubbard, and Mehan (2002). The work reported was supported by a grant from the Office of Educational Research and Improvement, US Department of Education, to the Center for Research on the Education of Students Placed At Risk (grant no. R-117D-40005) and a grant to the Center for Research on Education, Diversity, and Excellence under the Educational Research and Development Centers Program (PR/award no. R306A60001). However, any opinions expressed are the authors' own and do not represent the policies or positions of the US Department of Education. We are greatly indebted to the participants of our research studies who welcomed us into their schools, districts and offices and gave so freely of their time. We also wish to thank our colleagues who worked with us on some of these studies, most notably Sam Stringfield and Marisa Castellano.

REFERENCES

Anderson, S. and Stiegelbauer, S. (1994) 'Institutionalization and renewal in a restructured secondary school', *School Organization*, 14 (3), pp.279–93.

AVID (1996) *AVID Administrator Guide*, San Diego, CA: Advancement Via Individual Determination Center.

Berman, P. and McLaughlin, M.W. (1978) *Federal Programs Supporting Educational Change*, vol. 8, Santa Monica, CA: Rand Corporation.

Bodilly, S. (1998) *Lessons from New American Schools' Scale Up Phase*, Santa Monica, CA: RAND.

Bodilly, S. and Berends, M. (1999) 'Necessary district support for comprehensive school reform' in Orfield, G. and Debray, G.H. (eds) Hard Work for Good Schools: Facts Not Fads in Title 1 Reform (pp. 111–139). Cambridge, MA: Harvard University Civil Rights Projects.

Catalog of School Reform Models, Oak Brook, IL: Northwest Regional Educational Laboratory (www.nwrel.org/scpd/natspec/catalog).

Chicago School Reform Democratic Localism as a Lever for Change (1988), Boulder, CO: Westview Press.

Cuban, L. (1986) *Teachers and Machines: The Classroom Use of Technology since 1920*, New York: Teachers' College Press.

Cuban, L. (1992) 'What happens to reforms that last? The case of the junior high school', *American Educational Research Journal*, 29 (2), pp. 227–51.

Cuban, L. (1998) 'How schools change reforms: redefining reform success and failure', Teachers' College Record, 99 (3), pp. 153–77.

Datnow, A. (2000) 'Power and politics in the adoption of school reform models', *Educational Evaluation and Policy Analysis*, 22 (4), pp. 357–74.

7

Datnow, A., Borman, G. and Stringfield, S. (2000) 'School reform through a highly specified curriculum: a study of the implementation and effects of the core knowledge sequence', *The Elementary School Journal*, 101 (2), pp. 167–91.

Datnow, A. and Castellano, M. (2000) 'Teachers' responses to success for all: how beliefs, experiences, and adaptations shape implementation', *American Educational Research Journal*, 37 (3), pp. 775–99.

Datnow, A. and Castellano, M. (2001) 'Managing and guiding school reform: leadership in success for all schools', *Educational Administration Quarterly*, 37 (2), pp. 219–49.

Datnow, A. Hubbard, L. and Mehan, H. (1998) 'Educational reform implementation: a co-constructed process', technical report, Santa Cruz, CA: Center for Research on Education, Diversity, and Excellence.

Datnow, A. Hubbard, L. and Mehan, H. (2002) *Extending Reform: From One School to Many*, London: Routledge/Falmer Press.

Desimone, L. (2000) *Making Comprehensive School Reform Work*, New York: ERIC Clearinghouse on Urban Education.

Elmore, R. E. (1996) 'Getting to scale with good educational practice', *Harvard Educational Review*, 66 (1), pp. 1–26.

Fuhrman, S.H. and Fry, P. (1989) *Diversity Amidst Standardization: State Differential Treatment of Districts*, New Brunswick, NJ: Center for Policy Research in Education.

Fullan, M. (1991) *The New Meaning of Educational Change*, 2nd edn, New York: Teachers' College Press.

Fullan, M. (1999) *Change Forces: The Sequel*, Philadelphia and London: Falmer Press.

Fullan, M. and Hargreaves, A. (1992) *What's Worth Fighting for in Your School?*, New York: Teachers' College Press.

Hargreaves, A. (1994) *Changing Teachers, Changing Times*, New York: Teachers' College Press.

Hargreaves, A. and Fink, D. (2000) 'Three dimensions of educational reform', *Educational Leadership*, 57 (7), pp. 30–4.

Healey, F. and de Stefano, J. (1997) *Education Reform Support: A Framework for Scaling up School Reform*, Washington, DC: Abel 2 Clearinghouse for Basic Education.

Hubbard, L. and Mehan, H. (1999a) 'Scaling up an untracking program: a co-constructed process', *Journal of Education for Students Placed At Risk*, 4 (1): pp. 83–100.

Hubbard, L. and Mehan, H. (1999b) "Educational niche picking in a hostile environment', *Journal of Negro Education*, 68 (2), pp. 213–26.

Kirst, M. and Meister, G. (1985) 'Turbulence in American secondary schools. What reforms last?', *Curriculum Inquiry*, 15, pp. 169–86.

Lighthall, F. (1973) 'Review of Smith & Keith (1971), *Anatomy of An Educational Innovation', School Review*, 255–93.

Lipsky, M. (1980) *Street-level Bureaucracy: Dilemmas of the Individual in Public Services*, New York: Russell Sage Foundation.

Lusi, S. (1997) *The Role of State Departments of Education in Complex School Reform*, New York and London: Teachers' College Press.

Mehan, H., Hertweck, A. and Meihls, J. L. (1985) *Handicapping the Handicapped: Decision Making in Students' Educational Careers*, Stanford: Stanford University Press.

Mehan, H., Villanueva, I., Hubbard, L. and Lintz, A. (1996) *Constructing School Success*, Cambridge: Cambridge University Press.

Muncey, D. E. and McQuillan, P. J. (1996) *Reform and Resistance in Schools and Classrooms*, New Haven and London: Yale University Press.

Ross, S.M., Alberg, M. and Nunnery, J. (1999) 'Selection and evaluation of locally developed versus externally developed schoolwide programs' in Orfield, G. and Debray, E.H. (eds) *Hard Work for Good Schools: Facts not Fads in Reform*, Cambridge: Harvard University, Civil Rights Project, pp. 147–58.

Sarason, S. (1982) *The Culture of the School and the Problem of Change*, Boston: Allyn & Bacon.

Sarason, S. (1996) *Revisiting 'the Culture of the School and the Problem of Change'*, New York: Teachers' College Press.

Schorr, L. (1997) *Common Purpose: Strengthening Families and Neighbourhoods to Rebuild America*, New York: Doubleday, Anchor Books.

Silberman, C. (1970) *Crisis in the Classroom: The Remaking of American Education*, New York: Random House.

Slavin, R.E. and Madden, N.A. (1998) 'Disseminating success for all: lessons for policy and practice', revised technical report. Baltimore, MD: Center for Research on the Education of Students Placed At Risk, Johns Hopkins University.

Smith, L. and Keith, P. (1971) *Anatomy of an Educational Innovation*, New York: John Wiley & Sons.

Stringfield, S. and Datnow, A. (1998). Introduction: scaling up school restructuring designs in urban schools', *Education and Urban Society* 30 (3) pp. 269–76.

Stringfield, S., Datnow, A., Ross, S. and Snively, F. (1998) 'Scaling up school restructuring in multicultural, multilingual contexts', *Education and Urban Society*, 30 (3) pp. 326–57.

Tyack, D. and Cuban, L. (1995) *Tinkering Toward Utopia*, Cambridge, MA: Harvard University Press.

Tyack, D. and Tobin, W. (1994) The 'grammar' of schooling: Why has it been so hard to change? *American Educational Research Journal*, 31, pp.453–79.

Yin, R. (1989) *Case Study Research*, Beverly Hills, CA: Sage Publications.

Yonezawa, S. (1998) *Bay Elementary School Case Report*, Baltimore, MD: Center for Social Organization of Schools, Johns Hopkins University.

Yonezawa, S. and Stringfield, S. (2000) *Special Strategies for Educating Disadvantaged Students Follow-Up Study: Examining the Sustainability of Research-based School Reforms*, Baltimore: Johns Hopkins University CRESPAR.

7

CHAPTER 46

Sustaining the professional development of teachers: learning in networks

....

ANN LIEBERMAN AND DIANE WOOD

Over the past three decades, teacher networks have played a burgeoning role in efforts to reform public education in the USA (Lieberman and Grolnick, 1996). Such networks have coalesced around a range of educational change initiatives, including the restructuring and redesigning of schools, the teaching of specific content areas, the promotion of teacher research, and the challenges of assessment and accountability. The National Writing Project (NWP), one of the oldest – and arguably most successful of these networks – started as a 1974 summer institute for San Francisco Bay Area teachers interested in improving the teaching of writing. Since then, it has grown exponentially to include well over 100 sites at colleges and universities in all 50 states.

Intrigued with the NWP's capacities for both longevity and expansion, we launched a two-year study of two of those NWP sites, one based at the University of California at Los Angeles (UCLA) and the other at Oklahoma State University (OSU) in Stillwater, Oklahoma.[1] Over the period of the two years, we looked at the sites as a whole, tracking activities and events, holding focus groups and talking to site directors. In addition, we followed closely six teachers, three from each site, interviewing them about their NWP activities and observing them in their classrooms. As a result of our work, we are convinced that, despite ongoing challenges, the NWP makes a compelling case that teacher networks have the potential to foster significant professional learning, change teaching practices and affect students' learning experiences. In this chapter, we examine how the NWP attracts and sustains the enthusiastic participation of teachers, thus accounting for the remarkable spread of its influence, and describe some of its continuing challenges. In doing so, we hope not only to lay out the complexities of this particular network, but also to suggest how networks themselves may be a particularly significant vehicle for meaningful and lasting change in schools.

Perhaps most key to our understanding of networks is the notion that they offer teachers a 'third space' (Lieberman and Grolnick, 1996) – an in-between space with the capacity to address both local and distant educational concerns. Removed from the press of local bureaucracies and politics, such a space frees teachers to engage in genuine collaboration about serious classroom issues. The resulting dialogue widens professional perspectives without losing focus on classrooms. NWP teachers, for instance, expose one another to the challenges and successes they experience in their own contexts, and this process widens their horizons about educational issues writ large. NWP teachers come together from all grade levels (pre-K through to college) and subject areas, from both public and private schools, from diverse socio-economic contexts, and from rural, urban and suburban schools. Hence, their collaboration crosses the very boundaries that so typically divide K–12 school cultures. Perhaps most significant to the success of the NWP as a network is the grassroots nature of its 'third space', – a landscape explored, founded and settled on democratic principles. It is these principles that empower the network to resist orthodoxy, remain flexible and responsive, and yet rally teachers around a shared mission.

The model: the summer invitational

The National Writing Project began, as many teaching networks begin, in the midst of a perceived educational crisis. Administrators at the University of California at Berkeley (UCB), alarmed at what many believed to be the poor writing skills of their undergraduates, sponsored the founder of the NWP, James Gray, in his revolutionary idea to create a mutually respectful partnership between UCB and Bay Area teachers. It was Gray's contention (2000) that, if California students were to become better writers, then both knowledge constructed in the university and knowledge constructed in practice were needed. Thus Gray, then a supervisor of student teachers at UCB, argued that high-quality professional development must be grounded in authentic regard for the work of teachers. He envisioned successful teachers coming together under the auspices of the university to share and critique their best practices and to read current theory in the teaching of writing. From what they learned together, he proposed, teachers could then go out to their districts and schools and teach their colleagues – all in the name of improving writing instruction. Gray and a few trusted colleagues planned the first institute, invited teachers from the Bay Area to attend, and the seeds for a network were planted. Within four years, similar partnerships between universities and teachers were forged, not only throughout California, but also across its boundaries to other states.

Despite the rapid and continuing growth of the NWP over almost 30 years, the sites remain consciously faithful to what NWP insiders call 'the model'. Over time, we began to see that 'this model' essentially refers to the highly participatory, teacher-centred design for professional development that has evolved from Gray's original conception. It has three principle features (Gray, 2000):

- creating forums for successful teachers to teach one another;
- providing opportunities for teachers to write and share their writing in response groups;
- engaging teachers in reading and discussing relevant educational literature and research.

Disarmingly simple, these principles have spawned a professional development approach very unlike the mandated, isolated in-service workshops that are still pervasive in many schools. Such workshops instruct teachers in current educational strategies without tapping into what they already know or want to know. Far more democratic, the NWP model presumes effective teachers have constructed knowledge in and for practice and that this knowledge should be valued and disseminated. It also assumes that teachers who teach writing ought to be writing themselves, reflecting on the process, learning from it and incorporating that learning into their practices. Despite the emphasis on the expertise of teachers, the model also creates the space and time for K–12 teachers to read and discuss current educational research. Thus, it redefines the practices of K–12 teachers, not only in terms of pedagogical strategies, but also in terms of intellectual engagement (McLaughlin and Oberman, 1996). Teachers become responsible not only for the 'how' of practice but also for the 'why'. And, significantly, the model provides forums for teachers to make these practices public, immersing their ideas and strategies in collegial exchange and critique.

One of the national directors advised us that we would understand the model best by visiting the summer institutes – the five-week, annual invitationals that initiate new members to the NWP – because 'it all happens there'. We found she was right. Seeing the summer institutes first-hand brought the model to life. The institutes have a definite curriculum, shaped both by the expertise of institute fellows and by current knowledge in the field of literacy. Teachers prepare demonstrations of best practices and receive feedback on them. All institute fellows belong to writing response groups where they share and critique written drafts, and all choose a topic or a question of particular professional interest and pursue it in educational literature and research. Over the five weeks, they draft and revise four written pieces: three can be in any style or genre and on any topic of their choice; the fourth is a position paper on an educational topic they have chosen to research.

During the first few days of the institutes, some teachers are reticent to speak and/or reluctant to share their writing, while others can dominate. Over the five weeks, however, a vibrant learning community takes shape and participation equalizes. As teachers share their writing, get feedback on it and rework drafts, they create tangible evidence for the power of feedback and revision. They learn that individual perspectives are valuable for reconsidering and improving practice – whether it is writing or teaching. Through the demonstrations, discussions and writing response groups, teachers articulate their commitments and a shared mission emerges: to find ways collectively to make learning a meaningful, successful and enriching experience for all students. Participants bond, in other words, in shared purpose and mutual respect.

At the end of the institutes, fellows become NWP teacher-consultants (TCs), professionally authorized by the strength of their network's reputation – and their own enhanced sense of efficacy – to teach other teachers in their buildings and districts (Lieberman and Wood, 2001). Although not all institute fellows become active TCs, in fact many do, spreading accumulating insights and knowledge beyond the network itself. The following aspects of the design contribute to that success:

- Participation is voluntary. Those who are nominated as potential institute fellows are invited, undergo an application process and can choose whether or not to attend. In this way, the NWP establishes a form of quality control, seeking out already accomplished teachers, who are open and motivated to further learning (Gray, 2000). It is precisely these kinds of teachers whom they want eventually to become TCs, and they insist that the highest quality professional development is voluntary rather than mandated.

- Teachers receive recompense for their efforts. Institute fellows receive a stipend and frequently college credit in return for participation in the institutes. Once fellows become TCs, they are paid for in-services they provide colleagues. Perhaps most important to the TCs we interviewed, affiliation with the NWP in the UCLA and OSU sites proffers a measure of status and authority that enables them to exert influence.
- The NWP professional development activities involve multiple sessions. Unlike most one-shot professional development experiences, TCs return from the summer invitationals with opportunities to attend 'continuity' sessions that keep them learning, informed and connected. TCs who offer in-services to buildings and districts do so only if they can lead multiple sessions, allowing for practice, feedback and follow-through.

Again, the above guidelines fly in the face of most in-service approaches, which tend to be mandated, unrewarded and isolated. According to the teachers we interviewed, these attributes of the NWP deliver a strong message of respect for the teaching profession. Many, in fact, claimed that, during the course of the institutes, they began not only to think of themselves as 'authors', but to also see themselves as more professional. As one said, 'You get treated so much like a professional that you begin to think of yourself more as a professional'. This enhanced sense of authorship and professionalism empowers many to make their ideas and practices public. The six teachers we followed closely were all active TCs, including the two fresh out of their respective institutes. They were contributing regularly to the professional development of colleagues, writing essays and articles, and leading workshops in their buildings, districts and beyond.

Although the two site directors identified each of the six teachers for us because each was already an active TC or showed strong potential for becoming one, the directors claimed the choices were difficult because there were so many from whom to choose. And, indeed, as we interviewed TCs in the two sites, we met dozens who contributed frequently to the professional development of colleagues both inside and outside the NWP. Moreover, TCs we encountered tended to describe themselves as consumers of professional literature. In describing how her professional reading had ended after she left graduate school, a TC from the UCLA site then explained that 'the NWP has made me a reader again'. NWP teachers see themselves as located in a resource-rich professional context – in terms of both human beings and printed material – that supports them in meeting their classroom challenges.

The professional development experiences that TCs design for colleagues outside the network follow those they encountered at the institutes – the NWP model. The TCs themselves are 'teachers teaching other teachers' (Gray, 2000). They attempt to tap into the experience and knowledge of participants. They also insist that the teachers who participate do so voluntarily. Highly interactive activities unfold in multiple sessions, allowing opportunities for practice and feedback. Participants write they learn about relevant educational theories and they learn from the local knowledge and expertise of colleagues. Having experienced during the institutes the rewards of a non-hierarchical, more democratic 'third space' for learning, NWP teachers provide experiences that include both individual perspective and common purpose, both outside and inside knowledge, and both theory and practice.

The work: social practices in the NWP

Almost as frequently as we heard members of the NWP talk about 'the model', we heard them refer to 'the work'. At first, we conflated one with the other. Eventually, however, we came to realize that 'the work' refers to something apart. A national director described it this way: 'The work is the intellectual framing and building of the professional community in order to deepen knowledge and provide many occasions for doing it.' Ultimately, we came to see that the work is actually a set of social practices necessary for the implementation of the three-pronged NWP professional development model: collegial teaching and learning, writing in writing groups, and reading and discussing educational literature. These practices, in fact, 'enact a culture', as a national director explained to us. This culture, scholarly and dialogic, retains the grassroots pluralism originally intended in the design and practice of the first Bay Area institute.

We identified these social practices as follows.

Approaching every colleague as a potentially valuable contributor

During the summer institute, a key component of the curriculum emerges from teachers demonstrating their best practices. This process empowers TCs to define 'niches of expertise' (Gray, 2000) that they can share with other teachers. A TC who had developed such a niche told us:

> Being taught how to share your ideas with colleagues was so helpful to me. I was asked to do a presentation on mini-lessons [brief, on-the-spot skill instruction]. Even though for a long time I'd been doing them, to present I had to take a closer look at them. It helped me to become so much clearer about how I thought about them. It then helped me to get better in my actual use of mini-lessons in the classroom.

Teaching other teachers disseminates expertise while simultaneously strengthening it. Having teachers teach one another and learn from one another topples the hierarchical notion that authority lies with experts outside the field. Expertise is located in a community of knowers and learners who treat one another as valued equals because, as one TC told us, 'it may be the teacher right next to you who has found the answer you're looking for'.

Creating public forums for sharing, dialogue and critique

Again, during the summer institute the teachers learn the strength of making the knowledge and expertise of teachers public. They come away from the institutes equipped with new ideas and strategies gleaned from their colleagues' demonstrations. Because they have learned to value what other practitioners have to teach them, most begin to see themselves as having something of value to offer. But they also learn that bringing their professional opinions and practices to a public forum requires holding up those opinions and practices for critique. For some, this can mean relinquishing old habits. A new TC, for instance, told us she had been convinced by her colleagues during the summer institute that separating spelling instruction from writing instruction made little sense. When we visited her classroom, each of her third graders had created his or her own spelling book, comprised of words they discovered they needed in order to express their thinking.

Turning ownership of learning over to learners

The NWP makes a number of basic assumptions about learning to write. Good writers have a sense of purpose, which means they must have choices in what they say and how they say it. In fact, all learners, according to the NWP, need to see purpose in their learning, opportunities to develop their voices and exercise choices, and practise making their thinking transparent to others. Teachers are no exception. Professional learning requires purpose, voice and freedom. Under such conditions, teachers 'own' their own professional development and become invested in it:

> Because of the NWP I am constantly learning. It's not just a one-time workshop. Now I value my own learning like I value their [her students'] learning. I see what I need to know and I go after it. And that growth process that we all go through is so obvious in such a short time ... You watch it in the summer institute and then after that, it takes on a whole new life of its own. You're a writer; you're a learner.

Situating learning in practice and relationships as well as relevant knowledge

Repeatedly, NWP insiders spoke to us about the riveting learning experiences during the institutes. We heard comments like: 'It [being a part of the NWP] has changed my whole life. It's changed my life outside my teaching and inside my teaching ... It's given me a support system; it's given me friends; it's given me my writing back; it's given me my classroom back.' As this quotation indicates, the NWP provides opportunities for teachers to build strong collegial relationships and a sense of efficacy in their classrooms. They share what they have learned from practice and encourage one another to plot strategies for improved future practice. As institute fellows and TCs engage in the practice of collegial writing and teaching, they learn to serve as critical audiences for one another. In the give and take between author and audience and between colleague and colleague, the learning, which begins and ends with teaching practice, becomes intensely relational. Although NWP teachers explore relevant outside knowledge, they do it for the sake of informing professional practice and community.

Providing multiple entry points into learning communities

Remarkably, the NWP institutes and subsequent continuity meetings meet a wide range of professional needs. The relative newcomer to teaching takes his/her place beside the seasoned veteran, but a solid expectation is set: everyone teaches and everyone learns. When we asked TCs why they accepted invitations to the institutes, they gave a variety of reasons. Some wanted to improve their own writing, others sought new teaching strategies, some wanted intellectual stimulation, a few were looking for a clearer sense of purpose, still others longed for professional community. Despite the range of experience and interests, the teachers we interviewed claimed participation more than met their needs. Moreover, NWP teachers somehow avoid the ideological wars that threaten professional collaboration (Westheimer, 1998). We witnessed respectful exchanges between institute fellows committed to the teaching of phonics, grammar mechanics and great books and those committed to whole language, personal writing and student choice. These interactions, according to one TC, produce teachers who are 'flexibilists'.[2] As she puts it:

> *I don't want to fall into a category, not just in terms of falling on one side or the other, but in terms of where my kids need me to be. I don't want to just say this is my philosophy and then just stick with that. I need to look at everything when the kids need something, so I'll look, for example, at phonics and at whole language.*

Reflecting on teaching through reflection on learning

We were taken with the fact that, during the summer institutes, TCs keep a log of their ongoing activities and then take turns reading at the beginning of each day. This, coupled with an evaluation at the end of the institute, provides opportunities for participants to reflect on their learning. An assumption intrinsic to the NWP design is that the best teaching emerges from a solid understanding of how people learn. The best way to drive that lesson home is to ensure participants become critically conscious of their own learning as it unfolds. As one TC fresh from the institute put it: 'The learning is so powerful and it's made so transparent, you want to turn around and create that same kind of experience for your students in the classroom'.

Sharing leadership

A major purpose of the summer institutes is to build the capacity for leadership in teachers. Starting with the summer institute, when each individual fellow takes a turn sharing his/her writing, demonstrating a lesson, logging activities and so forth, the culture sets a norm for rotating leadership responsibilities. After the institute, TCs encounter more opportunities to continue the practice of leadership – both formally and informally. For example, some TCs come back to the summer institutes to coach fellows in preparing for demonstrations. TCs perform demonstrations of their own best practices to institute fellows and, of course, to colleagues in their districts and schools. A particularly strong leader told us what 'a growing experience' it had been for her to learn from TCs during the summer institutes. Their help on her presentation style and their confidence in her gave her a new sense of herself. She explained: 'It was very hard for me even to see myself as a leader until the Writing Project'.

Once having recognized their potential for leadership, many NWP teachers practise it enthusiastically. Some become leaders in their own buildings, like two elementary teachers who initiated and found funding for a writing camp for their low-achieving students. Some contribute to the professional development of colleagues in their schools and beyond, teaching effective approaches to literacy development. Some become involved politically, lobbying to ensure state and national policies friendly to 'the work'.

Adopting a stance of inquiry

A stance of inquiry is at the heart of scholarly activity and a prerequisite for meaningful learning. As we watched the proceedings of the institutes, talked to dozens of NWP teachers in the two years afterwards, interviewed site and national directors, and followed the six targeted teachers into their classroom, we recognized that NWP teachers relinquish a quest for certainty and replace it with a commitment to continuous inquiry. The processes of writing and critical dialogue so pervasive in the NWP model demand this. When NWP teachers share their drafts in order to improve them, they must be open to other perspectives and to critique. When they revise, they recognize the value of revisiting, rethinking and improving first efforts. These habits extend to their teaching, which they begin to see as perpetually in draft stages and always in need of public critique and further study.

Rethinking professional identity and linking it to professional community

A TC told us during an interview that she thought of writing 'as a bridge', enabling learners to make connections with content, their teachers and their colleagues. We saw the truth of her statement during the summer institutes when we witnessed how writing provides a bridge between individual fellows and the larger community. The self-disclosure necessarily involved in the sharing of writing creates a web of connections and draws the community closer. Because interactions are completely informed by the practice of 'teachers teaching other teachers', strong habits of collegial respect and interdependence are established. Hence, most NWP teachers quite consciously internalize the value of professional community over time and become dependent on it. They see professional responsibility as a shared responsibility. To be an NWP teacher is both to need a colleague and to be a colleague.

The role of the site directors

The site directors at both UCLA and OSU play key roles in the success of the NWP as a network. They are faithful to the NWP model as they plan and implement the summer institutes, and they go about their own work enacting the social practices that so effectively seal collegial relationships. In this way, they become carriers of the NWP culture. Besides being 'cultural carriers', directors are, at different times, teacher, facilitator, broker, fund raiser, entrepreneur, decision-maker, proposal writer, talent agent, organizer and professional developer. They communicate with principals, school districts, state officials and university personnel, while negotiating new relationships and new possibilities for their respective sites. Both the UCLA and OSU directors strive to reach out to underserved populations. At UCLA, for instance, second-language learners became a special focus for professional development. In a similar vein, TCs at the OSU site mobilized to find ways to support teachers working in remote, rural communities.

During the summer institutes, site directors watch fellows carefully, taking note of special talents and expertise that might be needed in the region. They work hard to keep TCs connected with one another through continuity sessions, special events and newsletters. It is not unusual for TCs to receive invitations to special writing retreats, which are usually designed to give them time and support to bring writing to publication. Besides brokering the individual talents of

TCs, directors also broker new networking arrangements with other sites. For example, TCs in both Washington and California have joined together to create state standards in language arts. Moreover, national and site directors have created collaborations on literacy standards across state lines.

Effective site directors must be knowledgeable about the local educational landscape and its political contexts, and they learn to exploit opportunities and defend against threats. For example, when the UCLA site faced a state policy suspending bilingual programmes and mandating English immersion only within a year, it created a professional development offering entitled 'Writing from Day One'. The sessions helped teachers to see how daily engagement in writing, whether in English or the student's native tongue, led more quickly and effectively to English fluency.

In part, because of this responsiveness, the local reputations of the UCLA and OSU sites are quite strong, as evidenced by the frequent calls from practitioners in the field asking for TCs to provide professional development. Because the site directors recognize and nurture the talents of TCs, they know whom to send to meet what needs – or they know whom to ask to find out. Despite occasional pressure to deliver an isolated in-service workshop in the old, one-shot mode, both site directors remain faithful to the model.

Learning from the NWP: the challenges of networks

The local networks created by the NWP are clearly having an impact on writing in the USA and continue to recruit teachers who are enthusiastic about their participation (Fancsali and Nelsestuen, 2001; St John et al., 2001). The network's continued growth attests to its viability and popularity. But networks as complex as the NWP also have their challenges. We highlight three major ones that the NWP faces: the complexities of school/university partnerships; the problem of quality control; and the tensions involved in developing commitments among participants without establishing a rigid orthodoxy.

School/university partnerships

Each NWP site, involving a university sponsor and a site director, is headquartered within a college or university. The site director oversees the day-to-day running of the regional network. Because true collaboration and respect for practitioner knowledge are core NWP beliefs, the work of the site requires independence from the university's regular programme of studies. Thus the site director must convince those in higher education that the starting place for teacher learning is classroom practice rather than university knowledge. In addition, directors must learn to navigate between the culture of the university and the growing culture developing in the sites. On the one hand, the site is dependent on the university for resources (office and meeting spaces) and for the status that university affiliation brings. On the other hand, the site needs support for its own independence or it risks its teacher-centred reputation. It is not surprising, then, that some partnerships flourish while others stagger through constant negotiations, attempting to nuance a position where they can rely on university support without having the mission derailed. Tensions inevitably arise around issues of control, resources, power allocation and the necessity for the NWP to have its own 'third' space.

Quality control

In all decentralized organizations, and in networks in particular, quality control can be problematic. Most teacher networks proceed on the assumption that their approach to professional development exposes participants to innovative alternatives, inspires changes in classroom practices and improves students' learning. Frequently, however, there is no system in place to determine whether or not this is actually happening. Taking this challenge seriously, the NWP has attempted a variety of strategies to ensure its effectiveness. For instance, the organization has developed special-interest networks to respond to unfolding issues and crises that make the work of the NWP sensitive to local sites. Annually, sites produce reports on their activities in relation to overall goals and determine targets for future growth and development. This reporting system serves as a troubleshooting strategy so that sites experiencing difficulties can get additional support. Finally, the NWP has commissioned an outside research group, the Academy for Educational Development, to conduct a three-year year evaluation of teacher assignments and student work. In the first year of the study it was found that (AED, 2001):

- NWP teachers spend far greater time on writing instruction than most fourth-grade teachers across the USA;
- teachers described many ways in which the writing project changed their philosophy about teaching and teaching practices;
- a majority of teacher assignments provided students with an opportunity to perform authentic intellectual work.

Commitment to ideals v. orthodoxy of thought

Yet another challenge involves the delicate balance between building shared commitments and establishing an orthodoxy. The teachers in our study share and defend certain values. For instance, they continually spoke to us of 'writing as a process'. When queried about what this meant, most talked about helping students to pay attention to the unfolding journey they undertake as they write. NWP teachers try to scaffold this process for those who struggle, helping fledgling writers to recognize that writing is essentially an interactive human endeavour involving communication between authors and audiences or authors and themselves. Good writing, NWP teachers maintain, cannot be conflated with following rules or examples. Good writing is fundamentally about high-quality thinking and the confidence to know how to express it. Accompanying this approach to writing is a fundamental belief in learners who, under the right circumstances, can make good choices and take ownership over their own learning.

Networks flourish to the extent that they provide a compelling idea to which participants make a commitment, yet they must avoid a constraining orthodoxy. A healthy network must win commitment from members to particular ideas and ideals while also providing opportunities for intellectual challenge and new membership and ideas. For instance, the NWP commitment to writing-as-process cannot afford to ignore perceptions that such an approach provides too little structure and too little intellectual rigour. Indeed, some who came to the summer institutes appeared to err in that direction. Ultimately, however, sentimental or superficial approaches to writing instruction simply cannot stand up to critical dialogue and reflection and scholarly research – all practised in NWP gatherings. This becomes increasingly true as the NWP has worked particularly hard – with notable success – to bring teachers of colour into its ranks (Fancsali and Nelsestuen, 2001), who raise challenging issues. By making room for intellectual diversity, the NWP guards against intellectual sloppiness.

The NWP and the promise of networks

The NWP has created an extra-institutional space for teachers to work together outside the hierarchical bureaucracies of their districts and schools. And yet the teachers bring to that space the primary concerns of teachers in their institutions. As teachers come together across the traditional boundaries of grade level, socio-economic contexts, subject matter and so forth, they create a pluralistic community characterized by multiple and diverse perspectives, priorities, concerns and interests. This pluralism results in an 'embracing of contraries' (Elbow, 1986) or an inclusion of seeming opposites that we have rarely experienced in educational settings.

For example, instead of debating whether to emphasize content or process, the NWP emphasizes both. For NWP teachers, writing is not simply a way to demonstrate what a student has thought and learned. It is itself learning and thinking made manifest and transparent and it involves the study of accumulated knowledge about genre, voice, audience, grammar, rhetoric and so forth. It is both process and content. Similarly, NWP teachers try to avoid other kinds of forced choices. Instead of privileging expository essays over personal writing or vice versa, they tend to teach both, recognizing that well-developed personal voices enhance analytic thinking and vice versa. Instead of choosing between community building and intellectual engagement, they see them in synergistic relationship. Their evolving social practices create strong relationships as a context for strong learning. Although the NWP focuses sharply on practitioner knowledge, the network avoids insularity by constantly drawing knowledge in from the outside and by working to increase the diversity in its ranks.

Perhaps a more difficult paradox involves teachers' time and their job descriptions. How can network involvement make sense when teachers already have too much to do? We were continually amazed at what NWP TCs managed to cram into their lives, despite the already demanding pressures of their classroom work. They led in-services, wrote for publication, attended meetings, participated in special projects, went to writing retreats. Whenever we broached the subject of teachers' time, we received the same two answers. First, they told us, NWP participation helps teachers work 'smarter not more'. For example, the emphasis on peer-to-peer teaching and assessment that TCs learn during the institutes they then incorporate in their own classrooms. A TC told us: 'We don't feel we have to grade everything any more, and in fact, we see it as counterproductive'. Second, when teachers become overwhelmed or their life circumstances preclude involvement, they simply back away for a while and re-enter when possible.

Another issue that hounded us during the study was local control. While the network provides a democratic approach to professional learning, many schools have strictly hierarchical governance structures and most are affected by outside mandates. When we pursued this issue with TCs, complaints poured out about standardized testing and English-only legislation. But we also heard firm resolve not to succumb passively:

> It [the network] gives you a sense of having control over the decisions you make and the actions you take for kids. And that's what we're supposed to be doing. This power comes from all the things the Writing Project does; it's like a support system. Being connected to people that help you express your thought gives you a way to do what you know is best.

Although NWP teachers admit to feelings of frustration, they do not surrender to helplessness. Resisting bad policies, they say, is possible if you have words, conviction and solidarity.

Networks have the capacity to transcend the local without ignoring it, to broaden and deepen understandings about education, to create relationships as enabling contexts for intellectual growth, to remain flexible and yet create shared purposes, to be responsive to a wide-ranging constituency, and to excite renewed compassion and enthusiasm among teachers. Despite its challenges, the NWP appears to be a new model of professional development that brings to the fore teachers' knowledge even as it introduces new understandings from research. Its democratic and inclusive ways of working, coupled with a network-like way of organizing, appears to provide teachers not only with opportunities to learn and to lead, but also to gain a professional community. It has made a difference in how teachers think of themselves and how they go about their work.

NOTES

1 Our study, sponsored by the National Partnership for Excellence and Accountability in Teaching, had a two-fold purpose: to investigate how the NWP facilitates professional learning in a network context, and to track possible influences on participating teachers' practices as well as possible impacts on their students' learning. Over the two-year study we interviewed national and site directors, as well as scores of NWP teachers, both individually and in focus groups, from the two sites. In addition, we documented the 1997 invitational UCLA and OSU summer institutes. Finally, we followed six teachers, three from each site, observing them in their classrooms and asking them to document closely their pedagogical strategies and the acacemic progress of from one to three of their students during the 1998–9 academic year. These teachers included two fresh from their respective summer invitationals and four NWP veterans.

2 Lisa Ummel-Ingram, a TC, coined this term during the 1998 OSU summer institute and later built an essay around it for the OSU Writing Project newsletter.

REFERENCES

AED (2001) *National Writing Project Evaluation. NWP Classrooms: Strategies, Assignments and Student Work. Year One Results, Spring*, New York: Academy for Educational Development.

Elbow, P. (1986) *Embracing Contraries: Explorations in Learning and Teaching*, New York: Oxford University Press.

Fancsali, C. and Nelsestuen, K. (2001) *Evaluation of the National Writing Project: Overview of Year Two Results*, New York: Academy for Educational Development.

Gray, J. (2000) *Teachers at the Center: A Memoir of the Early Years of the National Writing Project*, Berkeley, CA: National Writing Project.

7

Lieberman, A. and Grolnick, M. (1996) 'Networks and reform in American education', *Teachers' College Record*, 98 (1).

Lieberman, A. and Wood, D.R. (2001) 'When teachers write: of networks and learning' in Lieberman, A. and Miller, L. (eds) *Teachers Caught in the Action: Professional Development in Practice*, New York: Teachers' College Press.

McLaughlin, M.W. and Oberman, I. (eds) (1996) *Teacher Learning: New Policies, New Practices*, New York: Teachers' College Press.

St John, Dickey, M.K., Hirabayashi, J. and Stokes, L. with assistance from Murray, A. (2001) *The National Writing Project: Client Satisfaction and Program Impact: Results from a Follow-Up Survey of Participants at Summer 2000 Invitational Institutes*, Inverness, CA: Inverness Research Associates.

Westheimer, J. (1998) *Among School Teachers: Community Authonomy and Ideology in Teachers' Work*, New York: Teachers' College Press.

Wood, D.R. and Lieberman, A. (2000) 'Teachers as authors: the National Writing Project's approach to professional development', *International Journal of Leadership in Education*, 3 (3), pp. 255–73.

CHAPTER 47

Making it last: building capacity for sustainability

LOUISE STOLL AND LORNA EARL

A key challenge of school improvement, and educational reform more generally, is the issue of sustainability. Improvement and educational reform are fundamentally concerned with changing what already exists. It is relatively easy for some schools, at least, to get started on the road to improvement and to achieve considerable success. When they are visited a number of years later, however, there is frequently evidence of subsequent decline (Fink, 2000; Maden, 2001). The picture in relation to larger-scale reform efforts is even more gloomy. Revisiting the RAND Corporation Change Agent Study in the USA in the 1970s, McLaughlin (1990, p. 12) concluded: 'The net return to the general investment was the adoption of many innovations, the successful implementation of a few, and the long-run continuation of still fewer'. Why is it that changes are so very hard to sustain? We believe the answer lies in insufficient attention to building capacity. In this chapter we explore the concept of capacity – what it is and what influences it – and then discuss how it might be built and enhanced from within and from outside schools.

What is capacity?

Bringing about real and meaningful educational change requires much more than superficial tinkering with structures and practices in schools. Sustainable changes depend on an ongoing process of learning by individuals – singly and collectively – and by organizations. As society moves into this new century, there are compelling social forces that necessitate better learning and learning in new ways. As Darling-Hammond (1997) expresses it: 'Never before has the success, perhaps even the survival of nations and people been so tightly tied to their ability to learn'.

So what is it that makes schools and the people within them ongoing, capable learners? A number of researchers and theorists have offered definitions and conceptual frameworks for this notion of continuous learning as the 'capacity for change' or 'capacity for development'. While we agree that it can either help or hinder change and development, we believe this is the case because of its specific connection with learning, describing it elsewhere (Stoll, Fink and Earl, 2002, p. 161) as: 'The power to get involved in and sustain the learning of everyone within the school community with the collective purpose of enhancing pupil learning'.

Mitchell and Sackney (2000, pp. xiv, 12–15) also take learning communities as their starting point. They describe 'three mutually influencing and interdependent categories of capacity':

- personal: the active and reflective construction of knowledge;
- interpersonal: collegial relations and collective practice, building the learning community climate and team;
- organizational: building structures that create and maintain sustainable organizational processes, opening doors and breaking down walls, sharing leadership and sharing power, and making it happen.

King and Newmann (2001, pp. 88–90) offer a slightly different interpretation of the construct. They argue that what they call 'school capacity' helps to explain how the organizational features of a school influences the quality of instruction which, in turn, will then influence pupil achievement. Their three dimensions of school capacity parallel those of Mitchell and Sackney in some ways:

- the knowledge, skills and dispositions of an individual staff member;
- professional community among the staff as a whole – in 'an organised and collective enterprise';
- programme coherence within schools – such that programmes for both staff and pupils' learning are coherent, focus on school goals and are sustained over time.

In this chapter we refer to individual capacity and school capacity. We see the latter as comprising both the interpersonal, collective elements and the organizational structures.[1] These combine to create what we describe as 'internal capacity'.

Although the ways of expressing it might be different, capacity is a quality of people or organizations that allows them routinely to learn from the world around them and apply their learning to new and sometimes novel situations so that they continue on a path toward their goals, even though the context is ever-changing. It also helps them continuously to improve learning and progress at all levels, but particularly and ultimately that of pupils.

What influences capacity?

There are many influences on capacity. These influences operate at different levels and in complex ways, affecting how capacity engages in and sustains learning. The three influences are:

- influences on individual capacity
- social and structural influences on school capacity
- influences from the external context.

It is useful to depict schools and the individuals within them using amoeba-like shapes (Stoll, 1999a; Stoll, Fink and Earl, 2002). This representation emphasizes the dynamic and adaptive nature of individuals and schools. The breaks in the lines indicate that influences at each level (individual, school and external context) are not discrete and self-contained – rather, they blend in complex ways to create different patterns of relationships (see Figure 47.1).

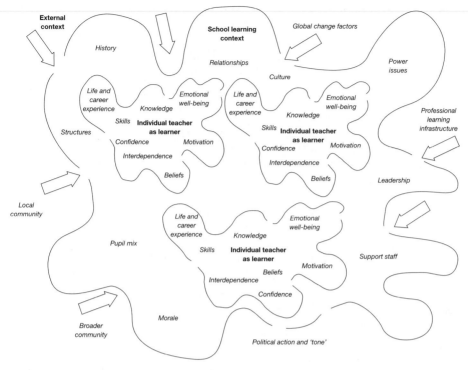

Figure 47.1 The Influences on internal capacity

Source: Stoll, 1999.

Individual Influences

Changing schools ultimately depends on changing individuals within schools. Eight interacting influences on individuals' capacity to sustain continuous learning appear particularly important:

- *Life and career experience*. People are influenced by what goes on in their lives, on a daily basis and over time. Their priorities, lives and career patterns are important influences on their desire to learn and readiness to engage in improvement activities.

- *Beliefs*. Individuals' perceptions and actions about changing and developing their teaching are influenced by what they believe. For example, some people believe ability is inherited – you have it or you do not – and, therefore, some children cannot learn. Others put more stock in effort and support for learning. They believe that with teaching and hard work, enormous learning is possible.

- *Emotional well-being*. Teaching is full of emotions (Hargreaves, 1998). Neglecting interpersonal and psychological processes leads individuals to behave defensively to protect themselves from innovations that might expose their inadequacies, whereas valuing individuals as people and their contributions enhances self-esteem, builds trust and creates receptivity to learning.

- *Knowledge.* Another influence is the detailed and deep knowledge individuals accumulate over time about their work. For teachers, this incorporates knowledge about their subject as well as about each student's strengths, weaknesses, home background, cultural experiences and learning styles.
- *Skills.* Individuals' capacity is influenced by the extent of their repertoire of pedagogical skills and their ability to use their experience to experiment with their own practice.
- *Motivation to learn.* Motivation is the starting point for learning (Biggs and Moore, 1993). For busy and often overworked individuals to devote effort to change and new learning, there has to be a good reason to change – a catalyst or 'urgency' (Earl and Lee, 2000) that 'what I'm doing doesn't seem to be working'.
- *Confidence about making a real difference.* Some individuals think that whatever they do can makes little difference in the face of, for example, students' deprived social circumstances and parents' low aspirations. Others are confident that what they do can and does make a significant difference.
- *Sense of interdependence.* Humans are social animals who need connections, relationships and social support to learn and sustain learning. The collective or distributed learning that influences organizational learning emerges from contexts in which colleagues work and think together.

School influences

To succeed in a world characterized by rapid change and increased complexity, it is vital that schools can grow, develop, adapt creatively to change and take charge of change so that they can create their own preferable future. Ability to take charge of externally driven change, rather than being controlled by it, has been shown to define schools that are more effective and more rapidly improving from ones that are not (Rosenholtz, 1989; Stoll and Fink, 1996; Gray *et al.*, 1999; Hopkins, 2001). The experiences, emotions, knowledge, skills, motivation, confidence and interdependence that affect individuals operate in the context in which they are located. This context is influenced by a set of social forces:

- *The particular mix of pupils.* The particular nature and mix of the pupil body in the school gives it its own 'flavour', through the nature of their background characteristics and their own student culture.
- *Relationships.* Working together productively in schools depends on positive relationships. When individuals come together as a whole staff, or even in departments, a dynamic of relationships is created. In some ways schools are like families: they can be happy or dysfunctional. Healthy relationships provide a secure basis for learning.
- *History.* Schools, like other organizations, go through life cycles. During some periods they are 'ripe for improvement'. At other times, there may be institutional 'inertia'. Schools also experience significant events, for example amalgamations, threatened closures or fires. In some schools, teacher mobility is high. Certain schools also develop particular traditions and reputations over time.

- *Culture.* Each school has a different reality of school life and how to go about its work because of the difference in basic assumptions and beliefs shared by its members; some schools also have several competing cultures. Culture shapes schools' capacity for change and improvement (Sarason, 1996; Stoll, 1999b).

- *Power issues.* Schools are influenced by internal politics (Ball, 1987); they are places in which control is a key issue. In secondary schools, for example, some departments sometimes view themselves as having higher status than others, leading to power struggles between departments. Sarason (1990) maintains educational reforms continuously fail because attention is not paid to the alteration of power relationships, including those between teachers and pupils.

- *Support staff.* These staff can play a significant role in the lives of a school. Many live in the local area and are connected to the local community. The extent of their involvement and interest in the school as a whole, and the ways in which they facilitate learning, are all potential influences on the school's internal capacity (Mortimore *et al.*, 1992).

- *Structures.* Schools are bounded by structures shaping their capacity to learn and respond to change. The size of the school and classes within it, the physical plant and how the school day is divided are all examples of structural aspects of a school's capacity. These types of structure may be perceived as 'givens', over which staff members have limited if any control (Mortimore *et al.*, 1988), but choices can be made about, for example, the location of different departments, classes or the staffroom.

- *Leadership.* Countless studies have found positive leadership to be a powerful force for school effectiveness and school improvement (for example, Mortimore, 1998; Teddlie and Reynolds, 1999).

- *Morale.* Sometimes morale is viewed as a trait of individual teachers (Evans, 1998). External factors also influence morale (Dinham, 1994). It can, however, be an internal school-level factor, influenced by quality of leadership and management of a school. Teachers certainly feel some schools are better places to work than others (McCall *et al.*, 2001).

External contextual influences

Argyris and Schön (1978) maintain that an organization's key challenge is not to become more effective at performing a stable task in the light of stable purposes, but to: 'restructure its purposes and redefine its task in the face of a changing environment'. This task is more complicated than it may appear. While the capacity of schools and the individuals within them is internally driven, the external contextual influences on a school's internal capacity cannot be ignored.[2] Central among these are:

- *The local community.* Schools serve very different communities. Pupils' background characteristics have an impact on their achievement. A school community's demographics can influence a school's internal capacity. Disadvantage, however, does not automatically inhibit internal capacity. Some schools in disadvantaged areas boost pupils' progress more than those in advantaged areas (Mortimore *et al.*, 1988). The extent of pupil mobility, the role and operation of the governing body, and location of a school are other influences. Parental expectations and aspirations can also vary. Educators wishing to change very traditional schools may find themselves up against a parent community with a strong notion of school being 'the one I attended when I was a child'.

- *The broader community.* Requirements of universities and workplaces influence curricula and assessments. Similarly, unions' policy and practices influence how at least some of their members respond to changes in school. Attitudes of the broader community to schooling can also affect teachers' motivation and belief that what they are doing is worthwhile.

- *Political action and 'tone'.* Policies, and beliefs about the purpose of education that underpin them, are central influences on schools. The amount of policy-oriented change is particularly significant. With the best will, teachers bombarded by unrelenting changes over a short time period tend to be exhausted and find it hard to maintain energy, enthusiasm and willingness for change (Helsby and McCulloch, 1998). As the pace of change quickens, teachers are increasingly faced with an excessive workload. In addition, the label of 'failing schools' can exacerbate and prolong problems of schools in difficulty, contributing to low teacher morale and feelings of impotence.

- *Professional learning infrastructure.* Some schools are located in areas or regions where the professional learning infrastructure is better developed than elsewhere. Infrastructure can be seen as 'a network or structure with a clear purpose ... infrastructure is just there. People count on it as they go about their work' (Fullan and Watson, 1997, p. 9). Difficulties arise when the infrastructure is weak, damaged, or missing.

- *Global change forces.* The fast-changing world, with its increasingly globalized social, economic, technological, political and ecological forces, is having major ramifications for all schools, and makes it more imperative that schools have the internal capacity to respond to such forces.

How can capacity be built?

Capacity is not static. Learning, individually and together, is dynamic, changeable and fragile. Learning with a particular group of people or in relation to a specific initiative does not guarantee that it will continue. Learning needs nurturing and nourishing to flourish; otherwise, the natural forces of entropy can take over.

Imagine two schools. In the first, pupils are learning, teachers are learning and leaders are learning. The second is a learning community. What has it got that is extra? We would argue that this school knows how to put it all together, involving everyone – including parents and the community – in a collective enterprise that ensures that individual learning adds up to a coherent whole, driven by high-quality pupil learning as its fundamental purpose. Teachers' and leaders' learning doesn't take place for its own sake; they are absolutely essential pieces of improving learning for pupils.

Building capacity from within

Harris (2001, p. 262) sees capacity building as being concerned with 'creating the conditions, opportunities and experiences for collaboration and mutual learning'. But, creating and maintaining communities of learners within schools is not an easy undertaking. Figure 47.2 shows a graphical representation of a number of internal processes that have been connected with building capacity. Some of the processes are individual, some are collective or organizational, some extend beyond the school, and some operate in several different spheres. Leaders at all levels, consciously and subconsciously, model and help others develop these processes because leadership is fundamentally concerned with capacity building (Stoll, Bolam and Collarbone, 2002).

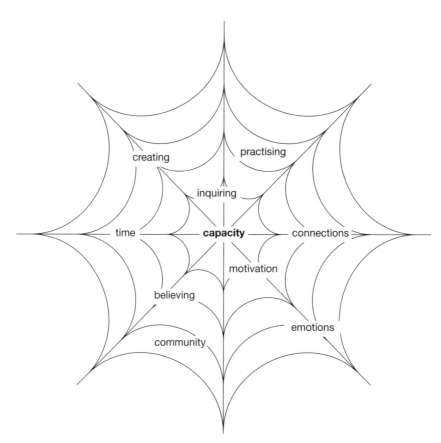

Figure 47.2 Processes connected with enhancing capacity

Source: Stoll, Fink and Earl, 2002.

Believing in success

Believing you can be successful is critical to capacity. Senge (1990) argues that schools create their own reality; so does each individual in schools. If individuals do not believe in themselves and their ability to be successful in what they set out to do, they can become locked in a cycle of despair and frustration. A moving school has a pervading 'can do' culture, a collective belief that it is possible to do better, no matter what difficulties it faces. It also feels it has the power to do so. It has a learning orientation; people believe that effort, rather than innate ability, leads to greater success.

Making connections

Successful schools depend on making connections at all levels. Connections are central to learning. Successful learners chunk together information into patterns. Working together, people also make connections between new information and old, develop new ideas, establish relationships that move beyond ones that exist in any one domain and organize their knowledge and ideas around significant concepts (see Brandsford, Brown and Cocking, 1999). At a whole-school level, more successful organizational learning involves understanding how each part of the system affects and is affected by other parts (Senge, 1997).

Attending to motivation

Motivation affects people's willingness to devote time to learning. Without commitment, openness and a sense of purpose, real learning can not take place. People may go through the motions and there may be an appearance of change but this change is likely to be shallow. In the learning-oriented school, the challenge of genuine learning is the ultimate goal, rather than purely performance or achievement. Such learning is more likely to be lasting because it is internally motivated – its rewards are intrinsic. It is not easily achievable and depends on the school focusing on the needs of each learner, whatever their age and role, and being oriented towards bringing out the best in all learners, individually and collectively.

Understanding and experiencing emotions

Emotion and learning have a powerful relationship. The human dimension of learning is critical. It is not just a bonus to have good relationships in classrooms, playgrounds, staffrooms and with parents; it is critical to fostering self-esteem and building the right climate for learning. There is also a link between positive relationships between teachers and pupils and greater academic progress (Mortimore *et al.*, 1988). While it may be right to be cynical about the dangers of managerial manipulation of emotion, the evidence from a range of sources is clear that experiencing and understanding emotions is essential to building capacity for learning.

Engaging in community

Learning in schools takes place within a social context – the school community. It can be seen in cooperative learning, collaborative planning, peer observation and mentoring, leadership teams and other teamwork, collective learning and understanding, working parties and shared vision building. As such, it depends on positive relationships, trust and respect relationships and, at its best, can lead to a sense of belonging to a professional learning community (Louis *et al.*, 1995).

Inquiring

Learning is about needing to know, even when what you find out is something you thought you did not want to know. Inquiring and developing 'inquiry-mindedness' (Earl and Lee, 2000) are key capacity-building processes. Inquiring means being open to new ideas, gathering necessary evidence, and questioning and challenging your own beliefs and perceptions. It involves such things as pupils assessing their own learning to promote deeper understanding, and teachers interrogating different teaching approaches to discover those most likely to promote real learning. It also involves finding out about the community to make necessary and meaningful connections with them.

Creating

Learning has the potential to foster creativity and creativity is an essential feature of learning. It is also critical in a changing world. Bentley (2000) describes creativity in much the same way as we have described capacity: as applying knowledge and skills in new ways to achieve a valued goal. A learning school is a creative school where new ideas and taking chances are encouraged and people 'practise fearlessness' (Fullan, 1992). They also feel empowered to take risks and 'think outside the box'. Essentially, the entire school community understands it is creating its own reality, has the power to change it and can influence the reality of those outside.

Practising

We never stop learning. It requires hard work, commitment and practice because new ways of learning or creating do not come easily. Learning often means coming to terms with different ideas and different ways of doing things. This usually necessitates trying something again and again, working at it, feeling uncomfortable for a while and experiencing new responses. Capacity depends on the opportunity to practise.

Finding time

Real change and learning are not straightforward. They depend on believing, making connections, attending to motivation, nurturing positive emotion, building community, inquiring, creating and practising, and all of these require devotion of time. Time for learning and development is so important that it cannot just be left to schools to find time.

Building capacity from outside

Schools and the people who work in them have the power to build their own internal capacity. However, our research and experience working in and with schools also tells us that they cannot do it alone. Given the external forces that influence capacity, to develop capacity, schools need an infrastructure of support from all groups with a responsibility for or interest in school improvement. Schools have many different kinds of partners, some of whom provide political support, some professional support, and others moral and emotional support. Some provide a combination. All the partners can assist in helping schools build and maintain their capacity for sustainable learning by supporting learning. They can:

Recognize the importance of learning for all

We are all learning for a different world. As the world becomes more complex, it is in societies' best interest to have well-educated citizens. Schools cannot afford to be sorting institutions to determine who can and cannot learn. They must be learning communities for one and all. To this end, it is important for the public to support the improvement of *all* schools and help enhance their capacity for learning as a way of keeping the culture strong and prepared for an uncertain future. As Hargreaves and Fullan (1998, pp. 65–6) assert, educational partnerships 'must be actively committed to social justice by agitating for changes that favour all students, not just the highest achieving or more privileged ones who promise the biggest success and corporate return'. Teaching and learning are collective responsibilities that will take concerted effort on everyone's part.

While there are common elements to learning, people bring their unique differences to the learning process. This means that, whether you are thinking about pupils, teachers, support staff, leaders, parents or anyone else, the keys to unlocking and enhancing the learning process of any individual varies from that of their peers. Just because something worked for you when you were at school, it does not mean that this will be right for all learners or for the current times. The importance of learning for all also includes the ongoing learning of those outside schools.

Respect and promote professionalism

Being a teacher includes more than teaching and related responsibilities. It also means working with others as part of a larger learning community; being collectively responsible for all pupils; engaging parents, carers and the community in meaningful, and sometimes different, ways; taking personal responsibility for continuing professional development, supported by the school; and being inquiry-oriented.

Teachers need time to learn and implement their learning; assess and evaluate; plan; and collaborate with colleagues, parents and others. They also need funded learning and administrative support so that they can focus on enhancing pupil learning. Most important, they need recognition that they are doing a good job, particularly those who work in challenging areas. Blame, from whatever source, does not reach the 'hearts and minds' of those needing to be reached for change to occur (Stoll and Myers, 1998 p. 5).

Supporting and promoting professionalism may also require a greater focus of unions' energies on the professional aspects of teachers' work that enhance learning. Louis and colleagues (2000) note that this 'new unionism', as they describe it, requires systemic effort: resources, individual advocates and leadership, as well as efforts to encourage and reward locally initiated change, and re-educate the membership.

Support continuous professional learning

All professions need to invest in development. If systems to support professional growth are intended to sustain the learning of teachers, leaders and support staff, they must also help schools develop as learning communities where educators collaborate to inquire critically about their own practice.

The best way to know how to support a school and its learning is to get to know it. There is a lot of information around about schools, but some of it may just be folklore. Information such as league tables of results provide a glimpse of a school but these reports may not take into account the background of the pupils who attend the school and the actual value the school has added. Schools are awash with data that can provide a first snapshot of what any school is about. To move beyond this to a sense of the dynamic video representation of a school means visiting schools, watching lessons and offering assistance. As outsiders consider what they read, see and hear, they can become part of the community of learners.

Understand all schools are not the same

It does not take long to realize that schools are all different from each other. They start their learning journeys from very different starting points: indeed, some find it enormously difficult to get started at all. Some are more 'ready' than others to deal with and work through challenges associated with learning. They have the resources, resilience and will to engage in and sustain continuous learning of teachers, leaders, support staff and the school itself, and have a clear vision of its primary purpose as enhancing pupil learning. Others have a long road ahead to build capacity for change. What works in one school, with a particular pupil population and at a particular stage of development, may not work in another. Some schools have greater need for extra external resources and support. Others may need greater external pressure for change, and they may not always be the schools highlighted by the media as schools in difficulty.

Network schools

Networking is increasingly seen as vital to extending and deepening the learning of teachers, support staff and leaders (Lieberman and Grolnick, 1996; Earl and Lee, 2000). Such networks enhance learning by bringing together people engaged in school improvement to share and discuss experiences, debate issues of mutual concern, reflect on their learning, solve common problems and further refine improvement strategies (Stoll, 1996).

Offer critical friendship

External eyes often pick up what is not immediately apparent to those inside a school. 'Critical friends' watch, listen, ask challenging questions, and help those in schools sort out their thinking and make sound decisions. What is particularly important to this relationship is that it is built on trust: critical friends do not bring vested interests. They will, however, say when they consider expectations are too low or interpretations are 'off-track'. These difficult messages – while uncomfortable and, sometimes, painful, to hear – are more likely to be accepted and addressed because those in the school know that the critical friend is fundamentally 'on their side'. This requires enormous sensitivity and diplomacy on the part of the critical friend (Doherty *et al.*, 2001).

Allow time for deep learning

Deep and meaningful learning is complex. Educators need time to think about, read about, talk about and argue about new ideas and new directions. This is the only way that they are likely to make changes that are dramatic digressions from their comfortable practices.

Conclusion

Capacity for change is all about learning: learning, in which teachers engage individually and collectively in continuous, challenging and purposeful consideration of their professional responsibilities, their beliefs, their skills, their motivations and their practices. Although we believe this kind of learning has inherent benefits for teachers, its real value in education is connected to sustainability: sustainability of honest appraisal of the conditions and outcomes that exist in the school, sustainability of inquiry and reflection, sustainability of conversations inside and outside the school, and sustainability of continuous learning designed to enhance the pupil's success. Sustainability is the goal; capacity is the engine that will ultimately power the sustainability journey.

ACKNOWLEDGEMENT

We would like to acknowledge our co-author Dean Fink. Some of the ideas in this chapter are based on our collective thinking for our book *It's About Learning (and It's about Time)* (2002).

NOTES

1 In secondary schools, it is also possible to talk of departmental capacity, but this is also a collective and organizational capacity.

2 It should be noted that the arrows in Figure 47.1 point outside towards the school. This is not to say that changing schools and changing teachers can have no influence on their external community and wider society – indeed, when students grow up, many (although not all) become the decision makers responsible for changes in their own lives, communities and society – but this particular model focuses on what is relevant to improving schools, not improving global conditions.

REFERENCES

Argyris, C. and Schön, D. (1978) *Organizational Learning: A Theory of Action Perspective*, Reading, MA: Addison-Wesley.

Ball, S. (1987) *The Micro-Politics of a School: Towards a Theory of School Organization*, London: Methuen.

Bentley, T. (2000) 'Learning for a creative age' in Crake, P. (ed.) *Education Futures: Lifelong Learning*, London: RSA and Design Council.

Biggs, J.B. and Moore, P.J. (1993) *The Process of Learning*, 3rd edn, Englewood Cliffs, NJ: Prentice-Hall.

Brandsford, J.D., Brown, A.L. and Cocking, R.R. (1999) *How People Learn: Brain, Mind, Experience, and School*, Washington, DC: National Academy Press.

Darling-Hammond, L. (1997) *The Right to Learn: a Blueprint for Creating Schools that Work*, San Francisco: Jossey-Bass.

Dinham, S. (1994) *Societal Pressures and Teaching*, paper presented to the Australian Association for Research in Education, University of Newcastle.

Doherty, J., MacBeath, J., Jardine, S., Smith, I. and McCall, J. (2001) 'Do schools need critical friends?' in MacBeath, J. and Mortimore, P. (eds) *Improving School Effectiveness*, Buckingham: Open University Press.

Earl. L. and Lee, L. (2000) 'Learning, for a change: school improvement as capacity building', *Improving Schools*, 3 (1), pp. 30–8.

Evans, L. (1998) *Teacher Morale, Job Satisfaction and Motivation*, London: Paul Chapman Publishing.

Fink, D. (2000). *Good Schools/Real Schools: Why School Reform Doesn't Last*, New York: Teachers' College Press.

Fullan, M. (1992) *What's Worth Fighting for in Headship*, Buckingham: Open University Press (first published in 1988 as *Whats Fighting for in the Principalship*, Toronto: Ontario Public School Teachers' Federation).

Fullan, M. and Watson, N. (1997) *Building Infrastructures for Professional Development: An Assessment of Early Progress*, final report submitted to the Rockefeller Foundation, Toronto: OISE/University of Toronto.

Gray, J., Hopkins, D., Reynolds, D., Wilcox, B., Farrell, S. and Jesson, D. (1999) *Improving Schools: Performance and Potential*, Buckingham: Open University Press.

Hargreaves, A. (1998) 'The emotional politics of teaching and teacher development: with implications for educational leadership', *International Journal for Leadership in Education*, 1 (4), pp. 316–36.

Hargreaves, A. and Fullan, M. (1998) *What's Worth Fighting for Out There*, Buckingham: Open University Press.

Harris, A. (2001) 'Building the capacity for school improvement', *School Leadership and Management*, 21 (30), pp. 261–70.

Helsby, G. and McCulloch, G. (1998) *Teachers and the National Curriculum*, London: Cassell.

Hopkins, D. (2001) *School Improvement for Real*, London: Routledge/Falmer Press.

King, M.B. and Newmann, F.M. (2001) 'Building school capacity through professional development: conceptual and empirical considerations', *International Journal of Educational Management*, 15 (2), pp. 86–93.

Lieberman, A. and Grolnick, M. (1996) 'Networks and reform in American education', *Teachers' College Record*, 98 (1), pp. 7–45.

Louis, K. S., Kruse, S. and Associates (1995) *Professionalism and Community: Perspectives on Reforming Urban Schools*, Thousand Oaks, CA: Corwin Press.

Louis, K.S., Seppannen, P., Smylie, M.A. and Jones, L.M. (2000) 'The role of unions as leaders for school change: an analysis of the 'KEYS' program in two US states' in Riley, K.A. and Louis, K.S. (eds) *Leadership for Change and School Reform: An International Perspective*, London: Routledge/Falmer Press.

Maden, M. (2001) *Success Against the Odds – Five Years On*, London: Routledge/Falmer.

McCall, J., Smith, I., Stoll, L., Thomas, S., Sammons, P., Smees, R., MacBeath, J., Boyd, B. and MacGilchrist, B. (2001) 'Views of pupils, parents and teachers: vital indicators of effectiveness and for improvement' in MacBeath, J. and Mortimore, P. (eds) *Improving School Effectivenes,* Buckingham: Open University Press.

McLaughlin, M.W. (1990) The RAND Change Agent Study: macro perspectives and micro realities', *Educational Researcher*, 19 (9), pp. 11–15.

Mitchell, C. and Sackney, L. (2000) *Profound Improvement: Building Capacity for a Learning Community*, Lisse, The Netherlands: Swets & Zeitlinger.

Mortimore, P. (1998) *The Road to Improvement: Reflections on School Effectiveness*, Lisse, The Netherlands: Swets & Zeitlinger.

7

Mortimore, P. and Mortimore, J., with Thomas, H., Cairns, R. and Taggart, B. (1992) *The Innovative Uses of Non-Teaching Staff in Primary and Secondary Schools Project: Final Report*, London: Department of Education and Science and Institute of Education.

Mortimore, P., Sammons, P., Stoll, L., Lewis, D. and Ecob, R. (1988) *School Matters: The Junior Years*, reprinted 1994, London: Paul Chapman Publishing.

Rosenholtz, S. J. (1989) *Teachers' Workplace: The Social Organization of Schools*, New York: Teachers' College Press.

Sarason, S. (1990) *The Predictable Failure of Educational Reform*, San Francisco: Jossey-Bass.

Sarason, S. (1996) *Revisiting the Culture of the School and the Problem of Change*, New York: Teachers' College Press.

Senge, P. M. (1990) *The Fifth Discipline: The Art and Practice of the Learning Organization*, London: Century Business.

Senge, P. (1997) 'Through the eye of the needle' in Gibson R. (ed.) *Rethinking the Future*, London: Nicholas Brealey Publishing.

Stoll, L. (1996) 'The role of partnerships and networking in school improvement' in Barber, M. and Dann, R. (eds) *Raising Educational Standards in the Inner Cities: Practical Initiatives in Action*, London: Cassell.

Stoll, L. (1999a) 'Realising our potential: understanding and developing capacity for lasting improvement', *School Effectiveness and School Improvement*, 10 (4), pp. 503–32.

Stoll, L. (1999b) 'School culture: black hole or fertile garden for improvement?' in Prosser, J. (ed.) *School Culture*, London: Paul Chapman Publishing.

Stoll, L., Bolam, R. and Collarbone, P. (2002) 'Leading for change: building capacity for learning, in Leithwood, K., Hallinger, P., Louis, K.S., Furman-Brown, G., Gronn, P., Mulford, B. and Riley, K. (eds) *Second International Handbook of Educational Leadership and Administration*, Dordrecht, The Netherlands: Kluwer Academic Publishers.

Stoll, L. and Fink, D. (1996) *Changing Our Schools: Linking School Effectiveness and School Improvement*, Buckingham: Open University Press.

Stoll, L., Fink, D. and Earl, L. (2002) *It's About Learning (and It's About Time)*, London: Routledge/Falmer Press.

Stoll, L. and Myers, K. (1998) *Schools in Difficulty: No Quick Fixes*, London: Falmer Press.

Teddlie, C. and Reynolds, D. (1999) *International Handbook of School Effectiveness Research*, London: Falmer Press.

PART EIGHT

School Improvement and Effectiveness

DAVID HOPKINS AND ALMA HARRIS

Introduction

DAVID HOPKINS

Over the past 20 years or so, a vast amount of evidence to support the common-sense notion that individual schools can make a difference to student progress has been accumulated. The school effects research, besides articulating the characteristics of effective schools, has demonstrated unequivocally that given the right conditions *all* students can learn. The research knowledge about the characteristics of those schools and classrooms 'whose pupils progress further than might be expected from considerations of intake' (Mortimore 1991, p. 216) is amongst the most robust there is in the quest for educational reform.

Running parallel to the specific application and development of the research on school effectiveness was the beginning of a widespread inquiry into and understanding of the change process and the school as an organization. The OECD-CERI project, Case Studies of Educational Innovation (Dalin, 1973), and the RAND Corporation Change Agent Study (Berman and McLaughlin, 1977), for example, highlighted the limitations of externally imposed changes, the importance of focusing on the school as the unit of change, and the need to take the change process seriously. Similarly, the research on schools as organizations, of which Sarason's study (1982), *The Culture of the School and the Problem of Change*, is an outstanding example, demonstrated the importance of linking curriculum innovation to the organizational culture of the school.

Given the constraints of this handbook format, the treatment here of the research literature on school effects and strategies for school improvement will inevitably be brief. The intention of this introduction is simply to outline the main contours of the knowledge base to illustrate the links between the two traditions and to provide a brief overview of the contents of Part Eight.

Surprisingly, until quite recently the ability of schools to make a difference to student learning was widely doubted. Even as late as the 1960s and 1970s, well known studies and 'blue riband' reports, many of which influenced national policy, looked to factors other than the school as predictors of a student's academic performance. The family, in particular, was regarded as being far more important. By the late 1970s however, the prevailing view began to change in the face of an emerging consensus that schools do make a difference. One of the earliest studies conducted in the UK was by Rutter and his colleagues (1979) who compared the 'effectiveness' of ten secondary schools in south London on a range of student outcome measures. The 'effective' schools were characterized by factors 'as varied as the degree of academic emphasis, teacher actions in lessons, the availability of incentives and rewards, good conditions for pupils, and the extent to which children are able to take responsibility' (ibid., p. 178). It was this constellation of factors that Rutter and his colleagues later referred to as the school's 'ethos'.

By the beginning of the 1980s, at a time when the cold winds of accountability were beginning to blow through most western educational systems, there came striking evidence that at last schools had something to be held accountable for. The 'effective schools' research makes it very clear that there are significant differences between schools on a variety of student outcomes, after full account has been taken of the pupils' prior learning history and family background at the time they enter the school. In terms of the contemporary debate over league tables, this is the 'value added' to pupils over and above what ability and socio-economic status would naturally bring them. This is not to say that an individual's learning history and family background are not important, but schools do contribute differentially to pupil achievement. The school a child goes to does matter.

In a similar way, school improvement as a field of study has evolved subtly but decisively over the past 50 years. This evolution has passed through five phases. The first was the contribution of Kurt Lewin, his formulation of action research and the application of his ideas on group dynamics to organization development. Second was the influence of organizational development strategies on education in the 1960s and 1970s. The third was the use of strategies for school self-evaluation, as a response to the increasing demand for school accountability in the late 1970s and early 1980s. Fourth, there was an emphasis on school-based development, and the management at the school level of complex changes and multiple innovations. The fifth phase of 'authentic school improvement' has only recently been entered. As will be seen in subsequent chapters, this phase is characterized by attempts to enhance student achievement through the use of specific instructional strategies that also have an impact on the organization and culture of the school.

Strategies for school improvement have become far more focused since the mid-1980s given that the amount of change expected of schools has increased dramatically. This increase in expectations has also been accompanied by fundamental changes in the way that schools are managed and governed. Although this has gone by different names in different countries – self-managing schools, site-based management, development planning, local management of schools, restructuring – the key idea of giving schools more responsibility for their own management remained similar. Two examples illustrate the point.

The Department of Education and Science (DES) project on School Development Plans (SDPs) in England and Wales was an attempt to develop a strategy that would, among other things, help governors, heads and staff change the culture of their school. Development planning provides an illustration of an authentic school improvement strategy, combining as it does curriculum innovation with modifications to the school's management arrangements. It is also a strategy that became widespread in British schools in the 1990s as teachers and school leaders struggled to take control of the process of change (see Hargreaves *et al.*, 1989; Hargreaves and Hopkins, 1991).

In a similar way, 'restructuring' efforts in the USA were attempting a more fundamental approach to educational reform by transforming the organization of the school in the quest for enhanced student achievement. Elmore (1990) suggested that there are three commonly agreed aspects to restructuring:

- changing the way teaching and learning occurs in schools;
- changing the organization and internal features of schools – the so-called 'workplace conditions';
- changing the distribution of power between the school and its clients.

Unless these three conditions or changes occur simultaneously, so Elmore argues, there is little likelihood of marked improvements in student outcomes or the achievement of the core goals of the school.

The experience with centralized change from the mid-1980s onwards also illustrated that simply devolving budgets, broadening the governance of schools or engaging in planning are no guarantees of school improvement. To be successful, models for school management and development need to achieve fundamental and lasting organizational change.

It may appear from this brief review of the school effectiveness research and the evolution of strategies for school improvement that the quest for the Holy Grail of educational reform is already at an end. Unfortunately, this is not the case. As will be seen throughout the contributions to Part Eight, there are a number of problems related to the way in which the school effectiveness research is conducted and the strategies for school improvement are implemented that inhibit the realization of their full potential.

This aside, the contribution of the effective schools research and the evidence of the impact of the strategies for school improvement has already been highly significant. Together they have transformed thinking about both the nature of school reform and student achievement. Murphy (1992), in his analysis of the 'real legacy of the effective school movement', has reformulated the debate in a very helpful way. He argued that the school effects correlates, and by the same token the strategies for school improvement are simply the means to an end – student learning. From that perspective it is not the correlates or strategies themselves that are important, but rather the principles that support them. Indeed the correlates and the strategies may look very different in the future; they certainly change in differing contexts at present, although the concepts of effectiveness and improvement remain the same.

Murphy has identified four aspects to the legacy (ibid., pp. 94–6):

- *The educability of learners.* At the heart of the effective schools and school improvement movements is an attack on the prevailing notion of the distribution of achievement according to a normal curve. There is a clear demonstration that all students can learn.
- *A focus on outcomes.* For a variety of reasons educators tend to avoid serious inspection of the educational process. Effective school advocates and increasingly those within the school improvement tradition argue persuasively that rigorous assessments of schooling are needed and that one can judge the quality of education only by examining student outcomes, especially that of learning. Equally important, they define success not in absolute terms, but as the value added to what students brought to the educational process.
- *Taking responsibility for students.* The third aspect of the legacy is the attack on the practice of blaming the victim for the shortcomings of the school itself. The effective school movement has been insistent that the school community takes a fair share of the responsibility for what happens to the youth in its care.
- *Attention to consistency throughout the school community.* One of the most powerful and enduring lessons from all the research on effective schools and school improvement is that the better schools are more tightly linked –

structurally, symbolically and culturally – than the less effective ones. They operate more as an organic whole and less as a loose collection of disparate sub-systems. An overarching sense of consistency and co-ordination is a key characteristic of our better schools.

This analysis represents a major contribution both to the effective schools literature as well as a challenge to school improvement. The legacy of the effective schools movement, as outlined by Murphy, leads away from the effective schools research *per se* into the territory of authentic school improvement. As a consequence, the argument made throughout Part Eight is for an integration of school effectiveness research and school improvement practice.

The contributions in Part Eight reprise the themes raised in this introduction. Pam Sammons, Karen Elliot and David Hopkins explore in more detail the foundations of school effectiveness and school improvement. Mel West and David Hopkins, in the spirit of integration and synergy, critique both traditions. In slightly different ways David Reynolds, David Potter and Chris Chapman, followed by Louise Stoll, illustrate how the research and practice from both traditions can be used to improve schools. Alma Harris reviews the contribution to both school effectiveness and school improvement to our understanding of departmental effectiveness. Finally, David Reynolds and Charles Teddlie point to the future of research and practice in both areas in their 'response to the critics'.

One of the most optimistic and well-supported conclusions from the school effects research was that of Rutter and colleagues (1979, p. 178), who commented that: 'the differences between schools in outcome were systematically related to their characteristics as social institutions', and that 'all of these factors were open to modification by the staff, rather than fixed by external constraints'. The social organization of a school and the consistent commitment of staff to a core set of educational principles provide the foundations for the value the school adds to a students' learning, progress and achievement and the inspiration for the strategies for school improvement.

It is from the synergy of the knowledge from the research on school effectiveness and the practice of school improvement that a coherent response to the contemporary world of rapid, centrally determined and externally enforced educational change can be developed. Some glimpses of that future are found in the contributions that follow.

REFERENCES

Berman, P. and McLaughlin, M. (1977) *Federal Programs Supporting Educational Change: Factors Affecting Implementation and Continuation*, Santa Monica, CA: RAND Corporation.

Dalin, P. (1973) 'Case Studies of Educational Innovation', in vol. 4, *Strategies for Educational Innovation*, Paris: CERI/Organization for Economic Co-operation and Development.

Elmore, R.F. (ed.) (1990) *Restructuring Schools*, Oakland, CA: Jossey-Bass.

Hargreaves, D.H. and Hopkins, D. (1991) *The Empowered School*, London: Cassell.

Hargreaves, D.H., Hopkins, D., Leask, M., Connolly, J. and Robinson, P. (1989) *Planning for School Development*, London: Department of Education and Science.

Mortimore, P. (1991) 'School effectiveness research: which way at the crossroads?' *School Effectiveness and School Improvement*, 24 (3), pp. 213–29.

Murphy, J. (1992) 'School effectiveness and school restructuring: contributions to educational improvement', *School Effectiveness and School Improvement*, 3 (2), pp. 90–109.

Rutter, M., Maughan, B., Mortimore, P. and Ouston, J., with Smith, A. (1979) *Fifteen Thousand Hours*, London: Open Books.

Sarason, S. (1982) *The Culture of the School and the Problem of Change*, 2nd edn, Boston: Allyn & Bacon.

CHAPTER 48

The underpinnings and contribution of school effectiveness research

PAM SAMMONS AND KAREN ELLIOT

This chapter explores the contribution school effectiveness research (SER) has made to our understanding of school performance. It examines the measurement of effectiveness and the relationships between school and classroom processes and effectiveness. There is a particular focus on the implications of the field for those concerned with promoting equity in education.

It is difficult to pinpoint the 'start' of SER exactly because many different sub-disciplines have studied schools and classrooms from a variety of perspectives. In the USA and UK the chief catalyst seems to have been the publication of work by Coleman *et al.* (1966) and Jencks *et al.* (1972). These studies claimed that the particular school attended by a pupil had little influence on their educational outcomes in comparison with factors such as IQ, 'race', and socio-economic status. The focus was thus on structural inequalities rather than on the influence of schools. These studies suffered from a number of limitations and subsequent research pointed to important school effects while acknowledging the strong influence of intake (Rutter *et al.*, 1979; Madaus *et al.*, 1979; Mortimore *et al.*, 1988; Smith and Tomlinson, 1989). In other countries, organizational theory, educational administration and instruction have been influential in promoting educational effectiveness research (Scheerens and Bosker, 1997; Teddlie and Reynolds, 2000).

Measuring school effectiveness

How can we try to measure the influence of schools, and by implication of teachers, on their students? This deceptively simple question lies at the heart of SER. The central focus of SER concerns the idea that, 'schools matter, that schools do have major effects upon children's development and that, to put it simply, schools do make a difference' (Reynolds and Creemers, 1990, p. 1).

In essence, SER seeks to disentangle the complex links between the pupils' 'dowry' (the mix of abilities, prior attainments and personal and family attributes), which any student brings to school, from those of their educational experiences at school and to explore the way these jointly influence their later attainment, progress and development. The main foci are:

- the impact of social institutions;
- characteristics that promote students' educational outcomes;
- the influence of contexts on outcomes.

SER seeks to provide empirical evidence to assist the evaluation and critique of classroom practice and educational policy. The use of quantitative methods, however, does not mean that SER is deterministic or mechanistic in nature. Indeed, it stresses the probabilistic nature of the findings and highlights the need to measure change over time and the impact of context. The subjective views of those involved (students, parents or practitioners) are seen as vital keys that help to illuminate school and classroom culture and the context of particular institutions.

Key features of SER methodology are that it:

- is mainly quantitative, but qualitative case studies are important;
- uses measures of student outcomes;
- emphasizes reliability and replicability and seeks to make generalizations;
- values the views and perceptions of teachers, students and parents.

Aims and goals of SER

In the USA the early effective schools movement was committed to the belief that children of the urban poor could succeed in school (Edmonds, 1979; Goodlad, 1984). Early SER research incorporated explicit aims concerned with equity and excellence and focused on the achievement in basic skills of poor/ethnic minority children in elementary schools. More recent research has studied more diverse samples of schools and students and is concerned with the concept of assessing progress over time, rather than cross-sectional 'snapshots' of attainment at one time point. In addition, more attention is paid to social and affective outcomes (Rutter *et al.*, 1979; Mortimore *et al.*, 1988; Ainley, 1994; Smyth 1999; MacBeath and Mortimore, 2001).

'Natural justice demands that schools are held accountable only for those things they can influence (for good or ill) and not for all the existing differences between their intakes' (Nuttall, 1990, p. 25). The use of 'raw' league tables of performance (published in England from 1992 onwards as part of a policy of bringing market forces to bear in education) increased pressure on schools to exclude disruptive students and to take older poor attendees or those unlikely to sit public examinations off-roll, since these have an adverse impact on their league table positions (Gray *et al.*, 1999).

SER provides a powerful critique of the use of raw league tables to monitor school performance through the concept of 'value-added' (Saunders, 1999). Value-added studies attempt to control statistically for intake differences between schools before any comparisons of effectiveness are made (Goldstein *et al.*, 1993; Mortimore, Sammons and Thomas, 1994; Hill and Rowe, 1998). An effective school is defined as one in which students progress further than might be expected from consideration of its intake (Mortimore, 1991). To assess value-added, measures of individual student prior attainment are needed to provide a baseline against which subsequent progress can be assessed. Other factors such as gender, socio-economic status, mobility and fluency in the majority language have been shown to affect progress and are often included in assessing school effects.

The need to interpret estimates of school effects (as in 'outlier' studies of highly effective or ineffective schools) by reference to their confidence limits is also now widely recognized (Goldstein *et al.*, 1993; Thomas and Mortimore, 1996). SER can distinguish only between schools where student progress (or other outcomes) is significantly better or significantly poorer than predicted on the basis of their prior attainment and intake characteristics. Studies suggest that the proportion of schools identified as significant outliers can vary between 15 and 33 per cent of those included in an analysis, depending on the outcome studied (Sammons, 1999). While patterns in overall results may be fairly stable from one year to another, subject results show more variation (Sammons, Thomas and Mortimore, 1997; Gray *et al.*, 1999). Only a small minority of schools or departments are likely to be identified as significant outliers over several years (under 10 per cent).

Choice of outcomes

The concept of what constitutes a 'good' school is highly problematic (OECD, 1989; Silver, 1994; Gray and Wilcox, 1995). The question of values in education and the purposes of schooling remain the subject of argument (White and Barber, 1997). Some critics of SER argue that, if the teacher–student learning relationship is right, then the educational outcomes will take care of themselves (Elliott, 1996). Against this, the need to gauge learning (which cannot be observed) by measuring its outcomes in some way, and to investigate how outcomes are influenced by teachers' classroom practices and school processes, is argued by proponents of SER (Sammons and Reynolds, 1997). In particular, the question of by whom or how it can be judged when such relationships are 'right' remains unclear if student outcomes are not measured in some way.

Rather than attempting to define 'good' and thus by implication 'bad' schools, SER focuses deliberately on the narrower concept of effectiveness, which concerns the achievement of educational goals using specific measures of student cognitive, social or affective outcomes. Effectiveness is thus seen as a necessary but not sufficient condition for any acceptable definition of a 'good' school.

A broad range of outcomes – cognitive, social and affective – is necessary to provide a satisfactory picture of school effects. Evidence indicates that attendance, attitudes, behaviour, motivation and self-esteem can act as intermediate outcomes that affect, and can themselves be influenced by, pupils' attainment and progress (Rutter *et al.*, 1979; Mortimore *et al.*, 1988; Lee, Bryk and Smith 1993; Smyth, 1999; Mulford and Silins, 2001). School 'connectedness' has been shown to reduce significantly adolescent emotional distress (Resnick *et al.*, 1997), while Battistich and Hom (1997) have drawn attention to the relationship between pupils' sense of their school as a community and lower involvement in problem behaviours, such as drug use and delinquent behaviour.

Equity and complexity

There is growing awareness of the issue of complexity in SER (Sammons, 1996; Goldstein, 1998). The question of whether schools are equally effective for different groups of students – girls or boys, those from different socio-economic or ethnic groups – is vital to the concept of inclusion. The study of differential effectiveness addresses such concerns (Mortimore *et al.*, 1988; Smith and Tomlinson, 1989; Goldstein *et al.*, 1993).

Sammons, Thomas and Mortimore (1997) explored internal variations in secondary schools' academic effectiveness, looking at departmental variations in terms of different subjects and for different student groups, and concluded that effectiveness is best seen as a feature of schools which is both outcome and time specific. For secondary schools the term needs to be qualified to incorporate both school and departmental effectiveness. The results also point to the importance of examining trends over time. (Harris, Jamieson and Russ, 1995; Harris, Bennett and Preedy, 1997, also highlight difference at the departmental level.)

The question of whether school effects differ between specific groups of pupils is of critical importance to the promotion of social inclusion. Scheerens and Bosker (1997, p. 96) assert: 'Schools matter most for underprivileged and/or initially low achieving students. Effective or ineffective schools are especially effective or ineffective for these students'. Their analysis of the evidence shows that:

- school effects for black students were almost twice as large as for white students in the USA;
- differences between public and private schools were almost twice as large for low-socio-economic-status students as for middle-class students, whereas the differences between schools for high-socio-economic-status students were small in the USA;
- school effects vary for pupils by race and low prior attainment in England;
- school effects were larger for initially low attaining and for black Caribbean pupils.

It must be stressed that SER does not suggest schools can, by themselves, overcome the powerful impact of social disadvantage (Mortimore and Whitty, 1997). Nonetheless, research by Mortimore *et al.* (1988) on primary schools illustrates that working-class children attending the most effective schools made progress over three years that resulted in higher final attainment levels than middle-class pupils in the least effective schools.

Size of school effects

Scheerens and Bosker's (1997) meta-analysis indicates that net school effects (after control for intake) are larger for mathematics than language, and largest for studies based on composite measures of achievement. On average, schools accounted for 8 per cent of the achievement differences between students after control for initial differences, but classroom level/teacher effects were substantially larger. Scheerens and Bosker conclude that the relatively modest size of estimated school effect in percentage terms should not be downplayed, given the average impact a school has on all its students. They suggest that effect sizes be considered in relation to the number of students in the school over several years. It should be noted that, in terms of percentage of total variance in cognitive outcomes, the school effect is larger than, for example, the effect of gender or other individual student characteristics, such as eligibility for free school meals

A further way of illustrating school effects is to consider the difference between outliers (significantly more or less effective schools) in terms of student attainment. Thomas and Mortimore (1996) show that, for a student of average prior attainment at age 11 years, the difference in total GCSE points score at age 16 was equivalent to obtaining seven grade B rather than seven grade D GCSEs, between the most and least effective schools .

Effectiveness is thus a relative concept dependent on the:

- sample of schools studied;
- choice of outcome measures and methodology, including adequacy of intake controls;
- timescale.

Judgements about effectiveness need to address three key questions, which are essential for the promotion of equity. Is the school effective:

- promoting which outcomes?
- for which student groups?
- over what time period?

School and classroom processes

To what extent can SER illuminate the black box of how school and classroom experiences combine to foster or inhibit student progress and their social and affective development? This is the focus of studies that seek to measure the relationship of school and classroom processes to student outcomes.

Reviews have identified common features concerning the processes and characteristics of more effective schools. Scheerens and Bosker (1997) distinguish eight aspects:

- productive climate and culture
- focus on central learning skills
- appropriate monitoring
- practice-oriented staff development
- professional leadership
- parental involvement
- effective instructional arrangements
- high expectations.

Teddlie and Reynolds (2000) distil SER findings into nine process areas, as shown in Table 48.1.

Ineffective schools have received much less attention than effective ones. Stoll and Fink (1996) reviewed studies of ineffective schools and noted four features:

- lack of vision
- unfocused leadership
- dysfunctional staff relationships
- ineffective classroom practices.

Ineffective classroom practices were characterized by:

- inconsistent approaches to the curriculum and teaching;
- generally lower expectations for students of low socio-economic status;

Table 48.1 *The processes of effective schools*

1	The processes of effective leadership	• Being firm and purposeful • Involving others in the process • Exhibiting instructional leadership • Frequent personal monitoring • Selecting and replacing staff
2	The processes of effective teaching	• Unity of purpose • Consistency of practice • Collegiality and collaboration
3	Developing and maintaining a pervasive focus on learning	• Focusing on academics • Maximizing school learning time
4	Producing a positive school culture	• Creating a shared vision • Creating an orderly environment • Emphasizing positive reinforcement
5	Creating high and appropriate expectations for all	• For students • For staff
6	Emphasizing student responsibilities and rights	• Responsibilities • Rights
7	Monitoring progress at all levels	• At the school level • At the classroom level • At the student level
8	Developing staff skills at the school site	• Site-based • Integrated with ongoing professional development
9	Involving parents in productive and appropriate ways	• Buffering negative influences • Encouraging productive interactions with parents

Source: Teddlie and Reynolds, 2000.

- an emphasis on supervising and communicating about routines;
- low levels of teacher–pupil interaction;
- low levels of pupil involvement in their work;
- pupil perceptions of their teachers as people who did not care, praise, provide help or consider learning as important;
- more frequent use of criticism and negative feedback.

The centrality of teaching and learning in determining schools' effectiveness is increasingly recognized (Creemers, 1994; Scheerens and Bosker, 1997). Sammons, Hillman and Mortimore (1995) argue that the quality of teaching and expectations have the most significant role to play in fostering students' learning and progress and, therefore, in influencing their educational outcomes. Nonetheless, school processes, including leadership, remain influential because they provide the overall framework within which teachers and classrooms operate (Sammons, 1999; Mulford and Silins, 2001).

Reviews (e.g. Joyce and Showers, 1988) identify a number of characteristics of effective teachers. These teachers:

- teach the class as a whole;
- present information or skills clearly and animatedly;
- keep the teaching sessions task-oriented;
- are non-evaluative and keep instruction relaxed;
- have high expectations for achievement (give more homework, pace lessons faster and create alertness);
- relate comfortably to students (reducing behaviour problems).

The features of 'structured teaching' have been reported as particularly relevant to promoting cognitive attainment in the basic skill areas, especially in schools serving higher proportions of socio-economically disadvantaged pupils. Stringfield (1994) has drawn attention to the need for special strategies, particularly the benefits of high expectations and structured teaching, for disadvantaged pupils. Curriculum coverage has also been shown to be important. In a study of ethnically diverse inner-city schools, Plewis (1998) showed that curriculum coverage was an important predictor of young pupils' mathematics progress. Mean curriculum coverage was lower in classrooms containing a substantial proportion of African-Caribbean pupils and it was concluded that African-Caribbean boys fell behind because they covered less of the curriculum.

Muijs and Reynolds (2000) studied classroom practice and found differences between experimental and control groups on nine measures of teacher behaviour. Mathematics progress was significantly higher in project classes; the most significant factors were effective interactive teaching, direct instruction and varied teaching. The benefits of interactive whole-class teaching were greater in classes where there were higher proportions of low ability and disadvantaged students. It was concluded that structured teaching methods are most effective for teaching basic skills and younger ages and disadvantaged pupils benefit particularly from such approaches.

Theories and models

There are a number of models of educational attainment that attempt to demonstrate the nature and direction of links between particular school processes and student outcomes. The framework of 'input-process-output' has been commonly adopted, and the importance of context has also been widely recognized.

Creemers (1994) argues that theories of learning and instruction are at the core of multilevel educational effectiveness models. Such models suggest school-level factors act as facilitating conditions for classroom-level factors. Hill and Rowe (1998) point to the importance of attentiveness, time and appropriateness of instruction as predictors of elementary students' achievement. They argue that these variables are closely related to the concept of 'effective learning time'.

SER research views schools as organizations made up of nested layers – students within classrooms, departments within schools. The most pervasive view on cross-level influences in nested (i.e. multilevel) models is that higher-level conditions (aspects concerning school leadership, policy and organization, for example) in some way facilitate conditions at lower levels (the quality of teaching and learning in classrooms), which, in turn, have a direct impact on students' outcomes (Scheerens and Bosker, 1997).

School culture

The creation of a positive school culture is highlighted in much SER. Sammons, Thomas and Mortimore (1997) point to the importance of three aspects of school and departmental ethos or culture (see also Smyth, 1999):

- order – behaviour, policy and practice
- academic emphasis
- student-focused approach.

Behaviour policy and practice, leading to a safe orderly working environment and an academic emphasis, are seen as necessary for task achievement (effective teaching and learning and thus students' progress), while a student-focused environment concerns social cohesion and helps create a positive climate for learning. An effective school manages to achieve an optimal balance between the social control task achievement and the expressive social cohesion domains (Hargreaves, 1995).

In the USA, Lee, Bryk and Smith (1993) found evidence that schools with a common sense of purpose and a strong communal organization (involving collegial relationships among staff and positive adult–student relationships) are more effective in promoting a range of student academic and social outcomes reflecting pupil engagement and commitment. Grosin's research (1995) in Sweden identified positive links between school climate and students' mathematics progress, reading comprehension and behaviour. In Australia, Mulford and Silins (2001) report research that reveals indirect links between school leadership and organizational learning, which impact on student outcomes via their influence on teachers' classroom practice and climate.

West and Hopkins (1996) propose a comprehensive model for the effective school, which focuses on four domains:

- student achievements
- student experiences
- teacher and school development
- community involvement.

Summary and conclusions

The last decade has seen a rapid growth in research, policy and practitioner interest in school effectiveness and its potential as a catalyst for school improvement. This chapter has sought to explore the aims and methods of SER, how such approaches can be used to promote fairer comparisons of school performance, and some of the issues involved in measuring effectiveness. Rather than attempting to define 'good' schools, SER focuses on the narrower concept of effectiveness. Key features of SER are identified:

- effectiveness is a necessary but not sufficient condition for any acceptable definition of a 'good' school;
- school effects are larger for disadvantaged and ethnic minority pupils;

- a focus on social and affective outcomes as well as cognitive progress is necessary to obtain a rounded picture of effectiveness;
- common features of effective schools and effective teaching characteristics have been identified in research conducted in a range of countries;
- the SER knowledge base is particularly relevant to schools serving socio-economically disadvantaged communities.

Mortimore (1998, p. 143) draws attention to the potential power of effective schools:

> *Although the differences in scholastic attainment achieved by the same student in contrasting schools is unlikely to be great, in many instances it represents the difference between success and failure and operates as a facilitating or inhibiting factor in higher education. When coupled with the promotion of other pro-social attitudes and behaviours, and the inculcation of a positive self-image, the potential of the school to improve the life chances of students is considerable.*

There are important connections at the pupil level between academic achievement, motivation, behaviour, attendance and self-esteem. These links are often reciprocal – poor attainment increasing the risk of subsequent poor behaviour and attendance and vice versa. Monitoring can be an important tool for effectiveness and improvement to help evaluate performance, set targets, assist in school development planning and provide evidence of any impact (Fitz-Gibbon, 1996, Elliot, Smees and Thomas, 1998; Elliot and Sammons, 2000). SER findings cannot provide 'quick fixes' for schools in difficulties (Stoll and Myers, 1997) and should not be treated prescriptively. They are best used to stimulate reflection and as tools to assist the development of schools as learning institutions (MacGilchrist, Myers and Reed, 1997; Harris, Bennett and Preedy, 1997).

Education is increasingly recognized by policy makers as essential for both economic prosperity and social cohesion. There is a particular concern to raise educational standards and widen participation, and especially to raise the achievement levels of disadvantaged groups. Education cannot remedy social exclusion but remains an important focus for policies intended to combat social disadvantage. Thus schools are now subject to greater pressures for accountability and improvement. The SER field can be seen as a threat by some because of the explicit focus on student outcomes, but it also provides a powerful antidote to crude attempts to compare schools in terms of raw results by showing the strong impact of intake. The knowledge base has important equity implications and can empower principals and teachers to reflect on their practice by providing valuable information about school and classroom processes and their impact on students. Moreover, SER has developed methods and approaches that are highly relevant to the design of improvement projects.

REFERENCES

Ainley, J. (1994) 'Multiple indicators of high school effectiveness', paper presented to AERA annual conference, New Orleans, April.

Battistich, V. and Hom, H. (1997) 'The relationship between students' sense of their school as a community and their involvement in problem behaviours', *American Journal of Public Health*, 87 (12), pp. 1197–2001.

Coleman, J., Campbell, E., Hobson, C., McPartland, J., Mood, A., Weinfeld, F. and York, R. (1966), *Equality of Educational Opportunity*, Washington, DC: National Center for Educational Statistics/US Government Printing Office.

Creemers, B. (1994) *The Effective Classroom*, London: Cassell.

Edmonds, R.R. (1979) 'Effective schools for the urban poor', *Educational Leadership*, 37 (1), pp. 277–90.

Elliott, J. (1996) 'School effectiveness research and its critics: alternative visions of schooling', *Cambridge Journal of Education*, 26 (2), pp. 199–223.

Elliot, K. and Sammons, P. (2000) 'Interpreting pupil performance information: knowing your PANDA from your PICSI!', *NSIN Research Matters*, No. 11, London: Institute of Education, University of London.

Elliot, K., Smees, R. and Thomas, S. (1998) 'Making the most of your data: school self-evaluation using value-added measures', *Improving Schools*, 1 (3).

Fitz-Gibbon, C. (1996) *Monitoring Education Indicators, Quality and Effectiveness*, London: Cassell.

Goldstein, H. (1998) *Models for Reality: New Approaches to the Understanding of Educational Processes*, London: Institute of Education, University of London.

Goldstein, H., Rashbash, J., Yang, M., Woodhouse, G., Pan, H., Nuttall, D. and Thomas, S. (1993) 'A multilevel analysis of school examination results', *Oxford Review of Education*, 19 (4), pp. 425–33.

Goodlad, J. (1984) *A Place Called School: Prospects for the Future*, New York: McGraw Hill.

Gray, J., Hopkins, D., Reynolds, D. and Wilcox, B. (1999) *Improving Schools: Performance and Potential*, Buckingham: Open University Press.

Gray, J. and Wilcox, B. (1995) 'The challenge of turning round ineffective schools' in Gray, J. and Wilcox, B. (eds) *Good School, Bad School*, Buckingham: Open University Press.

Grosin, L. (1995) 'School climate, achievement and behaviour in 21 compulsory comprehensive intermediate schools – report 1', paper presented at European Conference on Child Abuse and Neglect in Oslo, Norway, 13–16 May.

Hargreaves, D. (1995) 'School effectiveness, school change and school improvement: the relevance of the concept of culture', *School Effectiveness and School Improvement*, 6 (1), pp. 23–46.

Harris, A., Bennett, N. and Preedy, M. (eds) (1997) *Organizational Effectiveness and Improvement in Education*, Buckingham: Open University Press.

Harris, A., Jamieson, I. and Russ, J. (1995) 'A study of effective departments in secondary schools', *School Organization*, 15 (3), pp. 283–99.

Hill, P. and Rowe, K. (1998) 'Modelling student progress in studies of educational effectiveness', *School Effectiveness and School Improvement*, 9 (3), pp. 310–33.

Jencks, C., Smith, M., Acland, H., Bane, M.J., Cohen, D., Gintis, H., Heyns, B. and Michelson, S. (1972) *Inequality: A Reassessment of the Effects of Family and Schooling in America*, New York: Basic Books.

Joyce, B. and Showers, B. (1988) *Student Achievement through Staff Development*, 2nd edn, White Plains, NY: Longman.

Lee, V., Bryk, A. and Smith, J. (1993) 'The organization of effective secondary schools' in Darling-Hammond, L. (ed.) *Research in Education*, Washington, DC: American Educational Research Association, pp. 171–226,

MacBeath, J. and Mortimore, P. (2001) *Improving School Effectiveness*, Buckingham: Open University Press.

MacGilchrist, B., Myers, R. and Reed, J. (1997) *The Intelligent School*, London: Paul Chapman Publishing.

Madaus, G., Kellingham, T., Rakow, E. and King, D. (1979) 'The sensitivity of measures of school effectiveness', *Harvard Educational Review*, 49, pp. 207–30.

Mortimore, P. (1991) 'The nature and findings of school effectiveness research in the primary sector', Riddell, S. and Brown, S. (eds) *School Effectiveness Research: Its Messages for School Improvement*, London: HMSO.

Mortimore, P. (1998) *The Road to Improvement: Reflections on School Effectiveness*, Lisse, The Netherlands: Swets & Zeitlinger.

Mortimore, P., Sammons, P., Stoll, L., Lewis, D. and Ecob, R. (1988) *School Matters: The Junior Years*, Wells, Somerset: Open Books.

Mortimore, P., Sammons, P. and Thomas, S. (1994) 'School effectiveness and value-added measures', *Assessment in Education: Principles, Policy and Practice*, 1 (3), pp. 315–32.

Mortimore, P. and Whitty, G. (1997) *Can School Improvement Overcome the Effects of Disadvantage?*, London: Institute of Education, University of London.

Muijs, R. and Reynolds, D. (2000) 'School effectiveness and teacher effectiveness in mathematics: some preliminary findings from the evaluation of the mathematics enhancement programme (primary)', *School Effectiveness and School Improvement*, 11 (3), pp. 273–304.

Mulford, B. and Silins, H. (2001) 'Leadership for organisational learning and improved student outcomes – what do we know?', *NSIN Research Matters*, 15, London: ISEIC, Institute of Education, University of London.

Nuttall, D. (1990) *Differences in Examination Performance*, RS 1277/90, London: Research and Statistics Branch, ILEA.

OECD (1989) *Schools and Quality, An International Report*, Paris: Organization for Economic Co-Operation and Development.

Plewis, I. (1998) 'Curriculum coverage and classroom grouping as explanations of between teacher differences in pupils' mathematics progress', *Educational Research and Evaluation*, 4 (2), pp. 97–107.

Resnick, M.D., Bearmore, P., Blum, R., Bonman, K., Harris, K., Jones, J., Tabor, T., Beuhring, T., Sleving, R., Shew, M., Ireland, M., Biaringer, L. and Urdy, J. (1997) 'Protecting adolescents from harm findings from the national longitudinal study on adolescent health', *Journal of the American Medical Association*, 278, pp. 823–32.

Reynolds, D. and Creemers, B. (1990) 'School effectiveness and school improvement: a mission statement', *School Effectiveness and School Improvement*, 1 (1), pp. 1–3.

Rutter, M., Maughan, B., Mortimore, P. and Ouston, J., with Smith, A. (1979) *Fifteen Thousand Hours: Secondary Schools and their Effects on Children*, London: Open Books.

Sammons, P. (1996) 'Complexities in the judgement of school effectiveness', *Educational Research and Evaluation*, 2 (2), pp. 113–49.

Sammons, P. (1999) *School Effectiveness: Coming of Age in the 21st Century*, Lisse, The Netherlands: Swets & Zeitlinger.

Sammons, P., Hillman, J. and Mortimore, P. (1995) *Key Characteristics of Effective Schools: A Review of School Effectiveness Research*, London: Office for Standards in Education.

Sammons, P. and Reynolds, D. (1997) 'A partisan evaluation – John Elliott on school effectiveness', *Cambridge Journal of Education*, 27 (1), pp. 123–36.

Sammons, P., Thomas, S. and Mortimore, P. (1997) *Forging Links: Effective Schools and Effective Departments*, London: Paul Chapman Publishing.

Saunders, L. (1999) 'A brief history of educational "value-added": how did we get to where we are?', *School Effectiveness and School Improvement*, 10 (2), pp. 233–56.

Scheerens, J. and Bosker, R. (1997) *The Foundations of Educational Effectiveness*, Oxford: Pergamon.

Silver, H. (1994) *Good Schools, Effective Schools their Judgements and their Histories*, London: Cassell.

Smith, D. and Tomlinson, S. (1989) *The School Effect: A Study of Multi-Racial Comprehensives*, London: Policy Studies Institute.

Smyth, E. (1999) *Do Schools Differ? Academic and Personal Development among Pupils in the Second-Level Sector*, Dublin: Economic and Social Research Council.

Stoll, L. and Fink, D. (1996) *Changing Our Schools: Linking School Effectiveness and School Improvement*, Buckingham: Open University Press.

Stoll, L. and Myers, K. (eds) (1997) *No Quick Fixes*, London: Falmer Press.

Stringfield, S. (1994) 'A model of elementary school effects' in Reynolds, D., Creemers, B., Nesselrodt, P.S., Schaffer, E.C., Stringfield, S. and Teddlie, C. (eds) *Advances in School Effectiveness Research and Practice*, Oxford: Pergamon.

Teddlie, C. and Reynolds, D. (2000) *The International Handbook of School Effectiveness Research*, London: Falmer Press.

Thomas, S. and Mortimore, P. (1996) 'Comparison of value-added models for secondary-school effectiveness', *Research Papers in Education*, 11 (1), pp. 5–33.

West, M. and Hopkins, D. (1996) 'Reconceptualising school effectiveness and school improvement', paper presented at the School Effectiveness and Improvement symposium of the annual conference of the American Educational Research Association, New York, 8 April.

White, J. and Barber, M. (eds) (1997) *Perspectives on School Effectiveness Improvement*, London: Institute of Education, University of London.

8

CHAPTER 49

The foundations of school improvement

DAVID HOPKINS

During its relatively short history, school improvement as an approach to educational change has passed through three ages. Although the intellectual background to school improvement can be traced back to the work of Kurt Lewin in the immediate post-Second-World-War period, it was only in the late 1970s and early 1980s that it took shape as a practical approach to educational change. Many of the 'first age' of school improvement initiatives were 'free floating'. There was a focus on individual strategies, such as organizational change, school self-evaluation, the role of leadership and of external support. These initiatives were loosely connected to student learning, were too fragmented in conception and application, and therefore struggled to impact upon classroom practice. As a consequence, these first-age initiatives did not match the criteria previously outlined for authentic school improvement.

Many of the elements for a 'second age' of school improvement were, however, in place by the early 1990s. The catalyst for a qualitative move forward came from the beginnings of a merger of the two traditions of school effectiveness research and school improvement practice. By this time, the two traditions were in a position to give tools to practitioners that were directly applicable and useful in the new policy context. So, for example, 'value-added' measures of school performance provided schools with a methodology for gauging their effectiveness and in so doing sharpened the focus of reform efforts on student learning. Similarly the school improvement tradition was at last providing schools with guidelines and strategies for implementation that were sufficiently powerful to take educational change into the classroom. Approaches to staff development based on partnership teaching (Joyce and Showers, 1995), designs for development planning that focused on learning and that linked together organizational and classroom change within a medium-term time frame (Hopkins and MacGilchrist, 1998) are but two examples. In addition, the educational reform initiatives of the early/mid-1990s that reflected a more centralized attempt to reform schooling and impact on learning were beginning to bite.

Despite this, improvement on a national scale is very patchy. There is a lack of a strategic dimension to most national reforms and a consequent failure to accelerate significantly the learning of pupils. Success at the local level is often the result of either a strong and opportunistic leader or a happy series of serendipities. It is clear that neither the first or second ages of school improvement have made sufficient impact on the 'learning level'. Educational systems need not only to consolidate what has been learned from the second age of school improvement, but also to move on to a third that fully embodies what is referred to later in this chapter as the principles of authentic school improvement.

Many of the features of the first age of school improvement were outlined in the introduction to Part Eight. In this chapter what is known about the second age will be consolidated, and some indication given of what will make up the 'third age of school improvement', based on the authentic principles. The contours of the third age of authentic school improvement will become clearer as the discussion unfolds. This chapter therefore:

- describes the contribution of the OECD International School Improvement Project;
- assesses the school improvement response to educational change;
- proposes a framework for authentic successful school improvement.

The OECD International School Improvement Project

A major impetus to the development of school improvement as a strategic response to the challenge of educational change was given by the Organization for Economic Co-operation and Development (OECD) through its Centre for Educational Research and Development (CERI), which between 1982 and 1986 sponsored an International School Improvement Project (ISIP). ISIP built on previous OECD/CERI initiatives such as *The Creativity of the School* (Nisbet, 1973) and the in-service training (INSET) projects (Hopkins, 1986). Although school self-evaluation was regarded as an important strategy for school improvement, the ISIP took a more holistic and systemic view of educational change. At a time when the educational system as a whole faced not only retrenchment but also pressure for change, a project that focused on school improvement – at change at the meso-level, at strategies for strengthening the school's capacity for problem solving, at making the school more reflexive to change, as well as enhancing the teaching/learning process – was seen as both important and necessary. More detail of the knowledge that emanated from ISIP is found elsewhere (van Velzen *et al.*, 1985; Hopkins, 1987a, 1990).

ISIP proposed a very different way of thinking about change than the ubiquitous 'top-down' approach. When the school is regarded as the 'centre' of change, then strategies for change need to take this new perspective into account. School improvement for example, was defined in the ISIP as: 'A systematic, sustained effort aimed at change in learning conditions and other related internal conditions in one or more schools, with the ultimate aim of accomplishing educational goals more effectively' (van Velzen *et al.*, 1985, p. 48). School improvement as an approach to educational change, according to ISIP, therefore rested on what are now regarded as a well-known number of assumptions:

- the school as the centre of change
- a systematic approach to change
- focusing change on the 'internal conditions' of schools
- accomplishing educational goals more effectively
- a multi-level perspective
- integrative implementation strategies
- the drive towards institutionalization.

It was this philosophy and approach that underpinned the ISIP and laid the basis for further thinking and action. The ISIP also occurred at a fruitful time for the evolution of school improvement more generally. During this period some large-scale studies of school improvement projects were also conducted. The Study of Dissemination Efforts Supporting School Improvement (see Crandall, 1982) was particularly important. This mammoth study was responsible for the fine-grained analysis of Huberman and Miles (1984) and an analysis of policy implications (Crandall, Eiseman and Louis, 1986). Much was consequently learned about the dynamics of the change process during this period.

School improvement and the response to external change

If the nature of school improvement itself has been evolving over the past 20 years, so has the context of schooling changed since the OECD ISIP project first articulated school improvement as a strategy for educational change. Contemporary school improvement is now characterized by increasing complexity. On the one hand, school improvement approaches are becoming more sophisticated as they move through the three ages described here. On the other hand, the pressure for externally imposed change is also increasing. At the start of a new century it is not sufficient for school improvement to develop on its own terms; it also needs to be responsive to the changing demands of the external educational environment.

Research and experience illustrate a range of approaches that vary in their ability to address the challenge of external change. It is helpful to analyse these across two dimensions. The first dimension contrasts the response as either 'curricular' or 'organic'. A curricular response is self-explanatory, as it is a direct response to the curricular focus of many current policies. An organic response focuses on building a capacity within the school in order to manage change. The other dimension contrasts the response as either 'comprehensive' or 'diffuse'. In response to a particular curriculum-oriented policy a school may adopt an already well-developed, and tried-and-tested programme. This would be a comprehensive response. It is more usual, however, for the school to rely more on its own resources and to do more of what it has already done successfully. This could be termed a diffuse response.

	Curricular	Organic
Diffuse	The common curriculum of school improvement	The 'doors' to school improvement
Comprehensive	Success For All	Improving the Quality of Education for All

Figure 49.1 Examples of school improvement responses to external change

Some examples of this range of possibilities is given in Figure 49.1. This way of analysing school improvement captures not only the variety of responses that schools typically adopt in responding to external change, but it also provides a way of organizing and differentiating between a number of school improvement programmes and the associated literature.

A diffuse-curricular response to external change is the most common. Schools react as best they can, but often in an ad hoc and uncoordinated way. Detailed examples of this response are found in the case studies reported in Gray et al., (1999). The objective for the research was to explore how secondary schools become more effective over time; it found that different schools at differing levels of effectiveness and with different improvement trajectories exhibited contrasting 'routes to improvement'. All of the schools in the study, however, irrespective of being 'slow' or 'rapid' improvers, exhibited a diffuse-curricular response to external change. This tactical response was a direct reaction to the externally imposed target-setting agenda, in particular the pressure to raise examination results at age 16. These tactics included monitoring performance, introducing extra classes for certain groups of students, implementing 'codes of conduct', giving students greater responsibility, changing examination boards, and so on. They comprise what we termed the 'common curriculum' of school improvement (Gray et al., 1999).

This combination of tactics is powerful enough to raise the performance of low or slowly achieving schools up towards average levels of performance but no further. Although very popular such diffuse-curricular responses are by no means a panacea. There appears to be a ceiling on the amount of improvement such an approach can deliver. At best it can bring a school from a moderately low level up to an average level of performance. Also, it appears that the effect is short-lived; it usually plateaus or decreases after two years. Such a tactical response may be popular and in many cases necessary, but it is by no means a sufficient condition for authentic school improvement.

The diffuse-organic response is highly visible in Joyce's review (1991) of the 'doors' to school improvement. These are a series of individual approaches, which he describes as being 'doors' that can open or unlock the process of school improvement. Joyce concludes that each approach emphasizes different aspects of school culture at the outset – they provide a range of ways of 'getting into' school improvement. Each door opens a passageway into the culture of the school. His review reveals five major emphases (ibid., p. 59):

- Collegiality: the development of collaborative and professional relations within a school staff and with their surrounding communities.
- Research: when school staff studies the research findings about, for example, effective school and teaching practices, or the process of change.
- Action research: when teachers collect and analyse information and data about their classrooms and schools, and their students' progress.
- Curriculum initiatives: the introduction of changes within subject areas or, as in the case of the computer, across curriculum areas.
- Teaching strategies: when teachers discuss, observe and acquire a range of teaching skills and strategies.

Joyce argues that all these emphases can eventually change the culture of the school substantially. He maintains that single approaches are unlikely to be as powerful an agent for school improvement as a synthesis. The implicit assumption made by Joyce is that behind the door are a series of interconnecting pathways that lead inexorably to school improvement. In reality this is rarely the case. Most school improvement strategies tend to focus on individual changes and individual teachers and classrooms, rather than how these changes can fit in with and adapt the organization and ethos of the school. Because of their singular nature, they fail to a greater or lesser degree to affect the culture of the school. As a consequence, when the door is opened it leads only into a cul-de-sac. This partially accounts for the uneven effect of most of our educational reforms.

The broad conclusion from the analysis so far is that the diffuse responses to external change are inadequate. As will be seen, they do not match the criteria for authentic school improvement. If the problems of educational change are to be overcome then some way needs to be found of integrating organizational and curriculum change within a coherent strategy. To continue with Joyce's metaphor, the doors to school improvement need to be opened simultaneously or consecutively and the pathways behind them linked together. This would argue for the adoption of more comprehensive and well-specified approaches to school improvement.

The comprehensive-curricular response has a relatively long history, at least in terms of educational change. The 1960s has been described on both sides of the Atlantic as the 'decade of curriculum reform'. Although at that time many well-specified curricula were developed, few were sufficiently comprehensive enough to integrate both curriculum content and instructional strategies (Hopkins, 1987b). It is the integration of content and pedagogy that characterizes programmes that are associated with high levels of student achievement (Slavin and Fashola, 1998). Stringfield and his colleagues (Stringfield, Ross and Smith, 1996; Stringfield, Millsap and Herman, 1998), in their review of effective school improvement approaches, emphasize the need for carefully selected instructional strategies embedded within curriculum programmes that are designed to meet the particular learning needs of students. Unfortunately, within the field of school improvement at present, it is clear that few such strategies exist. An exception to this is the Success For All literacy programme that uses research-based approaches to curriculum, instruction, assessment and classroom management, with one-to-one tutoring being provided for those students falling behind in their reading (Slavin *et al.*, 1996).

Examples of the comprehensive-organic response are found in the various school improvement networks that are based on a particular philosophy or set of principles. They are a sort of school improvement 'club' where the rules of admission define a generalized approach to development work in schools. The Comer School Development Program (Comer, 1992); the Coalition of Essential Schools based at Brown University, which has evolved on the basis of the ideas of Theodore Sizer (1989); the League of Professional Schools at the University of Georgia led by Carl Glickman (1993); and the Learning Consortium in Toronto, including the Halton Project (Fullan, Bennett and Rolheiser-Bennett, 1990; Stoll and Fink, 1996), are all fine examples of this approach to school improvement. One of the weaknesses in such programmes is that the emphasis on principles, capacity building and whole-school processes is often at the expense of innovation at the classroom level. Without expanding the teacher's repertoire of instructional strategies, it is unlikely that such programmes will have any significant impact on student achievement. The Improving the Quality of Education for All (IQEA) project, however, provides one example of a comprehensive-organic approach that attempts to link whole-school development to enhanced classroom practice (Hopkins, 2001, 2002).

In terms of their contribution to enhancing the achievement of students, and to realizing the aspirations of national educational policies, it is the comprehensive approaches to school improvement that are the most effective. Despite the difference in focus and emphasis between comprehensive curricular and organic programmes, in practice they share many of the features of authentic school improvement.

The principles of authentic school improvement

As has already been seen, we now know enough about the theory and practice of educational change to successfully improve schools. Those engaged in such school improvement efforts do not just intervene in schools to carry through a particular change strategy; they are actively implementing improvement strategies that help both students and teachers to enhance their learning and achievements. They are also collaboratively researching the process in order to create new knowledge about schools, the change process and their own practice. More importantly, they are increasing the capacity of the school – the heads, teachers and students – to manage their own improvement process.

These approaches to school improvement have been referred to as 'authentic school improvement' (Hopkins, 2001). They stand in contrast to target-setting and high-stakes accountability reform strategies, and short-term quick-fix approaches, all of which are informed by different expectations, values and *modi operandi*. Reviews of successful school improvement efforts around the world suggest that they are based on a number of key principles (e.g. Hargreaves *et al.*, 1998). Taken together, these principles provide a framework for authentic school improvement and characterize the majority of successful school improvement programmes.

In general, authentic school improvement programmes are:

- Achievement-focused: they focus on enhancing student learning and achievement, in a broader sense than mere examination results or test scores.
- Empowering in aspiration: they intend to provide those involved in the change process with the skills of learning and 'change agentry' that will raise levels of expectation and confidence throughout the educational community.
- Research-based and theory rich: they base their strategies on programmes and programme elements that have an established track record of effectiveness, that research their own effectiveness and connect to and build on other bodies of knowledge and disciplines.
- Context specific: they pay attention to the unique features of the school situation and build strategies on the basis of an analysis of that particular context.
- Capacity building in nature: they aim to build the organizational conditions that support continuous improvement.
- Inquiry-driven: they appreciate that reflection-in-action is an integral and self-sustaining process.

8

- Implementation oriented: they take a direct focus on the quality of classroom practice and student learning.
- Interventionist and strategic: they are purposely designed to improve the current situation in the school or system and take a medium-term view of the management of change, and plan and prioritize developments accordingly.
- Externally supported: they build agencies around the school that provide focused support, and create and facilitate networks that disseminate and sustain 'good practice'.
- Systemic: they accept the reality of a centralized policy context, but also realize the need to adapt external change for internal purpose, and to exploit the creativity and synergies existing within the system.

Although these principles are based on an analysis across many programmes, obviously not all programmes will share all these characteristics. Even the most successful school improvement efforts will not necessarily embody all the principles, and there will be inevitable variation within the principles as well. That the principles share a high degree of intellectual coherence is not serendipitous. The principles, although empirically based, reflect an 'ideal type' of school improvement profile.

Table 49.1 represents a first attempt to define the influences on authentic school improvement. Although illustrative rather than exhaustive, the table identifies some of the wide range of influences that have helped determine this particular approach to school improvement. The table also serves to chart the intellectual history of 'authentic' school improvement. These principles therefore fulfil a number of important functions, since they:

- define a particular approach to school improvement;
- can be used to organize the theoretical, research and practical implications that define school improvement as a field of inquiry;
- provide a set of criteria that can be used to differentiate broad approaches to school improvement;
- can also be used more specifically to help analyse and define individual school improvement efforts or programmes;
- contain a series of implications for policy that could enable them to influence more directly the achievement and learning of all students.

Conclusion – towards the third age of school improvement

Authentic school improvement strategies focus both on how to accelerate the progress and enhance the achievement of students, and on establishing effective management practices within the school. This is the key characteristic of third-age approaches to school improvement and explains why previous strategies that tended to focus on either one or the other failed to enhance pupil progress and achievement. In this chapter the main characteristics of the second age of school improvement have been illustrated, and in the discussion of the more comprehensive and well-specified approaches some indication has been given of what third-age or authentic school improvement strategies look like.

Table 49.1 *The principles of authentic school improvement*

Principles	Examples of theoretical, research, policy or practical influences on school improvement
Achievement focused	The moral and social justice responsibility to enhance student learning, and the unrelenting focus on the quality of teaching and learning.
Empowering in aspiration	The moral imperative of emancipation, of increasing individual responsibility, the enhancement of skills and confidence (in the tradition of Dewey, Freire and Stenhouse).
Research-based and theory rich	The use of teaching and learning and organizational development strategies with robust empirical support for the developing of a variety of curriculum and teaching programmes or models; and the location of the approach within a philosophical tradition e.g. critical theory.
Context specific	The influence of the contemporary school effectiveness research that points to the importance of context specificity and the fallacy of the 'one-size-fits-all' change strategy.
Capacity building in nature	The necessity to ensure sustainability, the nurturing of professional learning communities, and the establishing of local infrastructures and networks.
Inquiry-driven	The uses of data to energize, inform and direct action; the influence of the 'reflective practitioner' ethic and a commitment to dissemination and utilization.
Implementation oriented	The research on the management of change, in particular the importance of individual meaning, the consistency of classroom effects and the creation of a commitment to active implementation.
Interventionist and strategic	The influence of 'Lewinian' action research and organization development principles and strategies, and the contemporary emphasis on development planning.
Externally supported	The centralization/decentralization polarity of most national educational policies, which places increasing emphasis on networking and external support agencies to facilitate implementation.
Systemic	The need to accept political realities and also to ensure policy coherence horizontally and vertically; the use of pressure and support to exploit the creativity and synergies within the system.

8

The new paradigm represents a new way of thinking, whose full ramifications have yet to be felt. In concluding, however, it is instructive to give an indication of the general character of third-age school improvement approaches (Hopkins and Reynolds, 2001):

- There is an enhanced focus upon the importance of pupil outcomes. Instead of the earlier emphasis upon changing the processes of schools, the focus is now upon seeing if these changes are powerful enough to affect pupil outcomes.

- The learning level and the instructional behaviours of teachers are increasingly being targeted for explicit attention, in addition to the school level. Specifications of curriculum and teaching are being adopted that extend current practice and that focus directly on the student learning goals that have been set.

- There is the creation of an infrastructure to enable the knowledge base – both 'best practice' and research findings – to be utilized. This involves an internal focus on collaborative patterns of staff development that enable teachers to inquire into practice, and external strategies for dissemination and networking.

- In addition there is an increasing consciousness of the importance of capacity building. This includes not only staff development, but also medium-term strategic planning, change strategies that utilize pressure and support, as well as the intelligent use of external support agencies.

- The adoption of a mixed methodological orientation – in which bodies of quantitative data plus qualitative data are used to measure quality, effects and deficiencies – is becoming more common. This includes an audit of existing classroom and school processes and outcomes, and comparison with desired end states, in particular the educational experiences of different pupil groups.

- There is an emphasis on the importance of ensuring reliability or 'fidelity' in the programme implementation across all the organizational members within schools – a marked contrast with the past when improvement programmes did not have to be organizationally 'tight'.

- There is an appreciation of the importance of cultural change in order to embed and sustain this approach to school improvement. There is a careful balance between vision building and the adapting of structures to support those aspirations.

REFERENCES

Comer, J. (1992) *For Children's Sake: Comer School Development Program*, New Haven, CT: Yale Child Study Center.

Crandall, D. (ed.) (1982) *People, Policies and Practices: Examining the Chain of School Improvement*, Vols 1–10, Andover, MA: The Network.

Crandall, D., Eiseman, J. and Louis, K.S. (1986) 'Strategic planning issues that bear on the success of school improvement efforts', *Educational Administration Quarterly*, 22 (2), pp. 21–53.

Fullan, M.G., Bennett, B. and Rolheiser-Bennett, C. (1990) 'Linking classroom and school improvement', *Educational Leadership*, 47 (8), pp. 13–19.

Glickman, C.D. (1993) *Renewing America's Schools: a Guide for School Based Action*, San Francisco: Jossey-Bass.

Gray, J., Hopkins, D., Reynolds, D., Wilcox, B., Farrell, S. and Jesson, D. (1999) *Improving Schools: Performance and Potential*, Buckingham: Open University Press.

Hargreaves, A., Fullan, M., Lieberman, A. and Hopkins, D. (eds) (1998) *International Handbook of Educational Change* (Vols 1–4), Dordrecht, The Netherlands: Kluwer Academic Publishers.

Hopkins, D. (ed.) (1986) *In-service Training and Educational Development*, London: Croom Helm.

Hopkins, D. (ed.) (1987a) *Improving the Quality of Schooling*, Lewes: Falmer Press.

Hopkins, D. (1987b) *Knowledge Information Skills and the Curriculum*, London: British Library.

Hopkins, D. (1990) 'The International School Improvement Project (ISIP) and effective schooling: towards a synthesis', *School Organization*, 10 (83), pp. 129–94.

Hopkins, D. (2001) *School Improvement for Real*, London: Routledge/Falmer Press.

Hopkins, D. (2002) *Improving the Quality of Education for All*, 2nd edn, London: David Fulton Publishers.

Hopkins, D. and MacGilchrist (1998) 'Development planning for pupil achievement', *School Leadership and Management*, 18 (3), pp. 409–24.

Hopkins, D. and Reynolds, D. (2001) 'The past, present and future of school improvement: towards the third age', *British Educational Research Journal*, 27 (4), pp. 459–75.

Huberman, M. and Miles, M.B. (1984) *Innovation Up Close*, New York: Plenum.

Joyce, B.R. (1991) 'The doors to school improvement,' *Educational Leadership*, 48 (8), pp. 59–62.

Joyce, B.R. and Showers, B. (1995) *Student Achievement through Staff Development*, 2nd edn, White Plains, NY: Longman.

Nisbet, J. (ed.) (1973) *Creativity of the School*, Paris: Organization for Economic Co-operation and Development.

Sizer, T.R. (1989) 'Diverse practice, shared ideas: the essential school' in Walberg, H. and Lane, J. (eds) *Organizing for Learning: Towards the Twenty First Century*, Reston, VA: NASSP.

Slavin, R.E. and Fashola, O. (1998) *Show Me the Evidence! Proven and Promising Programs for America's Schools*, Thousand Oaks, CA: Corwin Press.

Slavin, R.E., Madden, N.A., Dolan, L.J. and Wasik, B.A. (1996) *Every Child, Every School: Success for All*, Thousand Oaks, CA: Corwin Press.

Stoll, L. and Fink, D. (1996) *Changing Our Schools: Linking School Effectiveness and School Improvement*, Buckingham: Open University Press.

Stringfield, S., Millsap, M. and Herman, R. (1998) 'Using "promising programs" to improve educational processes and student outcome' in Hargreaves, A., Lieberman, A. Fullan, M. and Hopkins, D. (eds) *International Handbook of Educational Change*, vol. 4, Dordrecht, The Netherlands: Kluwer Academic Publishers.

Stringfield, S., Ross S. and Smith, L. (eds) (1996) *Bold Plans for School Restructuring*, New York: Lawrence Erlbaum Associates.

Van Velzen, W., Miles, M., Ekholm, M., Hameyer, U. and Robin, D. (1985) *Making School Improvement Work – A Conceptual Guide to Practice*, Leuven, Belgium: ACCO.

8

CHAPTER 50

Reconceptualizing school effectiveness and improvement

MEL WEST AND DAVID HOPKINS

Since Reynolds' observation (1992) that 'the disciplines of school effectiveness and school improvement need each other intellectually', we have seen a line of school effectiveness researchers and school improvement practitioners queuing up to make the same point. Those within the school effectiveness tradition (see for example Mortimore, 1991; Stoll and Fink, 1996; Teddlie and Reynolds, 2000) have made explicit their desire to see some merging of the two traditions. From those working within the school improvement tradition, Hopkins, Ainscow and West (1994), Fullan, Bennett and Rolheiser-Bennett (1990), Van Velzen et al. (1985), amongst others, have made similar overtures. There have also been a number of publications that have begun to celebrate this 'merging of traditions' (see for example Gray et al., 1996; Reynolds et al., 1996; Hopkins and Reynolds, 2001).

It seems unlikely, however, that some sudden fusing of the effectiveness and the improvement paradigms will transform our knowledge and understanding of what increases the quality of schooling. If all that was required was to enter into a 'meeting of minds' (Stoll, 1994), with eyes open and a clear appreciation of the strengths and weaknesses of the two traditions, then the desired fusion would have already been achieved, since the desire on both sides is strong.

As we know only too well from the history of science, the defining feature of a paradigm shift is that existing knowledge is re-orientated and extended in a way that is both inclusive and transformative, leaving the world looking a different place (Kuhn, 1970). If we seek such a shift, if we hope to establish a new paradigm within which to work towards more successful schools, then that requires a fundamental revision of existing views. Any fruitful marriage of the two traditions will require a fundamental reconceptualization of what is understood by the term 'an effective school' before rushing to consummate the union.

It is for this reason that we suggest that school effectiveness and school improvement require not just a merging of traditions or a meeting of minds, however attractive these seem. Rather, if we are to move beyond the rhetoric of aspiration we need the kind of paradigm shift that Kuhn has described.

Measuring school effectiveness: a critique

Undeniably, school effectiveness research over the past 20 years has increased our knowledge of schools and schooling. Useful as this knowledge base is, and Reynolds (1992) has described it as amongst the most 'robust' available, there remain a number of limitations that need to be acknowledged.

First, despite the extensive studies (mainly in the USA) that have been conducted, and the high levels of overlap between the correlates of effective schools that emerge, it is important to remember that correlates, by themselves, do not explain the nature of cause and effect. Indeed, it may well be that some correlates occur because they are outcomes of effective schools, not determinants of them.

A second area of concern relates to the somewhat narrow definition of an effective school that recently has tended to displace alternative definitions. The problem here is of two sorts, and can be illustrated by reference to Cronbach and Meehl's work (1955) on construct validation. In seeking a definition of an effective school that is amenable to verification, we need a construct that both reflects all (or at least a fair range of) those qualities that we associate with effective schooling, but is also amenable to measurement. Many would argue that the prevailing definition of an effective school falls far short of the rich and varied picture that the construct conjures in the mind. Consequently (as shown in Figure 50.1), the construct is not adequately captured in the definition. This becomes more obvious when we try to apply a measure, since we are likely to choose a measure that suits that part of the construct we have defined, rather than the parts that elude us. There will, however, typically be some area of overlap. Thus a measure such as the results achieved by pupils in public examinations does tell us something about one facet of our construct of an effective school. But since the match between measure and construct is far from complete (as for example, a thermometer might be when measuring temperature) two problems arise.

The first relates to the extent to which the selected measure fails to reflect the richness and complexity of the construct, and can be termed 'measurement deficiency'. A second, but related, problem concerns the extent to which there are aspects of the measure 'left over'. It can be observed that there is considerable reluctance to discard measurements, once taken, simply because they shed little light on the purpose (construct-related) for which were collected. Thus, for example, we may expect to find that public examination results at 16+ not only tell us little about the quality of schooling, but are nevertheless used to inform other purposes for which they were not designed, such as becoming a major determinant of the post-16 patterns of study that are offered to individual pupils, or even a method of ranking schools. This harnessing of measures for alternative purposes can be termed 'contamination'. In demonstrating a willingness to accept too narrow a definition of an effective school, many school effectiveness researchers have contributed to the levels of deficiency and contamination

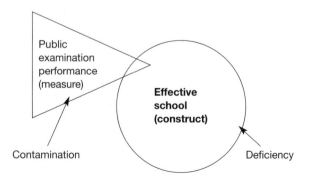

Figure 50.1 The mismatch of the construct and the measure of school effectiveness

associated with the league-table approach. Sadly, these failings are likely to have consequences for both schools and individual pupils.

Most recently, those working in this area have become interested in added-value approaches. However, this does not constitute a more representative index and is consequently a third area for concern. This is not to say that the replacement of a simple totting-up process by one that attempts to 'correct' the results achieved within a particular school (to reflect the differences in prior attainment, social and other factors) is misguided. Such scrupulousness is likely to lead to fairer comparisons between schools on that one particular measure – in effect it increases our confidence in the area of overlap between measure and construct. But it does not extend the measure in a way that makes it more representative of the other characteristics of an effective school. Value-added approaches therefore, though useful, will not resolve the problem of how we can fairly compare the performance of schools, though they may increase our understanding of the performance of pupils.

A fourth limitation of school effectiveness research has been the tendency for studies to highlight managerial behaviours and attitudes. Unsurprisingly, 'effective' management practice emerges from the research as a key correlate of 'effective' schools. However, there is relatively little parallel work available on 'ineffective' schools, and we have little reason to believe that the managerial solutions distilled from effectiveness studies will impact on failing schools.

A fifth concern is that the ranking of schools according to putative performance measures places enormous pressure on schools to maximize the reported results in the short term – as Sergiovanni (1992) points out, 'what gets rewarded gets done'. The consequences of adopting such a focus can include short-term thinking, restricted goals for the schools and its pupils, and increased tension and conflict amongst teachers, as they become increasingly afraid of 'failure'.

It seems then, that despite the recent increase in interest and activity, the school effectiveness movement may, as Murphy (1992) hinted in the early 1990s, have lost its way. Indeed, the current trend seems as much a response to the new possibilities for analysis as it is to any new vision of what an effective school looks like, or how a school might be made more effective.

School improvement: a critique

A commitment to work with the grain of schools notwithstanding, a number of limitations to school improvement approaches have also become more evident recently. In particular, the school improvement movement has in general found it difficult to grow away from its roots, which are essentially in staff development. And this is our first concern. Irrespective of the claims made for them, many school improvement initiatives tend in practice to be little more than glorified staff development activities.

A second area of concern is that improvement strategies have frequently adopted a rational technical approach that is difficult to sustain within the dynamics of a real school community. Collaborative school management (Caldwell and Spinks, 1988) is a well-known example. The introduction of self-management found the majority of schools unprepared to exercise control over their own futures. They simply do not have the structures, the experience or the strategies necessary to move the school systematically in a given direction, even where there is increased clarity about what the direction should be.

A third area of concern relates to the values that inform many school improvement models and practices. It is not surprising that those looking closely at school-level processes tend to be heavily influenced by the ways in which teachers construe schools. It is all well and good to start with the reality of teachers, but it is probably not moving the school too far forward when research ends there as well. Because school 'improvers' often spend significant amounts of time in school with teachers, they are susceptible in the conceptualization of their models to teacher values and concerns to a degree that is rarely approached in their assimilation of, for example, pupil or parent perspectives.

A fourth and contradictory concern is the degree of socialization sometimes assumed by school improvers as a result of their relationship with the senior management of the school. Although professing a 'whole-school' approach, it is almost always the case that entry into a school is governed by the head and/or the senior management team (SMT). Inevitably, school improvers are exposed first and then continually to SMT views of the world. Consequently, as hard as one tries, it is often difficult not to view the school through their eyes. As the relationship develops, it is also very tempting to 'pull punches' when it is necessary to give the headteacher critical or contentious feedback.

Fifth, there is the general problem of transferring 'recipes' from one school community to another. We have observed previously (Hopkins, Ainscow and West, 1994) that if school improvement is to be successful, it is necessary to move beyond a series of recipes that are produced in response to established problems and barriers to development. Rather, the school improvement 'ingredients' need to be selected from and combined in proportions that relate to the particular context and circumstances of the particular school. The prevalence of school improvement packages or models militates against classroom impact and encourages the overemphasis on staff development noted earlier. It is increasingly being realized that if we want to impact on student progress, then the school improvement strategy needs to be based on data about student performance.

This analysis of school improvement initiatives is also amenable to the same 'construct validation' critique that we made of the school effectiveness research. Here, however, the problem is a little different. With the effective school research there was in general a mismatch between construct (effective school) and the measure (lists of correlates); with school improvement initiatives, although they by and large work within the context of the construct of an 'improving school', they reflect a limited or stereotypical focus and only impact partially on the construct. The problem, of course, is that most school 'improvers' claim a whole-school approach, and although they may indeed be working within the reality of a school, often they are impacting only on small parts of it (inhibited by the 'socialization' process from offering hostile or contrary views).

This problem is illustrated in Figure 50.2. Claiming a whole-school approach and working within the realities of teachers may be a necessary, but is far from being a sufficient condition for school improvement. School improvers need a more profound understanding of the nature of the school and of the specific outcomes of their strategies if their work is to live up to the claims most make for it.

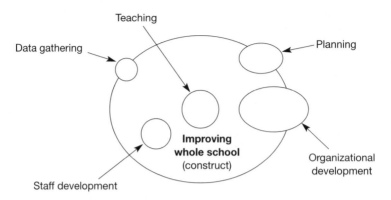

Figure 50.2 The school improvement 'whole school' illusion

Towards a reconceptualization

Though by no means a comprehensive critique, these limitations associated with the two dominant traditions argue that the time has come to reconceptualize the field. It is not sufficient simply to merge the two approaches by seeking out those areas on which the two groupings can agree – both because what can be agreed and what is right are not always the same thing, and because there is a need to transcend the vocabularies and question the 'truths' of both paradigms. In particular, as a prerequisite for meaningful dialogue, it is necessary to detach the term 'effective school' from the narrow and particular connotations it currently possesses. It is time to acknowledge that effective schools are the legitimate goal of all those currently involved in research and development work within the two traditions. But neither an 'academically successful school' (a much more accurate description of those schools that top the league tables) or a 'processes-approved' school (which seems to be what much of school improvement has been about) is necessarily effective, since to be truly effective a school must satisfy a series of different but equally valid criteria.

The more comprehensive model of the effective school that we are proposing attempts to capture in a constructive way the lessons we take from the critiques of school effectiveness and school improvement. It also reflects what we take to be the main challenge facing schools as we begin the new century – to rediscover the fundamental goals of an educational system.

Building on the critique we have offered, but also seeking to embrace the call for schools to meet the needs of democracy and community, we suggest that a model of school effectiveness must comprise four domains:

1. Student-experience-related: students' access to and the range and quality of experiences provided.
2. Student-achievement-related: the quality of the students' academic and other measurable achievements.
3. Teacher-and-school-development-related: the development and growth of teachers and of the school as an organization.
4. Community-related: the quality of involvement of the community of stakeholder groups, such as parents, governors, local education authorities (LEAs), government departments and employers.

The four domains are expressed in diagrammatic form in Figure 50.3. In the following section we outline what needs to be accommodated within each domain, and also suggest indicators that might be applied within each domain.

Figure 50.3 The four domains of school effectiveness

Domain 1: student experience

This domain is concerned with the development of the 'whole' student and all students. We believe with Murphy (1992) that the effective school is one that can educate all its students, and also concur with Rutter and his colleagues (1979) that the impact of the effective school is broader than scores on academic tests. It does not surprise us that of Gray's 'three performance indicators' (Gray and Wilcox, 1995, p. 27), two are related to pupil satisfaction and pupil–teacher relationships. Rudduck, Chaplain and Wallace (1996) also remind us that the pupils' perspectives on their own learning experiences often carry us beyond our somewhat limited assumptions about what constitute the important outcomes of schooling. We see a similar emphasis emerging in North America, where there are increasing arguments for the 'constructivist classroom' and a broader view of intelligence. Gardner's advocacy of 'multiple intelligences' (1991, 1993) is highly influential, as are his proposals for creating schools that promote broader learning. Joyce and his colleagues (Joyce and Weil, 1996; Joyce, Calhoun and Hopkins, 2002) despite some criticism of being too 'technicist', have also demonstrated that a wide range of personal, social, affective, as well as cognitive outcomes can be promoted by the use of a wider range of teaching models and styles.

It is considerations such as these that lead us to acknowledge student experience as a major and vital outcome of schooling. We need to legitimate that what is happening to students during their schooling matters quite as much as, and has a profound influence on, student achievement. In the student experience domain an effective school will therefore strive to ensure that its students have access to experiences that foster:

- high levels of self awareness and self-esteem;
- the ability to make relationships and to assume social responsibility;
- a concept of themselves as learners;

- an induction into a broad range of human experience (including cultural and sporting);
- an awareness of citizenship and their own role within community and society.

Domain 2: student achievement

This is the domain most closely related to the traditional model of school effectiveness. Certainly, an appropriate emphasis needs to be placed on pupil achievements within the overall model, although computing this can be problematic. The first priority for data about student achievement is their usefulness to individual teachers seeking to monitor the progress of individual students. This has particular importance in the early years and for students with poor learning histories or from disadvantaged backgrounds. If we are to increase equity within our system, then the effective school has to equip all its pupils with the basic skills necessary to survive in society.

In the light of these considerations, the time has come to embrace a wider definition of student achievement than has generally been associated with effectiveness research. Accordingly, in the student-achievement domain an effective school is likely to:

- offer a wide range of opportunities for study and accreditation, appropriate to the differing needs and interests of students;
- promote high levels of individual achievement, relative to the abilities and interests of students;
- reflect the expectations of employers and the further and higher education sectors in its curriculum and examination strategies, thereby increasing the utility value to the student of his/her own achievements.

Domain 3: teacher and school development

This is the domain most closely associated with those who work within school improvement tradition. There is clear empirical evidence to suggest that there is a strong connection between teacher development and student achievement. Rosenholtz (1989) writes evocatively about the school work cultures associated with effective schools. From her description we gain a clear idea of the teacher actions and school conditions that predispose the school to support the work of students through the work of teachers. Rosenholtz's 'moving' schools, for example, are characterized by high consensus, teacher certainty, high commitment, cohesiveness, collaboration, and are learning enriched. Joyce and Showers (1995) are even more explicit about the forms of staff development that relate to high levels of student achievement. This implies changes to the workplace and the way in which we organize staff development in our schools. In particular, this means the opportunity for immediate and sustained practice, collaboration and peer coaching, and studying development and implementation. We cannot achieve these changes in the workplace without, in most cases, drastic alterations in the ways in which we organize our schools. Yet we will not be able to transfer teaching skills from in-science training (INSET) sessions to classrooms without such changes. Effective schools pay careful attention to their workplace conditions.

Drawing on considerations such as these, in the teacher-and-school development domain an effective school would ensure that teachers:

- have a high level of mastery of basic teaching skills, subject knowledge, and a repertoire of teaching models and strategies;
- form collaborative partnerships and have other opportunities for professional development;
- work within a culture that promotes high levels of job satisfaction and motivation;
- take responsibility for the outcomes and experiences of their students;
- work in a structural/cultural environment able to respond innovatively and in empowering ways to the challenge of change.

Domain 4: community involvement

The notions of the school both as and within a community are not new, although the links made between these aspects of a school and its effectiveness for pupils have received little systematic attention. We feel that closer links should be made between the school community and the school's outcomes. There are a number of studies showing that parental involvement promotes school effectiveness (e.g. Henderson, 1981; Topping and Wolfendale, 1985). Our own work on school improvement programmes (Ainscow *et al.*, 2000; Hopkins, 2001, 2002) also points to the importance of positive strategies to involve key stakeholder groups in school improvement efforts. Such strategies are at their most powerful when the priority to be targeted and the strategy itself have been evolved in partnership with the appropriate group, rather than determined by school managers who then turn to stakeholders for support.

Real partnership implies that the school is willing to allow key groups to influence the discussion, and not simply seek external support for what are essentially internally determined policies. It is therefore important that we begin to conceptualize what an effective (as opposed to popular) school in the marketplace looks like. This leads us to suggest that the level and extent of community involvement will become an important 'check' within the system, as well as offering evidence of the school's wider effectiveness. In particular, in the community-related domain, an effective school will, at minimum:

- have a record of and strategies for working in partnership with parents, governors, LEA employees and government departments, for the benefit of students;
- develop the school itself as a community 'concentrating efforts and energies on their conceptions of what students should be and should know' (Sergiovanni, 1992);
- develop a rounded view of the educational marketplace and see 'marketing' as an opportunity to research the students' needs and preferences and to develop the school accordingly, rather than simply as a mechanism for attracting students and resources;
- develop specific policies and programmes that draw on the wider resources of the community (including employers and community groups) and draw them in to the school.

Conclusion

In this chapter we have proposed, on the basis of a critique of both school effectiveness and school improvement, a broader concept of the 'effective school' to which both traditions can contribute. Both the critique and the proposal assume a more fundamental re-alignment of work in both these areas than the merging of traditions or meeting of minds approach previously advocated by colleagues in these two traditions. We feel that nothing less than an abandonment of the secular orthodoxy proposed by advocates of the two traditions of the effectiveness and the improvement of schools is necessary if we are really to advance thinking about how to improve and how to measure school performance.

This means that school effectiveness researchers need to follow the example of Murphy (1992) and focus on the 'legacy' of their research tradition rather than squabble about the merits of one formula over another. In a similar vein, school improvers need to break out of their often cosy relationships with the teachers and senior staff of the schools in which they work. They urgently need to address the methodological issues implicit, but often ignored, in their work and seek to be explicit about the strategies they use and the impact that these have on the outcomes and experiences of students.

We believe that the limitations of both traditions outlined here offer reason enough for a new approach to school-development studies – an approach based on collaboration between the two groupings. Our proposal to reconceptualize what is meant by the 'effective school' provides a project worthy of our collective energies and different but complementary skills. The reconceptualization of school effectiveness and school improvement is timely, as well as philosophically appropriate. Let us not spend the next ten years arguing whether the league tables tell us more about school performance than the repertoire of teachers' classroom practice reveals. Let us rather begin to develop a more rounded picture of the effective school that draws on both traditions to create a new understanding.

REFERENCES

Ainscow, M., Hopkins, D., Southworth, G. and West, M. (2000) *Creating the Conditions for School Improvement*, London: David Fulton Publishers.

Caldwell, B.J. and Spinks, J.M. (1988) *The Self-Managing School*, Lewes: Falmer Press.

Cronbach, L.J. and Meehl, P.E. (1955), 'Construct validity in psychological tests', *Psychological Bulletin*, 52, pp. 281–302.

Fullan, M., Bennett, B. and Rolheiser-Bennett, C. (1990) 'Linking classroom and school improvement', *Educational Leadership*, 47 (8), pp. 13–19.

Gardner, H. (1991) *The unschooled mind*, New York: Basic Books.

Gardner, H. (1993) *Frames of Mind: The Theory of Multiple Intelligences*, 2nd edn, London: Fontana Press.

Gray, J., Reynolds, D., Fitz-Gibbon, C. and Jesson, D. (eds) (1996) *Merging Traditions*, London: Cassell.

Gray, J. and Wilcox, B. (1995) *'Good School, Bad School': Evaluating Performance and Encouraging Improvement*, Buckingham: Open University Press.

Henderson, A. (1981) *Parent Participation – Student Achievement: The Evidence Grows*, Columbia, MD: National Committee for Citizens in Education.

Hopkins, D. (2001) *School Improvement for Real*, London: Routledge/Falmer Press.

Hopkins, D. (2002) *Improving the Quality of Education for All: Progress and Change*, 2nd edn, London: David Fulton Publishers.

Hopkins, D., Ainscow, M. and West, M. (1994) *School Improvement in an Era of Change*, London: Cassell.

Hopkins, D. and Reynolds, D. (2001) 'The past, present and future of school improvement: towards the third age', *British Educational Research Journal*, 27 (4), pp. 459–75.

Joyce, B., Calhoun, E. and Hopkins, D. (2002) *Models of Learning – Tools for Teaching*, 2nd edn, Buckingham: Open University Press.

Joyce, B. and Showers, B. (1995) *Student Achievement through Staff Development*, 2nd edn, White Plains, NY: Longman.

Joyce, B. and Weil, M. (1996) *Models of Teaching*, 5th edn, Englewood Cliffs, NJ: Prentice-Hall.

Kuhn, T.S. (1970) *The Structure of Scientific Revolutions*, 2nd edn, Chicago: University of Chicago Press.

Mortimore, P. (1991) 'School effectiveness research: which way at the cross-roads?' *School Effectiveness and School Improvement*, 2 (3), pp. 213–29.

Murphy, J. (1992) 'Effective schools: legacy and future directions' in Reynolds, D. and Cuttance, P. (eds) *School Effectiveness*, London: Cassell.

Reynolds, D. (1992) 'School effectiveness and school improvement' in Reynolds, D. and Cuttance, P. (eds) *School Effectiveness*, London: Cassell.

Reynolds, D., Bollen, R., Creemers, B., Hopkins, D., Stoll, L. and Lagerweij, N. (1996) *Making Good Schools*, London: Routledge.

Rosenholtz, S. (1989) *Teachers' Workplace: The Social Organization of Schools*, New York: Longman.

Rudduck, J., Chaplain, R. and Wallace, G. (eds) (1996) *School Improvement: What Can Pupils Tell Us?*, London: David Fulton Publishers.

Rutter, M., Maughan, B., Mortimore, P. and Ouston, J., with Smith, A. (1979) *Fifteen Thousand Hours*, London: Open Books.

Sergiovanni, T. (1992) *Moral Leadership – Getting to the Heart of School Improvement*, San Francisco: Jossey-Bass.

Stoll, L. (1994) 'School effectiveness and school improvement: a meeting of two minds' in Hargreaves, D.H. and Hopkins, D. (eds) *Development Planning for School Improvement*, London: Cassell.

Stoll, L. and Fink, D. (1996) *Changing our Schools: Linking School Effectiveness and School Improvement*, Buckingham: Open University Press.

Teddlie, C. and Reynolds, D. (2000) *The International Handbook of School Effectiveness Research*, London: Falmer Press.

Topping, K. and Wolfendale, S. (eds) (1985) *Parental Involvement in Children's Reading*, London: Croom Helm.

Van Velzen, P., Miles, M., Ekholm, M., Hameyer, U. and Robin, D. (1985) *Making School Improvement Work*, Leuven, Belgium: ACCO.

8

CHAPTER 51

A review of research and practice

DAVID REYNOLDS, DAVID POTTER
AND CHRISTOPHER CHAPMAN

In this chapter we outline what we have found out from the research literature and the reports of practitioners about 'what works' to improve schools that face challenging circumstances. We concentrate upon the 'universals' of what seems to work across the very varied settings that this group of schools inhabit, but are very aware that the literature suggests that although many of the principles governing effective improvement are universals, some are context specific and must be tailored to the individual circumstances of each school. There is, however, very little evidence about this context specificity to review (see Teddlie and Reynolds, 2000).

We should begin by outlining the three phases or stages that the school improvement community of researchers and practitioners has passed through over the last 15 years, as a context to the literature that we review later, which mostly comes from the 'third age' of school improvement that has only been in existence for the last five or six years.

Although the intellectual background to school improvement can be traced back to Kurt Lewin, it was in the first phase – in the late 1970s and early 1980s – that the field took shape as a distinct body of approaches and scholars/practitioners. This first phase was epitomized by the OECD's International School Improvement Project (ISIP) (Hopkins, 1987), but unfortunately many of the initiatives associated with this first phase of school improvement were 'free floating', rather than representing a systematic, programmatic and coherent approach to school change. There was correspondingly, in this phase, an emphasis upon organizational change, school self-evaluation and the ownership of change by individual schools and teachers, but these initiatives were loosely connected to student-learning outcomes, both conceptually and practically, were variable and fragmented in conception and application, and consequently in the eyes of most school improvers and practitioners struggled to impact upon classroom practice (Hopkins, 2001; Reynolds, 1999).

The second phase of the development of school improvement began in the early 1990s and resulted from the interaction between the school improvement and the school effectiveness communities. Early voices calling for a merger of approaches and insights (Reynolds, Hopkins and Stoll, 1993; Hopkins, Ainscow and West, 1994, Gray et al., 1996) were followed by a synergy of perspectives in which both effectiveness and improvement researchers and practitioners made contributions to a merged perspective (see for example the contributions of Hopkins, Reynolds and Stoll in Gray et al., 1996). School effectiveness brought to this new, merged intellectual enterprise such contributions as the value-added methodology for judging school effectiveness and for disaggregating schools into their component parts of departments and teachers. It also brought a large-scale, known-to-be valid knowledge base about 'what works' at school level to potentiate student outcomes (Teddlie and Reynolds, 2000).

Third-age school improvement practice and philosophy, which came to prominence recently, attempt to draw the lessons from the apparently limited achievements of historical contemporary improvement programmes and reforms. They are various improvement programmes in the UK, such as the Improving the Quality of Education of All (IQEA) Project, the High Reliability Schools (HRS) Project and many of the projects associated with the London Institute of Education National School Improvement Network (NSIN). In Canada, they have been in evidence in the various phases of work conducted in the Halton Board of Education. In The Netherlands they are in evidence in the Dutch National School Improvement Project (further details of these programmes are available in Reynolds *et al.*, 1996; Teddlie and Reynolds, 2000; Hopkins, Ainscow and West, 1994; and Hopkins, 2001).

There are, of course, variations between these various programmes that make any global assessment difficult. Nevertheless, if one were to look at these examples of third-wave school improvement as a group, it is clear that there has been:

- an enhanced focus upon the importance of pupil outcomes – instead of the earlier emphasis upon changing the processes of schools, the focus is now upon seeing if these changes are powerful enough to affect pupil outcomes;
- explicit attention targeted on the learning level and the instructional behaviours of teachers, as well as the school level;
- the creation of an infrastructure to enable the knowledge base, both 'best practice' and research findings, to be utilized – this has involved an internal focus on collaborative patterns of staff development that enable teachers to inquire into practice, and has involved external strategies for dissemination and networking;
- an increasing consciousness of the importance of 'capacity building' – this includes not only staff development, but also medium-term strategic planning, change strategies that utilize 'pressure and support', as well as the intelligent use of external support agencies;
- an adoption of a 'mixed' methodological orientation, in which bodies of quantitative data plus qualitative data are used to measure educational quality, and variation in that quality – this includes an audit of existing classroom and school processes and outcomes, and comparison with desired end states, in particular the educational experiences of different pupil groups;
- an increased emphasis upon the importance of ensuring reliability or 'fidelity' in programme implementation across all organizational members within schools – a marked contrast with the past when improvement programmes did not have to be organizationally 'tight';
- an appreciation of the importance of cultural change to embed and sustain school improvement – there has been a focus on a careful balance between 'vision building' and the adapting of structures to support those aspirations;
- an increased concern to ensure that the improvement programmes relate to, and impact upon, practitioners and practices through using increasingly sophisticated training, coaching and development programmes.

This, then, is the intellectual context of school improvement that our review is situated within.

Findings from the literature: effective schools, improving schools and less successful schools

We have looked at a wide range of different types of studies to understand 'what works' and what schools could do in their drive for improvement, including:

- studies of schools that improved rapidly over time;
- studies of effective schools;
- studies of schools that were less successful, and those who had serious long-term difficulties;
- accounts of exemplary headteachers who 'turned round' their schools.

Some projects were aimed at whole-school improvement and some at improving student performance. Some were based upon one school – others were district or nationally based.

Generally, the material that we have looked at describes a set of processes, managed from within the school (Stoll and Fink, 1996), targeted both at pupil achievement and the school's ability to manage change (Ainscow *et al.*, 1994) – a simultaneous focus on process and outcome. All authors stress the self-managing nature of the improving school and that schools are most effective when they are organizations aided from time to time by external support, apparently taking control of an externally determined agenda – controlling, rather than the objects of, change. Improvement is seen as a sustained upward trend in effectiveness. An improving school is thus one that increases its effectiveness over time – the value-added it generates for pupils rises for successive cohorts.

There are certain general features of effective improvement programmes that flow necessarily from this concept of improvement:

- having a vision: since without a concept of where we are trying to get to, the verb 'to improve' has no meaning;
- monitoring: we must know where we are now in relation to the vision;
- planning: how will we get from where we are towards where we want to be?
- using performance indicators: to track progress over time in respect of the aspects we monitor.

Across all the various types of school the general internal pre-conditions for successful improvement (Gray *et al.*, 1999; Ainscow *et al.*, 1994) are shown in our review of successful improvement as:

- transformational leadership from the leadership team, offering the possibility of change;
- a school-wide emphasis on teaching and learning;
- a commitment to staff development and training;
- the use of performance data to guide decisions, targets and tactics;
- teamwork both within staff groups (collaborative planning, effective communication) and with stakeholders (involvement of teachers, pupils and parents in decision making);
- time and resources for reflection and research.

Turning to the specific, different groups of schools that were represented in the literature in our review, schools that succeeded 'against the odds' in improving against a background of significant pupil and community disadvantage (Maden and Hillman, 1996) shared the following characteristics:

- a leadership stance that embodies (in its leadership team) and builds a team approach;
- a vision of success couched in academic terms, which included a view of how to improve;
- the careful use of targets;
- the improvement of the physical environment;
- common expectations about behaviour and success;
- an investment in good relations with parents and the community.

Turning to another specific group, the characteristics of less successful or ineffective schools (especially from Reynolds in Stoll and Myers, 1998; Teddlie and Stringfield, 1993) have been shown in our review to be:

- At whole-school, including leadership, level:
  - a lack of the competences needed to improve;
  - an unwillingness to accept evidence of failure;
  - the blaming of others – pupils, parents, local education authority (LEA), etc.;
  - a fear of change and of outsiders who embody it;
  - being controlled by change rather than in control of it;
  - the presence of dysfunctional relationships, with cliques;
  - possession of goals that are not plausible or relevant;
  - a lack of academic focus, with principals who take no interest in curriculum and attainment;
  - being passive about recruitment and training;
  - the absence of longitudinal databases on pupils' progress;
  - valid improvement strategies being adopted but not carried through;
  - a governing body that may be passive, lack knowledge and have factions (may be political or ethnic).
- At classroom level:
  - a timetable that is an inaccurate guide to academic time usage;
  - the presence of inconsistency, including some high-quality teaching;
  - the possession of low expectations;
  - an emphasis on supervision and routines;
  - low levels of teacher–pupil interaction about work;
  - a perception by the pupils of their teachers as not caring, praising, etc.;
  - the presence of high noise levels and lots of non-work-related movement;
  - the use of negative feedback from teachers.

In these 'ineffective' schools, problems may be mutually reinforcing: since the agencies of effective change are synergistic (Hopkins and Harris, 1997), so is their absence. The scale of the intractability of problems in the long-term, serious-difficulty school cannot be ignored since these schools may have (O'Connor et al., 1999):

- lost public support;
- been vilified in the press;
- suffered multiple staff changes, including at senior management team (SMT) level;
- 'enjoyed' false dawns;
- lost numbers and therefore had to take other schools' excludees;

8

- a very challenging pupil population, with extremely high special education needs (SEN) of all kinds;
- huge budget problems;
- a community of extreme poverty and deprivation;
- a migrant population, many of whom have low literacy and/or EAL (English as an additional language) issues;
- a significant number of 'ghost' pupils who take up excessive amounts of time and who depress examination and attendance statistics;
- a history of factionalization and industrial unrest;
- a crumbling physical environment.

A persistent failure to improve argues that these schools cannot achieve the general school improvement processes above, since these are self-managed. There is a competence line (Myers, 1995) below which the school cannot use normal processes to avert decline or sustain improvement. The processes and intentions of conventional support programmes and the activities of school improvement projects provide appropriate help for schools that are functioning 'normally' – not these schools.

By definition, therefore, schools that are less successful need major programmes of intervention. Hopkins and Harris (1997) describe these situations as a 'Type 1' school – a failing school in which the intervenors are taking basic actions to establish minimum levels of effectiveness, involving high levels of external support and a clear and direct focus on a limited number of organizational and curricular issues. Most frequently, such programmes are provided or led by the LEA; LEAs have responsibilities for schools causing concern – these responsibilities are both *de facto* (such as in the judgements made in inspections by the Office for Standards in Education (OFSTED) of LEAs) and *de jure* (in the regulations governing Education Development Plans). In some cases, the failings of the LEAs themselves are major factors in the failings of the schools, and other support agencies need to be involved. If the school cannot manage improvement alone with normal levels of support, the activities of an intervention body must lie in a combination of:

- changing the chemistry by changing the people;
- training and supporting the new team, appropriate to the school context;
- withdrawing in a planned way as the level of on-site competence rises.

The principles of effective intervention (Fullan, 1992; Hopkins and Harris, 1997) are, in these kinds of schools:

- early and determined action;
- the investment of resources – lots of them – although these will not work without strong management in place;
- simultaneous action at whole-school (leadership), teacher and classroom levels;
- a balance of support and pressure;
- the coordination of internal and external processes, top-down and bottom-up.

Of considerable importance also is likely to be:

- managing the tension between a focus on a few things and the need to change everything;
- solving political wrangles at governor and LEA level;

- making tangible environmental improvements;
- using literacy as a Trojan horse to improve curriculum/teaching.

The stages of recovery in these two schools are described (Stark in Stoll and Myers, 1998) as:

- acknowledging failure, facing up to problems, preparing an action plan that is aimed at regaining commitment as well as re-establishing basic competence (three months);
- implementing action plans, restoring leadership, re-establishing sound management, improving teaching and learning (18 months), at the same time as re-establishing morale and self-esteem by early success with, for example, environment and/or behaviour;
- 'progressing towards excellence'.

One key finding in the work of many authors, but most clearly expressed by Stringfield (in Stoll and Myers, 1998) is that improvement gain varies more within projects owing to the level of implementation than the difference between projects – in other words, given that most projects are sensibly predicated, schools achieve greater gain by pursuing a project thoroughly than by choosing project (a) rather than (b). The originators of American improvement projects (for example, Slavin, 1996) talk about 'fidelity of implementation'. A senior officer of an English LEA, reflecting on a school in persistent serious difficulty, said aptly that everyone knew what was wrong and what needed to be done, but they did not do it consistently.

While reviewing the literature on the various kinds of schools, it is clear that the common challenging issues for managing school improvement and programmes are (from Stoll in Barber and Dann, 1996):

- deciding what to do with non-volunteer schools that need to improve but do not want to take part;
- managing the tension between ownership and accountability – how much action is 'done to' a school that it cannot do it to itself; how and when to enable the school to resume local decision making;
- the complexity of evaluation – how to assess what worked when everything is changing (attributability); poor baselining or success criteria in many projects;
- avoiding improvement attempts as 'bolt-on' rather than 'bloodstream' – an isolated event rather than an integral process;
- concurrent agendas – for example, development paralysis caused by OFSTED inspection in some schools;
- getting a school moving – how to start to move schools, when they have been 'stuck' or 'plateaued' or 'spiralling down' for some time.

Our final section draws together our findings on the general characteristics of schools that need to be changed for improvement to occur, together with the specific findings from different kinds of schools, and outlines our suggested model for improvement for all schools facing challenging circumstances.

A new school improvement programme

Our model has the following components:

- A multilevel approach that looks at schools, departments and classrooms but with the major improvement focus being on the classroom and on improving academic achievement.
- Strong leadership at headteacher level, which is secured before ...
  - building an effective leadership team, which is secured before ...
  - gaining staff commitment, which is secured before ...
  - a large input of resources.
- The understanding of, and preferably the involvement of, the community, especially parents.
- The characteristics of high-reliability organizations:
  - clarity of mission – a small number of clear, agreed and inflexible goals, with ambitious targets for pupils' academic achievement at their heart;
  - careful monitoring of key systems to avoid cascading errors;
  - data richness, with good benchmarking and openness about performance data;
  - standard operating procedures (SOPs), including an agreed model of teaching and consistent implementation of agreed actions in teaching, managing learning behaviour, attendance, etc.;
  - a focus on pupils at risk of failure;
  - proactive, extensive recruitment and targeted training, including the delivery of the agreed teaching methods;
  - rigorous performance evaluation to ascertain the rapid, early and continuous impact of initiatives;
  - maintenance of equipment in the highest working order.
- A 'club' structure with support networks – a learning network that may involve a higher education institute/LEA/other schools/consultants working as a multiskilled support team that provides pressure as well as support.
- Strong rules and processes about fidelity of implementation, which are in place at the start of the programme (and a recognition that fulfilling the rules is more important than the rules themselves!), with the school making greater input as confidence increases and the school begins to turn.
- A sense of early achievement, which is sought through a clean-up campaign and some improvements to fabric.

We believe these improvement components should be introduced through a two-stage approach. First, it is necessary to ensure schools understand that:

- every school can improve;
- improvement must ultimately be assessed in terms of improved pupil achievement outcomes;
- every individual in the school has a contribution to make to the improvement;
- there need to be the highest possible goals, but an acceptance that schools' start points are different;
- schools should help themselves and guard against creating dependency;
- everyone in the school should be learning from others.

Second, the improvement programme should encourage schools to work with partners in order to:

- take early, firm intervention to secure effective management and leadership;
- help the school identify its core issues through:
  - surveys of staff and student opinion;
  - gathering, analysing and presenting data on student achievement;
  - using these data to identify good practice;
- gain staff commitment through working with those staff unable or unwilling to change;
- introduce models of leadership and teaching quality:
  - building a leadership team, with appropriate contribution from the head;
  - introducing experienced new blood in the classroom;
- focus on dealing with issues in a phased manner in order to achieve a track record of success, while recognizing the importance of:
  - addressing any OFSETD key issues;
  - improving the cleanliness of the environment;
  - developing pride and self-esteem;
  - emphasizing attendance/punctuality/uniform.
- focus on teaching and learning:
  - establishing a set of core values and an agreed teaching model;
  - reskilling teams of teachers in a limited repertoire of teaching styles;
  - introducing a firm and consistent policy on behaviour (around the site as well as in classrooms);
  - supporting and building on models of excellent teaching.

Conclusions

We have outlined in this review the characteristics of successful improvement attempts for schools that face socially and economically challenging circumstances. We drew some general conclusions about the core principles that should underpin school improvement, such as ownership of the process of improvement, and then looked at the evidence concerning 'what worked' for different kinds of school. Clearly, for less successful schools a greater external input, and probably a more external locus of control, is suggested than would be appropriate for some of the schools that have already been improved or 'turned around'.

Notwithstanding the different kinds of schools that will be facing challenging circumstances, we have attempted to develop an improvement programme that can be relevant to all of them, although the particular focus of the various initiatives, the order of implementation of the various components and in particular the governance balance between external-to-the-school and internal-to-the-school authority and control will clearly need to vary according to the precise environment and conditions of each school.

This model of what successful improvement programmes may be a prompt for further detailed research on programme effectiveness, appropriateness and implementation in the different schools that serve the socially disadvantaged. While we hope we have generated here a 'normal science' of improvement, further progress will require major systematic programmes of research and practice to generate the further developments in knowledge and understanding that we need.

NOTE

This chapter is based upon Reynolds *et al.* (2001): a review of literature, commissioned by the Department for Education and Skills for the activities designed to help 'Schools Facing Challenging Circumstances', which was distributed to all the schools in spring 2001.

Schools Facing Challenging Circumstances is a categorization used by the DfES for those schools achieving 25% A–C GCSE or less. This group also includes all registered schools where 35% or more pupils are registered for free school meals.

REFERENCES

Ainscow, M., Hopkins, D., Southworth, G. and West, M. (1994) *Creating the Conditions for School Improvement*, London: David Fulton Publishers.

Barber, M. and Dann, R. (eds) (1996) *Raising Educational Standards in the Inner Cities*, London: Cassell.

Fullan, M. (1992) *Successful School Improvement*, Buckingham: Open University Press.

Gray, J., Hopkins, D., Reynolds, D., Wilcox, B., Farrell, S. and Jesson, D. (1999) *Improving Schools: Performance and Potential*, Buckingham: Open University Press.

Gray, J., Reynolds, D., Fitz-Gibbon, C. and Jesson, D. (1996) *Merging Traditions: The Future of Research on School Effectiveness and School Improvement*, London: Cassell.

Hopkins, D. (ed.) (1987) *Improving the Quality of Schooling*, London: Falmer Press.

Hopkins, D. (2001) *School Improvement for Real*, London: Falmer Press.

Hopkins, D., Ainscow, M. and West, M. (1994) *School Improvement in an Era of Change*, London: Cassell.

Hopkins, D. and Harris, A. (1997) 'Understanding the school's capacity for development: growth states and strategies', *School Leadership and Management*, 17 (3), pp. 401–11.

Maden, M., and Hillman, J. (1996) *Success Against the Odds: Effective Schools in Disadvantaged Areas*, for the National Commission on Education, London: Routledge.

Myers, K. (1995) 'Intensive care for the chronically sick', paper presented to the European Conference on Educational Research, University of Bath.

Myers, K. (1995) *School Improvement in Practice: Schools Make a Difference Project*, London: Falmer Press.

O'Connor, M., Hales, E., Davies, J. and Tomlinson, S. (1999) *Hackney Downs*, London: Cassell.

Reynolds, D. (1999) 'School effectiveness, school improvement and contemporary educational policies' in Demaine, J. (ed.) *Contemporary Educational Policy and Politics*, London: Macmillan, p. 65–81.

Reynolds, D., Creemers, B., Hopkins, D., Stoll, L. and Bollen, R. (1996) *Making Good Schools*, London: Routledge.

Reynolds, D., Hopkins, D. and Stoll, L. (1993) 'Linking school effectiveness knowledge and school improvement practice: towards a synergy', *School Effectiveness and School Improvement*, 4 (1), pp. 37–58.

Reynolds, D., Hopkins, D., Potter, D. and Chapman, C. (2001) *School Improvement for Schools Facing Challenging Circumstances: A Review of Research and Practice*, London: Department of Education and Skills.

Slavin, R. (1996) *Education for All*, Lisse, The Netherlands: Swets & Zeitlinger.

Stoll, L. and Fink, D. (1996) *Changing our Schools: Linking School Effectiveness and School Improvement*, Buckingham: Open University Press.

Stoll, L. and Myers, K. (1998) *No Quick Fixes*, London: Falmer Press.

Teddlie, C. and Reynolds, D. (2000) *The International Handbook of School Effectiveness Research*, London: Falmer Press.

Teddlie, C. and Stringfield, S. (1993) *Schools Make A Difference*, New York: Teachers' College Press.

CHAPTER 52

Using school effectiveness research to improve schools

LOUISE STOLL

These days school improvement is the much talked-about Holy Grail. It is also high stakes: high stakes in one sense because schools know the consequences for them if they do not raise standards but also, more important, high stakes because for their pupils, their time in school is precious time that cannot afford to be wasted. School improvement concerns all schools. It goes much deeper than raising standards and outsiders helping struggling schools get themselves out of difficulties. 'Real' school improvement (Hopkins, 2001) comes from within and is about the ongoing and sustainable learning of pupils and all those inside and outside schools who care about pupils' learning (Stoll, Wikeley and Reezigt, 2003). There is knowledge out there that can be used by schools on their improvement journey. Some of this knowledge comes from school effectiveness research. In this chapter, drawing on research and development work around the world, I first consider what school effectiveness research has to offer, also discussing limitations to this knowledge base. Next, I briefly summarize critical elements of school improvement research that need to be understood before school effectiveness research can be used. After highlighting a project in which school effectiveness and school improvement have been 'blended' in different forms, I conclude by suggesting ways in which those inside and outside schools might draw on the research to enhance school improvement.

What has school effectiveness research discovered?

Over the last nearly 30 years, school effectiveness research has demonstrated clearly that schools, departments and classrooms make a difference to pupils' progress and development and that decisions within the control of school leaders and teachers are linked with this progress. School effectiveness research offers two particularly important features to those involved in school improvement: a focus on pupils' progress and development – more commonly known as 'value added' – and an evidence base of those actions within schools and classrooms that are linked to better pupil progress. In describing these features, I highlight other contributions of school effectiveness research as well as neglected issues.

Effective schools focus on pupils' progress and development: they add value

The term 'value added' has become associated with school effectiveness. What does it mean to say a school adds value? I see five answers to this question.

First, a school adds value if it boosts pupils' progress over and above what they bring with them in terms of their prior attainment and background (Mortimore, 1991). The level of a child's reading at age seven (his/her prior attainment) is the best predictor of how that child will read at age 11 (Mortimore *et al.*, 1988). Home background also profoundly influences achievement. Taking prior attainment and background factors into account, the statistical technique – multilevel modelling – determines in which schools, classrooms and departments pupils make more progress. So, pupils in two schools with very similar intakes may show very different rates of progress.

Second, adding value means a school is promoting progress for all its pupils, not just a few. Effectiveness is, and must be, fundamentally concerned with equity (Murphy, 1992). A school is not truly effective if girls are making progress but not boys, or if it adds value for pupils of certain social class or ethnic backgrounds, or for its pupils with special needs but not its gifted and talented pupils, or vice versa. Some pupils do better than others within certain schools (Nuttall *et al.*, 1989), and there is a strong 'teacher effect', with pupils in some classes making more progress than in others (Teddlie and Reynolds, 2000). In secondary schools pupils also make more progress in some subjects than others – some departments add more value (Sammons, Thomas and Mortimore, 1997).

Third, the added value is sustained over time. A school's effectiveness needs to be considered over a period of several years (Gray *et al.*, 1999). Looking at progress in one year does not provide sufficient knowledge as to whether the school is able to sustain its effectiveness over time. This requires looking at a school's progress over at least three years, so trends become more apparent.

Fourth, each child or young person in that school is achieving the highest standards possible for them. For any parent, while the progress of the whole school may be a useful indicator, their own child's progress is of the greatest concern. While value-added analysis is a fairer way to analyse schools' effectiveness than looking at raw results, it is still important for schools to try to do all they can to help each child achieve their best.

Fifth, the school adds value to things that matter. What worked for us (or unfortunately did not work for some of us) at school may not be what is important for children and young people attending school at the start of the twenty-first century. Youngsters live in a very different world from the one in which we lived when we were at school, and global forces continue to change the world around them rapidly. In such times the inescapable questions are: 'What should education be for? What are its essential purposes?' Pupil learning outcomes need to capture the breadth of what it is likely to be needed to flourish in this century. While school effectiveness research has examined pupils' progress in the basic skills and, in some cases, aspects of their social development (such as behaviour, attitudes and self concept), the value added to some of the learning outcomes described is still to be explored.

Effective schools 'do the right things': they provide evidence on 'what works'

School effectiveness research not only helps to understand whether pupils are making good progress and developing socially, but also identifies what teachers, leaders and schools do related to these more positive pupil effects. A number of factors within the control of school leaders and teachers has been identified as being statistically related to greater pupil progress. These have been summarized into lists of effective schools factors (Sammons, Hillman and Mortimore, 1995; Teddlie and Reynolds, 2000) or characteristics, as they are better known, and further research has identified the characteristics of effective departments (Sammons, Thomas and Mortimore, 1997).

Figure 52.1 visually represents the effective school characteristics colleagues and I summarized for the Effective Schools Project in Halton, Ontario, which was a practical application of school effectiveness research in a Canadian school district (LEA) and its 83 schools (Stoll and Fink, 1996). The choice of a visual representation – in this case a wheel – is not insignificant. Discussing the characteristics with

Figure 52.1 Characteristics of effective schools

Source: Halton Effective Schools' Task Force, 1990; Stoll and Fink, 1996.

colleagues in schools, we found that lists did not have the same meaning or coherence for people who were trying to understand how things might fit together and how to connect different aspects of their work.

These characteristics are of interest to those searching for 'what works' in education, and there is now a policy drive in the UK for such research findings, in a move towards informing practice with evidence. For this reason, several 'health' warnings need to be offered:

- We cannot tell for certain that particular actions are responsible for certain outcomes: it may be that teachers teach certain ways because of children's particular level of reading, rather than the other way around.
- Classroom strategies and techniques associated with better progress in some subjects are not always the same as those linked with better progress in others, as we found in the School Matters Study (Mortimore *et al.*, 1988); indeed, the most effective teachers vary their approach to teaching.
- Most effectiveness studies resulting in the lists of characteristics have not looked at the influence of schools' external context on their effectiveness.
- Even if we accept that the identified characteristics of school effectiveness provide a picture of success in the here and now, this does not help understand the school and learning and teaching strategies needed for the future.
- 'What works' in one context is not always relevant somewhere else. Clearly, there are differences among inner city, urban and rural schools, primary and secondary schools, schools with varied pupil intakes, and schools in different countries. Even when the label used is similar across countries it may have very different meanings. For example, there is no word in the Portuguese language mirroring the word 'accountability', and effectiveness and improvement have a range of meanings in different European countries (Stoll, Wikeley and Reezigt, 2003).
- Within a school, what works with one group of pupils may not be effective with another group, although a proliferation of lists of characteristics for different groups of pupils and different subjects may prove no more helpful than an overall list (see next point).
- Some people assume that if a particular teaching technique is identified as being linked with greater effectiveness, you need only to tell people or show what to do them and they will put it into practice. This highlights a fundamental difference between school effectiveness and school improvement. Those involved in school improvement know it is not that straightforward. Deep change can be slow, requiring significant practice and colleagues' support (Joyce and Showers, 1995). As Little (2001, p. 33) notes: 'Reform environments tend to be volatile, fast-paced, and public, while learning may require sustained concentration, gradual development, and opportunities for relatively private ('safe') disclosure of struggles and uncertainties'.

This chapter focuses on using school effectiveness research to improve schools. School effectiveness research, however, will never provide all the answers. It is not the panacea to schools' 'problems'. Most crucially, a picture of current effectiveness – a snapshot in time – does not tell schools how to become successful, especially schools that are struggling, or necessarily persuade people that this is what they need to be doing. This is why knowledge from school improvement research is so important, because school improvement focuses on the journey to greater effectiveness and necessary conditions to support successful change.

School improvement research is critical to understanding how schools change and develop

While it is now much clearer that the ultimate aim of school improvement needs to relate to school effectiveness – school improvement should enhance pupils' progress – it is about more than just adding value and 'doing the right things'. School improvement is immensely complicated. It is about how the school develops the conditions and processes that support and enhance learning and the school's capacity to manage, take charge and sustain improvements. What knowledge, therefore, from school improvement research is needed before school effectiveness research can be used to greatest effect?

School improvement focuses on the process, not only the outcomes

While school improvement is outcomes-oriented, it is a process – a journey. An understanding of the change process is essential to school improvement. For example, serious change takes time, which means that quick-fix solutions (Stoll and Myers, 1998) or tactics (Gray *et al.*, 1999) rarely lead to deep and lasting change. School improvement research has highlighted the importance of developing the conditions that support and enhance school development (van Velzen *et al.*, 1985; Hopkins, 2001). Detailed case studies of improvement are important in helping to understand the complexity of the process, although even the richest of case studies cannot capture all the subtleties of how different schools go about their improvement journey.

School improvement focuses on learning and teaching

School effectiveness studies indicate that the classroom has a greater effect on pupils' progress than the school as a whole. More important, what interests teachers most is what goes on between them and their pupils. Focusing on teaching, and particularly learning, has become increasingly important within school improvement. Hopkins (2001, p. 68) argues that a major goal of school improvement: 'is to help teachers become professionally flexible so that they can select, from a repertoire of possibilities, the teaching approach most suited to their particular content area, and the age, interests and aptitudes of their students'.

Meaningful improvement comes from within

While 'urgency' for improvement (Earl and Lee, 2000) may be generated by mandating improvement strategies, it is internally driven improvement that is most likely to be meaningful and sustained (Barth, 1990; Hopkins, 2001). Ultimately, successful improvement depends on attention paid by those inside and outside to addressing internal conditions of improvement, and ensuring that the school's culture supports, rather than inhibits, improvement: in short, building and sustaining capacity for change.

8

School improvement depends on schools' readiness to engage in significant change and capacity to implement and sustain it

Determining a school's capacity to bring about and sustain change is extremely important (Stoll, 1999a; see also chapter 47 in this handbook). Briefly, capacity is vital to school improvement but harder to achieve in some schools than others. Facets of the climate of less effective schools need attention early on before people feel able to participate actively in improvement efforts and can concentrate on the real agenda. Without attending to these fundamental prerequisites for change at the earliest opportunity, real lasting changes impacting on teaching and learning are highly unlikely. In contrast, in more successful schools, capacity building is a 'habit of mind' (Hill, 1997). Such schools actively take charge of change, accommodating external ideas within their own context and needs, adapting policy mandates creatively to fit their vision: 'colonizing' external educational reforms (National Commission on Education, 1995; Maden, 2001).

Schools need external support, and sometimes pressure, for improvement

Even when governments move towards offering greater autonomy to schools, more successful schools do not operate as if they are isolated islands. Schools are part of a wider system that can help or hinder their improvement efforts (Reezigt, 2001). It has been suggested that a balance of pressure and support is necessary for successful improvement (Fullan, 2001). Whether all schools need external pressure to improve is unknown. There are, however, numerous studies highlighting the importance of external support for school improvement (e.g. Myers, 1996). To become and remain effective, schools need an infrastructure of support from parents and carers, governors (school councils), the local community, local education authorities (LEAs), businesses, unions, universities, the government and others.

Schools are different: one size of improvement strategy does not fit all schools

Anyone who has worked in two very different schools knows that each school has its own unique character and, therefore, 'identikit' improvement recipes do not work – which is why taking a list of characteristics and trying to apply them to all schools is inappropriate. Addressing the contextual differences among schools is one of the greatest challenges for school improvers. Over the last few years, researchers have begun to address this challenge (Hopkins, Harris and Jenkins, 1997; Slavin, 1998; Gray et al., 1999). For example, Fink and I have examined improvement in what we have described as the 'cruising school' (Stoll and Fink, 1998), and in Chapter 57 in this handbook, Reynolds, Potter and Chapman explore improvement for schools facing challenging circumstances.

Linking school effectiveness and school improvement

An increasing number of recent research projects have drawn on both school effectiveness and school improvement knowledge bases. Examples include the eight-European-country Effective School Improvement (ESI) Project (Reezigt, 2001) and the Improving Schools Project (Gray *et al.*, 1999). Evaluated development projects have also attempted to link the two knowledge bases: for example, the Halton Effective Schools Project in Ontario, Canada (Stoll and Fink, 1992); the Schools Make a Difference Project (Myers, 1996); the High Reliability Schools Project, based on Stringfield's analysis (1995) of high reliability organizations; and several other LEA, school and higher education partnership projects where pupil progress data are used as a basis for development work.

The Improving School Effectiveness Project (ISEP) (MacBeath and Mortimore, 2001), in which I was involved, is an example of a project combining a value-added model, examining pupils' progress and attitudes over two years in 80 Scottish schools, with qualitative case studies exploring improvement in 24 of these schools. It also incorporated intervention, where critical friends fed back pupil progress data and data on pupils', teachers' and parents' perceptions to the schools. They also supported the schools on chosen improvement themes related to ethos, teaching and learning, and school development planning, as well as working through leadership and management issues. This kind of research and development project offers useful insights to improvers wanting to use school effectiveness findings; this topic is discussed next.

Using school effectiveness research for improvement

Given knowledge of effectiveness and improvement, how can school effectiveness research best be used to improve schools? I would argue that what is needed is a 'connected' approach.

A difficulty of school effectiveness research is its linear nature. One way of describing it is, if you take a group of pupils (seen, in bald terms, as 'input', taking context into account), look at school and classroom processes in the middle ('process') and relate these to the pupils' progress at the end ('output'), you might be forgiven for thinking 'if you do X then Y automatically occurs'. This is the danger of translating school effectiveness research findings too literally when linking them with school improvement. What is needed instead is the blending and extending of insights from both sets of research into school-based designs for improvement, and evaluation of these designs as they are implemented in schools. This depends on researchers and others outside schools working to support schools' improvement efforts and help them understand how to enhance them. The key elements in the design are drawn from school effectiveness and improvement research and related to life in twenty-first century schools. Phrased as imperatives, they are:

- evaluate learning outcomes;
- emphasize learners, learning, and teaching;
- promote inquiry-mindedness;

- involve the whole community;
- facilitate 'deep learning' of teachers;
- distribute leadership and management;
- provide external support;
- ensure sustainability;
- adapt the design to suit the context.

Evaluate learning outcomes

Assessing outcomes is an essential feature of any improvement effort. It is, however, necessary to broaden the current domination of assessment of certain subjects to the range of necessary twenty-first century learning outcomes: in short, in preparing pupils for their future, we must also develop ways of assessing new learning outcomes. Success depends on considerably more than being literate, numerate and technologically competent. Given the pace and unpredictability of change, as well as the need to maintain and, in some cases, rebuild community, other skills are now equally important. These include flexibility, problem solving, collaboration, empathy, self-awareness, the ability to deal with complexity and a massive amount of information, and a love of learning. If young people are not able to keep on learning, their future options will be dramatically reduced. Serious school improvement efforts also need to evaluate other outcomes of improvement: for example, enhanced teacher learning and school capacity to sustain new learning and improvement.

Emphasize learners, learning and teaching

There is clear evidence from school effectiveness research that the classroom is the place where pupil progress is particularly demonstrated. Most work in this area and in teacher effectiveness research, however, has started with a behaviourist focus on the teacher's actions, and examined pupil learning as an outcome: hence the more common ordering of the phrase 'teaching and learning'. A parallel body of knowledge argues that effective learning involves processes as well as outcomes, and it is necessary to understand learners, how learning takes place, and what influences learning. This different approach suggests a shift in orientation towards improvement efforts that are learning and learner-centred, reversing the phrase so that it becomes 'learning and teaching'. Considerable research on learning exists, but more normally within the psychological literature than school effectiveness research.

Promote inquiry-mindedness

School improvers can draw on a wealth of evidence. School effectiveness research provides data as foci for inquiry, and critical questions to help interrogate data. For example, exploring pupils' results includes asking questions about differential effectiveness: is the school effective for all its pupils or just for certain groups or when they are studying certain subjects? School effectiveness research also provides indicators about factors related to better progress, providing starting points for dialogue about these factors – for example, 'What do teachers in our school mean by high expectations?' Greater attention, however, needs to be paid to exploring how schools use research findings, how they could most strategically be used, and how researchers might help them use the findings. Particularly, much more needs to be understood about how teachers respond to evidence about new ways of teaching. Drawing on evidence also means promoting research and evaluation across the school, in departments (in secondary schools) and by individual teachers, creating new knowledge and transferring it between situations and people as the school develops its intellectual capital (Hargreaves, 2001).

School improvement researchers increasingly conclude that inquiry and reflection are central to success (MacBeath, 1999; MacBeath *et al.*, 2000; Southworth and Conner, 1999). Not only should schools collect, analyse and use a range of data to monitor and evaluate the process, progress and outcomes of improvement efforts, but their very approach needs to be underpinned by reflective self-analysis and 'inquiry-mindedness' (Earl and Lee, 2000). This includes auditing influences on their capacity to engage in and sustain improvement. For example, questionnaires and other tools are used as a way of tapping into school culture (Hargreaves, 1999; Stoll, 1999b).

Involve the whole community

Involvement has been highlighted in both school effectiveness and improvement studies. Recently, greater attention has been paid to the pupil's voice in school improvement (Rudduck, Chaplain and Wallace, 1996; Fielding, 2001). Teachers' involvement in decision making has also been found to be critical in many studies of improvement, and relates to their commitment to school improvement. Similarly, while involving parents is more difficult in secondary schools and in deprived areas, improving schools in disadvantaged areas have developed a range of ways to involve their parents (National Commission on Education, 1995; Mortimore *et al.*, 2000).

Facilitate 'deep learning' of teachers

School effectiveness research emphasizes the importance of staff development, while school improvement researchers consistently stress teachers' commitment to change. Changing one's practice is notoriously difficult and requires considerable effort. What teacher learning will mean in the future – and the form that it will take – may be very different from the model practised today in many schools and education systems. Increasingly, the workplace is being highlighted as the key location for learning (Rosenholtz, 1989; Nias, Southworth and Campbell, 1992; Smylie, 1995; Day, 1999). Studies in the USA describe the benefits of developing school-based professional communities (Louis *et al.*, 1995). In such communities, attention is paid to structural conditions that inhibit progress and the social forces that so frequently constrain serious dialogue among teachers about their practice. Educational improvement and effectiveness depends on people learning collaboratively. It is not achievable individually. In such communities, teachers pursue a clear, shared purpose, engage in professional dialogue and open up their classrooms to colleagues. One key result of this process is improved pupil learning (Newmann and Wehlage, 1995).

Distribute leadership and management

School effectiveness and school improvement research in the UK and many other countries has consistently emphasized the importance of leadership and management. High value-added attainment in the ISEP primary schools was associated with greater teacher satisfaction with leadership and management in their schools. Leadership at the department level in secondary schools is also related to effectiveness (Sammons, Thomas and Mortimore, 1997) and plays an important role in improvement (Busher and Harris, 2000). In addition, several studies of improvement have highlighted the role of cadres or school improvement teams – leaders at all levels in the school who coordinate improvement efforts. Clearly, leadership and management in effective and improving schools are not just invested in one person. Further research remains to be done to understand how leadership and management at the different levels best operate together.

Provide external support

School effectiveness research has generally tended to neglect the role of those outside schools, although studies linking effectiveness and improvement have highlighted the importance of external support to improving schools (MacBeath and Mortimore, 2001; Reezigt, 2001). Reporting on their study of school improvement, Huberman and Miles (1984) commented: 'change-bearing innovations lived or died by the amount and quality of assistance that their users received once the change process was under way'. The ISEP found that outsiders offering schools critical friendship could be valuable external change agents. In their study of 22 schools involved in the Manitoba School Improvement Program in Canada, Earl and Lee (2000, p. 76) also found: 'critical friends are both critical (challenging critics) and critical (essential)'.

Networking is an increasingly popular form of support through which teachers or schools link up with each other to share ideas, good practice, discuss and resolve problems and challenge each other's thinking. Lieberman and Grolnick's study (1996) of 16 educational reform networks found that certain features created growth opportunities for participants: challenging rather than prescriptive agendas; indirect rather than direct learning; collaborative formats; integrated work; facilitative leadership; thinking that encouraged multiple perspectives; values that were both context-specific and generalized; and flexible structures.

Ensure sustainability

Schools embark on improvement from very different starting points: some find it extremely difficult even to get started. Some schools are more 'ready' than others to deal with and work through challenges that improvement efforts bring. They have the resources, resilience and will to engage in and sustain continuous learning of teachers and have a clear vision of its primary purpose as enhancing pupil learning . Working on developing supportive conditions – at individual, departmental, school and external context levels – is essential to any improvement effort because they influence the school's ability to sustain the improvement process and enhance outcomes over time.

Sustaining improvement is challenging. After schools decide to change, there is often a surge of energy as people become actively involved (Earl and Lee, 2000). Initial excitement, however, wears off as teachers are faced with other demands, as well as inevitable difficulties presented both by the change and the school's internal capacity: for example, overload, complexity, internal power struggles, or an impending inspection. These factors can lead to turbulence (Huberman, 1992). Without 'agency' – internal resources or access to appropriate and timely support (Earl and Lee, 2000) – entropy can ensue. Changing the school's culture – a powerful force in improvement – is usually necessary to provide the environment in which improvements can be sustained.

Adapt the design to suit the context

Looking at the varied routes more successful schools have taken to improvement, even if the right design elements are known, it is essential to understand how each element works in different kinds of schools. One size of improvement strategy does not fit all schools and we cannot simply 'improve' schools without an understanding of how each element connects with others in particular contexts. For example, aspects of leadership are different in schools in leafy suburbs from those in disadvantaged areas. Similarly, effective learning and teaching strategies may vary according to the nature of the pupils who attend a certain school. With such knowledge and insight we are more likely to move to an understanding of integrated learning and away from an individualized simplistic, piece-by-piece approach to reform.

Conclusion

School effectiveness research has played a significant role over more than two decades, validating the belief that schools make a difference, and helping discover many of the factors that can be found in effective schools, departments and classrooms. It has also sharpened the debate on the importance of the outcomes of schooling as well as its processes. On its own it does not provide a foolproof guide to improvement, but it can be useful when blended with the knowledge from improvement. However, we are now in a new era when what is currently considered effective – and the processes for achieving and sustaining it – may not serve learners well as they live in an increasingly complex and fast changing world. This means that even designs that are based on our best knowledge to date need to be sufficiently flexible and constantly evaluated to ensure that they are serving the needs of young people in times of rapid change.

REFERENCES

Barth, R. (1990) *Improving Schools from Within: Teachers, Parents and Principals Can Make the Difference*, San Francisco: Jossey-Bass.

Busher, H. and Harris, A. with Wise, C. (2000) *Subject Leadership and School Improvement*, London: Paul Chapman Publishing.

Day, C. (1999) *Developing Teachers: The Challenges of Lifelong Learning*, London: Falmer Press.

Earl. L. and Lee, L. (2000) 'Learning for a change: school improvement as capacity building', *Improving Schools*, 3 (1), pp. 30–8.

Fielding, M. (2001) 'Students as radical agents of change: "a minute correction to the essential is more important than a hundred accessories"', *Journal of Educational Change*. 2 (2) 123–41.

Fullan, M. (2001) *The New Meaning of Educational Change*, New York: Teachers' College Press and London: Routledge/Falmer.

Gray, J., Hopkins, D., Reynolds, D., Wilcox, B., Farrell, S. and Jesson, D. (1999) *Improving Schools: Performance and Potential*, Buckingham: Open University Press.

Hargreaves, D. (1999) 'Helping practitioners explore their school's culture' in Prosser J. (ed.) *School Culture*, London: Paul Chapman Publishing.

Hargreaves, D. (2001) 'A capital theory of school effectiveness and improvement', *British Educational Research Journal*, 27.

Hill, P.W. (1997) *Towards High Standards for All Students: Victorian Research and Experience*, IARTV Seminar Series No. 61, Victoria: IARTV.

Hopkins, D. (2001) *School Improvement for Real*, London: Routledge/Falmer Press.

Hopkins, D., Harris, A. and Jackson, D. (1997) 'Understanding the school's capacity for development: growth states and strategies', *School Leadership and Management*, 17 (3), pp. 401–11.

Huberman, M. (1992) 'Critical introduction' in Fullan, M.G. *Successful School Improvement*, Buckingham: Open University Press and Toronto: OISE Press.

Huberman, M. and Miles, M.B. (1984) *Innovation up Close*, New York: Plenum.

Joyce, B.R. and Showers, B. (1995) *Student Achievement Through Staff Development*, 2nd edn, White Plains, NY: Longman.

Lieberman, A. and Grolnick, M. (1996) 'Networks and reform in American education', *Teachers' College Record*, 98 (1), pp. 7–45.

Little, J.W. (2001) 'Professional development in pursuit of school reform' in Lieberman, A. and Miller, L. (eds) *Teachers Caught in the Action: Professional Development that Matters*, New York: Teachers' College Press.

Louis, K.S., Kruse, S. and Associates (1995) *Professionalism and Community: Perspectives on Reforming Urban Schools*, Thousand Oaks, CA: Corwin Press.

MacBeath, J. (1999) *Schools Must Speak for Themselves*, London: Routledge.

MacBeath, J. and Mortimore, P. (2001) *Improving School Effectiveness*, Buckingham: Open University Press.

MacBeath, J., Schratz, M., Meuret, D. and Jakobsen, L. (2000) *Self-Evaluation in European Schools: A Story of Change*, London: Routledge/Falmer Press.

Maden, M. (2001) *Success Against the Odds – Five Years On: Revisiting Effective Schools in Disadvantaged Areas*, London: Routledge/Falmer Press.

Mortimore, P. (1991) 'The nature and findings of research on school effectiveness in the primary sector' in Riddell, S. and Brown, S. (eds) *School Effectiveness Research: Its Messages for School Improvement*, London: HMSO.

Mortimore, P., Gopinathan, S., Leo, E., Myers, K., Sharpe, L., Stoll, L. and Mortimore, J. (2000) *The Culture of Change: Case Studies of Improving Schools in Singapore and London*, London,: Institute of Education, Universtiy of London.

Mortimore, P., Sammons, P., Stoll, L., Lewis, D. and Ecob, R. (1986) *The Junior School Project: Main Report Parts A, B., C and Technical Appendices*, London: Research and Statistics Branch, ILEA.

Mortimore, P., Sammons, P., Stoll, L., Lewis, D. and Ecob, R. (1988) *School Matters: The Junior Years*, Wells, Somerset: Open Books (reprinted 1994, London: Paul Chapman Publishing).

Murphy, J. (1992) 'School effectiveness and school restructuring: contributions to educational improvement', *School Effectiveness and School Improvement*, 3 (2), pp. 90–109.

Myers, K. (1996) *School Improvement in Practice: The Schools Make a Difference Project*, London: Falmer Press.

National Commission on Education (1995) *Success Against the Odds: Effective Schools in Disadvantaged Areas*, London: Routledge.

Newmann, F.M. and Wehlage, G.G. (1995) *Successful School Restructuring: A Report to the Public and Educators by the Center on Organization and Restructuring of Schools*, Madison, Wisconsin: CORS.

Nias, J., Southworth, G. and Campbell, P. (1992) *Whole School Curriculum Development in the Primary School*, London: Falmer Press.

Nuttall, D.L., Goldstein, H., Prosser, J. and Rasbash, J. (1989) Differential school effectiveness, *International Journal of Educational Research*, 13, (7), pp. 769–76.

Reezigt, G.J. (2001) (ed.) *A Framework for Effective School Improvement. Final Report of the ESI Project*, Groningen: GION, Institute for Educational Research, University of Groningen.

Rosenholtz, S.J. (1989) *Teachers' Workplace: The Social Organization of Schools*, New York: Longman.

Rudduck, J., Chaplain, R. and Wallace, G. (eds) (1996) *School Improvement: What Can Pupils Tell Us?*, London: David Fulton Publishers.

Sammons, P., Hillman, J. and Mortimore, P. (1995) *Key Characteristics of Effective Schools: A Review of School Effectiveness Research*, London: Office for Standards in Education.

Sammons, P., Thomas, S. and Mortimore, P. (1997) *Forging Links: Effective Schools and Effective Departments*, London: Paul Chapman Publishing.

Slavin, R.E. (1998) 'Sand, bricks, and seeds: school change strategies and readiness for reform' in Hargreaves, A., Fullan, M., Lieberman, A. and Hopkins, D. (eds) *International Handbook of Educational Change*, Dordrecht, The Netherlands: Kluwer Press.

Smylie, M. (1995) 'Teacher learning in the workplace: implications for school reform' in Guskey, T.R. and Huberman, M. (eds) *Professional Development in Education: New Paradigms and Practices*, New York: Teachers' College Press.

Southworth, G. and Connor, C. (1999) *Managing Improves Primary Schools: Using Evidence-based Management and Leadership*, London: Falmer Press.

Stoll, L. (1999a) 'Realising our potential: understanding and developing capacity for lasting improvement', *School Effectiveness and School Improvement*, 10 (4), pp. 503–32.

Stoll, L. (1999b) 'School culture: black hole or fertile garden for improvement?' in Prosser, J. (ed.) *School Culture*, London: Paul Chapman Publishing.

Stoll, L. and Fink, D. (1992) 'Effecting School Change: the Halton Approach', *School Effectiveness and Improvement*, 3 (1) 19–41.

Stoll, L. and Fink, D. (1996) *Changing our Schools*, Buckingham: Open University Press.

Stoll, L. and Fink, D. (1998) 'The crusing school: the unidentified ineffective school' in Stoll, L. and Myers, K. (eds) *No Quick Fixes: Perspective on Schools in Difficulty*, London: Falmer.

Stoll, L. and Fink, D. (1998) 'Effecting school change: the Halton approach', *School Effectiveness and School Improvement*, 3 (1), pp. 19–41.

Stoll, L. and Myers, K. (1998) *No Quick Fixes: Perspectives on Schools in Difficulty*, London: Falmer Press.

Stoll, L., Wikeley, F. and Reezigt, G. (2003) 'Developing a common model? Comparing effective school improvement across European countries', *Educational Research and Evaluation*.

Stringfield, S. (1995) 'Attempting to enhance students' learning through innovative programs: the case for schools evolving into high reliability organizations', *School Effectiveness and School Improvement*, 6 (1), pp. 67–96.

Teddlie, C. and Reynolds, D. (2000) *The International Handbook of School Effectiveness Research*, London: Falmer Press.

Van Velzen, W., Miles, M., Eckholm, M., Hamayer, U. and Robin, D. (1985) *Making School Improvement Work*, Leuven, Belgium: ACC.

8

CHAPTER 53

Departmental effectiveness and school improvement

ALMA HARRIS

It is now accepted wisdom that there are sizeable differences in effectiveness between and among schools. Researchers in the school effectiveness field have generated a substantial pool of evidence about the extent to which differential effectiveness can be measured and understood (Teddlie and Reynolds, 2000). These efforts over the past 20 years have proved to be very fruitful: there is now a better understanding of what creates and makes 'the difference' between schools and the weight of empirical evidence is consistent in describing and highlighting the reasons for variance in school effectiveness and performance. While the school effectiveness field has not been without its critics from both a methodological and ideological stance, the factors that influence school-level variation in achievement are widely known and generally endorsed (Sammons, 1999).

However, within the school effectiveness research field, the traditional emphasis on 'between school' differences has meant that it has tended to ignore, until relatively recently, differences within schools. Sammons, Thomas and Mortimore (1997, p.11) note that: 'perhaps a major limitation of the school effectiveness field during the early 1990s was the relatively small number of studies, particularly at the secondary level, which had examined the school and classroom processes'. Moreover, they point out that few research studies have attempted to investigate in detail the concept of secondary school effectiveness in relation to differential effectiveness, particularly at the departmental level.

This is a position that has changed over the last few years. A number of effectiveness studies have now been conducted at the departmental level, predominantly but not exclusively in the UK. These studies show that a substantial proportion of the variation in effectiveness among schools is due to differential effectiveness at the departmental level (Fitz-Gibbon; 1992 Sammons, Thomas and Mortimore, 1997; Harris, Jamieson and Russ, 1995; Harris, 1998). The emerging research base also demonstrates clearly that individual departments can and do make a difference to secondary students' school progress between the ages of 11 and 16 years (Sammons, Thomas and Mortimore, 1997 p. 208): although students' background characteristics exert a powerful influence, 'the quality of educational experiences at secondary school can significantly raise achievement levels and affect the subsequent life chances of students'. The conclusion from recent research is that the departmental level has a significant influence on the quality of teaching and by association upon student performance and achievement (Harris, 2001; Fullan, 2001).

The research base concerning departmental effectiveness suggests that to analyse pupil achievement school by school is to overlook much closer influences on individual pupil performance. It also suggests that the school is not the only unit of analysis for 'improvement' activities but that other levels, particularly the departmental level, need to be understood. Studies of departmental effectiveness have revealed that there are features or characteristics that effective departments or subject areas consistently display and that these can be modified and changed (Harris, 1999). The clear message from the research is that departmental effectiveness can be enhanced, as can school effectiveness, but that an important prerequisite for change is understanding the key characteristics of effectiveness at the departmental level (Harris, 2000).

Characteristics of effective departments

The two main research studies of departmental effectiveness in the UK demonstrate that there are consistent sets of characteristics displayed by effective departments. As comprehensive accounts of these studies already exist (Sammons, Thomas and Mortimore, 1997; Harris, Jamieson and Russ, 1995) the aim here is to highlight some of the key features of effective departments rather than offer a definitive account. Both studies cited show that effective departments emphasize high academic standards, reinforce a consistent approach to teaching, are well organized, monitor regularly and operate in a collegial way. Effective departments are student-centred and student-focused. They are departments that place a premium upon high-quality teaching and are constantly seeking new and better ways of engaging students in learning.

Both studies show that effective departments have a clear and shared sense of vision. This vision is influenced by the head of department and is a particularly important influence upon the quality of teaching and learning within the department. One of the most striking findings from the research studies into departmental effectiveness is the collegial vision adopted by effective departments. Effective departments tend to be 'talking departments', i.e. departments that are marked by a constant interchange of professional interchange both at a formal and informal level (Harris, Jamieson and Russ, 1995).

The research evidence shows that effective departments have the ability to organize key elements of teaching and learning in an optimum way. Within effective departments, monitoring and evaluation have been shown to be important dual processes. The mechanisms for monitoring student progress have been found to be tightly in place in departments that are improving (Harris, 1999). Information about the progress of individual students tends to be systematically collected within effective departments through a variety of means and is shared within the department. In addition, effective departments are those that keep detailed profiles of students to chart individual progress. These profiles often include detailed assessments of students' strengths and weaknesses in the subject area and are regularly shared with students.

The research evidence also shows that effective departments know their own strengths and weaknesses and collect systematic evidence of their progress towards departmental goals. Effective departments are departments that 'self-evaluate' and place a high premium on both the process and outcomes of self-evaluation. At the heart of any effective department is the effective organization of teaching and

8

learning. It is clear from the research findings that effective departments have set protocols in relation to teaching and learning taking a great deal of time and effort to select the most appropriate teaching strategies for their students.

In summary, the study by Harris, Jamieson and Russ (1995) found that effective departments displayed the following characteristics:

- a collegial management style;
- a strong vision of the subject, effectively translated down to the level of the classroom;
- good organization in terms of assessment, record keeping, homework, etc.;
- good resource management;
- an effective system for monitoring and evaluation;
- clear routines and practices within lessons;
- a strong pupil-centred ethos that systematically rewards pupils;
- opportunities for autonomous pupil learning;
- a central focus on teaching and learning.

Similarly, the study by Sammons, Thomas and Mortimore (1995) identified those features associated with greater departmental effectiveness at GCSE:

- high expectations
- strong academic emphasis
- shared vision/goals
- clear leadership
- an effective senior management team
- consistency of approach
- quality of teaching
- student-focused
- parental support/involvement.

Of all the characteristics of effective departments identified in the two studies, the style of leadership of the head of department was the most important contributory factor to the success of a department. Recent research has shown that giving others responsibility and developing others is at the core of effective departmental leadership (Harris, 2001). This form of leadership emphasizes the enhancement of self-worth and values individual members of the department. It suggests that leadership is a shared and collective endeavour that engages all teachers within the school or department (Lambert, 1998). It also implies that the context in which people work and learn together is where they construct and refine meaning, leading to a shared purpose or set of goals.

It is clear that departmental leaders are uniquely placed within the school organization to secure change and improvement. As middle-level leaders, they are key agents to school and classroom improvement because they have a direct influence over the professional practice of others. They are also in a position to create a culture and a set of values about teaching and learning within their department. As Hargreaves (1994, p. 54) points out: 'what the teacher thinks, what the teacher believes, what the teacher assumes … have powerful implications for the change process'. Consequently, the style and nature of departmental leadership is important because it influences the culture of the department and has a direct impact upon the quality of teaching (Busher and Harris, 1999; Harris 2001).

Departmental culture

Within secondary schools, heads of department not only face competing leadership demands but they also have widely differing arenas in which to exercise their power. As might be expected, departmental culture varies considerably because of the personalities and dispositions of those within it and the leadership style or approach of the head of department. Most recently, research activity has focused upon the relationship between departmental culture and departmental performance, illustrating how the size, configuration and the power base of departments in secondary schools influence the potential for development and change (Busher and Harris, 1999, 2000). This work has identified a range of organizational differentiation existing at the department level and has explored the micro-political tensions between departments.

It has been argued that unravelling the culture of a department will cast light on how teachers understand and engage with notions of collegiality and collaborative leadership. Departmental culture is understood as that manifestation of the moral relationships that exist both between or among the people in, for example, a subject department, and between that group of people and their surrounding institutional and socio-political contexts. It is constructed through the interactions of a group of people both with each other and with others outside the group and is visible in the rituals and symbols used by the group, as well as in the language in which they talk about key events and people. Departmental cultures represent the enacted views, values and beliefs of teachers and support staff about what it means to teach students in particular departments within particular institutional contexts. Departmental cultures may be collegial, autocratic, corporate, or demonstrate 'contrived collegiality' (Hargreaves, 1994) and, as Siskin (1994, p. 181) maintains:

> It is important to recognise that subject departments are not just smaller pieces of the same social environment, or just bureaucratic labels but worlds of their own, with their own 'ethnocentric' way of looking at things. They are sites where distinct groups of people come together and together share in and reinforce the distinctive agreements on perspectives, rules and norms which make up subject cultures and communities.

Subject departments, in terms of how they function in schools have been characterized by Goodson (1997) according to administrative and social relations functions. On the one hand, subject departments are administratively responsible for time and space in terms of students and staff. Consequently, subject departments provide a major communication link with distant colleagues working in the same area. These communication channels can contribute to the strength and bargaining power of department heads in their claims for increased resources. Subject departments therefore play an important mediating role between the subject demands and the demands of the organization.

On the other hand, subject departments also exhibit a very powerful social relations function. Subject departments represent the primary point of reference – or 'professional home' – for most teachers. Inevitably friendship groups will develop in an atmosphere in which teachers spend time together and work together. Conversely, subject departments can also provide a structure where interpersonal rivalry occurs and where conflict naturally arises. In this respect, the informal and formal relationships between teachers can create disparate working cultures between and within schools. In the case of the least effective departments, research has indicated how dysfunctional staff relationships within a department can negatively affect departmental culture and performance (Harris, 1998).

The realm of the department in secondary schools presents a considerable range of organizational differentiation that can be easily defined by size, configuration, staff-membership and subject expertise. Using these defining features of departmental structure, Busher and Harris (1999) have identified a range of departmental types and cultural states. Their typology highlights the potential challenge and inherent complexity of change at departmental level. Essentially, departments – like schools – reflect diversity rather than uniformity and therefore require a range of approaches to development and change.

School and departmental effectiveness studies have continuously shown that effective schools are structurally, symbolically and culturally more tightly linked than less effective ones. They operate more as an organic whole and less as a loose collection of disparate sub-systems. Within ineffective departments, dysfunctional relationships are frequently observed. One of the few studies of ineffective departments (Harris, 1996) in secondary schools highlighted that these departments have a particular pathology that contributed to their failure. In these departments communication had broken down severely and the departmental culture was at odds with the dominant culture of the school. These were departmental cultures where dissonant values emerged rendering them fragmented, separate and ineffective.

This reinforces a view of school and departmental improvement that embraces cultural change. Barth (1990, p. 6) suggests that 'what needs to be improved about schools is their culture, the quality of inter-personal relationships, and the nature and quality of learning experiences'. Implicit within this interpretation is a belief that school and departmental culture can be changed and that cultural change is achieved through changing the way in which teachers relate and interact. As Huberman (1990, p. 11) notes: 'I would rather look to the department as the unit of collaborative planning and execution in a secondary school ... this is where people have concrete things to tell one another and where the contexts of instruction actually overlap'.

Hopkins (2001) notes that 'much school improvement work assumes in practice that all schools are the same i.e. that a strategy will work as well in one school as another'. This would suggest that departments at varying levels of effectiveness, like schools, will require differential strategies for improvement and growth (Hopkins and Harris, 2000). The key message is that any improvement strategies selected need to reflect accurately and match the 'growth state' of the department or school in order to succeed. Consequently, differential improvement strategies will be required for schools and departments in varying socio-economic contexts. As Hopkins (2001, p. 3) suggests:

> Put simply, schools at different stages of development require different strategies not only to enhance their capacity for development, but also to provide a more effective education for their students. Strategies which are effective for improving performance in one context are not necessarily effective in another.

This implies that schools and departments will need to be highly discerning in selecting school improvement strategies and approaches. They will need to seek the 'best fit' between their departmental 'growth state' and the strategies for improvement they select. They will also need to ensure that any developmental activity addresses the real rather than perceived needs of the department for improvement to succeed and to be sustained (Harris, 2002).

Discussion

It is becoming increasingly apparent that the department is a crucial part of understanding the context of teaching in secondary schools. McLaughlin and Talbert's (2001) study of high schools in the USA illustrates the importance of the departmental level in explaining differences in school performance and student learning. This research shows how departments have dramatically different effects on the motivation and career commitments of teachers. They note (ibid., p. 18) 'when teachers from the English and social studies departments told us how they feel about their job, it was hard to believe that they teach at the same school'. This highlights the influence of the departmental context upon the structural, social and professional nature of teachers' work. Furthermore, it suggests that the departmental level is an important lever for change and improvement within the school because it is the place where collegial relations are fostered and flourish.

As Hargreaves *et al.* (2001, p. 1169) note, strong collaborative cultures and collegial relations within and among schools provide essential supports for implementing effective and sustained change. Research has shown that these are more likely to occur at the departmental rather than the school level as these 'realms of knowledge' are powerful influences upon the professional identities and practice of secondary school teachers (Siskin, 1994). Wenger (1998) suggests that individuals derive their understanding of their work from the 'community of practice within which they carry it out'. The members of the community have a shared understanding of the work and individuals are drawn into the community by a process of learning where the boundaries are that define the collection of tasks that make up the practice. Consequently, to operate simply on the basis of 'the school' as the unit of analysis is to ignore these potentially profound meanings in which individuals invest in their day-to-day actions.

While attempts have been made to generate theories of school improvement (Hopkins *et al.*, 1994) that reflect the complexity of organizational change, the department as a 'unit of analysis' rarely features. There is, however, a growing body of evidence which suggests that this omission is no longer justifiable and that long-term school improvement must be premised upon creating professional learning communities within schools, particularly at the departmental level (Harris, 2001). The development of individuals is not sufficient to secure school improvement, even though the knowledge, skills and dispositions of individual teachers can make a difference to individual classrooms.

A study of especially effective schools by Newmann, King and Youngs (2000) concludes that building school capacity is the key to success and that forging professional relationships between teachers where they work and learn together is central to sustaining school effectiveness. Consequently, it seems imperative that future efforts to improve secondary schools need to recognize the power and potential of departments to influence teachers, to generate change and to build professional learning communities. This is not simply to accept and endorse that such subject divisions are the best ways to organize the lives of students and teachers. Rather, it is to acknowledge that attempts at school improvement are more likely to succeed if development is undertaken at both the school and the departmental level, and, by implication, where change efforts are located much closer to the classroom.

REFERENCES

Barth, R. (1990) *Improving Schools From Within: Teachers, Parent and Principals Can Make a Difference*, San Francisco: Jossey-Bass.

Busher, H. and Harris, A. (1999) 'Leadership of school departments: tensions and dilemmas of managing in the middle', *School Leadership and Management*, 19 (3), pp. 305–17

Busher, H. and Harris, A. (2000) *Leading Subject Areas Improving Schools*, London: Paul Chapman Publishing.

Fitz-Gibbon, C.T. (1992) 'School effects at A level: genesis of an information system?' in Reynolds, D. and Cuttance, P. (eds) *School Effectiveness: Research, Policy and Practice*, London: Cassell.

Fullan, M. (2001) *Leading in a Culture of Change*, San Francisco: Jossey-Bass.

Goodson, I.F. (1997) *School Subjects and Curriculum Change*, London: Falmer Press.

Hargreaves, A. (1994) *Changing Teachers Changing Times: Teachers' Work and Culture in the Post-modern Age*, London: Cassell.

Hargreaves, A., Earl, L., Moore, S. and Manning, S. (2001) *Learning to Change: Teaching Beyond Subjects and Standards*, San Francisco: Jossey-Bass.

Harris, A. (1998) 'Improving ineffective departments in secondary schools: strategies for change and development', *Educational Management and Administration*, 26 (3), pp. 269–78.

Harris, A. (1999) *Effective Subject Leadership A Handbook of Staff Development Activities*, London: David Fulton Publishers.

Harris, A. (2000) 'Effective leadership and departmental improvement', *Westminster Studies in Education*, 23, pp. 81–90.

Harris, A. (2001) 'Department improvement and school improvement: a missing link?', *British Educational Research Journal*, 27 (4), pp. 477–87.

Harris, A. (2002) *Leading the Improving Department*, London: David Fulton Publishers.

Harris, A., Jamieson, I.M. and Russ, J. (1995) 'A study of effective departments in secondary schools', *School Organization*, 15 (3), pp. 283–99.

Hopkins, D., Ainsow, M. and West, M. (1994) *School Improvement in an Era of Change*, London: Cassell.

Hopkins, D. (2001) *School Improvement for Real*, London: Falmer Press.

Hopkins, D. and Harris, A. (2000) 'Differential strategies for school development' in Van Veen, D. and Day, C. (eds) *Professional Development and School Improvement: Strategies for Growth*, Mahwah, NJ: Lawrence Erlbaum Associates.

Huberman, M. (1990) 'The model of the independent artizan in teachers' professional relations' in Little, J.W. and McLaughlin, M.W. (eds) *Teachers Work*, New York: College Teachers' Press.

Lambert, L. (1998) *Building Leadership Capacity in Schools*, Alexandria, VA: Association for Supervision and Curriculum Development.

McLaughlin, M. and Talbert, J. (2001) *Professional Communities and the Work of High School Teaching*, Chicago: University of Chicago Press.

Newmann, F., King, B. and Youngs, P. (2000) 'Professional development that addresses school capacity', paper presented at the American Educational Research Association, New Orleans.

Sammons, P. (1999) *School Effectiveness Coming of Age in the Twenty First Century*, Lisse, The Netherlands: Sweits & Zetlinger.

Sammons, P., Thomas, S. and Mortimore, P. (1997) *Forging Links: Effective Schools and Effective Departments*, London: Paul Chapman Publishing.

Siskin, L. (1994) *Realms of Knowledge, Academic Departments in Secondary Schools*, London: Falmer Press.

Teddlie, C. and Reynolds, D. (2000) *The International Handbook of School Effectiveness Research*, London: Falmer Press.

Wenger, E. (1998) *Communities of Practice: Learning, Meaning and Identity*, Cambridge: Cambridge University Press.

CHAPTER 54

School effectiveness and its critics

DAVID REYNOLDS AND CHARLES TEDDLIE

The volume of criticism to which school effectiveness has been subjected (e.g. Thrupp, 1999, 2001; Hamilton, 1998; Slee, Weiner and Tomlinson, 1998), and the often highly personal attacks upon individual school effectiveness researchers, strongly suggest that the discipline has reached a position of some importance in educational discourse in several countries. After all, if this were not the case, there would be no point in these criticisms.

In this chapter we review the significant achievements of school effectiveness research over the last 20 years. We then want to go further by pointing out some of the cutting edges of current work in the field, much of it apparently unknown to our critics. We then want to look at, and hopefully refute, some of their criticisms in detail. We will conclude by arguing that far from being a convenient location for the ambitious, the compromised and the conservative, the school effectiveness movement is where liberal, or progressively inclined, educationists should situate themselves if they wish to bring about educational advance.

Significant achievements

Inventing a discipline

This discipline is probably the most successful academic educational 'invention' since that of teacher effectiveness in the 1960s. The journal *School Effectiveness and School Improvement* began publication in 1991 and (judged by citation counts) sits at the 'top of the middle' of the international rankings of journals, a remarkable achievement for such an infant publication. School effectiveness research has a professional association, the International Congress for School Effectiveness and Improvement (ICSEI), whose meetings now regularly command close to four-figure attendances. School effectiveness research now exhibits all the characteristics of mature 'normal science', especially with the publication of The *International Handbook of School Effectiveness Research*, an international review of the hundreds of studies that have been conducted in the last 35 years (Teddlie and Reynolds, 2000).

The reasons for this success are precisely those characteristics about which some critics complain. In the early stages of a field, there is much evidence that what generates rapid advance is the generation of a 'taken for granted' attitude in terms of an agreed world view. For example, in the nineteenth century physiology made rapid progress through its alliance with clinical medicine, which forced the discipline to concentrate upon the problems that needed solution, rather than indulge in philosophical speculation. School effectiveness has taken some things for granted, unlike British sociology of education whose values debate in the 1970s disabled it from disciplinary advance.

There are two further factors responsible for school effectiveness research's advance. First, a distinguishing characteristic of school effectiveness research is internationalization: around 50 countries regularly send delegates to the annual ICSEI meeting, and half a dozen countries have school effectiveness research communities of over 50 persons. Because the discipline started as a truly international group of persons, it has made progress from the interaction between persons, contexts and traditions. Second, disciplinary advance has been furthered by the possession of an agreed methodology, which can loosely be called mixed methods, that has generated a common framework to judge which knowledge is valid through the use of triangulation methods. This allows for a range of different kinds of data that can be collected and interpreted. What one will not find, however, is the belief that valid knowledge in the discipline should not be separated from invalid knowledge because of the relativized nature of all knowledge.

Generating a valid knowledge base

Our second achievement has been to generate an agreed set of findings concerning such issues as the size of school effects, their consistency, the processes within schools/classrooms associated with effectiveness and the 'context specificity' of these processes (e.g. Teddlie and Reynolds, 2000). After a promising start (e.g. Brookover, *et al.*, 1979; Rutter *et al.*, 1979) in the late 1970s, a redirection of research took place, generating more and better designed studies in many different countries. Progress has been made in the following areas:

- A range of outcome measures to measure school effects has been developed, not only in the cognitive domain, but also in other social and affective areas, although it should be acknowledged that the knowledge base on affective outcomes is still being developed. Connected with the cognitive domain has been the development of the concept and 'technology' of added value, and associated research on the stability and consistency of school effects.
- The size of the 'educational' effect has been studied in many research projects, especially related to different levels in the educational system (e.g. classroom, school). Useful discussion has taken place on how to present 'effect sizes' and how to show the relevance of the various levels in the educational system to the explanation of student outcomes.
- Most research studies have continued to focus upon the factors/variables at the different levels that contribute to effectiveness. Additionally, the possible differences between countries in the factors that explain the variance of outcomes have been investigated. Factors and characteristics have been codified into 'blocks' of similar factors that might be important (e.g. Levine and Lezotte, 1990, in the USA; and Sammons, Hillman and Mortimore, 1995, in the UK).
- The next step has been to develop models that are more theoretically based or oriented, or at least to generate more 'theoretical' explanations for the

differences in educational outcomes, both within nations and internationally. One way of doing this is to refer to learning theories, or to make use of classical sociologically oriented organizational theories.

- Major progress has also been made in school effectiveness research in the use of qualitative methodology within case studies, in order to come up with explanations and in-depth analyses of effectiveness. The development of multilevel and causal analyses has made it possible to test on larger datasets various models of effectiveness and to look for explanations of effects.

Encouraging educational advance

Our third contribution has been to improve the prospects of productive educational change by combating some of the pessimism that was generated in the 1970s and 1980s. We have convincingly helped to destroy the belief that schools can do nothing to change the society around them, and have also helped to destroy the myth that the influence of family background is so strong that children are unable to be affected by school. Some 30 years ago there was a widespread belief that 'schools make no difference' (Bernstein, 1968), which reflected the results of American research (e.g. Coleman *et al.*, 1966; Jencks *et al.*, 1972) and also the disappointed hopes that followed from the perceived failure of systemic reform, enhanced expenditure and the other policies that constituted the liberal dream of the 1960s.

We also took as our defining variables the key factors of school and pupil outcomes, from which we 'back map' to look at the processes related to these outcomes. For us, our 'touchstone criteria' concern is whether children learn more or less because of the policy or practice. We have continuously in our studies shown teachers to be important determinants of children's educational/social attainments and have, therefore, hopefully managed to enhance and build professional self-esteem. We have begun the creation of a 'known to be valid' knowledge base which can act as a foundation for training. With knowledge of school and of teacher effectiveness (e.g. Creemers, 1994), we can avoid the endless reinvention of the 'teaching wheel' and can move teachers to a more advanced level, conceptually and practically, more quickly than if they were left to discover good practice.

Why the criticisms?

It is difficult to square the volume of the criticisms with these positive achievements outlined. Certainly, those bodies of knowledge that purport to be of special relevance to professional educators should be subject to the most searching examination of all. However, the volume and the intemperate nature of the criticisms suggest that some other processes must be in play.

First, the criticisms may reflect simple ignorance. Many of them appear to come from people who have read very little school effectiveness research. Second, it may be that the criticism is because we are not 'club members'. The school effectiveness paradigm did not originate within the educational research mainstream; indeed, mainstream educational research was violently hostile to the initial Rutter *et al.* (1979) effectiveness insights (e.g. Acton, 1980; Goldstein, 1980).

Third, the criticisms may reflect the adherence of the critics to a very different view about what the nature of educational research should be. Most school effectiveness researchers hold to a 'technological' orientation to education and avoid a values debate about goals. Certainly none of us would deny the importance of this debate – indeed, it touches on a fundamental question, namely what should it mean to be 'educated'? However, it is important to realize that the obsessive concern about ends rather than means reflects national cultures that give more status to the pure than the applied, to the useless more than the useful and to the educational philosopher more than the educational engineer. Alexander's illuminating series of criticisms (1996, p. 6) about *Worlds Apart?* (Reynolds and Farrell, 1996) betrayed this academic snobbery when he talked patronizingly about school effectiveness research as the 'academic community's jet setting high-tech intellectual sharp dressers – the Essex men and women of educational research'. It may be that school effectiveness is simply victim to academic snobbery.

So much for the criticisms. We suspect that these will diminish as those within the education research community who have opposed school effectiveness lose their platforms. Indeed, we suspect that much of the criticism of school effectiveness is from people firing into the education room as they are, thank goodness, retreating through the door.

The detailed criticisms

In spite of our achievements listed above, recent criticisms of the field have been numerous. Here we look at the evidence for a number of them.

Misuse of findings

First, it is said school effectiveness research has had a pervasive impact on educational policy making and that school effectiveness researchers have been unable to 'control' negative uses of their findings. An illustrative quote argues: 'This book is offered as a considered interruption to the dominance of the school effectiveness juggernaught as it rides roughshod over educational policy-making and research' (Slee, Weiner and Tomlinson, 1998, p. 3).

However, the close relationship between educational policy makers and school effectiveness researchers is clearly overstated. In a review of Slee, Weiner and Tomlinson (1998), Daly and Ainley (2000, p. 140) rightly responded that:

> References to interrupting a 'school effectiveness juggernaught as it rides roughshod over educational policy-making and research' (p. 3) seems a somewhat exaggerated claim ... The links between school effectiveness research and market approaches in school systems ... appear to be exaggerated.

If the symbiotic link between government and school effectiveness research is occurring, it is doing so almost exclusively in the UK. The influence of school effectiveness research in the USA peaked in the late 1980s, while school effectiveness research literature has had little policy impact in The Netherlands.

We should note that school effectiveness researchers are not obligated to anticipate and eliminate the political misuse of their findings. Thrupp (1999, p. 192) wants school effectiveness researchers to censor their work for fear that it will fall into the 'wrong hands'. He contends that researchers should turn down projects 'which are tied to potentially dubious ends'. Are school effectiveness researchers to be blamed for policy makers' 'cherry picking' results to be consistent with their viewpoints? How does one effectively control for this, except by not doing any research?

Political agenda

Second, the field of school effectiveness research is said to have a well-defined political agenda. It has been portrayed as a monolithic enterprise: 'Effective schooling has become a global industry. Its activities embrace four processes: research, development, marketing and sales ... The school effectiveness industry, therefore, stands at the intersection of educational research and social engineering' (Hamilton, 1998, p. 13). However, the critics' reviews of the school effectiveness research literature are simplistic and skewed. Daly and Ainley (2000, p. 12) argue that: 'Much of the background ... in the book by Slee *et al.* (1998) appears to be based on a limited sampling of school effectiveness research'.

Additionally it is clear that there is a wide diversity of school effectiveness research: no single viewpoint prevails. School effectiveness research is a highly diverse academic specialization that has evolved considerably over the past 35 years. Teddlie and Reynolds (2000) concluded that there are three school effectiveness research strands:

- school effects research: studies of the scientific properties of school effects evolving from input–output studies to current research utilizing multilevel models;
- effective schools research: research concerned with the processes of effective schooling, evolving from case studies of outlier schools through to contemporary studies of classrooms and schools;
- school improvement research: examining the processes whereby schools can be changed utilizing increasingly sophisticated 'multiple lever' models.

Under the general heading of school effects research, there are at least seven different scientific properties, while there are at least nine processes that have been studied under the heading of effective schools research. The critical reviews touch on only a few of these topics. Perhaps the critics' tendency to see school effectiveness research as a monolithic enterprise has blinded them to distinctions within the literature?

Unrealistic claims

Third, critics argue that our school improvement models make unrealistic claims. One critic, Thrupp (1999, p. 4), concluded that: 'Nevertheless, the central theme of this book is that the "schools can make a difference" message has been thoroughly overplayed' (p. 4) and he mentioned that 'the impact of school mix will continue to undermine even our best efforts at schools reform' (ibid., p. 196).

However, the facts are that research evidence indicates that schools do have an effect on student achievement, which is enhanced longitudinally, and there is also ample evidence of successful school improvement projects. Such evidence comes from early studies conducted in urban settings in the USA (Levine and Lezotte, 1990); case studies of the application of the 'effective schools model' (Teddlie and Reynolds, 2000); specialized programmes enacted in Canada and the UK (e.g. Hopkins, 1987); and recent systemic school improvement projects (e.g. Bryk *et al.*, 1998).

Social class v. school influences

Fourth, critics argue that social class has a large impact on student achievement and that school effectiveness research has ignored, or downplayed, the impact of social class and overstated the importance of schools. The criticisms are summarized by Rea and Weiner (1998, p. 21): 'The Effective Schools Movement's … claim that schools can act independently of local or socio-economic contexts mirrors the instrumental and technical nature of much of school management'. However, numerous writers in the school effectiveness research literature have acknowledged over the past 35 years that the influence of the school is small, compared to individual student differences. For example, a recent synthesis led to the conclusion that only 12–15 per cent of the variance in individual student achievement is due to schools (Teddlie and Reynolds, 2000).

The difference is that writers in school effectiveness research believe that schools can have an impact beyond that of social class, and that educators should therefore try to influence what they can in their schools/classrooms. There is therefore an honest disagreement between school effectiveness researchers and their critics with regard to the influence of the school. The critics contend that school effectiveness researchers are deliberately duping their readers by downplaying the importance of student social-economic status (SES) and exaggerating the school's influence. School effectiveness researchers, while agreeing that social class has a large impact on achievement, conclude that this makes development of methods to improve lower-SES schools (and their classrooms) even more important.

Clearly, schools can have an important impact beyond that of social class:

- alternative measures of effect sizes demonstrate the practical significance of school effects: several authors have calculated alternative estimates of school effects, often in terms of standard deviations and/or grade levels (see Teddlie and Reynolds, 2000);
- school effectiveness research has documented the existence of schools serving low-SES students, which do quite well on student achievement: Teddlie and Stringfield (1993) presented data on a group of low-SES effective schools that outperformed a group of less effective middle-SES schools.

The critics perceive an 'either–or' dichotomy: either you believe that student achievement is determined by social class, or you believe that the two (student achievement, social class) are independent. School effectiveness research believes that social class and student achievement are closely linked, but also believes that many schools can (and have) weakened that link through various practices at the school/classroom levels.

Lack of redistribution policies

Fifthly, the critics argue low-SES schools will never be improved without 'redistributive' policies. Many critics repeatedly emphasize the power of social class in determining the educational outcomes of students. Thrupp (1999, p. 183) states: 'For policy makers it will mean grappling with the possibility that technical solutions will never be enough ... and that educational quality in low-SES settings will not be able to be substantially improved without redistributive policies of various kinds'. However, there is empirical evidence that good educational practices can occur in lower-SES schools that can result in higher student achievement, regardless of 'redistributive' policy.

School effectiveness research indicates that teachers in more effective schools demonstrate substantially superior classroom skills than teachers from less effective schools, when these schools are matched on SES. Slavin and his colleagues (1996) have demonstrated that the Success for All reading programme can have a large effect on the achievement of lower-SES students. His strategy for classroom improvement involves active learning and cooperative learning.

Why are the critics so relentlessly pessimistic, especially about teachers being able to make a difference, when there is ample evidence that teachers in more effective schools teach more effectively than teachers from less effective schools? Is this what the critic Thrupp (1999) meant when he refers to 'technical solutions' found in the school effectiveness research literature? On the contrary, these differences in teachers' behaviours occur at the very learning core of schools, and can hardly be seen as technical by the pupils they help.

Conclusions

It should be clear by now that while the critics have performed a useful service, many of their criticisms appear baffling when viewed rationally. Indeed, the discipline itself is undertaking a more searching self-examination of itself than it is being given by its critics.

In one final respect also, critics may be wide of the mark. They have always made it clear that they see a conservative orientation to school effectiveness research, presumably by comparison with their own activities. However, it is not always clear what their more radical alternative to school effectiveness is, unless they think that talking about outside school factors is change-producing. School effectiveness research believes not only in maximizing outcomes; it believes that the generation of more highly qualified young people is likely to produce a revolution of rising expectations that will change the outside school factors. Indeed, when school effectiveness started, the discipline attracted the more radical, who were distressed at the conservatism of those who researched outside-school factors.

Which is the more conservative act – to research and discuss how children are determined by the wider society, or to research and discuss how to change that society by generating children possessed of the intellects to change it? In its commitment to maximizing the educational quality of schools, both for its own merits and to generate wider social change, school effectiveness research is the discipline in which radicals should situate themselves. With their pessimism and inability to do anything more than talk about change, it is the critics who are the true conservatives now, as in the 1960s.

NOTE

This chapter is an abbreviated version of two articles: Teddlie and Reynolds (2001) and Reynolds and Teddlie (2001).

REFERENCES

Acton, T.A. (1980) 'Educational criteria of success: some problems' in the work of Rutter, Maughan, Mortimore and Ouston', *Educational Researcher*, 22 (3), pp. 163–73.

Alexander, R. (1996) *Other Primary Schools and Ours – Hazards of International Comparison*, Warwick: Centre for Research in Elementary and Primary Education, University of Warwick.

Bernstein, B. (1968) 'Education cannot compensate for society', *New Society*, 387, pp. 344–7.

Brookover, W.B., Beady, C., Flood, P., Schweitzer, J. and Wisenbaker, J. (1979) *Schools, Social Systems and Student Achievement: Schools Can Make a Difference*, New York: Praeger.

Bryk, A., Sebring, P., Kerbow, D. and Easton, J. (1998) *Charting Chicago School Reform*, Boulder, CO: Westview Press.

Coleman, J., Campbell, E., Hobson, C., McPartland, J., Mood, A., Weinfeld, F. and York, R. (1966) *Equality of Educational Opportunity*, Washington, DC: US Department of Health, Education and Welfare.

Creemers, B.P.M. (1994) *The Effective Classroom*, London: Cassell.

Daly, P. and Ainley, J. (2000) 'Recent critiques of school effectiveness research', *School Effectiveness and School Improvement*, 11 (1), pp. 131–43.

Goldstein, H. (1980) 'Critical notice – "Fifteen thousand hours" by Rutter *et al.*', *Journal of Child Psychology and Psychiatry*, 21 (4), pp. 364–6.

Hamilton, D. (1998) 'The idols of the marketplace' in Slee, R. Weiner, G. and Tomlinson, S. (eds.) *School Effectiveness for Whom? Challenges to the School Effectiveness and School Improvement Movements*, London: Falmer Press.

Hopkins, D. (1987) *Improving the Quality of Schooling*, Lewes: Falmer Press.

Jencks, C.S., Smith, M., Ackland, H., Bane, M.J., Cohen, D., Ginter, H., Heyns, B. and Michelson, S. (1972) *Inequality: A Reassessment of the Effect of the Family and Schooling in America*, New York: Basic Books.

Levine, D.U. and Lezotte, L.W. (1990) *Unusually Effective Schools: A Review and Analysis of Research and Practice*, Madison, WI: National Center for Effective Schools Research and Development.

Rea, J. and Weiner, G. (1998) 'Cultures of blame and redemption – when empowerment becomes control: practitioners' views of the effective schools movement' in Slee, R., Weiner, G. and Tomlinson, S. (eds.) *School Effectiveness for Whom? Challenges to the School Effectiveness and School Improvement Movements*, London: Falmer Press.

Reynolds, D. and Farrell, S. (1996) *Worlds Apart? – A Review of International Studies of Educational Achievement Involving England*, London: HMSO for Office for Standards in Education.

Reynolds, D. and Teddlie, C. (2001) 'Reflections on the critics and beyond them', *School Effectiveness and School Improvement*, 12 (1), pp. 99–113.

Rutter, M., Maughan, B., Mortimore, P. and Ouston, J. (1979) *Fifteen Thousand Hours: Secondary Schools and their Effects on Children*, Cambridge, MA: Harvard University Press.

Sammons, P., Hillman, J. and Mortimore, P. (1995) *Key Characteristics of Effective Schools: A Review of School Effectiveness Research*, London: Office for Standards in Education.

Slavin, R., Madden, N., Dolan, L., Wasik, B., Ross, S., Smith, L. and Dianda, M. (1996) 'Success for all: a summary of research', *Journal for the Education of Children Placed at Risk*, 1 (1), pp. 44–76.

Slee, R., Weiner, G. and Tomlinson, S. (1998). *School Effectiveness for Whom? Challenges to the School Effectiveness and School Improvement Movements*, London: Falmer Press.

Teddlie, C. and Reynolds, D. (eds) (2000) *The International Handbook of School Effectiveness Research*, London: Falmer Press.

Teddlie, C. and Reynolds, D. (2001) 'Countering the critics: responses to recent criticisms of school effectiveness research', *School Effectiveness and School Improvement*, 12 (1) pp. 41–82.

Teddlie, C. and Stringfield, S. (1993) *Schools Make a Difference: Lessons learned from a 10-Year Study of School Effects*, New York, NY: Teachers' College Press.

Thrupp, M. (1999) *Schools Making a Difference: Lets be Realistic*, Buckingham, UK: Open University Press.

Thrupp, M. (2001) 'Sociological and political concerns about school effectiveness research: time for a new research agenda', *School Effectiveness and School Improvement*, 12 (1), pp. 7–40.

PART NINE

The Teacher Career Cycle: The Role of Professional Development

PATRICIA COLLARBONE

Introduction

PATRICIA COLLARBONE

If one does not know to which port one is sailing, no wind is favourable.
(SENECA)

In recent years the relationship between teacher learning and raising the standards of pupil achievement has become better understood. As a result, continuing professional development (CPD) is viewed as a necessary and important aspect of the career cycle of a teacher. There is also a growing recognition that CPD opportunities come in many guises and that one of the most important is learning from each other – both formally and informally.

In many countries, there is a trend towards developing a career learning cycle based on individual needs, which are met in a variety of ways ranging from traditional taught courses to individual mentoring and coaching. There is, too, an increasing awareness of the role of new technologies and distance-learning techniques. The context within which the individual works is recognized as an essential element for the learning both of the person and of the organization. To support this process there is an increasing supply of highly skilled, experienced consultants, national and regional organizations, and government strategies directed towards facilitating this learning.

In Part Nine contributors describe a journey focused on the career development of the teacher. Ralph Fessler and Rochelle Ingram address theories of teacher development and how these reflect reform initiatives. They focus on different routes into teaching and how these affect the career cycle of the teacher. Sara Bubb extends these ideas with her focus on the significance of induction for long-term CPD and the retention of teachers. Drawing from her research in the UK, she highlights the importance of effective, fair treatment of newly qualified teachers and the need to consolidate their induction experience in the second and third years of teaching.

CPD can be taken to refer to the enhancement of professional and educational practice throughout a teacher's career. Agness McMahon examines the concept of professional development before moving on to discuss factors that influence teachers' learning, and the limitations of current CPD practices. She indicates a way forward for professional development, focusing on three trends: professional development standards, evidence-informed practice and the concept of the professional learning community.

Linda Evans begins by clarifying the nature of morale and job satisfaction and the relationship between them. She draws on her own research to consider the implications for policy and practice. She views the role of leadership and management as crucial and advocates the adoption of a 'teacher-centred' leadership philosophy – one that focuses on the individuals who make up a staff, rather than the staff as a whole.

David Clutterbuck considers the role of coaching and mentoring in professional development, and the importance of passing on the benefit of accumulated experience. He clarifies the skills required by the coach or mentor and the learner to make the relationship successful.

Finally, Vicki Phillips and Marilyn Crawford return to the theme of building learning communities by examining the developments in the school district of Lancaster, Pennsylvania. It is a case study of a system of continuous improvement that supports excellent teaching, which, the authors argue, is the key to raising standards.

Reflections

Five frogs are sitting on a log in the middle of a pond. Four decide to leap off the log into the pond. How many frogs are left on the log?

The changing and increasing demands placed on schools in recent years are beginning to take their toll on the work–life balance of the profession. The demands have been encapsulated in the drive to raise standards and to increase the transparency in accountability to the community. In some countries this drive has reached a critical point – where the demands on the lives of teachers pose serious threats to recruitment and retention. What has become obvious to all stakeholders is that we can no longer continue to do what we have always done. Across the world, education systems and schools are seeking to remodel in order to achieve a better balance for each individual between work and other responsibilities and interests. At the same time there is a requirement to benefit the educational organization for which teachers work by providing a better standard of education. It is, therefore, no coincidence that the spotlight has been turned both on to teachers, and, indeed, all staff who work within our organizations, as learners, and the nature of the role of CPD.

A number of significant, recurring themes surface in the chapters in Part Nine. The overarching theme is that of the career cycle of the teacher as a continuous learner. Consequently, CPD needs to be planned in a coherent manner, taking into account individuals, their experiences, the point they have reached in their career, their learning needs, their learning styles and the contexts in which they work.

The authors in Part Nine highlight the foundation aspects of the career cycle necessary for a successful induction into the teaching profession. These include:

- sound leadership and management, which provide a positive learning climate for all which motivates and sustains the workforce;
- professional learning communities, with adults learning from and contributing to the learning of others, leading to organizational learning;
- an expanding range of opportunities that focuses both on knowledge and skills acquisition and the emotional and spiritual needs of the individual.

How do we unleash the creative potential within our organizations to discover different ways of working that impact positively on the life chances of all pupils and restore a healthy life style for all staff? How do we enable our school leaders to lead and manage the necessary transformations from within? How do we enhance coherence and progression in a flexible range of CPD provision and nurture innovation, risk-taking and autonomy? What should be the guiding principles? How do we learn from global best practice and optimize new technologies for the benefit of all?

Five frogs remain on the log. Deciding to leap is not the same as leaping.

CHAPTER 55

The teacher career cycle revisited: new realities, new responses

RALPH FESSLER AND ROCHELLE INGRAM

During the contemporary era of school reform and redesigned teacher education, the concept of career development for teachers has become a topic of lively dialogue and debate. The two major questions that are raised in these discussions are: (i) to what extent do existing theories of teacher development reflect significant components of the recent reform initiatives in teaching, learning and teacher preparation? and (ii) to what extent are existing models of the teacher career cycle robust enough to describe the experiences of career-changers and others who are entering the profession of teaching in non-traditional ways? In this chapter we explore the thesis that teacher educators and staff developers need to analyse the complex dimensions of current educational environments and modify the theoretical frameworks they have used in the past to describe teacher development.

The problem: environmental changes

Since the late 1960s, many authors have proposed models to describe the knowledge, skills and dispositions needed by teachers as they progress through their careers. These models were highly dependent on the stability of the traditional mode of teacher training. They were built on a foundation of thought that separated 'pre-service' from 'in-service' teacher education. This view assumed that most teachers would pursue an undergraduate or graduate major in teacher education with coursework at a university/college and would eventually participate in a supervised clinical internship, usually referred to as 'student teaching'. Many programmes provided 'early field experiences' that prepared teacher candidates for the intensive student teaching experience that was the capstone event in the programme. Typically, early field experiences consisted of once- or twice-weekly observations in real K–12 classrooms. Sometimes they involved working with individuals or small groups of students. The philosophy that supports this type of programme is the belief that young adults pursuing teaching as their first careers should be provided with a solid theoretical foundation through university/college coursework and gradually be exposed to settings that allow them to apply theory to real life. Once teacher candidates completed their programmes, they sought employment in schools and periodically enrolled in courses and workshops to refresh their knowledge and skills. These courses and workshops were considered 'in-service' teacher training. In the USA, evidence of continuing professional development is required for state licensure and school district salary enhancement, and in recent years many US school districts have required a graduate degree for full professional licensure.

The explicit division between pre-service and in-service training has long been accepted within the educational professions. The clearly defined boundary between these two phases is the assignment of full-time responsibilities for a classroom. The teacher candidates' study of academic content, pedagogy and learning theory before becoming teachers is referred to as 'teacher preparation' or 'teacher education', whereas training after becoming a full-time school district employee is frequently called 'in-service' or 'staff development'. The transition phase is still seen by many teacher educators as the *sine qua non* of initial teacher preparation. It is commonly believed that the progression of skill and knowledge acquisition from theory to practice must culminate in a relationship with a master teacher who is present in the classroom with the teacher candidate, providing expert guidance and feedback. Ideally, the mentor teacher models techniques and supervises the teacher candidate as he/she attempts to apply the concepts, theories and strategies learned in the university/college programme.

Given the recent shortages of teachers in the USA and other nations, school systems often find the need to short-cut the system and hire teachers who have not experienced a comprehensive preservice teacher education programme. In some cases, such as Project SITE SUPPORT in Baltimore, Maryland, teachers are placed in their own classrooms with multiple layers of mentoring and support, as well as a redesigned and comprehensive teacher education programme delivered 'on the job'. In other cases, individuals are placed in their own classrooms with little or no support – left to succeed or fail on their own merits and survival capacity. In addition, even in the most supportive environments there may not be a sufficient number of master teachers who are willing and able to serve as full-time mentors for teacher candidates. Further, even when it is possible to enlist a sufficient number of experienced teachers to serve as mentors for teacher candidates, it is likely that only a small proportion of these teachers are experts in the emerging knowledge base in teaching and learning, which, in addition to content enhancement and pedagogy, has been expanded to include areas such as performance-based assessment, standards-based instruction and data-based decision making. The rapidity with which these trends have become installed as policy at the local, state and national level is astounding. They are now considered best practice by most professional associations, as well as the general public.

The view of teacher career development that divides pre-service from in-service also includes a phase of 'induction', during which novice teachers learn to function by themselves in a classroom. Some states and many school districts in the USA offer induction programmes for beginning teachers. These programmes are based on the premise that the highest attrition rates among teachers, especially in urban schools, occur during the early years of teaching. A proliferation of mentor programmes for new teachers has characterized the 1990s and beyond. In designing experiences for the beginning teacher, programme architects assume the traditional pre-service preparation pattern. Early career teachers are viewed as young adults preoccupied with survival in their new professions. Although this view may be appropriate for some new teachers, increasingly large numbers of them are pursuing teaching as a second career and are more mature and less fragile than their younger colleagues. The profile of the new teacher who has entered the profession via an 'alternative' path is very different from the profile of a young graduate of a four-year college programme.

Theories about teacher development

The early theories about teachers' career cycles borrowed heavily from the work of Frances Fuller (1969), who studied teacher education students at the University of Texas. She and her colleagues conducted many interviews and literature reviews that provided the basis for her Teacher Concerns Questionnaire. Her instrument reflects the primary concerns of student teachers as they progress through their teacher preparation programmes. The gradual evolution of the concerns of Fuller's student teachers moved from self to task to impact on students.

In the 1970s a number of authors proposed theoretical frameworks for teacher development. Among the most influential were Unruh and Turner's description (1970) of three career stages: initial, building security, maturing; and Gregorc's delineation (1973) of stages as becoming, growing, maturing, and fully functioning. Katz's labels (1972) included survival, consolidation, renewal and maturity. Five researchers at Ohio State (Ryan, Flora, Newman, Peterson, Burden and Mager, 1979) articulated a series of 'levels of experience' to describe teacher growth.

The 1980s was a decade of creative and prolific scholarship on teacher development, strongly influenced by the work of American scholars such as Feiman and Floden (1980), Burden (1982a, 1982b) and Burke, Fessler and Christensen (1983, 1984, 1987), as well as European scholars such as Vonk (1989) and Huberman (1989). Each of the theoretical frameworks developed by these researchers included distinctive phases or stages of development characterized by experience level, range of competence and/or psychological dispositions. Also in the 1980s the concepts of 'career ladders' and 'merit pay' became popular in some quarters. The various versions of these ideas had in common a differentiation of competence, roles, responsibilities and training that were connected to increased pay or status. An interesting alternative to the 'ladder' is described as the 'career lattice' by Christensen, McDonnell and Price (1988). The basic premise here is that teachers can assume a variety of differentiated roles while still occupying the core functions of the classroom teacher. The model includes roles such as learners, knowledge producers, coaches, teacher educators, mentors and leaders as descriptors of teachers' development. A similar model of teacher leadership and 'elastic career options' has been offered by Fessler and Ungaretti (1995).

A new view of teacher development

Fessler and Christensen (1992) presented a conceptualization of a teacher career cycle that progresses through stages not in a lock step, linear fashion, but rather in a dynamic manner reflecting responses to organizational and personal environmental factors. A supportive, nurturing environment can assist the novice teacher through early periods of adjustment and learning to extended periods of enthusiasm and growth as a teacher and facilitator of student learning. Conversely, a non-supportive environment that does not attend to early career confidence and competency building needs often results in a lack of sense of efficacy, job frustration and early career exit. Similarly, personal dispositions and life experiences can either support the emergence of enthusiastic and effective teachers, or contribute to a sense of despair, stagnancy and frustration. A summary of the dynamics of the teacher career cycle (TCC) model are presented in Figure 55.1.

The research and conceptual framework that served as the basis for the TCC model assumed a traditional route into teaching, where most teachers experienced a traditional undergraduate preservice programme, followed by school-based support for their in-service continuing professional development. As described earlier, the shortage of teachers and the emergence of alternative routes in teaching have changed the landscape over the past decade. Building upon the work of Fessler and Christensen (1992), a modern perspective on teacher development must be dynamic, taking into account the multiple internal and external influences on the developing teacher. To some extent, career stages are idiosyncratic, depending on the personalities and environments of the developing teachers. A new application of the Fessler and Christensen model is suggested by twenty-first-century trends in teacher development. It must be tested in the radically new environment of American public schools.

Many things have changed in recent years. First, as the severe teacher shortage of the late twentieth and early twenty-first century looms large, many school districts, colleges, and universities are delivering alternative programmes to train new teachers. Some of these alternative route programmes are robust, well conceived, content rich and conceptually sound, with multiple levels of mentoring and support to help new teachers adjust to the realities of their own classrooms. Others, however, are 'quick and dirty' minimalist programmes with little or no support offered – leaving candidates to sink or swim.

Second, a relatively large number of new teachers are career changers, who have had previous professional experience in business or governmental organizations. Unlike their predecessors, they have a rich repertoire of prior job knowledge from which to draw. Teaching is not their initial foray into the world of work.

Third, as a bi-product of the alternative route and previous work experience trends, many new teachers who are recruited to address the teaching shortage are older, with more life experience to draw upon. Many of these individuals have worked through the basic questions postulated by Fuller. For example, they may proceed more rapidly through concerns about 'self' and 'task' and concentrate their attention at earlier points in their careers on the 'impact' of their teaching.

Fourth, in today's schools, new and experienced teachers are all subject to stringent accountability for their students' academic achievement. Frequently, the performance-based evaluations of teachers are direct reflections of the progress and success of their students. In this atmosphere, teachers do not have the luxury of proceeding gradually through developmental stages. They are expected to produce results immediately. In the USA, for example, there is a profound sense of urgency associated with issues of teacher effectiveness and student achievement.

These new trends suggest the need for a more differentiated conception of development than in the past. Traditional pathways still exist, but they are accompanied by non-traditional routes – some of high quality – others of questionable appropriateness. Many career changers and other older candidates who experience robust and supportive alternative programmes may be more mature and proactive

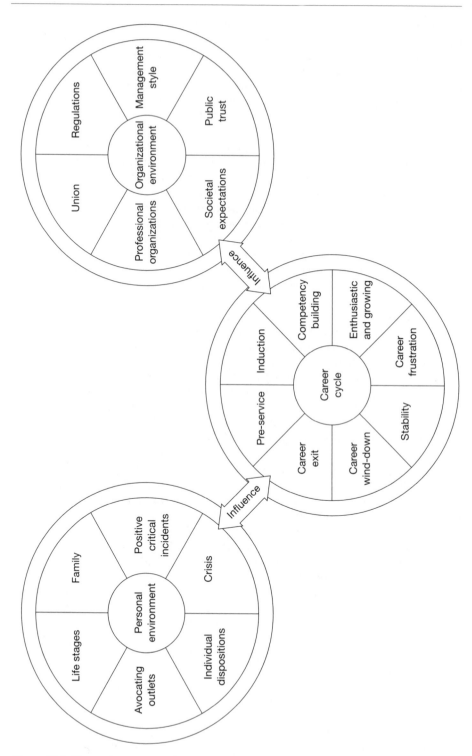

Figure 55.1 The teacher career cycle (TCC) model
Source: © Ralph Fessler 2003

than their traditionally prepared counterparts and often rapidly proceed to high impact, enthusiastic and growing career periods. Alternatively, poorly conceived, 'quick and dirty' programmes designed to address acute shortages of teachers with few support systems may create an environment that paves the way to frustration, failure and early career exit.

Conclusion

The teacher career cycle model developed in the early 1990s continues to provide a framework for viewing teachers' career paths, but it must be applied to the current and more complex context of teacher preparation and development practices and trends. The quest for a sound approach to teacher development inspires many more questions than answers. Given the diverse paths by which teachers now enter the profession and the school environments they encounter as they try to learn their craft, the following questions are paramount:

- How do the maturity and sense of urgency of non-traditional path teachers influence their career development?
- How can non-traditional path teachers be brought 'up to speed' quickly to become effective in results-based school environments?
- How should differentiated professional development experiences be designed to meet the needs of non-traditional as well as traditional path teachers?
- Which support systems (for example, mentoring formats) are most effective for traditional and non-traditional path teachers?
- As both groups of teachers advance in their careers, do differences in their professional development needs disappear?
- What is the impact of intense school reform agendas on the development of each group?

These questions and others provide a planning framework for policy makers, staff developers and university faculties who are responsible for supporting the next generation of successful teachers.

REFERENCES

Burden, P. (1982a) 'Developmental supervision: reducing teacher stress at different career stages', paper presented the annual conference of the Association of Teacher Educators, Phoenix, AZ, February.

Burden, P. (1982b). 'Implications of teacher career development: new roles for teachers, administrators, and professors', paper presented at the annual workshop of the Association of Teacher Educators, Slippery Rock, PA, August.

Burke, P., Christensen, J. and Fessler, R. (1983) 'Teacher life-span development: an instrument to identify stages of teacher growth', paper presented at the annual meeting of the American Educational Research Association, Montreal, Canada, April.

Burke, P., Fessler, R. and Christensen, J. (1984) *Teacher Career stages: Implications for Staff Development*, Bloomington, IN: Phi Delta Kappa.

Burke, P., Christensen, J., Fessler, R., McDonnell, J. and Price, J. (1987) 'The teacher career cycle: model development and research report', paper presented at the annual meeting of the American Educational Research Association, Washington, DC (ERIC document reproduction service no. ED 289 846) April.

Christensen, J., McDonnell, J. and Price., J. (1988) *Personalizing Staff Development: The Career Lattice Model*, Bloomington, IN: Phi Delta Kappa.

9

Feiman, S. and Floden, R. (1980) *What's All this Talk about Teacher Development?*, Research Series no. 70, East Lansing, MI: Institute for Research on Teaching, Michigan State University (ERIC document reproduction service no. ED 189 088).

Fessler, R. and Christensen, J. (eds) (1992) *Teacher Career Cycle: Understanding and Guiding the Professional Development of Teachers*, Needham Heights, MA: Allyn & Bacon.

Fessler, R. and Ungaretti, A. (1995). 'Expanding opportunities for teacher leadership' in Walling, D.R. (ed.), *Teachers as Leaders: Perspectives on the Professional Development of Teachers*, (pp. 211–22). Bloomington, IN: Phi Delta Kappa Educational Foundation.

Fuller, F. (1969) 'Concerns of teachers: A developmental conceptualization'. *American Educational Research Journal*, 6(2), pp. 207–26.

Gregorc, A. F. (1973) 'Developing plans for professional growth'. *NASSP Bulletin*, December, pp. 1–8.

Huberman, M. (1989) 'The professional life cycle of teachers', *Teachers' College Record*, 91(1), pp. 31–57.

Katz, L. G. (1972) 'Development stages of preschool teachers', *Elementary School Journal*. 73 (1), pp. 50–4 (ERIC document reproduction no. EJ 064 759).

Ryan, K., Flora, R., Newman, K., Peterson, A., Burden, P. and Mager, J. (1979) *The Stages in Teaching: New Perspectives on Staff Development for Teachers' Needs*, ASCD audio-tape.

Unruh, A. and Turner, H.E. (1970). *Supervision for Change and Innovation*, Boston: Houghton Mifflin.

Vonk, J.H.C. (1989) 'Becoming a teacher, brace yourself', unpublished paper, Vrije University, Amsterdam.

– CHAPTER 56 –

The induction of newly qualified teachers: treat them fairly

SARA BUBB

This chapter discusses the induction of newly qualified teachers (NQTs). Drawing on experiences of induction in schools in England since September 1999, it looks at how NQTs should be treated fairly in order for them to be as happy and effective as possible. After a discussion on general issues about induction, it examines some particular elements of treating NQTs fairly – their induction programme, contract, managing pupil behaviour, professional support and reducing variability of induction provision. The chapter ends with a consideration of how to support teachers in their second and third years.

The aims of induction

Most people would agree with the aims of England's policy (DfEE, 1999, para. 1) that induction should provide:

- all newly qualified teachers with a bridge from initial teacher education to effective professional practice,
- a foundation for long-term continuing professional development (CPD),
- well-targeted support ... which in turn helps them to ... make a real and sustained contribution to school improvement and to raising classroom standards.

In addition to making sure that all teachers are as effective as possible, the numbers of people coming into the profession – and staying – needs to be maximized. The number of people training but not going into teaching and those leaving in the first three years is high, and a huge waste of public money.

Initial training is not a total preparation for a career in teaching, but merely provides a platform on which further professional development will be built. The induction year is arguably the most formative period in a teacher's career. So we need to set high expectations and standards at this time of greatest receptiveness and willingness to learn and develop. However, the support of others is crucial if new teachers are to develop the competencies, the confidence and the attitudes that will keep them happy in the job and serve as the basis for ongoing professional development.

Therefore, knowing that there are induction arrangements should be an incentive to a career in teaching. NQTs should feel that they will be well supported, especially when things do not go smoothly. Induction should be a carrot. Indeed many aspects of England's induction policy are clearly attractive to new teachers. It is statutory, so that they know that all schools by law have to comply with it. They also have the following entitlement:

- a 10-per-cent lighter teaching timetable than other teachers in the school;
- a job description that does not make unreasonable demands, such as unduly difficult classes;
- meetings with a school 'induction tutor' (mentor), including half-termly reviews of progress;
- an individualized programme of support;
- objectives – informed by strengths and areas for development, as identified in the career entry profile – to help them meet the induction standards.
- at least one observation of their teaching each half term, with oral and written feedback;
- procedures to air grievances at school and local education authority (LEA) level.

This entitlement should give NQTs protection against the worst of experiences that others have encountered during their first year.

However, England has built into its induction policy a rigorous assessment and monitoring system. This is seen by some NQTs as beneficial in that they like to be told that they are doing well and to know that if there are concerns they will be raised. For many, however, the assessment component of induction is a stick that may threaten and potentially beat them. Formal assessment reports are written at the end of each of the three terms, placing considerable demands on the headteacher and induction tutor as well as the teacher. NQTs are judged on whether they meet the demanding standards for the end of the induction year. They have to demonstrate that they meet all the standards that they met during their initial training and the ten additional induction standards (DfEE, 1999, Annex A). These standards are demanding and the consequences of not meeting them severe. Unless they are successful in appeal, those failing to meet the standards will not be able to teach in a maintained school or non-maintained special school, despite still having qualified teacher status (QTS). These teachers would still keep QTS but are de-registered from the General Teaching Council. Thus, the only teaching they could do is in an independent school, a city technology college or as a private tutor. They cannot repeat induction or their initial training. Nor can they work as a supply teacher or classroom assistant. Is this 'zero tolerance of under performance' (DfEE 1998, p. 12) going too far?

Newly qualified teachers are a precious resource who have invested much time and effort into getting where they are – and the government has invested heavily in their training. They need to be treated well. They are agents of change and the profession's new generation – the headteachers of the future. Tickle (2000, p. 15) feels that induction policies such as those in England are predicated on a false picture of NQTs as deficient rather than seeing them as agents for change: 'an enviable resource', with 'creative potential'.

In my experience of meeting many new teachers, I would say that schools need to be prepared to cater for the full range of people who go under the NQT umbrella. The ease with which teachers settle into their first job will depend on:

- how well they met the QTS standards during training;
- the calibre of their initial teacher training and school placements;
- the new context of the school and class;
- the support during the induction period.

For those who only just passed their teaching qualification, a deficit model of induction is just what they need – an opportunity to develop from a low base. However, schools may be grateful for the protection of the assessment system to weed out people whose flaws identified during training turn out to have a detrimental effect on pupils' learning when tested in the workplace rather than on teaching practice.

At the other extreme, there are NQTs who are highly effective early on in their first year. Induction should meet their needs too. Tickle (2000, p. 9) feels the induction standards are 'an insufficient selection of teaching elements' and 'nothing more than a minor supplement' to those with QTS and would not challenge a high flier. He thinks that there should be a place for local or individualized specifications negotiated between induction tutor and NQT and is keen for NQTs to carry out practitioner research (ibid., p. 711). The fast-track programme (DfES, 2001a), which those who meet the rigorous entry requirements can join either on starting a PGCE or in the first few years of teaching, offers just that. It enables teachers to work in a school for two years with a particular remit in addition to class teaching. This should be a worthwhile task that moves the school on and that provides an appropriate challenge to the teacher.

Managing the NQT

Some elements of managing the NQT are especially important – the induction programme, the contract, managing pupil behaviour, professional support and reducing variability of induction provision.

An individualized induction programme

Schools need to treat NQTs in a professional manner and to provide a high-quality induction from which people will benefit not only in the first year of teaching but that will form a foundation for future professional development. Research on effective professional development by the Department for Education and Skills (DfES, 2001b) points to the importance of teacher collaboration; the role of mentoring, coaching and working alongside teachers in classrooms over a period of time; the opportunity to reflect on practice; classroom observation and feedback; and the chance to 'experiment' and to try out new ideas in a safe setting. There is also growing recognition of the need for differentiation in training and that different adults learn differently.

9

These issues need to be considered carefully when drawing up induction pro-grammes, which should be individualized but should exploit opportunities for NQTs to work together. A clear picture of the NQTs' strengths and development needs at the end of their initial training course is an essential foundation stone. This picture can come from the Career Entry Profile (TTA, 2001) and discussions with the NQTs about their experiences. It is crucial that this information does not overshadow, but contributes to, the picture of the NQTs' needs within their first school context.

Contracts

Research by the Office for Standards in Education (OFSTED) on the first year of induction found that up to 60 per cent of NQTs started work on temporary con-tracts in 1999–2000. If one assumes that temporary contracts should be given only to cover temporary positions, this figure is surely higher than it needs to be. It indicates that governing bodies may be using such contracts as a blanket insurance policy against NQTs they do not like. People on temporary contracts feel job inse-curity and low status. Without a permanent contract teachers find it well nigh impossible to get a mortgage or loan. In all respects, temporary contracts are demotivating and go against the principle of the induction year acting as a bridge from training into teaching as a career. With the current staffing crisis, it seems particularly unwise for schools to do anything less than offer permanent positions where possible. A permanent contract sends everyone the message that the invest-ment of induction is worthwhile, will be built upon and that staff are valued.

Managing pupil behaviour

In my role as 'agony aunt' for new teachers at *The Times Educational Supplement*, I come across many horror stories concerning the behaviour of pupils: 'I get so fed up with shouting at them to be quiet, and have walked out of the class three times. They have got me to the end of my tether' (TES, 2001). NQTs should not have to teach the very worst behaved pupils, which is an 'unreasonable demand' (DfEE, 1999, para. 28), though in practice some schools have little choice. NQTs need support of a very practical nature to deal with behaviour management. It seems to be the most common reason why teachers leave the profession in their first year and so must be addressed early on in any induction programme.

Professional support

Professional support is key to the success of the induction year. NQTs may need colleagues to take a range of roles, including:

- planning partner
- colleague
- friend
- supporter
- counsellor
- assessor

- helper
- disciplinarian of pupils
- adviser
- critical friend
- facilitator
- motivator
- expert practitioner
- organizer
- monitor of progress
- trainer
- protector
- parent.

Clearly, an induction tutor could not and should not take on all these roles. The whole staff is responsible for inducting a new teacher, and often people will take on certain roles naturally (Bubb, 2000a, p. 11). Problems may arise when key roles are not taken by someone in the NQT's life. Equally problematic is when one person takes on too many roles or when people assume erroneously that someone else is taking a role.

The induction tutor role is crucial. Here are positive comments that a group of NQTs made about their induction tutors (ibid., p. 14):

- They were always available for advice.
- They gave me a regular meeting time, even though they were busy.
- They were genuinely interested in how I was doing.
- They were honest and open, which encouraged trust.
- They listened to me – and did not impose their own views.
- They made practical suggestions.
- They shared their expertise, ideas and resources.
- They were encouraging and optimistic – they made me feel good.
- They stopped me working myself into the ground by setting realistic objectives.
- They weren't perfect themselves, which was reassuring!
- They looked after me, keeping parents and the head off my back.
- Their feedback after observations was useful – it was good to get some praise and ideas for improvements.
- They were well organized, and if they said they'd do something they did it.

More than anything, NQTs value someone who can give them time. This is a very precious resource. Induction tutors often have many other time-consuming roles and their time spent on induction is rarely funded. As ever, much has to be done on good will or it does not happen. Induction tutors should want to do the job and be suited to it, otherwise the NQT will suffer such as in this case: 'She is very seldom there for me. I don't feel that I can talk to her, she always seems to be looking down on me, she isn't a friend and certainly isn't a shoulder to cry on.'

9

Reducing the variability of induction experience

Research has highlighted the variability of new teachers' experiences (HMI, 1988; Earley and Kinder, 1994). One of the benefits of England's induction policy is that it should help standardize the provision that new teachers receive across and within schools. Though induction provision appears to have improved, there are still too many NQTs who do not get their 10-per-cent reduced timetable. This reduction is a crucial part of induction, without which other elements, such as observing other colleagues, cannot be achieved.

My own research (Bubb 2000b) found that schools' interpretation of what was a 'good enough' meeting of the induction standards varied and this was felt to be unfair by NQTs. It seems a flaw in the system that decisions are made so subjectively by induction tutors and headteachers with only limited input from LEA, university or OFSTED specialists in this field.

Although the government's induction circular (DfEE, 1999) makes clear that NQTs are responsible for raising concerns with their school and appropriate body, this is hard to do in practice. Complaining is always uncomfortable, and NQTs are in a particularly tricky situation, since the headteacher is responsible for recommending whether they pass or not. As one NQT wrote (Bubb, 2001, p. 19):

> It is very difficult to discuss problems. I want to pass my induction year and, if this means keeping my head down and mouth shut, that's what I'll do. The alternative is to highlight problems with my support and then have to face awkward times with my induction tutor or head, with the implications that might have on whether they pass or fail me.

Conclusion – the second and third years

The government's continuing professional development (CPD) strategy, launched in March 2001 (DfES, 2001b), emphasizes 'learning from each other and from what works'. An exciting part of this strategy is the Early Professional Development (EPD) pilot in 12 LEAs which targets resources towards teachers in their second and third years of teaching, in a similar way to induction. These teachers will have about £2100 in their second year and £1600 in their third year to spend on activities to help them become even more effective. It is hoped that this continued support and development will enhance the induction year and contribute towards greater teacher retention.

REFERENCES

Bubb, S. (2000a) *The Effective Induction of Newly Qualified Primary Teachers: An Induction Tutor's Handbook*, London: David Fulton Publishers.

Bubb, S. (2000b) *Statutory Induction – A Fair Deal for All?*, Viewpoint Series no. 12, London: Institute of Education.

Bubb, S. (2001) *A Newly Qualified Teacher's Manual: How to Meet the Induction Standards*, London: David Fulton Publishers.

Bubb, S., Heilbronn, R., Jones, C., Totterdell, M. and Bailey, M. (2002) *Improving Induction*, London: Routledge/Falmer Press.

DfEE (1998) *Teaching: High Status, High Standards*, Circular 4/98, London: Department for Education and Employment.

DfEE (1999) *The Induction Period for Newly Qualified Teachers*, Circular 5/99. London: Department for Education and Employment.

DfES (2001a) *Fast Track Teaching Programme*, London: Department for Education and Skills.

DfES (2001b) *Continuing Professional Development Strategy*, London: Department for Education and Skills.

Earley, P. and Kinder, K. (1994) *Initiation Rites – Effective Induction Practices for New Teachers*, Slough: NFER.

HMI (1988) *The New Teacher in School*, London, HMSO.

TES (2001) *The Times Educational Supplement* website www.tes.co.uk/staffroom/list_threads.asp?id=18085 (accessed 11 December 2001).

Tickle, L. (2000). *Teacher Induction: The Way Ahead*, Buckingham: Open University Press.

TTA (2001) *Career Entry Profile*, London: Teacher Training Agency.

9

CHAPTER 57

Continuing professional development for teachers

AGNES MCMAHON

Initiatives to increase pupil learning and improve the quality of schooling cannot succeed without the active support and cooperation of a skilled and dynamic teacher force. This fact is widely recognized and explains why the problem of how best to promote the continuing professional development of teachers is one that receives international attention. Yet, as Miles (1995) has noted, much professional development is unsatisfactory; indeed he argues that it is pedagogically naïve and does not lead to an increase in teacher knowledge, skills or commitment. This chapter examines what is understood by professional development, explores some of the limitations of current methods of provision and suggests how teacher professional development might be reinvigorated. The focus is on teachers rather than headteachers/school leaders but the implications for school leadership and management will be highlighted.

Changing contexts for teacher professional development

References to teacher professional development are usually now prefaced with the word 'continuing' in recognition of the need for ongoing development of teachers' knowledge and professional skills if teachers are to be effective in today's schools. Education systems internationally are striving to raise levels of student achievement and improve schools, and this effort has led to restructuring and multiple change at all levels and to increased monitoring of schools and teacher performance. Added to this are the challenges posed by the introduction of new technology and regular curriculum changes, which have led either to new forms of pedagogy (for example for literacy and numeracy) or to new subjects (for example health education, citizenship). Perhaps understandably, studies of teachers in the UK report that teachers are working long hours and are experiencing high levels of stress (Travers and Cooper, 1996; PricewaterhouseCoopers, 2001) and the government is increasingly concerned about problems of teacher recruitment and retention. There is some evidence that this pattern is replicated in other countries.

What is professional development?

Definitions of professional development vary in scope and may be contested. The statement that: 'By professional development we mean any activity that increases the skills, knowledge or understanding of teachers, and their effectiveness in schools' (DfEE, 2001, p. 3) is wide ranging but gives little sense of direction. In contrast, Bolam (2002) defines professional development as:

- an ongoing process of education, training, learning and support activities;
- taking place in either external or work-based settings;
- proactively engaged in by qualified, professional teachers, headteachers and other school leaders;
- aimed primarily at promoting learning and development of their professional knowledge, skills and values;
- helping them to decide on and implement valued changes in their teaching and leadership behaviour;
- enabling them to educate their students more effectively;
- achieving an agreed balance between individual, school and national needs.

Though comprehensive, all these points could be elaborated further. In particular the definition highlights the notion of individual commitment to learning by referring to a proactive engagement that implies a degree of personal choice. The need to clarify professional values is emphasized. Also, professional development is seen as an ongoing process that is achieved through different activities, education (acquisition of theoretical knowledge and skills through longer-term study), training (usually interpreted as being focused on the acquisition of specific knowledge or skills) and the learning and support that would normally be provided in the workplace.

Any discussion of professional development gives rise to debate about what it means to be a professional and the extent to which professionals should be able to exercise autonomy in their work. Although the focus here is on professional development, the answers to questions such as whether the individual teacher or the employer has the main responsibility for ensuring that staff receive professional development, what should be the focus and content of development activities and how they should be provided are clearly influenced by views about teachers as professionals. In practice some mid-point seems to be emerging, where definitions of the teacher as professional include that they take responsibility for their own learning, but receive appropriate support to do this within an accountability framework. One example is the professional code for teachers developed by the English General Teaching Council (2001), which has a model of teachers as reflective practitioners, enhancing their knowledge and skills so as to adapt their teaching to new knowledge and technologies.

Factors that influence teacher learning

Teacher learning is influenced by the characteristics of the individual learner, the context in which he/she works and the wider external educational context and policy framework (Stoll, 1999). The perceived significance of these factors will differ according to the theoretical perspective adopted, for example whether professional development is viewed in terms of an individual career journey or as something that is promoted or limited by the organizational context (Guskey and Huberman, 1995).

Characteristics of the individual learner

Learning is not an automatic process; at some level there has to be an individual decision to engage with the learning opportunity. Such a decision will be influenced by judgements about the perceived relevance of the learning experience, the effort and commitment that will be required and the consequences of failure. Learning can be a risky business and at particular times individuals may feel that they do not have the time or the confidence to engage. Individuals have a preferred learning style and the active, experiential approach that is enjoyed by one teacher may be rejected by a colleague who would prefer a more tightly structured didactic method. Teachers need specialized knowledge and a repertoire of pedagogical skills and, as Eraut (1994) reminds us, such professional knowledge is developed and refined in use. The concept of the teacher as reflective practitioner has been widely adopted and central to this is the need for teachers to develop the ability to reflect critically on their behaviour, alone or with the help of colleagues, so as to develop a deeper understanding of the learning process and gain insights about how it can be improved.

Individual development needs will also be shaped by factors such as length of experience, level of responsibility and possibly also gender and ethnicity. The professional development needs of a beginning teacher are likely to be very different from those of an expert teacher in mid-career who is taking on a senior leadership role.

The organizational context

A teacher's workplace will inevitably have a powerful influence on their attitudes to learning and professional development. The culture and ethos of the school, the quality of leadership and administration, the availability of resources, whether or not there is a calm and orderly atmosphere and the level of workload will in part determine whether teachers have any space or energy to devote to their professional development. Perhaps even more important is the attitude towards teacher learning demonstrated by school leaders. Tangible evidence that a school is aiming to promote professional development would include some procedures for reviewing individual needs (for example appraisal, classroom observation), regular support programmes (for example induction for new staff) and opportunities for staff to engage in development and training. Possibly even more important is whether teachers feel valued; if they are encouraged to adopt a questioning, critical approach to their teaching; and if innovation and experiment are supported or whether they are cautious about taking risks for fear of blame if unsuccessful.

The external context

The status of the teaching profession in any society is influenced by the national educational policy framework. Issues about teacher recruitment and retention, job satisfaction and teacher quality are largely shaped by policies on salary, hours of work, the nature of initial training and the level of support for continuing development.

Limitations of current approaches to professional development

Governments across the world have invested large sums of money in teacher development, yet the impact on teacher learning has often been regarded as disappointing. Why is this so? Two possible underlying reasons are that providers have paid insufficient attention to the needs of teachers as learners and, as a corollary, not all teachers have accepted that they should engage in continuing development. Experience in England and Wales is illustrative here. Although between the 1960s and 1980s provision of development activities was focused on meeting the needs of individual professionals, this approach was widely criticized because only a proportion of the teacher force participated and there was little perceived impact on learning and teaching in schools. Changes in the wider policy context and in funding procedures fostered a move to school-focused professional development, which targeted all teachers and prioritized organizational as well as individual needs. Significant features were the introduction of five compulsory training days for each teacher and the creation of a quasi-market in which schools received government funding to provide and buy training and consultancy services within a framework of national priority topics (Bolam, 2002).

This approach was intended to meet both individual and organizational needs but there is some evidence of shortcomings. A study of secondary school teachers' experience of professional development (McMahon, 1999) revealed that there were considerable differences between schools in the resources available for provision; that school procedures for supporting professional development were often inadequate (for example little induction for new staff, weak systems of staff appraisal, no classroom observation, little in-school support for teachers attempting to be innovative in their practice) and that the needs of the organization were given priority. So, for example, two or more of the professional development days were routinely allocated for whole-school administrative and planning tasks, and training for teachers in topics recognized as school development needs (for example information technology) was given priority over other requests (for example creative arts). School-based training events were normally presented to the whole staff with little or no account taken of differences among teachers in their existing knowledge and experience or their preferred learning style.

A further limitation has been in the nature of the development opportunities provided for teachers. Restructuring and the introduction of major curriculum innovations (for example a national literacy strategy) must be accompanied by training programmes for staff if they are to be implemented successfully. Unfortunately, however, these training programmes are often short briefing sessions that raise awareness of the innovation but are insufficient as a means of changing practice. If the aim is to enable people to master a complex new skill or teaching strategy, Joyce and Showers (1995) recommend that training should include:

- presentation of theory
- modelling or demonstration of the new approach
- practice in a workshop setting
- structured feedback
- direct coaching about how to use the new skill or approach.

9

Provision of all five training components would require a substantial input over an extended period of time, but this rarely occurs. However, professional development cannot be obtained solely through participation in training programmes. For example, Little (1993) has argued that, although training models intended to develop particular skills may work well for technical innovations or particular classroom practices, they are unlikely to help teachers develop the broader range of skills they now require.

Ways forward for professional development?

The core purpose of teaching is to enhance pupil learning. It follows from this not just that teachers should strive to enhance their knowledge and skills but that questions are raised about the impact of teacher professional development on student learning. Although such questions are problematic, given the number of variables influencing student outcomes and the difficulty of establishing any direct links back to the teacher's experience, it is likely that employers and teachers themselves will be more ready in future to consider the relevance and likely impact of particular development activities before making any commitment to participate. Three other trends are worthy of mention: professional development standards and codes, evidence-informed practice and the concept of the professional learning community.

Standards for professional development

The Teacher Training Agency in England and Wales has developed a framework of professional standards for teachers at four career stages: newly qualified teachers, special needs teachers, subject leaders and headteachers (TTA, 1998). This framework can be seen as a curriculum for professional development that specifies the knowledge, skills, tasks and responsibilities expected of teachers at the different career points and which is linked to qualifications at two points (initial training and for headteachers). Although there is little evidence to date about the impact of this framework on teacher learning, it is already influencing the content of professional development programmes and is being used to set benchmarks for teacher assessment. Prior to this, the National Board of Professional Teacher Standards in the USA had developed standards and assessment procedures for teachers based on five principles (NBPTS, 1993):

- teachers are committed to students and their learning;
- teachers know the subject they teach and how to teach those subjects to students;
- teachers are responsible for managing and monitoring students' learning;
- teachers think systematically about their practice and learn from experience;
- teachers are members of learning communities.

These are clear attempts to specify what teachers need to know and do and as such they can be used as guidelines that teachers can refer to when considering their own professional and career development.

Evidence-informed practice

Concerns about school effectiveness and school improvement have resulted in England and other countries in a focus on evidence-informed practice and with 'what works'. This approach has several implications for professional development; not least is the suggestion that teachers should adopt a more research-oriented approach to their work. There are several ways in which this could be implemented. School staff working individually or in groups could conduct research on their own practice, for example through an action research project. Greater use could be made of data about student, staff and school performance, using the information for diagnostic purposes and to inform practice. Although the collection and analysis of data about student learning has long been a routine activity in schools, it has been less common for teachers to reflect collectively about what the data can tell them about their own practice so that, in the term used by Joyce, Calhoun and Hopkins (1999), they become information-rich.

Professional learning communities

The concept of a school as a professional learning community is a powerful image for the future of teacher development. Increased awareness of the factors that influence learning, coupled with the realization that many professional development activities have limited impact, inform the vision of the school as a community where teachers could work more collaboratively with colleagues, students and parents with a resultant improvement in the quality of learning and teaching. King and Newman (2001) argue that teacher learning is most likely to occur when teachers:

- can concentrate on instruction and student outcomes in the specific contexts in which they teach;
- have sustained opportunities to study, to experiment with and to receive helpful feedback on specific innovations;
- have opportunities to collaborate with professional peers, both within and outside their schools, along with access to the expertise of researchers.

The concept of the professional community emphasizes the development of shared values and a mutually supportive culture in which teachers take joint responsibility for student learning. Much of the early research and writing about professional learning communities has taken place in North America, but other countries are now adopting these ideas.

Implications for school leaders

9

If the quality of learning and teaching in schools is to improve, then the school has to foster and encourage teacher as well as student learning. This is the key message that emerges from recent research and it has considerable implications for school leaders. It will not be sufficient just to provide the building blocks for a professional development programme (for example systems for identifying individual and organizational needs; support for and provision of professional development activities). Rather what is required is that leaders take the initiative in establishing a collaborative and supportive culture in the school in which teachers can share ideas about how best to improve learning and teaching and are encouraged to investigate and be innovative. Achieving such a culture will not be an easy task. Practical issues such as organizing the timetable so that teachers have time to reflect on their work and to meet with colleagues will be fundamental, but leaders also need to show that they value and celebrate teachers' work and learning and indeed lead by example by becoming active participants in the learning community.

Conclusion

The nature of the school as an organization is likely to change in the years ahead. Teachers have come to expect regular curriculum renewal, but other factors such as the widespread use of information technology and moves to employ more staff as aides or auxiliary helpers suggest that in future teachers will act more as facilitators of learning and managers of a team of support staff than as direct instructors. There is no evidence of a reduction in the pace of change and teachers will need to update their knowledge and skills through continuing professional development if they are to be effective. Furthermore, the image of the teacher as an autonomous professional is being replaced by the concept of the school as a learning community in which the teacher works collectively as a member of a wider group of staff in a joint effort to improve the quality of learning. However, as yet there is little or no research that has investigated the impact of teacher professional development on student learning and, until this issue has been addressed, questions about its relative importance will continue to be raised.

REFERENCES

Bolam, R. (2002) 'Professional development and professionalism' in Bush, T. and Bell, L. *Educational Management: Principles and Practice*, London: Paul Chapman Publishing.

DfEE (2001) *Learning and Teaching : A Strategy for Professional Development*, London: Department for Education and Employment.

Eraut, M. (1994) *Developing Professional Knowledge and Competence*, London: Falmer Press.

Guskey, T.R. and Huberman, M. (1995) 'Introduction' in Guskey, T.R. and Huberman, M. (eds) *Professional Development in Education*, New York: Teachers' College Press.

Joyce, B., Calhoun, E. and Hopkins, D. (1999) *The New Structure of School Improvement*, Buckingham: Open University Press.

Joyce, B. and Showers, B. (1995) Student Achievement through Staff Development, 2nd end, White Plains, NY: Longman.

King, M.B. and Newman, F.M. (2001) 'Building school capacity through professional development: conceptual and empirical considerations', *International Journal of Educational Management*, 15 (2), pp. 86–93.

Little, J.W. (1993) 'Teachers' professional development in a climate of educational reform', *Educational Evaluation and Policy Analysis*, 15 (2), pp. 129–51.

McMahon, A. (1999) 'Promoting continuing professional development for teachers: an achievable target for school leaders?' in Bush, T., Bell, L., Bolam, R., Glatter, R. and Ribbins, P. (eds) *Educational Management: Redefining Theory, Policy and Practice*, London: Paul Chapman Publishing.

Miles, M.B. (1995) 'Foreword' in Guskey, T.R. and Huberman, M. (eds) *Professional Development in Education*, New York, NY: Teachers' College Press.

NBPTS (1993) *What Should Teachers Know and Be Able to Do?*, Detroit, MI: National Board for Professional Teaching Standards.

PricewaterhouseCoopers (2001) *Teacher Workload Study: Final Report*, London: DfES.

Stoll, L. (1999) 'Realising our potential: understanding and developing capacity for lasting improvement', *School Effectiveness and School Improvement*, 10 (4), pp. 503–32.

TTA (1998) *National Standards*, London: Teacher Training Agency.

Travers, C.J. and Cooper, C.L. (1996) *Teachers Under Pressure: Stress in the Teaching Profession*, London: Routledge.

9

CHAPTER 58

Managing morale, job satisfaction and motivation

....

LINDA EVANS

Ask any member of the general public how to raise teacher morale and you are likely to meet with the response: 'Increase their pay'. There is a general assumption, reflecting conventional wisdom, that morale and motivation are influenced by what Nias (1981) calls 'extrinsic' factors – factors that are externally, and in many cases centrally, initiated and imposed, such as salary policies, conditions of service, and educational reforms. Indeed, it is this assumption that underlies the practice of performance-related pay, or merit pay, which is predicated on acceptance of the expectancy theory of motivation and productivity: individuals are more likely to put effort into their work if there is an anticipated reward that they value.

There is, however, considerable research evidence that identifies factors much closer to home – institution-specific factors – as the key influences on job-related attitudes (Ball, 1987; Chase, 1953; Farrugia, 1986; Hayes and Ross, 1989; Nias, 1989; Nias, Southworth and Yeomans, 1989; Veal, Clift and Holland, 1989). My own research corroborates these findings. Studies of morale, job satisfaction and motivation in school teachers (Evans 1998, 1999) revealed that, whilst externally imposed factors do influence job-related attitudes, their impact is considerably less potent than that of school-specific factors. In particular, it was found that leadership is a significant influence on how teachers feel about their work and about themselves at work: 'The most strikingly common factor to emerge as influential on teachers' morale, job satisfaction and motivation is school leadership ... the leadership effected by their headteachers was clearly a key determinant of how teachers felt about their jobs' (Evans, 1998, p. 118). 'My research findings revealed, categorically, that the greatest influences on teacher morale, job satisfaction and motivation are school leadership and management' (Evans, 1999, p. 17).

However, since making these assertions, I have moved on. Precisely how I have moved on and where my most recent analyses have taken me I explain in a later section of this chapter. First, to develop an understanding of morale, job satisfaction and motivation, I outline what research has revealed about these three concepts – about their nature and their relationship to each other.

Understanding morale, job satisfaction and motivation

Job satisfaction, morale, and motivation are not obscure terms. Everybody seems to know what they mean. There does not appear to be anything complex about them. But how many people could actually explain precisely what morale is, or what job satisfaction is, or what the difference between the two is? There is, of course, no real need for most people to be able to define these job-related attitudes, nor to develop anything more than an understanding of them that is perfectly adequate for day-to-day use. Yet for those who have made them the focus of serious academic study, morale, job satisfaction and motivation have been analysed as concepts, examined, discussed and defined.

Of the three, morale seems to have been the most difficult concept to get to grips with. One source of disagreement has been whether it may be applied to individuals, or whether it relates only to groups. My own work has led me to interpret morale as primarily an attribute of the individual, which is determined in relation to individual goals. Group morale certainly exists, but it is merely the collectivization of the morale of the individuals who form the group.

The distinction between morale and job satisfaction is also important to clarify. Although they are often used interchangeably, morale and job satisfaction are not the same thing. The distinction between them is that job satisfaction is present-oriented and morale is future-oriented. Both are states of mind, but satisfaction is a response to a situation whereas morale is anticipatory. The teacher who believes, for example, that the appointment of a new headteacher or principal to their school will improve the quality of their working life is manifesting high morale. The teacher who, on the other hand, is dissatisfied with their current headteacher is manifesting low job-satisfaction. Thus high morale may exist alongside dissatisfaction. Evaluations of the present constitute job satisfaction-related issues, whereas anticipation of the future constitutes morale.

What influences morale, job satisfaction and motivation?

Identifying what influences morale, job satisfaction and motivation is not straightforward. It is complicated by the combination of the multifaceted and multilayered nature of the influence and the individuality of the nature and level of response to these influences.

First, research has revealed job-related attitudes to be influenced primarily by institution-specific factors. This is not to say that externally imposed factors do not influence attitudes; merely that their influence is less potent than is often supposed. The reason why institution-specific issues, situations and circumstances evidently take precedence as influential factors is that these institution-specific issues, situations and circumstances constitute the reality and the substance of teachers' working lives. Centrally initiated conditions, or, indeed, any conditions that emanate from outside of the contexts in which teachers work, only become real for, and meaningful and relevant to, teachers when they become contextualized. Until they are effected within the real contexts in which teachers work, such conditions are, in reality, non-operational; they exist only in abstract form, as ideas, principles or rhetoric. They do not constitute reality.

Imposed reform does not, therefore, impact upon teachers' lives until it is introduced into their work contexts – their schools or colleges. The low status of teachers in
society does not, as an issue, encroach upon a teacher's life until it is introduced into it
– in the form of a derogatory remark, or a self-conception that reflects consciousness
of belonging to a profession that is held in low esteem, or a perception of being
unfavourably compared with other professionals. The problem of class sizes does not
become a problem for teachers until it occurs in their own schools. It is only within
the contexts of their own lives that things matter to people. However, sometimes this
contextualization may involve only consciousness, and may not be dependent upon
direct, activity-based experience. Under these circumstances, issues that, for example,
are at odds with ideologies, offend sensibilities, or conflict with values, constitute
introduction into people's lives, and, therefore, realization, through contextualization.

It is also important to recognize that it is within the contexts in which teachers
work that policy and initiatives that emanate from outside these contexts are,
through their realization, adopted, adapted, institutionalized and effected in ways
that may make them more, or less, acceptable to teachers than they were in their
conceptual form. It is at school or college level that government-imposed reforms
or district or local initiatives may be effected in ways that are either palatable to, or
that alienate, teachers and it is therefore at this level that teachers' morale, job satisfaction and motivation are affected.

But precisely what school or college-specific factors influence teachers' attitudes
to their work? The answer is that it depends – it depends on the individual teacher.
My research has revealed three interrelated factors to underpin the individuality
dimension of morale, job satisfaction and motivation: relative perspective, realistic
expectations and professionality.

Relative perspective

Relative perspective is the individual's perspective on her/his situation in relation
to comparable situations. In the context of work situations, for example, relative
perspectives may incorporate consideration of previous posts – in whole or in part
– or of other institutions, or of colleagues' situations. The current job-related situation is perceived and evaluated in relation to other jobs or occupations, former
jobs and knowledge of the situations of colleagues in other institutions or departments. Relative perspective also includes consideration of the work-related
situation in relation to the rest of one's life. This consideration includes the relative prioritization of work and personal life.

Realistic expectations

Realistic expectations are influenced by relative perspective. They do not necessarily reflect individuals' ideals; rather, they reflect what the individual realistically
expects from her/his work-related situation.

Professionality

Through an iterative process, professionality both influences and is influenced by
realistic expectations and relative perspective. Professionality is not the same as
professionalism. The term appears to have been introduced by Hoyle (1975), who

presented a continuum of teachers' professionality ranging from 'extended' to 'restricted'. 'Restricted' professionality is described as essentially reliant upon experience and intuition and is guided by a narrow, classroom-based perspective that values whatever is related to the day-to-day practicalities of teaching. 'Extended' professionality, at the other end of the continuum, carries a much wider vision of what education involves, values the theory underpinning pedagogy and generally adopts a much more reasoned and analytical approach to the job. I use the term 'professionality orientation' to relate to individuals' orientation towards either of these two extremes. Thus a 'restricted' professional would be less analytical, less reflective, less introspective and apply a less intellectual and developmental approach to their teaching than would an 'extended' professional.

Job-related ideals

Intra-institutional disparity is one of the key findings of my research into teachers' attitudes to their work, reflecting a complex combination of individuals' professionality orientations, realistic expectations and relative perspectives. Essentially, my research findings have led me to the interpretation that it is perceived proximity to their conception of their job-related ideal that underpins individuals' job-related attitudes. This ideal may not necessarily have been conceptualized as such, but its dimensions begin to take shape through individuals' conceptions of their preferences and priorities. Thus, without consciously conceptualizing his/her ideal job, a teacher who prefers teaching six-year-olds to 14-year-olds, who welcomes the challenges posed by working in a socially disadvantaged community and is uninterested in teaching in affluent suburbia, is indicating something of the nature of his/her ideal job.

The conception of one's ideal job is dynamic, being liable to fluctuation and modification. Job-related ideals – or ideal jobs – reflect individuals' current values, needs and expectations. These are influenced by relative perspective and they underpin professionality orientation and realistic expectations. Since these vary from individual to individual, what satisfies one teacher may not necessarily satisfy another, and the school that suits one may not suit another. An 'extended' professional may derive much satisfaction, motivation and sustain high levels of morale in a school that is 'on-the-ball' in relation to policy and practice, that presents him/her with professional challenges and that allows him/her to develop intellectually. The same school may provide a working environment that imposes stressful, unachievable and unwelcome challenges and standards on a 'restricted' professional.

The common thread

Cutting across the individuality of teacher morale, job satisfaction and motivation is a common thread. No matter what their professionality orientation, nor the specific nature of their realistic expectations and their relative perspectives, teachers achieve job fulfilment, high morale and motivation through a process that culminates in their feeling a sense of significant achievement (see Evans, 1998 and 1999 for details of the stages involved in the process whereby individuals experience job fulfilment). The individuality dimension means that there is much diversity in relation to precisely how teachers are able to feel a sense of achievement. For some, the source of a sense of achievement may lie in feeling that they have contributed to children's learning; for others, it lies in believing that they have contributed towards formulating an effective school policy.

A good teacher–school match provides greater opportunities than does mismatch for experiencing high levels of job satisfaction, morale and motivation, through the greater opportunities that it provides for feeling – and anticipating continuing to feel – a sense of achievement. A good match involves shared ideologies, values and priorities, which very often reflect shared, or similar, professionality orientations on the part of teacher and principal or headteacher – or other key leaders – and a shared vision of what the school or college should become and how it should develop. Yet, while the degree of match between teacher and leader is certainly important, my most recent analyses (Evans, 2001) have led me to identify teachers' work contexts as a more fundamental influence on morale, job satisfaction and motivation. Specifically, the degree of compatibility between teachers' professional and personal values and ideologies and the values and ideologies reflected in the contexts within which they work leads to the identification of a continuum of work-context compatibility in relation to the individual. My current definition of a work context is: 'the situation and circumstances, arising out of a combination and interrelationship of institutionally – and externally – imposed conditions, that constitute the environment and culture within which an individual carries out her/his job'. Leadership is not, fundamentally, in itself, an attitudes-influencing factor. Rather, it is the medium through which are transmitted the values and ideologies represented by the contexts in which people work. Leadership is seen to be an attitudes-influencing factor because it imposes considerable influence on these work contexts, either actively or – in the case of ineffective, *laissez-faire* leadership – by default.

The basis of a good match is an 'uncompromising context': a work context that does not require individuals to compromise their views, values and ideologies. A 'compromising context', on the other hand, is one that fails, to varying degrees, to accommodate teachers' views, values and ideologies. My research has revealed six specific issues that, in a work context, matter to people and which are incorporated into every conception of an 'ideal job'. Job-related ideals incorporate ethical, epistemological, affective, professional, economic and egocentric considerations to encompass views on:

- equity and justice
- pedagogy or androgogy
- organizational efficiency
- interpersonal relations
- collegiality
- self-conception and self-image.

Implications for policy and practice in educational management and leadership

Since it is at institutional level that morale, job satisfaction and motivation are influenced most of all, it is at this level that they are best able to be enhanced and improved. Institutional leadership and management can do much to foster positive job-related attitudes by helping to create and sustain work contexts that are conducive to high morale, job satisfaction and motivation. It is to the provision of work contexts that are congruent with individuals' values, ideologies and expectations in relation to the six issues identified above that leadership may most effectively contribute. This is not simple and straightforward to achieve because these values, ideologies and expectations vary from individual to individual. The leader who, in the interests of raising morale and increasing job satisfaction and motivation, wants to shape uncompromising contexts clearly has their work cut out. How, then, may work contexts be shaped in order to cater for diversity? How may individual, rather than simply a majority of, needs be met? I suggest what I refer to as a 'teacher-centred' approach to educational leadership.

Essentially, the teacher-centred approach parallels – and takes its name from – a child-centred approach to teaching. I present it as an educational management and leadership ideology that is predicated upon acceptance that leaders and managers have as much responsibility towards the staff whom they lead and manage as they do towards the pupils and students within their institution, and that this responsibility extends as far as endeavouring to meet as many individual needs as possible, within the confines imposed by having to consider more corporate needs. Teacher-centred leaders behave towards the staff whom they lead with as much care and solicitude and interest in their welfare as would child-centred teachers towards the pupils in their care. To become teacher-centred in their approach to staff management then, by applying a child-centred parallel, primary school headteachers need to consider themselves as, effectively, class teachers on a larger scale, their schools as their classrooms writ large, and their teacher colleagues as their classes of pupils, in a more mature state. This involves adopting a teacher-centred leadership philosophy and incorporating into their management an appropriate organizational structure.

Teacher-centred leadership focuses on the individuals that make up a staff, rather than a staff unit as a whole; it treats individuals differently and is responsive to the diversity that constitutes 'the staff'. The teacher-centred leader would try to develop a work context that, underpinned by a professional culture of tolerance, cooperation, compromise and consideration for others, is as uncompromising as possible for as many individuals as possible for as much of the time as possible. What is needed, in order to get the very best out of teachers, is leadership and management that acknowledges and respects the diversity of teachers' individual job-related needs. Managing morale, job satisfaction and motivation involves a recognition of the individuality that underpins teachers' attitudes to their work, an understanding of the nature of those attitudes, and a commitment to adopting radically different approaches that incorporate consideration of what matters to people in the contexts of their work.

It is time, too, to introduce changes to our conception of the nature, the role and the status of leadership. Traditionally, leadership is perceived within hierarchical decision-making structures as a high-status activity, and one that affords those who lead a position at the top of the hierarchy pyramid: leaders are generally accepted as those to whom others – namely, the 'led' – defer, and are accountable. A radical alternative to this traditional view, and one that builds on and extends the idea of teacher-centred leadership, recognizes leadership as a service provided by leaders to those who are being led. By extension, this idea incorporates acceptance that leaders are accountable to those whom they lead for the quality of the service that they provide. Such a conception of leadership would involve a shift of emphasis from leaders' authority over, to their responsibility towards, others. What is clear from research in this area, as well as much anecdotal evidence, is the need to address some of the problems with educational leadership policy and practice that create work contexts that fail to bring out the best in teachers. It is an idea that needs developing if it is to be seriously considered as a radically different policy. I present it here merely as food for thought.

REFERENCES

Ball, S.J. (1987) *The Micro-Politics of the School*, London: Routledge.

Chase, F. S. (1953) 'Professional leadership and teacher morale', *Administrator's Notebook*, 1 (8), pp. 1–4.

Evans, L. (1998) *Teacher Morale, Job Satisfaction and Motivation*, London: Paul Chapman Publishing.

Evans, L. (1999) *Managing to Motivate: a Guide for School Leaders*, London: Cassell.

Evans, L. (2001) 'Delving deeper into morale, job satisfaction and motivation among education professionals: re-examining the leadership dimension', *Educational Management and Administration*, 29 (3), pp. 291-306.

Farrugia, C. (1986) 'Career-choice and sources of occupational satisfaction and frustration among teachers in Malta', *Comparative Education*, 22 (3), pp. 221–31.

Hayes, L.F. and Ross, D.D. (1989) 'Trust versus control: the impact of school leadership on teacher reflection', *International Journal of Qualitative Studies in Education*, 2 (4), pp. 335–50.

Hoyle, E. (1975) 'Professionality, professionalism and control in teaching' in Houghton, V., McHugh, R. and Morgan, C. (eds), *Management in Education: the Management of Organisations and Individuals*, London: Ward Lock Educational in association with Open University Press, pp. 314–20.

Nias, J. (1981) 'Teacher satisfaction and dissatisfaction: Herzberg's "two-factor" hypothesis revisited', *British Journal of Sociology of Education*, 2 (3), pp. 235–46.

Nias, J. (1989) *Primary Teachers Talking: A Study of Teaching as Work*, London: Routledge.

Nias, J., Southworth, G. and Yeomans, R. (1989) *Staff Relationships in the Primary School: A Study of Organisational Cultures*, London: Cassell.

Veal, M.L., Clift, R. and Holland, P. (1989) 'School contexts that encourage reflection: teacher perceptions', *International Journal of Qualitative Studies in Education*, 2 (4), pp. 315–33.

CHAPTER 59

Coaching and mentoring in education

DAVID CLUTTERBUCK

Coaching and mentoring are complementary and often confused approaches to the management of learning. Their evolution in the world of education has paralleled that in other areas of society – in sport, in employment, the rehabilitation of offenders and even in managing the difficult (for many) transition into retirement. In this chapter, I attempt to sort out some of the confusion in terminology, explore some of the applications of mentoring within education (and particularly within the personal development of both junior and senior teaching staff) and look at some of the skills required by both coach/ mentor and the learner.

Because teachers make a vocation of stimulating learning in others, it is often easy to overlook the fact that the instinct to pass on the benefit of one's accumulated experience is a biological imperative. Our prehistoric ancestors apparently achieved their dominance of the Earth in large part as a result of this instinct, which ensured that the stock of knowledge and skills within a tribe was maintained and expanded. This urge to pass on, together with the equally powerful instinct of curiosity, lie behind the vast storehouses of knowledge that drive modern science and society. While one of the most obvious expressions, in higher education at least, is the near-obsession with publishing papers, the application of coaching and mentoring is equally pervasive.

Teaching, coaching and mentoring: core differences and similarities

Nonetheless, coaching and mentoring have a barrier to overcome within the teaching profession. Teachers teach. The behaviours required in teaching, coaching and mentoring are subtly different, but not always recognized as such. Look around you on any crowded beach or in any public gathering. It does not take long to identify the experienced teacher. The classroom manner projects through all the noise and clutter and transfers so easily to other environments. Effective teachers establish and maintain a relationship that is of necessity adult to child, even in a university environment – hence the insistence on building lecture theatres, which are designed to minimize the interaction between students and focus attention on the teacher. The primary flow in this context is one of information and concept, with the internalization of learning undertaken in separate activities, such as self-study, group work or tutorials. Moreover, this flow is essentially one-way – from the expert to the neophyte. The core of teaching, then, is the art of instruction.

The best teachers transcend this relatively sterile mode and find opportunities to operate in other modes, such as tutor, coach and mentor. They recognize that teaching is not the same as learning. Teaching is something you do to someone else; learning is something the individual does to and for him/herself.

In tutor mode, there is far less attention to and stress upon discipline (not least because of the smaller numbers) and a corresponding shift to a more adult-to-adult tone, albeit with a certain element of parent. The core skill and aim of the tutor is to help the learner acquire knowledge, which we can define as information made useful by being contextualized and relevant to the individual. In tutoring, the first beginnings of a genuine exchange of learning occur – good tutors relish sessions with their charges as an opportunity to add to their own store of knowledge.

Another approach to helping to learn that belongs in this list is that of role model. One reason this role so often gets missed out is that it is typically passive. The importance of role models in the development of young people has been increasingly recognized in recent years, particularly with respect to the development of positive attitudes towards learning and citizenship. Being an *active* role model is a skill that few people consider, let alone acquire, yet it is a critical component of leadership. Active role modelling seems to demand an ability for inclusion – for making the learner feel that, whatever their current level of ability, the meister recognizes their potential and is keen for them to exceed their competence. It also requires a high level of both self-awareness and insight into others. When the role model allows a parent–child relationship to develop, they become in effect a guru figure – a relationship that often leads to rejection and discord as the learner recognizes their guru's imperfections.

Finally, we come to the concept of mentoring, which draws upon or encompasses all of these other roles, but is distinct from them. Mentoring is about helping the other person develop their own fund of wisdom, although it may also sometimes be about sharing one's own accumulated wisdom. Wisdom is the highest level of understanding in a chain that starts with information (what you need to pass paper exams) and continues through knowledge (information organized to make greater sense of one's environment) and skills (knowledge applied to a specific task). Wisdom integrates all of these in a way that allows the learner to both personalize what information and knowledge they acquire, and to extrapolate from their own and other people's experience. Mentoring, again, is always adult-to-adult in tone, even though it may take place across a wide generation gap.

These various roles or styles of helping to learn differ in their closeness (from aloof to one-to-one friendship), the nature of the learning that occurs, the tone adopted, and where the discussions sit on a spectrum from explicit to implicit knowledge (*see* Table 59.1).

In general, the role that a helper adopts depends on three factors:

- The context: for example, it isn't possible to mentor 30 people at the same time.
- The capability of the helper in each of the roles: can the helper adapt from one to the other, with all the necessary changes in tone and style? (A successful mentor might not have the capability to manage a class of 14-year-olds.).
- The learner's need: in general, the less confidence and competence they have in the area of learning, the more structured and explicit the help people are likely to require. However, it is also observable that people who

Table 59.1 *Defining the differences of role types*

Role type	Relationship distance	Learning type	Tone (when effective)	Explicit to implicit spectrum
Mentor	● Close: often a professional friendship; one to one ● Minimal need for structure or discipline	● Wisdom ● High level of mutual learning	Adult to adult	Implicit, intuitive
Role model	● Variable, depending on whether the relationship is active or passive ● Provides example of self-discipline	● Mainly by observation ● Learning often one-way only	Adult to adult	Mixture of implicit and explicit
Coach	● Variable: can be one to one or one to group (e.g. team coaching) ● Helps learner develop own self-discipline and acts as a 'goad' where necessary	● Skills based ● Mostly one-way learning	Adult to adult	Mainly explicit, but encouraging the learner to *experience* for him/herself
Tutor	● Relatively distant: often one to small group ● Moderate requirement for structure and maintaining discipline	● Knowledge based ● Mostly one-way learning	Adult to adult	Mainly explicit, but encouraging the learner to *think* for him/herself
Teacher/ instructor	● Distant: often one to large group ● High requirement for structure and maintaining discipline	● Information based ● Mainly one-way learning	Adult to child	Mainly explicit

feel alienated from society are often highly resistant to a structured, disciplined approach. Coaching and mentoring (particularly the latter) have an excellent track record in helping such people establish a greater sense of self-worth and self-discipline, which enables them to take advantage of more structured learning opportunities.

The competencies issue

Most people have or develop the instinct to coach or mentor at some point in their lives. However, that does not make them any good at it, any more than the instinct to talk makes someone a great orator. The vast majority of coaches and mentors have a modest set of skills, which suffices in most situations. The growing cadre of professional coaches and mentors needs a different level of competence, which is gained from a mixture of study, practice and observation.

Although there are now a number of qualifications in coaching and mentoring, the basis upon which they are awarded is not standard and is in some cases questionable. If you wish to pursue a formal qualification in this area, it is advisable to check that it is:

- recognized or recommended by an appropriate, independent professional body, such as the European Mentoring Centre;
- recognized (depending on the level of qualification) by an appropriate academic institution;
- appropriate in its content and definition to the kind of coaching or mentoring you wish to do (this may seem obvious, but the term 'mentoring' has been applied to a variety of qualifications, not all of them with obvious connections to the subject);
- based on an appropriate mixture of theory, practice and personal reflection – more advanced courses should also involve an element of supervision from an experienced practitioner/facilitator.

Many people, who choose to develop their coaching and/or mentoring skills through some form of certification route, place greater value on the learning process and what they discover about themselves, than on the diploma or other award they achieve at the end. This runs counter to much of the normal academic ethos, but is a fundamental attitudinal competence for effective coaches and mentors.

Each of the roles we explored above has its own basic set of competencies, some of them shared with other roles. Coaches, at the most basic level, require three core skills – experience, observation and feedback. Experience is what allows the coach to assess the learner's current level of competence and confidence and to select:

- an appropriate task for the learner at this stage
- an appropriate style to adopt towards him/her.

Observational skills enable the coach to assess what the learner is doing, against the level of competence they could potentially demonstrate at this stage of skill development. Sub-skills of observation include analysis of visual and rhythmic data (the latter being particularly important in most sports and a surprising variety of jobs) and active listening.

Feedback skills involve sharing the coach's observations with the learner in a way that:

- motivates them to continue
- enables them to plan how to improve
- lets them focus on small elements one at a time.

More capable coaches go a major step further, however. They balance extrinsic observation and feedback (what they see and consider important) against intrinsic observation and feedback (helping the learner to develop the skills to observe, analyse and correct on their own). When the discussion between coach and learner explores a high level of intrinsic data, the pace of learning is typically much faster and the skills are better retained.

Mentors, in general, have little or no opportunity for extrinsic observation and feedback. In most cases, they do not even have third-party feedback on the mentee, because the confidentiality, upon which the relationship is based, would be compromised by discussing the mentee with, say, a teacher or social worker, both of whom might be seen by the mentee as an authority figure. Mentors have to work largely with the mentee's own perceptions and observations.

Mentor competencies therefore tend to be rather more complex. It helps to think of the competences as two sets – practical skills and personal attributes – although these are not totally distinct. Practical skills include:

- Rapport building: the ability to overcome differences in personality and background, to establish a sufficient level of mutual respect and, in many cases, friendship.
- Active, empathetic listening: seeking meaning beyond what is said.
- Analysis: help the mentee work out the logic of the situations they describe, showing how certain behavioural paths or life choices lead to fewer or more career options; identifying patterns of behaviour or outcomes that the mentee may wish to manage differently.
- Challenging: giving constructive challenge in a way that will be accepted by the learner; this is perhaps the most difficult skill to acquire, but it is frequently the one mentees value most.
- Networking: helping the learner develop a much wider support and learning net; it is difficult to do this if the mentor is not an adept networker him/herself.
- Guiding: giving practical advice if necessary, however, effective mentors recognize that they must control the instinct to solve the mentee's problems for them and instead use their practical experience to help the mentee work out their own solutions.

Personal attributes are equally varied, but we can usefully divide them into five pairs, as follows:

- Self-awareness and behavioural awareness: understanding your own strengths and weaknesses, and being open about them helps create rapport and respect. Some understanding of what makes others tick is useful in choosing how to approach their issues – for example, when to listen and when to challenge.
- Relevant experience and sense of proportion: the mentee needs to feel that you have shared or can understand some of the issues they face. The more open-minded the mentor is, the more willing to learn from the experience and the more they are able to place the mentee's issues in a broad context, the more valuable the relationship is likely to be.
- Openness and imagination: the mentor must be sufficiently self-confident to talk about his or her own failures and disappointments, as well as successes. S/he also needs a good conceptual imagination, to help the mentee understand the dynamics of situations they discuss and to develop alternative ways of looking at them.

9

- Commitment to their own learning and interest in developing others: altruistic mentors (people who see the role solely in how they can help the other person) tend to be much less effective than those who see the relationship equally as a significant learning opportunity for themselves.
- Goal clarity and sociability: having a clear idea of what the relationship should achieve and why gives it a shared sense of direction and purpose. At the same time, effective mentors value the relationship for itself – a gradually developing friendship that gives them new, sometimes very different perspectives.

In general, mentoring and coaching relationships deliver greater benefits when the mentee is relatively proactive and the mentor relatively reactive. The learner has to want to be there, to recognize the possibilities inherent in the relationship and to be committed to some form of change in their performance or circumstances.

Learners should be aware that they will get the most out of a mentoring relationship if they:

- take an active role in deciding what they want to discuss and why;
- prepare for each session, thinking through what they want to say and giving examples;
- be very clear about what sort of help they want at each point (for example direct advice or thinking an issue through);
- are prepared to challenge the mentor constructively, rather than simply accept what the mentor says (or worse, disagree silently);
- make the mentor aware of what they are getting out of the sessions together.

They will get more out of a coaching relationship if they:

- demonstrate enthusiasm;
- work with the coach to understand why things do not happen as planned;
- spend time practising and reflecting on their experience.

The future of coaching and mentoring in education

I have a personal vision – shared I think by most or all of my colleagues on the Learning Declaration Group – of a society where learning is valued more than education. Opportunities for learning abound in the twenty-first-century environment and a core skill for educators will (or should already) be the ability to help others develop a wide portfolio of learning approaches. The medium of learning – be it in a classroom or via the internet – is less important than the intimacy of learning. In other words, the information you require is readily available through many sources, but to what extent do you need it personalized to you? To what extent do you need to reflect on the information and contextualize it? Is this something best done alone, or by tapping the experience of other people? Can you learn more through an exchange of learning than through a one-way download?

In my idealized learning society, the process of mentoring will begin at a very early age, with infants first joining school being adopted by older peers. As children grow, they are encouraged in turn to become mentors to others. At each major transition – from junior to senior school, from school to further education, further education to work – the option to have a mentor (or several different mentors) is an automatic consideration. In between these life transitions, young people will be encouraged to use a coach, to develop particular skills areas, either for simple interest's sake or because they will be important in opening out career options.

Throughout the rest of the individual's life, being coached or mentored, coach or mentor (sometimes all of these at the same time) will be a commonplace and natural activity. Whereas companies, education and community institutions currently tend to run separate programmes of coaching or mentoring for their own specific audiences, the barriers will hopefully in future fall sufficiently so that each individual has a wide selection of coaches and mentors to call upon, whenever they need one.

Idealistic as it is, the seeds of this vision of the future are already planted. In industry and commerce the concept of the manager as a supervisor, with little responsibility for learning other than to send people on courses, is increasingly being replaced by the concept of the manager as coach or educator. In more advanced organizations the role has evolved further. Here the manager is becoming a facilitator of learning, responsible for creating the environment and the helping networks by which increased quality and quantity of learning can take place. The transition from educator to facilitator of learning ought, in theory at least, to be much easier, even in the context of curricular restraints. If it can be made, widely, then coaching and mentoring (already increasingly occurring in schools and universities) will shift from being a minor support for the disadvantaged to become an integral part of learning for the majority.

9

CHAPTER 60

Beyond alphabets and apples: in pursuit of quality teaching

VICKI PHILLIPS AND MARILYN CRAWFORD

What we want for children … we should want for their teachers: that schools be places of learning for both of them, and that such learning be suffused with excitement, engagement, passion, challenge, creativity, and joy.

(HARGREAVES, 1995, P. 3)

Of all the lessons learned from the education reforms of the twentieth century, one undeniable truth reigns supreme: in the end, it is the quality of teaching that matters most. It is impossible to be closely associated with schooling in any way and fail to know this. Every parent who greets the new school year with baited breath and fingers crossed while waiting for their child's classroom assignment knows that the quality of teaching matters most. Every principal who loses countless hours sleep over the 28 students assigned to Ms X; every reformer who has worked heart and soul to turn around a failing school or a group of schools; every student who has endured one, or two, or three years of their precious school lives assigned to marginal teachers knows this. No matter how technologically advanced we may become, no matter what precepts may underpin the next wave of education reforms, the quality of the teaching will lie perpetually at the heart of success or failure for districts, schools, and – most importantly – for each and every student who journeys there.

To achieve high levels of quality teaching with consistency and scale, we must look anew at how we prepare teachers, both novice and veteran alike, for the profession. Long gone are the days in which teachers were expected to come out of preparation programmes equipped with the skills and knowledge to complete a lifelong career in teaching with accomplishment. And long gone are the days in which teachers could close their classroom doors and disappear for years on end into the sacrosanct world of teacher autonomy. To be successful in the twenty-first century, teachers must open their classrooms, joining hands as learners themselves. To teach with success, they must live their instructional lives with intellectual vitality, working as active members of a 'spirited, reflective professional community that actually generates motivation to roll up one's sleeves and endeavor to meet the unfamiliar and often difficult needs of contemporary students' (McLaughlin, 1993, p. 98). In short, if we are to deliver the quality of teaching that lies at the heart of educational success, teachers must be energetic and continuous learners throughout their professional journey.

But nothing happens on its own. A key challenge for reformers the world over is to build and sustain the type of intellectual community that ensures the continuous learning necessary for high-quality teaching. In this chapter, we focus on two key strategies for making this happen. First, to ensure high-quality teaching these days means to ensure that teachers have access to an array of intensive, ongoing opportunities for improving their practice and for responding creatively and proactively to the changing needs of their students and community. Second, ensuring high-quality teaching also requires creating the conditions within which teachers thrive as learners. Woven together, these two strategies form a web of support that sustains quality teaching.

For educational leaders to meet this dual challenge successfully, both creating ongoing opportunities to improve teaching practice as well as establishing the conditions in which perfecting one's practice is an accepted norm, they must meet it intentionally. Certainly there are multiple paths, not just one foolproof trail, that lead to accomplishment of these two goals. Yet certain bedrock knowledge cuts across all successful conduits to success: knowledge upon which we can draw. It is knowledge born from the annals of research, from the wisdom of practice in places where there is serious improvement of schools, and from the confluence of the two.

In this chapter, we describe the work of the School District of Lancaster in Lancaster, Pennsylvania as an example of how creating both ongoing training opportunities as well as developing conditions that support teachers as learners can, in combination, improve the quality of teaching systemically. In this reform-minded district, the wisdom of practice and the insight of research has been gathered, blended, further developed and applied in order to create a system of continuous improvement that supports excellence in teaching. In addition to our successes, we also speak frankly about lessons we are learning along the way. Overall, we believe that our work is replicable in other places, largely because we have made it our practice to implement well what we have learned from research and experience elsewhere, as well as to capture what we are learning in sharable frameworks that contribute to increasing the knowledge base of the profession.

This chapter looks first at how the School District of Lancaster has developed a system of high-quality learning opportunities for teachers, including five specific core strategies. Next, we look at how the district is creating the conditions in which excellence in teaching thrives, focusing on the interplay between holding high expectations and providing high support. Used together, these two key strands form the backbone of a system that supports excellence in teaching – a system that can inform our collective work as we move together toward our international goal of quality teaching as the norm.

Creating intensive, ongoing, high-quality opportunities for teacher learning

9

The USA, like many other countries, has reached a crisis in teaching. Both the quality of teaching and the number of available teachers are at issue. After two years of study and debate, the National Commission on Teaching, a panel of public officials, business, community and education leaders, released a series of findings and recommendations designed to ensure that every child in every classroom has access to quality teachers. The panel essentially confirmed what we all know – that the single most powerful determinant of student achievement is the expertise and qualifications of teachers (Darling-Hammond, 1997, p. 38). Setting strong standards of practice and changing the way teachers are prepared, supported and compensated figure prominently in the Commission's recommendations. Moreover, a large-scale study found that every additional dollar spent on raising teacher quality netted greater student achievement gains than did any other use of school resources (Ferguson, 1991, pp. 465–98).

In the School District of Lancaster we have placed a premium on the professional development of our teaching staff, believing it to be an investment with serious dividends. We have reallocated dollars internally and sought additional external grants and funding in order to significantly increase teacher access to training. At the same time, we have been conscious that merely putting more dollars into training is not adequate: schools and districts have invested before with limited or no results. Rather, our focus is on the kind and quality of opportunities for teacher learning that we offer, conducting professional development in context of the teachers' reality. As Liberman (1995, p. 591) notes:

> *What everyone appears to want for students – a wide array of learning opportunities that engage students in experiencing, creating, and solving real problems, using their own experiences and working with others – is for some reason denied to teachers when they are learners.*

In Lancaster we are increasingly understanding teachers much better as learners, and, in response, are using a collection of key strategies that promote their development and build teacher capacity in every school.

While we have used a wide variety of strategies, the following five are enabling us to increase the capacity (i.e. quality) of our teaching staff:

- use of data and protocols to examine and adjust classroom practice;
- ongoing, intensive training via Content Institutes, forums, teacher networks, and study groups;
- on-site coaching and feedback via expert practitioners/consultants;
- school-based instructional facilitators;
- instructional and learning environment 'walkthroughs' and site visits to other places.

It should be noted that these strategies represent a collaborative effort between the district (i.e. the central leadership) and the schools. School leaders and staffs have a great deal of input into bringing these strategies to life, and much of the work is school-based. As a leadership team, consisting of central and site-level administrators, we believe these strategies are crucial to the long-term sustainability of our improvements.

These strategies reflect our desire not only to enhance core knowledge and skills of teachers but also to develop habits of practice that ensure focused attention on rigour and high-quality student work in the classroom. Our students need teachers who are assessment/data literate and who use those data continuously to monitor and adjust classroom practice as daily fare in every classroom. Our students need teachers who are excellent teachers of reading, writing and mathematics aside from (and perhaps in spite of) the *programme de jour* of the time. Our students need teachers who are not afraid to examine their work closely, both individually as well as collegially. As a system, we need teachers who are professional learners, instructors who take lifelong learning as seriously for themselves as they do for their students. Over a period of three years, four of the five aforementioned strategies have moved us a long way towards our goal of becoming a school district in which the habits that sustain quality teaching are routine rather than innovative practice. The fifth strategy, instructional and learning environment walkthoughs, is only now becoming part of our ongoing work.

In combination, these five key strategies are paying off. Even though they have only been in effect for a few short years, these strategies have moved the district light years ahead in building professional community, and collegial networking is fast becoming the norm in many of our schools. Yet these strategies have not occurred in isolation. We look next at the conditions necessary to support quality teaching – the environment that lets teachers put into practice what they learn via the five high-leverage strategies discussed above.

Creating the conditions in which quality teaching thrives

Australian principal Leoni Degenhardt (Degenhardt, 2001, p. 8) describes the need for teachers to become 'reheartened' – to have teachers exercise autonomy, to reclaim their power to make a difference, to restore a sense of idealism where it has become lost. She further asserts that teachers need to regain a sense of pride in their craft. Professionals, she says, 'sign their own work, stand by their professional judgement and exercise pressure on each other to ensure that no member damages the community's confidence in the profession'. To accomplish these dual goals, to develop teachers who are both engaged and competent, administration must create a healthy context that sustains teachers as they become perpetual students of their profession, learning both as individuals and as a collective.

If teachers are to become eager lifelong learners, they must first see teaching as important, since 'teachers' attitudes, beliefs, and feelings about their work play an important role in supporting or undermining effective practice' (McLaughlin and Talbert, 1990, p. 3). In addition, they must see quality teaching as possible, understanding that student academic performance 'reflects their own success at helping students find and develop themselves and their talent' (Darling-Hammond, Ancess, and Falk, 1995, p. 62). As leaders, this is a delicate balance to achieve. At the same time that we acknowledge the need to increase the quality of teaching, and indeed the accountability of teachers, we must also be conscious of the need to restore teachers' purpose, passion and joy in their work.

In Lancaster, we believe the context that supports quality teaching is based on the dynamic union of two fundamental strands:

- keeping the demand high – 'gentle pressure relentlessly applied';
- delivering the supports necessary for our staff and students to be successful – 'serious support intentionally delivered'.

This frame (see Barber and Phillips, 2000, pp. 9–15) leads to predictable results, as briefly outlined in Figure 60.1. The powerful combination of high expectations balanced by high support provides fertile ground for the seeds of professional community given root by the intensive, ongoing, high-quality opportunities for

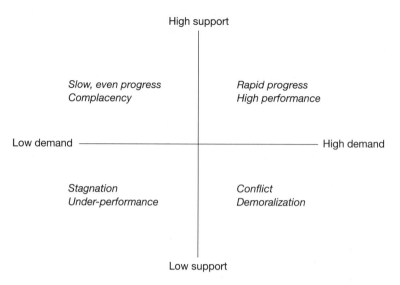

Figure 60.1 Balancing demand and support

teacher learning discussed in the previous section of this chapter. It is this frame that allows us to maintain this critical balance and, as leaders, to engage in thoughtful conversations among ourselves and with our staffs about creating the kind of professional culture in which quality teaching can thrive.

Holding high expectations – 'gentle pressure relentlessly applied'

The following are some of the key factors that we believe are instrumental in helping us hold high expectations as district culture, thus creating the conditions in which the quality of teaching has dramatically increased.

Holding the demand steady

We have set clear high standards for student achievement and professional practice, created a rhythm of assessments that gives teachers access to ongoing data about student performance, and established specific performance targets with which to hold ourselves accountable for steady and sustained improvements. Thus our goals are unambiguous at the policy level and are operationalized with the increased levels of clarity necessary for successful implementation.

Making practice public

We are setting an expectation that teaching should be inquiry-based, with teachers asking hard questions of themselves and of us as leaders. In addition, we are using strategies that require them to make their practice public, so they experience the benefits of developing joint solutions to common problems, do not receive the feared reprisals if the work is less than stellar, and so that their sense of isolation becomes a thing of the past. We want our teachers to experience first-hand what it means to be an intellectual community of learners pushing on one another's thinking and growing together over time. In fact, we openly discuss within the district the difference between creating an intellectual community of learners and maintaining social harmony, as teachers 'think, reinvent, and reflect on their work' (Lee, Smith and Croninger, 1995, p. 5).

Using experiences to shape beliefs and confidence

We believe in a teacher voice and seek teachers' input and feedback on many fronts. But there are times when we ascribe to the notion of Conners and Smith (1999) that you must change people's experiences in order to change their beliefs. When research and proven results are strong enough to support the implementation of a specific strategy districtwide, we make the decision as a leadership team and then give choice in the 'how'. Two good examples are our move to a full-day kindergarten programme and our adoption of a consistent K–12 mathematics programme across the district. While we mandated the programmes as a districtwide endeavour, we sought teachers' advice on various aspects (for example, which mathematics programme) and on the kinds of materials, training and support they would need to be successful and then delivered on their requests. As a result, teachers are the biggest champions of both programmes, because they have seen first-hand the benefits for their students. In these instances, many teachers had to experience first in order to believe. And the results are nothing short of astounding. For example, nine out of ten kindergardners (90 per cent) now go to first-grade meeting standards and our assessment scores improved in the first year of implementing new strategies for teaching mathematics.

Creating a change-oriented culture

According to Murphy *et al.* (2001, p. 123), 'In intellectual communities the work is never done' (p. 123). While our goals remain crystal clear, we expect the paths to achieving those goals to vary depending on a host of factors. For example, students leaving our elementary schools are increasingly successful in performing well academically, while all too many secondary students who have not had the same experiences continue to struggle. Thus our middle schools are indeed 'caught in the middle', and they have to develop programmes that fit the needs of two radically different groups. As more and more students enter sixth grade with success in basic skills, our middle schools will find continuous change the norm in order to meet the needs of the changing student body. This type of change culture – an essential backdrop for high–quality teaching – requires strong support so that teachers will jump in, 'focusing on new approaches to teaching, learning, assessment, and continuous problem solving' (Fullan, 1997, p. 46).

9

Providing high support – 'serious support intentionally delivered'

In addition to demanding high performance, we also provide high support as a backdrop for teaching excellence. The following are some of the additional factors that we believe are instrumental in helping us in providing high support as district culture, thus supporting teachers in providing quality teaching at scale.

Knowing every teacher as a learner

Among the standards for school leaders is the expectation that they know every teacher as a learner – their capabilities and their areas for improvement. More important, school leaders must be able to articulate the specific support being provided to a given teacher to ensure that they are moving from marginal to good or from good to excellent.

Creating enabling structures

Providing teachers with new means of teaching and doing business only adds to their frustration if they find themselves within organizational contexts that inhibit the implementation of those strategies. A keen lesson we have learned as leaders is that we must also do the hard work of reallocating resources and changing teacher loads, school schedules and staffing patterns. We have needed to rework time, so that large blocks of professional development time are the norm within the school day on a weekly basis, in addition to further training offered after school, on set-aside professional development days and during the summer. And we have had to be unflinching in addressing those issues, since they require confronting long-standing self-interests and past practices.

Providing necessary resources

According to Newmann (1997, p. 22), 'Schools may have competent teachers and still lack the capacity to boost student achievement significantly. Individual staff competence must be complemented by adequate ... resources.' While we use the SIP process to help teachers develop and select appropriate student assignments, we do not believe in recreating when excellent programmes and materials are available. Thus we select and adopt programmes with a proven track record to use as a spine for our work, then move beyond the limits of these programmes using strategies such as Education Trust's newly emerging work on replacement units and content landscaping to build as necessary.

Staging and phasing

With the daunting nature of the work at hand, there is a tendency to try to do everything at once – to take on the ills of history in one fell swoop. To create context that supports teachers as they journey toward excellence, we have very deliberately and thoughtfully picked high-leverage strategies, implementing them in a coherent sequence so that the system is not totally overwhelmed. For example, we first had to select critical standards in key areas – communication arts, mathematics, science, social studies, art, music, PE and world language – before we could demand and support high performance for students and staff. Once we selected these 'promotion standards' as the central driver of the system, we could then move on to select appropriate resources, external partners and training programmes for teachers. Only through staging and phasing can we keep the system moving forward at peak levels of performance in support of teacher excellence.

Harnessing the power of public will

If teachers are to be supported as lifelong learners, they must be supported and sustained by the public. Educators cannot work alone, separated from or even working in the face of public will. Reconnecting with community, indeed with all our various communities, has been a key role of central leadership in providing the teacher and school support necessary for quality teaching to emerge and continue. Our communication system, both formal and informal, is one of our most powerful tools for making this happen. By both 'listening' as well as 'talking' with our publics, we are developing a community context that will sustain and support teacher quality over time.

Acknowledging challenges

If teachers are to be sustained as learners, we believe it is key to be able to address challenges openly and productively as a team. To solve problems and move on rather than be hampered by our troubles, we put our issues on the table and work together as a team to solve them. In fact, we frame problems as the gift that lets us create intellectual community, harnessing the *esprit de corps* created by developing joint solutions to common problems to move us ahead. For example, we used the challenge of developing a standards-based report card system to move us ahead as a district in our understanding of the inherent complexities of assigning grades as well as reporting pure performance levels on meeting standards. By working collectively to resolve this problem, rather than blaming one another for inconsistencies in the two systems, we – teachers, administrators, and parents – drew together as community by crafting an acceptable solution to the challenge and learning together as we worked through the problem.

Honouring and celebrating the work

We make it a practice to celebrate progress – that of individual teachers, groups, school(s) and the district as a whole. Our motto is 'Together we can!' and we take every opportunity to share the good work that is happening in classrooms and schools across the district. Sharing progress helps teachers gain confidence that we are not only pursuing the right work, but that we have the ability to meet the rigorous targets we have set for ourselves.

In working to develop a context that both challenges and supports teacher quality, what we have 'rediscovered' is that teachers truly want to make a difference. It is why they entered this noble profession and it is what keeps many of them there, despite the increased demands, the rapid pace of change and the seemingly overwhelming challenges. And most teachers, we have discovered, do not mind (and even heartily embrace) the increased demands so long as they are given the tools, training and support they believe they need to meet those demands, and so long as they see progress where it counts – with their students.

Conclusion

As a district, we have come an enormous distance in three years, as have the majority of our individual schools. Student achievement has risen significantly after over a decade of stalled performance. Contributing to that rise are the dramatic improvements in the quality of teaching that have resulted from the implementation of these strategies, all of which are replicable. But we have a great deal of work yet to do to develop fully and sustain the pervasive professional learning culture to which we aspire. And a significant challenge facing us is finding the balance between providing teachers with continued opportunities to reflect on and deepen their practice around strategies they have already learned and pressing on to another needed skill set.

We in no way claim to have built fully the professional culture to which we aspire, but we believe we now know some the major ingredients. As indicated earlier, many of these are not new – you will find them in evidence in other places. What you might not find elsewhere is all of them in evidence at once. We believe that it is the simultaneous movement on many fronts, including the training and development described earlier, that has allowed us to regain teacher confidence in Lancaster. Just prior to current leadership initiatives in Lancaster, the teachers issued a 95-per-cent vote of no-confidence in the administration and the reforms, citing the lack of adequate training and support as the key factor in the vote. Our recent agreement with the teachers' association is rooted in professional practice (as opposed to the 'work rules' orientation of the past) and was approved 610 to 16. If teachers have a complaint, it is that the array of professional development opportunities is so rich that they cannot take advantage of it all. Part of our role as leaders is to help them to prioritize and to pace their growth and development, so that the knowledge and skills gain is deep and ongoing rather than surface and sporadic.

The point of this chapter is not to tout the work we are doing in Lancaster. Lancaster serves only as a current example of the successes and tribulations involved in the hard work of education reform and, in particular, in improving what matters most – the quality of teaching. Nothing we are doing in Lancaster could be categorized as 'rocket science'. Rather we are investing in and executing well what research and practice elsewhere indicates works. As leaders this is perhaps the most important lesson of the times – to remind ourselves that we do know what works in public education, just as we also remind ourselves that teachers want to make a difference. The job now is to garner the leadership and will to make it happen, and to work together as an international community to make teaching excellence the norm.

As we say in the School District of Lancaster, 'Together we can!'

REFERENCES

Barber, M. and Phillips, V. (2000). 'Fusion: how to unleash irreversible change. Lessons for the future of system-wide school reform', *Education Policy Studies Series*, 32, Hong Kong: Hong Kong Institute of Educational Research pp. 1–25.

Connors, R. and Smith, T. (1999). *Journey to the Emerald City: Achieve a Competitive Edge by Creating a Culture of Accountability*, Paramus, NJ: Prentice Hall.

Darling-Hammond, L. (1997) 'The quality of teaching matters most', *Journal of Staff Development*, 18 (1), pp. 38–41.

Darling-Hammond, L., Ancess, J. and Falk, B. (1995) *Authentic Assessment in Action: Studies of Schools and Students at Work*, New York: Teachers' College Press.

Degenhardt, L. (2001) 'Power, purpose and professionalism: teachers reclaiming the learning agenda', *Unicorn*, 27 (3), Australian College of Education.

Ferguson, R. (1991) 'Paying for public education. New evidence on how and why money matters', *Harvard Journal on Legislation*, 28, pp. 465–98.

Fullan, M. (1997) 'Broadening the concept of teacher leadership' in Caldwell, S. (ed.) *Provisional Development in Learning-centered Schools*, Oxford, OH: National Staff Development Council, pp. 34–48.

Hargreaves, A. (1995) 'Teacher development in a postmodern world', *The Developer*, Oxford, OH: National Staff Development Council.

Lee, V.E., Smith, J.B. and Croninger, R.G. (1995). *Another Look at High School Restructuring. More Evidence that it Improves Student Achievement and More Insights into Why*, Madison, WI: Center on Organization and Restructuring of Schools.

Liberman, A. (1995) 'Practices that support teacher development', *Phi Delta Kappan*, 76 (8), p. 591–6.

McLaughlin, M.W. (1993) 'What matters most in teachers' workplace context?' in Little, J.W. and McLaughlin, M.W. (eds), *Teacher's Work: Individuals, Colleagues, and Contexts*, New York: Teachers' College Press, pp. 79–103.

McLaughlin, M. and Talbert, J. (1990) 'The contexts in question: the secondary school workplace' in McLaughlin, M.W., Talbert, J.E. and Bascia, N. (eds), *The Contexts of Teaching in Secondary Schools: Teachers' Realities*, New York: Teachers' College Press, pp. 1–14.

Murphy, J., Beck, L., Crawford, M., Hodges, A. and McGaughy, C. (2001) *The Productive High School: Creating Personalized Academic Communities*, Thousand Oaks, CA: Corwin Press.

Newmann, F.M. (1997) 'How secondary schools contribute to academic success' in Borman, K. and Schneider, B. (eds) *The Adolescent Years: Social Influences and Educational Challenges*, (97th yearbook of the National Society for the Study of Education), Chicago: University of Chicago Press, pp. 88–108.

9

PART TEN

Schools of the Future

BRIAN CALDWELL

Introduction

BRIAN CALDWELL

Some writers assume that leadership and management are exercised in situations that are currently in evidence or at most may change in measured fashion in the years ahead. Other writers describe a future that is dramatically different and call for leadership and management of a high order to create that future and to sustain their organizations along the way. There has been sweeping change in schools in recent years and many significant reforms have been completed or are under way. However, a visit to most schools will reveal that, compared to many other organizations and institutions, they are still recognizably in much the same shape as they were a half-century or more ago.

The expert view presented in Part Ten makes it clear that leaders and managers in school education must prepare for a future that is radically different from the present. While generic approaches to leadership and management may still be relevant, the emphasis will be on a capacity to deal with transformation. It will not suffice to be able to manage change in the traditional sense. The challenge will be to bring about systematic, significant and sustained change – transformation – that will result in a future in 10 or 20 years time that differs in dramatic fashion to the current state of affairs. That future may well mean the demise of schools in some settings.

Hedley Beare sets the scene in his first sentence when he declares that 'from what we know already about the twenty-first century, it is clear that the traditional school has no chance of surviving in it'. While some are resistant to what is unfolding, there is broad acceptance that reform of school education is necessary. It is certainly continuing apace in most nations. It seems, however, that even the concept of 'reform' is out of date, and that transformation is the appropriate concept. Beare cites Perelman's conclusion that 'The nations that stop trying to "reform" their education and training institutions and choose instead to totally replace them with a brand-new, high-tech learning system will be the economic powerhouses of the twenty-first century'. Beare does not dream these thing; he is convincing in his account of how the seeds of the transformation are already in place, and that many of the characteristics of the future school are present in many settings.

The scenarios of the Organization for Economic Co-operation and Development (OECD) for the future of schools as devised in 2000 and 2001 are well known to those who move in OECD circles and to some scholars, but they are not familiar to most who lead and manage in schools and school systems. David Istance was an author of these statements and he provides a concise account here. Few will be attracted to two of the six scenarios that unfold from attempts to maintain the status quo. The continuation of bureaucratic systems will lead to an institutional-ization of current problems. Current difficulties in attracting and maintaining good teachers may lead to meltdown of school systems in some nations. More attractive are the 'reschooling' scenarios, with schools serving as either core social centres or focused learning organizations. Continued dissatisfaction with schools may eventually lead to the 'deschooling' scenarios, with learning occurring through networks in one, and a shift from public education to private education in the other. The reschooling and deschooling scenarios are consistent with Beare's view of the future for schools.

Judith Chapman and David Aspin provide a detailed account of networked learning in the broader context of lifelong learning as well as in school settings, in schools of the future. They argue that networks are 'a new vehicle for achieving educational change'. They warrant particular attention given the scale of the trans-formantion envisaged by Beare. In the following chapter in Cheong Cheng furnishes a concise account of his famous notion of 'triplization' in education, showing how globalization, localization and individualization are necessary and achievable. He provides a detailed listing of the many implications for those who lead and manage in schools and school systems. His contention that 'education will be triplized in the twenty-first century' is convincing.

The accounts of the school in the future set out in the first four contributions are exciting and daunting. These are made even more so by the analysis provided by Dan Gibton. Nearly every view of the future assumes that there will be signifi-cant authority, responsibility and accountability at the school level, no matter what form the school may take in the years ahead. Gibton describes the tensions and the dilemmas in systems where there is significant decentralization, but where centralization holds sway in many matters. The key to success is educa-tional leadership of high order at all levels, but those at the centre who have such high expectations for schools must gain an understanding of the 'mindscapes' of school leaders.

The integrating theme for Part Ten is that new 'mindscapes', a concept coined by Sergiovanni, are being created now and will be shaped and reshaped in the years ahead. The first step is to gain an understanding of what is in store, and Part Ten is intended to make a contribution to that endeavour.

– CHAPTER 61 –

The school of the future

HEDLEY BEARE

From what we know already about the twenty-first century, it is clear that the traditional school has no chance of surviving in it, at least not in the developed economies. Indeed, the gap between the countries that can afford the new forms of schools and those that stick with the old model is likely to widen alarmingly. Consider just two factors – population and technology.

World population trends

It took from the dawn of human civilization up to 1850 for the world's population to build to one billion people, but by the year 2000 it was 6.1 billion, and steepling towards about nine billion by 2050.

That human population now consists overwhelmingly of Third-World dwellers – where 97 per cent of the world's live births occur, where a majority lack essential services, are disease-ridden (as with AIDS), undereducated and lack access to new technologies. Half the world's people are under 25 and of child-bearing age. By 2050 fewer than one in ten will be white, and four-fifths will be crowded into Asia and Africa, with much relocating across national borders – some official, much of it illegal. The consumption and distribution of water, food, fish and forests will be in constant dispute. Pollution of the atmosphere, climate change and how energy is generated and shared will be international issues. Human and genetic engineering, access to health service and the use and occupation of space colonies will be major political issues. In countries where all women have more than three years of secondary education (and only there), the populations will be under control or in decline. The world's most widely spoken language will be Mandarin Chinese, its use already three times that of English.

There are many implications here for schools, for patterns of schooling, for the worldwide teaching service, for learning technologies, for the shape and content of the curriculum and for how and what make up the most efficient learning modes. We should already be asking questions about global educational resource usage. For the demand is huge, and many of the providers (such as schools with a world-class reputation) in developed countries will find themselves serving an international community where they will supply not merely student places, but training in the logistics of delivery, systems to produce professionally qualified teachers, 'capacity building' and internationalized curricula (UNICEF, 1995).

Formal schooling is still a luxury in many countries. A UNICEF study (Crossette, 1998) of 1998 revealed that in the world's poorest nations only a quarter of the children attend school at all. Illiteracy is directly related to high birth rates, and there are huge disparities internationally. In short, the traditional forms of schooling even now are incapable of meeting the demand.

The technology revolution and the knowledge-based society

The technology revolution is making much of the paraphernalia of conventional schooling obsolescent. Hammer and Champy (1994), the inventors of 'corporate reengineering', have said that 'the old ways of doing business – the division of labour around which companies have been organised since Adam Smith first articulated the principle – simply don't work anymore', and that includes the organizations called schools. Because information technology (IT) is developing at such incredible speed (Gates, 1999), international disparities are occurring in this domain too (Brittain and Elliot, 1996). In 1999 it was estimated that between 50 and 80 per cent of the world's population had never used a telephone; and that while a computer costs about a month's salary in the USA, its purchase price in Bangladesh would absorb eight year's income (Elliot, 1999, p. 53; Jones, 1997; Wertheim, 1999).

Yet IT brings huge advantages. The amount of material (both documentary and story) available through video, television and film presentation is astonishing. It is possible to replay it online, as often as one likes, and it uses a whole-of-frame, image-based, presentational format quite different from that of linear text. The e-book allows texts to be placed on one small disk or CD, and for printed books to be downloaded into a laptop computer. Students can create a workstation anywhere, including a home-learning station, whereby they can be on call, at call, or online from anywhere, with no need to be anchored on school premises in order to pursue a formal learning programme. Thus it may be a liability for a school formally to own obsolescent buildings. Networked systems enormously expand the power and versatility of learning programmes, for IT can link the home to an array of services delivered down-line where once they required physical delivery or a shopping excursion. The same facilities put academic and personal advice on tap 24 hours of the day, connect parent and school, allow e-mail and web-page communication, and provide serendipitous extensions to schooling (Brain, 1999).

The exponential production of information and databases means that very little has to be learnt by heart, but that it is essential to be able to locate material, to sift it intelligently, to test it for reliability, to synthesize it into meaningful chunks, to link it with other learning, to apply and to extend it in other contexts, and not least to solve problems and analyse issues with it.

Children in developed countries are quite at home with the knowledge society, picking up its implications and skills far more quickly than adults do. It also alters their perception of the world – automatically internationalizing them. Because people working inside knowledge-based enterprises conceive of their careers on fundamentally different lines from those who grew up inside a manufacturing-based economy, the new breed of students and workers comprehend that leveraging knowledge is the essential quality that gives them competitive edge, achieves results, and ensures them employment (*Management Today*, 1999).

Schools have already changed

For the whole of the twentieth century, school has taken students at age five or six, put them into class groups composed of children of the same age, put each class in charge of one teacher, and allocated students and teacher to a self-contained class-room. There the pupils were led through a curriculum based on the notion that human knowledge is divided into subjects, whose content has been graded from the elementary through to the very complex, with students advancing 'upwards' through it in lockstep over 12 years of study. The schools were ranked according to this upward progression – kindergarten or preparatory; elementary or primary; junior secondary or middle school; senior secondary; tertiary or higher or post-sec-ondary. The staff taught by transferring knowledge in which they had special expertise to learners who were relatively ignorant – a systematic and coherent transfer of knowledge from expert to novice. Some knowledge or subjects were valued more highly than others according to whether they were academic ('intel-lectual') or not.

Furthermore, the schools looked the same physically, and were set in school grounds fenced in to imply that these were self-contained institutions. Instruction was conducted in relatively large buildings consisting of rows of classrooms open-ing into long passageways designed to control student movement. If one allows for varying degrees of artifice and architecture, school buildings tended to look the same the world over.

But incremental, fundamental and far-reaching adaptations are under way – structural and framework changes, new ways of viewing knowledge, new ways of conceiving of planetary systems, new patterns of interactions across the world, new definitions for the world of work, new approaches to birth control, child-bear-ing and child-rearing, and powerful new technologies that have not only speeded up access to – and the volume of – information, but in many ways are superseding print materials and the traditional techniques of publishing. Schools have been remaking what is taught, the way teachers allow themselves to be employed, the way the school is managed, and how the school earns its operating revenue.

The school reform movement of the 1980s and 1990s showed that piecemeal adaptation of schooling was ineffective (Beare and Boyd, 1993; Caldwell and Hayward, 1998; Stoll and Fink, 1996; Stringfield, Ross and Smith, 1996; Townsend, Clarke and Ainscow, 1999), leading Perelman (1996, p. 20) to conclude: 'The nations that stop trying to "reform" their education and training institutions and choose instead to totally replace them with a brand-new, high-tech learning system will be the economic powerhouses through the twenty-first century'. Those schools and systems tend to have dispensed with large bureaucratic and central-ized structures, are collegial rather than hierarchical in the way they operate, have installed the new information systems and use them naturally in their learning programmes, accommodate a curriculum that is networked and branching rather than linear, foster digital as well as print literacy, use international rather than parochial benchmarks, encourage mobility and flexibility rather than static and standardized approaches, have professionalized their teaching teams, try to exploit the creativity of their best personnel, and have deregulated and freed up their operations wherever they can do so. What then does the new schooling paradigm look like?

10

The new paradigm for schooling

Technologically up-to-date schools have adopted the following mode of operation (Education Victoria, 1998). There is a whole-of-school approach to management through computerization. Its finances, budgets and student management system are on a school-wide database. It uses computerization for internal communication and information giving, making it in part a 'paperless site'. It has a school-wide IT plan, including a programme for updating software, for systematically replacing obsolete machines, for upgrading its staff and students, for inducting staff and students into the school's technology resources, and for familiarizing parents about how they can make productive use of IT.

It has reworked its teaching and learning programmes. Every teacher has a computer, whose software is compatible with that of the school, and teachers network regularly with professional colleagues in-school and across schools. There are computers in all classrooms and they are used routinely and daily for learning projects, group work, written composition and for accessing information in all subject areas. The rooms have been physically reconfigured to allow appropriate use of the computers by teachers and students during lesson time. Part of the space consists of learning alcoves and areas for group-based, round-table sessions. The whole school and every classroom can use the internet, the school's intranet and e-mail. Classrooms are connected to community resources like libraries, museums, and government offices and their websites. Some elements of the learning programme come from overseas. The school is wired for large-scale instruction or demonstrations, and has key lessons available online. Its pedagogic range enables some students to receive one-on-one instruction from a teacher, and to progress at their own rate. The school can supply its textbooks for the year on CDs or downlink. As well as books and other printed materials, the school's library has extensive digital materials. Every teacher keeps up with developments through release-time professional development activity.

The school has a huge databank on pupil achievements. Consistent, comparable and benchmarked data are collected on every student's academic progress, by every teacher in every key learning area. They are routinely stored in a database, which is accessible to every teacher at any time. The school regularly reports to its parents the trend lines in this body of consolidated data, and uses its website or homepage to keep parents informed with details about the school's learning programme, and what assignments, assessments and home study projects have been set. Some examinations and tests are conducted on and marked by computer, and there is an increasing tendency for students to take their tests when they are ready to do so.

The school day is reworked, because of the need for time flexibility and after-hours access to equipment like computers. Any good facility housing sophisticated equipment and amenities should be available around-the-clock, certainly after school, into the evening, and early in the morning, nor should it be closed for extended holiday periods, except for maintenance purposes. More staff are needed for an extended day, and most of them work in shifts.

The school's campus is enlarged, for new learning technologies release students from full-time physical attendance at school. The new technologies also change the reliance on textbooks and printed materials; demand literacy in digital as well as print materials and learning through imagery as well as words; give access to an array of people, places, and databases; extend learning styles; and put emphasis on skill development and knowledge production. Curricula become internationalized, and because students can find information that their teachers do not know about, the teacher role metamorphoses from that of expert and authority to that of mentor, adviser, learning strategist and wise friend.

Such schools, then, have become simply providers of the schooling process. The premises out of which they generate their learning programmes can vary enormously, and the process is not dependent on a stereotyped set of physical facilities. Formal schooling is no longer confined to a single, fenced-in property and schools are no longer merely 'places of learning' but rather articulators of learning – professional agencies that make schooling both accessible and systematic.

The twenty-first-century curriculum

Further, all the elements above tend to reconstruct the nature of knowledge itself. It is only partly correct to associate certain learning with certain ages. The twenty-first-century school has freed the curriculum of unnecessary or artificial straitjacketing. A learning programme for children and adolescents fed by technology involves a lot of spontaneous search, is partly serendipitous, and yet must still be systematic, coherent and cover key areas in which all young learners should become proficient.

The linear curriculum, then, with its apparent one-best-way approach and which sequences 'knowledge' into step-by-step gradations, is superseded by a curriculum that is nodular (chunks of learning that have to be unpacked with the help of a teacher or tutor) and modular (packages of intense learning that the student pastes together to form a coherent education). Some parcelling of knowledge into predetermined 'subjects' or 'disciplines' still occurs if only to conserve the time and energy of the learners, but overlaps and interconnections are regular, and the subjects themselves become hybridized. Students may travel by several paths through material, often handling complex matter before the simple emerges. The curriculum dwells on skills rather than on content, and emphasizes the capacities to identify and analyse a problem or issue, to devise solutions, and then to apply the findings in other areas of knowledge and skill.

In these transformations, education tends to function through an interconnected web of learning sites and resource people, and, as the brokers for learning, schools seek out and then buy, hire or lease the best modules of learning available. The problems and issues considered in the curriculum are increasingly borderless and transnational. What is to be 'learnt by heart' shrinks to a core of knowing called 'scaffolding knowledge', which is essential for negotiating one's way around the global community of knowledge. Learning how and where to access knowledge and how to handle it becomes a more productive use of a learner's time than committing a great number of facts to memory. The curriculum puts emphasis on learning 'how' as much as on learning 'what', on understanding underlying principles more than on committing information to memory, and on working jointly with others in a team on problem-solving as much as on individual learning.

10

Students, then, are virtual knowledge workers. 'Classwork' and 'school assignments' less often resemble factory jobs – a regular set of work, regular time in class or as a class, regular hours of the day committed to a subject, and a fixed place in which the work is done. The segments of the learning programme are likely to be differently organized, managed, accessed and assessed, and then used. Students may put the same number of working hours into their schooling, but in intensive chunks of time interspersed with leaner time as the workflows dictate (Handy, 1989, ch. 4). Their learning may not be acquired through one particular 'school', for their home school has become the facilitating base that enables them to access the learning appropriate to them at their stage of development. The best home schools are the networked and connected ones.

As a result, like knowledge workers elsewhere, students view their study programmes as a set of assignments and projects individually tailored to fit their own learning interests and pitched at an appropriate level of sophistication. These students understand that to be successful (and employed), they must remain learners for the whole of their lives – always reading, questioning, and intermeshing work and learning. Students understand that they themselves – not the school, nor the teacher – are responsible for their own learning career and for their progress. They know that they will be judged on learning outcomes, and that graduation or promotion depends on whether they are able to produce detailed evidence about their levels of performance and that they conform with the best standards being achieved elsewhere in the country and the world. 'Tests' are demonstrations by students of what they have learnt.

These developments are not startling to many schools or teachers. Most educators have internalized maps of the learning terrain in the form of syllabuses, core curricula or essential knowing, curriculum frameworks, and the skills and knowledge expected of the normal child at specified stages of their growth. They have a grid or matrix with subjects to be covered ('key learning areas' and 'scaffolding knowledge and skill') on one axis and the expected level of year-by-year attainments on the other axis. They can place every student in their care within that matrix, identifying what they have learned and where gaps exist (Gardner, 1999).

Educators as a group are therefore finding themselves responsible not so much for class teaching as for mentoring a group of learners, directing them sequentially into projects or modules of activities, and keeping track of progress and outcomes. It falls to them as educator-mentors, together with the student or students involved, to assess at the end of each learning project what skills have been acquired.

Modes of school management

The curriculum that incorporates centralized lockstep controls, standardized one-size-fits-all provisions, equalized access, homogenized quality and awards and regulations that impose conformity and consistency has been superseded; therefore organizational mode based on control and hierarchy, on bigness and standardization, on top-down, centralized command structures and on old-style supervision is also no longer suitable for schools.

Rather, schools will look like the knowledge-based, flexible conglomerates that centrally control only the essential and strategic areas but which allow entrepreneurial freedom to the operating units that make up the body corporate. Post-industrial organizations are radically different from those of the industrial society (Calas and Smircich, 1997; Handy, 1996; Hedberg *et al.*, 1997; Koch, 1998; Reich, 1992; Sadtler, Campbell and Koch, 1997; Senge, 1990; Townsend, Clarke and Ainscow, 1999). The new school models are flexible, allow for quick, strategic decisions to be made, encourage innovation and entrepreneurship, value creativity rather than conformity, give both students and teachers the power to take local decisions and to exercise initiative, and regard the people in or associated with the organization as partners rather than as property.

Indeed, the school is conceived of as a web of separable functions. These functions are divided into modules, and then contracted or franchised out to satellite units or subsidiary firms which supply services or components to the mother company, usually for a negotiated fee. The school therefore operates through a spider web of interconnecting, relatively autonomous, contractual units that deliver goods or services to school or student when they are needed – 'just in time'. It is not necessary for the modular operations to be performed by or within the school, nor is it necessary for the school to own all the subsidiaries that handle the modules. Some of them can be mini-schools, some operate as 'schools within the school', and others as independent entities (Horibe, 1999).

We have been used to regarding schools as permanent, solid, recognizable, unchanging organizations, which pride themselves in their longevity, history and old-scholar network, and which try to use these features as a selling point to attract able students. Schools in the knowledge society, however, are light-limbed organizations, more freewheeling, putting more faith in the staff's professionalism. They go in for teams and teamwork (Katzenbach and Smith, 1998); they try to gain maximum usage of the expertise and special competencies of staff, designing their operations around the staff rather than squeezing the staff into a predetermined mould; and they adopt collective decision making rather than the bureaucracy's pyramid of power. They work on assumptions about management as networking.

Savage (1996, p. 226) describes it as 'fifth generation management'. Schools using this approach succeed because they are 'founded on clear statements of mission' and they insist on everyone 'acting in accordance with their ideologies' (Sadler, 2001, p. 5). Because they consist primarily of people, they are thought of as a living entity; it is misguided to try to represent the educational enterprise in mechanistic terms. A more useful analogy, Sadler says, 'is to think of the structure as the anatomy of a living organism' with muscles and a skeleton (ibid., p. 13). Leadership never resides in just one person; it can be rotated or shared (Lipnack and Stamps, 1994, p. 57) and its main task is to define purpose, to maintain the culture, to keep the enterprise focused, to watch outcomes (fiercely!), and to make sure the units interact productively.

The professionalized teacher

Finally, with such curricula and management modes, the traditional view of teacher changes. The prescient Charles Handy (1979) indicated at the end of the 1970s that work would become more professionalized; management by contract and leadership by consent would be common; technologies would be harnessed to replace people-work as much as was possible; the worker would be paid for work done rather than for time spent on the job; work hours would be more flexible; workers would be attached to small, self-contained work units rather than to huge organizations; and 'organization villages' – clustering compatible enterprises in the same locality – would replace the megalopolis.

Since Handy's prediction was made, teaching has become a fully fledged profession – the most obvious indicator being that teachers in the developed world are now university graduates, all having successfully completed four years of tertiary education. They have the intellectual preparation, the career aspirations, the employment expectations and the same professional behaviour patterns of other graduates. Because their preservice courses are computer-intensive, they operate from the outset like members of the knowledge industries and are at ease in the knowledge economy. They now behave like Handy's workers, and do not function happily in traditional control-driven schools (Beare, 1998; Hargreaves, 1994).

Professionalized workers, like teachers, seek 'a deeper sense of meaning in their working lives'. The new work formats ask the employees 'to act like an owner', to forget about job descriptions (which are 'obsolete as quickly as they are written') and 'to do whatever needs to be done to make the [enterprise] a success' (Baker, 2000, p. 21). Professionalized workers see themselves as companies of one, as 'Me Inc.', trading their competencies and skills in a fluid mesh of cognate organizations and compatible openings (Jordan, 1999, p. 17).

So standard working hours (such as 9.00 to 5.00, Monday to Friday), a clock-on/clock-off work tradition, a set salary (which one receives regardless of productivity), award conditions for work (which tend to apply for one's physical presence on a site), and a defined work location may have been appropriate for an industrial economy where supervision was the principal control device of management, but they are increasingly unsuitable for the way the professions operate – and they will become progressively intolerable for professional teachers (Ransome, 1996). How we deploy and use the teacher corps will be a major consideration for the future's school.

Imagine, then, the world the students will inherit. Then picture the school geared up to prepare students for it – no longer imprisoned on an island site, but interacting with clusters of compatible enterprises, sharing its facilities and leasing its physical space; its teachers no longer necessarily employed by one school only, nor even working entirely in education, but carrying a portfolio of assignments and moving among school and other enterprises. Imagine the learners capitalizing on these synergies and the openings that their teachers engineer for them. Imagine, then, the school for the future.

REFERENCES

Baker, T. (2000) 'Not just a job', *Management Today*, June, pp. 20–2.

Beare, H. (1998) *Who Are the Teachers of the Future?* Jolimont, Victoria: IARTV, Seminar Series no. 76.

Beare, H. and Boyd, W.L. (eds) (1993) *Restructuring Schools: An International Perspective on the Movement to Transform the Control and Performance of Schools*, London: Falmer Press.

Brain, P. (1999) *Beyond Meltdown: the Global Battle for Sustained Growth*, Sydney: Scribe.

Brittain, V. and Elliott, L. (1996) 'Gulf grows between rich and poor', *The Guardian Weekly*, 155 (3), 21 July, p. 1.

Calas, M.B. and Smircich, L. (1997) *Post-Modern Management Theory*, Boston: Dartmouth Publishing Co.

Caldwell, B. and Hayward, D.K. (1998) *Future of Schools: Lessons from the Reform of Public Education*, London: Falmer Press.

Crossette, B. (1998) 'UN warning on global rise in illiteracy', *The Age*, 9 December, p. 10.

Education Victoria (1998) *Learning Technologies in Victorian Schools 1998–2001*, Melbourne, Victoria: Education Victoria.

Elliot, L. (1999) 'A new world disorder', *Good Weekend* (*The Australian*), 4 September, pp. 53–4.

Gardner, H. (1999) *The Disciplined Mind: What All Students Should Understand*, New York: Simon & Schuster.

Gates, B. (1999) *Business @ The Speed of Thought*, Harmondsworth, Middlesex: Viking (Penguin Books).

Hammer, M. and Champy, J. (1994) *Reengineering the Corporation*, St Leonards, NSW: Allen & Unwin

Handy, C. (1979) *Gods of Management*, Harmondsworth, Middlesex: Penguin Books.

Handy, C. (1989) *The Age of Unreason*, London: Business Books.

Handy, C. (1996) *Beyond Certainty: The Changing World of Organisations*, London: Hutchinson.

Hargreaves, A. (1994) *Changing Teachers, Changing Times*, New York: Teachers' College Press.

Hedberg, B., Dahlgren, G., Hansson, J. and Olve, N-G. (1997) *Virtual Organisations and Beyond*, New York: Wiley.

Horibe, F. (1999) *Managing Knowledge Workers*, Ottawa: John Wiley.

Jones, M. (1997) 'Beaming hope from the sky', *The Age*, 12 May, p. B2.

Jordan, J. (1999) 'Work in Y2K?', *Management Today*, July, pp. 15–19.

Katzenbach, J. and Smith, D. (1998) *The Wisdom of Teams: Creating the High-Performance Organisation*, Boston, MA: Harvard Business School Press.

Koch, R. (1998) *The Third Revolution: A Capitalist Manifesto*, London: Capstone Publications.

Lipnack, J. and Stamps, J. (1994) *The Age of the Network: Organising Principles for the 21st Century*, New York: Wiley.

Management Today, (1999) editorial (untitled), April, pp. 10–11.

Perelman, J. (1996) *School's Out*, New York: William Morrow.

Ransome, P. (1996) *The Work Paradigm: A Theoretical Investigation of Concepts of Work*, London: Avebury Press.

Reich, R. (1992) *The Work of Nations*, New York: Vintage Books.

Sadler, P. (2001) *The Seamless Organisation: Building the Company of Tomorrow*, London: Kogan Page.

Sadtler, D., Campbell, A. and Koch, R. (1997) *Break up: How Companies Use Spin-Offs to Gain Focus and Grow Strong*, New York: The Free Press.

Savage, C.M. (1996) *%th Generation Management*, Boston: Butterworth-Heinemann.

Senge, P. (1990) *The Fifth Discipline: The Art and Practice of the Learning Organisation*, New York: Doubleday.

Stoll, L. and Fink, D. (1996) *Changing Our Schools: Linking School Effectiveness and School Improvement*, Buckingham: Open University Press.

Stringfield, S., Ross, S. and Smith, L. (eds) (1996) *Bold Plans for School Restructuring: The New American Schools Designs*, Marwah, NJ: Lawrence Erlbaum Associates.

Townsend, T., Clarke, P. and Ainscow. M. (eds) (1999) *Third Millennium Schools: A World of Difference in Effectiveness and Improvement*, Lisse, The Netherlands: Swets & Zeitlinger.

UNICEF (1995) *The State of the World's Children 1994*, Paris: United Nations International Children's Emergency Fund.

Wertheim, M. (1999) *The Pearly Gates of Cyberspace*, Sydney: Doubleday

10

CHAPTER 62

The OECD schooling scenarios

....

DAVID ISTANCE

Permission granted: © David Istance OECD 2003

The Organization for Economic Co-operation and Development (OECD) at its Centre for Educational Research and Innovation (CERI) has a policy-oriented research programme, Schooling for Tomorrow, that began in the dying stages of the twentieth century with a focus firmly on the twenty-first century.[1] Having completed a first phase culminating in the scenarios described in this chapter, the endeavour continues with a new phase just beginning at the time of writing. This will develop both analytical tools to operationalize the scenarios and policy tools to promote forward thinking in education. The starting point for the completed and new work is the paradox that education is par excellence about long-term investment in people and society but is characteristically only short-term in its decision making. We lack not only longer-term perspectives in policy and practice, but also the tools and terminology to develop them.

It was to address this lack that the CERI/OECD work has engaged in an analysis of major trends and driving forces, on the one hand, and in constructing scenarios for schooling over the next 10 to 20 years, on the other (OECD, 2001a). It is useful at the outset to clarify what the scenarios are not. They are not predictions, since they represent alternative futures not single best guesses, and since they are meant to help shape, not forecast, futures. Nor are they visions of where we would like to be, for their value derives also from including plausible undesirable futures to give a wide range across which societal choices will be made. They are instead tools, which combine guiding policy ideas, key trends and plausible interrelationships. They are in 'pure form', and in reality complex mixes will emerge between these different possible futures. Their value is in helping to sharpen awareness of the long-term alternatives about what we do and do not want, and how probable these options are judged to be. As tools for this process of reflection, the OECD scenarios are already being used in policy debate and professional development in a number of countries.

To be of greatest use to the educational community we did not wish to begin with more general scenarios – economic, social, political and cultural futures – and then ask what education would need to be like to realize them. This approach would have led to a confusing multitude of scenarios, and risked assuming that education should simply be reactive to other concerns. Instead we sought scenarios addressing the future of schooling, albeit with the likelihood of each shaped by broad contextual factors. As such, the scenarios are about schooling arrangements overall, not models of individual schools. And, in the interest of focus and relevance, they are about young people from infancy to adolescence and their education – schooling – rather than the broad panoply of opportunities making up the lifelong learning picture.[2]

By constructing the scenarios around schooling we were not, however, biasing the options in favour of the institution called school, as demonstrated by the 'deschooling' scenarios. The six scenarios are clustered into three main categories:

- 1a and 1b: attempting to maintain the status quo
- 2a and 2b: reschooling
- 3a and 3b: deschooling.

Each scenario has been built around a common framework, described below in terms of learning and organization, management and governance, resources and infrastructure, and teachers.[3] They were constructed through an iterative process. Seminars and discussions began in the early stages of the programme on key trends and ideas about desirable and possible futures. This led in early 2000 to the first formulation of the scenarios (then four in number), which in turn were subject to further scrutiny by experts and policy-makers, partly but not exclusively drawn from the world of education.[4] The scenarios were then further elaborated and put before a major international conference on 'Schooling for Tomorrow' held in Rotterdam in November 2000. The feedback led to yet more revisions, and hence to the formulations found in OECD (2001a) and here. More intensive feedback and analysis will be part of the current phase but this is not envisaged to lead to any further revisions except as a possible final outcome towards 2004.

The OECD schooling scenarios in brief

Attempting to maintain the status quo

With the 'status quo' scenarios, the basic features of existing systems are maintained well into the future, whether from public choice or from the inability to implement fundamental change. In Scenario 1a, the future unfolds as a gradual evolution of the present, with school systems continuing to be strong; in Scenario 1b, there is a major crisis of the system, triggered by acute teacher shortages.

Scenario 1a: bureaucratic school systems continue

This scenario is built on the continuation of powerfully bureaucratic systems, strong pressures towards uniformity and resistance to radical change. Schools are highly distinct institutions, knitted together within complex administrative arrangements. Political and media commentaries are frequently critical in tone; despite the criticisms, radical change is resisted. Many fear that alternatives would not address fundamental tasks such as guardianship and socialization alongside the goals relating to cognitive knowledge and diplomas, nor deliver equality of opportunity.

- *Learning and organization.* Curriculum and qualifications are central areas of policy, and student assessments are key elements of accountability, though questions persist over how far these develop capacities to learn. Individual classroom and teacher models remain dominant.

10

- *Management and governance.* Priority is given to administration and capacity to handle accountability pressures, with strong emphasis on efficiency. The nation (state/province in federal systems) remains central, but faces tensions due, for example, to decentralization, corporate interests in learning markets and globalization.
- *Resources and infrastructure.* No major increase in overall funding, while continual extension of schools' remits with new social responsibilities further stretches resources. The use of information and communications technology (ICT) continues to grow without changing schools' main organizational structures.
- *Teachers.* A distinct teacher corps, sometimes with civil service status; strong unions/associations but problematic professional status and rewards.

Scenario 1b: teacher exodus – the 'meltdown' scenario

There would be a major crisis of teacher shortages, highly resistant to conventional policy responses. This is triggered by a rapidly ageing profession, exacerbated by low teacher morale and buoyant opportunities in more attractive graduate jobs. The large size of the teaching force makes improvements in relative attractiveness costly, with long lead times for measures to show tangible results on overall numbers. There are wide disparities in the depth of the crisis by socio-geographic, as well as subject, area. Very different outcomes could follow: at one extreme, a vicious circle of retrenchment and conflict; at the other, emergency strategies spur radical innovation and collective change.

- *Learning and organization.* Where teacher shortages are acute they have detrimental effects on student learning. There are widely different organizational responses to shortages – some traditional, some highly innovative – and possibly greater use of ICT.
- *Management and governance.* Crisis management predominates. Even in areas saved from the worst difficulties, a fortress mentality prevails. National authorities are initially strengthened, acquiring extended powers in the face of crisis, but weakened the longer crises remain unresolved. A competitive international teaching market develops apace.
- *Resources and infrastructure.* As the crisis takes hold, funds flow increasingly into salaries to attract more teachers, with possible detrimental consequences for investments in areas such as ICT and physical infrastructure. Whether these imbalances would be rectified depends on strategies adopted to escape 'meltdown'.
- *Teachers.* The crisis, in part caused by teaching's unattractiveness, would worsen with growing shortages, especially in the most affected areas. General teacher rewards could well increase, as might the distinctiveness of the teacher corps in reflection of teachers' relative scarcity, though established arrangements may eventually erode with 'meltdown'.

Reschooling

The 'reschooling' scenarios would see major investments and widespread recognition for schools and their achievements, including towards the professionals, with a high priority accorded to both quality and equity. In Scenario 2a, the focus is on socialization goals and schools in communities, in certain contrast with the stronger knowledge orientation of Scenario 2b.

Scenario 2a: schools as core social centres

The school here enjoys widespread recognition as the most effective bulwark against social, family and community fragmentation. It is now heavily defined by collective and community tasks and can be described as a 'social anchor' (Kennedy, 2001; see also the social capital literature in relation to schools, Coleman, 1988, and more generally, Putnam, 2000, as well as OECD, 2001c). This leads to extensive shared responsibilities between schools and other community bodies, sources of expertise, and institutions of further and continuing education, shaping not conflicting with high teacher professionalism. Generous levels of financial support are needed to meet demanding requirements for quality learning environments in all communities and to ensure elevated esteem for teachers and schools.

- *Learning and organization.* The focus of learning broadens with more explicit attention given to non-cognitive outcomes, values and citizenship. A wide range of organizational forms and settings emerges, with strong emphasis on non-formal learning.
- *Management and governance.* Management is complex as the school is in dynamic interplay with diverse community interests and formal and non-formal programmes. Leadership is widely distributed and often collective. There is a strong local dimension of decision making, while well-developed national/international support frameworks are drawn on, particularly where social infrastructure is weakest.
- *Resources and infrastructure.* Significant investments would be made to update the quality of premises and equipment in general, to open school facilities to the community, and to ensure that the divides of affluence and social capital do not widen. ICT is used extensively, especially its communication capabilities.
- *Teachers.* There is a core of high-status teaching professionals, with varied contractual arrangements and conditions, though with good rewards for all. Around this core would be many other professionals, community players, parents, etc., and a blurring of roles.

Scenario 2b: schools as focused learning organizations

Schools are revitalized around a strong knowledge rather than social agenda, in a culture of high quality, experimentation, diversity and innovation. New forms of evaluation and competence assessment flourish. ICT is used extensively alongside other learning media, traditional and new. Knowledge management is to the fore, and the very large majority of schools justify the label 'learning organizations' (hence equality of opportunity is the norm), with extensive links to tertiary education and diverse other organizations.

- *Learning and organization.* There are demanding expectations for all for teaching and learning, combined with widespread development of specializations and diversity of organizational forms. Research on pedagogy flourishes and the science of learning is systematically applied.

10

- *Management and governance.* 'Learning organization' schools are characterized by flat hierarchy structures, using teams, networks and diverse sources of expertise. Quality norms typically replace regulatory and punitive accountability approaches. Decision-making is rooted strongly within schools and the profession, with the close involvement of parents, organizations and tertiary education and with well-developed guiding frameworks and support systems.
- *Resources and infrastructure.* There are substantial investments in all aspects of schooling, especially in disadvantaged communities, to develop flexible, state-of-the-art facilities. Extensive use made of ICT. The partnerships with organisations and tertiary education enhance the diversity of educational plant and facilities.
- *Teachers.* Highly motivated teachers enjoy favourable conditions, with strong emphasis on research and development (R&D), continuous professional development, group activities, networking (including internationally). Contractual arrangements might well be diverse, with mobility in and out of teaching.

Deschooling

Rather than high status and generous resourcing for schools, the dissatisfaction of a range of key players leads to the dismantling of school systems, to a greater or lesser degree. In Scenario 3a, new forms of cooperative networks come to predominate, compared with the competitive mechanisms of Scenario 3b.

Scenario 3a: learning networks and the network society

Dissatisfaction with institutionalized provision and expression given to diversified demand leads to the abandonment of schools in favour of a multitude of learning networks, quickened by the extensive possibilities of powerful, inexpensive ICT. The de-institutionalization, even dismantling, of school systems is part of the emerging 'network society'. The longstanding critique of Illich (1971) is complemented by the more recent analyses of Castells (1996). Various cultural, religious and community voices come to the fore in the socialization and learning arrangements for children, some very local in character, others using distance and cross-border networking.

- *Learning and organization.* Greater expression is given to learning for different cultures and values through networks of community interests. Small group, home schooling and individualized arrangements become widespread.
- *Management and governance.* With schooling assured through interlocking networks, authority becomes widely diffused. There is a substantial reduction of existing patterns of governance and accountability, though public policy responsibilities might still include addressing the 'digital divide', some regulation and framework setting, and overseeing remaining schools.
- *Resources and infrastructure.* There would be a substantial reduction in public facilities and institutionalized premises. Whether there could be an overall reduction in learning resources is hard to predict, though major invest-

ments in ICT could be expected. Diseconomies of small scale, with schooling organized by groups and individuals, might limit new investments.

- *Teachers.* there is no longer reliance on particular professionals called 'teachers': the demarcations – between teacher and student, parent and teacher, education and community – blur and sometimes break down. New learning professionals emerge, whether employed locally to teach or as consultants.

Scenario 3b: extending the market model

Existing market features in education are significantly extended as governments encourage diversification in a broader environment of market-led change. This is fuelled by dissatisfaction by 'strategic consumers' in cultures where schooling is commonly viewed as a private as well as a public good. Many new providers are stimulated to come into the learning market, encouraged by thorough-going reforms of funding structures, incentives and regulation. Flourishing indicators, measures and accreditation arrangements start to displace direct public monitoring and curriculum regulation. Innovation abounds, as do painful transitions and inequalities.

- *Learning and organization.* The most valued learning is importantly determined by choices and demands – whether of those buying educational services or of those, such as employers, giving market value to different forms of learning routes. There is a strong focus on non-cognitive outcomes and values might be expected to emerge. Wide organizational diversity exists.
- *Management and governance.* There is a substantially reduced role for public education authorities – overseeing market regulation but with less involvement in organizing provision or 'steering' and 'monitoring' – and entrepreneurial management modes are more prominent. There are important roles for information and guidance services and for indicators and competence assessments that provide market 'currency'.
- *Resources and infrastructure.* Funding arrangements and incentives are critical in shaping learning markets and determining absolute levels of resources. A wide range of market-driven changes would be introduced into the ownership and running of the learning infrastructure, some highly innovative and with the extensive use of ICT. Problems might be the diseconomies of scale and the inequalities associated with market failure.
- *Teachers.* New learning professionals – public and private, full-time and part-time – are created in the learning markets, and new training and accreditation opportunities would emerge for them. Market forces might see these professionals in much readier supply in areas of residential desirability and/or learning market opportunity than elsewhere.

Likely and desirable futures?

It is useful to distinguish the different cycles of schooling in identifying possible ways ahead. To realize lifelong learning for all (OECD, 1996) may well call for reschooling in the earlier cycles, with both strong knowledge and social remits. But, it may also need more deschooling in the later years of schooling, permitting

10

powerful roles for markets, distance education, community networks and informal learning, as well as the public authorities.

When asked about their preferred alternative futures, many in education concur around the reschooling scenarios while condemning both the 'bureaucratic status quo' and the deschooling, especially market-oriented, options. If a broader public sounding were to be taken, not all would necessarily hold to such views, but this was the general consensus of the Rotterdam conference participants meeting in November 2000 (Hutmacher, 2001). What Hutmacher also found in their responses was a broad correspondence between what were desired as futures and what is expected actually to happen. He describes this as 'optimistic' – that many believe in the force of their dreams and are confident that their nightmares will be avoided. It may equally be indicative of an unwillingness to confront uncomfortable options.

If the future does lie with reschooling, however, some very powerful obstacles will need to be overcome. Some of the most evident problems for, and questions relating to, these particular scenarios include the following:

- *Bureaucracy*. Many agree on the need to reduce bureaucracy, and to increase innovation and professionalism. The contemporary push to increase accountability, however, which in part is driven by the difficulties of maintaining traditional forms of governance, may too often be resulting in the opposite – greater bureaucratic administration and diminishing room for experimentation. Can accountability and innovation be pursued together?
- *Resources*. The reschooling scenarios assume generous resourcing, to meet at the same time their highly demanding quality and equality requirements. While in some places (some of the Nordic countries and Korea), education accounts for some 7 per cent of GDP, in many others it is 5 per cent or less, and these figures drop markedly in relation only to school education. Is there room in the public purse and private initiative to make a significant new investment in education, especially in ageing societies facing growing health and pension bills? Are schools as a whole always doomed to lag behind the more expensive higher education sector, no matter how convincing the arguments for such investments?
- *Public attitudes*. On a related point, how near is the general consensus so important to reschooling – that schools are central societal institutions warranting high esteem and the end to carping criticism? Or will the underlying assumptions of the other scenarios prove to be more realistic – constant grumbling and the unwillingness to countenance significant change (status quo) or widespread dissatisfaction leading to flight and partial dismantling of school systems (deschooling)? In the context of an ageing society, there is also the open question of how an increasingly potent elderly population prioritizes education compared with, say, health policies.
- *Teachers*. The reschooling scenarios assume redefinitions of professionalism, high esteem and demand to enter the teaching force at the same time as greater flexibility about who counts as a 'teacher' and about what constitutes a career. All this will call for major shifts in viewpoint in many countries, both by practising teachers and others. And, while not all countries are necessarily facing the 'meltdown' of Scenario 1b, many systems are now confronting major problems of supply brought about by an ageing teaching force and the questionable attractiveness of the profession.

- *Knowledge management.* Between the two reschooling scenarios, education-ists often express particular favour towards 2b – schools as focused learning organizations. In this future, the large majority of schools would epitomize the tenets of organizations actively practising knowledge management, with constant learning and flexible reorganization, networking and the intense application of R&D. Yet a recent OECD analysis (2000b) argues that this remains very far from the typical school system. The struggle is clearly to be uphill.

- *Communities and social capital.* In the Scenario 2a version of reschooling – schools as core social centres – the proximity of schools to, and their inte-gration with, communities is viewed as an essential element of social and personal development in a fragmented world. Yet it is at least as plausible to argue that the opposite will occur – schools more closely reflecting their immediate communities might simply exacerbate existing socio-cultural inequalities. How could such a destructive lockstep be overcome?

The challenge for those responsible for shaping and managing the future will lie in their capacity to address such issues. Whichever path is chosen is likely to involve the willingness and imagination in the educational world to embrace far-reaching change.

NOTES

1 Its first main output was a report called *Innovating Schools* – a title intended to convey a focus both on making change happen and on schools that are already in the vanguard of change (OECD, 1999).

2 This is not to neglect the lifelong learning (LLL) objective, since the schooling focus allows the ques-tion of how LLL would be promoted (or not) in terms of the foundations of competence, values and motivation that would be laid for all young people within each scenario.

3 In the recent publication *What Schools for the Future?* (OECD, 2001a) these were elaborated as five dimensions: (i) attitudes, expectations, political support; (ii) goals and functions for schooling; (iii) organization and structures; (iv) the geo-political dimension; (v) the teaching force.

4 This was done in collaboration with the International Futures Programme (IFP), the unit within the OECD advising its secretary-general and other senior officials on futures for a broad range of social, economic and technological policies (see OECD 2001b and OECD 2000a).

REFERENCES

Castells, M. (1996) *The Rise of the Network Society. The Information Age: Economy, Society and Culture*, 1, Cambridge, MA: Blackwell.

Coleman, J.S. (1988) 'Social capital in the creation of human capital', *American Journal of Sociology*, 94, pp. S95–120.

Hutmacher, W. (2001) 'Visions of decision-makers and educators for the future of schools' in OECD (2001) *What Schools for the Future?*, Paris: Organization for Economic Co-operation and Development.

Illich, I. (1971), *Deschooling Society*, New York: Harper & Row.

Kennedy, K.J. (2001) 'A new century and the challenges it brings for young people: how might schools support youth in the future?' in OECD (2001a) *What Schools for the Future?*, Paris: Organization for Economic Co-operation and Development.

OECD (1996) *Lifelong Learning for All*, Paris: Organization for Economic Co-operation and Development.

OECD (1999), Innovating Schools, Paris: Organization for Economic Co-operation and Development.

OECD (2000a), *The Creative Society of the 21st Century*, Paris: Organization for Economic Co-operation and Development.

OECD (2000b), *Knowledge Management in the Learning Society*, Paris: Organization for Economic Co-operation and Development.

OECD (2001a), *What Schools for the Future?*, Paris: Organization for Economic Co-operation and Development.

10

OECD (2001b) *Governance in the 21st Century*, Paris: Organization for Economic Co-operation and Development.

OECD (2001c) *The Well-being of Nations: The Role of Human and Social Capital*, Paris: Organization for Economic Co-operation and Development.

Putnam, R. (2000) *Bowling Alone: The Collapse and Revival of American Community*, New York: Simon & Schuster.

CHAPTER 63

Networks of learning: a new construct for educational provision and a new strategy for reform

JUDITH CHAPMAN AND DAVID ASPIN

Networks provide a new construct for conceiving of educational provision and a new strategy for achieving reform. Across OECD (Organization for Economic Co-operation and Development) countries, networks have been seen as increasing relevant in the operationalization of lifelong learning. This chapter highlights the ways in which networks can be applied in the operationalization of lifelong learning and the creation of schools of the future and lays out a progressive programme of research designed to enhance our understandings of this important concept in the administration of education.

The importance of networks as a strategy in educational reform

In consideration of the operationalization of lifelong learning, a debate is emerging internationally on the need for a new strategy for learning provision and a new approach to innovation and change. The concept of 'networks' has begun to play an important part in these discussions. Networks provide a new construct for conceiving of educational provision and a new vehicle for achieving change. In recent times the restructuring of education has resulted in more decentralized systems of education. In such systems hierarchical and bureaucratic approaches to administration and management have become increasingly outmoded. In this context new approaches are being explored. The concept of networks provides one approach to navigating a way through issues associated with the decentralization of education systems.

Networks offer a means of assisting in the policy implementation process, especially in a time of changed centralization/decentralization arrangements. If we are going to raise standards in education there is a need to link policy both horizontally and vertically. Networks are one way of achieving this linkage. Networks provide a process for cultural and attitudinal change, embedding reform in the interactions, actions and behaviour of a range of different stakeholders in education and the community. They provide a multi-agency vehicle for reform that has the potential to be more supportive, cooperative, less costly and less disruptive than much of the wide-scale structural change of the past. Networks provide for an opportunity for shared and dispersed leadership and responsibility, drawing on resources in the community beyond members of the education profession. In so doing they can provide a more cost-effective, community-based reform strategy. Networks can also be capacity building, in so far as they are able to produce new knowledge and mutual learning that can then feed back and inform public policy.

A concern for networks moves attention away from recent preoccupations with micro-level change at the individual site. Networks are able to function at the meso-level to strengthen interconnections and spread innovation across all levels – the micro, meso and macro-levels. Through the dissemination of network knowledge, both policy development and practice may be enhanced in important areas of national concern. Networks have the potential to bring together the policy, resource and practice dimensions of educational reform. If networks are successful they hold the possibility of changing the environment in which policy makers operate. They provide the opportunity for the environment and the system to become 'recultured' in ways that are more cooperative, interconnected, and multi-agency. They have a capacity for evolutionary transformation and renewal in changing aspirations, ways of working together and providing learning opportunities. The commitment to working together that underpins networks incorporates the notion of working together at all levels, including government. In this way, networks provide an opportunity for more effective policy development and implementation at all levels through a wide array of agencies in the community.

The relevance of the concept of networks

The concept of networks differs in nature from other terms that have historically been used in association with educational institutions and with the organizational arrangements with which they are managed and through which innovation and change have typically been brought about. The idea of networks is distinct from traditional forms of grouping of educational organizations and systems, in which hierarchical structures and organizational approaches were most often adopted, and from the more recent emphases in which the market philosophy prevailed. In contrast to such approaches, the notion of networks stresses the idea of 'community' as the common element and principle of connection between institutions, organizations, agencies and people. In this approach, learning providers are not talked of as 'clusters', which simply connote geographical proximity, nor 'groups', which suggest an almost accidental agglomeration of disparate institutions. Rather they are seen as being overtly associated with each other in forms of connection and relationship that are deliberately established and worked upon in the pursuit of a commonality of interests, concerns and goals.

Networks are intentional constructions, linked together in a web of common purposes. They are self-conscious and deliberately established organic entities in which all the constituent elements are equal in the weight of enmeshment that they carry and the responsibility that they bear for making contributions towards the whole. An appropriate metaphor here is the worldwide web. In this, sites are set up and interlinking connections are made between them and then followed along filigrees of interlinked fields of interests and concerns. Here the operating principle is that inquiry in one area will lead on through interconnecting pathways and linkages to a congruent or contiguous area in and from which further avenues of inquiry can be opened up, explored and expanded.

There are sound grounds for the growth and adoption of this idea in organizational and institutional life and for understanding educational innovation and change. As opposed to more traditional views, based upon principles of disciplinary difference and demarcation, workers in the philosophy of science and language more recently have argued that the world of theory, knowledge and learning grows and develops holistically. Such learning is integrated in much the same way as the gradual construction and extension of the spider's web. Each strand of thought is capable of connection to neighbouring or even distant other strands, along a tracery of cognitive connections that constitutes an overall reticulation – a unified and unifying cognitive nexus – of the 'theory' we have about the world, the ways in which we cognize and think about it, and the moves we make when we are challenged to learn something new and so change it by expanding it further (Quine and Ullian 1970; Wilson 1998).

New lines of social, political and administrative thought have also functioned to provide an increasingly powerful basis for consideration of networks, arising from the envisioning of learning organizations and systems as communities and their conceptualization as important nodes in the evolution and establishment of learning networks. In recent years notions of the community, as articulated and developed by such writers as Sandel (1981), MacIntyre (1980), Etzioni (1996) and Gray (1997), have been enormously influential in revitalizing and redirecting social and political thinking. Notions of community have laid the basis for the establishment and elaboration of new ways of thinking about political morality, public policy and administrative relations, and the creation of new social forms, structures and interactions that have wide-ranging implications for education and its institutions. The notion of networks is an inherent part of these considerations.

The justification for networks in lifelong learning provision

Internationally, the concept of networks has been seen to be of increasing relevance in the operationalization of lifelong learning. A number of factors can be identified for this focus.

Educating flexible, networked workers

The OECD study on sustainable flexibility (OECD, 1997, p. 37) argues that, in the new information and knowledge-based economy of the twenty-first century, with rapidly changing technologies and markets for products, the nature of work will be transformed. This in turn will alter expectations regarding the kind of worker required. This transformation will be characterized by flexibility and networking, in which there will be a complex interplay between more highly educated workers prepared to learn more quickly to take on new tasks and to move from one job to another, and best-practice firms promoting increased flexibility through general training, multiple-task jobs, and employee decision making.

10

The OECD (ibid., p. 35) argues that the need to develop workers who have higher-order problem-solving skills and who can help organize more learning has profound implications for educational provision:

> *First it means that the standard forms of vocational education organised around specific skills for specific jobs are almost totally anachronistic, except in the sense that they can be used to teach problem-solving and organisational/teaching skills to students who have been alienated from more academic approaches to learning. Second, it suggests that learning should be increasingly organised in a co-operative fashion, where students study in groups, present group work, and often get evaluated as a group. Third, the curriculum should include the development of networking, motivational and teaching skills, so that students develop a clear understanding of human behaviour and the understanding of group processes.*

Creating optimal learning environments through teams and networks

In an examination of environments and infrastructures that will facilitate the flow of knowledge and ideas in the knowledge-based societies of the twenty-first century, Florida (1995, p. 535) concludes:

> *The industrial and innovation systems of the 21st Century will be remarkably different from those that have operated for most of the 20th Century. Knowledge and human intelligence will replace physical labour as the main source of value. Technological change will accelerate at a pace heretofore unknown: innovation will be perpetual and continuous. Knowledge-intensive organisations based on networks and teams will replace vertical bureaucracy, the corner stone of the 20th Century.*

The world-view of the late nineteenth and early twentieth centuries stressed the idea of learning as linear, sequential, generalizable and mechanistic, and organized approaches to learning were predicated upon that idea. Educational institutions became characterized by hierarchical organizational structures. Learning was arranged along the lines of rigid divisions and departments; knowledge was compartmentalized into discrete and manageable parts and sequences; assessment came to be based on the measurable and the quantifiable; and approaches to and methods of learning promoted the acquisition of facts and information constituting worthwhile knowledge.

Such assumptions concerning human mental processes, such approaches to learning and such models of the proper organization of schooling are no longer considered adequate, even if they were ever valid, to meet the demands of learners preparing for the changed economic and social conditions, cognitive climate and intellectual demands of the twenty-first century. It is now widely accepted that new thinking about the nature of learning and new conceptions of the styles of effective learning, which students find best suited to their own modes of cognitive progress and achievement, must lay the basis for learning. Approaches to learning constructed along such lines will more accurately reflect the findings and implications of current accounts of learning and the acquisition of knowledge and understanding worked out in accordance with the cognitive and meta-cognitive science of our times.

Griffey and Kelleher (1996, pp. 3–9) give an account of the history of learning theory and come forward with the following idea of an optimum learning environment consistent with most recent knowledge and understandings about learning. They recommend that the optimum learning environment is one where:

- learning is based on the provision of direct experience rather than indirect experience and the use of representational systems;
- learning takes place through action in the context in which the learning is to be applied;
- learning takes place in the presence of experts practised in the contexts in which the learning is to be applied;
- individuals become conscious of their implicit theories about learning;
- individuals view learning as under their control and as intrinsically rewarding;
- learners become conscious of their thinking and learning strategies;
- collaborative teamwork provides experience in learning to learn, facing problems, adapting to these in a practical context, and reflecting on problem formulation and problem-solving strategies;
- facilitators of learning themselves engage in learning.

Learning networks are aimed to embody such principles of optimal learning environments.

Learning networks beyond the formal learning provider

More fluid relationships and combinations of institutional-based learning and work, and formal and non-formal learning, are increasingly becoming a feature of the life and activity of organizations committed to the idea and principles of lifelong learning. This will necessitate the provision of innovative ways and means for young people to use the workplace and the community more widely as sites, opportunities and occasions for learning. Work-experience programmes can be regarded as an important way of enabling students to identify, understand and articulate their learning, career development and future professional needs. In organizations and systems committed to lifelong learning, young people will need to become active agents planning for and managing their formal and further learning opportunities, their work experience, and the unfolding and protraction of their careers.

Particular attention will need to be paid to the ways in which learning providers might assist students moving away from being 'at risk' to being 'on target' in respect of their future educational and career decision making and management. This will involve more effective career counselling to help prepare students for coping with and managing their own career pathways in an uncertain world of work and an often unstable and rapidly changing work environment. Work-based and community-based learning, and parallel learning programmes, will necessitate considerable inter- and intra-professional collaboration and organizational change.

10

Laying down a progressive programme of research

Networks have only recently emerged as a strategy for reform. There is now a need for a progressive research programme to study networks. Such a programme might include:

- sustained conceptual, analytical and empirical studies of networks as a construct and strategy for educational reform;
- clarification of the conceptual and practical issues relevant to the concept of networks and the role of networks in stimulating learning, innovation and change;
- consideration of what is new and specific about networks as a strategy for reform;
- identification of the values that underpin and pervade networks;
- an examination of the conditions that enable networks to be established and sustained: the opportunities, barriers and challenges to their operation; who are the stakeholders and what are their functions; what makes networks work and not work;
- studies of the individual and public impacts and outcomes of networks: how networks build a capacity to learn for individuals, agencies and organizations;
- consideration of the ways in which networks contribute to systemic change and improved policy and practice, and the ways in which policy can support networks.

Conclusion

Networks provide a new construct for conceiving of educational provision and a new vehicle for achieving educational change. Networks have the potential to raise educational standards through linking policy both horizontally and vertically. They provide a multi-agency vehicle for reform, drawing on resources in the community beyond the education profession to provide a more cost-effective, community-based reform strategy. They can be capacity building , in so far as they are able to produce new knowledge and mutual learning that can then feed back and inform public policy. If networks are successful, they have the potential to change the environment in which policy makers operate, since they provide the opportunity for the environment to be recultured in ways that are more cooperative, interconnected and multi-agency. In these ways they provide an opportunity for more effective policy implementation at all levels through a wide range of agencies in the community.

There is now a need for a progressive research programme focused on networks. Such a research programme will provide an opportunity to assess whether the potential of networks are realizable. If so, networks will provide policy makers, educators and member of the community with the opportunity to contribute in innovative ways to the international and national goal of making lifelong learning a reality for all and the creation of schools of the future.

ACKNOWLEDGEMENT

This chapter is informed by work undertaken by Judith Chapman in association with the OECD/CERI activity on Schooling for Tomorrow. Special acknowledgment is given to David Istance of the OECD Secretariat and to members of the Expert Meetings associated with that activity, held in Paris in 1999 and Lisbon in 2000.

REFERENCES

Etzioni, A. (1996) *The New Golden Rule: Community and Morality in a Democratic Society*, New York: Basic Books.

Florida, R. (1995) 'Toward the learning region', *Futures*, 27 (5), pp. 527–36.

Gray, J. (1997) *Endgames*, Cambridge: Polity Press.

Griffey, S. and Kelleher, M. (1996) 'How do people learn? Connecting practice with theory', *Training Matters*, 5, autumn.

MacIntyre, A. (1980) *After Virtue*, London: Duckworth.

OECD (1996) *Making Lifelong Learning a Reality for All*, Paris: Organization for Economic Co-operation and Development.

OECD (1997) *Sustainable Flexibility: A Prospective Study on Work, Family and Society in the Information Age*, Paris: Organization for Economic Co-operation and Development.

Quine, W.V. and Ullian, J.S. (1970) *The Web of Belief*, New York: Random House.

Sandel, M. (1981) *Liberalism and the Limits of Justice*, Cambridge: Cambridge University Press.

Wilson, E.O. (1998) *Consilience: the Unity of Knowledge*, London: Little, Brown & Company.

10

CHAPTER 64

Globalization, localization and individualization of education for the future

YIN CHEONG CHENG

Rapid globalization is one of the most salient aspects of the new millennium, particularly since the fast development of information technology in the last two decades. To different observers, different types of globalization can be identified, even though most of the attention is in the areas of economy and technology. In the new millennium there should be multiple globalizations, including technological globalization, economic globalization, social globalization, political globalization, cultural globalization and learning globalization (Cheng, 2000).

Triplization in education

Inevitably, how education should be responsive to the trends and challenges of globalization has become a major concern in policy making in these years (Green, 1999; Henry, *et al.*, 1999; Jones, 1999). As well as the effects of globalization, it is also necessary to consider localization and individualization in ongoing educational reforms (Cheng, 2000). All of these processes together can be taken as a 'triplization' process (i.e. triple+izations) to form a basis for paradigm shifts in planning educational reforms and developing new pedagogic methods and environments that will facilitate students' learning in facing the challenges of the new millennium. The implications of globalization, localization and individualization for education generally and educational management in particular are summarized in Table 64.1 and Figure 64.1.

Globalization refers to the transfer, adaptation and development of values, knowledge, technology and behavioural norms across countries and societies in different parts of the world. The typical phenomena and characteristics associated with globalization include the growth of global networking (for example, the internet, worldwide e-communication and transportation); global transfer and interflow in technological, economic, social, political, cultural and learning aspects; international alliances and competitions; international collaboration and exchange; the global village; multicultural integration; and the use of international standards and benchmarks. Implications of globalization for educational leadership and management should include maximizing the relevance of education to

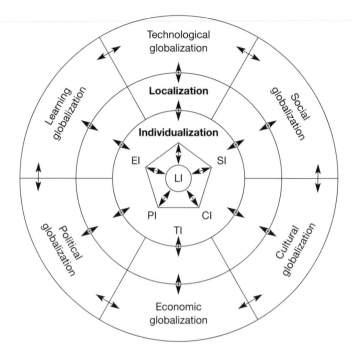

Figure 64.1 Globalization, localization and individualization of education

Note: TI, EI, SI, CI, PI, LI represent the development of technological, economic, social, cultural, political and learning intelligences.

Source: adapted from Cheng, 2000.

Table 64.1 *Implications of triplization for educational leadership and management*

Triplization	Conceptions and characteristics	Implications for educational leadership and management
Globalization	Transfer, adaptation and development of values, knowledge, technology and behavioural norms across countries and societies in different parts of the world:	To maximize the relevance of education to global developments and pool the best intellectual resources, support and initiatives from different parts of the world for learning and teaching:
	<ul><li>global networking</li><li>technological, economic, social, political, cultural and learning globalization</li><li>global growth of internet</li><li>international alliances and competitions</li><li>international collaboration and exchange</li><li>global village</li><li>multicultural integration</li></ul>	<ul><li>web-based learning</li><li>international visit/immersion programme</li><li>international exchange programme</li><li>learning from the internet</li><li>international partnership in teaching and learning at group, class and individual levels</li><li>interactions and sharing through video-conferencing across countries, communities, institutions, and individuals</li></ul>

10

Table 64.1 *Continued*

Triplization	Conceptions and characteristics	Implications for educational leadership and management
Globalization	• international standards and benchmarks	• curriculum content on political, cultural, and learning technological, economic, social, globalization
Localization	Transfer, adaptation and development of related values, knowledge, technology and behavioural norms from/to the local contexts: • local networking • technological, economic, social, political, cultural, and learning localization • decentralization to the local site level • indigenous culture • community needs and expectations • local involvement, collaboration and support • local relevance and legitimacy • community-based needs and characteristics • social norms and ethos	To maximize the education relevance to local developments and bring in community support and resources, local partnership and collaboration in learning and teaching: • community involvement • public-institutional collaboration • institutional-based management and accountability/school-based management • inter-institutional collaboration • community-related curriculum • curriculum content on technological, economic, social, political, cultural and learning localization
Individualization	Transfer, adaptation and development of related external values, knowledge, technology and behavioural norms to meet individual needs and characteristics: • individualized services • development of human potential in technological, economic, social, political, cultural and learning aspects • human initiative and creativity • self-actualization • self-managing and self-governing • special needs	To maximize motivation, human initiative and creativity in learning and teaching: • individualized educational programmes • individualized learning targets, methods, and progress schedules • self-lifelong learning, self-actualizing, and self-initiative • self-managing students and teachers • meeting special needs • development of contextualized multiple intelligences

the global developments and the pooling up the best intellectual resources, support and initiatives from different parts of the world for learning and teaching (Daun, 1997).

Some ongoing examples and common evidences of globalization in education are web-based learning; the use of the internet in learning and research; international visit/immersion programmes; international exchange programmes; international partnership in teaching and learning at the group, class, and individual levels; and interaction and sharing through video-conferencing across countries, communities, institutions and individuals. Many such examples of initiatives can be found in Hong Kong, Europe, Australia and the USA. Further, the development of new curriculum content on technological, economic, social, political, cultural and learning globalization is also important and necessary in new education.

Localization refers to the transfer, adaptation and development of related values, knowledge, technology and behavioural norms from/to the local contexts. Some characteristics and examples of localization include local networking; adaptation of external technological, economic, social, political, cultural and learning initiatives to local communities; decentralization to the community or site level; development of indigenous culture; meeting community needs and expectations; local involvement, inter-institutional collaboration and community support; local relevance and legitimacy; and concern for community-based needs and characteristics and social norms and ethos.

The implications of localization to education reform are to maximize the relevance of education to local developments and bring in community support and resources, local partnership and collaboration in learning and teaching. Some examples for the practice of localization include community involvement in education; privatization in education; public-institutional collaboration; assurance of institutional accountability; and the implementation of institutional autonomy, school-based management and community-based curriculum. More and more such examples can be found not only in developed countries like the USA, UK and European countries but also in many developing areas in the Asia-Pacific region. The development of new curriculum content related to localization in technological, economic, social, political, cultural and learning aspects of the society is also receiving growing attention.

Individualization refers to the transfer, adaptation and development of related external values, knowledge, technology and behavioural norms to meet individual needs and characteristics. The importance of individualization to human development and performance is based on the concerns and theories of human motivation and needs. Some examples of individualization are the provision of individualized services; emphasis on human potentials; promotion of human initiative and creativity; encouragement of self-actualization, self-managing and self-governing; and concern for special needs. The major implication of individualization to educational leadership is to maximize motivation, initiative and creativity of students and teachers in learning and teaching through such measures as implementing individualized educational programmes; designing and using individualized learning targets, methods and progress schedules; encouraging students to be self-learning, self-actualizing and self-initiating; meeting individual special needs; and developing students' contextualized multiple intelligences (CMI), including economic, social, political, cultural, technological and learning intelligences (for more detail, see Cheng, 2000).

10

Students, teachers and education institutions are 'triplized' (i.e. globalized, localized and individualized) during the process of triplization.

Paradigm shift in education

With these concepts of triplization in education, a paradigm shift of education for the future can be initiated from the traditional site-bounded paradigm to the new triplization paradigm.

The future of the world, human nature and development

In the new paradigm, the future of the world is assumed to be in multiple globalization, including technological, economic, social, political, cultural and learning globalizations. These globalizations are also increasingly interacting in the whole world. The world is moving very fast to become a global village, in which different parts of the world are rapidly networked and globalized through the internet and different types of IT, communications and transportation. All countries and areas have more and more common concerns. In addition, the interactions between nations and people become boundless, multidimensional, multilevel, fast and frequent. They become more and more mutually dependent with international collaborations, exchanges and interflows (Ohmae, 2000).

In the new paradigm, the human in the complicated social context of the new millennium is assumed to be multiple – as a technological, economic, social, political, cultural, and learning person in a global village of information, high technology and multi-cultures. Both individuals and society need multiple developments in the technological, economic, social, political, cultural and learning aspects. Lifelong learning individuals and a learning society are necessary to sustain the continuous multiple developments of individuals and society in a fast changing era. Society has to move towards being a multiple intelligence society that can provide the necessary knowledge and intelligence base and driving force to support the multiple developments. And individuals have to move towards becoming a CMI citizen who can contribute to the development of a CMI society.

In contrast, the traditional paradigm perceives that the need for lifelong learning or for a learning society may not be so important. That traditional society is an industrial or agricultural society emphasizing some types of intelligence or knowledge related to the existing stage of development of a society. Individuals are expected to be citizens with a bounded type of knowledge or skill that meets the need of society at a certain stage of development.

The education environment and aims of education

Following the assumptions about the world and its development, the new paradigm assumes that the education environment is inevitably characterized by triplization, including globalization, localization and individualization at the different levels and different aspects of the education system. As the education environment is very fast changing and becoming very complicated and full of uncertainties and ambiguities, the boundaries of higher institutions as well as the education system become unclear and disappearing. Students and teachers often interact frequently and intensively with the 'real world' in learning and teaching. Continuous educational reforms and developments are inevitable, owing to various local and global challenges emerging from this changing education environment. In such a context, the aim of education is to support students to become CMI leaders and citizens who will be engaged in lifelong learning and will creatively contribute to the building up of a CMI society and a CMI global village.

In contrast, the traditional paradigm assumes that the education environment is mainly characterized by the needs of the local community, which is slowly changing with moderate uncertainty and complexity. The aim of education in the traditional paradigm is to equip students with the necessary skills and knowledge to survive in a local community or to support the development of a society, particularly in the economic and social aspects at a certain stage.

Paradigm shift in learning

In the new paradigm, learning should be individualized, localized and globalized. (*see* Table 64.2).

Table 64.2 *Paradigm shifts in learning*

New triplization paradigm	Traditional site-bounded paradigm
Individualized learning	*Reproduced learning*
● Student is the centre of education	● Student is the follower of teacher
● Individualized programmes	● Standard programmes
● Self-learning	● Absorbing knowledge
● Self-actualizing process	● Receiving process
● Focus on how to learn	● Focus on how to gain
● Self-rewarding	● Externally rewarded
Localized and globalized learning	*Site-bounded learning*
● Multiple sources of learning	● Teacher-based learning
● Networked learning	● Separated learning
● Lifelong and everywhere	● Fixed period and within institution
● Unlimited opportunities	● Limited opportunities
● World-class learning	● Site-bounded learning
● Local and international outlook	● Mainly institution-based experiences

Individualized learning

The student is the centre of education. Students' learning should be facilitated to meet their needs and personal characteristics, and develop their potentials – particularly CMI – in an optimal way. Individualized and tailor-made programmes (including targets, content, methods and schedules) for different students are

10

necessary and feasible. Students can be self-motivated and self-learning with appropriate guidance and facilitation, and learning is a self-actualizing, discovering, experiencing and reflecting process. Since information and knowledge are accumulated at an unbelievable speed but are outdated very quickly, it is nearly impossible to make any sense if education is mainly to deliver skills and knowledge, particularly when students can find the knowledge and information easily with the help of information technology and internet. Therefore, the focus of learning is on learning how to learn, research, think and create. To sustain lifelong learning, learning should be enjoyable and self-rewarding.

Localized and globalized learning

Students' learning should be facilitated in such a way that local and global resources, support, and networks can be brought in to maximize the learning opportunities. Through localization and globalization, there are multiple sources of learning. Students can learn from multiple sources inside and outside their higher institutions, locally and globally, and are not limited to a small number of teachers in their institutions. Participation in local and international learning programmes can help them achieve the related community and global outlook and experiences beyond education institutions. Today, more and more examples of such kinds of programmes can be found in Japan, Hong Kong, France and the USA. The learning is a type of networked learning, and students will be grouped and networked locally and internationally. Learning groups and networks will become a major driving force to sustain the learning climate and multiply the learning effects through mutual sharing and inspiring. We can expect that each student can have a group of lifelong partner students in different corners of the world to share their learning experiences.

It is expected that learning will happen everywhere and is lifelong. Education is just the preparation for high-level lifelong learning and discovery. Learning opportunities are unlimited. Students can maximize the opportunities for their learning from local and global exposures through the internet, web-based learning, video-conferencing, cross-cultural sharing, and different types of interactive and multimedia materials. Students can learn from world-class teachers, experts, peers and learning materials from different parts of the world. In other words, their learning can be world-class learning.

Traditional paradigm of learning

In the traditional thinking, students' learning is part of the reproduction and perpetuation process of the existing knowledge and manpower structure to sustain developments of society, particularly social and economic developments. Education is perceived as a process for students and their learning is 'reproduced' to meet the needs of the manpower structure in the society. The profiles of student and learning are clearly different from those in the new paradigm (*see* Table 64.2).

Reproduced learning

In traditional education, students are the followers of their teachers. They go through standard programmes of education in which students are taught in the same way and at the same pace, even though their abilities may be different. Individualized programmes seem to be unfeasible. The learning process is characterized by absorbing certain types of knowledge: students are 'students' of their teachers, and they absorb knowledge from their teachers. Learning is a disciplinary, receiving and socializing process that makes close supervision and control of the learning process necessary. The focus of learning is on how to gain some professional or academic knowledge and skills. Learning is often perceived as working hard to achieve external rewards and avoid punishment.

Site-bounded learning

In the traditional paradigm, all learning activities are site-bounded and teacher-based. Students learn from a limited number of schoolteachers and their prepared materials. Therefore, teachers are the major sources of knowledge and learning. Students learn the standard curriculum from their textbooks and related materials assigned by their teachers. Students are often arranged to learn in a separated way and are kept responsible for their individual learning outcomes. They have few opportunities for mutual support and learning. Their learning experiences are mainly institutional experiences, alienated from the fast changing local and global communities. Learning happens only in school within a given time frame. Graduation tends to be the end of students' learning.

Paradigm shift in teaching

In the new triplization paradigm, teachers' teaching should be triplized: individualized, localized and globalized. (*see* Table 64.3)

Individualized teaching

Teachers and their teaching are facilitated in such a way that their potentials can be maximized to facilitate students' learning in an optimal way. Teaching is considered a process to initiate, facilitate and sustain students' self-learning, self-exploration and self-actualization, therefore, teachers should play a role as facilitators or mentors who support students' learning. The focus of teaching is to arouse students' curiosity and motivation to think, act and learn. Teaching is also about sharing with students the joy of the learning process and outcomes. To teachers themselves, teaching is a lifelong learning process involving continuous discovery, experimenting, self-actualization, reflection and professional development. Teachers are CMI teachers who can be models for students in developing their multiple intelligences. Each teacher has his/her own potential and characteristics, and different teachers can teach in different styles to maximize their own contributions.

10

Table 64.3 *Paradigm shift in teaching*

New triplization paradigm	Traditional site-bounded paradigm
Individualized teaching	*Reproduced teaching*
● Teacher is a facilitator or mentor to support students' learning	● Teacher is the centre of education
● Multiple intelligences teacher	● Partially competent teacher
● Individualized teaching style	● Standard teaching style
● Arousing curiosity	● Transferring knowledge
● Facilitating process	● Delivery process
● Sharing joy	● Achieving standard
● Lifelong learning	● A practice of previous knowledge
Localized and globalized teaching	*Site-bounded teaching:*
● Multiple sources of teaching	● Site-bounded in teaching
● Networked teaching	● Separated teaching
● World-class teaching	● Bounded teaching
● Unlimited opportunities	● Limited opportunities
● Local and international outlook	● Mainly site experiences
● World-class and networked teacher	● A site-bounded and separated teacher

Localized and globalized teaching

The new paradigm emphasizes that teaching should be facilitated in such a way that local and global resources, supports and networks can be brought in to maximize the opportunities for teachers' own developments in teaching and their contribution to students' learning. Through localization and globalization, there are multiple sources of teaching, for example, self-learning programmes and packages; web-based learning; outside experts; and community experiential programmes, inside and outside their institutions, locally and globally. Teachers can maximize the opportunities to enhance the effectiveness of their teaching from local and global networking and exposure through the internet, web-based teaching, video-conferencing, cross-cultural sharing, and different types of interactive and multimedia materials. With teachers' help, students can learn from the world-class materials, experts, peers and teachers in different parts of the world, so that teaching can become world-class teaching. Through participation in local and international development and research programmes, teachers can achieve a global and regional outlook and experiences beyond institutions.

Furthermore, this teaching is a type of networked teaching. Teachers are grouped and networked locally and globally to develop and sustain a new professional culture through mutual sharing and inspiring. They become world-class and networked teachers through localization and globalization. It is no surprise that each teacher can have a group of lifelong partner teachers in other parts of the world with whom they share and discuss their experiences and ideas of professional practice.

Traditional paradigm of teaching

As discussed in the traditional site-bounded paradigm of learning, teaching is often perceived as part of the reproduction and perpetuation process of the existing knowledge and manpower structure to sustain developments of society. As shown in Table 64.3, the characteristics of teaching are contrastingly different from the new paradigm.

Reproduced teaching

Teachers are at the centre of education. They have some technical, social and professional competencies to deliver knowledge to students. Teachers teach in some standard styles and patterns to ensure standard knowledge is taught to students, even though the students' own potentials and personal characteristics may be different. The teachers' major task is to transfer some knowledge and skills they have to students, and therefore teaching is often a disciplinary, delivery, training and socializing process. Teaching is also often perceived as working hard to achieve some external standards in examinations.

Site-bounded teaching

In the traditional paradigm, teaching is often bounded within the school. Schools are the major venues for teaching and teachers are the major sources of knowledge. Teachers are often arranged to teach in a separated way and are kept responsible for their teaching outcomes. They have few opportunities for mutual support and learning. Their teaching is often bounded such that teachers teach the standard curriculum with their textbooks and related materials approved by their schools or related authority. The teachers and their teaching are often alienated from the fast-changing local communities or international contexts. From this traditional perspective, teachers are clearly site-bounded and separated, and will rarely have any global and regional outlook to develop a world-class education for their students in the new century.

Conclusion

The triplization paradigm for rethinking and reengineering education is contrastingly different from the traditional thinking.

We expect education will be triplized in the twenty-first century. In fact, the ongoing education reforms in different parts of the world have already provided evidence that many countries are making strides in this direction. Various types of initiatives in globalization, localization and individualization of learning and teaching have been started with the help of the information technology and boundless multiple networking. Through triplization, we will create unlimited opportunities and multiple global and local sources for lifelong learning and the development of both students and teachers, and facilitate the students' learning process to become more interactive, effective, self-actualizing and enjoyable.

In the new millennium, educational leaders should be strategic and able to foresee the new trends and paradigm shifts in education and educational leadership. They must help all constituencies understand these shifts and prepare strategies to face up to the challenges and create a new future for school education. These leaders themselves should also be CMI leaders who create a CMI school environment that can facilitate teachers and students to achieve a higher level of multiple intelligence. To change education and the internal school process from the traditional mode towards the new mode, they should be transformational leaders who have the vision and capacity to make all the transformations and shifts technically, structurally and culturally possible. Since triplization is necessary to maximizing educational relevance and effectiveness for the future, school leaders should be triplization leaders who can initiate, implement and sustain globalization, localization and individualization of teaching and learning for their teachers and students (Cheng, 2003).

Clearly, the ongoing paradigm shift in education and functional shift in leadership are completely new and demanding and pose major challenges to our educational leaders. We need plenty of new initiatives in research, development and training to prepare for all these changes, shifts and trends in educational leadership and management in these few years ahead.

REFERENCES

Cheng, Y.C. (2000) 'A CMI-triplisation paradigm for reforming education in the new millennium', *International Journal of Educational Management*, 14 (4), pp. 156–74.

Cheng, Y.C. (2003) 'The changing context of school leadership: implications for paradigm shift' in Leithwood, K., Chapman, J., Corson, D., Hallinger, P. and Hart, A. (eds) *International Handbook of Research in Educational Leadership and Administration*, Dordrecht, The Netherlands: Kluwer Academic Publishers.

Daun, H. (1997) 'National forces, globalisation and educational restructuring: some European response patterns', *Compare*, 27 (1), pp. 19–41.

Green, A. (1999) 'Education and globalisation in Europe and East Asia: convergent and divergent trends', *Journal of Education Policy*, 14 (1), pp. 55–71.

Henry, M., Lingard, B., Rizvi, F. and Taylor, S. (1999) 'Working with/against globalisation in education', *Journal of Education Policy*, 14 (1), pp. 85–97.

Jones, P. W. (1999) 'Globalisation and the UNESCO mandate: multilateral prospects for educational development', *International Journal of Educational Development*, 19 (1), pp. 17–25.

Ohmae, K. (2000) *The Invisible Continent: Four Strategic Imperatives of the New Economy*, London: Nicholas Brealey Publishing.

CHAPTER 65

Educational leadership and the tensions and dilemmas of decentralization and centralization

DAN GIBTON

This chapter examines the links and tensions between what we know about educational leadership, and what we know about decentralization and centralization policy. The following case, regarding Ken, the principal of a large comprehensive secondary school in a rundown area in a large city in England, exemplifies some of these tensions:

> *I've been a head – I've seen the introduction of the national curriculum, and pupil behaviour management. I've gone all the way from being a 'headteacher' in the very strict and limited sense to becoming a true general manager of the school. I have little or no training for this new role, but every morning I remember when a simple thing like painting the school had to wait for a seven-year cycle run by the council. So I would never go back to my previous role – no matter how difficult things are now.*

Ken points at the crux of what educational leaders feel in these decentralized times: anxiety, sometimes fear, a lot of criticism, but a firm stand that decentralization does them good. He has been transformed into a powerful leader.

These findings now seem to be worldwide (Beare, Caldwell and Millikan, 1993; Caldwell, 1993; Davies and Ellison, 1997; Gibton, Sabar and Goldring, 2000; Hallinger, Murphy and Hausman, 1993; Seashore-Louis and Murphy, 1994). The fears and criticism are strengthened by research, especially on accountability (Adams and Kirst, 1998; Woods, 2000) and somewhat on issues of equity and equality (Gilborn and Youdell, 2000; Levačić and Woods, 2000; Whitty, Power and Halpin, 1998). However, decentralization contributes to the empowerment of educational leaders, as research on educational administration shows (Conley, 1997; Sergiovanni, 1995; Smith and Piele, 1997). As Ken's story enfolds, these contradictions are highlighted:

> *For example, the government is introducing sixth-form colleges.[1] This is a real threat to our school. Being in a troubled neighbourhood, getting good teachers, especially in maths, sciences and English, is very difficult. These last few years I've convinced several teachers with high academic degrees from good universities to come and teach here. One of the incentives I offer them is heading a department and teaching the sixth form [pre-college level]. Now the council receives government money to build a brand new sixth-form college. I am doubtful*

whether these teachers will remain in my school. Moreover, the sixth-form students are role models to younger students, and an asset to the school in issues such as violence control. So on the one hand you are your own boss, but on the other hand you are pinned down by these big policy initiatives. The government talks about inclusion, but such reforms actually weaken the idea of comprehensive schooling.

A model that links decentralization, school-based management and leadership

As the leading process in educational policy in many western countries, especially English-speaking ones, decentralization defines the extent, the scope and the areas to which authority and power are distributed among roles and sub-units in the system. Decentralization allocates responsibilities from national educational authorities to local authorities and sometimes directly to school boards and school principals (Brown, 1990; Whitty, Power and Halpin, 1998). The terms 'power', 'authority' and 'responsibility' typically refer to areas such as school finance, enrolment policy, curriculum planning, organizational decisions within the school and the county, and personnel management. This is also a socio-political and cultural process that relocates the moral or ideological base of power in education (Hill, Pierce and Guthrie, 1997; Chubb and Moe, 1990; Smrekar, 1996; Whitty, Power and Halpin, 1998). This process produces two forces, as can be seen in Figure 65.1.

The first force, along the left side of the triangle, is that of free-market ideology embodied in the mechanism of accountability. The second force, along the right side, is that of democratization, or what Chubb and Moe (1990) define as 'politics'. This is embodied in the idea of school autonomy. When translated into school structure, free-market ideology becomes school-based management (SBM). Democratization is implemented through restructuring.

Brown (1990, p. 89) maintains that SBM is 'a manifestation of decentralisation'. According to Caldwell and Spinks (1988, p. 5) it is a system: 'for which there has

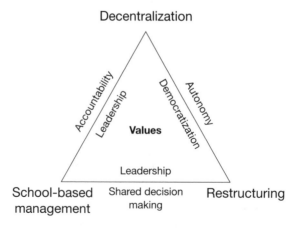

Figure 65.1 A conceptual model linking decentralization, restructuring and school-based management

been significant and consistent decentralisation to the school level of authority to make decisions related to the allocation of resources. This decentralisation is administrative rather than political'.

Restructuring is a realization of the decentralization process both in the educational system as a whole – sometimes also referred to as 'system restructuring' (Aspin and Chapman, 1994) – and within the school itself – referred to as 'school restructuring' or simply the 'restructured school'. It is a political and cultural phenomenon (Murphy, 1993; Conley, 1997), which is also sometimes labelled as 'reculturing' (Hargreaves, 1995; Woods *et al.*, 1997). Restructured schools redefine their relationships with their immediate surroundings, especially the parents and the community, and try to take charge of educational reform. The restructured school, rooted in socio-political global 'megatrends' (Caldwell, 1993), attempts to fulfil aspirations of democratization and cultural diversity in the school system (Dellar, 1994; Fullan, 1991; Hallinger and Hausman, 1994; Murphy, 1993; Muth and Segull, 1993; Murphy, 1994) through a democratic, decentralized innerstructure; a facilitative leadership style; a self-directed perception of the student; and a process, rather than result-based curriculum (Conley, 1997; Hallinger and Hausman, 1994; Murphy, 1994).

As research on decentralization deepens, the political, economic and legal aspects overshadow the pedagogical ones (Dimmock, 1993; Elmore, 1993; Hannaway, 1993; Whitty, Power and Halpin, 1998). There is substantive literature that points out that decentralization policy allows governments 'a complete abdication of responsibility by the state' (Whitty, Power and Halpin, 1998, p. 45), thus creating a form of insulation between the state and the education system (Weiler, 1993). Therefore, notwithstanding a contradictory decentralization policy, both declared and implemented, the state recentralizes certain factors or parts of the system so that it can keep some of its control (Elmore, 1993; McDonnell, 1991; Odden, 1991) or legitimacy (Whitty, Power and Halpin, 1998). This, coupled with public concern about the performance of public education and the practical need of consumers to acquire detailed information about schools so that they can choose between them, enhanced the appearance of the 'standards movement'. Numerous national evaluation bodies and agencies (for example, OFSTED in the UK, NAEP in the USA, and CMEC/SAIP in Canada)[2] in charge of auditing and assessing multiple aspects of school performance were established, their results published through league tables, benchmarking, government websites and similar mechanisms (Leithwood and Aitken, 1995; Levačić, 1995; McLaughlin and Shepard, 1995; Whitty, Power and Halpin, 1998).

Decentralization enjoys the support of various groups that are usually on opposite sides of the public debate on, and politics of, educational policy. These include mainstream, free-market capitalists and small ethnic communities; authorities and teacher unions; parents and various interest groups. This is perhaps why, as decentralization becomes stronger and more widespread, it is also perceived as a 'one-way-street' type of reform. Each time the state wants to change something in the system, the only thing it can do is decentralize it even more. However, when decentralization begins, the preliminary support that the various groups appeared to have voiced towards it changes, sometimes dramatically. First, everybody thinks power should be decentralised to them alone (McDonnell, 1991; Odden, 1991). Local authorities and municipalities think they should govern education. Parents think the school is theirs, in accordance with the legal concept of *in loco parentis*,

10

or simply as consumers (Harris, 1993; Booth and Bussell, 1999). Principals and teachers see decentralization as a form of professional empowerment. Ethnic and religious leaders have their say too. So the 'political' factor of the implementation process becomes very messy indeed. Moving on from decentralization into restructuring and school-based management is a difficult and tricky job. There are substantial contradictions between the two: restructuring is about the socio-political aspects of decentralization and school-based management is about the managerial ones.

The power shift that is at the heart of decentralization generated a whole new debate on accountability (Adams and Kirst, 1998; Cibulka, 1999; Radnor, Ball and Vincent, 1998; Ouston, Fidler and Earley, 1998; Woods, 2000). Questions include who is responsible for what, how capacity tools (Adams and Kirst, 1998) are allocated to those who now hold responsibility, and how are they utilized. It seems important to ensure that accountability will be spread evenly throughout the decentralized system, with a fair burden on schools, school and district boards and state-level officials and policy makers (Adams and Kirst, 1998; Bush, Coleman and Glover, 1993; Talbot and Crow, 1998). Adams and Kirst explain that accountability is connected to democratic control, because it hinders the use of arbitrary power by officials and institutions. Accountability strategies can focus on behaviour, performance or capacity, the last being the most compatible with the rationale of decentralization policy, because they include appropriate means through which the accountable agent will be able to carry out its responsibility. Such advance investment plays an important role in ensuring high motivation for building professional knowledge, and for building leadership and organizational autonomy, which are all necessary for successful and effective implementation of change. Ginsberg and Berry (1998) caution that a substantial gap lies between external accountability measures, taken by authorities, and internal accountability mechanisms, within schools.

A high level of accountability will be achieved when the agents have a clear definition of their obligation, attain direct control over results, have adequate resources to carry out the task, and are granted a high level of discretion in selecting between various courses of action. Unfortunately the consumerist factors of accountability have by far outweighed the democratic and political ones (Ouston, Fidler and Earley, 1998). Radnor, Ball and Vincent, (1998, p. 132), conclude that:

> The meaning and practice of accountability is now obscured ... some stakeholders can be held to account, others cannot. Some decisions are visible ... others are hidden from public view. 'Adhocracy' is considerably increased. Agencies like governing bodies have multiple allegiances and operate within contradictory definitions of their role and have unclear boundaries of their powers and responsibilities ... if democratic accountability is not to be lost ... new expressions of democratic practices at the local level need to be found.

This is not an optimistic note for educational leaders and leadership in a decentralized system.

The debate on decentralization, its targets, format and outcomes is rooted deep in fundamentals of democracy (Lewis, 1993; Weiler, 1993), especially in the ethics of equity and equality. The idea is that all people have the same potential and the same right to achieve self-fulfilment and authenticity, and to receive a fair share of society's valuable interests (Rawls, 1971). This is followed by the concept, or rather, fantasy, that if only the organizations that govern the lives of individuals in a democracy were replaced, this ethos could be achieved: 'the pervasive belief is that the institution is the problem and the community is the solution' (Lewis, 1993, p. 86). In the model presented in Figure 65.1, what brings together school-based management and restructuring, accountability and autonomy, is educational leadership. Leadership provides the links between the socio-political, moral and communal aspects at the school level (Seashore-Louis and Murphy, 1994) and the managerial level (Bottery, 2000). It would be therefore safe to say that successful leaders are recognized by their ability to combine both forces in their work, as this chapter explores further on.

Research on leadership and its relevance to studying and influencing decentralization policy

Research on educational leadership has changed quite dramatically during the last two decades or so, as can be seen in Table 65.1. Roughly between the 1960s and the 1980s, organizational psychology governed theories of leadership in education. The conceptual framework of these theories evolved around the idea of leadership as universal, standardized and typical – supposedly carrying certain similar traits across cultures, roles and organizations (White and Lippitt, 1960; Reddin, 1970). These studies focused on the leaders themselves, rather than their organizational environment, which, according to this conceptual framework, is quite irrelevant and unconditional. During the late 1970s and early 1980s this attitude gradually changed. Though leadership studies were still highly influenced by research in the business world, or in the military, leadership was no longer perceived as typical (Bennis, 1988). Leadership studies focused on organizational culture and knowledge (Schon, 1983).

This was also the beginning of work on educational leadership as a unique field, singling out school principals to be studied separately and specifically from other types of leaders. During this period, there was growing awareness of the dangers of managerialism and of the unequivocal adoption of leadership theories from the business world: 'Management is a powerful mechanism of exclusion. Through the application of management techniques problems or issues that may have value or ideological aspects can be translated into technical matters and thus depoliticised' (Ball, 1987, p. 138).

Such statements exemplify the rift that divides research on educational leadership in the 1980s and 1990s. The contradiction between the forces of managerialism and school-based management on the one hand, and the forces of school autonomy and restructuring on the other hand is at the core of this argument. The last two rows in Table 65.1 present the conflicts between these two forces. As Bottery (1992, p. 21) notes: 'when an area is weak in its own theory, it is prey to invasion from the theories of other, more thoroughly worked, areas'.

The movement of school-based management, which went hand in hand with that of school effectiveness (Bolam, 1993; Chapman, 1993), has had meaningful influence on educational leadership, so the results of this debate are not clear-cut at all. School-based management is responsible for a large chunk of the drive towards the empowerment of school principals, eventually allowing them to take part in real changes inside schools. It seems it has also given them a firmer

Table 65.1 Research on leadership, educational leadership and administration

Period	Movement	Theory/conceptual framework	Discipline/field of study	Focus	Research methods	Typical researchers
1960s	Scientific management	Leadership is universal, standardized and typical	Organizational/industrial psychology	Manager	Quantitative, statistical and laboratory-controlled experiments	Tyler; Blake and Muton; White and Lippitt; French and Raven; Reddin
Late 1970s to mid-1980s	Business administration	Leadership is universal but not standardized	Organizational/industrial psychology	Manager, peers, subordinates	Mixed methods and field work	Bennis; Nanus; Drucker; Peters and Waterman; Adijas
Mid-1980s	Organizational learning/culture	School culture	Sociology/urban anthropology	Manager versus organization Management by objectives (MBO); total quality management (TQM)	Qualitative; ethnography	Schon and Argyris; Sarason; Woods; Ball; Delamont; Hargreaves, A.; Lortie.
Mid-1980s to mid-1990s	Managerial effectiveness	School-based management	Business management and administration; organizational/industrial psychology	School infrastructure and environment	Mixed methods and field work	Mintzberg; Brown; Caldwell; Beare and Millikan; Leithwood; Lieberman; Mortimore; Cheng
Mid-1990s to 2000	Restructuring; accountability	Leadership as a moral and political phenomenon	Sociology; political philosophy; ethics; educational administration; educational management; educational policy	Leadership as social issue; values	Qualitative; ethnography	Murphy; Goldring; Rallis; Adams and Kirst; Conley; Giroux; Hallinger and Hausman; Sergiovanni; Hopkins; Hargreaves, D.; Bottery; Cibulka

foothold in influencing local decision making, and a much louder voice regarding educational policy. Indeed there is truth in the warnings that school-based management and effectiveness might widen gaps and encourage principals to exclude low-achieving students so as to boost up their school's results and statistics (Gibton, 2001; Gilborn and Youdell, 2000; Levačić and Woods, 2000), thus adopting 'outcome-based' rather than 'value-based' approaches.

But the movement towards school effectiveness has, despite and perhaps because of its managerial theoretical base, brought the whole concept of schooling and results out into the open and enhanced the debate on how schooling and education should be judged. Many age-old practices of exclusion and marginalization are now under tough public and professional scrutiny owing to the idea of school effectiveness (Caldwell, 2000). And on top of this, it seems that school-based management and effectiveness were in more than one way the predecessors of theories of accountability that themselves were translated into policies of educational standards (Leithwood and Aitken, 1995; Cibulka, 1999) and later into the drive towards quality education.

As theories and concepts of leadership changed, so have research paradigms and methods. At first, research on leadership was quantitative, somewhat manipulative, and experimental. When leadership was perceived to be universal, it is understandable why researchers thought it could be studied in well-controlled, 'sterile' laboratory experiments, in which participants were required to carry out abstract missions that allowed careful monitoring of dependent and independent variables. In the 1980s and 1990s theories of cultural and moral leadership were studied mainly through qualitative methods on small case-study type samples. These developments were consecutive, with the positivistic paradigm that perceives reality as rational, objective, and defined by constant correlation between variables, and later on with the naturalistic paradigm that perceives reality as holistic, unique, local and subjective (Densin and Densin, 2000). The shift in research paradigms and methods complicated attempts to compare theories and sets of findings. So research on educational leadership, which became primarily qualitative, and research on educational policy, which remained mainly quantitative, began to drift apart. While not so long ago, including in divisions of the American Educational Research Association (AERA), 'leadership' and 'policy' were both under the title of 'administration', during the 1990s they have separated, quite distinctively.

Today, one large body of knowledge summarizes the life of educational leaders – school principals (Ball, 1994; Gibton, Sabar and Goldring, 2000; Goldring and Rallis, 1993; Hallinger and Hausman, 1994; Leithwood, Jantzi and Steinbach, 1999; Murphy, 1994; Prestine, 1994; Talbot and Crow, 1998). Other research, on educational administration and policy, is either theoretical, or quantitative, or meta-analytical in character (Beare, Caldwell and Millikan, 1993; Bennett, Glatter and Levačić, 1994; Davies and Ellison, 1997). However, there is some research that attempts to utilize mixed methods (Gilborn and Youdell, 2000; Levačić, 1995; Whitty, Power and Halpin, 1998; Slavin, 1999).

10

Linking together research on leadership and policy through educational leaders' mindscapes

Oddly enough, decentralization has not created a large body of research that utilizes knowledge and stories told by educational leaders for crafting educational policy. After all, one justification for decentralization is allowing those who actually work in schools to acquire relevant knowledge and have a greater role in decision making. Sadly, most important issues that have substantial influence on life in schools and education systems in general are settled far from schools and from their leaders, just as before. Although school principals bear the heaviest burden of decentralization, many policy makers and policy-making agencies still view policy as a linear process (Ball, 1994; Cooper, 1996; Kennedy, 1999). They treat principals' opinions as biased, and the principals as people who at best lack an ability to grasp 'the big picture' (Gibton, 2002). According to Ball (1994, p. 23):

> *The effect of policy is primarily discursive, it changes the possibilities we have for thinking 'otherwise' ... policy as discourse may have the effect of redistributing 'voice' so that ... only certain voices can be heard as meaningful or authoritative.*

In short, discursive policy determines what can be said and by whom. In this sense, less has changed than meets the eye. Much of what Ken, the headteacher at the start of this chapter, says is written in academic texts and is discussed with graduate students in institutes of education. But does anyone listen to Ken himself? How aware are policy makers of Ken's insights, his thoughts, his dreams and his fears? How legitimate are these? How are they really useful for shaping high policy? How are they put to use?

So what should researchers and policy makers do in order to utilize the knowledge of educational leaders to change educational policy, and understand, in depth, what educational policy does to life in schools and to the work of school principals? One way to do this that can be presented here only briefly is by constructing and using actual maps that present mindscapes of educational leaders. According to Sergiovanni, mindscapes are like road maps, that 'provide rules, images and principles that define what the principalship is and how its practice should unfold' (Sergiovanni, 1995, p. 30). Connelly and Clandinin (1996, p. 25) use a related term: 'working landscape'. Although this term refers to research on teachers' knowledge, it is useful for studying the implications of policy among principals. 'Landscapes' is used to disclose teachers' 'secret, sacred and cover stories ... [that] provided a map useful for studying the dynamics of the relations between teacher's personal practical and professional knowledge'.

According to Bowman and Haggerson (1992, p. 8), interpretive inquiry can assist in connecting between 'informing policy' and 'informing practice'. While the first focuses on 'rules, written and unwritten, by which the educational institutions run, and on the problems that result from those rules' the latter is about 'the which doing his or her practice'. This is a process of demystification, which relates to Sergiovanni's 'mindscapes'. According to Sergiovanni, (1995, p. 30) there are three types of 'mindscapes': 'mystics', 'neats' and 'scruffies', shared by players in the field (for example principals) and researchers alike. 'Mystics' view educational administration as a tacit and intuitive occupation. 'Neats' see it as linked in a linear form to theory. To 'scruffies': 'educational administration resembles a craft-like science within which practice is characterised by interacting reflection and action episodes. Theory and research are only one source of knowledge ... designed to inform but not to prescribe practice'. The 'scruffy' point of view is useful when dealing with 'complex problems, that exist in turbulent environments under indeterminate conditions' (ibid., p. 33), such as decentralization policy in education and its implications for educational leadership.

In our work (Gibton, Sabar and Goldring, 2000; Gibton, 2001; Gibton, 2002) we have begun transforming such mindscapes into graphic maps. Figure 65.2 presents an example that summarizes the views of English principals on decentralization policy. According to this model, English school principals view the formally hierarchic and law-based educational system (Gibton and Goldring, 2002) as chaotic and unstable. While elaborate legislation throughout the 1990s, and especially in the later part of the decade, attempted to redefine the power structure of the system, the principals see the educational arena as a rather free-for-all, grab-all-you-can setting. Perhaps systematic use of such tools, and further work on principals' ideas regarding educational policy (Goldring *et al.*, 2002; Vogel *et al.*, 2002), can assist in the understanding of what educational leaders think about educational policy and create conditions that are more favourable for their work. Moreover, understanding the moral view of principals is important when deciding between alternative policies (Bottery, 1992; Giroux, 1992). Even when reading Ken's opening story, it is clear that such conditions have not evolved, though this does not necessarily mean that he and other leaders do not understand what is going on, or that their views are irrelevant.

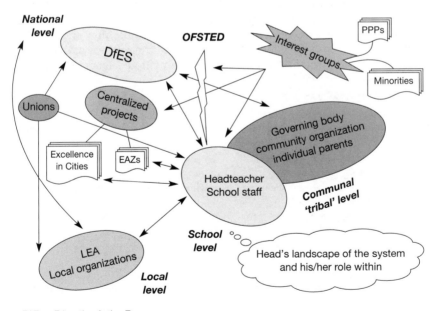

EAZs = Education Action Zones
PPPs = Public Private Partnerships

Figure 65.2: Headteacher's mindscape of the English school system and policy

10

Conclusion

Decentralization redefines the boundaries of leadership, but baffles school principals. Sometimes they feel that decentralization is an unfair trade-off that offers more empowerment than capacity tools, and is actually an opportunity to diminish government's responsibility for educational outcomes and for the maintenance of the education system. Governments place themselves side by side with citizens, moaning and groaning at the state of things in schools, concealing and blurring the fact that they are responsible for education. Principals are responsible too, of course, and certainly more than ever. But while there are now elaborate mechanisms that measure the achievement of schools and their staff, including making schools' failure and success public knowledge, hardly any such mechanisms measure the results of governments, including local authorities.

There is no real public debate on what government policies actually do to education. When there is such debate it is usually channelled towards headteachers, teachers and schools. Have governments ever really been held accountable for those characteristics in headteacher or teacher failure that are the result of inadequate training, insufficient salaries, nonexistent on-the-job professional support, reform and change that are introduced improperly, and budget-neutral policies? Seldom. Education audit-type agencies are never asked to review the work of government ministries of education, but are usually part of them. The popular answer would be that policy makers are judged at the ballot box, but the democratic political process is complicated enough so as to shield many of the shortcomings of policy makers and educational policies. Nevertheless, there is enough evidence to suggest that not only the role but also the leadership qualities of school principals have changed dramatically during the last 15 years or so. The main change is simply that they have become leaders. Decentralization policy should acknowledge this fact, and embrace educational leaders and their mindscapes more than it does today. This will benefit decentralization – and school leaders as well.

ACKNOWLEDGEMENT

With thanks to Naama Sabar (Tel-Aviv University), Ellen Goldring (Vanderbilt University), Peter Earley and Ros Levačić (University of London), from whom I've learned so much on leadership and autonomy.

NOTES

1 Sixth-form colleges or schools, also known as 16–19 schools, are an attempt by the government to improve academic achievement among secondary school students who reach GCSE level, by concentrating efforts in special schools.
2 Office for Standards in Education; National Assessment of Education Progress; Council of Ministers of Education of Canada/School Achievement Indicators Program.

REFERENCES

Adams, J.E. and Kirst, M.W. (1998) 'New demands for educational accountability: striving for results in an era of excellence', paper presented at the annual meeting of the American Educational Research Association, 13–17 April, San Diego.

Aspin, D.N. and Chapman, J.D. (1994) *Quality Schooling: A Pragmatic Approach to Some Current Problems, Topics and Issues*, New York: Cassell.

Ball, S. (1987) *The Micro-Politics of the School*, London: Routledge.

Ball S. (1994) *Education Reform: A Critical and Post-Structural Approach*, Buckingham: Open University Press, pp. 15–27.

Beare, H., Caldwell, B.J. and Millikan, R.H. (1993) 'Leadership' in Preedy, M. (ed.) *Managing the Effective School*, London: Open University Press/Paul Chapman Publishers, pp. 141–62.

Bennett, N., Glatter, R. and Levačić, R. (eds) (1994) *Improving Educational Management through Research and Consultancy*, London: Open University Press/Paul Chapman Publishers/Sage.

Bennis, W. (1988) 'Good managers are good leaders', *Across the Board*, 11 (10), pp. 7–21.

Bolam, R. (1993) 'School-based management, school improvement and school effectiveness: overview and implications' in Dimmock, C. (ed.) *School-Based Management and Effectiveness*, London: Routledge, pp. 219–34.

Booth, P. and Bussell, H. (1999) 'Parental choice of primary schools: the legal implications and parental perceptions', *Education and the Law*, 11 (4), pp. 295–308.

Bottery, M. (1992) *The Ethics of Educational Management: Personal, Social and Political Perspectives on School Organisation*, London: Cassell.

Bottery, M. (2000) *Education, Policy, and Ethics*, London: Continuum.

Bowman, A.C. and Haggerson, N.L. (1992) *Informing Educational Policy and Practice through Interpretive Inquiry*, Lancaster, PA: Technomic.

Brown, D.J. (1990) *Decentralisation and School-Based Management*, London: Falmer Press.

Bush, T., Coleman, M. and Glover, F. (1993) *Managing Autonomous Schools: The Grant-Maintained Experience*, London: Paul Chapman Publishing.

Caldwell, B.J. (1993) 'The changing role of the school principal' in Dimmock, C. (ed.) *School-Based Management and Effectiveness*, London: Routledge. pp. 165–84.

Caldwell, B.J. (2000) 'Local management and learning outcomes: mapping the links in three generations of international research' in Coleman, M. and Anderson, L. (eds) *Managing Finance and Resources in Education*, London: Paul Chapman Publishing/Sage, pp. 24–40.

Caldwell, B.J. and Spinks, J.M. (1988) *The Self-Managing School*, London: Falmer Press.

Chapman, J. (1993) 'Leadership, school-based decision making and school effectiveness' in Dimmock, C. (ed.) *School-Based Management and Effectiveness*, London: Routledge, pp. 201–18.

Chubb, J.E. and Moe, T.M. (1990) *Politics, Markets and America's Schools*, Washington, DC: Brookings Instution Press.

Cibulka, J.G. (1999) 'Moving toward an accountable system of K–12 education: alternative approaches and challenges' in Cisek, G.J. (ed.) *Handbook of Educational Policy*, San Diego, CA: Academic Press, pp. 184–213.

Conley, D.T. (1997) *Roadmap to Restructuring: Charting the Course of Change in American Education*, Eugene, OR: ERIC.

Connelly, M.F. and Clandinin, J.D. (1996) 'Teachers' professional knowledge landscapes: teacher stories – stories of teachers – school stories – stories of schools', *Educational Researcher*, 25 (3), pp. 24–30.

Cooper, H. (1996) 'Speaking power to truth: reflections of an educational researcher after four years of school board service', *Educational Researcher*, 25 (1), pp. 29–34.

Davies, B. and Ellison, L. (1997) *School Leadership for the 21st Century: A Competency and Knowledge Approach*, London: Routledge.

Dellar, G.B. (1994) 'Implementing school decision-making groups: a case study in restructuring', paper presented at the annual meeting of the American Research Association, New Orleans, April.

Densin, N.K. and Densin, Y.S. (2000) 'Introduction: the discipline and practice of qualitative research' in Densin, N.K. and Densin, Y.S. (eds) *Handbook of Qualitative Research*, 2nd edn, Thousand Oaks, CA: Sage, pp. 1–29.

Dimmock, C. (1993) 'School-based management and linkage with the curriculum' in Dimmock, C. (ed.) *School-Based Management and Effectiveness*, London: Routledge, pp. 1–21.

Elmore, R.F. (1993) 'School decentralization: who gains? who loses?' in Hannaway, J. and Carnoy, M. (eds.) *Decentralization and School Improvement*, San Francisco: Jossey-Bass, pp. 33–54.

Fullan, M. (1991) *The New Meaning of Educational Change*, London: Cassell.

Gibton, D. (2001) 'Once the government provided education. Now it provides information on education. Insights from what UK headteachers think of educational law regarding decentralisation policy, self-management and autonomy', paper presented at the annual conference of the British Educational Leadership, Management, and Administration Society (BELMAS), Newport-Pagnell, 5–7 October.

Gibton, D. (2002) 'The wild thoughts of principals in the UK: principals' graphic mindscapes on educational policy and law-based reform: a technique for second-degree qualitative data analysis on educational leadership', paper presented at the annual meeting of the American Educational Research Association, New Orleans, April.

10

Gibton, D. and Goldring, E. (2002) 'The role of legislation in educational decentralization: the case of Israel and Britain', *Peabody Journal of Education*, 76(3–4) pp. 81–101.

Gibton, D., Sabar, N. and Goldring, E.B. (2000) 'How principals of autonomous schools in Israel view implementation of decentralisation and restructuring policy: risks, rights and wrongs', *Educational Evaluation and Policy Analysis*, 22 (2), pp. 193–210.

Gilborn, D. and Youdell, D. (2000) *Rationing Education: Policy, Practice, Reform and Equity*, Buckingham, Open University Press.

Ginsberg, R., and Berry, B. (1998) 'The capability for enhancing accountability' in Macpherson, R.J.S. (ed.) *The Politics of Accountability: Educative and International Perspectives*, Thousand Oaks, CA: Corwin Press, pp. 43–61.

Giroux, H.A. (1992) 'Educational leadership and the crisis of democratic government', *Educational Researcher*, 21 (4), pp.4–11.

Goldring, E., Crowson, R., Laird, D. and Berk, R. (2002) 'Unmaking desegregation policy and 'going unitary": the loss of a sense of place', paper presented at the annual meeting of the American Educational Research Association, New Orleans, April.

Goldring, E.B. and Rallis, S.F. (1993) *Principals of Dynamic Schools: Taking Charge of Change*, Newbury Park, CA: Corwin-Sage.

Hallinger, P. and Hausman, C. (1994) 'From Attila the Hun to Mary had a little lamb: principals' role ambiguity in restructured schools' in Murphy, J. and Seashore-Louis, K. (eds) *Reshaping the Principalship: Insights from Transformational Reform Efforts*, Thousand Oaks, CA: Corwin Press, pp. 154–76.

Hallinger, P., Murphy, J. and Hausman, C. (1993) 'Conceptualising school restructuring: principals' and teachers' perceptions' in Dimmock, C., (ed.) *School-Based Management and Effectiveness*, London: Routledge, pp. 22–40.

Hannaway, J. (1993) 'Decentralization in two school districts: challenging the standard paradigm' in Hannaway, J. and Carnoy, M. (eds) *Decentralization and School Improvement*, San-Francisco, CA: Jossey-Bass, pp. 135–62.

Hargreaves, A. (1995) *Changing Teachers, Changing Times: Teachers' Work and Culture in the Postmodern Age*, London: Cassell.

Harris, N. (1993) *Law and Education: Regulation, Consumerism and the Education System*, London: Sweet & Maxwell.

Hill, P.T., Pierce, L.C. and Guthrie, J.W. (1997) *Reinventing Public Education: How Contracting Can Reform America's Schools*, Chicago: University of Chicago Press.

Kennedy, M. (1999) 'Infusing educational decision making with research' in Cisek, G.J. (Ed.) *Handbook of Educational Policy*, San Diego: Academic Press, pp. 54–81.

Leithwood, K. and Aitken, R. (1995) *Making Schools Smarter: A System for Monitoring School and District Progress*, Thousand Oaks, CA: Corwin Press.

Leithwood, K., Jantzi, D. and Steinbach, R. (1999) *Changing Leadership for Changing Times*, Buckingham: Open University Press, pp. 3–20.

Levačić, R. (1995) *Local Management of Schools: Analysis and Practice*, Buckingham: Open University Press.

Levačić, R. and Woods, P.A. (2000) 'The impact of quasi-markets and performance regulation on socially disadvantaged schools', paper presented at the annual meeting of the American Educational Research Association, New-Orleans, April.

Lewis, D.A. (1993) 'Deinstitutionalization and school decentralization: making the same mistake twice' in Hannaway, J. and Carnoy, M. (eds.) *Decentralization and School Improvement*, San Francisco CA: Jossey-Bass, pp. 84–101.

McDonnell, L.M. (1991) 'Ideas and values in implementation analysis: the case of teacher policy' in Odden, A.R. (ed.) *Education Policy Implementation*, Albany, NY: State University of New York Press, pp. 241–58.

McLaughlin, M. and Shepard, L. (1995) *Improving Education through Standards-Based Reform: A Report of the National Academy of Education Panel on Standards-Based Reform*, Stanford, CA: National Academy of Education.

Murphy, J. (1993) 'Restructuring schooling: the equity infrastructure', *School Effectiveness and School Improvement*, 4 (2) pp. 111–30.

Murphy, J. (1994) 'Transformed change and the evolving role of the principal: early empirical evidence' in Murphy, J. and Seashore-Louis, K. (eds) *Reshaping the Principalship: Insights from Transformational Reform Efforts*, Thousand Oaks, CA: Corwin Press, (pp. 20–56).

Muth, R. and Segall, R. (1993) 'Toward restructuring: developing cooperative practices in schools', paper presented at the annual meeting of the AERA, Atlanta, Georgia.

Odden, A.R. (1991) 'New patterns of educational policy implementation and challenges for the 1990s' in Odden, A.R. (ed.) *Education Policy Implementation*, Albany, NY: State University of New York Press, pp. 297–328.

Ouston, J., Fidler, B. and Earley, P. (1998) 'The educational accountability of schools in England and Wales' in Macpherson, R.J.S. (ed.) *The Politics of Accountability: Educative and International Perspectives*, Thousand Oaks, CA: Corwin Press, pp. 107–119.

Prestine, N.A. (1994) 'Ninety degrees from everywhere: new understandings of the principal's role in a restructuring essential school' in Murphy, J. and Seashore-Louis, K. (eds) *Reshaping the Principalship: Insights from Transformational Reform Efforts*, Thousand Oaks, CA: Corwin Press, pp. 123–53.

Radnor, H.A., Ball, S.J. and Vincent, C. (1998) 'Local educational governance: accountability and democracy in the United Kingdom' in Macpherson, R.J.S. (ed.) *The Politics of Accountability: Educative and International Perspectives*, Thousand Oaks, CA: Corwin Press, pp. 120–33.

Rawls, J. (1971) *A Theory of Justice*, Cambridge, MA: Belknap-Harvard.

Reddin, W.J. (1970) *Managerial Effectiveness*, New York: McGraw-Hill.

Schon, D.A. (1983) *The Reflective Practitioner: How Professionals Think in Action*, New York: Basic Books.

Seashore-Louis, K. and Murphy, J. (1994) 'The evolving role of the principal: some concluding thoughts' in Murphy, J. and Seashore-Louis, K. (eds) *Reshaping the Principalship: Insights from Transformational Reform Efforts*, Thousand Oaks, CA: Corwin Press, pp. 265–81.

Sergiovanni, T.J. (1995) *The Principalship: A Reflective Practice Perspective*, Boston: Allyn & Bacon.

Slavin, R.E. (1999) 'Success for all: policy consequences of replicable schoolwide reform' in Cisek, G.J. (ed.) *Handbook of Educational Policy*, San Diego: Academic Press, pp. 326–50.

Smith, S.C. and Piele, P.K. (1997) *School Leadership: Handbook for Excellence*, Eugene, OR: ERIC.

Smrekar, C. (1996) *The Impact of School Choice and Community: In the Interest of Families and Schools*, Albany, NY: State University of New York Press.

Talbot, D.L., and Crow, G.M. (1998) 'When the school changed, did I get a new job? Principals' role conceptions in a restructuring context', paper presented at the annual meeting of the American Educational Research Association, San Diego, April 1998.

Vogel, L.R., Rau, W.C., Ashby, D. and Baker, P. (2002) 'A decade of turbulence: the voice of principals caught in the middle of Illinois school reform' paper presented at the annual meeting of the American Educational Research Association, New Orleans, April.

Weiler, H.N. (1993) 'Control versus legitimization: the politics of ambivalence' in Hannaway, J. and Carnoy, M. (eds) *Decentralization and School Improvement*, San-Francisco, CA: Jossey-Bass, pp. 55–83.

White, R.W. and Lippitt, R. (1960) *Autocracy and Democracy*, New York: Harper & Brothers.

Whitty, G., Power, S., and Halpin, D. (1998) *Devolution and Choice in Education: The School, the State and the Market*, Buckingham: Open University Press.

Woods, P. (2000). 'Varieties and themes in producer engagement: structure and agency in the schools public-market', *British Journal of Sociology of Education*, 21 (2) pp. 219–42.

Woods, P., Jeffrey, B., Troman, G. and Boyle, M. (1997) *Restructuring Schools, Reconstructing Teachers: Responding to Change in the Primary School*, Buckingham: Open University Press.

10

Conclusion: the emerging agenda

BRENT DAVIES AND JOHN WEST-BURNHAM

No single study can hope to capture all the issues and debates surrounding a complex topic like educational leadership and management. Indeed, the very act of publication offers a false sense of coherence and completeness. The nature and purpose of education remains a highly contentious social, political and academic debate. Within that broader debate, there are specific topics, not the least of which is the nature and purpose of leadership and management in education. While this handbook offers a snapshot of the current debates, we are very aware of many issues that will come to play an increasingly significant role in the debate about future direction of education systems.

Equity and entitlement

No education system can yet claim to be fully confident that it operates on the basis of full equity and a guaranteed entitlement. While the 1990s was the 'decade of improvement', most education systems still reflect social inequality and a gap between aspiration and delivery. The role of educational leadership in securing full equity and ensuring that entitlement is achieved remains a fundamental ethical concern. It is an issue within systems and between systems; the responsibility of educators in the developed world for supporting education in the developing world has not yet been fully explored or realized. Closely linked to this are the continuing issues of racism, sexism, discrimination and exploitation that deny any notion of education. It may be that the role of educational leaders as advocates of social justice is only in the early stages of development.

Social trends

Closely related to the ethical basis of educational leadership is the need to develop educational responses to emerging changes in society. Changes in the nature of work and patterns of employment, the structure of the family, the nature of the community and fundamental changes in politics and the world order require responses from educationalists. The rapidly shifting view of the role of organized religion and the moral basis of society has profound implications for the content and delivery of education. A key question is the extent to which educationalists should be formulating responses to such changes or become active protagonists in the emergence of a new social order.

Policy and innovation

The 1980s saw the start of an era in which governments were increasingly willing to intervene directly in the organization and delivery of schooling. Policy moved from the historical model of being generic and enabling to being specific and controlling. The concept of professional accountability was replaced with management answerability. Increasing prescription of both the content of the curriculum and its delivery have resulted in central government moving towards the micromanagement of the classroom.

There is little doubt that this approach addressed many concerns about the effectiveness of school systems. However, it might be argued that it has diminished the capacity and motivation for radical innovation and creativity. Those who would seek to initiate change at institutional level may well feel constrained by the formal imperatives of central governments and the prevailing model of answerability. This inevitably compromises the ability of educational leaders to develop responses to major issues which policy might not be able to come to terms with. The political imperative (and the need to be re-elected), with its inevitable short-termism, militates against educational leadership addressing fundamental and vital issues.

Funding education

A classic example of short-term thinking relates to the funding of educational systems. Although education systems are better funded now than at any time in history (coincidentally with the end of the Cold War), there is little evidence of a strategic view of the need to secure long-term funding. This is a particularly critical issue as in many countries, where an ageing population will have the combined effects of switching political priorities to health and the care of the elderly and will also see a reduction in the proportion of the population paying tax, thus increasing the relative burdens of funding education.

State funding remains a vital component of education as a core social activity and responsibility. While the movement towards private funding and market forces has enhanced provision in some contexts, there cannot be social equity without economic equity. It may well be that our understanding of educational leadership will have to be extended to include social and economic entrepreneurship as well as skills in political lobbying.

The future of schooling

Much of the energy of educational leaders and managers has been focused on improving schools, making them more effective, etc. A fundamental issue facing educational leaders will be the extent to which schools, *qua* schools, are sustainable and justifiable. A key issue in many education systems centres on the long-term availability of qualified teachers to staff schools on the historic model. In most western educational systems a significant proportion of teachers currently in service are due to retire by 2010. On current projections, there is no guarantee that they will be replaced. In inner-city areas, there is already a crisis in terms of teachers and school leaders. This trend may force a fundamental reconceptualization of how schools might be staffed, if indeed it is still appropriate to struggle to maintain an essentially archaic system that is one of the very few organizational models that can be traced back to the nineteenth century.

The potential contribution of information technology offers an alternative way forward, but one that challenges prevailing orthodoxies and paradigms. If the potential of an information-based technology is fully realized and combined with emerging theories of learning then it becomes increasingly difficult to see how the current dominant models can be justified, let alone sustained.

It is impossible to speculate where the science of learning will eventually lead; discoveries in neurological science, cognitive and social psychology probably mean that the status quo is not an option. What they do seem to point to is an increasing individualization of learning, which will in turn call into question the present notion of what constitutes a curriculum.

The ethical and organizational implications of these changes point to radical and systematic reform, which requires a very different order of educational leadership that transcends being very good at running schools.

A changing world

It is probably not too melodramatic to argue that the world that we inhabit is going through a period of profound change in geo-political terms and in terms of the basic viability of life on Earth. Climate change, for whatever reason, is a reality, environmental pollution is largely unchecked, and the population of the planet, on current projections, will have increased by 50 per cent to 9 billion by 2050. This is all very remote from planning literacy and numeracy lessons or preparing a bid for specialist schools status. Yet if education is about preparation for life, then education systems need to focus on life as it probably will be lived, rather than as we fondly imagine it was lived.

The role of educational leaders in developing an appropriate response to an increasingly complex world is uncertain, but it would seem to be an area that requires leadership rather than management.

Conclusion

By most criteria, leadership is fundamentally concerned with the big picture, with values and with the future. This handbook has sought to explain and understand the implications of that approach. Just as important as any debate about the nature of leadership is the continuing and sophisticated dialogue centred on creating new models of leadership for the future. The editors and authors hope that this handbook will serve as a stimulus to that debate. What is clear is that educational leadership for the future will have to be fundamentally concerned with strategy, values and learning.

10

Editors and contributors

Main editors

Dr Brent Davies is Professor of International Leadership Development and Director of the International Leadership Centre at the University of Hull. He is also Special Professor at the University of Nottingham. He spent the first ten years of his career working as a teacher in south London; he then moved into higher education and now works exclusively on leadership and management development programmes for senior and middle managers in schools. He was Director of the International MBA in School Leadership at Leeds Metropolitan University, and moved to the University of Lincolnshire and Humberside to establish the first Chair in Educational Leadership and create the International Educational Leadership Centre. He moved to the University of Hull in 2000. He has published extensively and his recent books include *The New Strategic Direction and Development of the School* (Routledge/Falmer Press, 2003) and *School Leadership for the 21st Century* (Routledge/Falmer Press, 2003). His current research interests include strategic leadership, creating the strategically focused school and the emerging public/private sector in education.

John West-Burnham is Director of Professional Research and Development at the London Leadership Centre, Institute of Education, University of London. He was previously Professor of Educational Leadership, International Leadership Centre, University of Hull. He worked in schools, further and adult education for 15 years before moving into higher education. He was a part-time Open University tutor for 15 years and has worked at Crewe and Alsager College, the University of Leicester and the University of Lincolnshire and Humberside. He was also Development Officer for Teacher Performance for Cheshire LEA. He is author of *Managing Quality in Schools* (1997, Pearson Education), co-author of *Effective Learning in Schools* (1997, Pearson Education), *Leadership and Professional Development in Schools* (1998, Pearson Education) and co-editor of *Performance Management in Schools* (2001, Pearson Education) and has written 12 other books and over 30 articles and chapters. He has worked in Australia, Israel, New Zealand, the Republic of Ireland, Singapore, South Africa, UAE and the USA. He is coordinator of the European School Leadership Project and is a consultant to the National College for School Leadership in England. His current research and writing interests include transformational leadership, leadership learning and development and educational leadership in the community.

Section editors

Dr Mike Bottery is a Professor of Education and Head of the Centre for Educational Studies at the University of Hull. He has taught and lectured in North

America, the Far East, the Caribbean and in various parts of Europe. His current main interests are in the effects of global and national changes upon the management of educational institutions. He has published six books including *Education, Policy and Ethics* (Continuum, 2000).

Dr Brian Caldwell is Professor and Dean of the Faculty of Education at the University of Melbourne. He served previously as Head of Teacher Education and Dean of the Faculty of Education at the University of Tasmania. His main interests lie in the areas of leadership education finance, and the management of change, especially where significant authority, responsibility and accountability have been decentralized to schools. His co-authored trilogy on the self-managing school has helped shape developments in several countries, and he has had professional assignments in 29 nations over the last 20 years. In 2001–2 he served as Visiting Professor at the National College of School Leadership in England.

Dr Patricia Collarbone is the founding Director of the London Leadership Centre based at the Institute of Education, University of London. She has been a special adviser to the Department for Education and Employment on leadership aspects linked to the Green Paper 'Teachers Meeting the Challenge of Change' and was charged by the Minister of State to develop the new programme for the National Professional Qualification for Headship. She is a member of the vision group for the National College of School Leadership and is currently Project Director of the Pathfinder Teacher Workload Change Management Programme. In January 1998 she received the honour of Dame Commander of the British Empire (DBE) for services to education.

Dr Dean Fink is an international educational development consultant. He is also an associate of the International Centre for Educational Change at the Ontario Institute for Studies in Education, and the Centre for Educational Leadership, Learning and Change at the University of Bath, and a Visiting Fellow of the International Leadership Centre at the University of Hull. He is a former principal and superintendent with the Halton Board of Education in Ontario, Canada. He has authored *Changing Our Schools* (with Louise Stoll of the University of Bath, Open University Press, 1996, *Good Schools/Real Schools; Why School Reform Doesn't Last* (Teachers' College Press, 2000) and *It's About Learning and It's About Time* (with Louise Stoll and Lorna Earl of the University of Toronto, Routledge/Falmer Press, 2002).

Dr Andy Hargreaves is the Thomas More Brennan Chair in Education at the Lynch School of Education, Boston College. Prior to that, he was Professor in Residence, National College for School Leadership, University of Nottingham, and Co-director of and Professor in the International Centre for Educational Change at the Ontario Institute for Studies in Education of the University of Toronto. He is holder of the Canadian Education Association/Whitworth 2000 Award for outstanding contributions to educational research in Canada. He is the author or editor of more than 20 books in the fields of teacher development, the culture of the school and educational reform. His book *Changing teachers, Changing times* (Cassell, 1994) received the 1995 Outstanding Writing Award from the American Association of Colleges for Teacher Education. Among his other recent books are *Learning to Change: Teaching Beyond Subjects and Standards* (with Lorna Earl, Shawn Moore and Susan Manning, Jossey-Bass, 2001).

Dr Alma Harris is Professor of School Leadership and Director of the Leadership, Policy and Improvement Unit at the Institute of Education, University of Warwick. She has published extensively on the theme of leadership and school improvement and her latest books include: *Building Leadership Capacity for School Improvement* (with L. Lambert, Open University Press, 2002), *Effective Leadership for School Improvement* (Harris, A., Day, C., Hopkins, D., Hadfield, M., Hargreaves, A. and Chapman, C. (2002) London, Routledge), *School Improvement: What's in it for Schools?* (Routledge/Falmer Press, 2002) and *Leading the Improving Department* (David Fulton Publishers, 2002). Her most recent research work has focused upon improving schools facing challenging circumstances and the relationship between teacher leadership and school improvement. She is currently working with Department for Education and Skills, National College for School Leadership, General Teaching Council and National Union of Teachers in a research and development capacity.

Dr Guilbert Hentschke is holds the Richard T. Cooper and Mary Catherine Cooper Chair in Public School Administration at the University of Southern California's Rossier School of Education, where he served as Dean from 1988 to 2000. Prior to 1988 he served in professorial and administrative capacities at the University of Rochester, Columbia University, and in the Chicago Public Schools. Currently he directs programmes in the business of education, including at the Galaxy Institute of Education (California, USA) and on the school business management programme. An author of numerous books and articles on school reform and charter schools, he teaches graduate courses dealing with markets, regulation and performance in schooling and serves on several boards of education businesses, including the Aspen Education Group, the National Centre on Education and the Economy, the Education industry Association, Excellent Education Development and WestEd Regional Educational Laboratory. He earned his bachelor's degree in history and economics at Princeton University and his masters and doctorate in education at Stanford University.

Dr David Hopkins prepared this section of the handbook while Professor of Education at the University of Nottingham, where he served as both Head of the School and Dean of the Faculty of Education between 1996 and 2001. During this time he was also Chair of the Leicester City Partnership Board and a member of the Governing Council of the National College for School Leadership. His professional interests are in the areas of teacher and school development, educational change, teacher education, and policy implementation and evaluation. He has published over 30 books on these themes, including *School Improvement For Real* (Routledge/Falmer Press, 2001), *A Teacher's Guide to Classroom Research*, (3rd edn, Open University Press, 2002), *Models of Learning – Tools for Teaching* (with Bruce Joyce and Emily Calhoun (2nd edn, Open University Press, 2002) and *Improving the Quality of Education for All* (2nd edn, David Fulton Publishers, 2002). In February 2002 he took up his appointment as Director of the Standards and Effectiveness Unit at the Department for Education and Skills, and in that position succeeds Michael Barber as the Chief Adviser to the Secretary of State on standards issues. He is also an International Mountain Guide and has climbed in many of the world's great mountain ranges.

Dr Barbara MacGilchrist is Professor of Education and Deputy Director at the Institute of Education, University of London. She has developed a deep understanding of school improvement and the role of leadership and management in that process through

10

being a primary teacher, headteacher, local authority chief inspector and a researcher. She has directed and been involved in a wide range of research and development projects, all of which have had a particular focus on improving the quality of learning and teaching in classrooms. Her publications include *Planning Matters* (co-authors Jane Savage, Peter Mortimore and Charles Beresford, Paul Chapman Publishing, 1995) and *The Intelligent School* (with K. Myers and J. Reed, Paul Chapman Publishing, 1997).

Dr Janet Ouston has recently retired from the Institute of Education, University of London where she was Head of the Management Development Centre. She currently works as an educational consultant and for the Open University. Her publications include books and papers on educational leadership and managements, the management of change, school effectiveness and school improvement and the impact of OFSTED (Office for Standards in Education) inspection on secondary schools. She is also chair of governors of an inner-London comprehensive school, and trustee of an educational centre for excluded students.

Contributors

David Aspin is Emeritus Professor and formerly Dean of the Faculty of Education at Monash University. Prior to his moving to Australia he was Professor of Philosophy of Education at King's College, London. He has published widely in the area of philosophy of education, particularly epistemology, ethics and the mind. His current interests are in the field of values and values in education, especially in relation to policy and administration.

Greg Barker is Head at St Vincent's Primary School, Warrington. OFSTED described his school as having: 'excellent leadership and vision' and that 'the quality of teaching and learning is strength of the school'. The school has been awarded the Basic Skill Quality Mark with the recommendation that 'This school is a beacon of good practice in the field of effective teaching and learning styles'. Greg's work in promoting effective teaching for learning takes him beyond his own school and he is currently working with several schools throughout the UK. He is President of the Warrington Branch of the National Association of Head Teachers and is studying for an international MBA in Educational Leadership and Management with the University of Hull.

Dr Len Barton is a Professor of Inclusive Education at the Institute of Education, University of London and is the Director of the Inclusive Education Research Centre. He is the founder and editor of *Disability and Society* and has published extensively on issues relating to socio-political perspectives on disability and inclusive education. He is particularly committed to both teaching and supervision of research degrees. One of his key interests is in developing an informed understanding and appreciation of the fundamental importance of cross-cultural ideas and links.

Dr Hedley Beare is Emeritus Professor in Education and a part-time Principal Fellow in the Centre for Applied Educational Research at the University of

Melbourne, where he taught educational administration and policy. In the 1970s he was the foundation permanent head (CEO) of the only two new public school systems established in Australia in the twentieth century. He has crystallized his well-known commentaries on education policies and the future of schooling in his latest book, *Creating the Future School* (Routledge/Falmer Press, 2001). He has degrees from Adelaide, Melbourne and Harvard Universities. He was a Harkness Fellow from 1967 to 1970 and a Senior Fulbright Scholar in 1979, and has been a Visiting Scholar at Oregon, Stanford, Bristol, Penn State, Harvard, London and Aoyama Gakuin Universities.

Dr Les Bell is Professor of Educational Management and Director of the Doctorate of Education Programme at the Centre for Educational Leadership and Management, School of Education, University of Leicester. He trained as a teacher at Goldsmiths' College, London and has taught in both primary and secondary schools. He joined the Education Department at Coventry College of Education and subsequently became a member of the Education Department at the University of Warwick after the College merged with the University. In 1994 he left Warwick to become Director of the School of Education and Community Studies at Liverpool John Moores University. He was appointed to the Chair of Educational Management at Leicester in 1999. He has written extensively on educational management and his research interests include the impact of government education policy on primary school headteachers, the nature of schools as organizations and cultural diversity in educational management.

Dr Paul Black is Emeritus Professor at King's College London. He directed the departments at Chelsea and then at King's from 1976 to 1989 and retired in 1995. In the 1980s he helped direct national surveys (for the APU) in school science performance. In 1987–8 he was chair of the government's Task Group on Assessment and Testing which set out the basis for national testing. More recently, he has served on four advisory groups of the USA National Science Foundation and is currently Visiting Professor at Stanford University. His recent research with colleagues at King's has focused on teachers' classroom assessments.

Sara Bubb is an education consultant specializing in induction. She speaks nationally on induction and runs NQT (newly qualified teacher) and induction tutor programmes for local education authorities, Jersey and at the University of London Institute of Education, where she also lectures. In 2000–1 she co-directed a national research project on induction in England. She has written several books on the subject and writes a weekly advice column for new teachers in *The Times Educational Supplement* and gives advice on its website.

Christopher Chapman is Research Fellow at the Institute of Education, University of Warwick, where he is engaged on a number of externally funded projects in the areas of leadership and school improvement. Current projects include Variations in Teachers and their Effectiveness (VITAE) and Attainment in Former Coalfield Areas. He has recently co-directed an investigation into leadership in challenging circumstances and researched on an exploration of 'capacity building' in schools for the National College for School Leadership. Other recent projects have involved research and evaluation in Schools Facing Challenging Circumstances. In addition to research, he teaches on MA courses at the Universities of Warwick and Nottingham.

10

Judith Chapman is Professor and Dean of Education and Director of the Centre for Lifelong Learning at Australian Catholic University. She has published widely in the field of educational policy and administration, lifelong learning and school-based decision making and management. She is a Member of the Order of Australia for services to tertiary education as a teacher and researcher.

Dr Yin Cheong Cheng is Professor and Director of the Centre for Research and International Collaboration of the Hong Kong Institute of Education. He is also the Head of the Asia-Pacific Centre for Education Leadership and Education Quality and the founding Vice-President of the Asia-Pacific Educational Research Association. His major research interests include educational effectiveness, school-based management, educational reforms, teacher education and paradigm shifts in education. He has published eight books and over 150 book chapters and academic journal articles internationally. Some of his English publications have been translated into Chinese, Hebrew, Korean, Spanish and Thai languages. His research has won him a number of international awards, including the Awards for Excellence from the Literati Club in the UK in 1994, 1996–8 and 2001. He has been invited as keynote speaker at numerous international conferences in education.

David Clutterbuck is Visiting Professor at Sheffield Hallam University, where he is a member of the Mentoring and Coaching Research Group. A founder Director of the European Mentoring Centre, he has been involved in the design and implementation of hundreds of mentoring schemes around the world. His many books include: *Everyone Needs a Mentor* (CIPD, 2001), *Leadership Alliances* (CIPD, 1998), *Mentoring in Action*, with David Megginson (Kogan Page, 1995), *Mentoring Executives and Directors*, with David Megginson (Butterworth Heinemann, 1999) and *Mentoring Diversity*, with Belle Rose Ragins (Butterworth Heinemann, 2002).

Keith Collar is Vice-President of the Education Entrepreneurs Fund and manages the Fund's programmes, policies, investment processes and fundraising activities. He is responsible for identifying promising partnerships, negotiating strategic alliances and providing business support for internal and external development initiatives. He worked for 11 years in banking, including as a Senior Vice-President in Fleet Bank's Sports Lending Group. He was also a Managing Director for a financial advisory firm providing services to the professional sports industry. He holds a master's degree with a concentration in school leadership from Harvard Graduate School of Education (2000), having graduated *cum laude* from Harvard College (1986).

Dr Marilyn Crawford is a career educator who has spent 30 years working in the public schools both in teaching and leadership roles. As a national participant in school reform efforts, she focuses on developing secondary schools that demand high performance of all students while providing a wide range of paths for achieving what is required of them. With a Ph.D. in educational leadership from Vanderbilt University, she currently serves as the Strategy and Resource Co-ordinator for Secondary Education in the School District of Lancaster, Pennsylvania. She also continues her work as a national consultant for middle and high-school reform.

Michael Creese formerly a secondary headteacher and local education authority governor training coordinator, now works as a freelance consultant/researcher. He was member of the Institute of Education team undertaking research into effective school governance (Scanlon, M., Earley, P. and Evans, J. *Improving the Effectiveness of School*

Governing Bodies, DfEE, 1999 and, more recently, has published with Peter Earley) *Improving Schools and Governing Bodies: Making a Difference* (Routledge, 1999). He is currently undertaking historical research into the Indian army.

Carmel Crévola is Director of Building Essential Literacy, Mondo Publishing, New York, and a Fellow of the Faculty of Education at the University of Melbourne.

David Crossley began teaching history in 1978. In 1991 he became Head of Cirencester Deer Park School, a large comprehensive school, one of the first in the UK to gain the then new national standard for staff development and training: Investor in People status. The school became one of the first specialist Technology Colleges in 1995. In 1997 David was invited to be Principal of Jerudong International School in South-East Asia. The school served students from 29 nationalities from ages 2–19. The school grew from 50 to almost 900 in its first three years and had almost unparalleled access to leading-edge information technology. In May 2000 David took up the post of Principal of Kings College for the Arts and Technology in Guildford, the UK's first privately managed state school, which operates in partnership with the not-for-profit company 3Es and Surrey County Council. He is also a member of the Executive of the UK Technology Colleges Trust's Vision 2020 think-tank.

Dr Amanda Datnow is Assistant Professor in the Department of Theory and Policy Studies at the Ontario Institute for Studies in Education of the University of Toronto, where she teaches in the educational administration and pre-service teacher education programmes. Her research focuses on the politics and policies of school reform, particularly with regard to the professional lives of educators and issues of equity.

Barbara Davies has extensive experience in primary school leadership and management. After graduating from Oxford University, she taught in primary schools in Oxfordshire, West Germany and West Sussex. She took up her first headship in West Sussex, followed by her second in North Yorkshire. She was Senior Lecturer at Bishop Grosseteste College in Lincoln, working in initial teacher education, before specializing in leadership and management in the primary sector at the University of Lincolnshire and Humberside, where she was a course leader for a masters degree in leadership and learning. Subsequently she returned to primary headship in Nottinghamshire before taking up her current post as Headteacher of Washingborough Foundation Primary School in Lincolnshire. She gained a masters degree in educational management in 1994 and is currently completing her doctorate in educational leadership at the University of Hull. Her thesis is focused on strategic leadership and planning in schools. She has published a number of books and articles in the field of educational leadership.

Dr Christopher Day is Professor of Education and Co-director of the Centre for Research on Teacher and School Development at the School of Education, University of Nottingham. He has worked as a schoolteacher, teacher educator and local authority adviser. He has extensive research and consultancy experience in England, Europe, Australia, South-East Asia and North America in the fields of teachers' continuing professional development, action research, leadership and change. He is

10

editor of *Teachers and Teaching: Theory and Practice*, and co-editor of *Educational Action Research*. He is a Board Member of the International Council for Teacher Education (ICET). In addition to *Leading Schools in Times of Change* (Open University Press, 2000), recent publications include *The Life and Work of Teachers: International Perspectives in Changing Times* (co-editor and contributor, Falmer Press, 2000), *Educational Research in Europe: Yearbook 2000* (co-editor, Garant, 2000), *Developing Teachers: Challenges of Lifelong Learning* (Falmer Press, 1999).

Pauline Dixon lectures in economics at the University of Northumbria and is completing her Ph.D. studies on an Austrian economic approach to regulation of private schools in developing countries at the University of Newcastle-upon-Tyne. Prior to taking up economics, she was a jazz pianist and organist.

Dr Lorna Earl is an Associate Professor in the Theory and Policy Studies Department and Co-Director of the International Centre for Educational Change at the Ontario Institute for Studies in Education, University of Toronto. Prior to this, she was Research Director with the Scarborough Board of Education and the first Director of Assessment to the Education Quality and accountability Office of the province of Ontario. She has worked for over 20 years in schools and school boards and, as a leader in the field of assessment and evaluation, has been involved in consultation, research and staff development with teachers' organizations, ministries of education, school boards and charitable foundations.

Peter Earley is a Reader in Education Management at the Institute of Education, University of London. His research interests include school leadership, professional development, school improvement, self-evaluation and inspection, school management and governing bodies. He is a school governor himself and is increasingly involved in working with schools, governing bodies and local education authorities on school improvement and governor development projects. He is currently co-directing a research project on school leadership funded by the Department for Education and Skills. His most recent book (with Neil Ferguson, Brian Fidler and Janet Ouston) is *Improving Schools and Inspection: The Self-inspecting School* (PCP/Sage, 2000).

Karen Elliot is a Research Officer in the Curriculum, Pedagogy and Assessment School and Research Associate of the International School Effectiveness and School Improvement Centre (ISEIC) at the Institute of Education, London. She is currently involved in the Effective Provision of Pre-School Education Project and the national evaluation of New Community Schools in Scotland. Her research interests include value-added measures, pupil performance data and the effective feedback of data to schools.

Linda Evans is Senior Lecturer in Education at the University of Warwick's Institute of Education and Co-director of the Institute's Development Research and Dissemination Unit. Before becoming an academic she spent 15 years as a primary school teacher working in socially disadvantaged areas in the north of England. She has researched and published widely in the fields of teachers' attitudes to their work, teacher professionalism and professionality, school-based and school-centred initial teacher training, and teaching and learning in higher education. Her books include *Teacher Morale, Job Satisfaction and Motivation* (Paul Chapman Publishing, 1998) and *Managing to Motivate: A Guide for School Leaders* (Cassell, 1999).

Dr Ralph Fessler is Professor and Dean of the School of Professional Studies in Business and Education at John Hopkins University in Baltimore. He holds a Ph.D. in educational administration and supervision. He is a former public school classroom teacher in Wisconsin and Illinois. His research and programme development specializations have included teacher career stages and development, alternative approaches to teacher education, integration of K–12 and teacher education curricula and alternative approaches to leadership development. He has been involved in numerous partnership projects with school systems, with a particular emphasis on the implementation of teacher education reform initiatives.

Dr Nick Foskett is Professor of Education and Head of School in the Research and Graduate School of Education at the University of Southampton. He has taught and held leadership posts in secondary schools, further education and universities. His main research interests lie in strategic planning and external relations management in education, and he has published widely in these fields as well as providing consultancy and professional development for schools, colleges, local education authorities and government. In 1994 he founded the Centre for Research in Education Marketing, which undertakes funded research in the UK and internationally on young people's choice processes in education and on strategic marketing in schools, colleges and universities.

Jeffrey Fromm is founder and President of KnowledgeQuest Education Group LLC, a New York-based professional service and financial advisory firm focused exclusively on the education and training industry, specializing in the K–12 and higher education sectors. Previously, he served as Vice-Chairman and General Council of an international Pepsi-Cola bottling company and as an attorney at O'Sullivan, Graev & Karabell, a New York-based corporate law firm. He is a frequent author and speaker on education and training industry topics, an elected member of the Education Division Board of the Software and Information Industry Association (SIIA) and a Senior Fellow at the Centre for Digita Education organized by *Converge* magazine. He received a BA degree from the UNiversity at Albany, a JD degree from New York University School of Law and an MBA degree from Columbia University Graduate School of Business. He is an Adjunct Faculty member at Columbia's Executive MBA programme, where he regularly supervises education-related project courses.

Dr Michael Fullan is Professor and Dean of Ontario Institute for Studies in Education of the University of Toronto. He participates as researcher, consultant, trainer and policy adviser on a wide range of educational change projects, working with school systems, teachers' federations, research and development institutes and government agencies in Canada and internationally. He has published widely on the topic of educational change. His most recent books are *The New Meaning of Educational Change*, (3rd edn, Teachers' College Press, 2001) and *Leading in a Culture of Change* (Jossey-Bass, 2001). He has also published *Change Forces: the Sequel* (Falmer Press, 1999), *Change Forces: Probing the Depths of Educational Reform* (Falmer Press, 1993), and the *What's Worth Fighting For* series (Teachers' College Press). He is currently leading the evaluation team conducting a four-year assessment of the National Literacy and Numeracy Strategy in England.

10

Dr Dan Gibton teaches educational administration, law and policy at the Department of Educational Policy and Administration, School of Education, and is Adjunct Lecturer at the Faculty of Law, Tel-Aviv University, Israel. He is course leader for the MA in educational leadership at the University. His areas of interest include trends in educational leadership and law-based policy and reform. Currently he is using qualitative research methods to study how educational law and policy influence the leadership, roles and work of school principals. During 2000–1 he was Visiting Fellow with the Policy Studies Group, Institute of Education, University of London and recipient of the British Chevening Award Scholarship.

Peter Gilroy is Professor of Education at Manchester Metropolitan University's Institute of Education and is currently the elected Chair of UCET. He first worked as a school teacher and then held posts at Clifton College of Education, Manchester and Sheffield Universities. He has researched and published widely in the area of continued professional development, and is the joint editor of the international *Journal of Education for Teaching*. He is at present seconded to the post of Acting Head of his university's Research Development Unit.

Dr Ron Glatter is Professor of Education Management in CEPAM, the Centre for Educational Policy and Management, at the Open University, UK. He was Director of CEPAM for several years. He is currently a Vice-President of the British Educational Leadership and Management Society (BELMAS), of which he was founding Secretary and later national Chair. He has contributed to the work of a number of international bodies, including the OECD's Centre for Educational Research and Innovation (CERI). His major interests and publications are in educational governance, leadership and management, in particular the impact of reform initiatives on educational provision.

Dr Stephan Gorard is a Professor at the Cardiff University School of Social Sciences, having previously been a secondary school teacher and deputy headteacher for 14 years. His research interests include widening participation (*Creating a Learning Society*, Policy Press, 2002), the role of technology in lifelong learning (*The Information Age*, University of Wales Press, 2002), informal learning ('Adults learning at home', ESRC grant 2001–4), the role of targets ('Privileging the visible', *British Educational Research Journal*, 28 (2), 2002), and developing international indicators of inequality (Socrates grant, 2001–3). His main task at present is to direct the Research Capacity-building support network for the ESRC Teaching and Learning Research Programme.

Peter Gronn is Associate Professor in the Faculty of Education, Monash University, Melbourne, Australia, where he coordinates and teaches a number of masters degree programmes on aspects of leadership and management. His work on leadership is used extensively in courses in Australasia, North America, the UK and Europe. He has published numerous books and refereed journal articles. His most recent books are *The Making of Educational Leaders* (Cassell, 1999) and *The New Work of Educational Leaders: Changing Leadership Practice in an Era of School Reform* (Paul Chapman Publishing, 2002). Current research projects include distributed leadership in Australian schools, co-principalships and school principal recruitment. He has recently been appointed to the Editorial Board of the *Leadership Quarterly*.

Dr James Guthrie is Professor of Public Policy and Education, Chair of the Department of Leadership, Policy and Organizations, and Director of the Peabody Center for Education Policy at Peabody College, Vanderbilt University. He also is Chairman of the board of Management Analysis & Planning Inc. (MAP), a private sector management consulting firm that specializes in education finance, management and litigation support. Previously a Professor at the University of California at Berkeley for 27 years, he has had wide experience in the private sector, in government, with foreign nations and international agencies, in public schools and in higher education. He holds a BA, MA and Ph.D. from Stanford University, and undertook postdoctoral study in economics and public finance at Harvard. He was also a postdoctoral Fellow at Oxford Brooks College. He currently is serving as Editor-in-chief of the *Encyclopaedia of Education* (Macmillan, 2002).

Frank Hartle is a Director of Hay Group, which he joined in 1985. Currently he is head of the education consulting business, offering a range of services and programmes to national bodies, local education authorities, education action zones, schools, further education colleges and universities. Since 1999 he has been Hay Group Project Director for the Leadership Programme for Serving Headteachers and for a research project into the characteristics of teacher effectiveness (research commissioned by the Department for Education and Skills). His education team has developed an online professional development service to headteachers and teachers (Transforming Learning).

Dr Stephen Heyneman is Professor of International Education Policy at Vanderbilt University. His interests include issues pertaining to the commercial provision of education and to the international trade in education goods and services. For two years prior to joining the Vanderbilt faculty in 2000, he was the Vice-President for International Operations for the International Management and Development Company, and education consulting firm in Alexandria, Virginia. Between 1976 and 1998 he served in three different education research and policy-making positions at the World Bank in Washington, DC. His undergraduate work in political science was at the University of California, Berkeley, his graduate work in African area studies was at UCLA and at the University of Chicago, where he received his Ph.D. in comparative education in 1975.

Dr Peter Hill is currently Director of Research and Development with the National Center on Education and the Economy, Washington, DC, having taken leave from his position as Professor of Education (Leadership and Management) withing the Faculty of Education of the University of Melbourne.

Russell Hobby is a Senior Consultant at Hay Group and a manager on the Transforming Learning project – Hay's online professional development service. Today, the Transforming Learning project caters for over 5000 teachers in more than 500 schools in the UK and abroad. Prior to joining Hay in 1997, Russell worked in information technology security and project management. At Hay, he is an education specialist and was a project manager on the research project into teacher effectiveness. He has co-authored several reports on leadership in education, including the *Lessons of Leadership* (2000).

10

Dr Suzanne Hood has more than six years' research experience with the Social Science Research Unit, Institute of Education, University of London. Her research interests include parental involvement in schools and education, children's participation in service development, and inter-agency and multidisciplinary work. She combines research experience in these areas with a background in social work management and practice. Her most recent studies include research into the impact of an innovative school-based after-school agreement initiative. She has also researched and written the first *State of London's Children Report*, for the Children's Rights Commissioner for London.

Dr Lea Hubbard is an Assistant Research Scientist in the Sociology Department at the University of California, San Diego. Her work focuses on educational reform and educational inequities as they exist across ethnicity, class and gender. She is currently involved in a comprehensive study of the educational reform of a large urban school district.

Dr Rochelle Ingram is Associate Dean and Director of the Graduate Division of Education at Johns Hopkins University, Baltimore. She has held teaching and administrative positions in various school districts, the University of Maryland and the Maryland State Department of Education. She presents regularly at annual meetings of national organizations and has published in areas relating to teacher development. Her professional interests include teachers' professional development and preparing teachers and administrators for culturally diverse settings. She has been a consultant to school districts and colleges of education and serves on state and national committees related to innovations in teacher education.

David Istance is a project leader in OECD's Centre for Educational Research and Innovation (CERI). He is currently responsible for the CERI project 'Schooling for Tomorrow', writing the 2001 report *What Schools for the Future?*. One of his long-standing interests is lifelong learning and he co-edited with Tom Schuller and Hans Schuetze *International Perspectives on Lifelong Learning* (The Society for Research into Higher Education and Open University Press, 2002). Other interests include equity, teachers, and the economics and sociology of education. He spent several years in academic life in Wales in the 1990s, researching *inter alia* into excluded teenagers, and he maintains an attachment to the School of Social Sciences, Cardiff University.

Renée Jacob is the Managing Director of Investment Services of the Education Entrepreneurs Fund (EEF), making and monitoring strategic investments in education organizations committed to raising student achievement through high-quality school improvement programmes. Prior to joining EEF, she worked at the Non-profit Finance Fund (NFF), providing financial and advisory services to various non-profit organizations in New York City. She has also worked with the National Cooperative Bank Development Corporation in Washington, DC on strategic charter school financing initiatives. She earned her MBA from the Yale School of Management and holds an AB in American history from Harvard University.

Todd Kern is Executive Vice-President and Principal of KnowledgeQuest Education Group LLC. Previously he served as the Acting Director of the Institute on Education and Government at Columbia University Teachers' College. Prior to joining Teachers' College, he managed programme-evaluation activities for the Institute for Learning Technologies, worked for the Chicago Panel on School Policy, served as an education policy consultant to the Chicagoland Chamber of Commerce, served as the Legislative Associate for the Council of Chief State School Officers, and worked for the Committee for Education Funding. He holds undergraduate degrees in political science and psychology from Miami University and a master's degree in public policy from the University of Chicago.

Dr Linda Lambert is Emeritus Professor and founder of the Center for Educational Leadership at California State University, Hayward. Previously, she was a teacher, principal, district director and coordinator of leadership academies. During the past decade her work in leadership and leadership capacity has taken her to Egypt, Asia, Australia, Canada and Mexico. She is the lead author of *The Constructivist Leader*, 2nd edn, (Teachers' College Press, 2002), *Who Will Save Our Schools?* (Corwin Press, 1997), *Building Leadership Capacity in Schools*, with Alma Harris (ASCD and Open University Press, 2002) and *Developing Sustainable Leadership Capacity in Schools* (Association for Supervision and Curriculum Development, 2002).

Denis Lawton is Professor of Education at the Institute of Education, University of London. He is internationally known as an expert in the field of the curriculum. He has taught in secondary schools in the UK and was the Institute's Director from 1983 to 1989. He has acted as consultant for UNESCO and OECD. His most recent publications include *Royal Education: Past, Present and Future,* with P. Gordon (Frank Cass Publishers, 1999) and *Education for Values: Morals, Ethics and Citizenship in Contemporary Teaching*, edited with R. Gardner and J. Cairns (Kogan Page, 2000).

Dr Kenneth Leithwood is Professor of Educational Administration and Associate Dean of Research for the Ontario Institute for Studies in Education of the University of Toronto. He has published more than 60 refereed journal articles and authored or edited two dozen books on school leadership and organizational change. He is the senior editor of the *International Handbook on Educational Leadership and Administration* (Kluwer Academic Publishers, 1996). Some of his other recent books include *Understanding Schools as Intelligent Systems* (JAI Press, 2000), *Changing Leadership for Changing Times* (Open University Press, 1999), *Organizational Learning in Schools* (Sloets Publishers, 1995), *Expert Problem Solving: Evidence from School and District Leaders* (SUNY Press, 1995), *Making Schools Smarter* (Corwin Press, 1995). Currently he is co-principal investigator (with Lorna Earl, Michael Fullan and Nancy Watson) of the external evaluation of the UK's National Literacy and Numeracy Strategy. He is also the external evaluator for the Durham Board's Together We Light The Way Program, and the Greater New Orleans School Leadership Center. His current research is focused on the effects of accountability policies on schools and students.

Dr Ben Levin is Professor of Educational Administration at the University of Manitoba in Winnipeg, Canada. He has recently completed a three-year second-

10

ment as Deputy Minister (chief civil servant) for Education for the Government of Manitoba. His research interests are in education policy, politics and economics and he is working on a new book on governments and education policy.

Dr Ann Lieberman is Emeritus Professor of Teachers' College, Columbia University. She is now a Senior Scholar at the Carnegie Foundation for the Advancement of Teaching and a Visiting Professor at Stanford University. She was President of the American Educational Research Association (AERA) in 1992. She is widely known for her work in the areas of teacher leadership and development, collaborative research, networks and school–university partnerships, and the problems and prospects for understanding educational change. Her recent books include *Teachers: Transforming their World and their Work*, with Lynne Miller (Teachers' College Press, 1999) and *Teachers Caught in the Action: Professional Development that Matters* (Teachers' College Press, 2001). She is currently writing a book with Diane Wood entitled *Inside the National Writing Project: Network Learning and Classroom Teaching, a New Synthesis*.

Dr Agnes McMahon is Senior Lecturer in the University of Bristol Graduate School of Education, teaching and researching in the field of educating management and policy. Her current research focuses upon the continuing professional development of teachers and how schools can create and sustain effective professional learning communities.

Dr Hugh Mehan is Professor of Sociology and Director of the Center for Research on Educational Equity, Access and Teaching Excellence at the University of California, San Diego. He has studied classroom organization, educational testing, tracking and untracking, computer use in schools and the construction of identities. He has worked closely with K–12 educators to make informed decisions to insure that excellent educational opportunities are available to all children.

Dean Millot is President of the Education Entrepreneurs Fund which is affiliated to New American Schools (NAS), where he leads a $15-million social investment programme. Before joining the NAS staff in 1997, he was a senior scientist at the Rand Corporation. In that capacity, he provided strategic planning support on the challenge of transforming eight design teams of NAS from grant-based research programmes to sustainable providers of comprehensive school reform services. At NAS he led the effort to move that organization from grant-making to lending and equity investment in social enterprises, combined with technical assistance in business operations. To focus NAS expertise in social investment, he formed the Educational Entrepreneurs Fund in 1999. He received his undergraduate degree from American University, did graduate work at Tufts University and earned his law degree from George Washington University.

Dr John Novak is a Professor of Education at Brock University in St Catharines, Ontario, Canada where he has been Chair of the Department of Graduate Studies in Education, Chair of the University Faculty Board and a member of the Board of Trustees. An active lecturer and writer, he has been an invited keynote speaker on six continents and has addressed groups north of the Arctic Circle and in the southern part of New Zealand. His most recent book is *Inviting Educational*

Leadership (Pearson Education, 2002). His forthcoming publications deal with inviting online success and creating inviting schools.

Dr Alan Odden is Professor of Educational Administration at the University of Wisconsin-Madison. He also is Co-Director of the Consortium for Policy Research in Education (CPRE), a national centre studying how to improve state and local education policy. He was formerly Professor of Education Policy and Administration at the University of Southern California (1984–1993) and Director of Policy Analysis for California Education (PACE), and from 1975 until 1984 held various positions at the Education Commission of the States. He was President of the American Educational Finance Association (AEFA) in 1979–80 and received AEFA's distinguished Service Award in 1998. He is currently directing research projects on school finance redesign, resource reallocation in schools, the costs of instructional improvement and teacher compensation. He has written widely, publishing over 200 journal articles, book chapters and research reports, and 25 books and monographs.

Dr Jenny Ozga is Professor of Educational Research and Director of the Centre for Educational Sociology at the University of Edinburgh. Her main research interests are in education policy and governance and policy for the teaching profession. Her most recent book is *Policy Research in Educational Settings: Contested Terrain* (Open University Press, 2000).

Vicki Phillips is the Superintendent of the School District of Lancaster. The district has a student population of 11 500 and an aggressive, standards-based reform agenda. She has served in key leadership roles in the implementation of systemic education reform agendas and has experience at virtually every level – school, district, state and national. Before her move to Lancaster in 1999, she was the Director of the Philadelphia Partnership for Reform and the Executive Director of the Children Achieving Challenge – a $150-million programme organized and funded to assist the School District of Philadelphia, Pennsylvania to implement its ten-point school reform agenda.

David Potter is an education consultant interested mainly in the management of teaching quality – helping schools, especially those causing concern, assure quality and plan for improvement. After 17 years of teaching, during which he ran two departments, was a pastoral head and deputy head, and led a large secondary school, he worked in local education authorities, eventually as Chief Adviser and Assistant Director of Education. He was a member of the Curriculum and Assessment Committee of the Qualifications and Curriculum Authority and works for the Department for Education and Skills to support schools facing challenging circumstances. He is an OFSTED Registered Inspector, Performance Management Consultant, Threshold Assessor and External Adviser. In addition to working widely in the UK, he works as a consultant to education departments in South Africa and Russia.

Dr David Reynolds is Professor of Education at the University of Exeter, and has been researching in the areas of school effectiveness, school improvement and teacher effectiveness for 30 years. His most recent books are in the area of school effectiveness (*The International Handbook of School Effectiveness Research*, with Charles Teddlie, Falmer Press, 2000) and teacher effectiveness (*Effective Teaching* with Daniel Muijs) He is currently writing up the findings of an innovative school improvement

10

programme: the High Reliability Schools Project. He is also involved in national (UK) educational policy making as an Adviser to the Department for Educational and Skills, and as a board member for the Teacher Training Agency (TTA) and the British Educational Communications and Technology Agency (BECTA).

Dr Pam Sammons is a Professor of Education in the Curriculum, Pedagogy and Assessment School and Co-ordinating Director of the International School Effectiveness and Improvement Centre (ISEIC) at the Institute of Education, University of London. She is a leading authority on school effectiveness and improvement research and also has interests in the development of educational indicators, assessment, teaching and learning and evaluation. She is currently working on a five-year study of Effective Provision of Pre-School Education (EPPE) funded by the Department for Education and Skills (DfES) and is Co-director of the three-year national evaluation of New Community Schools in Scotland, commissioned by SEED. She is also Co-director of the new VITAE longitudinal study of teacher effectiveness funded by the DfES.

Michael Sandler founded Eduventures Inc. in 1993. Eduventures is the leading independent market research and advisory firm serving the for-profit education and training markets worldwide. A lifelong entrepreneur, Michael has built a career in both business and education. A graduate of the Wharton School at the University of Pennsylvania, he has served as a trustee of the university and as an overseer of its School of Arts and Sciences. He has established several successful businesses, including Marsan Industries, which merged with ITT Corporation, and Auto Parts Distributors, which was sold to Rite-Aid Corporation. In 1989 he was appointed a fellow at the John F. Kennedy School of Government at Harvard University, where he researched the relationship between business and education. He is founder and chairman of A Different September Foundation, a non-profit organization that supports the Boston University/Chelsea Public Schools Partnership. He is Vice-Chairman of the advisory board of the David T. Kearns Program on Business, Government and Education at Harvard and is Chairman of the Education Industry Leadership Board of the Association of Education Practitioners and Providers.

Dr Thomas Sergiovanni is Lillian Radford Professor of Education and Administration and Senior Fellow, Center for Educational Leadership at Trinity University, San Antonio. Prior to joining the Trinity faculty he was for 18 years Professor of Educational Administration and Supervision at the University of Illinois (UC), Among his recent publications are *Moral Leadership: Getting to the Heart of School Improvement* (Jossey-Bass, 1992), *Building Community in Schools* (Jossey-Bass, 1994), *Leadership for the School House: How Is It Different? Why Is It Important?* (Jossey-Bass, 1996), *The Lifeworld of Leadership: Creating Culture, Community, and Personal Meaning in Our Schools* (Jossey-Bass, 2000), *The Principalship: A Reflective Practice Perspective* (4th edn) (Allyn & Bacon), *Leadership: What's in it for Schools?* (Routledge/Falmer Press, 2001).

Kim Smith is Co-Founder and CEO of the New Schools Venture Fund, a non-profit venture philanthropy fund created by technology venture capitalists and entrepreneurs to improve public K–12 education by supporting education entrepreneurs. She began her career as a consultant specializing in business–education partnerships and in 1989 became a Founding Team Member of Teach For America (TFA).

Following TFA, she was the Founding Director of BAYAC AmeriCorps, a consortium of 20 non-profits serving youth across six Bay Area. Her business experience includes marketing with Silicon Graphics' Education Industry Group, where she focused on the online learning industry, and her role as Founding Director of a new trade show venture. She holds a bachelor's degree in political science and psychology from Columbia College, and an MBA from the Stanford Graduate School of Business. She was featured in *Newsweek's* edition of 'Women of the twenty-first century' as 'the kind of woman who will shape America's new century'. She is a member of the 2002 Class of Henry Crown Fellows of the Aspen Institute.

Rosanne Steinbach is a senior research officer at the Ontario Institute for Studies in Education of the University of Toronto. Her research interests are administrative problem solving, shared decision making, team learning and effective school leadership. Recent publications include 'School leadership and teachers' motivation to implement accountability policies' (with K. Leithwood and D. Jantzi, *Educational Administration Quarterly*, 2002) and *Changing Leadership for Changing Times* (with K. Leithwood and D. Jantzi, Open University Press, 1999).

Dr Louise Stoll is Professor in Education and Director of the Centre for Educational Leadership, Learning and Change at the University of Bath. She is also President of the International Congress for School Effectiveness and School Improvement (ICSI). Her national and international research examines effective school improvement practice and policy, with an increasing focus on schools' capacity for learning and change. She has worked with schools and local education authorities around the UK, presented and consulted internationally, and published widely in the field of school effectiveness and school improvement.

Dr Chris Taylor is a researcher at the Cardiff University School of Social Sciences, having completed a Ph.D. on the *Geography of the New Education Markets* (Ashgate, 2002) and postdoctoral research on the impact of the Education Reform Act 1988 on patterns of inequity (www.cf.ac.uk/socsi.markets). He is now the manager of the £700 000 Research Capacity-building support network for the ESRC Teaching and Learning Research Programme.

Dr Charles Teddlie is the Jo Ellen Levy Yates Distinguished Professor of Education at Louisiana State University (LSU). He has also taught at the University of New Orleans and has been a Visiting Professor at the University of Newcastle-upon-Tyne and the University of Exeter in the UK. He has been awarded the Excellence in Teaching Award from the LSU College of Education. He has published over 100 chapters and articles and is the co-author or co-editor of nine books, including *Schools Make a Difference: Lessons Learned from a 10-year Study of School Effects* (with Sam Stringfield, Teachers' College Press, 1993), *Mixed Methodology: Combining the Qualitative and Quantitative Approaches* (with Abbas Tashakkori), *The International Handbook of School Effectiveness Research* (with David Reynolds, Falmer Press, 2000) and *Handbook of Mixed Methods in Social and Behavioral Research* with (Abbas Tashakkori).

Dr James Tooley is Professor of Education Policy at the University of Newcastle-upon-Tyne, and author of *Reclaiming Education* (Continuum, 2000) and *The Global Education Industry* (IEA/IFC, 2001). He directed the International Finance Corporation's global

10

study of private education, and has held research positions at the Universities of Oxford and Manchester and at the National Foundation for Education Research. He gained his Ph.D. from the Institute of Education, University of London. Prior to taking up educational research he was a mathematics teacher in Zimbabwe.

Jason Walton is an advanced doctoral student at Peabody College, Vanderbilt University, where he is studying school administration. He holds a both a BA and an M.Ed. from the University of Mississippi. He currently serves as the student editor of the *Peabody Journal of Education*.

Keiko Watanabe is Deputy Director in the Financial Affairs Division of the Elementary and Secondary Education Bureau, Ministry of Education, Culture, Sports, Science and Technology, Japan.

Dr Mel West has worked with schools and education authorities both in the UK and abroad on school improvement and school leadership issues, and is presently Consultant to UNICEF's School Improvement initiative in China. While at the University of Cambridge, he directed the Improving the Quality of Education for All (IQEA) Project, and he is currently working on a number of other projects, including the preparation of a desk study on headship for the National College for School Leadership and the coordination of leadership practice within (Excellence in Cities) EiC partnership at the Faculty of Education, the University of Manchester and the Manchester Business School, where he is also Dean of Education Faculty.

Dr Dylan Wiliam is Professor of Educational Assessment and Assistant Principal at King's College, London. His teaching on masters and doctorate programmes includes courses on educational assessment, research methods and the use of information technology in academic research. He divides his research time between mathematics education and research in educational assessment and evaluation, where his main interests are the interplay between meanings and consequences in conceptualizations of validity, and formative assessment.

Derek Wise was appointed as Head of Cramlington Community High School, Northumberland in 1990. OFSTED describes his school as 'strikingly successful' and its innovative teaching and curriculum has led to excellent examination results with 'a success for all' culture. In 1999 the under-16 soccer team was the national ESFA champion and in 2000 the school received awards for Internationalism and the Basic Skills agency Quality Mark. In 1999–2000 Derek was seconded for a year to the Newcastle Education Action Zone as Project Director. He currently chairs the Northumberland Association of Headteachers and serves on the BBC Secondary Education Committee. He has recently published, with Mark Lovatt, *Creating an Accelerated Learning School* (Network Press, 2002) and is currently engaged on two projects: *An Introduction to Accelerated Learning* and *The Learning Focused School*, both for Network Press.

Dr Diane Wood is an Assistant Professor in the College of Education and Human Development at the University of Southern Maine. Having spent 20 years as a teacher and administrator in high schools, her present work focuses on professional development of veteran teachers, narrative inquiry as a method for understanding teaching, and democratic change in public school cultures. Her articles have appeared in the *Harvard Educational Review, Anthropology and Education Quarterly*, and the *International Journal of Leadership in Education.* She is co-editor of and contributor to *Transforming Teacher Education: Lessons in Professional Development* (Bergin & Garvey, 2001). Currently she and Ann Lieberman are writing a book on the National Writing Project to be published by Teachers' College Press.

10

INDEX